BOOKS BY SANFORD J. UNGAR

Estrangement: America and the World (Editor, *1985*)
Africa: The People and Politics of an Emerging Continent (*1985*)
FBI: An Uncensored Look Behind the Walls (*1976*)
The Papers & The Papers:
    An Account of the Legal and Political Battle Over
    the Pentagon Papers (*1972*)
The Almost Revolution: France—1968 (*1969*)

AFRICA

REVISED AND UPDATED EDITION

The People and Politics
of an Emerging Continent

SANFORD J. UNGAR

A TOUCHSTONE BOOK
PUBLISHED BY SIMON & SCHUSTER, INC. · NEW YORK

Touchstone
Simon & Schuster Building
Rockefeller Center
1230 Avenue of the Americas
New York, New York 10020

10 9 8 7 6 5 4 3 2 1 Pbk.

Library of Congress Cataloging in Publication Data
Ungar, Sanford J.
  Africa : the people and politics of an emerging continent
Sanford J. Ungar.—3rd rev. ed.
    p. cm.
  "A Touchstone book."
  Bibliography: p.
  Includes index.
    1. Africa—Politics and government—1960– 2. Africa—Economic
conditions—1960– 3. Africa—Social conditions—1960– I. Title.
DT30.5.U54 1989   88–29043
960'.32—dc 19   CIP
ISBN 0–671–67565–6 Pbk.

We have made every effort to trace the ownership of all copyrighted material and to secure permission from copyright holders. In the event of any question arising as to the use of any material, we will be pleased to make the necessary corrections in future printings. Thanks are due to the following authors, publishers and publications for permission to use the material indicated:
   Permission to quote from Inside Africa *by* John Gunther *has been granted from Harper & Row, Publishers, Inc.*
   Permission to quote from Along the Africa Shore *by* Russell Warren Howe *has been granted by Barnes & Noble Books.*
   Permission to quote from The Forum, 1901, *has been granted from Current History Inc.*
   Permission to reprint portions of "Dilemma in the Horn of Africa" by Sanford J. Ungar has been granted by Saturday Review *magazine.*
   Permission to quote from Harold Isaacs' article in Saturday Review, 1953, *has been granted by* Saturday Review *magazine.*

Portions of this book appeared originally in The Atlantic, Foreign Policy, The New Republic, Saturday Review *and* Foreign Affairs.

Acknowledgments

I WAS INTRODUCED to one part of Africa by Tertius Myburgh and to another by Beth Ungar; without them this book truly would not have been possible.

Along the way I have been tutored, coached, and constructively criticized by Gerald Bender, Peter Vale, Fleur de Villiers, Jean Herskovits, John de St. Jorre, Alison Rosenberg, Hilary Ng'weno, Helen Kitchen, and Joel Barkan; others to whom I am grateful prefer, for various reasons, not to be mentioned. Thanks, too, to Hans Hielscher and Nicholas Spiliotes, as well as my patient colleagues at *The Atlantic, Foreign Policy,* and National Public Radio, and my friends at the *Economist.*

For research assistance at various stages, I am indebted to Marilyn Rouvelas, Terrell Lamb, Tandi Stern, and the staff of the library at the Carnegie Endowment, especially Jane Lowenthal and Monica Yin. Gladys Bostick prepared the manuscript with great skill, and Sara Goodgame performed a few miracles.

Peter Shepherd was my guide and defender on this project, as he has been on many others. Alice Mayhew showed an interest in the subject when Africa was not in the news and, along with David Masello, kept me on the straight and narrow. Tom Hughes gave me shelter from the storm, and David Weiner was utterly indispensable. Lida Ungar learned to say "Africa" at an absurdly early age, and her brother Philip is working on it now. Their mother put up with a whole lot that I won't go into here.

S.J.U.

Washington, May 1985

FOR THE REVISED, PAPERBACK EDITION of this book, I have attempted to take account of the key events on the continent during the past year, while correcting a few misimpressions that may have been created in the first edition. I have had the benefit of one further journey to Africa, as well as research help from Melissa Berger and Daniel Cutler. My new colleagues at The American University have been particularly supportive, and Jane Isay of Touchstone Books has helped find ways to get this introduction to Africa to a broader audience. From the moment this book was published in August 1985, Henry Ferris has looked after it as if it were his own, and I am especially grateful for his sensitivity and skill.

S.J.U.

Washington, July 1986

FOR THE THIRD EDITION of *Africa,* new developments and major events have necessitated changes throughout the text, but I would call the reader's attention especially to the new chapter on AIDS in Africa and to the expanded Epilogue; the Appendix, with data on all sub-Saharan African countries, has also been completely updated. I am grateful to Greg Pearson for his painstaking research, and to Carole Hall and James Nichols at Touchstone Books for maneuvering this book through the shoals once again. Cerita Wilson and Jessica Freedman have also helped make this edition possible.

S.J.U.

Washington, February 1989

FOR LIDA AND PHILIP

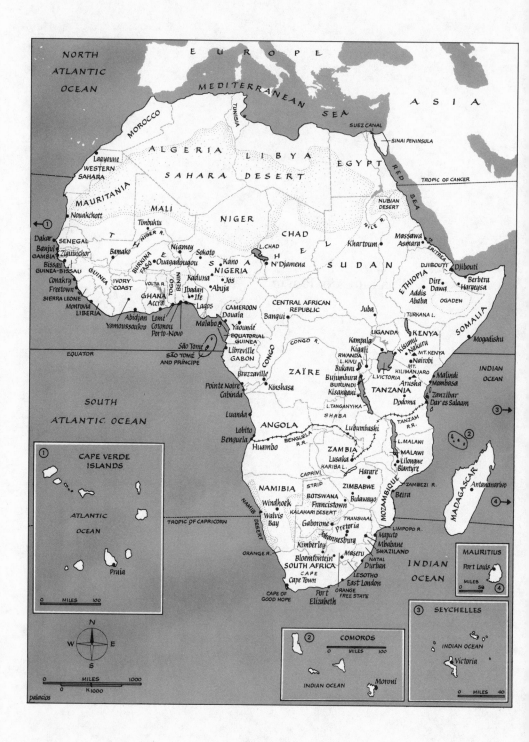

Contents

_____IV. THE CRISIS AHEAD

Introduction

AFTER KOMLA AGBELI GBEDEMAH became finance minister of the newly independent West African nation of Ghana in 1957, one of his first duties was to travel to the United States for meetings with officials of the United Nations, the American government, and the World Bank and International Monetary Fund. Pausing en route between New York and Washington in Dover, the capital city of Delaware, Gbedemah walked into a restaurant and ordered a glass of orange juice. He was denied service, because he was black. Change might have been sweeping through the African continent at the time, as dozens of European colonies moved toward independence, but in the United States, only three years after the Supreme Court's most important desegregation decisions, change was slow. Just ninety-six miles from a city that liked to call itself the capital of the "free world," Gbedemah came face to face with certain harsh realities.

The African official complained, loudly and publicly, and within two days he had an invitation for breakfast at the White House with President Dwight D. Eisenhower and Vice-President

Richard M. Nixon. Gbedemah had entertained Nixon during his visit to Accra for Ghana's independence ceremonies earlier that year, and Nixon wanted to demonstrate that the embarrassing incident was not typical of American attitudes or hospitality. Along the way, Ghana got some badly needed attention and publicity, and the American public consciousness about Africa was raised one small notch.

Three decades later, a visiting African would be unlikely to encounter such a blatant act of discrimination. In fact, in Washington he could be greeted by a black mayor, eat at one of several Ethiopian or West African restaurants (some of whose owners arrived in the United States as penniless immigrants and are now millionaires), and spend an evening at a fashionable club called the Kilimanjaro. And yet, he would still find it difficult to meet Americans who know his country well or have even the vaguest acquaintance with general African affairs. He would find that in the government bureaucracy and on Capitol Hill, Africa has low priority until it is the scene of a crisis relevant to American interests.

It is not hard to find the African antecedents of many current cultural phenomena in the Western world. The *macumba* cults that have swept through all strata of society in Brazil, their ceremonies and paraphernalia mingling with more orthodox religious practices and artifacts, can be traced directly to Africa, as can the voodoo religion and art of Haiti. Americans and Europeans may flock to exhibitions of newly appreciated carvings and other works of art from Nigeria or Cameroon, but few recognize that much of the music and dance they enjoy is directly descended from traditional African sounds and movements. The most remarkable aspect of all this is that African art forms and cultural influences were resilient enough to survive the holocaust of the international slave trade. Repression, displacement, violence, and an astonishing assault on human dignity took a profound toll. But the people who were put in chains and shipped off to alien lands brought their cultural baggage along. It was not only passed on to subsequent generations of black people, but also envied, imitated, and absorbed by nearly everyone else.

Indeed, there are many respects in which traditional African societies have dealt successfully with issues and problems that still baffle advanced Western civilization. For example, the San of southern Africa (also known as the "Bushmen") have apparently avoided heart disease, high blood pressure, and other stress-related illnesses through the development of unusually rich and significant human relationships. Part of their health and longevity is undoubtedly due to their low-fat diet, but researchers have also found that the San's strong group identification and social support system help them cope particularly well with the frustrations and conflicts of daily life. For generations, the San have practiced an effective form of birth control, using an oral contraceptive made from roots. A vast number of the San were destroyed during the past three hundred years, following the arrival of settlers and diseases from Europe, but those who remain continue to talk through and laugh about their difficulties in a way that has important lessons for more sophisticated, modernized people in the industrialized world.

Westerners are often surprised by what they learn from Africa. The much-neglected and often-persecuted Falasha, the indigenous black Jews of Ethiopia, arrive in Israel in rags after a long and harrowing journey, only to find that they have much to teach their new countrymen about traditional, fundamentalist religious observances. The Dogon people of Mali are one of the rare civilizations in the world that have managed to preserve their ancient culture, with its own unique mythology and numerology. They still live in remote villages along the sides of vertical cliffs and tend their onion fields, almost entirely free of external influences.

Paleontologists exploring desolate areas of Kenya continue to turn up new fossils, at least seventeen million years old, some of primates previously thought to have existed only in Asia. It is in the African wilderness that the search continues for the common ancestors of the great apes and of humans, and one new theory has it that a substantial piece of North America, from Alabama to the Carolinas, was once part of Africa. Griots from Senegal tell stories that have come down through their families over seven centuries or more, accompanying themselves on twenty-one-string instruments that produce sounds totally unfamiliar to the Western ear. Folktales that seem to encompass all there is to know about the relationships between people and governments and machines and nature emerge from every part of Africa.

Africa sometimes appears to be the world's last natural frontier, where the most fundamental issues of environment and ecology have yet to be confronted. It is a continent where a commodity as basic as firewood is running out, where scarce, exotic animals like the black desert rhinoceros are threatened with extinction. It is a place where a simple battery for a radio or a flashlight can still make all the difference between ignorance and awareness, by extending an individual's horizons beyond the village limits. It is a part of the earth where millions of children die every year for lack of basic nourishment.

There are places in Africa where, when you are there, many things happen every day that relate to fundamental issues of life and death, to humanity's effort to organize and improve itself. And yet, it is as if these events are a secret, as if nobody in the rest of the world is paying attention. This book is intended to introduce the general reader to the complexity, the fascination, and the tragedy of Africa.

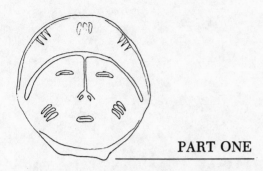

PART ONE

WORLDS APART

1

Ignorance
and Insults

IT WAS DECEMBER 1978 in the torrid port of Dar es Salaam, the capital of Tanzania. Hardly anything stirred except a few palm leaves. The ordinary business of the city had come virtually to a halt, and the only local news was of shortages; mainlanders were begging travelers to the offshore island of Zanzibar to bring back butter and other staples for them. The talk of strategies of development, theoretical discussions of African socialism, even the drumbeats on the need to liberate the black majority in southern Africa from white oppression had stopped, as Tanzanian soldiers—young, callow, and frightened—headed northwest to the border with Uganda to liberate their neighbors from the black oppression of Idi Amin. They went in trucks, and they were cheered as they passed through villages.

Floating in the harbor and lying along the quiet, sultry beaches of Dar es Salaam were plastic bags. They bore the legend, "Gift to the people of Tanzania from the people of the United States," alongside the insignia of USAID, the United States Agency for International Development. Once, the plastic bags had contained enough powdered milk to nourish thousands of villagers for months. But the American gift had never reached its intended beneficiaries. Through a failure of coordination, communication, or internal distribution systems, the bags had sat in boats or on the docks and had eventually fallen or been pushed into the sea. A few ugly chunks of white powder still floated in the water, along with the seemingly indestructible plastic bags, as a reminder of American good intentions. A few miles away, even a few blocks away, people went hungry.

American intentions in Africa have frequently been good, to the extent that there have been any at all. From colonial times to the present, the United States has almost ignored the African continent, maintaining a childlike innocence about the second largest land mass in the world, 11,635,000 square miles with a population now estimated to be approaching 625 million. Those parts of the continent that did attract American interest—Egypt, for example—were really part of another world, the more obviously fascinating Middle East. When American attention was diverted occasionally to the rest of Africa, it was temporary, faddish, disorganized, and often obtuse. Even the fact that at least 12 percent of the American people trace their roots to Africa made little difference until very recently.

There are now more than fifty independent countries in Africa, but most Americans would be hard-pressed to name half a dozen. Even those that are individually almost a third the size of the continental United States (Sudan, Zaïre, and Mali), the one that for ten years was the second-ranking foreign supplier of crude oil to the United States (Nigeria), or those that are viewed as potential bases for the U.S. military forces occasionally deployed to deal with crises in the Middle East (Kenya and Somalia) are little known in America. Indeed, Africa, for some Americans, is one vast exotic place, perhaps a single gigantic country, where wild animals roam and where the people cannot resist killing and perhaps even eating each other. For others, the only part of the continent that truly matters is South Africa, a purported bastion of white Western civilization, holding out against what are seen as the hordes to the north and fighting communism.

It is only a small minority of Americans who pay careful attention to Africa. They find a continent of rich, varied cultures and enduring civilization—indeed, the birthplace of humankind as we know it. They recognize plenty of trouble and turbulence, but also see a source of vast human, economic, mineral, and agricultural potential. Africa is critical to American interests in the world, they argue, a site of political and social drama that may eventually become issues in domestic American politics and society as well. But the gap between these specialists—the "Africanists"—and the general public is enormous.

In some respects, Africa never had a chance to be taken seriously by America and Americans. From the earliest references in literature, both scholarly and popular, the continent suffered from the vision of "darkest Africa"—a place of savages, jungles, and chaos. The Puritans made much of the negative connotations of dark skin, and they were among the first to invoke biblical support for theories of black inferiority, including such devices as Noah's Curse. Then the ideas arose about Africans' closeness to the "natural life," their similarity to apes and other dark animals, their tendency toward promiscuous sex and other sins. All of this pseudoreligious and pseudoscientific analysis gained currency in the United States during the late nineteenth and early twentieth centuries. As Melville Herskovits, an anthropologist who became a preeminent American student of Africa, explained at a 1961 conference, Africa's "people were held to have fallen behind in the march of progress, with ways of life representing early stages in the evolution of human civilizations."

It was not as if those who denounced Africa knew it well. European colonization had not really begun in earnest by the turn of the century, and few outsiders had deeply penetrated the continent, except in South Africa. Even in Angola, the largest European settlement outside South Africa, there were barely two thousand Portuguese, mostly soldiers, traders, administrators, and exiled convicts. Only one white settler had arrived in the Kenya highlands by 1895, and about 125 Europeans were living in the area of Dakar, Senegal.

Many observers held Africa to be a lost cause purely on the basis of climate, which was blamed even for the mistreatment of the local population by the colonial powers. In an article in the March 1910 issue of the *Atlantic Monthly*, James M. Hubbard noted:

With the exception of a small tract on the east coast, it is a land in which no white man can live for any length of time and retain his faculties in a normal condition. There can be no doubt that much of the misgovernment of the Congo native is due to the terrible influence upon the Belgian official of the climate and the unnatural surroundings. More than one traveler has called attention to the fact that some of the officials in the isolated stations are practically insane.

But there was hope for the white man's adjustment to these difficult conditions, Hubbard said, and one thing was certain: "In thirty years . . . the civilization of Europe will have poured into the barbarism of Africa."

Hubbard happened to believe that Africans would eventually come to control their own land, but more typical was the view expressed in 1901 by Samuel Phillips Verner, a missionary-explorer from Alabama, in the *Forum:*

It is interesting to consider the exact means by which the white control and direction of Africa will be carried out . . . the fact that Africa is to be a white man's land is now a foregone conclusion . . . the high, mountainous, healthful, and invigorating parts of Africa are on the slopes of the mountain ranges and on the watersheds of the great rivers; these regions being distributed all over the continent, instead of massed together in any one part. In these regions the Caucasian can live and labor. From them he will govern and direct all the rest.

Verner's attitude was, of course, racist. But that kind of racism was pervasive in the West at the time, and it was rarely questioned. In 1899, Sir Harry Johnston, one of Britain's foremost empire builders, had said that "the Negro has been marked out by his mental and physical characteristics as the servant of other races . . . a born slave." There was constant reinforcement of this view in respectable publications by people of high standing and good reputation, not to mention staunch religious beliefs.

The refrain continued well into the twentieth century. "It would be as insane to give [Africans] a smattering of our involved religious beliefs and so-called education as it would be to give our children sticks of dynamite with which to play," wrote Major Frederick Russell Burnham, a pioneer in the Boy Scout movement, in a book of tales from Africa. "Only as the blacks' skulls grow thinner and their brains heavier will they absorb our ways and standards," he said. "At present they are at the stage of development equal to that of children eight or ten years old."

When Westerners encountered the rich tradition of African sculpture, woodcuts, music, and other art, they sometimes incorporated its characteristics into their own work, but they could not accept it as an accomplishment in itself. Invariably, it was measured against Western standards. European ethnologists were among the worst offenders. Leo Frobenius, for example, who on the whole contributed a great deal to Western understanding of African societies when he visited them at the turn of the century, sometimes contemptuously mocked what he found. Describing one discovery in a West African tomb as "strange and mysterious . . . delicious," he added that as for style and content, it was "typically African trash."

Prejudice toward Africa was just as strong in the United States as in Europe, and was related to the virulent racism in American society toward its own black citizens, especially in the South. It had taken the United States longer than most to do away with slavery. American white supremacists who had never been to Africa spoke the same language as colonists and missionaries. U.S. Senator "Pitchfork" Ben Tillman of South Carolina, for example, in a 1907 Senate speech, defended the lynching of blacks as a punishment for their alleged rape of white women:

> Look at our environment in the South, surrounded, and in a very large number of counties and in two states outnumbered, by the Negroes—engulfed . . . in a black flood of semi-barbarians. . . . For forty years these have been taught the damnable heresy of equality with the white man. . . . Their minds are those of children, while they have the passions and strengths of men.

Decades later, when many Southerners were looking for an intellectual justification for their resistance to integration of their public schools, they fell back on the old canards about Africa. As Henry Garrett, once the head of the psychology department at Columbia University, put it in a booklet published by the Patrick Henry Press of Richmond, ". . . over the past 5,000 years, the history of black Africa is blank." How could black children study alongside whites, he asked, when "the Black African had no written language; no numerals; no calendar or system of measurement. He did not devise a plough or wheel, nor did he domesticate an animal; he built nothing more complex than a mud hut or thatched stockade." Though denying centuries of African culture, religion, political sophistication, and productivity, such prattle had its effect.

Negative stereotypes of blacks were presented to generations of American schoolchildren in their mostly segregated classrooms. The unfavorable depiction of Africans in English literature goes back at least as far as the plays of Elizabethan times, but new and insidious examples appeared again in the late nineteenth century. The most notorious offender was *The Story of Little Black Sambo*, written by Helen Bannerman, an Englishwoman living in India, and first published in Britain in 1898 and in the United States in 1900. Its caricature of the black child as lazy, slow, and stupid—loyal to his white master, but liable to lie and steal—did incalculable harm; yet it remained on the standard American lists of recommended children's books through the late 1960s.

American films set in Africa took the stereotypes further. *The Nun's Story*, released in 1959 and considered one of the most profoundly religious films ever made in America, relied for part of its success on the heroine's conversion of an idol-worshiping "native" after another nun has been murdered by an African "heathen." The script is laced with references to "native boys" who wear fetishes around their necks and attack white women at the slightest opportunity.

The rich American comic tradition, on stage and screen, often used Africa as the butt of its jokes. In *Animal Crackers,* one of the high points in the development of the Marx Brothers' slapstick style, George S. Kaufman and Morrie Ryskind wrote a part for Groucho as a madcap African explorer called Captain Jeffrey T. Spalding (perhaps inspired by Henry Morton Stanley). Spalding's grand entrances included scantily clad African bearers, and he continually confused Africa with Harlem.

It was inevitable that these images would have a profound influence on all Americans. Black preachers in particular spoke of the need to redeem and enlighten this distant pagan continent of their origin. The "addresses and discourses" of Alexander Crummell, rector of St. Luke's Church in Washington, published in

1891, contain many such references. "The redemption of Africa cannot be effected through the influence of trade and commerce," he said. "In every instance that we know of, where men have been morally elevated, they have always had the missions, from superior people, of either letters or grace, as the origination of such elevation." Charles E. Silberman pointed out in his classic study, *Crisis in Black and White,* published in 1964, that black Americans had no defense against the consistent picture of Africans as inferior savages; they "had no way of knowing that the picture happened to be false." It would be understandable if all this induced in them shame about their origins and, in many instances, a sense of worthlessness—only to be followed by anger, when they later learned the truth about Africa.

Twenty years after Silberman's study, however, prominent white Americans were still playing on the distinction between Africans and American blacks. William K. Coors, the head of a Colorado brewery firm, for example, told a group of black businessmen at a seminar in Denver in 1984 that the problems of black-ruled countries in Africa resulted from "a lack of intellectual capacity." Coors added that "one of the best things [the slave traders] did for you is to drag your ancestors over here in chains."

Africans have been trying to attract American attention for more than two centuries, but especially since the late 1950s and early 1960s, when their newly independent nations began to command greater notice on the world scene. For most African states, a connection with the United States was valued more than any other. They embraced the American claim to stand for liberty and justice for all, and they believed that if they could establish an American friendship, they might also be able to tap into the enormous reserves of American wealth to help with their problems of self-definition and development.

The Africans have been unable to help focus American attention. Their inability to do so has its roots in a failure to understand the open, fluid, American political system, and in a deep sense of frustration and disillusionment. As one junior officer in the Washington embassy of a former British colony in Africa said, "We learned so much in school about Western cultures, and we made the naive assumption that you were learning about us, too—

especially with all your media. . . . Alas, that turns out not to be the case. Finally I learned that part of my job was to try to educate Americans."

In one of his earliest educational efforts, this young African spent weeks preparing for his first visit to Capitol Hill, where he was to explain his country's position on several international issues to a congressman with some responsibility for African affairs. When the long-awaited moment came, he was told the congressman was busy and so a member of the staff would see him. After a time, the aide emerged, but he insisted on holding their conversation while standing in the office's busy reception room, with ringing telephones, frenetic typing, and visiting constituents in the background.

The sub-Saharan African diplomatic community in Washington includes about 340 people, spread among the 40 missions of countries with which the United States has diplomatic relations.* They are a lonely crowd, often lost in a sea of policy and protocol. They reside near the seat of American power, but tend to feel remote from its exercise and impact.

In most African countries, as in many other parts of the world, the position of ambassador to the United States is reserved for only the most senior or best-connected person. It is the custom in some African and other developing countries to send off people who are out of favor as envoys to other small countries where they cannot make trouble. But often an African ambassador in Washington is related to the head of the government at home or is an old school friend or political crony; he is assumed to have direct and prompt access to the highest officials in his capital. However, his connections in Washington, with rare exceptions, are something else entirely. Typically, after he has presented his credentials on arrival—usually in an impressive, if brief, ceremony in the Oval Office—an African ambassador fades into oblivion. Unless his chief of state or another high official from his country visits Washington during his tenure, he never sees the inside of the White House again, and he rarely meets with the top-ranking people at

---

* At this writing the United States has relations with forty-five independent sub-Saharan African countries, all but Angola. Four of them, Equatorial Guinea, Guinea-Bissau, São Tomé and Principe, and the Comoros conduct their minimal business with the American government through their missions to the United Nations in New York.

the State Department unless there is a crisis that concerns his nation. The most effective way to reemerge in recent years, in fact, has been to represent a country under attack by Libyan leader Muammar al-Qaddafi or "threatened" in some way by communism. Then an African embassy's phones begin to ring.

Interviews with a number of African ambassadors and other diplomats in Washington reveal that most of them get to know very few Americans during their stay and have few friends even among their own African diplomatic community. The one universal measure of their success seems to be the attendance at the receptions they hold every year on the occasion of their country's national day celebration. There are exceptions, of course—the ambassadors of Zaïre, Somalia, and Sudan have had a high profile in recent years, because of the extent of U.S. aid to their governments. There are others who, because of the countries they represent, might be expected to achieve a certain prominence, but do not. One recent long-term ambassador from Kenya rarely ventured forth, apparently out of a fear that if he became too well known he would soon be resented at home and recalled. According to sources close to him, he did not properly spend the entertainment allowance provided to him by his government in Nairobi, and he declined to share it with other officers in the embassy; instead he used the money for his own personal expenses. Chief Abudu Yesufu Eke, a prominent Nigerian educator and journalist who represented his country in Washington for two and a half years, took to watching soap operas, game shows, and other daytime television in his office rather than becoming heavily involved in complex Nigerian-American relations. On one occasion when I visited him to discuss the African impact on American foreign policy, Eke's attention was riveted on a hotly contested television game show over my shoulder; as our conversation proceeded, he turned the television volume louder.

Occasionally, an African ambassador is caught up in an incident that raises questions about his activities in the United States. Take the case of Mamady Lamine Conde, who was ambassador to the United States from Guinea, one of Africa's poorest countries, whose government was one of the first on the continent to espouse Marxism. He brought a lawsuit in superior court of the District of Columbia, blaming Air France for the loss of a briefcase that he said contained a kilogram of gold worth $16,000 and other articles worth almost $2,000, along with "secret diplomatic papers." Conde had entrusted shipment of the briefcase to the airline, after he forgot to bring it with him to the airport in February 1982 for a trip from Washington to Paris.

According to one African ambassador in Washington, some of his colleagues—especially from francophone countries—soon give up going to their offices at all and simply withdraw from diplomatic activity. "They end up sitting in their houses, consuming all the liquor their governments will buy for them," he said. Indeed, although exact statistics are difficult to obtain, alcoholism has become a severe problem among African diplomats in the United States, and several ambassadors were called home in recent years for that reason. Others have dealt with their idleness and feelings of uselessness by becoming students at Washington-area universities. One ambassador from a small country enrolled in classes in "information science" at the University of Maryland, and another, from Senegal, completed a master's degree in international relations at the Johns Hopkins University School of Advanced International Studies.

Information science might be an appropriate field of study for these diplomats, for their embassies' press relations are poor, if they exist at all. Generally, the spokesmen for African embassies are uninitiated in the ways of the Western press, unfamiliar with the organizations and individuals in the United States who take an interest in their countries' affairs. Approached by journalists to comment on breaking news stories that involve their nations, they often react quizzically, if not rudely, demand questions in writing and reply days or weeks later, or simply fail to respond to telephone messages. After the story in question appears, they write letters to the editor, complaining of mistreatment and parroting an official line. Occasionally, African press attachés band together and attempt to get more attention for their continent in the American media, but they are quickly squelched by their ambassadors. On the twentieth anniversary of the Organization of African Unity in 1983, for example, a number of African embassy spokesmen sought out their contacts in the Washington press corps and lined up about a dozen interviews with their ambassadors about the organization and its problems. At the last minute, however, all of the interviews were cancelled for fear that "controversial" questions would be asked. The ambassadors contented themselves, instead, by marking the occasion with a lavish reception at the Kenyan embassy residence in the far suburbs of Washington. The fact that Secretary of State George Shultz made a cameo appearance at the party assured it some mention in the social pages, but the American public certainly learned nothing new about Africa and its needs.

Some African embassies in Washington have come to be regarded as such unreliable sources of information about their own countries that the congressional subcommittees dealing with African affairs no longer bother to ask for their comments. Instead, congressional staff members call the various African desk officers at the State Department with their questions. Thus do Africans lose an available opportunity to try to influence the course of American policy. The desk officers for certain African countries—often relatively junior foreign service officers—tend to be besieged from the other side as well; their African "clients," ignorant of the American political process and independent sources of information, depend on them for the answers to even the most routine queries from their home governments (not to mention nongovernmental and personal matters). African governments, through the laziness or ineptitude of their own representatives, thereby lose the benefit of the many available alternatives to the official American point of view on the issues of the day.

It was in response to these problems that the U.S. Information Agency began a program of seminars in 1982 for African diplomats who seemed to be "especially unfamiliar" with the ways of Washington and the formulation of American foreign policy. Guest speakers were invited to explain "how the government works" and how to deal with the American press. The ambassadors were taken on a tour of several American cities they might otherwise never have seen during their time in the United States, because some of them have no travel budget. The idea was to demonstrate the domestic influences on foreign policy, as well as the internal "reverberations" of foreign policy decisions. The Congressional Black Caucus has also sought to reach out to African ambassadors in Washington and urge them to be more ambitious and aggressive in their contacts. After attending the "foreign affairs workshops" during the caucus's annual legislative weekend, a few ambassa-

dors began to regard the black congressmen as their court of first
resort on Capitol Hill, asking them to press for greater drought relief and other aid and to call attention to African issues.

The lack of a travel budget is the least of the problems of
some African ambassadors, who have to operate with woefully inadequate facilities. The chancery of the embassy of Lesotho, a
small mountain kingdom surrounded by South Africa, is a case in
point. Located two floors above a pizza parlor in the Dupont Circle section of Washington, it has threadbare green carpeting left
behind by a prior tenant, and often its telephones go unanswered
because of a shortage of personnel. The map in its waiting room
is a faded old Rand-McNally edition on which Zimbabwe is still
Rhodesia and Western Sahara still belongs to Spain. There 'M'Alineo Tau, whose last job was as the librarian of the national university of Lesotho, headed a staff of five people in a futile attempt
to get the American government to acknowledge her country's
existence.

Tau, who had long been associated with Lesotho's ruling party
and says she had previously "done errands for the government
overseas," was sent to Washington because she had experience
with Americans from her time as a student at the Pratt Institute
in New York. Her first task upon arrival in 1980 was to patch
things up with the State Department, which had become agitated
over the fact that Lesotho had suddenly established diplomatic
relations with the Soviet Union after years of behaving like a
solidly pro-Western ministate. (What Lesotho had done, in effect,
was to make a belated discovery that even a country its size could
play the superpowers off against each other.) She was treated to
an early dose of the diplomatic deep freeze, finding it almost impossible to get appointments and to talk with officials at the
Agency for International Development (AID) about her pet project concerning "women in development" and her country's particular needs for assistance.

Once she had mended the United States–Lesotho fences, however, Tau developed a special technique for getting help for her
country that made her a quiet legend in Washington. 'M'Alineo
Tau went on the prayer breakfast circuit, recruiting one church
group after another to extend private help to a place they'd never
heard of before. It all began in 1979, when she was invited to a
prayer meeting at the home of Representative Don Bonker, a

Democrat from Washington State, whom she had met at a conference. She found the people there surprisingly interested in hearing about Lesotho, and they in turn put her in touch with others.
By January 1981, in the last days of Jimmy Carter's presidency,
she found herself addressing a high-powered prayer breakfast in
Baltimore, which was also attended by Carter and a number of
black congressmen. "Since then, I've been going around with
the AME [African Methodist Episcopal] Church," Tau explained
proudly. During one weekend visit to Oklahoma City, for example, she persuaded a number of individual churches to make it
possible for several small villages in her country to have new wells
(and she made a local bishop an honorary consul of Lesotho in
the bargain). On a subsequent trip to Buffalo, she did the same.
Her church contacts helped her find an American company that
makes boreholes and the other necessary equipment for the wells,
and she persuaded businessmen to pay for the shipping. For the
embassy of Lesotho, there was no exchange of cash, no bureaucracy to deal with, and unlike many government-to-government
assistance programs, little prospect of "loss"—corruption—along
the way.* (Tau later lost her job after a coup in Lesotho.)

Many African embassies in Washington take an alternative
route to the promotion of their countries' interests. Instead of trying to beat the American system, they join it, in effect, by hiring
lawyers, lobbyists, and public relations experts. The services are
usually quite expensive, the results often mixed.

Public filings at the U.S. Justice Department, required under the Foreign Agents Registration Act of 1938, reveal that at
least sixteen independent sub-Saharan African countries employed
American agents during 1982. The people representing Malawi

* Another small African country that benefited from American church and
other private efforts was the poor, overpopulated Central African nation of
Burundi. The family of the American ambassador there in the early 1980s,
Frances D. Cook, a career foreign service officer who at thirty-four was the
youngest American ambassador in the world, took great interest in the welfare of the nation. Cook's parents, who lived in southern Florida, put together a slide show after visiting their daughter in Burundi and routinely
made presentations at local churches and service clubs. Afterward, they
would pass the hat on Burundi's behalf, raising as much as $300 in an eve-
ning and sending it off for use in development projects. A cousin of Cook's
set up a booth at a county fair in North Carolina that raised money to wrap
and send bandages to a rural hospital in Burundi. To get such a project
approved by AID might have taken years.

and Swaziland, among others, lobbied with the Office of the President's Special Trade Representative and the departments of State and Agriculture for an increase in their sugar quotas. One man reported receiving $12,500 for holding meetings or making phone calls on fourteen occasions on behalf of the Republic of Cape Verde. (His list included a "chance meeting" in an airport with a Massachusetts congressman who has many Cape Verdean constituents and a "brief encounter" with the assistant secretary of state for African affairs at a convention of the African Studies Association.) Another received $90,000 for helping arrange "for American companies to establish processing and manufacturing facilities in Somalia." Nigeria paid one Washington law firm $55,000 over a ten-month period, in part for assessing trends in U.S. policies, encouraging private investment in Nigeria, and monitoring congressional and administrative actions involving southern Africa—all jobs that one might have expected an embassy with forty-six diplomats (the largest African mission in Washington) to be able to do for itself. Nigeria also paid a Washington public relations firm $26,000 to arrange a single media reception in the capital.

From the euphemisms used in the official filings, it was clear that some African countries were paying tens of thousands of dollars a year for services that amounted to little more than the clipping of newspapers and magazines and the monitoring of television programs. Zaïre, however, paid a Washington law firm more than $140,000 to advise it on financial and commercial matters, to prepare for visits to the United States by President Mobutu Sese Seko and by some of his detractors, and "to encourage stronger relations between the U.S. and Zaïre." A New York law firm received $60,000 for helping Mobutu restructure the country's foreign debt, and a public relations firm there reported spending $550,000 to promote "public interest in Zaïre" and to persuade U.S. government officials to enact "favorable policies towards Zaïre." The latter firm subcontracted part of its work to another group of Washington lawyers, who, for $73,000, "communicated" with the State Department, the Pentagon, and members of the House of Representatives "regarding the mutual interests of the two governments." Even Mobutu's leading critic, his former prime minister, Nguza Karl-I-Bond, got into the act. From his exile in Belgium, Nguza paid $17,000 to a Boston firm to publicize "corruption and mismanagement" in Zaïre and to fight for a decrease in appropriations for American aid to that country.

Gabon, an oil-rich, underpopulated nation along the Atlantic coastline of central Africa, spent an enormous amount of money to have outsiders handle its affairs in the United States, yet it remained one of the countries least well-known to the American public. Long under French influence, the autocratic ruler of Gabon, President Omar Bongo, gradually became unhappy over the coverage of political and economic scandals in his country by the French media, and he resolved to diversify Gabon's international contacts. In one statement, Bongo compared Gabon to "a very beautiful girl whom all men wish to woo," and he proclaimed that "when France says, 'No, I cannot give you that,' we will go to other countries." Even before this new friendship offensive, which also extended to Canada and Japan, Gabon was spending a veritable fortune to increase American awareness of its attractive investment climate. In 1982 alone, it paid at least $800,000 to various American agents to do the job—for a country with a population of barely a million.

There are few countries anywhere in the world, however, that could claim to have equaled the extraordinary efforts of the tiny French-speaking West African nation of Togo to attract attention among Americans. Togo, which has two and a half times as many people as Gabon but a much smaller land area (56,600 square miles), no oil, and a treasury chronically in debt, spent more than half a million dollars on representation in the United States in 1982, most of it through the Washington public relations firm of David Apter & Associates, Inc.

The Apter firm put together a promotional effort so aggressive and so thorough that it won an international award for effective public relations. Asked to encourage tourism on the beaches of Lomé, Togo's capital, and in its varied interior, Apter first sent a crew to West Africa to produce a slick fourteen-minute color film about the country. Armed with the results, the firm persuaded ten major tour operators to market voyages to Togo in the United States and Canada. (Only three tour operators had done so previously.) Dealing with an issue that seemed to irritate both the tour operators and their customers, Apter also persuaded the Togolese government to become the first in West Africa to eliminate the requirement of visas for American and Canadian visitors. A young American woman with an interest in African affairs (the daughter of a former U.S. ambassador in the region) was dispatched to Togo to provide a constant flow of photographs and feature articles that could be distributed to the press, and she also helped arrange the itineraries of travel writers who flocked to Togo, at the Apter firm's suggestion, to write about its charms and attractions.

To reach an affluent audience of Americans who might be able to afford to take vacations in Togo, Apter arranged for all-expenses-paid trips to be offered during broadcast auctions used by American public television stations to raise money. (This cost the Togo government nothing extra, inasmuch as the plane fare, hotel rooms, and meals were donated by Air Afrique and one of Lomé's luxury hotels.)

David Apter's son Marc, who personally handles the Togo account, claims that the concrete benefits to that country of its promotional campaign far outweigh the $426,000 a year that it costs. During the first two years that Apter represented Togo, visits by Americans and Canadians increased by 30 percent, yielding at least $600,000 in new tourist revenues. The Apter firm also literally became the "Togo Information Office" in Washington—with a plaque attesting to that fact on its door—and worked assiduously to establish a favorable image for its client in the American press. By putting out fires as they arise, including stories about corruption in Togo, Apter functions as a semiofficial arm of the Togolese government and probably has a more effective impact on its international reputation than could the government in Lomé or its formal representatives in Washington. To the extent that this encourages greater private investment and further improves Togo's relations with the United States, it could also have a long-range positive effect on the country's stability and its standard of living.

Yet, in scope and sophistication, nothing could match the efforts of the South African government in the United States. In 1982, it spent well over two million dollars on legal and promotional work in Washington and New York. Its state-run tourist corporation alone spent more than a million dollars. One private U.S. firm arranged tour itineraries in South Africa for travel writers. Another set up a conference where South African business leaders could meet high officials of the American government, and a third

lobbied for the elimination of import restrictions on various products of the South African metals industry. One Washington consulting group charged $63,000 just for helping the South African
embassy select the names of people to be included in seminars
and on mailing lists, and another collected $35,000 for updating
"an educational kit, sound track, and wall map" for the South African consulate in New York. South Africa spent $625,000 for a
year's worth of services from a Washington law firm whose partners included John Sears, the former director of Ronald Reagan's
presidential campaign. Another law firm, headed by two prominent Democrats, former Florida Senator George Smathers and
former Missouri Congressman James Symington, looked out for
South Africa's interests on the other side of the political aisle; it
received $306,000 for monitoring and working against legislation
pending in Congress that would stiffen U.S. policy toward the
apartheid state. Smathers and Symington had no trouble getting
appointments with the Democratic congressional leadership for
visiting dignitaries from South Africa.

Separately, the South Africa Foundation, funded by business
interests in that country, spent almost $200,000 sponsoring South
African visitors to the United States and otherwise seeking "to
promote international understanding of South Africa's achievements, problems, and potential." One of the more effective, low-
key promoters of any country's interests in any other, the foundation routinely sends its staff on tours around the United States to
explain its belief that "change [in South Africa] is best effected in
a situation of economic and political stability." In a typical visit
to a midwestern state, a representative of the South Africa Foundation is interviewed on local radio stations, meets with prominent members of the local chambers of commerce, and addresses
world affairs councils. The impact is hard to measure precisely,
but the foundation seems to be uniquely successful at spreading
a sympathetic attitude toward the South African government at
the American grass roots.

In the past, the South Africans exercised another, surreptitious influence on the American political system, by funneling
money into campaigns to elect candidates who were favorable to
the Pretoria government and to defeat those who were not. In the
1970s, for example, secret contributions from funds maintained by
the South African Department of Information are thought to have

played an important role in the defeat of two Democratic senators who opposed the South African (and, at the time, American) position in Angola, John Tunney of California and Dick Clark of Iowa. Officially these activities have ended, but through intelligence agents and private organizations, the South African government has found other ways to direct funds to the American candidates of their choice.

In addition to the work done directly on behalf of the South African government, several of the "homelands" within that country that have accepted "independence" from Pretoria have representatives in Washington paid to try to persuade Americans of their legitimacy. One man, employed for $156,000 a year, actually issued visas to one of the homelands, the Transkei, along with giving speeches at various colleges, universities, and fraternal organizations. A colleague of his, a former employee of Ian Smith's white minority regime in Rhodesia, spent his time on Capitol Hill, discussing "Transkei's distinctive constitutional position and its strategic significance to Western defense." Up against all this, the efforts by the rest of Africa to put its views across fade into insignificance.

2

An Undistinguished History

THE FLEDGLING American republic of the late eighteenth century was not alone in its mishandling of its early contacts with Africa. It was simply farther away from the continent than were the European powers, poorer, less experienced at diplomacy, and disinclined to develop a colonial empire, having just been bruised by the colonial experience itself. It did not know what to expect or want from Africa.

For centuries—probably beginning in the early fifteenth—the Europeans carried on a lively slave trade along the West African coast, as the Arabs had done much earlier. The Portuguese, newly independent, arrived first and set about exploiting the gold and other treasures, not to mention the people. The British, French, and Dutch soon joined them. Eventually, the Portuguese managed to seize control of the East African coast from the Arabs and, for a time, had competition in that arena only from the Turks. But when Portugal temporarily lost its independence to Spain in 1580, the trade in African goods and people opened up to others, and the New World was an obvious market.

By 1618, just eleven years after the first settlement at James-
town and two years before the *Mayflower* sailed to Massachusetts, the first African slaves were introduced into Virginia. The
transatlantic business would grow steadily. The British were optimistic about its profitability; the New Royal African Company
was formed in 1672 and granted a monopoly on all trade from
Morocco to the Cape of Good Hope for a thousand years. (The
company actually lasted only a few years.) Over the centuries,
somewhere between ten and thirty million African people were
sold into slavery. One estimate is that more than two million of
them were imported into the British colonies in the West Indies
and North America between 1680 and 1786, and for some aboli-
tionists in the American colonies this became an early point of rebellion against the king.

The slave trade was the first of many African issues on which
the United States would display ambivalence and hypocrisy. It
was a question of moral scruples versus economic advantage, and
the latter often prevailed. Some states, including Rhode Island,
Massachusetts, New York, and Pennsylvania, passed specific laws
prohibiting their citizens from engaging in the slave trade, and in
1790 Congress voted by a narrow margin to assert its right to reg-
ulate slavery at the federal level. However, as late as the first
years of the nineteenth century, South Carolina (facing a constitutional deadline of 1808) permitted the importation of almost
forty thousand slaves from Africa into its borders. They arrived
in the holds of some two hundred ships that kept the port at
Charleston booming.

After a time, the slave trade—and the belated American decision to try to suppress it—became one pretext for a more or less
permanent U.S. presence on the West African coast. It was also
the reason for the creation, in the mid-1800s, of the "U.S. African
Squadron," which was to police ships carrying the American flag.
The Stars and Stripes was then a flag of convenience for shippers
who wanted to avoid stringent inspections (like the Panamanian
and Liberian flags in later days), and the U.S. flag was often used
to conceal the continuing traffic in slaves on Spanish and other
vessels. The squadron had little success. It was mostly left to the
British to patrol the Atlantic sea-lanes. They often embarrassed
the United States by capturing and hauling slave ships, flying the
American flag, into New York harbor.

Earlier American contact with Africa related to the new nation's clumsy attempts to establish foreign commerce. One of the first treaties the United States signed with any nation was with Morocco in 1786, and it is theoretically still valid. The treaty contained a pro forma military alliance—still suffering from the hostility of Britain, the United States was willing to make friends and allies wherever it could find them—but more important, it provided that American ships and commercial transactions were entitled to privileged treatment from Morocco. The main effect was the establishment of a U.S. consulate in Tangier, a safe haven for Americans compared to hostile European ports.*

The American government based in Philadelphia signed a similar, but less successful, treaty with Algiers in 1795, and the next year the United States began to pay an annual tribute to the pasha of Tripoli for the protection of its shipping from the pirates along the Barbary coast.† However, when the United States refused to increase its remittance to the pasha in 1801, it found itself fighting a slow and inconclusive war with Tripolitania; after it was over, the trouble with the pirates resumed. Even after winning a similar clash with Algiers in 1815, American officials had to pay bribes to protect U.S. shipping interests on the Mediterranean coast of Africa.

On the west coast things were easier. Europe began to recognize a special American interest there after 1816, when the American Colonization Society was formed for the purpose of repatriating impoverished freed slaves to Africa. A British settlement for freedmen (and others rescued in midpassage from slave ships) already existed at Freetown, Sierra Leone; the American group selected a somewhat less congenial site for what would become Liberia a few hundred miles down the coast. The first few dozen

---

* The American consul in Tangier for ten years beginning in 1793 was James Simpson; he was shunned by most of his European counterparts, was perpetually in debt, and had trouble paying off his bills from his meager budget. (One of Simpson's local contacts wrote directly to George Washington to try to collect his fees.)
† Thus "the shores of Tripoli" in the Marine Corps hymn, written in 1847, during the Mexican-American War, by an unknown soldier-poet. The payment of tribute, or bribes, to further American interests overseas was a controversial issue in the early days of the republic. "Millions for defense, but not one cent for tribute," said Congressman Robert Goodloe Harper of South Carolina, in a toast to John Marshall at a banquet in 1798.

emigrants arrived in 1821 and built a settlement at Cape Mesu-
rado. It would later be named Monrovia for President James Monroe, a supporter of the repatriation scheme.

Despite an Anglo-American agreement of 1815 that forbade
U.S. trade with British possessions in Africa, before long American
mercantile relationships in the region were flourishing. To serve
these interests, a consulate was established in the Portuguese-held
Cape Verde Islands in 1818, and four years later the French-
dominated island of Gorée, off the coast of Senegal, became an official American trading post. By 1834 the United States had a
consular agent at Bathurst in Britain's Gambia enclave, and the
U.S. dollar soon began to be accepted as legal tender in West African ports.

An American consulate had also been established at Cape
Town in 1799, primarily to deal with the New England whaling
ships operating in the area. Other American traders, restricted by
the British around the Cape, turned to East Africa. A roving
American consul with responsibility for the Indian Ocean signed
an agreement in 1833 with the sultan of Muscat, Oman, and Zanzibar, which led to the establishment of a formal American diplomatic post on Zanzibar, "the spice island." (It remained in business
almost continuously until 1979, when the Carter administration,
in an economy move, closed it down.) Zanzibar boomed as a center for American trade, especially for the sailor-merchants from
Salem, Massachusetts, but sensitive American feelings sometimes
hampered governmental relations. When the sultan cancelled a
public salute to the Stars and Stripes on the Fourth of July in
1850, the insulted American consul closed up shop. An American
warship was dispatched to the area and threatened to bombard
Zanzibar unless the sultan apologized. He did, and the consulate
soon reopened under more conciliatory management.

The Europeans and Americans conducted these commercial
activities almost exclusively along Africa's coasts. Little was known
of the continent's interior. An internationally renowned geogra-
pher, publishing his definitive map of Africa in 1802, could establish clear outlines only of Morocco and Algeria in the North, British
and Dutch settlements in the South, and the Portuguese possessions in the East and West; the middle was a blank. But exploration was something that Americans, imbued with a frontier spirit,

liked to do, or at least to sponsor. One of the earliest to become known for his U.S.-funded exploits was Paul Belloni du Chaillu, a Frenchman who grew up in Gabon and later became an American citizen. On the first of his "scientific" journeys to equatorial Africa in 1853, he discovered the gorilla. Confronted by doubting experts, he brought back a dead gorilla from his second excursion in 1863, during which he also encountered pygmies.

The best known of the men who carried American curiosity to Africa was Henry Morton Stanley. An Englishman who was orphaned and abandoned as a child, he became a naturalized American under the influence of his foster father, who came from New Orleans. Eventually he would fight on both sides of the American Civil War. Perhaps the most important assignment in Stanley's subsequent journalistic career came when James Gordon Bennett, publisher of the *New York Herald*, sent him in 1871 to find Dr. David Livingstone, the British medical-missionary-turned-explorer, who had not been heard from in some time. That expedition made Stanley the subject of fame and legend.* He later embarked on a trans-African journey that took 999 days and led to his book, *Through the Dark Continent* (a term that stuck and was still making Africans angry a century later). Stanley also worked for the International African Association of Belgian King Léopold II in the Congo for six years, and he led a relief expedition to find the German explorer known as Emin Pasha between 1887 and 1889.

Stanley's vivid dispatches from Africa, also published in the *Daily Telegraph* of London, had a profound impact on the attitudes and policies of the Americans and the British in the last part of the nineteenth century. It is possible that Stanley's behavior and his writings also influenced the feelings of Africans toward the West. He cut an absurd and sometimes grotesque figure, setting out into the jungle in military fashion with hundreds of men (whereas Livingstone had made do with only a few dozen on each of his trips). Stanley held himself aloof from the other Europeans and the Asians who accompanied him, but he had better, if paternalistic, relations with the African servants he took along. If any of his retinue stepped out of line, however, he punished

---

* On encountering another white man at Ujiji in Tanganyika, Stanley is reported to have said with cool detachment, "Dr. Livingstone, I presume?"

them severely, even to the point of hanging murderers on the spot.

Stanley has been variously described as extravagant, brave, ruthless, and foolishly urgent about his travels. Certainly he was presumptuous in his evaluation of the African peoples he encountered. He tended to categorize them as "fierce" or "docile" simply on the basis of the reception they gave his caravan of ragtag intruders. Yet Stanley sometimes did some good as he swept through the uncharted wilds, arguing for a halt to the Arab- and African-run slave trade and sometimes, by invitation, mediating in local intertribal disputes.

Stanley shared all the classic biases against Africa. "I do not think I was made for an African explorer," he said at one point early in his efforts, "for I detest the land most heartily." When he wrote about the people, his words were often tinged with haughtiness and superiority. "Our tame, mild manners were in striking contrast to their bullying, overbearing, and insolent demeanour," he wrote of an encounter on Lake Victoria with "the inebriates of Ugamba." Of another group, he said:

> I skirmish in their streets, drive them pell-mell into the woods beyond, and level their ivory temples; with frantic haste I fire the huts, and end the scene by towing the canoes into midstream and setting them adrift.

On one occasion Stanley observed that "Natives are so wild here . . . they will not stay to be questioned, they are only to be captured by stratagem and made friends by force."

Ultimately, Stanley would portray himself as a friend and promoter of Africa. He argued that the continent's riches and resources should be tapped, that God had intended that Africa "should be reserved until the fullness of time for something higher than a nursery for birds and a store-place for reptiles." He was deeply disappointed when he failed in the late 1870s to convince British government and business figures to become more involved in Africa.

It was then that Stanley, desperate to have some role in the great scramble for Africa, turned to Belgium. He entered the personal service of King Léopold, who regarded the large Congo basin (almost one-fourth the size of the United States) as his private property. Stanley signed treaties on the king's behalf, established outposts in the bush, and openly competed with the aggressive French explorer Count Savorgnan de Brazza. But in November 1884, Stanley turned up as an adviser to the American delegation at the Berlin Conference, which was convened, at German and Belgian instigation, to settle disputes over the Congo. Ultimately, that meeting carved up much of Africa and distributed the pieces among the European powers; it created new entities out of unrelated territories and tribes—a convenience for the colonists, a source of future trouble for the Africans themselves.

The United States played two roles at the Berlin Conference. Publicly it took the high road. The chief American delegate, John Adams Kasson, a diplomat-politician from Iowa, proposed that war be outlawed in much of Africa and that all African disputes be submitted to an international court of arbitration. He also suggested that the rights of African people to "dispose freely of themselves and their hereditary territory" be respected universally, and he advocated the prohibition of alcoholic beverages in Africa, just as he had in the United States. (That proposal had a certain irony to it, inasmuch as one of the earliest American exports to Africa was rum.) The other American role was played out behind the scenes, where Stanley and another member of the U.S. delegation, Henry Shelton Sanford, who had also been in the employ of King Léopold, dealt with the Europeans' political and territorial disputes. Not surprisingly, they saw to it that the United States was on Belgium's side on most of the issues. This seemingly uncritical pro-Belgian attitude engendered criticism from Congress and the American public, especially since Kasson and Sanford represented a lame-duck Republican administration. Grover Cleveland's election as president in 1884 doomed American accession to the treaty that Kasson and Sanford had signed in Berlin. The United States never formally ratified the results of the Berlin Conference, but Washington did soon recognize a new "independent" Congo state (still under Belgian control).

It was not long before the forced labor, official thievery, and other atrocities of Léopold's administration in the Congo became known internationally. There were those in the United States who were embarrassed that their country had been pulled into the orbit of an ugly colonialism. From this, many drew the lesson that America should stay out of things that did not directly concern it. The situation in Africa seemed to be one; the continent did not appear to be a place where American goodwill and high principle could be usefully brought to bear.

After one last grandiose voyage to Africa, Henry Morton Stanley decided his adopted country was hopeless. He gave up his American citizenship and became a British subject again. He was knighted and elected to Parliament, but denied his last wish, which was to be buried next to Livingstone in Westminster Abbey. The reason given was that Stanley was not important enough to deserve that honor.

While the United States observed from a distance, the European powers continued to fill in the African colonial map at the end of the nineteenth and beginning of the twentieth centuries. They adjusted boundaries, traded favors, and recognized each other's spheres of influence without much regard for the sensibilities or needs of the Africans. Germany established its control over Tanganyika, Ruanda-Urundi, Togoland, part of the Cameroons, and South-West Africa. Italy took over Eritrea and its own chunk of Somalia (other parts of "Somaliland" going to France and Britain). The British extended their authority over Gold Coast and parts of Nigeria, and they sent settlers out to East and South-Central Africa—Uganda, Kenya, Rhodesia, and Nyasaland. The French, meanwhile, gained dominance in Dahomey, Ivory Coast, and Madagascar, and as they expanded into the Sahara and Sahel, took over ancient African cities such as Timbuktu. The Portuguese consolidated their borders in East and West Africa, while the Belgians struggled to improve their reputation in the Congo.

Whether colonialism had a positive or a negative effect on Africa in the long run is an argument that may never be settled. What is development to some is exploitation to others. Mining and other enterprises removed valuable resources, but they also established a wage economy and, in some instances, spread wealth more evenly among the people. Years later, Americans would question the merits of colonial rule. President Franklin D. Roosevelt, after two wartime visits to Gambia, observed in 1944 that "the natives are five thousand years back of us." Where did he place the blame? "For every dollar that the British . . . have put into Gambia, they have taken out ten. It's just plain exploitation of those people. There is no education whatsoever." But his distant cousin who had occupied the presidency a generation earlier had not felt the same way. "On the whole the African regions which during the past century have seen the greatest cruelty, degradation, and suffering, the greatest diminution of population," said Theodore Roosevelt in 1909, "are those where native control has been unchecked. The advance has been made in the regions that have been under European control or influence."

Theodore Roosevelt was second to none in his condescension toward Africans—"the porters are strong, patient, good-humored savages, with something childlike about them that makes one really fond of them," he wrote. Yet, as a public figure, he gave Africa a kind of respectability in America simply by going there. Roosevelt thought Africa was a good place for missionaries, as well as adventurers like himself, and the turn of the century saw an increase in U.S. missionary activity, including many black emissaries from the African Methodist Episcopal (AME) Church. The Americans translated the Bible into African languages and occasionally pressured colonial administrators to have a more benign attitude toward the local population.

Americans were beginning to pay attention to events in Africa, and when the Portuguese authorities seized a railroad line owned by an American, there was an uproar. During the Anglo-Boer war in South Africa, fought between 1899 and 1902, many Americans spoke out about the need for self-determination and the outrages of British rule there. However, the objects of their concern were not the subjugated Africans, but the Boers, the descendants mostly of Dutch settlers who had first come to South Africa in the seventeenth century, who had their own legitimate grievances. American consular officers and journalists working in the area displayed open pro-Boer sympathies—something that the Afrikaner people (as the non-British whites in South Africa came to be known) would remember decades later, when they looked for international support. Nonetheless, it was only after the British victory in the Boer War that American investment in South Africa became substantial. The American presence in the South African economy would fluctuate—after World War II it would be more significant—but beginning in the early twentieth century the white majority in the United States began to have important links, public and private, with the white minority who ruled South Africa.

The idea spread that there were social, intellectual, and emotional ties between these two countries where white pioneers had conquered a hostile, dangerous frontier.

Two other nations in sub-Saharan Africa, which happened to be ruled by minorities within their black populations, also developed early special relationships with America. They were the only two that were never European colonies, Liberia and Ethiopia.

The American ties with Liberia were complicated and tortuous. That country owed its very existence to the well-intentioned whites who formed the American Colonization Society for the purpose of repatriating freed slaves. When Liberia declared its independence (from no one in particular) and drew up a constitution (modeled on the American one) in 1847, the State Department served notice on the British Foreign Office that this new nation was of "peculiar interest to the United States," which was "very unwilling to see it despoiled of its territory." Yet, while Britain and France granted immediate diplomatic recognition to Liberia, the United States waited fifteen years, until 1862. (Congress had been reluctant to recognize a black republic, given the possible domestic political repercussions.) When Liberia had financial problems—as it often did, in part because of corruption— Washington was quicker to advise than to help. Finally, in 1909, an American commission went to Monrovia and reported back that the United States was "the only country which can give [the Liberians] effective aid." But having lost 44 percent of its original territory to the British (in Sierra Leone) and the French (in Ivory Coast) between 1847 and 1910, Liberia wanted more than aid; it sought an American guarantee of its independence and territorial integrity to back up the advice on its foreign and domestic policies.

American officers eventually did go to Liberia, and U.S. warships anchored off the coast to help that country deal with border disputes. Beginning in 1915, the United States assisted in putting down bush revolts against the government in Monrovia. Three years later, having made some internal reforms and pledging others, the Liberian government got a promise of a $5 million American loan and additional U.S. advisers. But what President Woodrow Wilson had agreed to, his successor, Warren G. Harding, was unable to deliver. Then, as in later years, Congress was sensitive on aid questions; after heated debate, the Liberian loan

died in a Senate committee. The Liberians received temporary
help from American bankers, but finally they turned to the millionaire industrialist Harvey S. Firestone and made a business deal
for the production of rubber that would permanently alter the
country's landscape and economy.

There were to be plenty of other problems between the
United States and Liberia, even a four-year suspension of relations
over financial and political issues (including evidence of a system
of forced labor bordering on slavery run by the Liberian elite).
However, by the mid-1930s Washington was again protecting the
regime in Monrovia. In 1936, in the midst of the appeasement
period in Europe, the Roosevelt administration vetoed a British
government suggestion that Nazi Germany be allowed to take
over the administration of Liberia. That transfer had been proposed as a way to satisfy Hitler's desire for new colonies to com-
pensate for what Germany had lost after World War I.

Ethiopia, also known as Abyssinia, was another matter. An
ancient kingdom, it had a reputation for uncanny strength and independence, and in 1896 it redeemed that reputation by defeating
an Italian expeditionary force in a battle at Adowa. The Italian
army lost half its power in that clash, and Ethiopia came to be
known in many corners of the world, including the United States,
as a stalwart defender of black people everywhere; some black
churches in Africa and America added the word "Ethiopian" to
their names. An "Ethiopianist Movement" swept through some
African Christian sects, including in South Africa. Under its influence, African churches asserted their independence from blatantly
racist European missionaries. (Later Ethiopia would become a
center of pan-Africanism, and eventually, the headquarters of the
Organization of African Unity.)

Theodore Roosevelt authorized the first official American
diplomatic visit to Ethiopia in 1903. The American delegation, led
by the consul-general in Marseilles, took nearly two months to
reach the new capital of Addis Ababa, but it was dazzled by the
court of Emperor Menelik when it got there. Menelik proved to
be a shrewd negotiator, well aware of events in the world despite
his physical isolation from them. (News reached him in this manner: Reuters dispatches received in Aden were typed and sent by
weekly boat to Djibouti, then by train to Dire Dawa, where they
were translated into French and taken by messenger to Addis.)

He was also an obsequiously gracious host, sending back to Roosevelt two eight-foot-long elephant tusks and two lion cubs.

Subsequent American dealings with Ethiopia were symbolic of official Washington's indifference toward Africa. Despite the expanding U.S. commerce with the country, the State Department maintained only on-again, off-again representation there. A new commercial treaty was signed with Menelik's son and successor in 1914. Amazingly, however, President Wilson forgot to put it into effect, and the treaty was found in a drawer at the State Department in 1920, by which time it had expired. Ras Tafari, at first regent for the royal Ethiopian court and later its ruler as Emperor Haile Selassie I, was initially hostile to American companies that wanted to prospect for oil and do other business in Ethiopia. But he soon saw the light, and beginning in the 1920s and 1930s, he sought a closer relationship that would include American arms and military advisers. Congress resisted the embrace, at one point denying President Calvin Coolidge the appropriation necessary to open a legation in Addis Ababa.

In 1935, Benito Mussolini sent his army and air force into Ethiopia, to avenge the humiliation at Adowa of four decades earlier and to satisfy fascist Italy's dream of a new colony with great agricultural potential. The Italian assault was brutal and indiscriminate; the invaders bombed hospitals, persecuted missionaries, and rounded up educated Ethiopians. Despite the pleas of the chief American diplomat on the scene, Cornelius van H. Engert, for an angry reaction from Washington, the State Department instead followed the advice of its ambassador in Rome and tried to avoid offending Mussolini. Engert was reprimanded by Secretary of State Cordell Hull when he formally expressed U.S. outrage over the Italians' execution of Ethiopian resisters outside the gates of the American legation. The United States embargoed arms deliveries to both sides (thus helping the Italians, who had plenty of other sources), but it would not participate in any other sanctions against Italy. As the Italians, using poison gas, marched on Addis Ababa, it was the British who evacuated Haile Selassie, and instructions from Washington advised American representatives in Europe to discourage him from seeking refuge in the United States. Still, many Americans were moved by the emperor's dramatic plea for help before the League of Nations in Geneva, and the State Department resisted subtle Italian efforts to obtain American recognition of its African "empire."

When Haile Selassie triumphantly returned to Addis in 1941, he did so with British help and American blessings. Those blessings, later converted into substantial aid, would be a significant factor for the rest of his reign, which the United States endorsed without critical examination.

But for those special cases, the United States did not worry about events in Africa during the early years of the twentieth century. The First World War, of course, had profound African implications for the European belligerents—Germany lost all of its colonies, to Britain, France, Belgium, and South Africa (a grievance that would figure in the rise of Hitler)—but not for the United States. Woodrow Wilson's "Fourteen Points," enunciated at the end of the war, with all their talk about self-determination, seemed to be defined as not applying to Africa and other parts of the non-Western world. (There was a "Pan-African" delegation to the Versailles Peace Conference, led by the black American philosopher and activist W. E. B. DuBois, but it had little effect.)

Wilson was instrumental in preventing South Africa from simply annexing South-West Africa after the war, but otherwise he showed little interest in Africa. At home, Wilson was never particularly sensitive to the needs and attitudes of blacks. He initiated, and declined to modify, a system of segregating black and white employees in the federal civil service. When a delegation of blacks protested, he felt insulted and insulted them back. Wilson also sent an emissary to France during World War I to warn black Americans fighting there, who made up 13 percent of the U.S. forces, not to get any ideas about equal treatment with whites on their return.

Although the United States never ratified the Versailles treaty or joined the League of Nations, it did subscribe to the Convention of Saint-Germain-en-Laye, negotiated at the same time. That document reaffirmed the need to suppress slavery in Africa, guaranteed freedom of religion and missionary activity there, and offered protection to all religious and charitable institutions "which aim at leading the natives in the path of progress and civilization." Most important, it endorsed once again the rights of the colonial powers who had won the war to their slices of Africa.

Marcus Garvey held his "Convention of Negroes" in New York in 1920, where he was elected "Provisional President of Africa." Garvey, a Jamaican, had come to the United States four years earlier, preaching black pride and promoting a new back-to-Africa movement. His slogan was "Africa for the Africans"; but although he recruited millions of black Americans to join his United Negro Improvement Association and collected $10 million in small contributions for his effort, Garvey failed to get any significant number of people to move back to the continent of their origins. (He was himself later deported to Jamaica, after spending two years in jail on a mail fraud conviction and having his sentence commuted by President Calvin Coolidge.)

Apart from Garvey's oratory, and the various controversies surrounding Liberia, Americans scarcely heard about Africa during the interwar period. To be sure, the tone of what little popular comment there was began to change. "There are historic, humanitarian, and material reasons in favor of [American] association in any international effort to promote African welfare," wrote Raymon Leslie Buell in *Foreign Affairs* in the autumn of 1927. He argued for a greater American presence in Africa and pointedly observed that "it will be futile if the white governments in Europe and America attempt to stamp out the Negro's aspirations."

In 1930, the United States had three full-scale diplomatic posts south of the Sahara, in Addis Ababa, Monrovia, and Pretoria, plus a consulate-general in Cape Town. There were consulates in three other South African cities (Johannesburg, Durban, and Port Elizabeth), plus Dakar, Lagos, Nairobi, and Lourenço Marques, the capital of Portuguese Mozambique. Because of recriminations in Congress over U.S. participation in World War I and because of a resurgence of isolationist sentiments among the American public, Washington was generally content to follow the lead of its European friends on Africa policy. Despite assurance in the Saint-Germain convention and other treaties that the United States had equal commercial rights with its allies, American trade with Africa declined again.

But no sooner had World War II begun than American officials suddenly recognized Africa's strategic significance. The decision of French Equatorial Africa to stand with Charles de Gaulle's Resistance, rather than following the lead of the collaborationist government based in Vichy, opened up significant transport routes across Africa to Egypt for the Allies. "Not one American in fifty thousand has any idea of the potential strength of Africa," wrote Eugene Wright in *Harper's* in December 1941; he warned that German control of the continent would be a disaster, and he called Dakar, which was in Vichy hands, the "key to Africa." (Earlier that year, elaborating peace terms with France and looking ahead to the conquest of Britain, Nazi Germany proposed taking over the British dependencies of Nigeria, Gold Coast, and Sierra Leone, and adding them to the existing French African empire as a vast German sphere of influence.) Another analysis, published in 1943, observed that "the combination of powers able to hold Africa will be well on the way to ultimate world victory." Africans were themselves convinced on that point, and various English-speaking African colonies and protectorates, from Gold Coast to Uganda to Basutoland, collected substantial sums of money for the Allied cause, especially to pay for aircraft.

American officials, unknowledgeable about a place they still considered "the dark continent," had a great deal of catching up to do. Secretary Hull was especially weak in his grasp of geography, and he frequently made embarrassing public errors in the pronunciation of African place names. But gradually, U.S. diplomacy—and intelligence—became more proficient in Africa, especially in the Arab North, where an Allied invasion was an important turning point and subsequent battles were crucial to the defeat of Germany. The United States also made commitments, such as the construction of Robertsfield, a major airport, in Liberia, that opened the way for a more lasting American presence on the continent. By sponsoring Liberian and Ethiopian participation in the emerging United Nations, Washington also set an important precedent and sent a clear message to the rest of the world.

The Atlantic Charter, issued by Franklin D. Roosevelt and Winston Churchill in 1941, like other grand pronouncements before it, proclaimed the right of all peoples to choose the form of government under which they would live. Roosevelt seemed to intend that this and his own declaration of the "Four Freedoms"—freedom of speech and expression, freedom of religion, freedom from want, and freedom from fear—apply to the developing world along with the rest. As Cordell Hull put it in 1942, "We have always believed . . . that all peoples, without distinction of race, color, or religion, who are prepared and willing to accept the responsibilities of liberty, are entitled to its enjoyment." That language left a few definitions to be worked out.

By the end of World War II, the United States was irrevocably involved in Africa. The eighteenth-century days of bartering *merikani* cloth for gum, palm, and other raw materials were long gone, and so was the period when American government representatives in Africa could be part-time, free-lance troubleshooters. It was time to formulate a policy toward Africa, and to recognize the fact that Africans expected America to help them survive and prosper in the postwar world.

The war had brought a dramatic increase in the number of black Africans who traveled and served overseas. What they saw— including black Americans organizing to demand equality—gave them ideas. Some of these Africans obtained an advanced education abroad, many in the United States. Education only intensified aspirations of self-determination and independence. America, with its own history of rebellion against a colonial power and its widely promulgated gospel of democracy, was perceived as a natural supporter, even a leader, of those aspirations.

Franklin Roosevelt, had he lived past the end of the war, probably would have tried to follow through on the promises of the Atlantic Charter. Even while the wartime alliance with Britain was still the overriding principle of American foreign policy and Anglo-American unity was a fundamental need, FDR criticized the British for their record in Africa. Roosevelt held out the example of the American administration of the Philippines as something the British might follow—encouraging self-government by gradual steps—and he urged American blacks to take a special interest in the African situation. (One of his unspoken motives may have been to defuse black concern about civil rights at home.) He also suggested that an early postwar task of the United Nations be to inspect Europe's colonies and evaluate their progress toward self-determination.

That suggestion upset America's wartime allies and also ran into opposition in the United States. Churchill rejected it out-of-hand as meddlesome and foolish. For other British, and especially for the French, it revived old suspicions about American imperial and commercial designs in Africa—as if nations that became free with American encouragement would somehow automatically fall under American influence. European leaders were also horrified by Roosevelt's attitude because they were counting on the continued exploitation of colonial resources as part of their own postwar economic recovery. Roosevelt's unofficial "assistant president" for the home front, James Byrnes, a former governor of South Carolina who was conservative on racial issues, had his own doubts, too; he felt skeptical of Liberia and contemptuous toward the rest of black Africa.

After Harry Truman succeeded to the presidency on Roosevelt's death, Byrnes was named secretary of state and U.S. policy in Africa was brought back in line with European thinking. Truman tended to follow Churchill's lead, and Dean Acheson, the man who later became Truman's secretary of state, saw Africa as a pawn in the Cold War, but one that was Western Europe's job to control. In the classic struggle between *realpolitik* and idealism, *realpolitik* was the winner. The United States would feel no breeze from the "winds of change" blowing through the African colonies until or unless Europe sent a weather report.

In a sense, sub-Saharan Africa was better off out of the limelight during the early part of the Cold War period, when—by comparison to the dramatic events in Europe and Asia—African affairs were thought by American policymakers to have little strategic significance. Once the doctrine of "containment" came to the fore in the early 1950s, Africa's distance from the Soviet Union and its satellites made the continent seem irrelevant. For the moment, geography protected African nations from becoming an arena of East-West struggle.*

Dwight D. Eisenhower, in his first inaugural address in 1953, did not mention Africa. His State Department, under John Foster Dulles, cut U.S. diplomatic representation in Africa by nearly 40 percent. Africa (like Central America) traditionally had been a place of nonpreference in the foreign service, and this was re-

---

* The only exception to this new phase of Washington's benign neglect of Africa was a quiet one: a mutual defense assistance agreement signed with Ethiopia in 1953, which provided for modernization of Haile Selassie's army and development of an air force. It also gave the United States a base in Asmara, on the Eritrean high plateau, for the conduct of electronic intelligence. (The Allies had encouraged Ethiopia to annex the Italian colony of Eritrea at the end of the war.)

flected in the diplomats stationed there. When Democratic statesman Chester Bowles toured Africa in 1955, he was alarmed by
what he found in the U.S. diplomatic missions; among the fewer
than fifty American representatives in all of colonial Africa, he
noted, almost none had "a significant background in African affairs." Many of them seemed to Bowles to be racially biased and
considered their responsibilities to consist only of day-to-day contacts with the colonial administrations. They neglected people
who might be inclined to challenge the status quo. Out of four
consulates he visited, Bowles found that only one had ever had an
African to dinner. Of 680 people registered to borrow books from
the U.S. Information Agency library in Leopoldville at the time,
only 12 were Africans. The library had just 280 books in French,
compared to 4,020 in English, although the educated Congolese
generally spoke French (or perhaps Flemish).

The pool of Americans eligible to serve knowledgeably in
Africa was small. Indeed, the first African Studies program at any
American university began only in 1948 at Northwestern; eight
years later there were only two others, at Boston University and
Howard University in Washington. At that time, African studies
was regarded as a field of low academic prestige for American
scholars, thought to be attractive only to those who could not
compete well in the more mainstream areas of international relations.

American aid to Africa, though channeled through the colonial powers, did increase substantially in the mid-1950s. Whereas
loans and grants to Africa reached a total of $120.3 million for the
years 1953–57, for fiscal year 1958 alone the figure was about $100
million, and more than twice that figure in 1960, the last year of
the Eisenhower administration. Congressional interest in Africa
finally began to develop, too, led by Democratic Senator Theodore
Francis Green of Rhode Island and Republican Representative
Frances P. Bolton of Ohio. In 1958, both houses of Congress established African affairs subcommittees. The first chairman in the
Senate was an enterprising politician who knew a good issue when
he saw it, John F. Kennedy of Massachusetts.*

---

* The chairmanship of the African Affairs Subcommittee of the Senate Foreign Relations Committee came to be regarded as a mixed blessing. Albert
Gore of Tennessee, who succeeded Kennedy in that slot, gave it up in 1963

Also in 1958, the State Department established a separate bureau to handle African affairs. (In the same week the Soviet foreign ministry set up an Africa bureau, too.) Responsibility for Africa had previously been divided up and traded back and forth between the State Department's European and Near East bureaus. The achievement of a separate bureaucratic entity was a symbolic victory for those few who had struggled for years to obtain recognition of Africa's significance and potential. It also put the American dilemma over decolonization into sharper focus. Aides to Dulles had been acknowledging openly that America felt pulled in two directions, but now the pull on Africa's side—on behalf of what the Africanists considered the inevitable forces of self-determination—would be stronger than before.

There was already substantial pressure on Africa's behalf from outside government. The African-American Institute began to publish *Africa Report* in 1955 to help fill in the gaps in public awareness. Paul Nitze, widely respected for his roles in government and business and later a key player in the debate over U.S.-Soviet arms control, wrote in 1955 that

> the test of a nation's greatness is whether it can adjust from a position where it once disposed to a position where it must deal with problems. . . . At one time the West disposed with respect to Africa. Today it is necessary to deal with Africa. The basic challenge is whether the West can do this imaginatively and constructively.

One prominent foreign policy commentator, Harold Isaacs, complained in a special issue of *Saturday Review* devoted to Africa in 1953 that the European colonizers had driven Africans in such places as Kenya and South Africa "to react with desperation." Isaacs argued that the longer the United States displayed ambiva-

---

out of concern that his interest in Africa could become a liability in his reelection campaign the following year. Thereupon Mike Mansfield of Montana took the chairmanship, because no one else wanted it. That was still true a decade later, when Dick Clark of Iowa, who knew nothing about Africa, became chairman as a relatively junior senator. The more he learned, the more he became involved in African issues, and resentment over that involvement (not to mention South African aid to his opponent) was a clear factor in his failure to be elected in 1978. When his successor as Africa chairman, George McGovern of South Dakota, was targeted by conservative groups for defeat in 1980, his positions on African issues were also part of the bill of particulars.

lence on these matters, the more it would simply be assumed to have taken the side of white supremacy:

> The political, social, economic, and moral ramifications of the gathering crisis in Africa are immense. But it should at least be clear that the days of European empire in Africa are coming to an end. . . . If not out of high moral need, then at least out of the crudest kind of self-interest, Western men had better be asking themselves if they are serving their own survival by what they do in Africa or assisting in their own destruction.

Perhaps the greatest challenge to American patience and understanding was the concept of "nonalignment" in the developing world, which was enjoying particular popularity in Africa. One argument on behalf of development aid that was widely understood and accepted in Congress was that the United States had to prevent the emerging nations from "going communist." Now the Africans were joining others and saying they did not want to choose sides in the global struggle, because their feelings of nationalism deserved to be understood in their own right. Many Americans responded by saying, in effect, "If you're not for us, you're against us." But as Melville Herskovits, head of the African Studies program at Northwestern, warned in a landmark report to the Senate Foreign Relations Committee in 1959, "Friendship cannot be bought; we might remember that this is as true in the case of Russian aid, extended for political and military reasons, as it is in the case of our own aid." Herskovits stressed that "it is essential for us not to confuse communism and African nationalism," and he decried the American tendency to count the Communists or try to calculate Communist influence at every African gathering.

The event that became a watershed of modern African history was the transformation of the British colony Gold Coast into the independent nation of Ghana in 1957. Ghana was not especially large in geographical area or population, unusually wealthy in resources, or in the long run a likely power in African politics; but the nation demonstrated, initially at least, that independence was possible without disaster. When its nationalist leader and first prime minister, Kwame Nkrumah, appeared on the cover of

Life magazine, it was a sign that Africa had arrived. Ghana was a symbol and an inspiration to other African colonies that sought independence, and Nkrumah quickly became a renowned world figure. In his opening address to the All-African People's Conference in Accra the next year, he proclaimed that Africa wanted "to develop our own community and an African personality. Others may feel that they have evolved the very best way of life, but we are not bound, like slavish imitators, to accept it as our mold."

Vice-President Richard M. Nixon attended the Ghanaian independence ceremonies in 1957 and seemed to understand the issues at stake in Africa. "The importance of Africa to the strength and stability of the free world is too great for us to underestimate," he said upon his return from a trip that included visits to Liberia, Ethiopia, and Sudan (which had achieved independence from its unusual status as an Anglo-Egyptian condominium in 1956). Nixon viewed Africa through a Cold War lens, but he presciently observed in his report to President Eisenhower that African trade unions were an important point of contact and object of concern for the West. He urged American efforts to cultivate the union leaders and other potential statesmen of independent Africa.

Another set of observations that were crucial to American policy in the period came from Julius C. Holmes, a senior career official in the State Department. After traveling extensively in Africa during 1957, Holmes reported that independence would come much sooner and more widely than U.S. policy at the time anticipated, and he recommended that the United States put pressure on Britain and France to accept the inevitable. "The greatest factor making for instability" in Africa, he predicted, would be modernization, the process of abandoning tribal folkways and methods in favor of the mechanisms of statehood. Holmes pointed to the widespread distrust of Africans toward whites, and he predicted violent explosions in South Africa. (Herskovits would echo the theme two years later when he told the Senate that "for the newly self-governing peoples of the world, as for those who remain under tutelage, colonialism is something a white nation does to a darker people.") Holmes called for more careful planning of American policy in Africa, in order to "avoid the need to engage in expensive and inefficient rescue operations."

Africa was achieving greater prominence among Americans. John Gunther, who had already written major works about Europe, Asia, and Latin America, produced a tome on Africa in 1955 that became a best seller. *Inside Africa* contained many misperceptions and mispredictions, but this survey of the continent greatly increased the amount of popular literature about Africa accessible to the nonspecialist. (Many chapters were published in advance in *Reader's Digest.*) Only two American newspapers of general circulation, the *New York Times* and the *Christian Science Monitor*, routinely covered Africa during the 1950s, but other journalists began to be attracted to the continent.

Still, for all the expanding awareness and the warnings about the future, American policy through the late 1950s followed the lead of the Europeans. In 1958, Charles de Gaulle, newly in power in France, conducted a referendum in the French colonies in Africa; the choice was between continued association with France or immediate independence. Only Guinea opted for the latter course. The French, furious with Guinean nationalist leader Sekou Touré, departed virtually overnight, even pulling the telephones out of the walls. De Gaulle threatened to leave NATO if Washington recognized the new government in Conakry, but he had nothing to worry about. The United States ignored Touré's pleas for assistance, and so he appealed to the Soviet Union instead. Moscow was only too glad to help.

Nineteen-sixty was known as "the year of Africa." In a short space of time, seventeen more African colonies became independent. On a single day, September 20, sixteen African countries were admitted to the United Nations, substantially increasing the volume, if not necessarily the effectiveness, of the continent's voice in world affairs.

During its last months in office, the Eisenhower administration tried to catch up with events. Speaking to the United Nations General Assembly just two days after so many new African members had been admitted, Eisenhower proposed a five-point program for Africa—including a pledge by all UN members to respect the Africans' right to self-determination; a UN effort to help African countries "maintain their security without wasteful and dangerous competition in armaments"; UN help with long-term modernization efforts; a UN-sponsored effort to improve education in Africa; and support for the UN role in the unfolding Congo crisis.

Eisenhower emphasized the need to develop multilateral rather than bilateral aid to developing countries—an idea whose time had not yet come—but other decisions he made that year were disheartening to those Africans who had high hopes of America. He chose, for example, not to name an individual ambassador to each of the newly independent African states. Coming from a country with the vast resources of the United States, this was taken as an insult, a pronouncement that these little-known African nations with exotic names and uncertain leaders did not deserve full rank in the world family. In the meantime, Eisenhower's aides worried about the importance of South Africa's strategic minerals to American defense and made agreements that would assure access to them; they also arranged for a tracking station for the new American space program to be located safely in South Africa. (United States–South African cooperation on space-related matters has continued ever since, with a brief interruption after the Apollo missions ended in 1975.)

In December 1960, the lame-duck Eisenhower administration abstained on a general vote in the United Nations condemning colonialism. The American vote was withheld at the last-minute request of British Prime Minister Harold Macmillan, who was himself edging many British colonies toward independence at the time. The United States seemed at worst duplicitous, or at best confused. After that symbolic parting shot from Eisenhower, the Africans were especially pleased with the arrival of John F. Kennedy in the White House in 1961.

Kennedy had a reputation for being on Africa's side. As early as July 1957, he had taken the bold step of supporting Algerian independence from France, warning that colonies "are like fruit that cling to the tree only till they ripen." His speech on the issue, entitled "Facing Facts on Algeria," scarcely attracted attention at home, but it created a major sensation overseas. African nationalists immediately adopted JFK as a hero, and few of them considered a visit to Washington complete without a call on his Senate office. Although Kennedy only convened three meetings of the Senate African Affairs Subcommittee during his year and a half as chairman, the fact that such a prominent figure would take on that assignment played well not only among Africans, but also among

American blacks. (Indeed, it may have helped him win the black votes that were important in his victory over Richard Nixon in the 1960 presidential election.)

Kennedy advocated a new, progressive policy on African issues. Addressing the American Society of African Culture in June 1959, he spoke of Africa as "a land of rich variety—of noble and ancient cultures . . . of vital and gifted people." Kennedy mocked Nixon's statement that the United States should be "winning the battle for men's minds" in Africa. He asserted that "the people of Africa are more interested in development than they are in doctrine. They are more interested in achieving a decent standard of living than in following the standards of either East or West." That could have been Kwame Nkrumah talking. A few months later, speaking at Nebraska Wesleyan University in Lincoln, Nebraska, Kennedy proposed the establishment by the United States of an Educational Development Fund for Africa. (All told, there are 479 references to Africa in the index to his 1960 campaign speeches.)

In his first foreign aid message to Congress as president, in March 1961, Kennedy warned that many new nations in Africa and elsewhere in the developing world were under "communist pressure." But he insisted that

> the fundamental task of our foreign aid program in the 1960s is not negatively to fight communism [but] to help make a historical demonstration that in the twentieth century, as in the nineteenth—in the southern half of the globe as in the north—economic growth and political democracy can develop hand in hand.

Beyond the rhetoric, Kennedy did change American policy in Africa. Total economic assistance to Africa more than doubled between the last year of the Eisenhower administration and the first year of Kennedy's reign, when it reached $459.6 million. It was not just direct loans and grants that went up, but also allocations of "Food for Peace" aid and financing guaranteed by the Export-Import Bank. By 1962 Kennedy would be increasing military aid to Africa as well.

Kennedy named ambassadors to all the independent African countries, and as assistant secretary of state for African affairs he selected G. Mennen "Soapy" Williams, the former Democratic governor of Michigan, who had a strong record on civil rights issues. Williams' deputy was J. Wayne Fredericks of the Ford Foundation. Between them, they set out to forge a new image for the United States in Africa. For example, in 1963 they ordered American diplomats in South Africa to flout segregationist laws and local custom by inviting multiracial groups to official functions for the first time. That same year, the Africa bureau at the State Department persuaded the White House to announce a voluntary, self-imposed embargo on arms shipments to South Africa, just days before the UN Security Council adopted a similar international measure. Kennedy was even willing to insult a NATO ally, Portugal, by speaking of independence for its African colonies. The United States supported an (unsuccessful) UN Security Council resolution urging reforms in Angola, and the president's brother, Robert F. Kennedy, met with the leader of the Mozambican resistance movement, Eduardo Mondlane, in a public display of interest in his efforts; he later arranged CIA funding for Mondlane's early activities against the Portuguese.

Williams traveled frequently to Africa, spreading the administration's philosophy of "Africa for the Africans." He gave twenty-three major speeches on Africa in 1961, according the continent a much higher profile in American foreign policy. Perhaps the most important representatives of a new attitude were the young Peace Corps volunteers sent into African villages (and elsewhere in the Third World). Africa was much in demand as an assignment by prospective volunteers, and in its earliest days, the Peace Corps seemed to be the embodiment of American idealism. The liberal arts graduates who went to Africa helped amend the image of America as a place of unbridled racism and materialism. One side effect was the spread of American popular culture and its artifacts—from rock music to blue jeans to news magazines—into some of the most remote African communities. To this day, those symbols of America can be found in humble homes in the tiniest African villages. So can pictures of John F. Kennedy.

African heads of state were suddenly welcome in Washington; during Kennedy's nearly three years in office, twenty-six presidents and prime ministers traveled from Africa to visit him at the White House. Through governmental and private programs, thousands of African students and potential leaders also came to the United States, some of them staying for years.

Altruism and idealism were part of the reason for this astonishing shift in the American attitude toward Africa. Kennedy's
keen pragmatic, even expedient, political sense was also engaged.
But there was a third element: however well disguised in charm
and sincerity, Kennedy's Africa policy was one way of carrying on
the Cold War with the Soviet Union. As the confidential report of
an advisory committee told the new president, "We see Africa
as probably the greatest open field of maneuver in the worldwide
competition" between the Communist bloc and the Western
world. Kennedy and many of his advisers believed that the United
States could court the emerging nations with kindness, decency,
and demonstrations of the success of the American free-market
economy and open society. They thought that nonalignment could
be given a pro-American character, just as Nikita Khrushchev
thought it could go the other way.

Two events caused profound disillusionment for the Kennedy
team, and brought about important changes in American tactics
in Africa. One was the sustained, seemingly intractable crisis in the
Congo, which captured the attention of and caused consternation
in much of the world. The other was an overnight coup d'etat in
the sliverlike West African country of Togo; it went almost unnoticed by the general public.

If there was one place in Africa of which the outside world
had at least a rudimentary knowledge, it was the Congo. Henry
Morton Stanley had spent much of his time there. Mark Twain had
published his little-noticed but eloquent "King Leopold's Solilo-
quy" in 1905, to call attention to the appalling conditions in the
Congo. By the late 1950s and early 1960s the Western countries
had other reasons for paying attention: they were getting 69 percent of their industrial diamonds and 49 percent of their cobalt,
plus significant quantities of other strategic materials, from the
Congo. The territory was a very important piece of real estate, a
single country that served as a connector among the various regions of Africa. It bordered on Sudan, which was on the fringes of
the Middle East, but also on Zambia (then Northern Rhodesia),
the gateway to the troubled South. It reached from the Portuguese
colony of Angola to British- (once German-) controlled Tanganyika, and it also had borders with five other territories that eventually became independent nations.

The Congo came to independence under most inauspicious

circumstances. The Belgians, never really anticipating the end of their colonial rule, had done nothing to prepare the country for a successful transition. In 1960 there were only sixteen Congolese college graduates in a nation the size of the United States east of the Mississippi; the Belgians and other Europeans who lived there disdained and feared the local people. Tribal rivalries and hostilities had been encouraged, and the Belgians were shocked when they discovered almost universal support among the Congolese for independence, as evidenced by riots early in 1959. A year later they convened a conference in Brussels, and within six months the country was cut loose, although many of the colonial institutions and personnel were still in place. A few days later, Congolese soldiers rebelled against their Belgian superiors, with the tacit encouragement of their new prime minister, Patrice Lumumba, a charismatic nationalist who was a protégé of Kwame Nkrumah. Before long the country had disintegrated into civil war, and Moïse Tshombe, leader of its richest province, Katanga, was attempting to secede, with Belgian and other Western support. When Belgian troops intervened to try to restore order and prevent the massacre of whites, they massacred blacks.

Lumumba's first instinct was to appeal to the United States for help, but the Eisenhower administration sent him to the United Nations instead. In the Security Council both Washington and Moscow voted to establish a UN peacekeeping force, over West European objections. Lumumba still hoped for U.S. assistance in getting the Belgian troops out of the Congo. He made an impromptu three-day visit to Washington during which he met with high State Department officials, who failed to satisfy him. They came away convinced of Lumumba's irrationality, reinforced in their view that they were dealing with "uncivilized people" in this new country. (American officials had been repelled by lurid and graphic accounts of the rape of white women by Congolese soldiers, provided by the Belgian foreign ministry. Lumumba's request to the Congo desk officer at the State Department for a white female companion while he was in Washington only fueled the racial and sexual components of the U.S. reaction to him.)

When Lumumba returned home empty-handed, he turned to the Soviet Union to accept a standing offer of help. Nikita Khrushchev, in the first of many such Soviet adventures overseas, happily obliged, adding military equipment to the food shipments he had already been sending to the Congo. The reaction in Washington was one of hysteria. Eisenhower took the matter personally, perceiving the United States as being forced out of the strategic Congo by a Soviet-supported madman. The worst American prophecies about Lumumba were being fulfilled. Allen Dulles, then director of the Central Intelligence Agency, called him "a Castro, or worse," and—it became known many years later—the CIA hatched a plot to assassinate him by poisoning his food or his toothpaste. The poison was delivered from CIA labs to agents in the Congo but not in time, because in January 1961 Lumumba fell into the hands of Tshombe, who had him brutally murdered. The news of his death, when it became known a month later, set off a wave of bitter anti-Western feeling all across Africa, where Lumumba was regarded as an inspirational figure.

There were indications at the time that Eisenhower knew about—and perhaps even directly authorized—the CIA effort to kill Lumumba. When Kennedy came into office, he renounced the use of such tactics against Congolese leaders (although not against others, such as Fidel Castro). He took an important interventionist step, however; he chose an American candidate to lead the Congo, just as the Soviets had sided with Lumumba. Many American officials, including senior statesman Averell Harriman, had been supporters of Tshombe, who was especially adept at dealing with the Western business community and believed in splitting the Congo into several different states. But Kennedy went at first with a self-effacing labor leader, Cyrille Adoula, and later with the head of the Congolese forces, Joseph Désiré Mobutu, a former journalist who had been one of Lumumba's aides in the early days but eventually became a favorite of the CIA. Mobutu seemed like a viable moderate alternative to the various extremes, and he was content for many years to assert his—and American—power behind the scenes.

But Kennedy's experience in the Congo was full of other pitfalls. At one point, when Lumumba's political heir, Antoine Gizenga (aided by the Soviets and recognized by Nasser's Egypt*

---

* Gamel Abdul Nasser played a complex and important role in Africa during the decolonization period. The brief section about sub-Saharan Africa in his book, *Egypt's Liberation*, published in 1955, was an Arab version of the "white man's burden." In "the interior of the dark continent," he said, the African people would look to the Egyptians, "who guard their northern gate,

and Touré's Guinea), appeared to be on the verge of winning control, the U.S. ambassador made a unilateral decision to bring a naval task force off the Congo's shores. Later, when Tshombe came close to winning a war of secession in Katanga, the Pentagon prepared a plan to ship American combat troops to the Congo, but Kennedy vetoed it.

UN Secretary General Dag Hammarskjold died in a plane crash in the midst of the Congo crisis (perhaps with Soviet or Katangan connivance), and the Congo crisis was a turning point—a public relations disaster—for postcolonial Africa. Although this was probably the worst laboratory in which to judge the decolonization process, that is what many people, especially Americans, did. After all the hoopla and fanfare about self-determination and independence, they said, here was a bloody and tragic demonstration that the Africans could not handle it. Here, too, was a new precedent for regarding Africa as an East-West battleground; the Congo was the opening round in an intense competition between Washington and Moscow for influence among the new nations of the continent. After the early stages of the Congo crisis, the United States and the Soviet Union seemed always to be on opposite sides in Africa. One of the guiding principles of American foreign policy in the developing world became, "The enemy of my enemy is my only sure friend."

The names of Togo, the former German colony in West Africa that came to be administered by the French, and of its first president, Sylvanus Olympio, are hardly mentioned in most historical reviews of Africa in the early 1960s. But Togo, although tiny, was significant. Olympio's insistence on the setting of an early date for Togo's independence had been a major factor in convincing de Gaulle to hold a referendum in French Africa in 1958. He was the kind of pragmatic, pro-Western nationalist who came to be regarded as an alternative to the socialist firebrand type represented by Nkrumah. Early in 1963, however, Olympio was overthrown and murdered by Togolese soldiers who had served with the French army in Algeria and were angry over Olympio's refusal to expand his own tiny army and accept financial responsibility for

---

and who constitute their link with the outside world." Nasser pledged that Egypt would support "the spread of enlightenment and civilization to the remotest depths of the jungle." What he did spread, ultimately, was an increasingly pro-Soviet and anti-American version of neutralism.

them. They assassinated him when they discovered him trying to take refuge at the American embassy.

Before long there was a string of similar military coups in other African countries, creating the impression of a violent continent where power was transitory and respect for authority slight. From then on, even if a country's name was hardly known in the American media, any change of government that occurred in that country tended to be reported in graphic detail. A coup was news. This produced a new, unenviable kind of attention to Africa, and it led many Americans, in and out of government, to feel a sense of disgust and horror toward a place with so little capacity for law and order. The apparent willingness of African citizens and commentators to go along with this here-today-gone-tomorrow way of life, to revere a leader one day and exult over his corpse the next, only made the image worse.

Theoretically, Lyndon Johnson shared the Kennedy administration's interest in African affairs. As a Southerner, he had a sympathetic understanding of American blacks and perhaps a human, as well as political, appreciation for their affinity with Africa. Johnson referred to Africa's revolutions as the natural successors to America's, and when he became president after Kennedy's assassination, he left G. Mennen Williams's activist team in place in the Africa bureau at the State Department. The United States continued to cast votes at the United Nations that pleased the African bloc, including one in June 1964 establishing a committee to look at ways to bring about change in South Africa.

But later in 1964, just after he had been elected to a full four-year term in his own right, Johnson had an initiation in African affairs that would have been enough to sour anyone. In the Congo, President Joseph Kasavubu, pro-Western but weak, was confronted with a new rebellion in the northeastern part of the country. He called Moïse Tshombe back from European exile to be his new prime minister. Tshombe was anathema to other African leaders, but his American connections were still excellent. When Mobutu's army was unable to put down the revolt, Tshombe managed to arrange for American planes, piloted mostly by anti-Castro Cuban exiles with CIA connections, to bring his old Katanga gendarmes and newly recruited white mercenaries to the scene. But the U.S. involvement, small-scale and clandestine at first, soon

escalated and became public. In November, with the rebels holding some sixteen hundred foreign hostages (including American
officials and missionaries) in Stanleyville, Johnson agreed that
the United States would fly Belgian paratroopers to the scene.
Most of the hostages were rescued successfully, but many were
found dead or were killed during the raids.

The mission was a failure for other important reasons. As the
Belgian military team left, Mobutu's troops and Tshombe's mercenaries moved into Stanleyville and executed thousands of the
Congolese rebels. Not surprisingly, the United States shared in
the blame handed out by the Africans and others in the Third
World. Johnson was not a man who responded well to criticism,
and he was furious when the Africans failed to understand that
he had been acting out of humanitarian, rather than racist or imperial, motives.

The next year, after Kasavubu dismissed Tshombe, the solidly
pro-American and seemingly uncomplicated Mobutu in turn overthrew Kasavubu in a bloodless coup. The complications would
come later. For now, Mobutu was someone the United States
could understand and count on, and when he consolidated his
dictatorial power by banning all Congolese political parties in
1967, no one in Washington complained. By that time, the Africa
bureau at the State Department was under the reticent leadership
of Assistant Secretary Joseph Palmer II, who had warned ten
years earlier against "premature independence" for African colonies and had argued that the United States should keep its distance from the racial crisis in South Africa.

For most of Johnson's five years in the White House, Africa—
like much of the rest of the world—suffered from the president's
preoccupation with the war in Vietnam. Domestic critics who
urged Johnson to prosecute the struggle in Vietnam more deci-
sively did not want the country to be distracted by the even more
confusing crises in Africa. But neither did those who favored an
American withdrawal from Vietnam; they argued that the United
States should be less entangled overseas generally, less involved
in the internal affairs of Third World nations. These tendencies
were reinforced by the American concern in the mid-1960s with
domestic issues—civil rights legislation and Johnson's "war on poverty," for example—and even black Americans who had shown an
interest in Africa now backed off.

Two African issues did manage to intrude on the American consciousness during the mid and late 1960s. One was the unilateral declaration of independence from Britain of the white-minority settler regime in Southern Rhodesia, renamed Rhodesia. The white Rhodesian rebels, with the help of a well-orchestrated public relations campaign, found a small but influential corps of sympathizers among American whites, including businessmen with interests in southern Africa. They claimed that it was Ian Smith's stubborn white band, not various black African radicals, who were successors to the American revolution, and they pressed for American violation of United Nations sanctions against the breakaway Rhodesian regime. This vocal American lobby hurt American diplomacy in the rest of Africa.

Many Americans also seemed to have a mysterious fascination with the eastern region of Nigeria, which broke away in 1967 and called itself "Biafra." The U.S. government formally stayed neutral in the two-and-a-half-year-long Nigerian civil war, although it and many private American groups contributed food, medicine, and other relief to victims on both sides. (When the United States refused to provide arms to the Nigerian federal government, Nigeria turned to the Soviet Union, which added to the widely held American impression of growing Soviet influence in Africa.) The pro-Biafran lobby in the United States, composed mostly of representatives of business and industry who saw profitable opportunities in Biafra, came close to convincing American officials that Washington should intervene in the war on the rebels' side, as some other Western capitals had, overtly or covertly. (France, for example, was persuaded by its former colony, Ivory Coast, to favor Biafra.) Certainly the American press gave an unusual degree of coverage to this dramatic African story. Correspondents based in Nairobi, who had experienced difficulty getting their editors interested in anything African, suddenly found themselves flying across the continent every few months to provide an update on the war.

Yet, the overall American attitude toward Africa in this period of general disillusionment with foreign policy was once again indifference verging on contempt. As a general retrenchment set in, Congress became convinced that aid was working no better in Africa than anywhere else. Indeed, once the Kennedy flair was gone, it seemed as if the Africans no longer paid attention to

America's noble votes in the United Nations, not even to the difficult ones that alienated the Europeans. Nor did they give credit
to America's mostly good intentions. Instead they seemed only to
notice the negatives—the U.S. concern about access to Portuguese
bases in the Azores, for example, which led to some votes on
Portugal's side in the UN—and they directed more and more of
their obligatory anti-imperialist rhetoric against the United States.

As American development aid shrank further (measured as
a percentage of gross national product), an emphasis on regional
and multilateral efforts sometimes meant that certain countries,
especially the smaller, less well-known ones, were neglected altogether. And as Africa came once again to seem less central to the
global struggle, African countries could not even get away with
threatening alignment with "the other side" as a method of attracting attention and help. No one was listening.

The next several changes of administration in Washington—
from Lyndon Johnson to Richard Nixon to Gerald Ford to Jimmy
Carter to Ronald Reagan—seemed calculated, from an African
point of view, to render the United States incomprehensible. Some
aspects of African policy shifted as mysteriously and arbitrarily as
the sands of the Sahara.

During his first term, Nixon, too, was almost entirely preoccupied with Vietnam. When he issued his personal blueprint on
"U.S. Foreign Policy for the 1970s" early in 1971, Nixon devoted
only five out of some 230 pages to the African continent. He did
send his first secretary of state, William P. Rogers, on a tour of
African capitals, but that was because he considered Rogers expendable on marginal tasks. Rogers did not really influence what
Nixon regarded as the important areas of foreign policy; that role
fell to Henry Kissinger, originally Nixon's national security adviser and later his secretary of state as well.

Kissinger knew little about Africa—it had no place in his writings on the international strategic balance—and he complained
about the difficulty of formulating a policy toward a continent
with fifty different countries governed by regimes of every possible ideological stripe. In an effort to educate himself, Kissinger
asked his National Security Council staff early in 1969 to review
American policy alternatives in southern Africa. The result, National Security Study Memorandum (NSSM) 39, offered five op-

tions, three of which involved softening American pressure on the white minority regimes, including South Africa (and Namibia), Rhodesia, and the Portuguese colonies of Angola and Mozambique. Kissinger selected one of those three, commonly known as the "tar baby" option because its critics said it would stick the United States to those regimes. The national security adviser instigated a less critical position toward the white governments at the United Nations and reduced American pressure on the Portuguese, but he also arranged for $5 million in aid to the black-ruled countries in the area. Except for the last part, none of the new policy was made public, although the South African government was given private hints of the intended shifts. Kissinger and other Nixon administration spokesmen denied that the American posture had changed, even while communicating instructions to diplomats in the field to change it.

Soon the new tilt became apparent. Nixon sent millionaire Texas oilman and rancher John Hurd as his ambassador to South Africa, and Hurd bathed the white rulers there in expressions of warmth and support from 1970 to 1975. He particularly angered South African blacks with a gesture of singular insensitivity: he went hunting on Robben Island in Cape Town Bay, where most of South Africa's political prisoners were kept; black inmates were required to fetch the birds Hurd shot, as if they were hunting dogs.

Elsewhere in Africa, the record of U.S. diplomats was still a mixed one. Senator Stuart Symington, Democrat of Missouri, complained in 1969 after a trip to Africa: "Our representatives do not understand other cultures. . . . I went into a country which we have probably lost to communism . . . and found that nobody in our Embassy there understood any of the tribal languages. I went to the largest base in North Africa. Out of thousands of officers there, one officer could speak Arabic."

Perhaps the most controversial element of the Nixon/Kissinger policy was its sympathy for Portuguese colonialism. It was based in part on Portugal's status as a member of NATO and continued American access to Portuguese facilities in the Azores.* Portu-

---

* In the Portuguese colonies, the impact of the Kennedy contacts with the nationalists had long since worn off. Indeed, in the still-Democratic year of 1968, of the more than four hundred guests invited to the Fourth of July party at the American consulate in Luanda, Angola, not one was black.

gal's administration of its five-hundred-year-old African empire had been brutal and crass. There was none of the strict official separation of the sort practiced by South Africa. (Indeed, it was a time-honored practice for South African white men to go off to Lourenço Marques to do something they could not do at home, consort with black women.) But opportunities for the African residents of Angola and Mozambique—and Portugal's other, smaller African colonies, Guinea-Bissau, São Tomé and Principe, and the Cape Verde Islands—were virtually nonexistent. In 1954, when the proportion of Portuguese to Africans in Mozambique was one to a hundred, there were eight hundred European students and five Africans in the high school in Lourenço Marques.

All Portuguese territories were designated "overseas provinces" in 1951, and even the Europeans living there were forbidden to engage in political activities. They became a hostile, angry band, regarded as second-class citizens back home and fearful of the black people they treated as third-class citizens in the colonies. All necessary decisions were taken in Lisbon, and as Portugal's long-time dictator, Antonio Salazar, once put it, "Africa is the complement of Europe, indispensable to its defense, a necessary support for its economy." Overseas control was necessary, he said, lest "Europe be defeated in Africa." If there was an African revolution underway, according to Salazar, it was prompted by external forces rather than African nationalism.

Salazar was gone by the time Henry Kissinger began to dominate American foreign policy, but his successor, Marcello Caetano, did little to alter the situation in the colonies. Now the Portuguese were fighting a costly guerrilla war against liberation movements in Angola, Mozambique, and Guinea-Bissau. The official American view, as expressed in NSSM-39, was that "there is no hope for the blacks to gain the political rights they seek through violence," so the United States substantially increased its military aid to Portugal—even though it was an open secret that American-supplied weapons, including napalm, were being diverted for use in Africa, despite explicit promises to the contrary. After Portugal permitted U.S. planes to refuel in the Azores during their resupply missions to Israel in the midst of the 1973 Yom Kippur war, Kissinger supported a deal to provide Lisbon with missiles and other sophisticated offensive weapons for use in Africa. But before that deal could go through, the socialist-oriented Portuguese military overthrew the Caetano government in April 1974. One of the grievances that led to the coup was that the unwinnable war of attrition in the African colonies had been draining national resources and wasting lives. Portugal's "overseas provinces" were suddenly set free, with as little preparation as the Congo.

The ensuing events in Angola were almost as perplexing as those in the Congo a decade earlier. Nixon, his presidency fatally weakened by the Watergate scandal, did nothing to stop Kissinger from compounding the American mistakes in the Portuguese colonies. Nor did Gerald Ford, Nixon's accidental successor, who relied totally on Kissinger in the foreign policy arena. The United States had long had secret contacts with the National Front for the Liberation of Angola (FNLA), in part because its leader, Holden Roberto, was a brother-in-law and protégé of the Congolese leader Mobutu. Kissinger chose to back the FNLA in the coming Angolan civil war—not so much because he agreed with its goals or admired its leader, but because the Soviet Union was on the side of (and had long been helping) another faction, the Popular Movement for the Liberation of Angola (MPLA) of Agostinho Neto. Apparently afflicted with the "enemy of my enemy" syndrome, the Chinese also backed the FNLA and its eventual ally, a third force called the National Union for the Total Independence of Angola (UNITA), led by a charismatic figure named Jonas Savimbi.

Beginning early in 1975 Kissinger approved CIA requests for covert support of the FNLA, on the grounds that this was the way to confront and check Soviet interventionism in southern Africa. Gerald Ford authorized at least $14 million to finance the shipment of arms through Zaïre (Mobutu's new, Africanized name for Congo), while UNITA recruited American mercenaries. (Savimbi also had Europeans and South Africans advising and fighting alongside his forces.) Each subsequent development raised the stakes on all sides. In response to the American buildup of the FNLA, the Soviets shipped massive quantities of arms to the MPLA. This was followed by the entrance of foreign troops on both sides, South Africans and Zaïreans on the side of the FNLA and UNITA and Cubans to shore up the MPLA.

There is a bitter, unresolved debate among government officials and scholars over what came first in Angola during this period and who is responsible for escalating the conflict. It seems clear, however, that at the time of the initial, relatively limited South African entry into Angola, in August 1975, there were only a few hundred Cubans with the MPLA, most of them still involved in training rather than combat. But the leaders of the MPLA panicked and asked for more Cuban help. Another thousand troops were dispatched by Havana, arriving at about the time of a major South African invasion of Angola in October 1975; after that invasion, much larger contingents of Cuban forces arrived and took up arms on the MPLA's behalf. South Africa has claimed American encouragement for and cooperation with its move into Angola, but Kissinger has repeatedly denied that.

Only late in 1975 did the extent of CIA involvement in Angola begin to emerge publicly, and two Democratic senators, Dick Clark of Iowa (then chairman of the Senate African Affairs Subcommittee) and John Tunney of California, pushed through legislation, known as the "Clark amendment," to deny funding for any U.S. covert operations there. Once American—and, more important, South African—interference became known, moral and diplomatic support for the MPLA solidified elsewhere in Africa. Kissinger continued to reject a diplomatic solution to the conflict that would permit the various factions to share power, but early in 1976 the MPLA, with Cuban help, won a tentative victory in the war. The introduction of Mobutu's troops was no help at all to the pro-Western side, and they had to retreat hastily. The FNLA essentially dropped out of the picture, but UNITA managed to keep up the struggle in the countryside for years, with Savimbi continuing to receive substantial material and logistical support from the South Africans. But the MPLA was strong enough in the region surrounding the capital city, Luanda, and in other parts of the country, to be able to govern and to receive international diplomatic recognition.

In the end, the events in Angola were widely interpreted overseas as a fiasco for the Ford administration, for Kissinger, and for the United States. Angola, a country hardly known to most Americans, became a cause célèbre, a stumbling block in United States–Soviet relations. Washington declared it could never grant diplomatic recognition to Angola as long as the Cubans remained there; but even though the Cubans began to wear out their welcome, the Angolans found it necessary to keep them as a counterweight to American hostility and possible further South African intervention. An irony of the situation was that the Cubans protected Gulf Oil and other American corporate interests from attacks by purportedly pro-Western guerrillas.

Beneath all this lay the symptoms of utter chaos in the formulation of American policy toward Africa from 1969 through 1976. As in many other areas, Kissinger felt contempt for the established bureaucracy in the State Department that had developed some expertise in African affairs. During the Angolan civil war alone, he had four different assistant secretaries of state for Africa. One of them, Donald Easum, was fired for trying to get the United States diplomatically, instead of militarily, involved in Angola. (He was exiled to Nigeria as American ambassador, where he would ultimately have his own revenge through the improvement of relations between Washington and Lagos.) Another, Nathaniel Davis, resigned rather than implement a policy he did not support.

There were new pressures on behalf of a different American attitude and role that would be popular in black Africa—for example, from the newly formed Congressional Black Caucus and the lobbying group, TransAfrica—but legislation that required the United States to continue trading with Rhodesia, sponsored by Senator Harry F. Byrd, Jr., of Virginia, repeatedly sailed through Congress with the tacit approval of Kissinger and his presidents.

Toward the end of his service as secretary of state, with his Angolan policy in shambles, Kissinger showed signs of rethinking the American options in Africa. As if to repudiate NSSM-39 publicly, he traveled to a conference of the British Commonwealth nations in Lusaka, Zambia, in 1976, and said that the United States identified with the aspirations of the black majorities in the southern part of the continent after all. Some Africans believed him, but most did not.

It was left to the new reformist Southern president, Jimmy Carter, to implement the latest American change of heart. Initially Carter took a moralistic approach to foreign policy in Africa, as elsewhere. He revived much of the substance of Kennedy's Africa policy, but with little of the form that had made it successful.

In southern Africa, which he believed could learn from the experience of the American South, Carter followed the advice of the liberal wing of the Democratic party, represented by his vice-

president, Walter F. Mondale, and of the black community that
had been so crucial to his election, represented by his ambassador
to the United Nations, Andrew Young. His first secretary of state,
Cyrus Vance, a New York lawyer with substantial experience in
earlier Democratic administrations, tended to agree with them
that Africa should be regarded as a distinct region with its own
unique problems. But Carter was also powerfully influenced on
foreign policy issues by his national security adviser, Zbigniew
Brzezinski, who had been a kind of tutor in international affairs
for this obscure governor of Georgia while he was striving to be
president. Despite a professed interest in and substantial writings
about the Third World, Brzezinski tended to see Africa much the
way his academic rival Henry Kissinger had—as another battleground in the East-West struggle. The competition between these
two points of view within the Carter administration, often waged
in public, created an American image of inconsistency and confusion in Africa.

One of the Carter administration's earliest and most dramatic
gestures concerning Africa was the message delivered by Mondale to the South African prime minister John Vorster at a meeting in Vienna in March 1977. The South Africans could not count
on the United States to help them deal with the crisis bound
to be created by the policy of apartheid, Mondale warned, and
friendly relations between the two countries could be maintained
only if South Africa made progress toward full participation in
national affairs by the nonwhite majority of its population. This
was an application of the new American human rights policy—at
first forced on Ford and Kissinger by a Congress eager to become
involved in making foreign policy, later picked up by Carter as a
major campaign theme—and it foreshadowed substantial U.S.
pressure on the Pretoria regime to reform itself or face greater
isolation.

The effectiveness of Mondale's mission would be debated for
years. Critics claimed that it resulted in a gain of more than a
dozen new seats by South Africa's ruling National Party in parliamentary elections a few months later, but supporters said it was
imperative to place the United States on the proper side of a historic issue.

Carter also distanced his administration from the rebel white
regime in Rhodesia, which was facing increased resistance from

black guerrillas. He pressed for, and obtained, repeal of the Byrd amendment, so that the United States could again be in compliance with United Nations sanctions against the government of Ian Smith. Through Mondale, Young, and Richard Moose, assistant secretary of state for African affairs, Carter made his administration accessible to influential black African leaders. Carter was willing to see almost any African figure who wished to come to Washington, and he struck up a particular friendship with Julius Nyerere, the socialist president of Tanzania who was a leader among the "front-line states" concerned with southern African conflicts. Carter himself traveled to Nigeria early in 1978 and spoke to a throng assembled at a stadium in Lagos. He declared that "this departure from past aloofness by the United States is not just a personal commitment of my own, but I represent the deep feelings and the deep interest of all the people of my country." The president assured the Nigerians that "we share with you a commitment to an Africa that is at peace, free from colonialism, free from racism, free from military interference by outside nations, and free from the inevitable conflicts that can come when the integrity of national boundaries is not respected." For the Africans, Carter was saying all the right things.

Yet in other respects the Carter policy differed little from that of previous administrations. Brzezinski, like Kissinger, was very bothered by the Cubans in Angola, and later in Ethiopia. They had become a point of special protest by the American right wing. Despite contrary views expressed by Vance, Young, Moose, and others, Brzezinski felt that United States recognition of the MPLA government in Luanda was out of the question. His view prevailed.

Pressure grew to find a way to check the apparent growth of Soviet influence in Africa. When the Shaba province of Zaïre (formerly Katanga) was invaded in 1977 by exiles based in northern Angola, a Congress still smarting from the Vietnam experience prevented the Executive Branch from becoming involved. The Pentagon did supply Mobutu's beleaguered troops with Coca-Cola and other American treats, but it was left to the French and Belgians to react militarily. When the same thing happened again the next year and the invaders—still Tshombe's old Katanga gendarmes, by now middle-aged and even more bitter—took over the mining center of Kolwezi and massacred European workers and

missionaries, the situation was considerably different. By this time
the Soviets were increasingly involved in the Horn of Africa, and
indirectly in the conflict over Western Sahara; Afghanistan was also
beginning to worry American strategists. It seemed to Brzezinski,
among others, that the United States had to prove its mettle somewhere in Africa. In 1978 the Carter administration provided aircraft and logistical support for French, Belgian, and Moroccan
troops that came to Mobutu's rescue in Shaba. The administration
also loudly blamed the Soviet Union and Cuba for the trouble in
Zaïre, although there was never any hard evidence to back up the
charge.

Even Mobutu reached a reconciliation with Angola later in
1978, recognizing that he could not cope with any more invasions
from the south and that access to the Benguela railroad through
Angola would make it much easier to get Shaba's copper and
other minerals to their markets. Despite the fact that the reconciliation had been arranged in part by Donald McHenry, Young's
deputy at the United Nations and later U.S. ambassador there in
his own right, Washington was still unyielding on the issue of recognition for the MPLA.

The progressive half of Carter's team working on Africa policy, including Young, Moose, and McHenry, urged that the United
States gradually disengage itself from Mobutu, whom they regarded as an embarrassment on grounds of human rights abuses
and personal corruption. They believed that Mobutu was bound
to fall from power, and that Washington had to prevent its prestige and honor from falling with him. Career diplomats in the
State Department, however, for once in agreement with Brzezinski's National Security Council staff, argued that Mobutu was no
worse than many other less visible African leaders. He was certainly preferable to the notorious Idi Amin of Uganda or "Emperor" Bokassa of the Central African Republic, both of whom
the Soviets were then supporting. And besides, they argued, a
Mobutu who was pro-American was a safer bet than some unknown successor whose politics were unpredictable. Carter settled
for pressing Mobutu to institute internal reforms.

Carter also took sides in the regional conflicts in the Horn
and Western Sahara. America's long-standing connections with
Ethiopia had dissipated greatly after the aging, out-of-touch Haile
Selassie was overthrown in 1974 by leftist military officers. The

Soviet Union had been buttressing the regime of Mohammed Siad Barre next door in Somalia, trading advanced weapons for the right to use the Somali naval base at Berbera and supporting Somalia in its centuries-old dispute with Ethiopia over the Ogaden desert. But when the military regime in Ethiopia began to move further left, Moscow saw a better opportunity: in perhaps one of the most cynical moves ever taken by a European power in Africa, the Soviet Union simply switched sides overnight. Whereas one day the Somalis were invading the Ogaden with Russian weapons, the next day they were being repelled by Ethiopians with Russian weapons and eventually with Soviet and Cuban soldiers at their side. Carter responded to Somali entreaties and began to pick up on that side where the Soviets had left off. The new enemy of America's old enemy was now an American friend. Although the United States declined to become as deeply involved as Siad Barre intended, U.S. aid to Somalia increased steadily, and before long the Pentagon was negotiating for the use of the Berbera base as a staging ground for its new rapid deployment force. Meanwhile, Ethiopia was colored red on the American map of Africa.

The United States knew little of Western Sahara, a scarcely populated piece of desert in northwestern Africa, Spain's last colony. The Spaniards abruptly pulled out in 1975, ceding the northern two-thirds to Morocco and the southern third to Mauritania. Once Morocco ignored a World Court decision that the people of Western Sahara were entitled to settle their own future, the Polisario (an acronym for the Popular Front for the Liberation of Saguia el-Hamra and Rio de Oro) launched a guerrilla war, backed by Morocco's adversaries in Algeria and Libya. Mauritania gave up its claim and dropped out of the war in 1979, but King Hassan II of Morocco fought on. Carter felt grateful to Hassan for his help elsewhere in Africa, so he continued the policy of shipping U.S. arms to Morocco, on the unenforceable condition that they would not be used in the Sahara (which they were). After he pronounced his "Carter doctrine" in response to the Soviet invasion of Afghanistan—drawing his own line on Soviet expansionism—the president became even more permissive and forthcoming with Morocco, which therefore felt encouraged to continue its inconclusive struggle in the desert.

The Soviet action in Afghanistan, combined with the overthrow of the shah of Iran and the seizure of American hostages in

Tehran by Islamic fundamentalists, had the Carter administration talking about an "arc of crisis" that extended from South Asia across Africa. Carter yielded to the hard-liners among his advisers. So it was that when South Africa invaded Angola again in June 1980, the same president who had taken such a tough stance with Pretoria three years earlier did not support a UN Security Council resolution condemning the attack. When it came time to vote, the United States abstained, along with Britain and France.

One of Carter's fondest hopes had been to be a peacemaker in southern Africa, to contrive an African equivalent to the Camp David accords signed by Egypt and Israel. For the first two and a half years of his presidency, many people in his State Department devoted almost full time to working with the Labour party government in Britain for a reasonable settlement in Rhodesia. But those efforts bogged down, and it was Lord Carrington, foreign minister in a British Conservative party government, who finally moved Rhodesia to majority rule by convening a constitutional conference in London. The Democratic administration in Washington was intimately involved in that process, but Carter was denied the diplomatic and public relations advantage he had hoped for in Africa.

Having encouraged black Africa's greatest expectations of the United States when he took office, Carter left the White House having failed to fulfill them. Critics complained that it would have been better to promise less and deliver more.

Ronald Reagan promised little to or for Africa during the campaign that led to his election in November 1980. He did, however, voice support for a new American involvement in Angola on the side of Jonas Savimbi, to strengthen his ability to challenge the Cuban-backed MPLA government in Luanda. Also, early in his term, in an interview with Walter Cronkite of CBS, Reagan referred to South Africa as "a friendly nation" that "has stood beside us in every war we've ever fought" and "strategically is essential to the free world." It was difficult to tell whether Reagan truly intended to change policy or whether he, like Margaret Thatcher in the campaign that made her British prime minister in the spring of 1979, was saying the things considered obligatory by some of the party faithful.

Black Africa braced for the worst; the annual conference of

the African-American Institute, held in Sierra Leone in January 1981, just two weeks before Reagan's inauguration, was somber; Reagan sent no one to that meeting to offer reassurances about his Africa policy. Meanwhile, in South Africa, his election was celebrated as a breakthrough.

Some of Reagan's most conservative supporters, such as Senator Jesse Helms of North Carolina, who worried about the "loss" of Rhodesia to a black Marxist leadership and wanted the United States to treat South Africa as a valued friend and strategic asset, tried to dictate Reagan's choice of a right-wing activist as assistant secretary of state for African affairs. When they did not have their way, they made the man who was selected by Reagan, Chester A. Crocker, wait months for Senate confirmation.

Crocker, a political moderate who enjoyed the personal confidence of Reagan's first secretary of state, Alexander Haig, from their days together on the National Security Council staff under Nixon, was unusually well qualified for the job; he had an academic background in African affairs. Still, Crocker worried some Africans and American Africanists when, in an article published in *Foreign Affairs* shortly before his appointment, he advocated an American policy of "constructive engagement" toward South Africa, in contrast to the gradual disengagement of U.S. interests that had been threatened previously. Crocker was not advocating a retreat from American principles—"sustained and orderly change" in South Africa would still be the goal—but it was easy to perceive him as proposing a return to the Nixon/Kissinger policy of siding with the white minorities. "In South Africa . . . it is not our task to choose between black and white," Crocker told the annual convention of the American Legion in Honolulu in August 1981. "The Reagan administration has no intention of destabilizing South Africa in order to curry favor elsewhere."

What Crocker had in mind was building enough mutual respect and dialogue with the South Africans to permit some internationally acceptable plan for the independence of Namibia, or South-West Africa. But it was some time before the Namibian negotiations bore fruit, and for nearly three years there was little to show the domestic or African public. One sticking point was the linkage in the discussions between a South African departure from Namibia and a Cuban departure from Angola, a linkage suggested by the Reagan administration in 1981 and enthusiastically accepted by the South Africans. Meanwhile, the United States continued casting votes in the United Nations (for example, refusing to condemn South African incursions into Angola) that seemed to have the effect of protecting and encouraging South Africa. Also, when South African police, enforcing the "Group Areas Act," set fire to a pathetic squatters' camp outside of Cape Town in 1981, leaving thousands of Africans homeless in the midst of winter—an incident that drew worldwide attention and condemnation—the Reagan administration's criticism was measured and restrained.

After a time, the State Department was able to point to a few developments in South Africa that were arguably the result of America's new quiet diplomacy. Vice-President George Bush persuaded the South African government to lift restrictions on Bishop Desmond Tutu, then secretary general of the South African Council of Churches, so he could travel to the United States. The National party government decided not to enact a law severely restricting the domestic and foreign press in South Africa, after Reagan's ambassador, journalist Herman Nickel, showed his concern by attending an all-night parliamentary debate on the issue. The Reagan administration also encouraged and congratulated a new South African constitution that gave a limited share in government to the country's mixed-race and Asian minorities (although not to its black majority).

But it was a series of developments involving South Africa and its neighbors in late 1983 and early 1984 that led many people to credit "constructive engagement," and Crocker in particular, with major influence in the region. With the State Department playing the role of intermediary, the South Africans and Angolans began to negotiate directly; eventually they met in Lusaka to sign a cease-fire and establish a joint commission that would monitor the withdrawal of South African troops from a large section of southern Angola and try to prevent the South-West Africa People's Organization (SWAPO) guerrillas from continuing to infiltrate into Namibia. (The United States had observer status on the commission and briefly established a liaison mission in Windhoek, the Namibian capital.) The actual withdrawal moved ahead slowly, but the implication of the agreement was that within time UNITA might end its struggle against the Angolan government, the Cubans might leave Angola, and Namibia might at last become independent through negotiation rather than warfare.

Equally dramatic was the "Nkomati Accord," named for the river that forms the border between South Africa and Mozambique. Each country agreed not to allow its territory to be used as a sanctuary for insurgent groups seeking to overthrow the other's government. That meant South Africa had to withdraw its support for the Mozambique National Resistance (MNR), and Mozambique had to expel prominent members of the African National Congress (ANC) and their offices from its capital of Maputo. In scenes reminiscent of Portuguese colonial times, South African and Mozambican officials met to talk about trade, investment, and other exchanges. A similar public pact between South Africa and Swaziland soon followed (a secret one had already been in force for two years), and with other nearby countries adopting a tamer attitude toward Pretoria, increasingly it looked as if South Africa had achieved its goal of peace and stability along its borders. It was becoming a regional superpower.

The American role in all of this was controversial. The Reagan administration—frustrated in its dealings with the Soviet Union, in the Middle East, and in Central America—pointed to southern Africa as an arena of foreign policy success. But there were other ways to view it. One interpretation was that the United States had been tricked into lending its diplomatic imprimatur to what was essentially a series of South African military successes; another was that Washington had been badly used by the South Africans, who contrived to exclude American representatives altogether from another conference on Namibia that took place under the sponsorship of Zambian President Kenneth Kaunda. (State Department officials were left to scurry through the halls, along with journalists, in order to find out what was happening in the conference room.) Ultimately, the test of the American role would be whether the various peace agreements in the region held, and whether the calmer situation on its borders led the South African government to make further concessions internally. Racial strife increased within South Africa in 1984 and 1985, however, and the Reagan administration found itself in the uncomfortable position of being identified with repressive South African government actions by critics of that government in both South Africa and the

United States. Also, in April 1985, ignoring American and other international protests, the South African government went ahead with a plan for Namibia's independence that included only the "internal" parties and ignored the United Nations, thereby frustrating one of the major goals of the Reagan policy of "constructive engagement."

When the Reagan administration looked north of the southern African cauldron, it searched for anti-Communist leaders it could support. Mobutu knew how to play to that instinct—he also knew he would be watched less critically for human rights violations—and the Reagan administration was less self-conscious than its predecessor about backing him. Morocco got new encouragement—and more weapons—from the United States for its war in Western Sahara, although the majority of the OAU was now backing the Polisario. The Reagan State and Defense departments also bolstered the military regime of Samuel Doe in Liberia, who had initially flirted with Libya but then returned solidly to the Western camp. Support for Doe was consistent with Carter administration policy, but now the United States became more generous with its military and economic aid. Another anti-Communist government that benefited from intensified American support under Reagan was that of Jaafar el Nimeiry in Sudan, which was overthrown in 1985; Libya, once considered a menace to Sudan's stability, soon became the country's main arms supplier.

Indeed, much of the Reagan administration's attention to Africa north of the Limpopo consisted of ferreting out the schemes of Libya's leader, Colonel Muammar al-Qaddafi, and advising the more vulnerable nations on the continent about how to protect themselves from him. It was the Qaddafi factor that engaged American concern in the summer of 1983, when the old civil war in Chad flared again and Washington rushed aid to the nominally (and perhaps temporarily) pro-Western regime of Hissene Habre. But Chad was one place where the French interest was easily rearoused, and President François Mitterrand sent forces there to limit Qaddafi's advance, just in time to spare the United States an overcommitment to a place it hardly knew.

Returning to an old American trait—an institutional version of the judgment process employed by Henry Morton Stanley a century earlier—the Reagan administration tended to evaluate African nations primarily on the basis of their warmth or hostility to the United States. It counted votes in the United Nations on such issues as the Soviet downing of a South Korean civilian airliner and the American invasion of Grenada, and when a country like Zimbabwe was found wanting, its quotient of American aid was cut sharply. When a severe drought struck many African countries in 1983, Washington sent some emergency aid, but not as much as many congressmen and voluntary agencies advocated. (American governmental and private aid increased dramatically in 1984 and 1985, as a result of greater awareness of the widespread African famine, particularly in Ethiopia.) By putting a strict ceiling on American contributions to the World Bank and International Monetary Fund, the Reagan administration caused other Western nations to reduce their shares proportionally, thus cutting back the amount of multilateral aid that would be available to African nations (and others) at a time of economic and human crisis. Many African leaders were faced with a choice of pleading with the United States for help, or adapting their personal and national philosophies in such a way as to attract American admiration. It was an unappealing dilemma.

With rock stars recording a song intended to promote international sympathy for African drought victims and even American school children raising money for relief—and with a new wave of protest against South African policies gaining momentum—Africa became a popular cause in the United States. But it was not clear how long that attention would last, and in the effort to attract the interest of the United States government, Africa still had a difficult time competing with other parts of the world. Conflict in El Salvador and Nicaragua, the disastrous commitment of an American peacekeeping force to Lebanon, the Iran-Iraq war, a new arms-control treaty with the Soviet Union—all made it unlikely that the average American would learn much about population pressures in Kenya, the corruption-induced collapse of democracy in Nigeria, or the refugee crisis in the Horn and other areas of Africa. The Africans would have to wait.

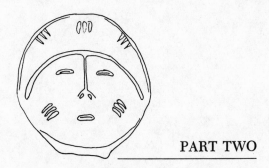

PART TWO

FOUR COUNTRIES

3

Liberia: American Stepchild

On March 10, 1980, George Boley was arrested on the street in Monrovia. Boley, in his early thirties, was one of Liberia's promising young men, an outsider who was becoming a provisional member of the ruling establishment. That establishment consisted almost entirely of "Americo-Liberians," the descendants of freed American slaves who settled the country early in the nineteenth century. Boley, however, was one of the "country people," or "aborigines." (The latter term was used in the Liberian constitution to describe those who did not have roots in America.) He had managed to get to the United States for an education, and won a Ph.D. from the University of Akron. With his American wife, he returned to Liberia and soon became an assistant minister of education in the government of President William R. Tolbert, Jr. But Tolbert's agents kept an eye on Boley and found that, even as he was working for the government, he was quietly associating with its opponents, members of the new Progressive People's party, which was challenging the established order in Liberia. Joseph Chesson, the minister of justice, charged Boley with treason and sedition and locked him up, along with some twenty other suspicious characters, in the post stockade at the Barclay Training Centre, a military base on the Atlantic Ocean in downtown Monrovia.

For a month Boley did not see his family. He was given twenty-five lashes every morning. He had no bath the entire time, and he slept on the bare cement floor of the cell, which he shared with several others. Eating only one scant meal a day, he lost fifty pounds and became very weak. Then he became frightened. There was a rumor that on April 14, 1980, the first anniversary of nationwide riots to protest a sudden, large increase in the price of rice, Boley and the other political prisoners would be executed.

Tolbert was serving his term as chairman of the Organization of African Unity in 1979–80, and to protect his reputation, he had waffled on the issue of dissent. At first, he had responded to the rice riots of April 1979 with force, calling the organizers "wicked, evil, and satanic men" under the influence of the Soviets and other subversive elements, and ordering the police to fire into the protesting crowds. Dozens were killed and hundreds injured in the confrontation. Most of the shops in Monrovia were looted, and some foreign investors panicked and began to withdraw their capital. Tolbert realized he could not count on his own army to put down the uprising, and order was restored only with the arrival of troops lent by President Sekou Touré of Guinea.

But later, following the advice of one-half of his entourage, Tolbert rescinded the price increase (from which he and other wealthy rice growers stood to gain personally), released most of the arrested demonstrators, and seemingly liberalized the political system. Then the president vacillated. As soon as he realized that his opponents were more defiant than grateful, Tolbert, on the advice of the other half of the team, reverted to repression. It was at this point that Boley and his cohorts were arrested. Tolbert wanted to use the anniversary of the rice riots to teach an important lesson, by having some of his most articulate opponents shot.

On April 12, 1980, two days before their scheduled execution, George Boley and the other activists were released from prison. A group of young army enlisted men—hungry, angry, illiterate soldiers—had killed the president, announced over Liberian radio that they had charge of the country, and then unlocked the gates of the post stockade. To the surprise of the intellectuals who had long tried to weaken Tolbert, guns now succeeded where reason had failed.

The soldiers wanted the intellectuals to help them run Liberia. Their leader was Master Sergeant Samuel Kanyon Doe, then twenty-eight, a native of the same region of the country as Boley, and one of Boley's former English students in night classes at the Marcus Garvey School in Monrovia. Doe, who had never finished high school, had never been outside Liberia, and spoke only halting English, asked his mentor to become his minister of state for presidential affairs.

For ten months, George Boley sat in an office next to Doe's in the executive mansion. He gained back his weight, and he wore stylish suits hand-tailored from locally woven cloth. In the top drawer of his desk, he kept a revolver and thick files of documents detailing the corruption of the Tolbert regime. He was a man in power; "the Chief" rarely made a move without consulting him. Then, in February 1981, while Boley was in the United States, others who resented his power persuaded Doe to demote him. He became minister of posts and telecommunications, a relatively unimportant position. Eventually, he worked his way back into Doe's favor and became minister of education and still later, having fully ingratiated himself, he became secretary-general of a new political party created by Doe. George Boley's experiences—his roller-coaster rise and fall and rise again—are a metaphor for the recent, bizarre adventures of Liberia, a small country whose stability was taken for granted until the old order collapsed in 1980.

Liberia is the oldest "republic" in Africa, the only country on the continent never to have been a colony or part of an empire, a staunch American friend with the strongest possible cultural and financial ties to the United States. That is why Liberia has always been regarded by the rest of Africa as a different, even peculiar place. And that is also what made Liberia's coup special. Few outsiders—especially Liberia's friends in America—thought it was likely that this sophisticated African political dynasty, so schooled in the ways of the West, would be overthrown. Liberia had a reputation as an outpost of stability in a continent of chaos. It purported to have given the world "a new black man." Its American-style institutions and the familiar idiom in which the country

conducted its business made it easy for Americans to have confidence that Liberia would avoid the crises so many other African
nations faced.

Yet, in retrospect, the explosion was inevitable. For 133 years,
a black-settler elite, which made up no more than 5 percent of Liberia's population, had monopolized all political power and controlled access to the country's resources. A class of perhaps forty-
five thousand people, almost all of them members of the three
hundred or so Americo-Liberian extended families, made the decisions controlling the lives of a million and a half others. Outsiders were admitted into this class only by marriage or by gradual
sponsorship, beginning as "wards" of their settler patrons. The
elite's brutal and selfish methods and its almost medieval subjuga-
tion of the unwitting peasants made the later-arriving white-settler
elite in Rhodesia seem gentle by comparison. With the humiliation of the indigenous people so complete, Liberia was a time
bomb that was bound to explode.

The events of 1980 revealed the rage felt by the country's
majority. In a brutal sequence that became a national legend, the
angry band of soldiers broke into the executive mansion, rushed
upstairs, and surprised Tolbert in his luxurious quarters. They
shot and killed the president, disemboweled him, stuck a bayonet
through his head, and after displaying his body in the morgue at
the John F. Kennedy Hospital, buried it in a mass grave with
twenty-seven others.

Ten days later, the international press was invited to a grue-
some ceremony and encouraged to record it in words and pictures
and on film. The army took thirteen of the wealthy Americo-
Liberian officials who had been arrested (including Minister of
Justice Joseph Chesson), marched them nearly naked through the
streets of Monrovia past jeering citizens, tied them to seaside
posts at the Barclay Training Centre, and executed them at point-
blank range. A crowd of thousands gathered at the beach to watch
and cheer as the officials—some whimpering and collapsing, others faintly smiling—were cut down with rifle shots and their limp
bodies sprayed with machine-gun fire. By all accounts, there was
jubilation throughout the country, literally dancing in the streets.

The executions took place within sight of Master Sergeant
Doe's new home, the enormous seven-story executive mansion,

and about a hundred feet from his old one—a roofless hovel the size of a toolshed, with no door, no plumbing, a dirt floor, and windows without glass. There he had lived with his wife and four children and, just a few nights before the coup, had found no shelter from the rain. The run-down barracks room became a symbol of Liberia's "revolution," one that Doe and his associates liked to show off to visitors.

Many other soldiers who had lived in similar places suddenly felt released from their condition. A self-appointed elite of the previously dispossessed moved into the palatial homes of Americo-Liberians who had fled—sometimes three or four military families to a single house—and in the name of the revolution confiscated their Mercedes-Benzes and other possessions. They harassed businessmen and merchants and freely brandished weapons to get their way. For a time, the soldiers' reign of unorganized terror brought the country to the brink of paralysis. It seemed as if Liberia would be permanently changed, and no one knew what to expect.

"The love of liberty brought us here." That was the motto of the early settlers of Liberia, who believed they were not only leaving behind the bonds of slavery in America, but also undertaking a civilizing mission by returning to the continent of their origins and imparting Western knowledge. Liberia was a creation of the American Colonization Society, a quaint institution founded in 1816. The Society sought to emulate Sierra Leone, just to the west of Liberia, which was developing as a haven for freed British slaves (including blacks who had fought on the British side during the American Revolution and later retreated to Nova Scotia). Some members of the Colonization Society were motivated by humanitarianism, but others were simply practical; American slave owners wanted former slaves out of sight, lest they provoke discontent on the remaining plantations. The civilizing mission was taken very seriously indeed by successive waves of black emigrants to Liberia.*

---

* Alexander Crummell, a New Yorker whose grandfather had been a chief in Sierra Leone before being sold into slavery, argued in 1870 that there was a need to bring "the genius of free government" to Africa, "this seat of

Encouraged by President James Monroe, the first group of adventurous freedmen landed at a West African harbor in 1822 and obtained some land from local "native kings," in exchange for a collection of weapons, trinkets, utensils, and drink. Those who survived the many diseases they suffered formed a community that was at first ruled by white governors on behalf of the Colonization Society but in 1847 became the Republic of Liberia. "We the people of the Republic of Liberia were originally the inhabitants of the United States of North America," began the constitution promulgated that year, leaving out what was then some 97 percent of the country's population.

In the early 1850s, the first president of Liberia, Joseph Jenkins Roberts (said by some to be a son of Thomas Jefferson), traveled to Europe and was received with honors by the reigning monarchs, thus establishing Liberia's dignity as a nation. The dignity was soon enshrined by the "honorables" in the True Whig party, American in its organization and character, but distinctly authoritarian in its circumstances; for most of the century during which it ruled Liberia, it was the only party in this showcase African "democracy."

For many decades—even well into the twentieth century—the government of Liberia actually controlled only a narrow strip of land along the coast. The coastal strip flourished, while the Hinterland (as it was officially known), still in the hands of traditional chiefs, was pitifully poor and chronically neglected. President Edwin Barclay made news in the early 1930s when he journeyed deep into the countryside, borne in a hammock by porters, bringing word of the Monrovia government. When Graham Greene made his pilgrimage by foot through Liberia in 1935, which he described in *Journey Without Maps*, he found himself welcomed in some areas "because I was a white, because they hoped all the time that a white nation would take the country over." If this enthusiastic reception was not precisely a yearning for colonial rule of the sort practiced across the border by the French in Guinea and Ivory Coast or by the British in Sierra Leone, it may have been a genuine sign of contempt for the self-perpetuating regime

---

ancient despotism and bloody superstition." Challenged about the rights of those already present in Liberia, settler-politician Crummell answered as a true colonist: "Both our position and our circumstances make us the guardians, the protectors, and the teachers of our heathen tribes."

in Monrovia, which loved its own liberty more than that of its subjects. So appalled was American writer John Gunther by the conditions he found during his visit to Liberia in the early 1950s that he called it "a kind of perverse advertisement for imperialism, since, although the country is free, the [Liberian] people are so badly off compared to those in most French and British colonies."

One Liberian president, Edward J. Roye, a native of Ohio, ended his term in jail after negotiating a gigantic loan in 1871 to keep the country afloat, and he drowned while trying to escape Liberia in a canoe. Another, Charles Dunbar Burgess King, was implicated in the slave trade on the offshore island of Fernando Po and also in appalling labor practices within Liberia, among them the custom of forcing country people to "pawn" their children or other relatives, if necessary, in order to obtain the money to pay fees and fines levied by the government. A League of Nations investigation, instigated by U.S. Secretary of State Henry Stimson, found that in the interior of Liberia young boys were hunted down like animals, herded to the ports, and shipped off on Spanish and German ships; others were sent to another part of their own country, forced to work without pay, and, if uncooperative, subjected to such torture as being smoked over a fire. All of this took place with government knowledge and, sometimes, participation.

One of the worst offenders was King's vice-president, Allen N. Yancy, who murdered people at will and had rural chiefs flogged in front of their tribesmen if they did not meet their quotas for shipment to Fernando Po. The League of Nations report revealed these practices to the world in 1931, recommending that Liberia be deprived of its independence and colonized. That did not happen, but Yancy was impeached and King was forced to resign. After seventeen years in "retirement," however, King was finally rehabilitated, sent to Washington as a Liberian diplomat, and subsequently returned to conduct a lucrative private law practice in Monrovia.

King's and Yancy's lawyer during many domestic and international legal proceedings was William Vacanarat Shadrach Tubman, who eventually succeeded Barclay (who had himself succeeded King). Tubman served as president from 1944 until his death in 1971. In a sense, it was Tubman who brought Liberia— or the Americo-Liberian part of it—into the modern age. He established an "open door policy," attracting foreign capital to Liberia under unusually favorable conditions. Investors could obtain eighty-year leases for tracts of undeveloped land, and the flow of profits and dividends out of the country was not restricted. Machinery imported for industrial use was exempt from customs duty, and other taxes were low. This did little for the improvement of agriculture, and while the policy did have some beneficial effects in the countryside, overall it intensified the contrast between the industrialized coast and the backward Hinterland. In the long run, the open door policy produced what outside analysts called "growth without development."*

Tubman did recognize the political and economic disparities in Liberian society, and he purported to do something about them. He provided for representation of the Hinterland in the Liberian House of Representatives for the first time, but his so-called "unification policy" was largely a sham. Although Tubman would occasionally confiscate property and distribute it more evenly, for the most part his reign was a time of growth for the great Liberian fortunes. He himself lived in a country chateau and sometimes traveled abroad on a presidential yacht whose upkeep required more than 1 percent of the national budget. Under Tubman, an Old (American) South antebellum architectural style flourished, and Monrovia became a place of elaborate and pompous ceremony, complete with top hats and morning coats, brass bands and honor guards. (The appropriation for ceremonial bands at one point surpassed the expenditure on public health.) Meanwhile, as roads and transportation improved, the ruling elite began to buy up—or simply steal—land in the interior that had supposedly been reserved for the tribal people.

Liberian foreign policy under Tubman was eclectic. The country developed a close relationship with the right-wing regime of Generalissimo Francisco Franco of Spain, and Tubman traveled

* That was the title given to a book that grew out of an economic survey of Liberia done by four American and English economists in 1961–62. They found that "the rapid growth in production between 1950 and 1960 has had little developmental impact on Liberia or Liberians," and they could scarcely conceal their outrage over the country's economic, political, and social system. As they said, "In Liberia, political form differs radically from political substance." (Robert W. Clower et al., *Growth Without Development: An Economic Survey of Liberia* [Evanston: Northwestern University Press, 1966]).

there to visit him. Yet, he also perceived the appeal of pan-Africanism, became an early champion of Ghana's Kwame Nkrumah, and was a cofounder with him of the Organization of African Unity in 1963. In 1960, Liberia joined Ethiopia in bringing a case against South Africa in the World Court, one of several initiatives that led eventually to revocation of Pretoria's old League of Nations mandate over Namibia (South-West Africa). But economically and culturally, Liberia was a loner in Africa, for many years a member of no free-trade bloc or regional association of states. Thus, the original dependence on the United States was perpetuated.

It was after Tubman's death that William Tolbert, the grandson of freed slaves from South Carolina, an ordained Baptist minister who had been vice-president for twenty years, came to power. (The two men were also linked in a kind of Liberian royal family, as one of Tubman's sons was married to one of Tolbert's daughters.)

Appearing publicly in sport shirts open at the collar, Tolbert was less given to absurd formality than Tubman, and so the life style of the Americo-Liberians became more relaxed, if no less exclusive and ostentatious. Tolbert made the usual obligatory promises about better integrating Liberia's sixteen up-country tribal groups with the elite into one national family, and while he was president more opportunities were available for outsiders in government, if not in business. Ironically, this attempt at gradual reform may have hastened Tolbert's own undoing. After a century of unabashed repression and exploitation, even a slight loosening of the constraints had a profound effect. Liberia began to experience more frequent labor disputes and other signs of political discontent.

But Tolbert's foreign reputation was almost unblemished. Relying heavily on his religious background, he cultivated a role as a peacemaker and mediator. Particularly significant in the context of African politics was the rapprochement that Tolbert effected in 1978 among the three senior statesmen of francophone West Africa—Léopold Senghor of Senegal, Félix Houphouët-Boigny of Ivory Coast, and Sékou Touré of Guinea. Though he could not speak to them in French, he persuaded them all to come to Monrovia for a summit on neutral ground, where it was possible for them to overcome various personal and philosophical quarrels.

Tolbert astonished his black African neighbors and friends by hosting South African Prime Minister John Vorster for a brief visit to Monrovia in 1975, supposedly extracting a promise that Namibia would soon be free. Later, when he felt that Vorster had reneged on the deal, Tolbert proclaimed "one hundred thousand percent" support for the South-West Africa Peoples Organization (SWAPO) and gave it minor financial aid for its guerrilla war against the South Africans in Namibia. In another demonstration of erratic political behavior, he got the Israelis, who had trained some of the Liberian police and military, to build a $6 million executive mansion to his specifications in the early 1970s; but then he essentially switched sides (like many other Africans) and became an ardent defender of Arab causes, in order to assure an oil supply for Liberia after the 1973 Middle East war.

Especially important to Tolbert was his term as head of the OAU. To spruce up Monrovia for the 1979 summit that would mark the beginning of his chairmanship, he spent well over $100 million of the government's money, constructing special chalets to house visiting heads of state, putting in new streetlights, and hiring a retired ocean liner to provide extra conference facilities in the harbor. He broke the bank to enhance his own prestige. (The finance minister at the time was dismissed after many thousands of dollars that came in during the OAU meeting disappeared.)

The Monrovia summit went well enough—although it characteristically failed to solve any of the intra-African disputes outstanding at the time—but soon afterward Tolbert's domestic difficulties resumed. It was said that he was weary and that at the end of his year of OAU responsibilities, Tolbert planned to begin thinking about stepping down, perhaps in 1983, to take on some grander international role. Instead, he made history as the first African statesman to be overthrown or killed while serving as chairman of the OAU.

Throughout Liberia's history, whether it was being ruled by slave traders or benevolent despots, the country had particular importance for American blacks, many of whom had relatives there. But the contrast between the official egalitarianism enshrined in the Liberian constitution (written at the Harvard Law School) and laws (codified at Cornell) and the harsh realities of life in Liberia was cause for shame and embarrassment. This was a small black country that thrived on its status as a quaint, almost comic-opera imitation of the powerful white one where its founders had been enslaved. The imitation went so far as to include a property qualification for voting, an insistence on Anglo-Saxon rather than African names, and the cultivation of an upper-crust American accent and manner of speaking which few ordinary Liberians, who spoke tonal dialects, could understand, let alone imitate. Liberia became a society where some of the most personal decisions of the ruling elite, such as marriage and divorce, were taken largely on the basis of efforts to retain social, economic, and political control. Yet many who wished Liberia well, because it was a proudly independent black nation, ignored these painful truths.

Part of Liberia's pose as a black republic was its racist rule that only blacks could be citizens and own land. Practically speaking, that meant that a small number of people in the aristocracy owned enormous amounts of land and, at the expense of their fellow Liberians, made outrageous deals for its use and exploitation by outside, generally white-controlled economic interests. The agreement that brought the Firestone Tire and Rubber Company into Liberia in 1926 gave it the right to lease up to a million acres for ninety-nine years at six cents an acre. Meanwhile, a specially established Firestone subsidiary lent the Liberian government large sums of money at the then-substantial interest rate of 7 percent. (Tubman finally announced that the Firestone loan had been paid off in 1951.)

Admittedly, Firestone's arrival in Liberia was a mutually beneficial event. The country was desperate for money, having defaulted on several major loans and then having been disappointed repeatedly by American congressmen and bankers. Firestone, faced with restrictive trade practices in Malaya, Ceylon, and elsewhere in the British empire, was itself desperate for new sources of rubber, and Liberia seemed the ideal answer.

The terms of the company's presence did improve over time—Firestone eventually agreed to pay a higher royalty on the land it used, as well as Liberian income taxes—but until the 1970s, few indigenous Liberians could hope for good jobs on the rubber plantations. Americans were brought over instead, with only a few Americo-Liberians employed as window dressing. Firestone also failed to teach small-scale local growers how to tap their own rubber trees, and it frequently undercut their prices and tried to drive them out of the market. The company did nothing to help Liberia develop the industrial capacity to process the raw material into finished goods with a higher market value. Thus Liberia, one of the world's richest sources of rubber, still imports tires and pays top dollar for them.

Over the years, Liberia's most obvious priority was to keep business booming. During the OAU meeting in Monrovia in 1979, the government distributed a brochure designed to entice multinational corporations into a new "industrial free zone." Its anti-Marxist message: "Industrialists of the World Reunite in Liberia to Experience Freedom." The caption of a photograph of a worker in a hard hat implored, "Hire me! I am skilled, hard-working, reliable and inexpensive, and there are many like me in my country. Give us a chance to help you make good profits in Liberia." One feature of the "free zone" was that corporations which located there would be exempt from income tax for at least five years. The Liberian elite felt no pressure to negotiate better arrangements so long as they were comfortable. While proclaiming dedication to religious principles and African decolonization, they lived a decadent, colonial life, which could be preserved only as long as the flow of money continued but the country did not develop too far or too fast.

One old Liberian money-making scheme was the registration of ships according to notoriously loose rules and regulations. It did not cost much to win the right to fly the Liberian flag of convenience at sea, and inspections were lax. If enough shippers took advantage of the system, Liberia earned millions of dollars in fees every year. A third of Liberia's commercial fleet is made up of U.S.-owned tankers and bulk carriers; at least 75 percent of American-owned ships fly the Liberian flag. It was no surprise that most of the major oil spills that provoked international outrage in the 1960s and 1970s came from ships—such as the *Torrey Canyon* and the *Amoco Cadiz*—registered in Liberia.

Successive American governments of both parties knew of the flaws and the exploitation so central to the Liberian system, but they looked the other way, and took advantage of the special relationship to build Voice of America transmitters, sophisticated navigation stations, and the like, on Liberian soil. The United States failed to use its substantial influence to good ends, for example to promote equal access to education. Indeed, American officials were unfailingly obsequious toward Liberia and deferential to the wishes of its leaders. "Liberia was born out of mankind's eternal desire for freedom, and you have achieved it here," crowed President Jimmy Carter on his arrival for a visit of just a few hours in 1978. Carter, having spent several days in Nigeria, had been persuaded that it would be an insult to one of America's best friends if he did not also stop in Liberia while he was in the neighborhood. The Liberians, for their part, said that a call at Robertsfield airport for fuel and ceremony would not do; Carter would have to make the long journey into Monrovia for a working lunch. In his toast to Tolbert, Carter developed the familiar theme of Liberia as a place where "individual human freedom" and "the liberty of the human soul" flourished. Having talked with Tolbert, a fellow Baptist, Carter said he was impressed by "how much he knew intimately and personally about the needs of the average citizen in Liberia who has not yet been blessed adequately."

In the autumn of 1979—six months *after* the rice riots in which so many Liberians had been massacred—Tolbert made an official visit to the United States. He was warmly received in Washington and honored at a reception by the black lobbying group, TransAfrica.

In terms of corruption, Liberia became a leader in Africa and the Third World. Under Tubman's benign dictatorship, there were limits; it is an old saw of Liberian politics that "when Tubman stole a dollar, he would give ninety cents back to the people" in the form of food or minor amenities. Tolbert, however, "would return ten cents." His son, Adolphus B. Tolbert, a lawyer, set an example of excess and exploitation for many other Americo-Liberians in and out of government. One of Tolbert's daughters, an assistant minister of education, controlled the sale of all textbooks in Liberia. Another, a representative in Monrovia for the World Health Organization, was in the pharmaceutical business on the side. The president himself was thought to have as much as $200 million stashed away in the United States. His brother Frank, who was president pro tempore of the Liberian Senate at the time of the coup, acknowledged assets of more than $500,000, plus seven homes and seven apartment buildings in Monrovia. His residence in the family compound at Bensonville (renamed

"Bentol" in order to enshrine one syllable from the family name on the map) was even more plush than that of the president. The husband of Tolbert's niece Charlotte, Frank J. Stewart, budget director in the old regime, owned twenty-eight city lots, five houses, and a rubber plantation. The Tolbert family's greed was a key factor in the downfall of a system that might otherwise have survived for another generation.

Documents in the possession of the new Liberian government trace the outright sale to foreigners, especially Germans, of dozens of Liberian diplomatic passports (which would permit the holders to travel around the world without having their baggage opened or inspected). In one instance, a woman paid half a million dollars for her title of "financial consultant" to Liberia and for other unspecified favors. One man paid $150,000 for an eight-year appointment as Liberia's honorary consul in Rome. Others established "foundations" in their own names in Monrovia, to which they would send "contributions" whenever they wanted something from the Liberian government. As far as can be determined, these payoffs went directly into family, rather than government, coffers.

Astonishingly, the Tolberts left behind substantial evidence of their wheelings and dealings. They kept photocopies of the passports they sold, issued receipts for many of the payments they received, and in some cases even made surreptitious videotapes of the transactions that took place in the executive mansion. In one extraordinary letter, handwritten on an airplane during an international journey and then photocopied for the files, Adolphus Tolbert told one European business associate who had recently been in Liberia: "I expect to meet you in London during the first week in June to discuss the gold, diamond, and uranium project . . . Bring along the Rolls-Royce. . . . Please transmit the balance on that amount given to me last night. Also send the papers for the two cars. . . . Make sure that a secretary is awaiting my arrival in London."

In 1977, William Tolbert published his personal economic theory. He called it "humanistic capitalism"; under its terms, rich Liberians were to distribute their excess income to poor Liberians, through the traditional African extended-family system. It was a way to combine unbridled free enterprise with a sense of responsibility. By that time, Tolbert was one of the wealthiest men in

Liberia, perhaps in all of Africa. When he was deposed, three
years later, the average annual per capita income of Liberians
was still $419. The average monthly wage was between $70 and
$80. Illiteracy was around 85 percent.

Americans go to Monrovia mostly for reasons of business or
family ties, or by mistake. Nearly all of Pan Am's African itineraries used to include a stop at Robertsfield, the gigantic American-
built international airport, some forty miles from town but adjacent to Firestone Rubber's 77,863-acre Harbel plantation. Some
American travelers have thought that Monrovia might be a restful
interlude on the way to or from the difficult cities of Lagos and
Kinshasa or the tourist paradise of Nairobi. It is not.

Monrovia is a steamy, grimy, torrid port city, where the poorest of the poor are less escapable than in some other African capitals. Malaria is endemic and rampant—nearly every Liberian is
thought to have the disease at some point in his life—the air is
dense with industrial and automobile pollution, and one is liable
to be mugged or robbed, night or day. The youngsters who have
streamed into the capital from the underdeveloped countryside,
where few villages have electricity and few huts have running water, look as if their expectations have dwindled into a constant
search for the next meal.

While the Americo-Liberians still held sway, much of this
was concealed by an overlay of elegance and pomp: piazzas and
limousines, pillared mansions and debutante balls, a marble Masonic temple that would look right at home in an American small
town. Some of the most important political horse-trading was
done in secret meetings of the Masonic lodge, to which all the
truly important people belonged. The temple was sacked and its
statuary destroyed during the 1980 coup, but its shell still looms
on a hill at one end of Monrovia, a monument to the ancien ré-
gime and its values. It became a home to squatters, but the American ambassador suggested it might make an appropriate museum
of Liberian history.

Symbols of American influence abound in the capital. The
country's red, white, and blue flag—a single star and eleven stripes—
looks as if it were designed by some Liberian relative of Betsy
Ross. Monrovia's police wear hand-me-down summer uniforms

from the New York City Police Department. The Roxy Theatre is next door to the Travolta Boutique, and bacon cheeseburgers are on nearly every menu. Videotapes of old episodes of "Sanford and Son" are very much in demand. There is a "strip," on Gurley Street, where nightclubs and discos with American names (the "California," the "Phoenix") blare Donna Summer and Diana Ross; outside, prostitutes parade and young toughs alternately jostle strangers and offer to protect them for a price. As a counterpoint, the Baptist church remains strong, and Monrovia has a religious radio station on which evangelists Oral Roberts or the Reverend Ike would come as no surprise.

The Americo-Liberian regime built a remarkably faithful rendition of the U.S. Capitol, complete with House and Senate chambers and committee rooms in which a charade of the American system could be practiced. It stands on "Capitol Hill." The official currency of Liberia is the Liberian dollar; but in fact, until recently there were no Liberian paper dollars, only American ones, and so every financial transaction in the country was carried out in greenbacks, the oldest, most worn bills extant, ready for shipment back to the (U.S.) treasury. (Tolbert did have some silver dollars minted that carried his image, as did Doe in his time.) The biggest bank in Monrovia is the Chase Manhattan, and any government of Liberia must maintain the confidence of Chase and other private American financial institutions if it is to stay afloat.

During World War II, Liberia's unusually large supply of natural rubber was so important to the United States that there was a virtual American occupation of the country. In fact, the U.S. military built the port of Monrovia, so that war matériel and raw materials could be shipped in and out more easily. Rubber now ranks second to iron ore among Liberia's exports, but it is still important. Harbel—with more than 9 million trees, the largest single rubber plantation in the world—is like a rural American company town (or county) tucked away on the great bulge of West Africa. There Firestone maintains 597 miles of road (forty-one miles paved), two hundred and fifty hospital beds, twenty-eight school buildings with almost six thousand students, eight Christian churches, a hundred and ten athletic teams using thirty-five playing fields, four Scout troops, and sixteen community organizations. But, so far, no union.

●

Liberia's coup brought to power an odd combination of forces. On one side was the People's Redemption Council (PRC), composed of the twenty-seven soldiers who claimed to have helped plan or execute the events of April 1980. They were a ragtag group, mostly in their twenties and semiliterate, ranging in character from Doe (the best educated of the lot) and a few others who, for a time at least, seemed genuinely interested in the public welfare, to Harrison Pennue, who built his notoriety and power on the basis of his boast that it was he who disemboweled Tolbert. Although some of them stated in their official biographies that they were descendants of famous "warriors," the members of the PRC were mostly the children of rural laborers and market women, and as typical Liberian soldiers, they had joined Tolbert's army to improve their chances for a decent life. But in the army they lived in squalid conditions and were usually required to kick back 10 percent of their meager salaries to their officers. Before the coup and after, they were an angry bunch.

On the other side was the mostly civilian cabinet. Some of its members were anomalies, such as Doe's first information minister, Gabriel Nimeley, who used to do play-by-play broadcasts of soccer games for Liberian radio and happened to be on duty when Master Sergeant Doe came to the studio on that night in April to announce his coup on the air. After promptly surrendering the microphone to Doe, Nimeley joined the government. Most, however, like George Boley, were highly educated people in their thirties or forties who had obtained American doctorates and worked in junior positions under the old regime, but got into trouble when they spoke too freely about the need for change. While the members of the PRC gave bold speeches and made rash promises, especially in the early days after the coup, the ministers worried about how to deliver from a virtually bankrupt treasury.

The first major clash in the coalition came only days after the coup. Togba-Nah Tipoteh (Ph.D., University of Nebraska), founder of the Movement for Justice in Africa (MOJA) and for a time the minister of planning and economic affairs, along with several of his civilian colleagues, stayed awake for four straight days and nights, pleading with the PRC to heed the advice coming from Washington and elsewhere—to stop the summary trial and execution of former officials and wealthy Americo-Liberians, lest the new government be completely ostracized from the Western community of nations. After about thirty people had been put to death, Doe agreed, and he announced publicly that the executions were over.

Later it fell to the ministers to persuade the soldiers that they could not possibly carry out all their promises. They could not freeze the price of gasoline if the cost of imported oil was going up; they could not keep increasing the salaries of the military and the civil servants if the government had no new revenues; they could not offer free primary and secondary education throughout the country if they had few teachers and poor classrooms; they could not even freeze the price of ever popular Coca-Cola, because if they did, the local franchise-holder, a subsidiary of Firestone, would simply stop producing it.

But some members of the PRC resisted instruction. Intoxicated with their newfound authority, they were inclined to call news conferences, during which they detailed their travels around the country, delivered harangues on the duty of the ministers to correct various problems, and then upbraided the reporters in attendance, Liberians and foreigners alike, for publishing or broadcasting things they did not like. (One article in *Newsweek* that particularly offended Doe became a cause célèbre in Liberia, the subject of official speeches, and a pretext for keeping other journalists out and limiting the access of those who got in.) One of the chief showmen was Thomas Weh Syen, cochairman of the PRC and Doe's "vice head of state" for almost a year and a half after the coup. Before he began his tirade at one news conference, called to berate the ministers, Weh Syen and several military colleagues behaved like teenagers at play, mugging for pictures they took of each other with a Polaroid camera and then giggling over the results. All the while, the reporters summoned for the occasion watched these preliminaries in wonderment.

The PRC issued a regular newsletter of its own following the coup. It included everything from stern warnings on the correct spelling of members' names to homilies against "antirevolutionaries." The PRC's early behavior tended to embarrass the civilian ministers, who wanted to establish international respect for a new Liberia and felt that buffoonery, combined with confiscation of personal property and a lack of respect for due process, would further damage the country's reputation. But while the council needed the ministers to keep Liberia functioning, in times of crisis the sophisticates with the American Ph.D.s could be easily over-ruled by the people who came to work in their military fatigues. Doe dealt with the standoff in July 1981 by drafting all twelve civilians remaining in the cabinet into the army, a move that made them less likely to speak openly against the PRC and subjected them to military discipline—potentially including secret trials—if they stepped out of line.

Although the PRC took over the Capitol building and constituted itself as a legislature of sorts, complete with speaker and committees, the real government headquarters remained in Tolbert's old seven-story executive mansion. Bullet holes in the heavy metal doors on some floors served as reminders of the events of April 1980, but gold-leaf settees and quaint antique tables still sat under thick oil paintings of Liberia's former presidents in plush drawing rooms and antechambers. It was as if nothing had changed, although now the settees were occupied not by Americo-Liberians of high social standing, but by the ubiquitous petitioners, men and women with weary faces, bearing grievances, suggestions, or most likely job applications, hoping that some tenuous connection with the new regime would bring them a break in an economy where unemployment was staggering.

The man who presides over the new Liberia, Samuel Doe, looks less like a genuine "head of state" (as he insisted upon being called at first) than a student who has won the role of president in the school play and has decided to act and dress the part with particular originality. For a time Doe wore only camouflage fatigues, with a gold-script pin on his collar that said "Chairman" (of the PRC). He affected yellow sunglasses and, sometimes, a tilted cowboy hat in place of his army beret. He carried a machine gun or a two-way radio, and most of his formal pictures showed him behind a desk that had nothing on it but a Lucite pen set.

In the early days after the coup, Doe was careful about his image, keeping his military rank of master sergeant while others playfully promoted themselves to general, and preferring to drive a beat-up old Chevrolet or a Honda Civic instead of using the leftover limousines from the Tolbert era. But the trappings of power became irresistible. Doe promoted himself from master sergeant to "commander in chief" of the army. He moved up to three-piece dress suits and took to having himself driven around Monrovia in a black Mercedes-Benz. He engaged a personal hairdresser to come by the executive mansion every morning to coif him. His wife, Nancy, is routinely called the "First Lady" of Liberia, and she is frequently photographed officiating at dedication ceremonies or announcing her involvement in education projects. She is chauffeured on her rounds in a powder-blue Lincoln Continental with a white top.

The PRC took care of itself, too. It preferred to use Tolbert's old presidential jet, rather than selling it at a profit, and it was profligate in the use of limousines and other government cars. During its first year in office, the PRC spent well over $1 million on travel, more than twice the amount spent by Tolbert's government in its last year. Doe himself decided to build a luxury home in the countryside with funds from unspecified sources—nothing on the scale of Tolbert's extravagant palaces, but still something that would stand out for its opulence and (some would say) its betrayal of the revolution's aims.

Doe insisted on being treated as if he were the fount of all wisdom, and he quickly developed a distaste for dissent. Liberian government offices, including overseas embassies, routinely distribute collections of Chairman Doe's thoughts and sayings.

Because of the violent beginnings of his regime, Doe initially had trouble establishing credibility outside Liberia. It was not so much the number of people killed that seemed to upset outsiders—many rulers had come to power elsewhere in Africa through coups that killed more—but the manner and method and public display. Some other African heads of state worried that they might be vulnerable to the same sort of uprising. A number of them, old friends and associates of Tolbert's, would not even let an airplane carrying Doe land in their capitals for meetings. Eventually, the modest, soft-spoken man charmed them, and persuaded them that he was a moderate, restraining influence within the PRC. Even Sékou Touré of Guinea, who had been a staunch friend of Tolbert despite their ideological differences, rallied to Doe's side and helped him achieve respectability in Africa; he needed access to Liberia's ports for Guinea's exports and could not afford to quarrel over niceties.

Crucial to the initial improvement of Doe's image were two speeches, drafted with the encouragement and direct involvement of the International Monetary Fund and the American embassy in Monrovia. The first, delivered in November 1980, warned of

Liberia's grave economic situation and criticized excesses among the military. Doe put a freeze on government hiring, required every Liberian wage-earner to forgo at least a month's salary in order to buy new national savings bonds, and removed the "PRC coordinators" who had been supervising the affairs of private businesses. Finally, he declared that

> the meaning of the Revolution is misunderstood by many of you. Even after half a year, people are still hoping and dreaming of the impossible. They are thinking that the Revolution means instant prosperity; plenty of new jobs; big cars; big houses; and all of the fine things of the world. In other words, they feel that this is a Revolution of Entitlement. While recognizing the growing wave of your rising expectation, I should let you know that the PRC government cannot solve all the nation's problems overnight. . . .

In the second speech, on Christmas Eve of the same year, Doe announced the release of many of the political prisoners held since the coup and, declaring that the PRC remained "committed to our pledge to return to the barracks," promised that the council would appoint a national commission to draft a new constitution for Liberia.

The commission was appointed on the first anniversary of the coup, but initially it was not able to work as openly and freely as promised. One of its members, Patrick Seyon, vice-president of the University of Liberia, was arrested and accused of plotting with two other civilians and thirteen soldiers to overthrow the PRC government. Seyon was severely beaten during three days in jail, but then released "for lack of evidence." The soldiers, however, confessed and were executed in June 1981.

Two months later, Doe's deputy, Thomas Weh Syen, and four of the other original members of the PRC—a kind of opposition bloc within the council—were accused of planning to kill Doe and take charge themselves. Doe had them tried and convicted by a secret military court, put in the post stockade at the Barclay Training Centre, and on their first night there shot or beaten to death in their cells.* Although the method of Weh Syen's demise

---

* One thing that the viciously independent Weh Syen had done during his final months in power was to dispose of the military regime's most controversial political prisoner, Adolphus B. Tolbert, a figure of great notoriety

could hardly be condoned, his departure from government was greeted with relief by American officials, private investors, and others concerned about Liberia's shattered economy.

Liberia's economic circumstances make it unlikely that the country will be able to survive on its own anytime soon. The monthly bill for oil (100 percent of it imported from Saudi Arabia) is at least $12 million, and each time it comes due, the lights burn late in the American embassy as U.S. advisers try to help the Liberians juggle their accounts. At least $30 million in capital, one-fourth of Liberia's entire currency base, left the country after the coup, mostly in the hands of either Americo-Liberians escaping to the States or Lebanese merchants who controlled much of the local retail trade, but who also had operations and havens in other nearby countries. (A survey by Liberia's new National Investment Commission several years after the coup found that 75 percent of the country's small businesses were still owned by Lebanese and Indian businessmen.) Liberia's external debt was estimated at $800 million and growing at the time of the coup, and some economists have feared a total economic collapse. A drop in the price of iron ore on the world market did not help, and production cuts by LAMCO, the country's largest iron ore company, made it clear Liberia would be buffeted by the sagging world demand for steel. Like many other West African countries, Liberia prayed for an offshore oil discovery that would bring overnight prosperity. The World Bank financed a study of the prospects, but there has been no sign of a commercial bonanza from oil.

The combination of capital flight, a decline in Liberia's terms of trade, the general world recession, and the crisis in investor confidence growing out of the coup made the first several years of the Doe regime an economic disaster. From 1979 through 1982, Liberia's per capita gross national product declined, possibly by as much as 8 percent a year. (One contributing factor was that

and resentment. The late president's son had initially found refuge in the French embassy in Monrovia, in the hope that he might escape to Ivory Coast and gain the protection of his father-in-law, Ivorian President Félix Houphouët-Boigny. But after two months, Liberian troops burst into the French embassy compound and took the younger Tolbert to the Barclay Training Centre; one night, several months later, Weh Syen and his cohorts went there and shot him to death before he could be put on trial.

Firestone closed down its second biggest rubber plantation, putting another seventeen hundred people out of work.) As a result, the standard of living went down, further exacerbating some of the problems that brought about the coup in the first place. Even when the economic situation began to improve late in 1983 after rubber prices had gone back up, the most that anyone seemed to hope for was a return to positive growth of about 1 percent a year.

Meanwhile, the most obvious place to turn for emergency aid, governmental or commercial loans, and new private investment was Liberia's traditional guardian, the United States. That was not easy for Doe at first, given the revulsion over the coup among Liberia's American constituency (not to mention an influx of Americo-Liberian exiles in the Virginia suburbs of Washington and in several other cities). But within months, a consortium of New York banks was pitching in to help Liberia avoid insolvency. Help was also forthcoming from the International Monetary Fund, especially as Doe began to agree to austerity measures. He even instituted a 20 percent increase in the price of rice and raised taxes, demonstrating that he could get away with things that Tolbert could not. Workers on the public payroll, having previously had their salaries doubled, found them cut, late in 1982, by amounts ranging from 16 to 25 percent, and free gasoline allowances and other privileges that drained the coffers were eliminated for many government officials.

The first country to recognize the PRC government after the coup was Libya, and Colonel Muammar al-Qaddafi—who at the time had his troops in Chad and his eye on other West African nations—launched an immediate friendship offensive, inviting members of the cabinet and the PRC to Tripoli. There were stories of people being offered suitcases full of cash as an enticement. Several members of the new regime did go to Libya, but the U.S. State Department apparently weighed in just in time to persuade Doe himself not to accede to the Libyan blandishments. Indeed, Washington later convinced him to expel the Libyan "People's Bureau" from Monrovia altogether, and early on Doe also expelled nine Soviet diplomats on suspicion of espionage. Later he required the Soviet ambassador and the *chargé d'affaires* of the Ghanaian embassy to leave, because of "conduct incompatible with their diplomatic status." Doe did visit the leftist military regime in

Ethiopia early in his tenure, but he returned unimpressed with its system or the accomplishments of Cuban aid there. He also found that promises of aid from Libya and other Arab states quickly faded when it became clear that he did not intend to comply with their policy wishes.

Gabriel Baccus Matthews, founder of the Progressive People's party and Doe's original foreign minister, argued for a more independent, truly nonaligned Liberian foreign policy. He said it was fine for Liberia to accept American warnings against a change in international orientation, but only if Washington backed up those warnings with substantial contributions to the country's well-being. Matthews told U.S. officials that considerable aid would be necessary to protect America's "important interests" in Liberia, including the complex communications facilities and other installations that the U.S. military has built. Matthews's boldness toward Washington, and his status as an articulate potential civilian leader of Liberia, help explain why he was removed from the cabinet by Doe in 1982. Another advocate of an independent course, Tipoteh, who was a Marxist and a leading intellectual in the new regime, sought asylum in Ivory Coast in August 1981.

Americans who feel that aid to Liberia is important argue that the country's position on the coast of West Africa is strategic and that political and economic instability there would tempt international interference. The Reagan administration took a symbolic step toward maintaining U.S. influence in Liberia by sending a hundred Green Berets and a naval destroyer there on a training exercise in April 1981 on the first anniversary of the coup. After staging a celebratory parachute jump, the Green Berets stayed on to run a one-month basic training program for the Liberian infantry, a stint that was later credited with a substantial effect on the discipline and morale of Liberian soldiers. Reagan also carried out previously existing plans for some $2 million in military aid to the Doe regime in fiscal year 1981 and granted an additional $25 million in economic support funds over the $7 million the Carter administration had budgeted. Subsequently, despite overall cutbacks in the American foreign assistance program, U.S. aid to Liberia grew even further, to a total of some $75 million a year. The Peace Corps contingent was expanded to two hundred volunteers, food aid was substantially increased, and the

United States brought large numbers of Liberian soldiers to train at American military schools.

The Reagan administration went out of its way to give Doe the kind of high-level attention he wanted. He made a full-fledged state visit to the United States in 1982, and when he returned to address the UN General Assembly in 1983, Reagan met with him again in New York.

U.S. advisers were quietly brought into virtually every department of the Liberian government, maintaining a low profile but having a significant influence on policy. "Sometimes I feel like we're running the Colonial Office," said one State Department official with responsibility for Liberia. "We expect Liberia will continue to require our support and that of its other friends for some time," U.S. Ambassador William Lacy Swing noted in a speech in Houston in October 1981, "but we are encouraged by the efforts which Liberians in the private sector, as well as the public sector, are making to restore confidence in their country and to restore its image as a friendly partner of private enterprise." One thing that did not change was that shipping registry fees—the use of the Liberian flag of convenience—continued to provide 6 or 7 percent of the nation's revenues. Shippers could still count on the fact that as long as they paid their money, the Liberians would not hold them to high safety and environmental standards.

It is ironic that Liberia, despite a violent upheaval aimed at a class that epitomized the country's American ties, should end up as close to and dependent on the United States as ever, if not more so. The Americo-Liberian bias was finally being eliminated from Liberia's history textbooks, and other symbolic measures were taken to promote the idea of equality regardless of ethnic origin. But probably the only way for Liberia to avoid some of the agonies and indignities experienced by Ghana or Uganda is to draw upon its American connection and stay on good terms with the United States. It is as if Liberia had attempted to tamper with its destiny and failed. To this day, Liberian officials are jealous and resentful if they believe the United States is paying too much attention to Nigeria or other African states, at the expense of its oldest African friend and ward.

To consolidate his own power and to reestablish Liberia's reputation, Doe found it necessary to bring his coconspirators and other members of the military under control. The excesses did continue for some time. For example, Harrison Pennue, the soldier who disemboweled Tolbert, was known to flog people just for passing his car on the street (a throwback to the days of Tubman, who sometimes personally shot out the tires of cars that did the same). But before long, the soldiers had virtually disappeared from downtown Monrovia; those still in evidence mostly gave up their machine guns and instead carried walky-talkies as signs of their status. In 1984 Doe actually disbanded the PRC as a step toward the return of civilian rule, naming all of its remaining members to a new interim national assembly. He established a Bureau of Reacquisition to administer the return of properties confiscated at the time of the 1980 coup, and he ordered all soldiers illegally occupying the homes or other property of private citizens to move out or enter into proper leases with the owners.

Eager to put the best gloss on his regime, Doe lifted the onerous curfew that had caused some foreign officials to spend the night at the airport and had promoted a lively extortion business at roadblocks throughout the country. And he demonstrated an unusual, at times amusing, political savvy.*

For all the talk of change, corruption soon became a major problem in Liberia again. Western diplomats claimed to know exactly which members of the People's Redemption Council were in charge of the illicit drug trade and other profitable illegal operations. In one notorious incident, the crew of a Liberian-registered tanker supposedly carrying oil to South Africa was arrested in Senegal and later transferred to a jail in Monrovia. The crew members were released without any judicial proceedings, and the suspicion was that several officials of the new government were paid off; they simply refused to comment. Bribes and other illegal payments are more widespread and obvious in Liberia now than before. The man named finance minister in one cabinet reshuffle had previously been fired for malfeasance by both the finance minis-

---

* After one corruption trial, the three defendants who had been found guilty, including two policemen, were sentenced to death. Thereupon, Doe asked the minister of justice to form a firing squad to carry out the sentence, composed entirely of honest policemen who would volunteer for the job. When the minister of justice reported back that he was unable to assemble such a group, Doe fired him and the chief of police and set the guilty parties free, on the grounds that they were probably no worse than their peers.

try and the Chase Manhattan Bank. One Monrovia banker said that a member of the government involved with bank regulation unabashedly approached him and several other bankers with a demand that they buy him a car. This banker suggests that the total financial burden of the corruption may be as great under Doe as it was under Tolbert, but the difference is simply that many more people are now sharing in the payoffs.

In most other respects, the Liberian economy has drifted back to normal operations. The traditional food markets function smoothly again, although there are some shortages. The inflation rate shot up over 20 percent (compared to 14 percent in Tolbert's last days), but that compares favorably with the situation in many developing and developed nations. One early problem was that other people became jealous of the soldiers and civil servants, the immediate beneficiaries of the coup. Dock workers in Monrovia went on strike, and Doe's government responded harshly, jailing the strike leaders and firing others from their jobs. A nurses' strike, supported by doctors, was handled with similar harshness, and Doe found other occasions to prove how tough he was; he even threatened to lock up the Liberian national soccer team if it lost a match with Ghana. (The result was a tie, so his resolve did not have to be tested.)

Violent crime increased in Liberia, especially in the country-side, and Doe promised that anyone convicted of murder would be executed. In this and other respects, Doe's government seemed willing to defy the theoretically independent civilian court system. Liberia's chief justice complained that members of the military and officials of the Ministry of Justice were taking matters in their own hands, "arresting people and confining them in our prisons without any reference to the judicial authority of this government." One reason for the substantial tension in the countryside is that life there has not changed significantly from the old days. There has been little in the way of agricultural development, and none of the rural cooperatives or land distribution efforts favored by Tipoteh and his MOJA has been instituted.

A few Americo-Liberians, especially the less wealthy, have managed to continue their lives relatively free of harassment, and others have returned or been released from prison and resumed normal routines. Virtually all of the original political prisoners were set free, although some new ones were arrested, including prominent Liberian journalists. For those who do end up in the Barclay Training Centre, government officials say, conditions are much improved; but they do not permit outsiders to verify that claim.

Doe's government was constantly alert to the threat of another coup. It used that excuse to suppress dissent, and it regularly accused former officials, including the former vice-president under Tolbert, Methodist Bishop Bennie Warner, of planning one. Warner was at a religious gathering in Indiana at the time of the 1980 coup, and his behavior then (and later) was peculiar. At first, he let it be known that he thought Tolbert deserved to be overthrown, but then he quickly turned against the new regime. Warner held a news conference in Abidjan to rally opposition to Doe, but a few days later at another news conference in Houston, he denied that it had been he who spoke out in Ivory Coast. He finally acknowledged both, but when he failed to establish credibility as an opposition figure, he faded from prominence. The various exile groups that took shape in the United States seemed capable of little more than rhetoric. One of them, the "Save Liberia Organization," adopted as its motto, "Achievement comes slowly and steadily through peace, diligence, and honesty"—hardly a call to arms. Its newsletter, written by chairman James Benedict Mason, consisted primarily of diatribes against the military government.

Liberians are still debating whether their society has undergone a revolution or just another garden-variety African coup. Many people—including Ellen Johnson-Sirleaf, who was minister of finance under Tolbert, ran the Liberian Development Bank for a time under Doe, and then returned to an old job with the World Bank—feared that the lot of the average Liberian would not change much at all, that one elite would simply be replaced by another—different, but no less selfish and ruthless. The Americo-Liberians (now sometimes derisively called "the Congo people") had lost their automatic access to power, but the technocrats and the soldiers who found themselves in the right place at the right time proved to be equally insensitive and harsh, and Americo-Liberians who were clever about it worked their way back into important positions.

One popular effort by Doe was the encouragement of indigenous cultures, tribal dress, and a simpler manner of speech. But at the same time, there was a risk that this would cause a surge of tribalism. The old Americo-Liberian aristocracy had avoided that African ailment by not favoring any one of the country's sixteen tribes over the others and by belittling all their traditional folk-ways. Now Doe has been accused of favoring his own Krahn tribe (a relatively small one) with government largesse and jobs, at the expense of others, such as the Nimba, who were known as sup-porters of the old Progressive People's party. Indeed, tribal ten-sions were at the heart of some of the alleged coup plots that Doe uncovered and punished. Before long, Doe himself had given up tribal dress for American-type three-piece suits, and he was proudly developing a speaking style that his U.S. sponsors could under-stand.

In Monrovia, there was serious concern over Doe's slide to-ward authoritarianism, especially in his dealings with student pro-testers and with opposition elements in the press. At one point Doe put a student activist under the same sort of banning order that is commonly used in South Africa against government oppo-nents considered dangerous. He shut down a new independent newspaper, the *Daily Observer*, and jailed its entire staff for ten days for printing letters critical of the ban. Later it was closed al-together. Even the government-owned *New Liberian* was rou-tinely scrutinized and its staff harassed. In 1984 Rufus Darpoh, a well-known Liberian journalist, was arrested after writing un-signed articles exposing the plans of some members of the military to try to remain in power; government agents accused him of "transmitting news clandestinely against the interests of the gov-ernment." Darpoh was released after five months in Liberian pris-ons, after torture had prompted him to confess that he was the author of the controversial articles. Doe also ordered the censor-ship of all incoming publications on Africa, with the aim of re-moving anything considered "derogatory" to Liberia.

Yet the constitutional commission finally got a $350,000 bud-get (provided by the United States) and a promise of freedom from persecution. It delivered a draft constitution to Doe on March 30, 1983, which was not much different from the original charter suspended after the 1980 coup. After many postponements, the ban on political activity was lifted in July 1984. Legislative elections were scheduled for October 1985 and the presidential election a month later. Inauguration of Liberia's new civilian

government was set for January 1986, almost six years after
the coup. Doe nipped a number of potential political careers in
the bud when he declared that anyone (excepting himself) who
planned to run for civilian office would have to resign from the military government. Some of the most prominent officials, whether
or not they planned to run for office, seemed to fall in and out of
favor from one day to the next. Brigadier General Thomas Quiwonkpa, for example, a key figure in the 1980 coup and then army
commander under Doe, was abruptly shifted to the obscure position of secretary-general of the PRC, but dismissed altogether
when he resisted the change. Doe banned everyone, including
diplomats, from having any contact with Quiwonkpa. The popular
officer went into hiding, then exile in the United States, finally
returning to attempt a coup in November 1985. When it failed,
Quiwonkpa was shot and killed by Doe's bodyguards. Another
of the original group that overthrew Tolbert, Nicholas Podier,
having been elevated by Doe to vice-chief of state and later
speaker of the interim national assembly, was suddenly arrested
and charged with participating in a plot to overthrow his boss.
He was eventually pardoned, but stripped of his military rank
and privileges.

Doe returned home early from a European trip in mid-1984
when he heard of one of many alleged attempts to get him out of
power. This time the target of his suspicions and anger was Amos
Sawyer, the principal drafter of the new constitution and would-be
presidential candidate of the new Liberian People's party. But
Sawyer, a professor at the university in Monrovia, was a popular figure, and his arrest provoked more reaction than most. Some
two thousand students took to the streets to protest, and—in an
eerie echo of Tolbert's days—troops fired into the crowd to disperse them. Dozens were injured, and according to Liberian exile
groups, as many as fifty people may have been killed in the
clashes; the government admitted only that many students had
been flogged or raped by the undisciplined soldiers who were
called out in the emergency. Doe angrily shut down the university,
warning that his enemies were planning to burn down Monrovia
and set up a socialist state. A few months later, however, he relented, reopened the university, and released Sawyer and other
opponents from detention. But early in 1985 a group of uniden-
tified men attempted to burn down Sawyer's house in Monrovia,

and he was banned from participating in politics pending an audit of the constitutional commission's finances.

It became increasingly clear that Doe intended to manipulate the new constitutional process to confer civilian legitimacy on himself. He quietly changed his own age, growing older just fast enough to be thirty-five, and thus constitutionally eligible for the presidency, in 1985. Finally he made it official and declared his candidacy in mid-1984, establishing his own National Democratic party that he hoped would sweep the elections. The "Special Elections Commission," a creation of the Doe regime, found excuses to refuse to certify one after another opposition party, and independent politicians who were persistent in their criticism of Doe's maneuvers found themselves silenced under "Decree 88A," intended to protect the Liberian public against "rumors, lies, and disinformation." Some disappeared for months at a time and were shipped off to the notorious Belle Yallah prison in the country's interior. When leaflets began to circulate that were signed by an unknown "Revolutionary Action Committee," Doe's National Security Agency launched a witch-hunt to find the authors. Ironically, the most serious threat to Doe's domination of Liberia seemed to come from his military comrades. That is why, even in the face of other glaring needs, Doe proceeded with his multimillion-dollar, American-aided program to build new barracks for the soldiers. Still, in April 1985, the deputy commander of Doe's personal bodyguards led a public assassination attempt, ambushing a jeep in which the head-of-state was returning to the executive mansion. Doe escaped unharmed and began new efforts to suppress opposition to him.

Doe traveled abroad to such symbolically important countries as Egypt, China, and South Korea (a major trading partner and investor in Liberia). He came home from Korea with an honorary doctorate and began to encourage people to call him "Dr. Doe." He also fulfilled a lifelong dream with his first visit to the United States. The Washington leg of Doe's American journey was actually a private success and a public failure. He held his own in a White House session with Ronald Reagan, and he convinced others in the Executive Branch and on Capitol Hill that he had a firm grasp of his country's problems and prospects. Unfortunately, President Reagan mistakenly introduced Doe to the White House press corps as "Chairman Moe," and in the absence of substantive information about his visit the press focused on that detail.

During his American tour, Doe had opportunities to reach the American public through extensive interviews, but when he became upset over an article about him in the *Washington Post*, he cancelled all his other scheduled contacts with the press, including one at the Voice of America, a favorite source of news in Liberia. He dropped many other appointments, too—among them, a meeting with scholars at the African Studies Center of the University of California at Los Angeles—pleading fatigue or demonstrating peevishness. Nonetheless, Doe impressed some of the businessmen he met, and he spent considerable time with officials of the Firestone Tire & Rubber Company in Akron, Ohio, seeking to avoid further cutbacks in its Liberian operations.

Liberia's interest in business—its "traditional enthusiasm for the free enterprise system," as government documents put it— again became the theme of its domestic and foreign policies. In a bizarre twist, the new Liberia seemed to outdo the old, its officials turning up at overseas conferences and pleading for no-holds-barred foreign investment. A speaker at a conference on Liberia at Georgetown University in 1983 said it "is one of those rare countries in the world least inhibited by internal economic controls and constraints, and an ideal place for the embrace of private investors." Some of the investors and deal-makers would once again have the opportunity to become Liberia's "honorary consuls" overseas; one shrewd Louisiana businesswoman obtained that title to help her plan a Liberian pavilion at the 1984 New Orleans World's Fair.

In a characteristic bit of overkill, Doe returned from his overseas trip in 1983 so full of enthusiasm for the free enterprise system that he ordered his ministry of education to be on the lookout for people who might promote "socialistic doctrine" in Liberia's schools; they were, he said, enemies of the state. Of course, many Liberian devotees of capitalism who had started their own small businesses were complaining that the scarcity of capital inside the country and harassment by the military were still preventing them from succeeding.

With its American connection firmly in place, Liberia set

about trying to carve out a new leadership role in Africa. One step in that direction was Doe's appointment of an old-line Americo-Liberian civil servant and diplomat, Ernest Eastman, as his new foreign minister. (Another of the original radicals in Doe's cabinet had rotated through that post and been dismissed by the head of state for subscribing to "an ideology contrary to Liberia's interest.") Eastman, a fluent and persuasive spokesman, argued that Liberia could "work to influence the economic orientation and development of Africa, particularly in West Africa, as the socialist economic model proves to be a disillusionment."

But first Liberia had to achieve better relations with some of its immediate neighbors. There were almost constant quarrels with Sierra Leone, whose aging president, Siaka Stevens, regarded Doe skeptically and worried that a similar person might emerge in his own country. When a Sierra Leonean newspaper erroneously reported that Doe had killed his own wife, Doe was so angry that he closed the border between the two countries and moved twenty-four hundred troops north to police it. Stevens put the offending editor in prison, and he detained other journalists in an effort to assuage Doe's feelings. Still, other factors interfered with neighborly good will, including the presence of some four thousand Sierra Leonean refugees in Liberia, whom Doe said his government could not afford to shelter and feed indefinitely. Some observers believed that Doe wanted to maintain tension between the two countries for his own domestic political purposes; his frequent references to the fact that Liberia had originally owned the parts of Sierra Leone where oil finds were now considered a possibility were especially ominous.

In a gesture that provoked controversy within his own government, Doe reestablished diplomatic relations with Israel and traveled there in August 1983 for talks on trade, military and technical aid, and an exchange of intelligence information. Convinced that Qaddafi was bitter over Liberia's rejection of his overtures after the 1980 coup and now sought to undermine the Monrovia government, Doe was eager for Israeli help in monitoring Libyan activities in West Africa. Israel was delighted to have a toehold there—it sent advisers back to Liberia on the same plane with Doe—and to be able to cite another example of a new diplomatic success in Africa. (Zaïre was the first.) To those who criticized Doe's move as a misplaced effort to curry favor with the United

States, he cited Liberia's long history of friendship with Israel, pointing out that Liberia had cast a decisive vote for establishment of the Jewish state during the United Nations debate on that issue in 1948.

Before long, Eastman and others developed a sophisticated revisionist history of modern Liberia for international consumption, asserting that the 1980 coup was really just one event in a consistent stream. Before it was disbanded, the PRC, for its part, declared that "the April 12, 1980, revolution was not directed against any particular segment in the Liberian society; rather it was intended to correct a system which prevented the majority of the people from participating in the affairs of the state."

To declare such conciliation to be in effect, however, did not necessarily make it true. There were new, serious problems on the horizon, including a startling rise in Islamic fundamentalism in the rural areas of Liberia. (Some estimates put the Moslem percentage of the population as high as 50 percent, despite official claims that Liberia has no significant Moslem population.) There was also a troubling increase in the number of ritual murders reported in the countryside—presumably conducted by the so-called "heart men" who were asked to provide body parts for mystical ceremonies on behalf of people seeking election to public office. No such developments were about to be acknowledged or discussed by Doe or his government, for the slightest indication of potential unrest or other trouble would deal a further blow to Liberia's economic recovery.

Yet the corruption and economic mismanagement of the Doe regime became so severe by 1987 that the International Monetary Fund, the World Bank, and the African Development Bank stopped spending money in Liberia. Public services, including telephone, water, and electricity, were virtually suspended. Finally, after reports that huge amounts of American aid were being stolen, the United States agreed to send, and Liberia agreed to accept, seventeen "operational experts" to run the country's economy.

"In the cause of the people, the struggle continues," according to Doe's slogan, which appears on every document and at the close of every letter written by a government official—a flashback to that revolutionary moment in 1980. But Doe, like William Tolbert, seemed to have ever less doubt about the true source of his own authority. "God is the one who chose me to be here," he said flatly in an interview; "God knows I can better help the people."

4

Nigeria: Black Power

It was a hot, steamy night in the summer of 1982 in Washington. At Woodrow Wilson House, a grand old brick mansion in the "Embassy Row" section of town, the languid capital came back to life for a few hours for an unusual event. It had been planned by two public relations firms—one new and black-owned, the other old-line with good bipartisan political connections—and by the standard measure of turnout, it was a great success. Senator Edward M. Kennedy of Massachusetts, not an easy person to produce for such an occasion, made a fleeting appearance, accompanied by his foreign policy adviser, and addressed the crowd. Potential Democratic presidential candidates, including Senator Gary Hart of Colorado, wandered from room to room hoping to be recognized. Members of Congress were everywhere, as were many of their former colleagues, now working as lawyers or lobbyists. Andrew Young, former ambassador to the United Nations and now mayor of Atlanta, had flown in for the evening. Other well-known figures in the black community were also on hand. So was Donald Easum, the former ambassador to Nigeria and now the head of the African-American Institute. Corporate representatives from Lockheed and other giants moved about efficiently, taking care of their business.

The event was more than just another Washington cocktail party. Although the Nigerian foreign minister was there—direct from Lagos by way of the United Nations—it was not really a diplomatic occasion. It was more political in nature. Officially it was a book party, intended to mark the publication of an authorized biography of the man who was then Nigeria's president, Alhaji Shehu Shagari. He had won the 1979 election that brought that country back to civilian rule for the first time in almost fourteen years and would soon be running for reelection. No one could anticipate at the time that Nigeria's democracy would collapse again a year and a half later.

Actually, the evening was a celebration of Nigeria and its relationship with the United States. Few people among the hundreds at the reception would ever read the Shagari biography. In fact, it was not available for purchase in America. Some of the party-goers did not even know Shagari's name, let alone how to pronounce it; but all of them probably shared one strong conviction: that Nigeria matters, and Americans had better learn to know and care about what happens there.

It was not always so. The precarious rise of Nigeria and the growth of the Nigerian-American connection make one of the more intriguing stories in modern African history.

One out of every six Africans is a Nigerian. In population (probably upward of 100 million), Nigeria is larger than any other country in Europe and Africa except the Soviet Union. At that moment, in 1982, it was the world's fourth largest democracy, and the eighth largest oil producer. For the United States, it was the third largest foreign supplier of crude oil (after Mexico and Saudi Arabia); the American balance-of-payments deficit with Nigeria was second only to that with Japan. U.S. investment in Nigeria had reached nearly half a billion dollars. Indeed, Nigeria was—and remains—black Africa's biggest market for Western goods; Western trade with Nigeria is about double the commerce with South Africa. As a result, Nigeria's stability has become important to the United States and the rest of the Western world. Its point

of view has won limited, if grudging, consideration in the making
of American foreign policy.

Nigeria may well be growing, and otherwise changing, as fast
as anyplace else in the world. At last count, it had nine thousand
miles of highway under construction. The government promised
comprehensive health care and a free primary education—and a
secondary one, too, if possible—to everyone. That meant that 3
million new students arrived in Nigerian schools at the same moment in the late 1970s, half of them in first grade. (Nigeria produced more university graduates during the 1970s than did all of
Africa during the colonial era.) The Nigerian government, at the
federal and state level, employs at least a million people. A new
capital city is being constructed in the wilderness, much as Brasília
was in Brazil, at an estimated cost of $30 billion. During the
1970s private consumption in Nigeria increased by 473 percent
compared to the 1960s. The country was transformed from a relatively backward agricultural-based society to a relatively wealthy
capitalist-oriented one. Oil was the fuel for most of the change;
until the price of oil plunged, it accounted for more than 80 percent of total federal and state government revenues and at least
90 percent of the nation's foreign exchange. Nigeria was home to
an increasing number of millionaires, but also to an increasing
number of people who live in squalor and poverty.

All demographic and economic statistics about Nigeria are
vague. There has been no reliable census in at least twenty years,
and every effort to count Nigerians during that time has resulted
in controversy, even violence. That is because census figures, logically enough, are the basis for the distribution of political power
and the allocation of government revenues among the various regions of the country. This process is complicated everywhere, but
especially so in Nigeria because regional rivalries coincide with
fundamental ethnic divisions and disparities.

At least 250 separate tribal groups live in Nigeria, and recent
research has revealed that 395 different, mutually unintelligible
languages are spoken there. They all happen to be in the same
country by colonial accident. Out of the Berlin Conference of
1885 emerged the Royal Niger Company, based in London, which
had exclusive trading rights in the basin of the Niger River. Like
other such institutions of the period, including Belgian King Léo-

pold's International African Association in the Congo, the trading company functioned as a government; it granted a sort of protection to the missionaries and explorers who ventured into its territory. But in 1900, as the great scramble for Africa was proceeding, the British government took over the Royal Niger Company's domain and expanded it in every possible direction to head off the French and the Germans. It was not easy, given the ravages of malaria, yellow fever, sleeping sickness, and other diseases, but eventually the British pulled together a vast and diverse land into a single colony. It was named Nigeria at the suggestion of the wife of its first governor-general, Sir Frederick Lugard.

Even after Lugard "amalgamated" the northern and southern sections of Nigeria in 1914 and began to administer them jointly, they remained two distinctly different places. There was also a standoff within the South, between East and West, the eventual cause of a brutal civil war in the 1960s. But the North-South rivalry was the first to develop. The North was almost entirely Moslem, the home most notably of the Hausa and Fulani people, a traditional society where slavery persisted into the early twentieth century and women were denied the vote until the 1960s. The South was primarily Christian (the Ibo in the Southeast) or the bastion of traditional African religions (the Yoruba in the Southwest), but above all a place that revered education and welcomed evolution to a modern society. The northerners tended to be more numerous and xenophobic, the southerners more inclined to want to reorganize and dominate the entire country.

The tension was made worse by the fact that these cultures, and the others that coexisted with them, were very old. More than two thousand years ago, the Nok culture was smelting iron and creating terra cotta sculpture in the area that is now central Nigeria. In the northern city of Kano, written records go back as far as 900 A.D., and the kingdoms of Kano and Katsina are thought to have had an important role in the early caravan trade across the Sahara. In the kingdom of Oyo, the Yoruba developed a highly sophisticated political structure, which flourished between the seventeenth and nineteenth centuries. Bronze work was done at Igbo-Ukwu in the East by the ninth century A.D., at Ife in the West in the twelfth century, and at Benin in the Southwest in the thirteenth. To this day the old Benin bronzes are among the most prized art objects in the world. (Most of them were carried off by the British, and Nigeria is still in the process of buying them back.)

The slave trade took its toll on all of these cultures. The stretch of the Atlantic coastline near Lagos came to be known as "the slave coast" (as distinct from the Gold Coast or the Ivory Coast), because of the ease and profitability of the human trade there. Warring tribes willingly sold their captives into bondage, and as one Portuguese explorer wrote in the late fifteenth century, the kingdom of Benin traded its prisoners for "12 or 15 brass bracelets each." By the eighteenth century, about twenty thousand people from the area were being sent every year to servitude on plantations in Brazil, the West Indies, and North America. Around the time that the U.S. Constitution was being written, a slave could be purchased along the coast for two pounds sterling and sold in America for more than thirty times that amount.

Somehow Nigeria survived all of this degradation better than most. It was poor and battered, and it emerged into the colonial era divided, but Nigerians were proud and politically resourceful. There was never a settler class, black or white—probably for reasons of climate, very few whites came to live in Nigeria during British rule—and although this deprived nationalists of an easy target, it made it easier for them to organize openly and achieve respectability. Outsiders who traveled to Nigeria were surprised by the absence of the "color bar" so common in other African colonies, and they found that black Nigerians were generally treated with respect by the white colonial administrators. After a certain point, earlier than in most other places, it seemed to be universally acknowledged that Nigeria would become free without having to wage a military struggle.

Political parties began to form in the South as early as the 1920s, after Britain conceded a few urban seats in an advisory legislative council to Africans; before World War II was over, an articulate and intellectual Nigerian independence movement was taking hold. "We all overseas soldiers are coming back home with new ideas," wrote one recruit, Theo Ayoola, stationed with the British forces in India, in a typical letter to Herbert Macaulay, the father of Nigerian nationalism, in 1945. "We have been told what we fought for," he said. "That is 'freedom.' We want freedom, nothing but freedom."

It would take a little longer. Many Nigerians had hoped to

beat Ghana out of the starting gate by attaining independence in
1956, but that was too soon for the North, which feared domination by the better-organized and -educated southerners. Predictably, three strong parties emerged in Nigeria during the 1950s:
one in the North, dominated by the Fulani and Hausa; one in the
West, catering primarily to the interests of the Yoruba; and a
third, really the oldest, with its greatest strength among the Ibo
of the East. (The original leaders of the latter two parties, Chief
Obafemi Awolowo and Nnamdi Azikiwe respectively, were still
very much on the scene and were both presidential candidates
during the 1979 and 1983 elections.) It seemed as if these parties
could agree on nothing, and a dispute over the date for independence led to a walkout from the colonial legislature in 1953, followed by riots and killings of southerners living in the northern
city of Kano.

Some argued that the creation of new and smaller political
units would help defuse sectarian and sectional tensions, as well
as protect the minorities within each region. But the British said
that would only delay independence, so Nigeria became free on
October 1, 1960, as a federation of three large regions, each suspicious of the other two. The first ruling coalition in the parlia-
mentary-style government was composed of the eastern party and
the northern one. Abubakar Tafawa Balewa of the Northern People's Congress became the prime minister, confirming the worst
fears of some westerners, who imagined themselves being over-
run by the Islamic forces in the North.

The first five years of Nigerian independence were chaotic
and bloody, the climate one of plotting and conspiracy. Aspirations vastly exceeded know-how, and the divisions within the
country were dramatized by the fact that there was not a single
paved road that connected the North with either region of the
South. Having declared itself a republic, Nigeria stumbled from
one unsuccessful census to another and held elections whose results few people respected. Rather than spurring development or
improving communication, the government fell to tinkering with
the country's structure. One of its first major decisions was to split
the western region—then thought to be the richest part of the
federation, because of its cocoa exports—into two. Awolowo's
angry protests against this tactic were interpreted by the courts as

treason and conspiracy, and he and many of his supporters were put in prison.

The army took charge in January 1966, assassinating Balewa and other influential northerners. For six months Ibo officers and civil servants dominated the country, attempting to cure regional discord by abolishing the regions altogether and rashly creating a unitary state. Once again, in reaction, northern mobs massacred southerners. Then a second coup, in July 1966, resulted in the death of the leader of the first, and it brought to power a northerner who was not a Moslem but a member of a Christian minority group, an unusually gifted and charismatic thirty-one-year-old lieutenant colonel named Yakubu Gowon.

Gowon immediately sought to build a broad, multiethnic power base, releasing people like Awolowo from prison. The new ruler went beyond reestablishing the regions that his predecessors had abolished; he created twelve new states in an attempt to guarantee more effective minority representation. Before that innovation could take effect, however, the military governor of the eastern region, Odumegwu Emeka Ojukwu, having failed to persuade Gowon to turn Nigeria into a loose "confederation," declared on May 30, 1967, that his region of the country was a separate, sovereign nation, the "Republic of Biafra." Ibo came home from all other parts of the country and from overseas to defend their honor; many fierce Nigerian nationalists, including government officials and well-known literary figures, overnight became fierce Biafran "freedom fighters."

For nearly three years Nigerians battled each other in a bloody and costly civil war. An estimated six hundred thousand people were killed. Many people and nations that had never given Nigeria two minutes' thought felt obliged to choose sides. The outnumbered and overwhelmed Biafrans, generally cast as the underdogs, picked up an unusual assortment of friends. For example, in the United States, Eugene McCarthy, a liberal antiwar candidate for the Democratic presidential nomination in 1968, joined the conservative Republican candidate, Richard Nixon, in accusing Nigeria of "genocide." Widely distributed photographs of children who were starving because food shipments could not get through the Nigerian lines seemed to prove the point. But the official position of the Johnson administration was one of detached

neutrality. Secretary of State Dean Rusk infuriated the Nigerians
when he observed that the civil war was a "British responsibility,"
as if Nigeria were still a British colony.

Most other African nations identified with Nigeria's plight—
knowing that they too could easily break apart if sectionalism got
out of hand—but Ivory Coast, Gabon, Tanzania and Zambia recognized Biafra's independence. Tanzania's move came first and
was a major breakthrough for the separatists. Tanzanian President
Julius Nyerere, taking a characteristically philosophical approach,
believed that not all secessions were equally grave events (he had
supported some of the leftist mischief in the Congo in the mid-
1960s), and he apparently thought that recognizing Biafra would
call attention to the human suffering there and dramatize the
futility of the military conflict. Ivory Coast acted out of somewhat
less pure motives. President Félix Houphouët-Boigny did not like
large, potentially powerful federations generally, and he was suspicious of Nigeria in particular as a rival for influence in West
Africa. (The French also worried about Nigeria as a threat to
their own continuing role in Africa, and they exerted considerable
influence on Ivory Coast.) Zambia followed Tanzania's lead, and
Gabon acted because of Ivorian influence there. Some other African countries took a perverse pleasure in Nigeria's trouble, but
never took the step of recognizing Biafra. In fact, the only other
country in the world to do so was Haiti, apparently on the basis
of President François Duvalier's belated discovery that the Ibo
who ran Biafra were black Roman Catholics like himself.

Ultimately, Nigeria prevailed, with the help of British arms,
Soviet weapons and planes (flown by Egyptians and East Germans), and an army that grew to be a quarter-of-a-million strong.
Gowon pulled the postwar pieces together surprisingly well. He
offered an amnesty to all who had rebelled and fought on Biafra's
side (except Ojukwu, who fled to Ivory Coast), and he swore to
work toward the economic development of the entire country and
a return to civilian rule.

On the one hand, Gowon had an important advantage: Nigeria's growing oil revenues—by 1972 it was the world's ninth
largest producer—made it easier to pay off war debts and dream
up ambitious new schemes. But on the other hand, Nigeria's
young ruler, still only thirty-five after the war, faced enormous
problems; the country needed everything, from schools and hos-

pitals to water pipes and telephones. The quickening internal migration from the countryside to the cities shifted the burdens and made the needs more acute, and progress was frustrated by the overt corruption of the military governors of the various states.

Gowon began to renege on the schedule for returning to civilian government. In 1974 another attempt to take a census failed—the results were rejected by the six states in the South, because they showed the six in the North to have twice as many people. Things began to fall apart again.* In July 1975, while Gowon was out of the country, he was overthrown by a reformist group of young military officers.

By all accounts, the man who took charge after that coup, a war hero from the North named Murtala Muhammed, was remarkable for his decisiveness and conciliation. He launched investigations of corruption and retired some ten thousand people from the civil service. On the fifteenth anniversary of Nigerian independence, October 1, 1975, he announced a precise schedule and process for returning to a constitutional, popularly elected civilian government, to culminate exactly four years later. It is difficult to verify or refute Muhammed's reputation, because after barely six months in office he was assassinated in a countercoup attempted by disgruntled military elements. But he was instantly replaced by his chief of staff, Olusegun Obasanjo, also a wartime celebrity, a Baptist member of the Yoruba tribe, who pledged to carry out Muhammed's program and promises. Obasanjo held on to power throughout the transition to civilian rule and stepped down only after Shagari's election and inauguration.

Since the early 1970s, everything about Nigeria—its domestic and international affairs alike—has been profoundly affected by oil. The first shipment of crude oil from under the Niger delta to refineries in Rotterdam took place in 1958, but no one dreamed at the time that petroleum would play a major role in the soon-to-be-independent country's economy. Indeed, the only real busi-

* *Things Fall Apart*, the title of the first novel by Ibo writer Chinua Achebe, has become a popular phrase to describe the recurring sense of crisis in modern Nigeria. That book, published in 1958, deals with the first encounters between missionaries and tribal chiefs at the turn of the century; for Achebe, their conflict is a symbol of the continuing clash between traditional and modern ways.

ness of Nigeria in the 1950s seemed to be agriculture; 80 percent of the labor force was engaged in farming, often under primitive conditions. Manufacturing was inconsequential, and largely backward. The United Africa Company and other large foreign firms controlled commerce and high finance; foreign merchants, especially Lebanese, Greeks, and Indians, ran most of the small businesses. Few Nigerians were involved in the professions. In the early 1950s Nigeria still had only 150 black lawyers, 160 black doctors, and 786 black clergymen. But the country did grow 95 percent of its own food, and it exported large quantities of cocoa, palm products, cotton, peanuts, and rubber. In 1964, in fact, Nigeria made just as much from exporting peanuts as it did from exporting oil—$90 million each. As late as 1965 Nigeria was still a dependent former colony. It received more aid from the United States than any other African country, and it was host to the largest contingent of Peace Corps volunteers on the continent.

Nigerians began to play a major role in the commercial sector of their own country only in 1970, after the civil war had ended, but especially beginning in 1972, when the military government issued an "indigenization decree," reserving some business endeavors to Nigerian citizens and requiring foreign companies to sell off at least 40 but sometimes 60 or 80 percent of their interests to local people. That made a major difference; for one thing, it created a wealthy class of Nigerians known as "Forty-Percenters." But it was in the following year that a historic change occurred.

At the time of the oil embargo that followed the Yom Kippur war between Israel and the Arab states in 1973, Nigeria was already moving from third to second place in the ranks of foreign oil suppliers to the United States. Nigeria had joined the Arab-dominated Organization of Petroleum Exporting Countries (OPEC) in 1971, but at the crucial moment after the Mideast war it decided not to participate in the Arab-led, anti-American boycott. Although it was not openly acknowledged by Washington at the time, that decision made a great difference in America's ability to weather the crisis. In effect, the United States depended on Nigeria.

The lessons were significant on both sides. The United States— or at least the inner circles of foreign and energy policy makers— realized that Nigeria could assure a stable supply of oil and, in the process, help the United States avoid becoming a victim of international economic blackmail, especially in the Middle East. For its part, Nigeria saw an opportunity to build a new relationship with the United States. More important, if they were not previously aware of certain economic facts of life, Nigerians now realized that oil was the wave of their future. It was a resource that could utterly transform the prospects of a developing country. It could create a fantastic boom overnight.

But transformation is not always a smooth or orderly process. In Nigeria it occurred with a degree of chaos that has since become legendary. One graphic symbol is that at one point in 1975, as the oil boom gained momentum, Nigeria had orders pending outside the country for 20 million tons of cement. That is an astonishing quantity of cement, enough to build whole cities. But in this case, no one had stopped to realize that the annual cement-unloading capacity of all Nigerian ports taken together was less than 2 million tons. As a result, Lagos harbor became jammed with some four hundred ships, weighed down with cement, all waiting their turn to be unloaded; the queue extended to the horizon and beyond. How to use or store so much cement at once was a problem in itself. Meanwhile, the immobilized ships levied storage charges, and virtually nothing else could get in or out of the clogged harbor.

The capital city became a symbol of Nigeria's growing pains. Lagos is a vast laboratory of helter-skelter expansion, a fount of confusion and frenzy perhaps unequaled anywhere else in the world. Nobody who has visited there since Nigeria's oil boom began can easily forget the experience. For diplomats, journalists, businessmen, and the few tourists brave enough to try it, Lagos has become the embodiment of the "WAWA" syndrome ("West Africa Wins Again"), the conquest of external circumstances over personal will.

In 1965 Lagos had a population of perhaps three hundred thousand. By the early 1980s it had more than ten times that number, and in the entire extended metropolitan area there may now be ten million or more. A tiny minority of those people live extremely well, in villas or plush apartments, and they go to work in gleaming skyscrapers that sit awkwardly next to traditional marketplaces. A vastly larger number of people live in appalling slums, where open sewers may run under disintegrating floorboards. Many of those people do not go to work at all. In fact, they have no place to go, unless they embark on a life of crime, by day or night, victimizing the people who walk on the streets or sit endlessly in traffic jams.

The traffic jam, or "go-slow," is a fact of life in Lagos, and as a result much of the everyday commerce that is conducted in more conventional ways in most other places occurs in this city through the windows of cars, trucks, and other vehicles. While sitting in your car in Lagos, tempers flaring and horns blaring all around you, it is possible to buy fruits and vegetables, meat and fish, clothing and shoes, cameras and jewelry, even lamps and pieces of furniture, from the hawkers who stroll by. So persistent are they, in fact, that it is difficult not to buy from them while you wait to proceed a few feet or try to find a place to leave your car and walk.

The trip between downtown Lagos and the airport has been known to take half a day when things are at their worst, and accidents are a major menace. One estimate is that at least three hundred people are killed in auto-related accidents in Lagos every month. Virtually every attempt to solve the problem ends in frustration and failure. For a time, the completion of a belt of highways around the city seemed to help, but soon the congestion returned. One official restriction, permitting only cars with odd-numbered license plates on the road on odd-numbered days and those with even-numbered ones on even-numbered days, was easily rendered meaningless. Resourceful but thrifty citizens arranged to have two sets of license plates; the wealthier people simply bought an extra car. Seemingly, no one is immune from the outrages of Lagos traffic; General Murtala Muhammed, head of state after the military coup of 1975, was shot and killed by rebel soldiers while stuck in a Lagos go-slow.

Hotels in Lagos, whether new or old, are among the most frustrating on the African continent. Reservations are often meaningless, and guests have been known to be expelled from their rooms in the middle of the night when someone with better connections arrives at the reception desk. Hotel rooms that fall into disrepair are often left unattended for months. In hotels and elsewhere, electricity and water come on and off again with no discernible pattern, and progress on the city's overburdened telephone system has been extremely slow. It is sometimes easier to fight the traffic and the tumult than to get a phone call through.

Arrival at or departure from the Lagos airport is a memorable adventure. Until a partially successful government crackdown, the airport was, in effect, managed by "touts," burly, crafty young men who charged high fees for guiding travelers through the un-moving lines at customs, the health station, and the baggage claim area. As often as not, it is impossible to get a seat on an airplane leaving Lagos without a substantial "dash," or bribe, to the right person at the right time. It is not just that the planes are over-booked (as they can be anywhere in the world), but that board-ing passes, rather than being routinely distributed to ticket hold-ers, may be for sale.

An astonishing number of handguns and other weapons are in private possession in Lagos—a characteristic that makes it quite different from most other major African cities. In the smuggling that thrives in the harbor and at the airport, the weapons trade is one of the most successful and growing businesses. Many of those weapons fall into the hands of gangs of brigands and outlaws, as large as a hundred strong, that rob and terrorize entire neigh-borhoods at a time. Sometimes they announce their intentions in advance, even posting notices of when and where they will strike; their raids may last four or five hours, but they are rarely appre-hended by the police. Nor are ships in Nigerian ports immune from attack. Pirates have been known to arrive in motorboats, board ships at anchor, assault the crew, and loot the cargo. In one notorious case in 1978, a Danish ship's captain was thrown over-board into shark-infested waters, after a raid that seemed to have been precisely planned and skillfully executed.

Nigerian military governments have sometimes resorted to a kind of frontier justice. People convicted of serious crimes like armed robbery would be publicly executed by firing squad, and spectators would be encouraged to attend in the hope of creating a deterrent to other criminals. In many instances, vigilantes or angry mobs took matters into their own hands, carrying out arrest, trial, and death sentence in the space of a few minutes. All of this had little positive result, however, and Lagos seems perpetually in the grip of a chronic crime wave. To this day, the most common and successful form of auto theft does not involve breaking into parked, empty cars and stealing them, but pointing a gun at the head of a driver, forcing him to get out, and driving his car away. Some victims later buy their own cars back from the thieves, and they avoid contacting the police out of a fear of retribution. A few people have told stories of policemen in uniform carrying out just such car thefts, but the more typical culprit is a former soldier who has been unable to find new work, but has held on to his old weapons.

Although some of the urban problems, including electricity shortages and strained public facilities, are national, most Nigerian cities are quite different from Lagos. Heavily populated though they may be, Kano, Kaduna, and Sokoto in the North are typified more by the eerie silence of their mosques than by the noise and frenzy of Lagos. Indeed, Kano at dusk could be in another universe entirely. The dominant sound in the city is of the mullahs using loudspeakers to summon the faithful to prayers. Thousands of people may be in the central square at that moment, and if Kano has traffic jams they are more of people and pack animals than of cars and trucks. In the eastern part of the country, by contrast, the cities are smaller frontierlike outposts built on the swamps and river deltas; in the place of skyscrapers or mosques, there are oil rigs. The western part of Nigeria, outside of cities like Lagos and Ibadan, is forested and unrelentingly hot, like much of the rest of West Africa. Yet the country also has a few uniquely serene spots like Jos, high up on a plateau, near the home of an ancient civilization, cool and seemingly removed from the ordinary world below.

But it is Lagos, with all its problems, that has somehow come to symbolize Nigeria for outsiders. That is probably unfair to the capital and the country. Few cities, after all, could handle gracefully the strains that have been put on Lagos. Originally established as a fishing station by a powerful Yoruba chief, the village later became a slave-trading center for the Portuguese. The British established themselves in the nineteenth century, and because they made it clear they would grant protection to freed slaves, thousands of people who were looking desperately for their old homes in West Africa or fleeing inland tribal wars flocked to Lagos; so did European traders and missionaries. At first, Lagos was administered as a separate British colony, but it was proclaimed to be the capital of Nigeria in 1914, when the northern and southern parts of the country were "amalgamated" by Lugard. Some parts of the city, such as Victoria Island, were reclaimed from the sea and built on for the first time as late as the early 1960s. The improvisational aspect of the development of Lagos is symbolized by the fact that its newest port facility in the harbor is on "Tin Can Island," so named because until recently it was used as a dump for tin cans and other refuse.

Nigerians generally react with anger and insult when outsiders talk negatively about Lagos. But the government itself, in a report explaining why its new capital city should be built at Abuja, in the interior of the country, referred to Lagos as a city of "perennial traffic jams, intolerable congestion, chaotic sanitary situation, inadequate social amenities, an alarming crime rate." It is unclear whether Lagos will get any better or easier when the federal government headquarters is moved away. It is also uncertain whether the chaos and corruption will extend to Abuja, if and when it is finally completed.

Beyond its astonishing effects on Lagos, the oil boom profoundly changed the Nigerian economy and society. Perhaps the most noticeable phenomenon was inflation, which ran as high as 50 percent a year or more. Housing costs soared for all sectors of the population. (Foreign businessmen or wealthy Nigerians may pay upward of $75,000 or $100,000 a year to rent their villas, with several years' rent often demanded in advance.) Simple foods like rice cost far more than ever before, and yams, once a basic element in the Nigerian diet, have been known to go for as much as $7.50 apiece. Visitors often found that food and clothing, not to mention hotel accommodations, were more expensive in Nigeria, and especially in Lagos, than in New York or other major American and European cities. (According to Business International Corporation, a Geneva-based consulting firm that advises companies establishing overseas offices, at the peak of the boom Lagos was the most expensive major city in the world.)

Another part of the country's transformation, and a cause of many of its problems, is the oil-related decline of Nigeria's agricultural sector. Nearly three-fourths of the Nigerian labor force still works in agriculture, but it produces a diminishing share of the country's gross national product. Farming has become even less efficient than before, in part because of the increase in absentee-landlord situations, and Nigeria now imports some of the same commodities it used to export, such as peanuts and palm oil. Almost all of its sugar, dairy products, and grain come from overseas, and its total food imports exceed food exports by about $2 billion a year. The United States alone sells perhaps half a billion dollars' worth of food a year to Nigeria. Successive governments have insisted that agricultural development is their priority, but improvement is slow. Although rice production has increased faster than the population has grown, all other crops have lagged. It now seems clear that Nigerian agriculture is moving in the direction of depending upon, and imitating, European and American "agribusiness," with uncertain implications for Nigeria's ability to feed and employ its own people at home.

As for the manufacturing and construction that have taken the place of agriculture in the Nigerian economy, there are major problems in those sectors, too. Everything has happened so fast that the country's infrastructure—its roads, power supply, and regulatory mechanisms—has virtually collapsed from the burden. As a result, many projects are not adequately planned, much of the construction is shoddy, and some investments and businesses simply fail before they really get off the ground. What is more, the much-vaunted "indigenization" program is often a farce in practice. Most of the major road-building and other construction in Nigeria has been done by foreign firms, especially the Julius Berger construction company of West Germany. And many of Nigeria's own highly visible government enterprises are actually run by foreigners. KLM, the Dutch airline, keeps Nigeria Airways flying, for example, and another Dutch consortium operates the harbors and inland waterways. Nigerian Railways are run by a group from India.

The most profound effect of the reliance on oil has been to give Nigeria a permanent seat on the roller-coaster of the international oil market, with all its ups and downs of price and supply. Nigeria was initially one of the "price hawks" within OPEC, arguing for higher and more frequent increases, largely because of the country's insatiable need for foreign exchange to pay for its ambitious development efforts. The higher the price, the greater the income, or so it seemed. But international oil gluts—one in 1977–78, another in 1981–82, and a third beginning in 1983—let Nigeria know just how fragile its new wealth really is.

As long as Nigeria stuck with the high OPEC price, some overseas customers began to go elsewhere, especially to North Sea producers, Mexico, and the then cheaper spot market, or else they relied on reserves and postponed new purchases. That caused Nigeria to accumulate an oil surplus and, in turn, to cut production. In the midst of the second glut, the country saw its output plunge from a high of 2.3 million barrels a day to a low of 707,000 barrels a day. Nigeria's oil production in 1981 was almost 30 percent lower than in 1980. Finally Nigeria cut its price by 10 percent, or $4 a barrel, and the combined effect was a loss of billions of dollars for the national treasury. In its frantic effort to regain its lost customers, Nigeria had the help of Saudi Arabia, which pressured some of the major oil companies to continue their purchases from Nigeria or face cuts in Saudi production levels. The Saudis were trying to establish two points: that oil companies could not simply break their contracts to purchase oil from OPEC members, and that the consuming countries could not go after the OPEC cartel by taking advantage of one of the economically weaker links in the chain.

Nigeria is a weak link precisely because it is so dependent on its oil income. Countries like Saudi Arabia and Libya can cope far more easily with oil gluts, because they have vast reserves of hard currency to spend and relatively small populations to satisfy. Nigeria did rebound briefly from the crisis of the early 1980s. By the summer of 1982 it was increasing its oil output again, and work resumed on certain development projects, such as a new steel mill and an additional oil refinery. But the improvement came only after the Nigerian government had taken the drastic step of imposing a freeze on almost all imports, as the reserves in its central bank dropped to critically low levels. That meant immediate cutbacks in industrial production, housing construction, and social welfare programs, with all the inevitable economic, social, and political consequences. Immediately there was a dramatic increase in labor unrest. In Kaduna state, one of several that simply ran out of their budgeted share of reduced oil revenues, teachers walked off the job because they had not been paid for several months. Employees of the Nigerian Electric Power Authority went on strike when they did not receive a scheduled bonus, halting much of the nation's business and causing a health crisis as well.

Once again in February 1983 Nigeria had to cut its oil price by $5.50 a barrel in order to try to preserve, if not enlarge, its share of the international market. That decision produced new disarray within OPEC and nearly caused Nigeria's expulsion from the organization, but the Nigerian authorities argued that they had no choice; again in 1984 and 1985 they refused to be forced back into compliance with OPEC pricing. Some income from oil had to be assured, just to sustain the flow of raw materials and spare parts to those Nigerian industries that were still functioning. The country's central bank ran far behind in its payments of bills for imports already received; in June 1983, for example, the Peugeot assembly plant in Kaduna had to be shut down because the central bank was unable to transmit millions of dollars owed to the company.

Even in the worst of crises, import controls can be only partially successful in Nigeria, because of the extent of the smuggling problem. Certain commodities, such as fine European lace and French champagne—particular status symbols in Nigeria—have long been available only on the black market, because they could not be legally imported; additional controls simply served to lengthen the list of such goods and to increase their illicit price (as well as the profits for smugglers). Indeed, the United Africa Company, black Africa's largest publicly held corporation, and such American businesses as Johnson Products Company of Chicago (which built a plant in Nigeria to manufacture its cosmetics for black consumers) have lost millions of dollars in the competition with smugglers. One Japanese textile firm closed its Nigerian subsidiary altogether rather than try to compete. Union Carbide and other local manufacturers of batteries resorted to full-page advertisements warning Nigerians not to buy illegal goods, because of their effect on the economy and on job opportunities.

"You can smuggle a train into Nigeria today if you are ready to pay the right bribe to customs," said General Theophilus Danjuma, once chief of the armed forces and later the head of a shipping company. He contended that employees of the Department of Customs and Excise actually promote smuggling, and that some of these public officials, acting in the true spirit of Nigerian free enterprise, have organized a private service to advise smugglers and to help deliver contraband goods. Insulted customs officers responded to his charges by purchasing expensive newspaper advertisements—which they never could have afforded with their meager civil service earnings—revealing that $5 million worth of illegal goods had been seized from boats connected with Danjuma's own firm.

The smuggling and other blatant corruption inside and outside government have served to deepen and exacerbate old inequities in Nigerian life. True, the money from the oil boom has "trickled down" to the point that Nigeria's middle class has grown; many more people are today able to think about buying such former luxuries as cars, television sets, and air conditioners. That alone sets Nigeria apart from most other African countries. But at the same time, many more people are also complaining that they cannot comfortably pay their bills for such basics as food and rent. And the rest are too poor to complain; they are thinking about how to survive beyond the next meal. Urban unemployment in Nigeria is estimated at more than 35 percent.

These contrasts have produced disillusionment about the process of decolonization. If the 1939 level is taken as a base of 100, the Nigerian index of real wages was at 144 in 1965, but had fallen to 112 by 1970. A government commission lamented that year that there was "intolerable suffering at the bottom of the income scale, because of the rise in the cost of living." It went on to say that this suffering was made "even more intolerable by manifestations of affluence and wasteful expenditure" at the other end of the income scale that could not be explained by salary levels or other legitimate income. Again, in 1976, as a constitutional committee set down the "fundamental objectives" for civilian rule in Nigeria, it said the country's economic system must not be operated in "such a manner as to permit the concentration of wealth or the means of production and exchange in the hands of a few individuals or a group." Studying the Nigerian economy in 1981, the International Labor Organization said that after more than twenty years of independence and rapid economic growth, "there should be by now signs of substantial improvements in the living conditions of the majority of the Nigerian people. These are not evident."

Good intentions abound in Nigeria, but most observers believe that the disparities have only become worse, especially during oil gluts and domestic economic crises. One incident in May 1981 served as a poignant symbol of the problem: just at the moment when national labor unions were on strike, demanding a minimum wage of $500 a month (which the government rejected as excessive), powerful leaders of the ruling National party of Nigeria and wealthy businessmen who supported it and President Shagari gathered in Lagos for a fund-raising reception and dedication of the NPN's new $3 million headquarters. In half an hour, they raised $8 million, with one man, the chairman of ITT Nigeria, donating a fifth of the total.

Few have ever spoken up to disagree with the astounding statement in 1977 by Obasanjo, then the head of the military government, that Nigeria "is still a place where people are prepared to destroy anything, to cover up any crime, if doing so promotes their economic interest or might." Indeed, the lengths to which some people were willing to go was demonstrated in recent years by a rash of fires in government buildings where investigations of corruption were taking place. Before Shagari's election in 1979 a blaze gutted the accounting department of the Ministry of Communications; similar fires occurred subsequently at the Ministries of Education and External Affairs, as well as other federal offices. Typically they began in the accounting office, and then spread to envelop an entire building. Investigations of the arson, in turn, have not been notably successful.

For all its economic crises and social tension, Nigeria did a remarkable job of repairing the wounds from its civil war. The story of this rehabilitation went largely untold in the Western press. That was partially the fault of the Nigerians themselves, who were badly insulted by the pro-Biafran slant of much of the war coverage and, as a result, made it more difficult for outside reporters to enter and cover postwar Nigeria. Often Western correspondents were expelled soon after arrival, on the basis of old grievances found in some government official's files. Then, too, many news organizations that had devoted so much attention to the war found the peace less interesting and, to their own surprise, suddenly found other important stories to attend to in Africa. When they did get around to asking to reopen bureaus in Lagos in the mid or late 1970s, they found a new array of obstacles in their path, frequently including a demand for enormous rents on offices and houses, to be paid several years in advance, with no prospect of a refund even if the correspondents in question were expelled. (Many Western media thus established their bureaus in Abidjan, the capital of Ivory Coast, instead.)

Those who did look found that reconciliation in Nigeria was surprisingly fast and thorough. The federal government was slow to return some of the property it had confiscated, and many roads and other bombed-out public facilities went years before they were repaired. But very little war damage remains today, even in cities that were nearly destroyed during the civil war, and most of the industries in the eastern part of the country have returned to or begun to exceed their prewar levels of production. The Ibo people have not been openly discriminated against in public or private life (at least not noticeably more than other non-north-erners), and they have actually returned to what some would consider a disproportionate influence in national affairs. In 1980, ten years after the civil war had ended, Shagari announced that he was restoring federal pension rights to thousands of civil servants who had worked for Biafra rather than the federal government during the war.

Postwar reconciliation was very much tied up with Nigeria's much-vaunted, but ultimately unsuccessful, return to civilian rule, a process that seemed for a time to energize the country and give it a new spirit. The characteristic that most distinguished the Muhammed-Obasanjo regime from its Nigerian predecessors and its counterparts elsewhere in Africa was that its number one priority seemed to be to retire itself. Gowon, in particular, had never come to terms with the issue of how to reduce the size of an army that, at 230,000 in 1976, was vastly larger than anything Nigeria needed or could justify. Obasanjo put a lot of people out of work in the process, but within three years the army was down to 150,000.

As for the political side of the transition, the effort to find a new governmental system for the country took on the characteristics of a jamboree that everyone wanted to attend. A steady stream of Nigerians came home from self-imposed exile, in fact, just to see how they could help. They had a sense—an arrogant one, perhaps—of doing something that all of Africa was watching and might want to imitate.

A constitutional drafting committee first came up with proposals, including "truly national" parties, an independent judiciary, and an American-style "executive presidential system." Then a 232-member constituent assembly, partly elected and partly appointed, minutely debated each provision of the draft constitution. The discussion was raucous and sometimes tense, especially on such issues as whether *sharias*, or Islamic courts in the North that made judgments based on Koranic doctrine rather than secular laws, would be recognized by the federal government. The delegates argued over a formula to govern the creation of new states (the military government already having created seven more, for a total of nineteen, on the theory that this would provide for better representation of minorities). With Nigeria's dozens of aggressive and competitive newspapers joining in, the drafters quarreled over whether to enshrine an American-style guarantee of freedom of the press. What emerged was a remarkable replica of the U.S. Constitution, complete with a federal House and Senate (but Nebraska-style unicameral legislatures at the state level) and procedures for impeachment.

A year-long election process got underway at the local, state, and federal levels in 1978, and the Federal Election Commission (FEDECO) accepted only five political parties (out of fifty-two that applied) as being plausibly "national." In reality, even they appealed to regional loyalties. The United party of Nigeria had its base primarily among the Yoruba of the West and was led by one of the most familiar old names in Nigerian politics, Chief Awolowo, by then seventy years old. Azikiwe, at seventy-four, emerged with his own party, too, and, not surprisingly, it was strongest among the Ibo of the East. Another party, led by another famous figure, Aminu Kano, was especially popular in the North. It looked and sounded like the old ethnic politics all over again, with hardly even a change of personnel, and some rules had to be bent to accommodate the principal figures. Azikiwe and Kano, for example, were allowed to run only after the high court overruled FEDECO's refusal to certify them on the grounds that they could not prove they had fully paid their income taxes.

There was one party, however, with a more credible claim to national status: the National party of Nigeria, which had the most money and at least some element of competition within its ranks, rather than a single obvious figure, for leadership. In a closed convention, it selected Alhaji Shehu Shagari as its presidential candidate for 1979. He was a Fulani from near Sokoto in the North. The first person from his ancestral village to obtain a secular education, he became known for his poetry in the Hausa language. Shagari had been in the civilian government during the First Republic, but also served under Gowon's military regime.

The elections for lesser offices were held on four successive Saturdays in July 1979; and for president, two weeks later in August. The campaign had been hard-fought, a kind of parody of an American political race with an overlay of the confusion endemic to a developing country. In the end, Shagari won, although his party fell far short of a majority in the national legislature. Even his assumption of the presidency required a creative interpretation of the new constitution, which said that a president must receive a quarter of the votes cast in each of at least two-thirds of the nineteen states. Shagari had a large plurality, but a full quarter of the vote in only twelve states, not thirteen, as presumed to be necessary. FEDECO, upheld by the high court, found a different way to calculate the fractions and ruled that Shagari had enough votes in the thirteenth state to squeak by. He was sworn in, and Nigeria's Second Republic officially launched, on October 1, 1979.

For Nigerians who were expecting immediate change, Shagari was a disappointment. During an initial period of negotiations over his cabinet, he virtually disappeared from public view, finally emerging with a legislative coalition with Azikiwe's party and several of its members in his cabinet. (One complicating factor was the constitutional requirement of at least one representative from each of the nineteen states in the federal cabinet.) The new president seemed genuinely popular with the public, but he had a hard time obtaining a verbal cease-fire from competing politicians, especially Awolowo, who saw his lifelong dream of running the country fading with his age. Awolowo, in fact, believed that he had been cheated out of the presidency.

Nigeria's new constitutional system was put to many early tests. The Senate asserted its independence by rejecting half of Shagari's original twenty-four cabinet appointments. (Later it backed down.) The courts imposed a fine of $658,000 on the executive branch for expelling a state legislator from the country on the grounds that he was not a Nigerian citizen. The supreme court also struck down the formula for the allocation of oil revenues and other funds between the federal and state governments. Shagari pushed his own authority to the limit when he established "presidential liaison officers" in all the states except Lagos and filled each one of those jobs with defeated candidates or factotums from his own party. The legislature tried to deny the $3 million budget for the liaison officers, claiming they would only usurp the governors' power, but Shagari in turn found another way to pay them. A presidential advisory body meanwhile cut the salaries the legislators had voted for themselves. Demands were pressed almost immediately for the creation of still more new states.

One early improvement under Shagari was in the Nigerian government's respect for civil liberties. The Nigerian Security Agency, once feared and prone to abuses, was brought under control and more carefully supervised. In the area of freedom of the press, however, Shagari's record was not so pure. Nigeria's press is the liveliest in Africa. Its newspapers, in particular, are unabashedly partisan and seek out scandal at every turn. Matters of national policy are treated side by side with, and in much the same tone as, sex-related stories and tales of crime and violence. The style and approach of most of the papers resemble that of the *National Enquirer* in the United States.

As this liveliness and partisanship inevitably began to be turned on the president himself, he resorted to authoritarian tactics. When the *Nigerian Tribune* published a front-page story accusing Shagari of bribing opposition legislators, armed riot police raided its offices in August 1981 and arrested its two top editors; after being detained for twenty-four hours, they were charged with sedition and publishing false statements that would disturb the peace. In the following week, three more editors on two other newspapers were subjected to the same treatment, because of controversial reports they had published. The president's office disavowed the tactics of the police, but did nothing to discourage the notion that Shagari was cracking down on dissent.

It was in the North that the new Nigerian democracy was most fragile. The governors of Kano and Kaduna states fell into bitter disputes with the national head of their own party, and the Kaduna governor was impeached by his state legislature, which was under the control of Shagari's party. The left-leaning governor of Kano made the mistake of confronting the emir of Kano, the traditional religious leader there, and accusing him of improprieties; in reaction, the emir's followers rioted. They burned down the state radio station, the legislative assembly, and other public buildings, killing at least two people and causing $300 million worth of damage. Kano was the scene of other riots, too, including one explosion in December 1980 apparently instigated by members of a fundamentalist Islamic cult; before it was over, at least a thousand people had died. Again in October 1982, an estimated 450 people died in sectarian violence—further confirmation that national unity was an elusive goal.

By mid-1981 the political alliance that Shagari had constructed with Azikiwe's party had collapsed (although several cabinet ministers from that party, including the foreign minister, Dr. Ishaya Audu, refused to resign). The four major opposition parties held a summit in the spring of 1982 and talked of offering a single challenger to Shagari the next year; but one of the parties soon backed out. The political jockeying had the effect of getting the Nigerian presidential campaign underway even earlier than its American counterpart might have been. The copy risked exaggerating the excesses of the model.

Political conflict, coupled with what critics called "the Shagari malaise"—the president's apparent inability to act forcefully—had the Nigerian military watching events closely once again. There were rumors of restiveness in the ranks; one or two small provincial mutinies were quickly suppressed. But some officials from the last military regime indicated their faith in the system by running for civilian office, especially as candidates of Shagari's party. The president himself pursued a strategy of conciliation. In May 1982 he went so far as to pardon Odumegwu Ojukwu, the leader of the Biafran rebellion, who returned from Ivory Coast to a hero's welcome. He too joined the president's party. Shagari also extended the olive branch to his most formidable political opponent, Awolowo, by honoring him as a "Grand Commander of the Federal Republic"—a sort of Nigerian knighthood—during 1982 ceremonies marking the twenty-second anniversary of independence.

The National party of Nigeria held American-style primaries to select its candidates for the 1983 legislative elections. Another American-inspired innovation—this one not necessarily beneficial— was the expenditure of vast amounts of money on Shagari's campaign, including television advertising. The NPN even hired a political promotion firm from New York to design its commercials, and Gerald Funk, a former adviser on Africa policy from the staff of the U.S. National Security Council, also worked on the effort. Shagari treated the oil-revenue crisis as a national cause rather than a political liability, and he benefited from a rearrangement of the election process; this time the presidential poll was held first, and the federal legislative and state elections followed.

Aminu Kano's party barely survived his death and won only one governorship in 1983, but both Awolowo and Azikiwe again mounted serious presidential campaigns. Between them, however, they took only 45 percent of the vote, and Shagari was declared the winner with his own 47 percent. His party also claimed a majority of the seats in both the 95-member Senate and the 450-member House, and it took control of eleven out of the nineteen states (as compared with only seven the first time around).

Awolowo once again insisted that he had been cheated, and he was not alone. There was widespread suspicion of an advance voter registration effort that produced some improbable figures, and there were claims of rigging in several states during the election itself. Rioting, arson, and political assassinations occurred in some areas, along with charges that FEDECO had manipulated the results to help Shagari's party, especially in several state elections. At least a hundred people died, and many more were arrested, in election violence. Ojukwu at first seemed to lose his race for a Senate seat from Anambra state (in the area that was once Biafra), but a court overturned the results, claiming he was the victim of false voting booths and fraudulent tallies.

Shagari was inaugurated as president again on October 1, 1983, and this time he presented an image of decisiveness by selecting his cabinet and his personal advisers quickly. But as it happened, he would serve barely three months of his second term. Early in the morning of New Year's Eve, a group of military officers announced that they had bloodlessly deposed the civilian regime and reestablished a "federal military government." Explaining the suspension of the 1979 constitution and the need for yet another coup, Brigadier Sanni Abacha, a spokesman for the officers, cited economic chaos, a declining standard of living, and rampant corruption. "There is inadequacy of food at reasonable prices for our people," he said in an initial radio broadcast. "Health services are in shambles. . . . Our educational system is deteriorating at an alarming rate . . . workers are being owed salary arrears of eight to twelve months. . . . Yet our leaders revel in squandermania."

Selected by his colleagues as leader of the new regime was forty-one-year-old Major General Mohammed Buhari, another Hausa-Fulani from the North who had fought in the civil war and, as a young colonel, had helped overthrow Gowon in 1975. At that time Buhari managed investigations of official corruption and became the military governor of one of Nigeria's states. Later he served as minister of energy and chairman of the Nigerian National Petroleum Corporation under Obasanjo. Thus he was familiar with the dependence on oil that had sent the country into an economic tailspin. In early interviews and declarations, Buhari sought to assure Nigerians and concerned outsiders that the latest military government was committed to reform and conciliation, but he was not sanguine about the prospects for democracy in Nigeria. "The economic mess, the corruption, and unacceptable level of unemployment could not be excused on the grounds that Nigeria was a practicing democracy," he said; "democracy at that price was certainly not in the interest of the people of this country."

Even in Nigerian terms, corruption had reached epic proportions during the latest experiment with civilian rule, and efforts to deal with it proved meaningless. Shagari had called for an "ethical revolution" prior to his reelection, and he created a "Ministry of National Guidance" that was supposed to help carry it out. But the drive hardly got off the ground before the coup; even if it had, no one expected it to touch powerful figures like Shagari's reelection campaign manager and former minister of transport, Umaru Dikko, who was widely regarded as one of the most corrupt people in the country. Named to head a presidential task force charged with controlling illegal distribution of rice, Dikko himself hoarded rice to drive its price up. There were many other instances of a blatant disregard for standards of decent conduct. Within a few weeks of the coup, for example, a ship was intercepted in Lagos harbor carrying tons of illegally imported tires; the designated recipient of the contraband freight was the former attorney general, and it was addressed to him at the Ministry of Justice.

Such abuses seemed all the worse in the context of Nigeria's drastic economic circumstances. During the nearly four and a half years of civilian rule, foreign currency reserves shrank from about $8 billion to less than $1 billion and Nigeria's external debt increased threefold, to an estimated $15 billion. The need to spend the dwindling reserves to import food made it ever more difficult to afford the raw materials and semiprocessed goods necessary for Nigerian industry. The IMF and private lenders were pressuring the Nigerian government to introduce austerity measures, including an end to food price subsidies and a devaluation of the national currency, as a condition of assistance, but those were unpopular actions and for political reasons Shagari had resisted. Ironically, the president had finally announced a "structural readjustment" of the Nigerian economy just two days before the coup.

In reality, the domestic and foreign policies of the new military government were not greatly different from those of the Shagari regime. Buhari's economic decisions were more stringently enforced, however, and if Nigeria still did not formally satisfy the IMF, it moved in the direction required by international critics; Buhari's first budget provided for a 40 percent cut in federal spending and stricter controls on the government contracts and other financial transactions that were the source of so many abuses during civilian rule. With a flair for public relations and sloganeering, Nigeria's new leader announced a "War Against Indiscipline," or "WAI," which had the initial effect of convincing many ordinary Nigerians that they could do things in their everyday lives that would have the patriotic result of helping the nation. Buhari also sought an increase in Nigeria's oil-production quota from OPEC.

A "Supreme Military Council" was named that closely mirrored the one that had been the highest authority during the Obasanjo regime. Buhari selected a cabinet with a majority of civilian members, some of them well known and widely respected, for example, Ibrahim Gambari, of the Nigerian Institute of International Affairs, who became foreign minister. Joseph Garba, the foreign minister under Obasanjo, went to the United Nations as Nigeria's ambassador. The major elements of Nigerian foreign policy, including its membership in OPEC, remained intact, and there was every indication that the country would continue to cultivate its American connections.

Although political parties were abolished and the national assembly was shut down, the independent judiciary survived. One major change, of course, was a new—perhaps more sincere and effective—drive against corruption. Some four thousand elected officials and political appointees from the years of civilian rule turned themselves in, as required, after the coup. Many were freed after the military government had seized what it said were illegally obtained assets, but in mid-1985 there were still several hundred people, including Shagari and other key former officials, in custody; a number of different military tribunals were investigating them, along with others who had managed to escape detention. The minimum sentence for those convicted of corruption was twenty-one years in prison, and some, including former governors, were sentenced to as much as seventy-two years.

At the top of the military government's "most wanted list" was Dikko, who was living in luxurious exile in London and keeping up a steady stream of invective against Nigeria's new rulers. In an incident that nearly led to a break in diplomatic relations between Britain and Nigeria, officials of the Nigerian embassy in London and others, including several Israelis, were implicated in a scheme to kidnap Dikko and bring him back to Lagos for trial. The plot was aborted when the former minister was discovered drugged and unconscious inside a crate at an airport outside of London, about to be shipped off to Nigeria as diplomatic baggage.* That sort of tactic did not help the new regime's credibility. And for all the military government's high-minded rhetoric and promises of a new way of life, reports began to filter out of Nigeria that corruption, albeit on a smaller scale, had already emerged within the Buhari regime.

Other Nigerian problems remained consistent. Once again there were uprisings by Islamic fundamentalists, and in February and March of 1984 in the city of Yola, militant members of one sect fought against local vigilantes who were trying to repress them. The official death toll was five hundred, but some sources said that twice that many people died in the clashes. Ethnic and regional rivalries seemed intact, and one interpretation of the coup held that the "Kaduna Mafia," a subterranean network of powerful Moslem soldiers, civil servants, and businessmen from the North, was worried that Shagari was allowing too much influence to Christians and might actually have permitted himself to be succeeded by an "infidel."

At least for an initial period, the coup seemed to be a popular development within Nigeria and the new military government's promises to get the country back on track were taken seriously. If nothing else, Buhari benefited from a public disgust with corruption and a willingness on the part of ordinary citizens to trust anyone who made a plausible promise to improve their daily lives.

---

* One Nigerian military officer implicated in the effort to smuggle Dikko out of Britain later escaped prosecution by exactly the same ploy—shipping himself home in a crate.

The soldiers did reestablish some semblance of order in Nigeria's national life, albeit at a considerable cost: many decrees were harshly enforced, and Nigerians gave up some of the personal freedom they had enjoyed previously even in the hardest times. The press was dealt with much more severely than it had been under Shagari; when other tactics failed to squelch criticism, the government simply restricted the amount of newsprint that opposition newspapers could bring into the country. Buhari claimed to be repaying a substantial part of the country's foreign debt, and he reported a significant improvement in the balance of payments. In an attempt to shift priorities, he increased the budget for agriculture from 6 percent of government spending to 10 percent. Predictably enough, however, before the new regime had been in office a year, it was executing some forty soldiers for allegedly planning another coup. Another group, including some of Buhari's closest colleagues, tried and succeeded in August 1985. The new military ruler was forty-four-year-old Major General Ibrahim Babangida, a popular war hero.

It was outside of Nigeria that the collapse of civilian rule was taken as an especially great disappointment. Although most African leaders were hardly in a position to criticize the return of military rule in Nigeria, a few—most notably in Kenya and Zimbabwe—worried that the end of this experiment in Africa's most populous nation would be taken as a powerful symbol that weakened their own legitimacy as elected leaders. In the United States and other Western countries, the events in Nigeria were regarded as a grave and lamentable sign that democracy was in retreat in the developing world. For some, they confirmed the worst stereotype of the African continent as an unruly, ungovernable place. If Nigeria, with its intelligentsia, its resolve, and its oil, could not make it, then who could?

Nigeria's political and economic evolution has focused new attention on its role within Africa and in the Third World generally. The main trend in Nigerian foreign policy in recent years has been to forge close political, economic, and even philosophical links with the United States, all the while reasserting Nigeria's adherence to the principles of nonalignment and African unity. As political scientist Ali Mazrui has said, "the giant of Africa" and "the giant of the West" have somehow "entered into a strange social contract without fully realizing it. Something from Nigeria is needed for the economic health of the United States. Something from the United States seems to be needed for the political health of Nigeria."

Although it was slow in coming, there is a greater popular awareness in America now that Nigeria has been a reliable source of oil. The fact that Nigeria tried to adopt the American constitutional model (and might well try again) and has built a capitalist economy flattered some U.S. officials and businessmen. In a period of American adversity in the world, Nigeria seemed unusually appreciative of American examples. In fact, there are striking similarities between the two countries that few people have acknowledged: important regional differences and rivalries that can take decades (or centuries) to heal; a strong ethnic strain in political life; a seemingly endless debate over the relationship between national and local government and the levels in between; and even a recent tradition of violence and assassination that threatens the integrity of governmental and political processes.

An estimated fifteen to twenty thousand Nigerians were studying in the United States at any given moment in recent years; by 1983 that number was up to fifty thousand. Although there are notable exceptions, most of those who have returned home have found that their American training and experience are an advantage in Nigeria. And they have tended to carry with them a balanced appreciation of America's strengths and weaknesses.* There have also been many more Americans in Nigeria in recent years, mostly working in oil and other businesses. Some have learned a great deal about Nigeria—and Africa—but most live in such an insulated bubble that they gain little understanding of

---

* Yet there is a long tradition of Nigerians who have spent time in the United States turning haughtily against the country where they trained. John Pepper Clark, a Nigerian poet and writer, published a book recounting his experiences while he held a fellowship at Princeton University in the 1960s and scoffed at Americans for their materialism, insularity, elitism, and obsession with sex. T. Obinkaram Echewa, who returned to Nigeria in 1982 after twenty years in the United States, took a parting shot in a column he wrote for *Newsweek*. "Living successfully in modern America takes more than a little Philistinism," Echewa said. "American social and intellectual life is so bathed in clichés that it is nearly impossible to think a fresh or original thought. . . . America blunts one's finer sensibilities by insisting that life is a grabfest, a jungle, a dog-eat-dog fight."

where they are and what is going on around them. When a *New York Times* reporter polled twenty-four Americans working on an oil rig off the Nigerian coast in 1981, for example, not one of them could name the president of Nigeria.

Certainly there were rough spots along the way in the development of this new Nigerian-American relationship. The standoff when Henry Kissinger was conducting American foreign policy has became legendary. The Nigerians were offended at the time by the increasingly obvious American tilt toward the minority white regimes in southern Africa. Joseph Garba, who was foreign minister in the Obasanjo government, likes to tell the story of how Nigeria three times refused Kissinger's proposals to stop in Lagos in the course of his shuttle diplomacy efforts. On one of those occasions, when Kissinger would have been arriving from Europe, Nigeria almost relented. But then Kissinger brought up the subject of the notorious traffic jams between the airport and the city, and he said he had heard that Nigerian government officials sometimes avoided them by using helicopters. Could he bring along a helicopter or two from an American base in West Germany? Garba replied that Nigeria had good helicopters and good pilots of its own, which Kissinger would be welcome to use. The secretary of state insisted that he would fly only in American equipment with American crews. Garba's final answer was, "If you bring your own helicopters, we will impound them and they will never leave Nigeria." Kissinger did not visit.

The major change came during the Carter administration, when UN Ambassador Andrew Young, in particular, cultivated a friendship with the Nigerians. Young and the then-American ambassador in Lagos, Donald Easum, patched things up so thoroughly that an American president was willing and welcome to visit Nigeria in the spring of 1978. For Jimmy Carter, a Nigerian rapprochement had many advantages. It was bound to be popular with his black constituency. Carter was sure he could relate well to Africans, because of the parallels he drew between African issues and those he had faced in his own political career in Georgia. There was also a religious component to the feeling. Carter seemed to perceive himself as a missionary of sorts when he went to Africa, and it was truly appropriate that a fellow evangelical Baptist, Olusegun Obasanjo, was waiting for him at the other end.

Carter said things the Nigerians wanted to hear—including a

warning that "the hour is late" for achieving majority rule in southern Africa—and Obasanjo assured him that "the whole of Africa"
was paying attention. Even if Nigerians generally reacted to Carter's presence with a classic haughty reserve (the state-owned
television network broadcast a tennis match at the time Carter
was giving his major address), it was clear that Nigeria appreciated getting such high-profile attention from the United States.

American officials were delighted to hear Nigeria joining in
the protests against the Soviet and Cuban presence in Africa. In
a hard-hitting address to the annual summit meeting of the Organization of African Unity in Khartoum in 1978, Obasanjo warned
Moscow that Africa was "not about to throw off one colonial yoke
for another." The next year, the Nigerians ordered the Soviet
Union to cut its contingent of military advisers in Lagos from
forty to five.*

The Nigerian intelligentsia bristled at such closeness with
America and pressed for a more even-handed approach to Washington and Moscow. "Neither of the superpowers has interests
which are legitimate in terms of African aspirations," argued
A. Bolaji Akinyemi, then director-general of the Nigerian Institute
of International Affairs (and later foreign minister), in a speech
he gave in the mid-1970s. "While the interplay of the policies of
the superpowers may be a matter of life and death to the African
state involved, to the superpowers, the interests of the African
states are expendable in the cause of a higher goal called détente
now or whatever name may become fashionable in the future."

That attitude found justification for some Nigerians after the
election of Ronald Reagan in 1980. Shagari, speaking at a moment
when Nigerian clout seemed to be at its peak, warned the Reagan
administration—and the Conservative party government of Margaret Thatcher in Britain—that there would be severe repercussions if they took too soft a line with South Africa or in any way

---

* Ironically, just at the time when the Nigerians were making it difficult for
American journalists to work in their country, they were paying no attention
to the activities of Soviet news representatives in Lagos, even though some
of them were allegedly intelligence agents and were writing mischievous dispatches. One official in the Nigerian foreign ministry suggested at the time
that the Soviet "journalists" were being left alone only because the Nigerian
foreign ministry had no one who was able to read and evaluate the Russian-
language reports they filed.

intervened to help South African-aided, pro-Western rebels in Angola. A senior political adviser to the Nigerian president openly described Reagan's Africa policy as "retrogressive" and said Nigeria might ultimately resort to the "oil weapon" as a means of exerting pressure on the United States and others in the West.

Nonetheless, the change of American presidents and Africa policy did nothing to impede the development of commercial relations and technical cooperation between the United States and Nigeria. The two countries signed agreements in 1981 for American assistance in training Nigerian technical educators and for joint public health projects. The Nigerians agreed to make it easier for American business to enter Nigeria and deal with complex licensing procedures. At the same time, they set up trade and investment centers in several U.S. cities. Convinced that something had to be done to improve Nigeria's image in the United States, the government in Lagos also purchased lengthy advertising supplements in American newspapers, portraying Nigeria as a place almost without flaws, an investor's paradise.

Often the Nigerians and Americans who tried to do business found themselves at odds with each other. The Americans were generally looking for markets, for trade opportunities that would help balance off the enormous flow of U.S. dollars to pay for Nigerian oil. The Nigerian desire, on the other hand, was for investment on the host country's terms, especially if it would help implant technological know-how and promote the long-range development of the Nigerian economy. American (and other western) businessmen were frustrated by red tape and by "Nigerianization" rules requiring a significant local stake in every new enterprise. But these requirements arose out of bitter experiences in colonial days, when the foreign-owned United Africa Company, for example, came to control nearly 60 percent of Nigeria's agricultural exports. The Nigerians had no objection to capitalism, but they were determined that some of the profits go to African, rather than outside, capitalists.

Increasingly, Nigerian-American ties could be described as a love-hate relationship. Many well-intentioned Americans, including government officials, simply could not understand the hate side of it. It seemed unfair to hold present-day America responsible for its own and others' wrongs of the past. But it was a fact of life that if Nigeria became too closely identified with the United

States, it would risk losing credibility elsewhere in Africa and the Third World. Washington must realize, political scientist Ali Mazrui warned, that if it wants to enhance the stature and influence of its best new friend in Africa, it must not attempt "to seduce Nigeria to the bosom of Uncle Sam." It must leave Nigeria room to assert its independence from, and its right to criticize, the United States.

Nigeria did seem to win a special place in the U.S. firmament and the American popular consciousness. On a continent so full of violence and radicalism, Nigeria came to seem from afar like a calm, trustworthy, even conservative nation. For all its domestic turmoil, it did not have a significant movement that advocated a Marxist or even a mainstream socialist solution to the country's problems.* Ironically, in some parts of the American press—and especially in the American academic community—Nigeria achieved a special status, almost free from criticism. Indeed, when one university professor interested in Third World affairs mounted a frontal attack on Nigeria in the American liberal weekly, *The Nation,* he did it under a pseudonym, apparently to preserve his access and his reputation as a friend of Nigeria.

There were other reasons for a Nigerian tendency to identify with the United States. Nigeria has come to have a role in sub-Saharan Africa roughly comparable to the American role in Europe after World War II. It is the most powerful country in black Africa, the most influential, the one of whom friends and allies expect the most. It tends to be watched more closely than any other country in its arena, and its missteps or embarrassments sometimes provoke an unseemly joy among its supposed partners. Nigeria has even had the character-building experience, so familiar to the United States, of having the recipients of its aid act ungrateful and contemptuous. Under the circumstances, the Nigerian ego turned out to be just as fragile as the American ego.

Apart from its vast population, its early devotion to African nationalism, and its sometime oil wealth, Nigeria based its claim to leadership in Africa on its militancy toward South Africa and,

---

* Some of the people out of power actually went on to study the science of government, as if to learn what they had done wrong. Yakubu Gowon turned up as a student at the University of Warwick in England, and Joseph Garba, between service in military governments, went to Harvard for a degree in public administration.

previously, white-ruled Rhodesia. A country's stridency on southern African issues is often directly proportional to its distance
from the actual crises and its ability to avoid direct involvement.
Nigeria's four thousand miles of remove do make it easier to tell
others what they should be doing to deal with the devil next door.
The Nigerian government hardly sent an expeditionary force to
fight in Namibia or to infiltrate into South Africa, but it did offer
more than rhetoric. For years, it provided financial support to
groups like the African National Congress, and more recently, Nigeria took more dramatic steps.

In 1978, after Barclays Bank in Britain announced it had
purchased South African government bonds, the Nigerian military
government moved against its local subsidiary, withdrawing all
government deposits and ordering two-thirds of Barclays' expatriate staff out of the country. The next year, after a defiant Barclays
subscribed to a South African defense bond issue, the Nigerians
nationalized the bank altogether. Also in 1979, Nigeria nationalized the British Petroleum Company's interests, in retaliation for
BP's alleged sale of oil—perhaps Nigerian oil—to South Africa. Nigeria also excluded British companies from bidding on a $200 mil-
lion port construction contract. These actions probably damaged
the prospects for new British investment in Nigeria. (At the same
time, without public knowledge, Nigeria continued to buy South
African goods whose origin had been conveniently concealed.)

Nigeria could hardly afford to use its "oil weapon" on the
South African issue at a time of oil gluts and other economic
stresses. But at one point the civilian government startled its
American and other friends by launching a "nuclear program"
of unknown scope. One hot-headed adviser to Shagari warned
that although Nigeria had signed the Nuclear Non-Proliferation
Treaty, it would not hesitate to try to build a nuclear bomb "if it
is necessary to bring South Africa to the negotiating table." With
all its other problems and urgent priorities, it is hard to imagine
Nigeria developing nuclear weapons. Still, that kind of talk wins
points for Nigeria in other black African countries, where the external issue of South Africa, for all its moral force, is also the
most convenient and constant device available to distract attention and discontent away from troubles at home. (Soon after the
military returned to power at the end of 1983, Mohammed Buhari

warned that domestic problems would probably require Nigeria to reduce its activist role in Africa.)

Even in the worst of times, Nigeria is more prosperous than most of its neighbors. As a result, there is a steady stream of immigrants from other countries, such as Ghana, Togo, Benin, Niger, and Cameroon. Nigeria long had mixed feelings about the immigrants (and often blamed them for conditions in Lagos); but for years it was reluctant to do anything about them, since the charter of the Economic Community of West African States (ECOWAS), of which Nigeria is a chief promoter, guarantees freedom of movement within and between the member countries.

The reluctance dissipated, however, as the decline in oil prices hit the Nigerian economy and social fabric. In January 1983 the Shagari government took the startling step of expelling all illegal aliens from Nigeria. The mass exodus of a million or more Ghanaians and other foreigners—no one seemed to know the exact number—in a period of two weeks was reported widely in the western press. Some drowned while desperately trying to board ships; others died in traffic accidents or violent confrontations on the highways; and still others were victims of hunger or exposure during the confused rush for the borders. The situation was all the more pathetic because of the ambiguous legal status of most of the people who were expelled from Nigeria. They were not technically refugees, and so they did not qualify for various forms of bilateral or international assistance (although the United States and other western nations did ship some emergency help, especially to countries like Togo, which had to cope with their needs as they passed through). Those returning to Ghana knew there was little hope for a decent life when they got home, because their own country was in a dreadful economic state.

Nigeria took substantial international criticism for the expulsion. At home, however, the move was quite popular as a means of dealing with the country's new hardships, and it probably contributed to Shagari's reelection in 1983. Ironically, though, Nigeria could not really afford this self-righteous bit of economic nationalism. The Nigerian economy suffered from the sudden departure of factory and construction workers (many of whom were employed at lower wages because of their illegal status). The operations of the port in Lagos were adversely affected, and the departure of many Ghanaian teachers caused chaos in Nigerian schools. All of these problems were mitigated some months later when the foreign workers began to slip quietly back into Nigeria.

In better economic times, Nigeria's neighbors had hopes that the flow of humanity across the borders would be a two-way affair. They wanted to draw Nigerians to their countries—not jobseekers, but well-to-do tourists. Indeed, the beaches up the coast in Togo are an attraction for Lagosians trying to escape the chaos, and other nearby countries dreamed of developing tourist industries geared to Nigerian tastes.

Nigeria does have another claim to prestige in Africa: it is the African country that has done the most to preserve and honor traditional arts and culture. Other nations, such as Senegal and Kenya, have had the same inclinations, but fewer resources. The national museum in Lagos is a monument to the country's determination to show off its past; it has been a place for Nigerian art to come home from its dispersal around the world during the colonial era and the Biafran war. Traveling exhibitions of Nigerian antiquities have helped to make an important point: that far from fitting into the old stereotypes of primitive art useful primarily for black magic or other pagan ceremonies, the masks and sculptures and other pieces demonstrate great achievements on the part of complex civilizations. By exposing a vast lay audience around the world, instead of just the usual specialists, to African art, Nigeria has gone a long way toward exploding Eurocentric myths about what is valuable and sophisticated.

In civil as well as artistic life, Nigeria has demonstrated a reverence for the African past. Unlike some other countries, such as Uganda, Nigeria has permitted, and even encouraged, traditional forms of leadership, including tribal monarchies, to coexist with its modern governmental system. Except in some parts of the North, where there have been tense confrontations between religious and secular authorities, this has generally worked well. Although the *obas*, or tribal kings, have less actual power and prestige than they once did, some of them, in places like Benin and Oshogbo, still mediate local disputes and preside at tribal rituals. A few traditional chiefs have used their standing to launch successful business or political careers.

The practical and psychological conflict between tribal traditions and the requirements of modern life is a prominent theme in some of the best modern Nigerian literature, such as *Death and the King's Horseman*, a play by Wole Soyinka. Indeed, Nigerians have stood out among African writers as not only the most prolific (almost a quarter of the books in the African Writers Series, published in England, are by Nigerians), but also the most willing to confront the painful issues of modernization and to admit the failings of their country in the postcolonial era. Their work is often politically controversial, but prominent Nigerian writers have generally not been subject to the same kind of governmental restrictions as their counterparts in Kenya, South Africa, and elsewhere.

As Americans know all too well, learning how to handle a role of leadership and influence with one's friends and adversaries is not easy. Nigeria's efforts in this regard have had mixed results. It was certainly impressive when Shagari managed to convince Pope John Paul II, during his visit to Nigeria, that he should grant an audience at the Vatican to the leaders of two southern African guerrilla organizations, Sam Nujoma of the South-West Africa People's Organization and Oliver Tambo of the African National Congress. Nigeria also scored points for principle when, during the Angolan conflict in the mid-1970s, it first stood neutral among the various nationalist groups, but finally threw its support to the Marxist MPLA because the South Africans had become involved on the side of other factions. Nigeria's alignment with the MPLA was enough to tip the balance and win it the endorsement of the OAU.

But on other occasions Nigeria has been accused, especially by francophone African states and by France itself, of seeking to establish hegemony in West Africa. The cliché of "the ugly Nigerian" has begun to be heard in Africa in much the same way that "the ugly American" was once complained about in Southeast Asia. Nigeria made no new friends in 1977 when it fought its French-speaking neighbor, Niger, for a seat on the United Nations Security Council and won. Niger had been designated by the OAU as next in line for an unofficial "Africa seat" on the council, but the Nigerian government decided it did not care to wait for some supranational body to designate its turn for such honors; it wanted to exercise what it regarded as its own legitimate influence in world affairs. In putting together their victory, the Nigerians stepped on many toes. They were also accused of foolish consistency when, in the name of the principle of territorial integrity, they voted in the OAU to condemn Tanzania's invasion of Uganda in 1979 to overthrow Idi Amin.

Perhaps the clumsiest Nigerian attempt to assert regional influence came during the prolonged crisis in Chad, its neighbor to the northeast. In 1979, the Nigerian military government sponsored a conference near Kano of the four principal factions embroiled at that point in the old Chadian civil war. The cease-fire agreed upon there did not hold, however, and the next year some twelve thousand Libyan troops poured into Chad's capital of Ndjamena and other parts of the country to fill the vacuum left by the departure of French forces. A Libyan presence so near to Nigeria, and to other less stable West African countries, caused considerable alarm in Washington, London, and Paris, not to mention Lagos. But Muammar al-Qaddafi of Libya resisted Nigeria's efforts at friendly persuasion. He said he had no intention of withdrawing his troops from Chad just to please Nigeria, because Libya had a border with Chad, too, and Qaddafi felt Chad was within his own sphere of influence.

Nigeria also found itself embroiled in a crisis with its neighbor to the east, Cameroon, in 1981. Originally a German colony, Cameroon was divided after World War I between France and Britain, and so it had (and still has today) two distinct parts, each influenced by its own colonial culture and language. At the time when Cameroon was attaining independence, Nigeria entertained the hope that the anglophone part of Cameroon would opt to attach itself to the eastern region of Nigeria rather than staying with the francophone part of Cameroon; but except in a small section of anglophone Cameroon, that did not happen, and the two countries came into independence with unresolved bad feelings toward each other. During the Nigerian civil war, in an attempt to prevent Cameroon from helping next-door Biafra, Gowon quietly made frontier concessions that seemed to give Cameroon sovereignty over a seabed rich in oil deposits; subsequent Nigerian governments never ratified Gowon's agreement with Cameroon or accepted the new frontier that Cameroon claimed.

The border dispute flared in May 1981, when five Nigerian soldiers were killed in a clash with Cameroonian troops. Both in the Nigerian military and in the popular press there was a fiercely nationalistic, even jingoistic reaction. "We must march on Yaoundé and sack the banana government there," cried one newspaper. Another called Shagari "chicken-livered Shehu" for his refusal to order an attack on Cameroon and his failure to take a harder line against Libya in Chad. But the president insisted on handling the conflict with Cameroon by diplomatic means, asserting that Nigeria's "leadership and mediatory role" in Africa were inconsistent with a quick resort to military force. That approach became a grievance for the Nigerian military against the civilian regime. (Ultimately, Cameroon helped Shagari out of his fix by agreeing to pay reparations for the soldiers' deaths.)

There is nothing approaching a consensus in Africa today that Nigeria should lead the continent as it would like to do. That cannot happen until Nigeria makes genuine progress in dealing with certain fundamental national problems: corruption in government and business; a gigantic foreign debt; general economic decline; ethnic tensions; and grave inequities in society. It must also demonstrate an economic competence and resilience that provide an immunity to the ups and downs of the oil market, and find some system other than occasional military coups to achieve political stability and continuity. The humbling experience of returning to poverty after a period of great prosperity has taught Nigeria some bitter lessons. For the country in Africa that has, in important respects, come the farthest, there is still far to go.

5

Kenya:
Frayed Paradise

THE CROWD of tens of thousands of people assembled in Jamhuri Park on the outskirts of Nairobi could have swung either way, toward jubilation or rage. It was a classic postcolonial African gathering: modern, Westernized folks stood elbow-to-elbow with traditionals whose ears had been elongated or cheeks scarred in tribal rituals. Some looked proud and others hungry; many were in tattered clothes and wore no shoes; others, in suits and elegant dresses, seemed vaguely frightened. On the fringes were a few whites and Asians, human souvenirs of another era.

It was December 12, 1978, Jamhuri (Swahili for "republic") Day, the fifteenth anniversary of Kenya's *uhuru* ("freedom") from British rule. As a commemorative postage stamp proudly boasted, they had been "15 great years" for Kenya. The country had ostensibly made a smooth transition from a colony stained by a bloody rebellion to a stable and moderately prosperous developing nation, the showcase of East Africa.

But recent events had also made this independence day an occasion of uncertainty and tension. For it was late in Kenya's fif-

162

teenth year that Jomo Kenyatta, the father of the nation and one of Africa's revered elder statesmen, died in his mid-eighties. To Kenyans, the absence of "Mzee" ("old man," a term of respect) from this event was almost a violation of the natural order of the universe. Admittedly, in Kenyatta's last years the dreams that accompanied *uhuru* had seemed to fade. Yet with his piercing leonine gaze, his booming voice, and his fly-whisk, Kenyatta had been a steady symbol, and no one knew what to expect of his successor, a former schoolteacher named Daniel arap Moi, who, during twelve years as Mzee's vice-president, built no clear public image. Unlike Kenyatta, who was a member of the Kikuyu, Kenya's largest ethnic group, Moi was from the tiny Tugen tribe, part of the Kalenjin group, which had been allied with, but always distinct from, the Kikuyu.

The ceremonies were replete with symbols of the old and the new. The military and police marching units were composed entirely of blacks, yet their style was thoroughly British. But the colonial flashback was mitigated by traditional dancers, dressed in monkey skins and carrying spears, who alternated with school choirs before the reviewing stand. Old-fashioned military transports flew slowly overhead, creating a vapor trail of Kenya's red, green, and black flag (and permanent red, green, and black splotches on the clothes of everyone present). They were followed by a squadron of American-supplied F-5E fighter jets, which squealed past, doing acrobatic twists and turns and calling attention to Kenya's growing military might.

After a moment of silence in memory of Mzee, Moi, who had been in office barely three months, delivered his ceremonial address, stilted in tone but packed with surprises and gifts for the citizens: a program to eliminate illiteracy within five years, an instant increase by 10 percent of the number of people employed in the private and public sectors, free milk daily to all primary school children beginning in mid-1979, and an additional year of universal free primary education (bringing it up through the sixth grade).

Moi saved the bombshell for last: the release of all twenty-six political detainees then held by Kenya, including Ngugi wa Thiong'o (formerly James Ngugi), a literature professor and internationally recognized novelist, and several politicians who had dared to challenge or disparage Kenyatta's leadership. The crowd exploded into thunderous cheers, hardly noticing the president's warning that "my government will not hesitate in taking immediate and firm action against anyone whose activities threaten our peace, unity, and stability."

The joke around town was, "Today Kenya is the only country in the world without political prisoners. We'll see about tomorrow." At the University of Nairobi, students poured into the streets to demonstrate in favor of the government—a first in Kenyan history. When Ngugi suddenly appeared on campus in his car, they lifted him, car and all, on their shoulders and paraded him around in celebration.

Kenya is a country the size of France, with a population of about 20 million. Because it straddles the Equator, it experiences only a few minutes' variation in the length of its days and nights in the course of a year. And except for two annual periods of intense rain—the "long rains" from March through May and the short ones in October and November—the weather varies little. This can be tedious for those accustomed to the changing seasons, but in Nairobi, at an elevation of more than a mile above sea level, it translates into a moderate, easy climate, permitting a comfortable life style almost year round. Still, July and August are usually an especially pleasant and optimistic time in this capital that often seems like a bit of paradise; the daytime sky is particularly blue and unclouded, the nights crisp and cool. It is winter, of a sort. Visitors seem less frantic than at other times, and the local people more relaxed and welcoming. On the surface, it is hard to imagine much of anything going wrong.

But in 1982 this characteristic optimism was missing. Three and a half years after Daniel arap Moi's first Jamhuri Day as president, it seemed as if there was something very wrong. It was not just that tourism was still suffering as the result of a terrorist (Middle East–related) bombing at the Norfolk Hotel on New Year's Eve of 1979 and the world recession. Nairobi was now a different place. There was a feeling of malaise and alienation.

The euphoria of Moi's initial months in office, when Kenya was still enjoying the economic and political proceeds of a "coffee boom" (the unexpected dividend from a failed Brazilian harvest), had worn off. Many ordinary Kenyans, normally respectful toward authority figures, were grumbling about the president—blaming him for sudden shortages of food and other goods, complaining that corruption had gotten out of hand, and worrying that the tangible progress so many people had experienced since independence was now slipping away. Rival politicians were scheming. The students were again demonstrating in the streets, this time, more characteristically, against the government, denouncing the mishandling of their grants by the bureaucracy and publicly daring to call themselves Marxists. Even in the rural high schools there were signs of rebellion, protests against an oath of allegiance to the president that students were required to take twice a week. One popular chant complained, "Moi gives us milk, and it causes diarrhea." In one school, a class turned on a teacher known as a supporter of the government and beat him up. In another incident, young girls went on a rampage and caused tens of thousands of dollars' worth of damage to their school.

Moi had refused to help prominent former political prisoners find new livelihoods, and he had begun to detain his political opponents without trial. At least seven of them were behind bars, and when the editor of a Nairobi newspaper editorialized his protest, he was fired at the prompting of the government. Oginga Odinga, or "Double O," an early nationalist figure and later briefly vice-president of Kenya, who had eventually become a thorn in Kenyatta's side, was again under restrictions. Odinga had been in London, talking with Labour party members of the British Parliament about the need to form a socialist party in Kenya. When his remarks became known, Moi was infuriated and felt threatened; he rushed a constitutional amendment through the Kenyan Parliament in less than two hours, formally converting Kenya into what it already was informally—a one-party state.

Ngugi had been in trouble again. His new musical, *Mother, Sing for Me,* containing more than a hundred songs, seemed at first to be a mainstream account of colonial oppression; but when the onstage villain exploiting the peasants turned from a white man into a black man, the authorities began to catch on to his message. This and another play of his, *I Will Marry When I Want,* represented an intolerable challenge to the established order, especially because they were performed in the Kikuyu tribal language for a peasant audience, using some peasants as actors. The productions were banned and the open-air theater Ngugi had built in his home village demolished. Finally Ngugi, having failed to get back his job at the university, went into exile in Britain.

There had been rumors of stirrings within the Kenyan army, fears of a right-wing effort to seize power and punish Moi for being too lenient and failing to take the necessary steps to protect domestic and foreign business interests. His shifts of personnel in the civil service had begun to anger powerful Kikuyu, who saw power slipping away from them. Despite warnings that something untoward might be brewing, Moi felt comfortable enough, on the weekend when July turned to August, to venture forth to Nyeri for the annual Mount Kenya Agricultural Show. There the air force performed one of its impressive overhead displays for the assembled dignitaries. The president was on his way back to Nairobi by car when he learned, on the Voice of Kenya radio, that the country's "armed forces" had allegedly taken power and would soon be announcing the makeup of a "redemption council" that would be running things. Members of parliament were to report to the nearest army commander.

Astute listeners realized immediately that the announcement was not credible. The man on the air spoke with the accent of the Luo tribe, and there were few Luo in the army. Indeed, the troops who took the radio headquarters played no martial music, the stock in trade of such a coup d'etat—apparently, they could not find any—but instead broadcast first a song popular in the western part of the country (home of the Luo) and then American jazz and Jamaican reggae music.

That was the tipoff that the takeover was being attempted by the Kenya air force, a rare African military service in that a majority of its members had an advanced education; many were university graduates and some had been trained in the United States. Better paid than the army, members of the air force were not confined to barracks or bases, but allowed to live where they pleased while on duty. Thus they often spent their free time with disgruntled university students in Nairobi and joined them in deploring the plight of the growing ranks of Kenya's urban poor. Moi's government had recently angered the air force by taking away some of its special privileges, such as an exemption from drill and other routine aspects of training; it was natural for the young air force cadres to find kindred spirits, and possibly coplotters, among those who themselves felt mistreated by and unsympathetic to the regime. And it is easy to imagine that on the basis of their day-to-day contacts and philosophical discussions, the rebels in the air force thought they could easily touch off a nation-wide popular uprising that would lead to a more equitable political and economic system.

In the event, the university campus erupted in a spontaneous burst of support for the air force. Moreover, during the time when it seemed as if the coup had been successful, some of the poorest people of Nairobi took to the streets and looted. They stole bags of meal, bolts of cloth, and electronic equipment, and they turned their special anger on the shops owned by Kenyan Asians, the tiny mercantile minority that controls 55 percent of the nation's industry and 90 percent of its commerce. At least $50 million worth of goods were taken.

Within a few hours, however, the government regained control. The rebels had neglected to seize the Voice of Kenya transmitter, and so when the plug was pulled, control of the radio studios became meaningless. The air force had no discernible support from the army and, therefore, no armored vehicles or heavy weapons to help them hold on to those installations they had seized. Although much of the army was off on maneuvers near Lake Turkana in the northwestern part of the country at the time of the coup attempt, enough units were available to save the day for Moi and restore order. Hundreds of people were killed or injured in the brief fighting, and some three thousand more—including many students and all members of the air force who had survived—were arrested. The university was closed.

Because two of the key ringleaders of the revolt commandeered an airplane and escaped to Tanzania, the origins and evolution of the plot were mysterious. Although those two were indeed Luo, it seemed clear that many Kikuyu in the air force had been involved, too, or at least aware of what was coming. Theories abounded: that prominent politicians had participated in the planning; that a coup with broader military support had actually been scheduled for a few days later, when Moi was to be in Libya for an OAU meeting, but when word leaked out, the air force went ahead on its own; that a right-wing army coup really had been in the offing, but air force officers, having had word of it, moved to preempt it from the other side; that key figures in the army had actually egged on leftists in the air force, just to give themselves a chance to put down a coup and, in the process, enhance their own power by keeping Moi in office.

The courts-martial and other trials would continue for years, although within days the Asian shops were back in business and in other respects Nairobi was functioning normally. Moi asked Western nations for $125 million in special assistance to help repair the damage, and he got most of what he wanted. But the overall reaction abroad and at home—even, in retrospect, among some of the students who had participated in the coup attempt or felt sympathetic to it—was one of shock. It was hard to imagine that this seemingly calm, comfortable country had arrived at such a sorry state. "Well, that's it," said one Western diplomat based in Nairobi; "Kenya has finally become part of Africa."

It is doubtful that anyone could truly replace Jomo Kenyatta; the position of charismatic, untouchable leader that he occupied is simply not transferable in the ordinary sense. Originally an orphan named Johnstone Kamau—there is dispute over whether he took his new name from that of his country or from the beaded tribal belt that he wore as a young man—Kenyatta became outraged over colonial rule while working as an interpreter in Nairobi, and he was an early member of what became the Kikuyu Central Association. It gained influence originally as a defender of traditional Kikuyu customs and a promoter of ethnic identity, but it evolved into a political organization that protested the treatment of all Africans in this settler colony. After decades of living side by side with the Kikuyu, the Englishmen who ruled them still refused to learn their language, let alone treat them as a highly developed, sophisticated indigenous culture.

Although he had been well known before he left (and indeed had been sent previously to present a petition of grievances to the British), Kenyatta really became a broadly accepted nationalist leader only during a fifteen-year stint abroad that began in 1931. He studied anthropology in Britain and the Soviet Union, published his landmark work on the Kikuyu, *Facing Mount Kenya*, and often took menial jobs to support himself as he tried to promote Kenya's cause among European governments. He returned in 1946 as the unquestioned leader of the Kenya African Union (KAU), but soon clashed with the colonial government and the white settlers over issues of land ownership and African political representation.

Most of Kenyatta's influence was demonstrated at mass meetings attended by as many as thirty thousand people; yet as violent
opposition grew in the countryside, the British held Kenyatta and
some of his colleagues responsible for that, too. They detained
him in 1952 when they declared a state of emergency and charged
him with managing the so-called "Mau Mau" rebellion.* Even if
he did not lead Mau Mau, the British asserted, Kenyatta could
have stopped it, because he had so much prestige in the colony.
As a form of protest, he had persuaded Kenyans to stop drinking
British beer and stop wearing British hats, but the authorities believed he had double-crossed them when he agreed to help them
stem the violence. They thought that while he spoke openly
against terrorism, he was giving secret signals to continue it.

The trial at which Kenyatta was convicted, lasting for months,
became one of the landmark events of modern African history.
Some of the witnesses later acknowledged that they had been
paid to lie, so that Kenyatta would be out of the way. He was imprisoned for nine years altogether, the duration of "the Emergency." Although many of the fighters surrendered after he was
released, it seems clear in retrospect that Kenyatta had little or
nothing to do with them, but was actually the moderate, nonviolent politician he claimed to be. As a good politician, of course, he
later did nothing to disabuse Kenyans of the notion that he was
responsible for their freedom, and he named streets and other
public facilities for some of the best-known Mau Mau fighters.

From the time of his election as leader of the new Kenya African National Union (KANU, the successor to KAU)—at first *in
absentia,* while he was still detained and restricted to a remote
district near the Somali border—Kenyatta was Kenya's paramount
leader. He was voted prime minister before independence, and
then president, after he converted the country into a republic with

* Mau Mau has been a subject of great misunderstanding in the West.
While it was aimed at defeating colonial rule, fewer than a hundred Englishmen (including soldiers) were actually killed by these fighters who hid in
Kenya's forests. Thousands of Africans, and especially Kikuyu, were brutally
murdered, however, for refusing to take traditional oaths and join up. Subsequent research has led to uncertainty over whether there was any formal
"Mau Mau" organization at all, or just loosely connected units of guerrilla
fighters. See, for example, *The Myth of "Mau Mau,"* by Carl G. Rossberg, Jr.,
and John Nottingham (Stanford: Hoover Institution Press, 1966).

a mixed presidential-parliamentary system. He commanded an extraordinary following among the common people. Both inside and outside his country, Kenyatta was given credit for putting Kenya on the western side of the geopolitical map, building it into a mecca for tourists and multinational corporations alike. Toward the end, Kenyatta was vain, greedy, arbitrary, and often wrong-headed, but he was forgiven these faults by most of his blindly loyal countrymen. His picture is still on the wall of many homes in Kenya, however humble; his thoughts and actions—his aphorisms for daily life—for a time enjoyed a status roughly equivalent to those of Mao Zedong in China.

Kenyatta's legacy is mixed. On the positive side was his unusual ability to rally the *wananchi* ("the masses") in terms they could understand. Often he would deliver three separate speeches at a single rally: the first, in English, stressed economic stability and the need to avoid bitterness over past suffering; the second, in Swahili, which is understood by most of Kenya's black population regardless of tribe, emphasized national unity and the need to Africanize the economy; and the third, in a colloquial form of the Kikuyu language, reassured his own people that if they were patient, the foreigners would soon be gone and their places taken mostly by Kikuyu. Typically, he would end with a piercing shout of *"Harambee!,"* a Swahili work chant that translates roughly as "Let's All Pull Together!" (One practical result of Mzee's relentless exhortations is that the country is dotted with a vast number of *harambee*, self-help development projects ranging from high schools to cattle dips and community centers to livestock pens.) Then he would twirl across the platform with tribal dancers and bask in the applause and approving shouts of the audience.

Part of Kenyatta's message, rare for the head of a new African state, was realism and restrained expectations. As he warned in his independence day message in 1963:

> Many people may think that, now there is Uhuru, now I can see the sun of Freedom shining, richness will pour down like manna from Heaven. I tell you there will be nothing from Heaven. We must all work hard, with our hands, to save ourselves from poverty, ignorance and disease. . . .
>
> . . . You and I must work together to develop our country, to get education for our children, to have doctors, to build roads, to improve or provide all day-to-day essentials.

Before long, it became clear that certain rewards of freedom would be especially available to the Kikuyu, who represented about 20 percent of the people, but had a share of the power and the spoils far beyond that percentage. Kenyatta appointed so many of his fellow tribesmen (and members of closely related tribes) to important positions, and he so concentrated the benefits of nationhood in the Kikuyu areas of central Kenya, that other large groups, such as the Luo and the Luhya, with about 14 percent of the population each, emerged early on as potential sources of opposition. For most of his presidency, Kikuyu held at least a third of the cabinet jobs, including all of the major portfolios. They also controlled the civil service. To be sure, not all Kikuyu were in an equally advantageous position. An inner elite, whose members frequently called on Mzee at his official residences to demonstrate their loyalty, enjoyed particular privileges; among other things, they were uniquely able to buy up available land and to make profitable business deals with presidential blessings.

In one major respect, Kenyatta was very much like other African leaders: he did not want to attend to the issue of succession, and he discouraged everyone from discussing it. At one point, when there was widespread public speculation about who might eventually take over from Kenyatta, Charles Njonjo, then his attorney general, issued a statement reminding Kenyans that "it is a criminal offence for any person to compass, imagine, devise, or intend the death or the deposition of the president." The mandatory sentence for commission of such a crime, he pointed out, was death, and any accessories to the crime might be jailed for life. "Anyone who raises such matters at public meetings or who publishes such matters does so at his own peril," Njonjo added.

No formal case was ever brought against anyone on these grounds, but at least two men who were seen as potential successors to Kenyatta suffered the ultimate penalty.

During the early years of independence, the Kenyan who was probably best known, after Kenyatta, in the outside world was Tom Mboya, the head of the Kenya Federation of Registered Trade Unions, who had close ties to the American labor movement and traveled widely on behalf of his country and his government. Mboya, a suave, debonair man who enjoyed wearing custom-tailored suits and driving a white Mercedes-Benz, was the organizational genius of Kenyatta's party, KANU. He was a Luo, but was typical of a new generation of Kenyan politicians who seemed able to surmount tribal rivalries and become genuine national figures. There was no obvious reason to doubt Mboya's loyalty to the president, but several of Kenyatta's old confidants, who were resentful of the younger man's life style and suspicious of his long-range political motives, waged a surreptitious campaign against him. Under circumstances that have never been fully understood or explained, Mboya, then minister for economic planning and development, was assassinated in broad daylight on a Nairobi street in mid-1969. The man charged with killing him, a Kikuyu who had studied for a time in Bulgaria, was little known to the public; only much later was it learned that Njonjo had arranged for payment of the expenses connected with the assassin's legal defense.

Kenyatta was more obviously and understandably offended by Josiah M. Kariuki, a former Mau Mau fighter and a Kikuyu member of Parliament who emerged as a populist figure during the early 1970s and openly broke with the president to plead the cause of the poorest people of Kenya. "J.M." Kariuki had none of the urbanity and polish of Mboya; nor was he poor or in any respect ascetic. He was more in the mold of Adam Clayton Powell, the black American congressman from Harlem who cut a flamboyant figure and manipulated the political system, sometimes corruptly, but always insisted he was doing so on behalf of the underprivileged minority. Early in 1975, Kariuki was kidnapped and brutally murdered. The government later rejected a parliamentary investigative report implicating the paramilitary General Service Unit in his demise; ministers who criticized the government's handling of the Kariuki affair soon found themselves demoted, fired, or even jailed.

For reasons mostly of style and generation, the Luo politician Odinga was probably not regarded by very many people as a genuine alternative to Kenyatta. Still, the president made sure of that by detaining Odinga and several colleagues and banning his old opposition party, the Kenya People's Union, during a period of unrest that followed Mboya's assassination in 1969. Odinga was never a serious political contender again. Indeed, in his declining years, Kenyatta centralized so much power in himself that he almost functioned as an executive, a legislature, and a judiciary all rolled into one. Some compared his power to that of the pope.

Anyone else who enjoyed and exercised authority did so only on the basis of a direct delegation from the president. Even the very title "president" was sacrosanct; no business or organization in Kenya was allowed to have one, lest there be some confusion with Mzee.

Perhaps the most intriguing episodes of Kenyatta's last years were the efforts by various members of his political "family"—some of them actual blood relatives, others connected more by geographic or business ties—to subvert the Kenyan political system and assure that the presidency would be passed to an acceptable Kikuyu after Kenyatta's death. In its early stages, the attempt took the form of clandestine "oathing" ceremonies (described in chilling detail by Ngugi in one of his most controversial books, *Petals of Blood*), in which Kikuyu villagers would be virtually kidnapped, forced to drink blood, and then required to swear their fealty to the "family"; in exchange they became members of a secret tribal society, GEMA.* Eventually GEMA went public, in a manner of speaking. Some of its leading figures were responsible for launching the "Change-the-Constitution Movement" in the late 1970s, after Kenyatta's health had deteriorated to the point that he had occasional lapses during which he was incapable of making decisions. The movement's goal was to revise the constitution of KANU and, if possible, of the country, so that Moi would not automatically succeed to the presidency on Kenyatta's death. For a time it held well-attended meetings and rallies to press its point, until Njonjo, presumably acting with Mzee's knowledge and authority, put a stop to them. (Later the government formally banned tribal organizations like GEMA.)

Another, more secret effort to control the succession took the form of a clandestine paramilitary police commando unit that was formed in the Rift Valley area of Kenya during the 1970s. Called the "Ngoroko," for a small pastoral tribe that is known for cattle thievery and for fierce attacks on other neighboring tribes, the unit masqueraded as part of a legitimate battalion whose job it

---

* GEMA was an acronym for the Gikuyu Embu Meru Association. The title used the traditional way of writing the word Kikuyu in English and also the names of two smaller, ethnically and politically related tribes whose traditional homelands were adjacent to that of the Kikuyu. GEMA had extensive holdings in property and business, and some of the dues paid by peasants were used to enrich the association's leaders.

was to control stock theft in a vast section of the country. In fact, however, it stockpiled large quantities of arms that had been obtained from Israel and other sources; looking ahead to the day of Kenyatta's death, when they would supposedly carry out their ultimate mission, members of the Ngoroko meanwhile harassed various public figures who were not certified members of the true Kikuyu "family." Even Moi, as vice-president, was often stopped at road blocks when he was on his way to perform official duties. According to a later government investigation, the unit had a list of fifteen people it planned to assassinate immediately upon Kenyatta's death, including Moi, Njonjo, and other ruling figures, and hundreds more soon thereafter. Within two days, the Ngoroko paratroops would have taken over the country, and according to some, they might have instituted a reign of terror comparable to what Idi Amin had visited upon Uganda.

As it happened, Kenyatta, gravely ill, insisted upon making a trip to the Indian Ocean coast in August 1978, and thus he died during the early hours of August 22 in Mombasa, rather than in Nakuru (in the Rift Valley) as had been anticipated. Having been alerted quickly, Moi traveled from his own farm to Nairobi before dawn and before the Ngoroko could intercept him and put their plans into action. Within a few hours Moi was sworn in for a ninety-day term as acting president. A few days later, the Ngoroko approached leaders of the army and asked them to stage a coup, but the army remained loyal to Moi. So did a number of prominent Kikuyu politicians who were quietly asked to push him aside, but refused. Moi soon obtained KANU's nomination for a full five-year term as president. By October 1978 he had uncovered and dismantled the secret commando force; more than two hundred of its members were arrested.

The standard line among the leaders and intellectuals of more socialist-oriented countries in Africa is that Kenya is a typical example of how and why capitalism is doomed to failure on the continent, that the gap between the rich and the poor is growing dramatically, and that a revolution is inevitable. But returning repeatedly over the years to Ngecha, a Kikuyu village in the highlands north of Nairobi, one finds evidence for at least a tentative refutation of the conventional wisdom—a sign that economic growth rates of more than 4 percent a year (which Kenya achieved in the early 1980s) can make a difference in people's lives.

Ngecha, like many other villages in the area, was originally populated mostly by homeless people resettled after the Mau Mau emergency of the 1950s. In the late 1960s, it seemed a thousand miles away from the bustle of the capital. It was poor in almost every respect, and its people were, for the most part, discouraged and gloomy about the future. Individual progress seemed to come only through luck or good connections, and many of the local *harambee* projects, to which the villagers were constantly being asked to contribute, were poor substitutes for genuine development. Ngecha's unpaved dirt roads made it difficult to get in or out, especially during the rainy seasons, when they turned into a mass of red mud.

Although it still has a long way to go, Ngecha today is a study in rural African prosperity. Many of those who lived for years in one- or two-room huts made of mud, wattle, and thatch have moved into larger wooden dwellings with tin roofs. Some have even built stone houses and erected fences. Most families now have running water in their homes, and many who were once virtually cut off from the world outside the village now have radios.*

The village church, long abuilding, was finally finished in the late 1970s, right down to the stained glass windows. The *harambee* high school had not yet been completely taken over by the Ministry of Education as a government school (a step that would assure village children better teachers, free secondary education, and a remote chance for a place at the university), but the addition of a science lab improved its accreditation prospects and helped it obtain partial government funding. The children playing in the village streets are better clothed and look better fed and healthier than they used to be, although there are so many more of them now that it is hard to imagine Ngecha being able to keep up with its population explosion indefinitely. Even the livestock appear to be less scrawny than before.

---

* As more and more villages around the country have obtained radios, Kenya has become an important test case for efforts to teach English and other basic subjects by radio. In some classrooms, broadcast lessons have been used to supplement the limited skills of untrained teachers.

Village commerce is booming. There are many new shops and cafes, a few additional drunks in the streets, and even a local branch office of KANU. Statistics are elusive and unreliable, because much of the economic activity here and in other rural areas is carried on by self-employed entrepreneurs who are not necessarily taken into account in the official reckoning; but it is clear that more money is in circulation, and ordinary people with no special connections seem to be doing relatively well compared to the past.

One man with a large family, who came home only rarely from his job as a domestic servant at a foreign embassy in Nairobi during the late 1960s, now keeps hundreds of chickens on his small property. He runs a booming egg business of his own, making daily runs in his car to supply hotels and restaurants in the city. Soon he will construct bigger, better chicken coops, and he is shopping for an incubator that will help him expand production. His son-in-law has helped him buy a small farm in Nakuru, where he will build a modest house, probably with his own hands and those of his many sons, and keep a growing number of animals. Already one of the man's sons, having failed in his quest for a higher education, is living in a makeshift shelter on the land in Nakuru, taking care of a few animals and preparing for the day when the rest of the family arrives.

Capitalism is surely not good for everyone, admits one Kenyan professor at the university grudgingly, but in villages like Ngecha, "it's not doing badly. . . . No one can understand exactly how this happened."

Ngecha has lost none of the characteristics of a small, rural African village. It still has the unique smell that comes from a blend of dust, cattle dung, and wood fires. The air is thick with flies, and swarms of youngsters still gather around any visitor from the outside world, dancing in his path, tugging at his clothes, looking in his eyes dolefully. (In this case, the ritual is often accompanied by chants of "mazungu," the Swahili word for "white person," which is used to describe other outsiders, too.) The visitor will be treated as a guest of honor in any home where he is known. In traditional Kikuyu fashion, he will be left to sit alone in the house's largest room, while the mother of the family and her neighbors cook up a feast that will be bigger than any one person could ever imagine eating in a single sitting. On a special occasion, such as a return after many years' absence, a goat may be slaughtered and cooked in the visitor's honor.

What is different now is a sense that it is feasible and plausible for these rural Kenyans to feel some connection with the world beyond the village limits. There are several telephones in Ngecha, and new roads have made access to the village much easier. There are also several people from Ngecha who have made it in Nairobi, but still come back home and serve as a model for the aspirations of others. And that, after all, in a country with Kenya's legacy and its social system, is still the dream: to get out of the village, to do whatever is necessary to get a job where you are entitled to wear a coat and a tie or a skirt and a blouse.

For all the optimism and surface prosperity it is possible to feel in rural Kikuyuland, other parts of the Kenyan countryside can be dry, bleak, and pessimistic. And one can make a case that Nairobi is a powder keg. Beneath the capital's glitter, opulence, and Western veneer, out of sight of its skyscrapers and chic shops and the headquarters of international organizations, is a stratum of society that aches with poverty and violence. Here the gap between the haves and have-nots sometimes does seem impossible to bridge. Some of the have-nots are routinely sent out on display to the visitor. Cripples and amputees of all ages lurk outside every office building, movie theater, and resturant, begging for a few shillings. The "parking boys," teenagers with no idea who or where their families are, emerge at dusk to badger the wealthy and the tourists, demanding money to dust off and protect the cars parked in public spaces along the street. Some of their older sisters eke out a living as prostitutes. The younger ones scamper on the sidewalks barefoot, begging for coins. The number of these children in the city has grown steadily, and they are an embarrassment to a government that claims to be taking care of its people; but repeated attempts to round them up into halfway houses or other welfare institutions have had little effect.

The vast majority of Kenya's hard-core urban poor are better shielded from public view—in the slums of Nairobi, such as Kariobangi and Muthare Valley, where many live in tar-paper shacks with only the most elemental social services. When shortages hit, they are the first to be affected, and sometimes they will have to stand in line for hours just to buy enough paraffin to fill a small container. Safety standards are minimal, and from time to time these teeming settlements are hit by fires that kill dozens of people at a clip and leave hundreds homeless. The slums are where Nairobi grows (with a birthrate just over 4 percent a year) and where new arrivals from the countryside (an estimated inward migration of at least another 4 percent annually) go while looking and waiting for jobs. Their wait will be a long one indeed, for among Kenya's estimated 19 million people, unemployment is now thought to be at least 30 percent. That makes programs like the approximately 94,000 jobs created by Moi's Jamhuri Day proclamation in 1978 seem desperately inadequate.

Long a quiet, provincial spot, Nairobi has recently expanded at an uncharted, breakneck pace, and like the country of which it is the capital, it has suddenly become more convincingly a part of its continent. In contrast to many other places in Africa of comparable importance, Nairobi is not an old city. At the turn of the century it was still a swamp—its name is a Masai word meaning "place of dampness"—and it originally developed on its current site only because that was a convenient way station for the British, who were building a railroad from Mombasa, on the coast, to the shores of Lake Victoria. They pitched tents while they waited for supplies to catch up with them. Many of the amenities the British later provided for themselves remain today; Nairobi still has rugby teams and squash courts, a properly genteel race track, and country clubs. Expatriates, businessmen, and government officials can still live in suburbs like Muthaiga in luxurious circumstances. That stratum of Nairobi society does not often intersect with the rest, but one place where it does is at the cinema. Nairobi is movie-mad. Its fifteen theaters, including two drive-ins, present almost every popular film ever made in Britain or the United States, plus Indian imports to serve the Asian community, and kung-fu movies. Anyone who can scrape together a few shillings for a ticket goes often. The government uses this as an opportunity, reaching a captive audience with slickly produced short subjects that extol the accomplishments of its development efforts in the remote areas of Kenya.

But the context is changing. Despite the gentility of its luxury hotels and other Western-style institutions, Nairobi is becoming an ever noisier, more chaotic and dangerous place. The crime rate has skyrocketed to the point where it far surpasses the ability of the police to control it, and so vigilante or mob action often substitutes for the normal legal process. (Kenya has the dubious distinction of being one of the seven countries in the non-Communist world with the largest prison populations.) In certain parts of town, a nonstop cacophony is produced by the drivers and the horns of the *matatus,** or bush taxis. Nairobi's public transportation system has long since proved inadequate, and so these privately operated cars and minibuses have become the most common means of travel to the outlying areas of the city; rarely, if ever, subjected to inspection, they generally suffer from broken taillights and bad brakes, they invariably carry more passengers than is safe, and they leave behind a trail of suffocating exhaust. It does not help that many of the roads they travel were last resurfaced by Italian prisoners of war during World War II. (At the end of 1983, Moi impounded all of the *matatus* on the grounds that many were unsafe. The result was chaos, and soon they were back on the street.)

It would be foolish to believe that Nairobi could remain indefinitely the gracious, civilized, colonial-style capital that it was for so long. But the fear among moderate and responsible officials is that Nairobi is now virtually out of control, and that its problems are becoming a metaphor for all of Kenya.

The government can pull off small successes from time to time, but it cannot possibly keep up with Nairobi's real growth rate, which some people now estimate to be as high as 13–15 percent a year. The widely accepted conclusion is that the armies of unemployed can never be successfully accommodated in the city, even if there is an explosion of industrial development, that the only way for them to fit satisfactorily into the economy is to return to the countryside. Thus the frequent references by Moi to those who "loiter in the cities while farmers in the country are looking for workers," and his threat that "we may eventually have to use force like other countries." Privately, and less subtly, cabinet ministers speculate on the feasibility of creating work camps

---

* The name derives from the Swahili expression for "give me three (*tatu*) coins." A ride in one originally cost three Kenyan ten-cent pieces, but inflation and a sellers' market have since affected the *matatus*, the ultimate example of Kenya's free-enterprise system.

to clear vast new areas for agricultural development and of employing other methods of coercion borrowed from quite different economic and political systems.

Kenya's economy has been healthier over the years than many others in independent Africa, but its health came as much from lucky breaks and loyal tourists as from steady, methodical exploitation of natural resources. Next to Nigeria's oil, Zaïre's copper, and Zimbabwe's chrome, in fact, Kenya has relatively little to sell besides coffee and tea, although there are occasional flurries of excitement about discoveries of gemstones, graphite, and other minerals in remote areas of the country. Its largest producer of income is still agriculture, which was responsible for more than 38 percent of the gross domestic product in 1977, the year of the great boom in coffee prices (and of an 8.8 percent growth rate), still remembered as the last year of plenty for Kenya. Agriculture continues to account for more than 30 percent of the national economy.

But agriculture is fundamentally unreliable in Kenya, since only about 15 percent of the country's land is arable and a third of that has only moderate potential. Seventy-five percent of the population lives on 10 percent of the land, and in the best farming areas the population density has reached more than a thousand per square mile. Soil erosion and depletion are the result. Hazardous chemicals, imported for use as pesticides without proper safeguards, have also taken their toll on the land and on the streams once rich with fish. Moreover, Kenya is typically vulnerable to adverse climatic conditions. When the rains fail, so do the coffee and tea and pyrethrum (used in insecticides); even when the weather is ideal, there is no guarantee that Kenyan crops will not be overwhelmed and underpriced in a worldwide glut.

Kenya's fourth development plan, for the years 1979–83, gave the highest priority to improving agriculture and developing a more sturdy, self-reliant industrial base, while counting on continuing tourist business. Nearly half a million people traveled to Kenya in the peak year of 1978, for example, spending $13 million and comprising the second largest source of income. The numbers rise and fall each year with international economic conditions and events inside the country (the 1982 coup attempt scared many people away), but the government has worked and spent steadily to expand tourist income.

Increasingly, though, tourism has come to be regarded as a mixed blessing. No country could have a tourist industry on the scale of Kenya's and escape profound effects on the landscape and the society. The impact has been obvious in Nairobi for many years, and busloads of touring Japanese no longer attract special attention in the big city. But now game hunts and poaching have hastened the depletion of some of Kenya's storied wildlife. The illicit ivory trade is a serious and tragic problem that has devastated Kenya's elephant herds, while enriching many government officials and members of the Kenyatta family, including Mzee's fourth wife and widow, "Mama Ngina" Kenyatta.

Now the tourist influx has thoroughly saturated Kenya's Indian Ocean coast. The visitors there are a new breed for Kenya, more than half of them Germans and Swiss, who fly on cheap jumbo-jet charters from Europe straight to Mombasa. Although a few go on safaris into the countryside, most stay put on the relatively unspoiled, temperate beaches of the coast, where their currency purchases first-class accommodations and European-style food about as cheaply as anywhere else in the world. In the once-quaint coastal village of Watamu, which has been virtually taken over by tourism, hardly a sign remains in English or Swahili. The advertisements for everything from souvenirs to laundry service are in German, with some translations into French and Italian, and some people complain that Kenya's pride and self-respect have been compromised along the way.

Industrial development and the improvement of export earnings are essential, because Kenyans' modern tastes have run far ahead of the current capacity to satisfy them at home. After the good year of 1977, which only fueled those tastes, the balance-of-payments deficit for 1978 shot up to about $300 million, prompting calls for new emergency measures to protect the fragile economy. By 1980, that figure was almost $1 billion. The government began borrowing heavily to balance the books, and by 1983 Kenya, seemingly so well fixed a few years earlier, had a foreign debt of $2.9 billion, in part because it had become a net importer of food. As the four-year development plan was slashed by 25 percent, the effects began to be felt across the board. The budget for

school construction, for example, plunged by 60 percent, and the
minister in charge of that department told Kenyans they would
have to build more *harambee* schools themselves instead of counting on the government. The prices of basic foods, such as maize
and bread, were increased by 20–25 percent, and crude oil imports
were cut by 10 percent in an attempt to preserve dwindling foreign exchange.

Some Kenyan and foreign economists warned at the time of
the coffee boom that hard times lay ahead, but they were generally laughed at by people who were enjoying the prosperity of the
moment and, in many cases, making an extra windfall on the side.
At one point in the midst of the boom, recalls a government official, "We had so much money, we didn't know what to do with
it." Some of that money apparently left the country at the time of
Kenyatta's death. So did some of the surplus food that had been
gathered into warehouses; it was sold off at lower prices than
necessary by officials who thought the good times could be indefinitely extended. The next year, 1979, Kenya's maize crop
failed, and food reserves sometimes fell so low as to cover only one
month's needs at a time.

Kenya has never fully recovered from that economic low
point. The shortage of foreign exchange became a chronic problem, leading to draconian restrictions on import licenses and frequent depletion of the raw materials and spare parts necessary to
keep industry operating. Gasoline fell into such short supply at
times that Nairobi taxis could not always find enough to make a
round trip to the airport, and many arriving or departing passengers had to plan on a stop at a gas station en route (and on advancing part of the fare to the driver so that he could pay for the gas).
The Kenya branches of companies like Firestone and Union Carbide had to shut down intermittently, as did the local toothpaste
factory. The supply of imported cork ran so low that the brewers
of Kenya's excellent domestic beers almost had to close at Christmas 1982 for a lack of bottle caps. Imports of fertilizer fell, too,
affecting domestic agricultural production.

Indeed, for the first time since independence, profound anxiety developed over the availability of adequate food supplies in
Kenya. One reason was the maintenance of an old, inefficient and
corrupt distribution system, which made it illegal to transport

food across the boundaries between districts and provinces. The government tried to improve its capacity to keep track of food shipments, out of fear that the scarce supplies would be smuggled to Uganda, Tanzania, and other neighboring countries, but tighter control only served to make some commodities seem even less available. Once that perception spread, individual families that could afford to do so began to hoard food, in order to be sure that they would be able to feed their children.

An unexpected surge in world tea prices caused a mini-boom in late 1983 and early 1984, and with government-mandated increases in the prices paid to farmers, Kenyan agriculture seemed poised for another takeoff; but the bubble burst again when the long rains failed to appear in 1984. Suddenly Kenya had to be added to the list of African countries afflicted by a disastrous drought. By June, six hundred thousand people needed help to avoid starvation, and the government estimated it would have to import at least 1.5 million tons of corn and other grains over a fifteen-month period to fight off famine. One bizarre result of the drought was that farmers who could find no good grazing land began to sell off their cattle at a panic rate; there was a temporary surplus of meat at low prices, but with the certain prospect of a meat and milk shortage looming on the horizon. The political fallout included expressions of bitterness that wildlife had been protected and preserved to assist tourism (animals were now raiding farms), possibly at the expense of hungry people. To calm fears of manipulation and exploitation of food stocks, the government banned all grain exports.

The number of children to be fed continues to grow geometrically, and economists who look into Kenya's future envision a Malthusian nightmare. By the early 1980s, Kenya had the fastest growing population in the world. One estimate put the growth rate at 4.2 percent a year. Half of all Kenyans were under the age of fifteen; the combination of a declining infant mortality rate, a longer average life expectancy (at fifty-six, one of the highest in Africa), and an ever-growing birthrate made it look as if Kenya's population would probably double by the year 2000 (as it already had since independence), and then double again early in the twenty-first century. (One World Bank study said Kenya might have 120 million people by 2050.) The average number of children borne by a Kenyan mother was more than eight, and government family-planning programs were barely having an effect. The problem was not simply ignorance and suspicion of contraceptive methods, but also deep-rooted cultural practices. For most people in rural areas, a large family was a sign of status. More children meant greater security—more help working on the family's land or tending its animals, plus a greater likelihood of being cared for in old age. That the opposite would eventually be the case, because of acute shortages and worsening prospects for future generations, did not really sink in.

The tolerance of polygamy among many tribes made the problem worse. According to one view, the Christian missionaries who attempted to stop polygamy in Kenya early in the twentieth century only fueled the baby boom. Although men traditionally had many wives, they tended to have just a few children with each wife, because of strict rules concerning cohabitation and the spacing of children. Among some tribes, for example, sex was forbidden as long as a woman was nursing a child, which she tended to do for four or five years; and it was also frowned upon for her to have another child after her oldest one had already married. The missionaries thought that if they encouraged more permissive cohabitation in defiance of tribal customs, that would help defeat polygamy; on the contrary, the polygamy continued, but each relationship produced more children than before. A 1978 government survey showed that a third of Kenya's marriages were still polygamous.

Meanwhile, the breakdown in respect for traditional rules has hastened the advent of the sexual revolution in Africa. The average first pregnancy is occurring in Kenya at age fifteen, and the average age of marriage for women is seventeen; but the same 1978 survey found that only 6 percent of Kenyan women were using birth control and that 12 percent had never heard of it. For a government to make family planning a major issue, in Kenya as elsewhere in Africa, would require a degree of political courage that has been lacking.

Population growth also aggravated another fundamental Kenyan economic problem, a scarcity of productive land that was one of the central issues in the Mau Mau rebellion. Kenyans have what many observers have called a "land mania," a fundamental feeling that unless they have a piece of ground they can call their own, their financial and personal security cannot be assured. That is one reason that a socialist system of communal ownership, of the sort that President Julius Nyerere has tried to introduce in Tanzania, could probably never succeed in Kenya. Even educated people who live in the city dream of owning land in the countryside, preferably near their birthplace or another place of ancestral significance; once they obtain it, they may go there only a few times a year, but those visits have enormous significance. One young doctor who lives and works in Nairobi, a member of the Meru tribe, is a case in point: he has bought a small farm in the Meru district. His wife and children rarely go there—she is from another African country—but one weekend every month he makes a quiet pilgrimage, pitches a tent, and sleeps on his own land. Later, when he can afford to do so, he will build a small structure on his property, in the hope that one day he can retire and live there.

It is already clear that the vast majority of Kenyans will never be able to satisfy this longing for the land. Although there are more than 1.2 million small landowners in the country who till their own soil, most of them are really engaged in subsistence agriculture. Overall, land redistribution in Kenya has had a limited effect. Only about fifty of the largest farms are still owned by white settlers or their descendants (as against fourteen hundred at independence), but thousands of others, located in the most fertile areas of the country, have been transferred almost intact into the hands of a few wealthy black men, some of them civil servants and politicians who run the farms over the telephone from the capital. Their estates are symbols of the new elite, objects of resentment and hatred for many still landless peasants.

There is a parallel in other parts of the economy, where the vast majority of businesses are still owned by Asians and whites, who may employ African managers but show few signs of trusting them. Some of these businesses are controlled from overseas. When the Kenyan economy was booming and new jobs were being created at a fairly rapid rate, these circumstances were often ignored; but in hard times, the anger felt by the *wananchi* becomes more apparent. "People have shouted *uhuru* long enough," said one professional in Nairobi, who feels uncomfortable with the poverty around him; "now they want the goods delivered." That the very richest and the very poorest people both generally tend to be Kikuyu complicates, rather than simplifies, the problem. It only intensifies the pressure on Moi to deliver more of the goods and distribute them fairly, to make necessary changes in the structure and the profile of the modern Kenyan economy, without scaring off the foreign investors who have played an important role in the relative prosperity that Kenya has enjoyed to date.

Apart from population growth and the pressure it creates, Kenya's biggest social and economic problem, which affects and aggravates every other problem, is the pervasiveness of the corruption that developed and flourished under Kenyatta. It extends from the policeman who accepts a twenty-shilling bribe when he stops a motorist to the members of the black elite who have private arrangements with bank officials for unsecured loans and illegal overdrafts. One reason for corruption in government ranks is that civil servants and politicians are permitted, even encouraged, to engage in private business. The rationale is that these public officials, with their education and know-how, are among the few blacks in a position to reclaim economic power from the numerous Asian shopkeepers and the white-run multinational corporations. It happens too often, however, that cabinet officials and bureaucrats spend more time at making money privately than at performing their government duties.

Moi himself holds the East African distributorship for International Harvester, and it seems to be beyond the acceptable limits of political discourse for anyone to suggest that he give it up. While the president talks often about the need to deal with corruption, he has rejected the idea of appointing an ombudsman with broad investigative powers. Instead, the attack on corruption has taken place mostly at the lower levels, and the Nairobi newspapers are full of stories about minor officials caught taking payoffs for work permits or trading licenses. How high up the campaign will reach remains to be seen. For all the talk of investigating her, for example, Ngina Kenyatta has seemed immune from prosecution; many people wonder how she obtained an interest in so many service stations in Central Province, but the government has not been eager to provide answers.

Occasionally an incident will arise that offers proof of the public's intent to establish limits on what corruption is acceptable and what is not. Four prominent citizens of Nairobi finally brought a private prosecution in 1982 against Nathan Kahara, the mayor of the capital, and several members of his city council, when it became clear that the government was not going to take its own steps against them for selling off city land for personal profit. How these outraged private citizens were able to afford the substantial costs of the legal case against public officials was not entirely clear, but finally they managed to have them removed from office. Yet there are other examples of extraordinary greed and callousness that are routinely overlooked. It was well known, for example, that one member of Moi's cabinet took government funds that were intended to help handicapped children and used them instead to build a housing project that would enrich himself; nothing was done about it.

A standard technique in Kenyan politics is for public figures to build up their reputations by appearing at *harambee* meetings and rallies around the country and making personal contributions to self-help projects. The amounts contributed by individual politicians in a single year often far exceed the total of their known public and private income, before living expenses are deducted. One Kenyan journalist estimates that among the more than two dozen members of the cabinet, at any given time, perhaps four or five are "relatively honest"; the rest, he says, are undoubtedly stealing substantial amounts of money.

Corrupt public officials in Kenya tend not to put the proceeds in foreign bank accounts or overseas property, as do, say, those in Zaïre or Nigeria, where the problem is far more serious. The Kenyans are more likely to accumulate property at home and flaunt their wealth before their compatriots. One government official, who is himself alleged to be corrupt but denies it, indulges in an old prejudice about Kenya's Asian community, in trying to explain the widespread cheating at every level: "As a matter of principle," he says, "the Asians believe you must bribe for things," and so other people have gotten used to it and followed suit. But a foreign diplomat insists that Kenya's political leaders are to blame. Corruption has not deepened so much as it has "broadened," he says; "the guy who takes your letter at the post office has seen his bosses get away with it for years, and now he's just decided to get his share, too."

It is easy to imagine the effect of corruption on the political tensions and the moral fiber of Kenyan society, but difficult to know whether it plays a major role in the country's economic well-being. Intuitively, however, it seems logical to suppose that if Kenya has survived relatively well with corruption, it would have done far better without it.

The Kenyans who are usually most visible in Nairobi are the urban poor and the black power elite, wealthy and refined gentlemen, mostly graduates of the prestigious Alliance High School and foreign universities, some of them married to white women from Britain or the United States.

But there is also in Kenya today an emergent, upwardly mobile middle class that is less noticeable and more difficult to meet, yet that may have a significant role in the future leadership of the country. These Kenyans are struggling to balance their traditional, conservative tribal upbringing in the countryside with the modern ideas and habits they have learned in school and at work in the city. They are, in a sense, the shock absorbers of the economy and the political system, the people who will help cushion the pressures and ease the tensions. But they are not easy to satisfy, and Moi's success or failure in doing so will have a major effect on his and the country's future. The lives of these people and their role in society are a microcosm of Kenya's effort to establish stability at home and respect on the African and world scene.

One couple in their mid-twenties, he a former bank officer, who is now running his own paint manufacturing business, and she a secretary in a government ministry, illustrate the point. Peter and Naomi (not their real names) still speak to each other in Kikuyu at home, though they both, in their outside lives, speak mostly in Swahili and English. They had a long courtship, but were finally married, according to Kikuyu custom, only after she had become pregnant. Their wedding was an elaborate affair, and the festivities lasted for days; some friends presented them with cows and goats, others with a television set and furniture. They bought a small house in Nairobi, but before they had even moved in, it was decided by their families that they were rushing things a bit. Peter is an oldest son, and he was said to be needed at home to help control and give guidance to his siblings, so a tiny cabin was constructed for the newlyweds and their infant daughter on his father's large farm about thirty miles from the city. On this farm are two separate houses for two distinct households, one for each of Peter's father's two wives and her children; the wives co-exist peacefully, although the two sets of children (a total of fifteen altogether) have little to do with each other.

Naomi was assigned a *shamba*, a small plot where she could grow vegetables, as her traditional role dictates she do. But the land was actually tended most of the time by someone else, because she went to work in the city every weekday—a requirement to pay back the government for her partially subsidized secretarial education. On the weekends she must do laundry and other traditional women's work, and this routine, plus nursing her baby, so exhausted her that she had to rely on her sisters-in-law for help. Eventually she found a teenage girl to work as a servant. True to the strong family ties of the Kikuyu, the couple were also expected to help various sisters and brothers find places in secondary schools or jobs.

With the arrival of a second daughter, the small cabin became inadequate, and so Peter and Naomi built a larger home on a substantial piece of land, about ten miles away but still near Nairobi, which was also a wedding gift. They are proud of this place, despite its general lack of furnishings. In the back there is room for a much larger garden, a hedge against inflation and food shortages; between it and the chickens wandering around the property, the young family would probably be able to raise all of its own food if that became necessary. There is a major drawback to life in this country setting, however. Crime has increased substantially in the belt around Nairobi, and at night it is difficult to feel safe and secure. Indeed, like all the other men who live in the area, Peter takes his turn one night a month going out on patrol with the police, as a means of both helping them out and keeping them honest. But these self-help law-and-order efforts were to little avail; one night early in 1983 a "panga gang" (named for the fearsome, machete-like tools they wield, made famous during Mau Mau) struck, harming no one but stealing all of the couple's hard-earned possessions.

Business has been a struggle, too, for Peter, who has had to learn that the practice does not always correspond to the theory he learned as a student at Makerere University in Uganda. He has had to pay bribes not only to obtain import licenses for raw materials that he needs to make his paint, but also to convince government ministries and others that they should buy his products.

Some potential customers, including civil servants and purchasing agents for private firms, insist that they be taken off on weekend trips and entertained by women before they will agree to sign contracts that may ultimately not even be honored.

Peter and Naomi also found that they had to grease palms in order to obtain telephone and electrical service. For three months they sat in the dark, refusing to pay the twenty-thousand-shilling "tip" demanded by the men who controlled new electrical connections. Eventually the men said they would accept half that amount as a payoff, but Naomi, who felt angry and betrayed, refused those terms. She went directly to "the white boss," an expatriate working in the government department that handles rural electricity, and protested. The family obtained service within a week, after paying a standard connection fee of three hundred shillings.

Once she gave birth to her third child—the boy considered necessary in every Kikuyu household—Naomi felt some easing of the pressure to have a large family. Still, when she goes home to the village where she was born, her mother and other relatives taunt her about having only three children. "Those girls will get married and leave you," they say as she walks through the village streets with her daughters, "and then you'll only have one son to comfort you." Even if Naomi does not want to have the standard eight children, they implore her, "How about seven? Or at least six?" Determined not to replicate the circumstances in her own family, which could barely feed all of its children even in prosperous times, she shakes her head persistently. So far, despite similar pressures from within his own family, Peter has been supportive. But what if he should decide to emulate his own father and take a second wife, in order to have more children? "I have thought about that," Naomi says. "I would not put up with it. I would leave him." (Other angry first wives have been known to take more severe steps. When the deputy registrar of the University of Nairobi took a second wife several years ago, the first wife burned down their house with her husband inside.)

The conflict between tradition and modernization takes many forms in Kenya today. On one issue, the female circumcision rituals that have long been practiced by some Kenyan tribes, the controversy goes back to the 1930s. British missionaries, appalled by the practice, were attempting to wipe it out at the time, and Jomo Kenyatta used this as one of many rallying points against the colonial influence on Kenyan life. In recent years, however, the dangers and abuses of such operations—usually performed in nonhygienic circumstances—and their effect on women's dignity have become much better known in Kenya and other nations in Africa and elsewhere in the Third World. In 1982, after learning of the deaths of fourteen young girls who had undergone clitoridectomy in tribal ceremonies, Moi banned the practice nationwide and threatened to prosecute anyone who insisted on preserving this particular tradition.

Other transitions have occurred only with great difficulty. One high-ranking Kenyan official, schooled at Oxford and Iowa State University, in the midst of a long discussion about the country's political evolution, pointed out that Kenyan society was still emerging from a traditional system in which "the elders' word was final." Complaining about challenges to the president, he said, "We are still learning this new type of life, where there are complicated laws and courts. . . . Why, now even a son can take his father to court and obtain a judgment against him. That is sacrilege."

One issue on which this tension often comes into focus is detention without trial. Discussing the case of an officer in the security police who had been detained without formal charges, on suspicion of stockpiling firearms for a challenge to the government, this official complained that the officer's wife, in filing a *habeas corpus* action in the Kenyan courts, seeking the release of her husband, had resorted to "a Western trick" that would do no good. "I'm not saying it's wrong," he went on, "it just isn't African."

Nothing aggravates the Kenyan government more than being singled out for criticism on human rights grounds, especially since it believes that other nearby countries, including Tanzania, tend to be judged less harshly. "Just because we have a few guys in detention, Amnesty International makes a great fuss," said the official. "You do other bad things. . . . You go to Vietnam and kill a whole lot of people. Why is that not worse than anything we have done? . . . We cannot maintain this society unless we take certain measures. You have to be cruel in order to be kind."

The accession of Daniel arap Moi to Kenya's presidency, decisive event that it was, did little to end the scheming and intrigue that had characterized the country's political process during Kenyatta's last years. On the contrary, during Moi's early time in office the Byzantine maneuvering only intensified. Various cabinet ministers, seeking to demonstrate their intimacy and influence with the new president, would routinely make appointments with Moi for each other, on the theory that it is one thing to be able to schedule a visit with the head of state for yourself, but quite another if he trusts you so much that he will take your advice on seeing others. In the wake of the attempted air force coup of August 1982, a new device became available that politicians could use to bedevil each other: anyone could stoke Kenya's already overactive rumor mill by letting it be known that certain others—namely, his enemies—had somehow been involved in the plot, or he could say that he understood such an allegation had surfaced during the official investigation. For months, as courts-martial and other prosecutions proceeded, many prominent politicians held their breath in the hope they would not be falsely implicated. Eventually, a severe political crisis did develop out of all this, but it took a course rather different from what most people expected.

The first public manifestation of serious tension in the inner circles of Kenya's government came in October 1982, during a choral concert at State House in Nairobi presided over by Moi. The man in charge of music in the president's office made a habit of composing songs with a political message to be sung by a mass choir on just such occasions, but ordinarily they consisted of the stock exhortation that the people must work together for the good of the nation. This time, however, the songs were more controversial. In one of them, as the choir looked straight at the president and sang about "a traitor, a Judas Iscariot," the composer-conductor pointed to the members of the cabinet, who were arrayed on either side of Moi. The ministers shifted uneasily in their seats and began to mumble and stare at one another. The expectation of the choirmaster, if no one else, seemed to be that if someone had been disloyal to the president, he would, like the proverbial thief in a crowd, suddenly reveal himself and get up to leave. That did not happen—not the first time and not when Moi, after hearing two other songs, demanded that the "traitor song" be repeated a second time. But as one of the ministers later said, "Everyone thought it was Charles" that the choir was singing about.

"Charles" was Charles Njonjo, who now held the formal position of minister for constitutional affairs, but enjoyed power that extended far beyond a single ministerial portfolio. Having been attorney general, he had enormous influence over the legal and judicial departments of the government; it was widely assumed that he could give orders to many of Kenya's judges, and that it was he who generally decided on whom to serve with detention orders. Over the years he had also put his imprint on the police, and the man who was in charge of Kenya's substantial civil service, a former defense ministry official named Jeremiah Kiereini, although he reported directly to Moi, was known to be intensely loyal and responsive to Njonjo. By squelching the "Change-the-Constitution Movement" and rallying to Moi after Mzee died, Njonjo had also become uniquely close to the new president and, according to some sources, he easily manipulated Moi to do things his way. When Njonjo was off in Britain (and sometimes South Africa) on one of his frequent business trips, he kept in almost constant telephone contact with his cohorts in Nairobi and, it was said, pulled the strings of Kenya's government from afar.

Invariably dressed in Savile Row suits, with a rose in his lapel, Njonjo stood out from—and held himself above—the pack. The son of a Kikuyu chief who remained particularly loyal to the British during the Emergency, he was married to an English-woman. He was openly contemptuous not only of Kenyans with a lower social and economic standing, but also of the leaders of other African countries. His analysis of the population problem extended to telling Kenyans to "stop breeding like rabbits." Njonjo surrounded himself with expatriate whites in his government offices and had a reputation for treating those Africans who did work for him very badly. According to one rumor that had wide circulation and credence, he actually helped create a food shortage in Kenya at one point, by manipulating supplies to maximize profit for his own enterprises and those of his friends. Njonjo was notorious for provoking the anger of Kenya's neighbors, for example, by telling parliament that the day the East African Community collapsed in 1977 was the "happiest day" of his life, an occasion he toasted with fine champagne. "Who is this man Obote?" Njonjo asked when Uganda's president, Milton Obote, complained about the political attacks being launched against him by Ugandan refugees living in Kenya. When Njonjo publicly derided Tanzania as a "poor country," Tanzanian officials replied that Kenya was a "man-eat-man society." Njonjo's rejoinder was that Tanzania was a "man-eat-nothing society."

Njonjo's alliances with other Kenyan, and especially Kikuyu, politicians shifted often, but in the period following Kenyatta's death he emerged as a particular rival of another Kikuyu, the new vice-president, Mwai Kibaki, a more populist figure who nonetheless had substantial business interests of his own on the side. Having helped institutionalize the succession process, Njonjo and his allies were now agitating to get him elected as vice-president of KANU and the country in Kibaki's place, and there were suspicions that he would then try to push Moi aside and take over the presidency himself. It was no doubt those efforts and the growing suspicions of Njonjo that lay behind the incident at the State House concert. So concerned were his rivals about Njonjo's machinations that they postponed party elections rather than risk a test of his strength. One astute observer of the Kenyan political scene said at the end of 1982 that power could not be shared indefinitely by three such strong figures—Moi, Njonjo, and Kibaki (who, as a former finance minister, had his own extensive political organization, with loyalists well placed throughout the government)—that someone would have to go.

Finally, in May of 1983, Moi went public with the accusation that there was "a traitor" in the government's midst, who, in league with a foreign power (presumably Britain), was plotting to take control. Most members of the cabinet tripped over each other on their way to the press to issue pledges of loyalty to Moi and to demand that he publicly identify and eliminate the culprit. Having failed to flush him out voluntarily, Moi finally named Njonjo publicly, in July 1983, and stripped him of all his positions in the cabinet, Parliament, and the party. The president then appointed a formal commission of inquiry to probe a host of allegations against Njonjo. He was accused of everything from conspiring to overthrow the government of the Seychelles and compromising Kenya's opposition to South Africa, to holding illegal political meetings, covering up illegal business transactions, and contributing to "the unlawful disturbances" of August 1982.

A public inquest into Njonjo's activities became Nairobi's longest running show. Lasting seven months, it featured a daily torrent of evidence about this suave operator's public and private life. All three of Kenya's English-language daily newspapers car-

ried extensive coverage of the hearings before a commission of
three judges, but one, *The Daily Nation,* published almost ver-
batim accounts. (The record was 18,612 words on the Njonjo
affair in a single edition of the newspaper.) It was clear from the
start that Njonjo was unlikely to end up in prison, if only because
he was privy to so much derogatory information about other public figures—a kind of Kenyan J. Edgar Hoover. And there was a
risk that by pushing so hard against Njonjo, the government
would convert this former villain into a hero for the Kikuyu. In
the end, having suspended all the rules of evidence and admitted
every available rumor into the judicial record, the commission
found Njonjo guilty of corruption and abuse of office. Among other
things, it found that Njonjo had stolen money from the Association
of the Physically Disabled of Kenya. Moi formally purged him and
fourteen of his political associates from KANU in September 1984,
but then three months later, on Jamhuri Day, pardoned Njonjo of
all formal charges. The former attorney general was thus dis-
graced, but not deprived of his liberty.

With Njonjo pushed aside, Moi was able to establish a much
clearer political identity for himself, but he still remained an
enigmatic, remote figure, far from the image of the charismatic
African politician who, like Kenyatta, could unite and inspire his
people. Moi was stolid-looking and spoke in a slow, methodical,
unemotional manner. Having lived and worked in Kenyatta's long
shadow for so many years—his most important public appearances
consisted of ceremonies and dedications—he was actually little
known to most Kenyans when he first came to power. If he had
strong views on domestic or international issues, few people
knew what they were; his typical stump speech consisted of a
homily on the virtues of milk as compared to alcohol, or an attempt to shed light on current problems by quoting extensively
from biblical passages that he had memorized in early childhood.
Typical of his policy initiatives was a crackdown on *Playboy* and
other "pornographic" magazines (whose main effect, in free-market Kenya, was to boost their price by more than 500 percent).

Moi's personal life held little interest or inspiration. Separated
from his wife, he rarely exposed his children to the public glare.
Even those who worked closely with him had no idea how many
children he had and knew of no special interests or outside hob-
bies that he enjoyed. By all accounts, he was a man who got up

early in the morning, went to bed early at night, and did little but work methodically in between.

Early in his tenure, Moi came across as a humble figure who was genuinely interested in communicating with people at the grass roots. He would travel often to his home constituency in the Rift Valley and talk to the "little people" about national affairs, as well as receiving them when they came to Nairobi. It was not long, however, before the presidency and all of its prerogatives seemed to go to his head and he wanted to be treated as the fount of all wisdom. The fact that some of the people around him— especially Kibaki and Njonjo—were better educated, more sophisticated and worldly caused him to assert himself all the more. He substituted his own likeness for that of Mzee on Kenya's currency, and he even shut off the four eternal flames on Kenyatta's tomb in downtown Nairobi. In trying to demonstrate his strength and his mastery of all issues, Moi mostly demonstrated his feelings of personal insecurity. "He wants to be able to talk about everything and prove he knows it all," said one Kenyan commentator. "Every day, every time he opens his mouth, he wants to issue a major political statement or directive. But since we don't have the resources to follow through on everything, a lot of what he says becomes laughable."

But Moi did not react well to laughs, or to the slightest hint that he was not really in charge or did not know what he was doing. When one of Nairobi's daily newspapers, for example, reported KANU's denunciation of a doctors' strike at Kenyatta Hospital in 1981, it referred to the party's statement as "anonymous" because it carried no signature. That enraged Moi. "Since the president is the head of KANU, it is Moi they are calling anonymous," he declared, ordering the arrest of the newspaper's editor and five other staff members. They were released a few days later in exchange for a front-page apology to the president and the country.

At the start, Moi named his governing philosophy *Nyayo* —literally translated from Swahili as "footsteps"—to indicate that he would not depart from the main lines of policy as defined by Kenyatta. His subthemes were reasonable enough: "Love, Peace, and Unity." "All of this is very abstract," conceded one top government official when asked to elaborate, "but basically he wants to work toward a society that is integrated politically, culturally, and economically . . . a circumstance in which any citizen of this country could go and live in any village in the country."

What *Nyayo* soon came to represent was the concept of absolute loyalty to Moi, and the people closest to him came to be known as "the *Nyayo* group." Moi explained his evolving attitude late in 1984 in a speech at Kenyatta Airport on his return from a visit to Ethiopia: "I would like ministers, assistant ministers and others to sing like a parrot after me," he said. "That is how we can progress." To drive the point home, the president required all government civil servants to join KANU by the beginning of 1985 as a condition of keeping their jobs; future vacancies would be filled, he declared, exclusively from the party ranks.

It was understandable that Moi, having neutralized and divided the old Kenyatta courtiers, would want to dilute the power of the Kikuyu establishment. Inevitably, though, he created another power elite of his own, and in it were a disproportionate number of people from his own Kalenjin ethnic group. They gained ground not only within the president's office, but also within the military, the foreign ministry, and other departments. There were once again complaints about tribalism and widespread favoritism, but this time from different quarters, from the people who had been favored before.

As this shift within the national balance indicates, Kenya is still far from being a place where any person can live and work anywhere, without regard to tribal affiliation. Tribal stereotypes abound in Kenyan life, even in conversations with government officials about the need to achieve ethnic equality and national unity. The Luo are particular targets of derision by the Kikuyu, who have an especially strong work ethic and a free-enterprise orientation that has been taken on by the nation. "The Luo just want to talk, talk, talk. They make good lecturers and artists," complained a senior civil servant, a Kikuyu himself, "but they don't know how to be agriculturists or businessmen." Touching on an especially sensitive issue from the past, he added that the Luo "took no real part in the struggle [for independence], yet they laid an immediate claim to all the benefits."

These ongoing strains and the need to alleviate them are the most important evidence that can be adduced on behalf of Kenya's one-party system. It seems clear that if the country had multiple political parties, they, like the early parties in Nigeria, would

invariably be tribally based and defined. Indeed, many of the
groups now favored politically by Moi, including the Kalenjin and
various small tribes from the highlands and the coastal areas of
Kenya, were originally united, before independence, in the Kenya
African Democratic Union (KADU), which was founded and led
by Moi, among others, but later folded into Kenyatta's KANU,
whose membership was at first composed primarily of Kikuyu and
Luo. Nothing can prevent the emergence of factions within a
gigantic political organization like KANU, and nothing has done
so, but the party has substantially reduced tribal rivalries. It is the
single national institution that cuts through the labyrinthine network of ethnic and socioeconomic groups. Despite one-party rule,
there is usually competition for parliamentary seats, sometimes
as many as eight or ten candidates in a single constituency; but
the competition tends to be more on substantive political, rather
than explicitly tribal, grounds. If MPs do not deliver on their
promises, they generally are defeated. Indeed, KANU itself is so
weak that Kenya is sometimes said to have a "no-party system."

Moi called parliamentary elections for September 1983 to
"clean the system," after he had purged Njonjo and most of the
court cases growing out of the 1982 coup attempt had been resolved. Although the voter turnout was unusually low for Kenya—
less than 50 percent in some areas—it was clear that the country's
political system was still healthy and competitive. The campaign
was more nearly free of violence than any other in the country's
history, although one cabinet member was charged with murder
after a nineteen-year-old supporter of an opposing candidate was
shot to death during a street fight. (The MP was reelected anyway, but dropped from the cabinet and later acquitted.)
Altogether, a total of 991 candidates stood for the 158 elected
seats in the legislature, and about 40 percent of the incumbents
were defeated—a substantial turnover, but smaller than the 58
percent who lost in the 1979 elections and the 64 percent voted
out in 1974. Five cabinet members lost their parliamentary seats,
and Moi took the opportunity to shrink the cabinet and change it
substantially. He reduced the Kikuyu presence, but he also selected an apolitical mathematics professor from the University of
Nairobi to be finance minister and, for the first time, named a Kenyan Somali to a cabinet-level job, as a minister of state in the

president's office.* (He was the brother of an army general who played a key role in creating a new air force loyal to Moi.) In addition, he brought an independent African businessman into the cabinet. Moi was generally praised, especially by nations that aid Kenya, for appointing a cabinet designed more to solve the country's problems than to preserve political alliances. Unaware that a new drought was coming, the president promised that Kenya would repay its substantial foreign debts and, in the future, not borrow more than it could afford.

As if to demonstrate that he now felt more secure in his job, Moi followed his inauguration for a second five-year term with another release of many of Kenya's best-known political prisoners, including Oginga Odinga. On Jamhuri Day 1983, the twentieth anniversary of Kenya's independence from Britain, he pardoned seven thousand petty criminals from the country's crowded jails.

But the most dramatic post-election development was Kenya's reconciliation with Tanzania and Uganda, its former partners in the East African Community, a step that probably would not have been possible while Njonjo was still in the picture. After six years of squabbling, aided by a mediator from the World Bank, the three countries agreed on a formula for dividing up the community's assets, and they pledged to enter into a new era of cooperation with each other. Only a few common institutions or services remained, including a flying school, a regional development bank, and a library exchange, but there was some hope that new joint endeavors might evolve.

One significant and immediate change, announced after a summit meeting of the three countries' leaders in the northern Tanzanian city of Arusha, was that the border between Kenya and Tanzania, closed since 1977, was reopened. The closing of that frontier had caused hardships of many different kinds. Kenya's overland trade with countries south of Tanzania was substantially cut off. Tanzania's tourist industry, which had depended heavily on overseas visitors who crossed over from Kenya, was virtually destroyed. Unless they had special permission for charter flights, diplomats, journalists, and other travelers who wanted to get to

* The Somali people, however, remained the victims of some of the most severe discrimination and mistreatment in Kenya. At least three hundred pastoral tribesmen were massacred in February 1984 during an army operation 320 miles northeast of Nairobi.

both countries had to divert themselves by hundreds or even thousands of miles to travel through Rwanda, Zambia, or the Seychelles. The closed border had also stood as a poignant symbol of the quarrels and the bitterness that beset independent Africa; with their frequent harsh words, neither Kenya nor Tanzania did any good for itself, but each managed to harm the other. There were risks in the decision to reopen the border, especially for Tanzania, but as Julius Nyerere put it, "If risks are to be taken, it should be the risk of trusting each other. The risk of mistrust has been too costly for East Africa."

There was another side to the Kenyan-Tanzanian reconciliation that was not made public initially. Even before the summit meeting in Arusha, Moi and Nyerere quietly agreed to an exchange of prisoners and exiles from each other's territory. The bonanza for Kenya was the return of the two Luo air force officers who had been ringleaders of the August 1982 coup effort; the Tanzanians had previously sneered at Kenya's request for their extradition. But Kenya also got back some others, including a former member of Parliament who had criticized the way the government handled the investigation of J. M. Kariuki's disappearance. Tanzania obtained the return not only of dissidents who had been responsible for various plots against Nyerere's regime, but also of former Tanzanian politicians who had lived in Nairobi for years and routinely extended help to young exiles passing through.

On both sides, some of the returnees were obvious candidates for legitimate prosecution, but others were clearly headed for indefinite detention without trial on political grounds as soon as they got home. (The two leaders of the Kenyan coup proclaimed their innocence, but were convicted and sentenced to death. Some of the other dissidents who were sent back to Kenya were not prosecuted, however.) There were many Ugandan exiles in Kenya who feared they would soon be shipped home, too. The potential for abuse of this agreement was so great that the United Nations High Commissioner for Refugees launched an investigation into whether the exchange of prisoners had violated any existing international accords. A number of Nyerere's critics noted that this idealist, who had just been given an international award for his help to refugees, found it easy to compromise his principles when he had a chance to lock up some opponents.

The East African reconciliation certainly went a long way toward dealing with Kenya's fears of isolation. For at least half a dozen years Kenya had had no other country in the region that it could truly call a friend. Nyerere's smugness and his doctrinaire socialism had posed almost as many problems as Idi Amin's barbarism. The arms buildup in Somalia, first with Soviet and then with American help, made irredentist elements in that country seem all the more threatening. Ethiopia, under the Soviet- and Cuban-influenced military regime of Mengistu Haile Mariam, was unpredictable, and unlikely to respect Kenya's capitalist system. Sudan, while ideologically compatible, had serious internal problems that precluded any meaningful outside relationships.

All of this made Kenya rely increasingly on its burgeoning friendship with the United States, which, under Republicans and Democrats alike, admired Kenya's economic choices and appreciated its pragmatism and moderation on international issues. Pan-African and Third World solidarity aside, the Kenyans did not automatically vote against the West on every issue at the United Nations, and they were, from Washington's point of view, appropriately wary of the Soviet Union. The relationship was mutually satisfying, because Kenya under Moi, as under Kenyatta, was a comfortable friend for the United States to have—more comfortable, say, than the controversial regime of Mobutu Sese Seko in Zaïre. (Moi sometimes responded well to American "advice," for example, following suggestions from the U.S. ambassador that he not come down too hard on the university after the 1982 coup attempt.)

It was inevitable, then, that the United States would become Kenya's primary supplier of arms. Former Foreign Minister Munyua Waiyaki tells with great relish of how Kenya obtained its first F-5E jets in 1976. Notwithstanding his reputation for pro-Palestinian sympathies, Waiyaki says, an Israeli diplomatic friend in New York advised him that he would have to lobby personally on Capitol Hill if Kenya was to have any serious chance of success with its request for the American planes. According to Waiyaki, the Israeli set up his first appointment for him, with then Senator Jacob Javits, Republican of New York. Then the foreign minister saw several other influential members of the Senate Foreign Relations and Armed Services committees. "By the end of the day," recalls Waiyaki, "Henry Kissinger was looking for me. He called and said, 'Okay, I got your message. You can have the planes. What else do you want?' "

Kissinger may have been joking with his open-ended offer, but the Kenyans have received plenty more since. The Carter administration increased military aid to Kenya from $10 million in fiscal year 1979 to $26 million (more than half of all U.S. military assistance in Africa at the time) in fiscal year 1980. This figure included money for thirty-two Hughes helicopters equipped with sophisticated air-to-ground antitank missiles, which the Kenyans argued could be necessary to defend themselves against an invasion from Somalia or Uganda. By fiscal year 1982, the total of annual U.S. aid to Kenya, loans and grants, economic and military, had reached $92.4 million, and soon it went over the $100 million mark.

In return, Kenya welcomed an ever larger American presence beginning in the late 1970s, including routine use of the port at Mombasa by ships of the U.S. Navy, which, by that time, did not have many other places to call in the Indian Ocean. Before long, the United States had agreed to renovate the port at a cost of about $50 million, and, along with bases in Somalia and Oman, Mombasa loomed large in American arrangements for its "rapid deployment force" intended to respond quickly to crises in the Persian Gulf region. Gradually Mombasa's unique tropical calm, which had evolved during centuries of Portuguese, Arab, and eventually British influence, took on an overlay of American popular culture—navy baseball caps, T-shirts, and other paraphernalia. Normally lackadaisical street vendors were stirred to new heights of marketing, as they dealt with the influx of sailors. During a major visit, as many as six thousand might come ashore at one time. Drug abuse and prostitution flourished in the port, Kenya's second largest city, and at one point a twenty-one-year-old American sailor was charged with killing a young Kenyan woman.

The most extraordinary aspect of the growing U.S. military stake in Kenya was that Moi tried to prevent it from becoming a matter of public record. When Kenyan and American forces (including eighteen hundred U. S. marines) conducted joint maneuvers off the northeast Kenyan coast in 1984, they were treated as a national security secret; they went unmentioned in the Kenyan press. Virtually everyone knew that the American navy had access to Kenyan bases and other facilities, but the president refused to permit the issue to be discussed in Parliament. Apparently concerned that open debate would make him vulnerable to political attack from the left or lead to demands for greater American compensation, Moi kept the terms of the bases agreement so secret that he managed to stir rumors of even more complex and sinister U.S. involvement in Kenyan affairs. Some people actually believed that secret American bases had been constructed in remote areas of the country, and government officials who owned land along the coast occasionally approached U.S. officials in Nairobi, offering to sell their holdings to the Pentagon so that more such bases could be built. Those approaches were turned away with amusement, but at one point at least nine U.S. government agencies working in Kenya were trying to expand their representation in the country.

After the number of U.S. officials in Kenya had passed 250, one of the main jobs of the American ambassador in Nairobi came to be fighting the further growth of the mission. One unfortunate aspect of the American image in Nairobi was that the new embassy building there—one of the first U.S. overseas posts built after the Iran hostage crisis of 1979–80—was like an armed fortress. Kenyans and others trying to enter it were subjected to stringent, sometimes demeaning, security precautions.

What only the most savvy American officials understood was that there were liabilities for both sides if the American presence grew too far and too fast, that it was not in the interest of either country for Kenya to be regarded by other African nations as an American client or Moi as Washington's puppet. "You know," said one young physician in Nairobi, "there are times when Kenya seems like a pro-Western island surrounded by more radical states. . . . The connection with the U.S. can be an embarrassment for us, especially when the West has done so little to support the liberation struggles to the South." There was particular dissatisfaction among educated Kenyans during the Reagan administration over the policy of so-called "constructive engagement" with South Africa.

Kenya, of course, had a long-established reputation for pragmatic, if sometimes furtive, dealings with South Africa, especially during the time when Njonjo had substantial influence over government policy. One open gesture was that European airlines were permitted to stop in Nairobi to refuel and pick up and discharge passengers on their flights to and from Johannesburg; that practice had obvious benefits for Kenyan, as well as South African, tourism and other commerce.* Organizations of Kenyan doctors and other professionals sometimes quietly invited their South African counterparts to attend conferences in Nairobi, in the hope of not only learning something from the interchange, but also demonstrating that black-ruled countries could function smoothly and successfully. South African heart specialist Christiaan Barnard even paid a visit, brought in by Njonjo to examine Kenyatta during the last year of his life.

Other African countries that felt economic pressure to make compromises with principle on the South Africa issue often turned to Kenya for moral support. For example, when Zambian President Kenneth Kaunda found it necessary to reopen his country's rail link with Rhodesia while the civil war was still raging there, in order to bring food in and ship Zambia's copper out, he consulted with Kenya before Tanzania. Kenya approved, while Tanzania emphatically disapproved. As Waiyaki later recalled it, "We told [Kaunda] we would do the same thing in his position. It is ridiculous for a man to fight other people's wars when his own people are starving."

Moi has talked about carving out a new, more activist role in Africa for Kenya. He has a vague "French connection," a relationship with some of the leaders of francophone West Africa that Kenyatta never encouraged or cultivated himself. And unlike Mzee, who did not like to fly and in his last years rarely left home, Moi enjoys attending OAU and Commonwealth summit meetings and other conferences. There have been no signs, however, of his acceptance as a major pan-African leader in an era of great disarray on the continent.

As long as Kenya is in severe economic straits and Moi feels at all insecure politically, the country's American ties are bound to remain the central element in Kenyan foreign policy. Kenya's

---

* Most other black-ruled countries were more strict and ruled out direct flights to or from South Africa, in the name of isolating the Pretoria regime. Some, like Liberia under Samuel Doe, preferred simple subterfuge; it permitted Pan American to stop at Robertsfield between New York and Johannesburg, but the plane's arrival from or departure to South Africa was never announced or acknowledged.

relations with Britain are often a touchy matter, given the violence and bitterness of the struggle for independence and the lingering resentments on both sides. The British government was outraged by Moi's suggestion that it was scheming with Njonjo to overthrow him, but that incident was an exception to an otherwise steadily improving relationship. Both sides benefited from annual training exercises that British military units held in the north of Kenya, and the British continued to maintain a generous aid program in Kenya, including funds for low-cost housing and the training of teachers and public works employees. Some fifty thousand Britons live in Kenya today, about twice as many as at independence. The two countries' trade with each other remains substantial. When Queen Elizabeth II made a sentimental return visit to Kenya in November 1983 (it was in Kenya thirty years earlier, as a princess, that she had learned of her father's death and her accession to the throne), she was greeted enthusiastically by thousands of people everywhere she went.

Kenya is capable of some diplomatic surprises from time to time, such as the establishment of relations in recent years with Communist-ruled Albania, which has few ties with the world outside its borders. However, despite substantial informal trade, Kenya seemed unlikely to imitate Zaïre and Liberia by reestablishing relations with Israel.

A number of issues cloud Kenya's future. One is the new visibility and influence of the country's military, particularly the army. After saving Moi's regime, at the time of the 1982 air force coup attempt, army officers felt entitled to a greater role in national affairs, and one committee of colonels met routinely for a time to pass along its views on the issues of the day to the president through the chief of staff of the armed forces. There was no particular reason to believe that the army was unhappy with Moi, but some observers perceived an implicit threat of another coup— the next one, presumably, by the army and, in that case, more skillfully executed—if the president strayed far from what is regarded as acceptable policy. One policy that Moi seemed bound to accept was a steady growth in Kenya's defense budget and its arms purchases overseas. According to one unpublished estimate, he was committed to spending at least $750 million over a period of five years, an enormous amount for a developing country with such severe problems in other spheres. Whether that money would be subject to corruption through padded purchasing contracts was not clear.

The Kenyan army was traditionally dominated by members of the Kamba tribe, and while that is still the case, there is apparently little ethnic friction in the army of the sort that characterizes so many other institutions in the country. What worries some people is that Kenya's army has had little contact with the general public during the years since independence, less than in most African countries. "We really don't know a thing about the army," said one journalist; "traditionally, they've had no contact with the press at all." Thus, it is difficult to know what sort of policies it might advocate.

Kenya still has a long way to go before it can truly call itself a well-integrated society. The role of pastoral groups, such as the still semi-warlike Masai, in the modern nation has yet to be resolved. To be sure, a few Masai have achieved prominence in government, business, and academia; some have become cabinet ministers. But the vast majority live a nomadic existence along the Kenya-Tanzania border, excluded from most of the benefits and advantages of Kenyan political and economic development. Many argue that the best thing would be to leave the Masai alone, to permit them to live according to the dictates of their ancient culture as long as they see fit; the question is whether the Masai, and others similarly situated, would really prefer it that way if they had more awareness of the alternatives.

At a completely different point on the socioeconomic and cultural spectrum are the Kenya Asians, about sixty thousand in number. Some of them are from families that have been in East Africa for centuries, others came from Bombay to work on building the railroad, and a large percentage arrived more recently. They, along with the resident British, are the main component in Kenya's claim to be a tolerant multiracial society; but the Asians are frequent scapegoats when anything goes wrong in the country. Moi has often blamed them for Kenya's economic difficulties and threatened to deport even those who are Kenyan citizens if they are involved in illegal currency transactions. The Asians' fears that their businesses or property might be seized increased after Njonjo fell from grace; he had been their main protector in government circles. As a result, many wealthy families have sent representatives to Britain, Canada, or the United States to prepare the way for them to emigrate, and so there probably has been an increase in currency outflows.

The truth is that Kenya could not get along without its Asians—they include about half the country's doctors and most of its shopkeepers—and Moi could not risk the domestic and foreign repercussions of a repression and expulsion of the sort imposed on Uganda Asians by Idi Amin. But the self-inflicted separateness of Kenya Asians and the continuing resentment felt toward them by many Africans are inevitably destabilizing factors.

Another problem that must be addressed urgently in Kenya is education. It seems obvious that the country cannot afford to spend the 25 percent of its budget on education that it once did, yet the nature of the educational system will probably have to change as well. With tens of thousands of people already trained for white-collar jobs they will never find, it would be irresponsible to continue the trend. The role of polytechnical education will have to be enhanced, and the government will have to devise incentives for new generations to stay on or return to the land. The pressures on Nairobi and smaller cities cannot be tolerated indefinitely. One small step was taken in 1984 with the launching of Moi University in Eldoret, with a curriculum intended to produce agricultural graduates who remain in the rural areas.

How Moi handles Kenya's complex political tensions will obviously be an issue of profound importance. Given his record of sensitivity to criticism, he might be expected to strike out against the lively, often irreverent Kenyan press, which has frequently served as a sort of safety valve in moments when dissent was not bubbling up through the formal party structure. Ironically, foreign ownership may have helped assure that Nairobi's newspapers function as some of the freest in Africa. The largest publication, the *Daily Nation*, is owned by the Aga Khan, leader of the Isma'ili sect of Moslems; it has gotten away with publishing articles disparaging the political leadership that might have posed more problems for local investors, and it has also served as a training ground for many of Kenya's sophisticated journalists.

One of the *Nation's* most prominent alumni, American-educated Hilary Ng'weno, publishes the *Weekly Review*, perhaps the best news magazine in Africa, which often conceals a brutal frankness beneath a surface idiom of adulation for nation-building and other popular themes. Ng'weno had also published a daily newspaper, the *Nairobi Times*, but it suffered crippling financial hardships, and in 1983 the government took it over and converted it into the *Kenya Times*, an official organ of KANU. There was obvious concern that this might foreshadow pressure on the other independent newspapers, but some Kenyan journalists predicted the contrary; now that there was a guaranteed outlet for the official point of view, they argued, the other publications might actually have greater latitude.

Other potential avenues of dissent are liable to have less tolerance from Moi and his government. The university, for example, remained a cauldron. The president complained that it had fallen into disrepute because of a student body that was vulnerable to the "crudest stupidities of dialectical subversion." After another spate of student unrest early in 1985—including a rally at the university's athletic fields that drew more than two thousand protesters and was brutally broken up by the police—Moi closed the university again and sent the students home. He claimed that foreigners, particularly from Eastern Europe, were responsible for fomenting the trouble. One of Moi's aides suggested that "Marxism is outdated and irrelevant to the Kenyan situation and as such, it should be removed from the university schedule." The very term "lecturer" became a synonym for "troublemaker" in the Kenyan political lexicon; one government minister estimated that the greatest challenge to Moi comes from "the thinking group"—the people, mostly young, who believe that Kenya's economic system is not socially and intellectually justifiable. So long as they do not find new allies like the ones they had in the air force, these dissidents can create little trouble of a practical nature, but they are certainly able to push the country to be morally more self-searching than it tended to be while resting on the laurels of its early success.

In the long run, Kenya cannot possibly avoid the chaos that has beset so many other African countries unless it finds better means of distributing its wealth and its income and, at the same time, controls the growth of its population. Another coffee boom of sorts appeared to be developing in 1986—once again benefiting from crop problems in Brazil—and it promised to give Kenya at least a temporary economic reprieve; but the fundamental challenges remained the same. Can Daniel arap Moi handle these gigantic challenges indefinitely, or will he make a statesmanlike decision, along the lines of Léopold Senghor in Senegal, to step down after a reasonable period and make room for others? Although they dare not say so publicly, many Kenyans believe that former Vice-President Mwai Kibaki, while no less corrupt, would be able to lead the country with more imagination and subtlety than Moi. But Kibaki has been ill, and Kikuyu aspirations to regain power now focus on younger men, such as Kenneth Matiba, a wealthy businessman who entered the cabinet as minister of culture and social services.

As Moi moved toward his automatic election to a third five-year term in 1988, he began to look more and more like a typically repressive African leader, and the human rights and political development of Kenyans suffered gravely. Persuasive evidence emerged that dissidents—especially the members of *Mwakenya*, a clandestine Marxist opposition group—were being jailed without trial and, in some cases, tortured. Gibson Kamau Kuria, an Oxford-educated lawyer who filed a lawsuit on behalf of three alleged torture victims, was himself detained for nine months without trial.

Perhaps the most serious blow to Kenya's democratic reputation came in the parliamentary elections of 1988, when Moi did away with the secret ballot and reverted to an old colonial practice of having voters line up publicly behind photographs of their preferred candidates; the result was a widespread boycott of the election. Later he pushed through new laws giving himself the power to fire at will judges and members of Kenya's Public Service Commission, and extending the length of time a suspect can be held in police custody without being brought to court, from twenty-four hours to two weeks.

6

South Africa:
White Nightmare

WALKING INTO THE LOBBY of the Carlton Hotel in Johannesburg at midnight, one could imagine being in Vienna during the 1930s. Music wafts through the air, while gracious white gentlemen and their handsome ladies chatter over drinks. They move about smoothly and laugh heartily over small amusements. They appear to be utterly unaware, or unwilling to admit, that they are living on top of a volcano, and that there are severe rumblings below.

On the surface, it seems as if there has been a change in South Africa, an adjustment that has made a certain degree of coexistence possible. Now blacks and whites occasionally walk on the street together, chatting casually, and in the parks on Sunday afternoon, mixed groups of teenagers play soccer and look as if they have been friends for years. But the level of tension and anxiety just beneath the surface is extraordinary, almost unbearable. Whereas it used to take at least half an hour before the subject of race and politics crept into a conversation between a white South African and a foreign visitor, it now takes perhaps half a minute. Cut off from any genuine knowledge of what the blacks in their own country are thinking and feeling, whites immediately press a new arrival to share his first impressions: How bad do things look? Are the blacks becoming Marxists? Does the revolution seem imminent? Everyone is welcome to become an instant expert.

Telegraphing her own answer to those questions, one South African friend confides that she has made a major change in her vast and beautiful garden: she no longer plants anything that will take more than a year to mature. Another, an older woman deeply involved in politics, mourns the disillusionment and dispersion of an entire English-speaking generation—young, well-educated white professionals who despair of change in their own country and many of whom take a chance on a better life as exiles. Their parents stay behind with the Afrikaners (descendants of the original Dutch and other early European settlers) and the "non-whites"; few of them have anyplace else to go.

But for the people who really run the country, for the Afrikaner establishment, life goes on with an astonishing consistency. There is tinkering here and there with the system, perhaps an argument with an old friend who has become conscience-stricken and rebellious, even an occasional terrorist explosion that temporarily affects the electricity or brings about some roadblocks. The servants may be uppity, and some days they do not appear for work at all. And yet, extravagant vacations at the beach continue. Plenty of flashy new cars are available, and while there has suddenly been a surge of inflation—a problem that South Africa somehow avoided for years—almost everything still seems affordable. Dinner parties go on far into the night.

So undisturbed is the traditional way of doing things that the entire administrative branch of the national government, the cabinet and bureaucracy, still moves back and forth between Pretoria and Cape Town every year (a practice originally instituted to minimize regional and ethnic rivalries). In every government office in Pretoria each December, files are packed into fine old wooden trunks for the trek, along the route of the Blue Train, South Africa's most luxurious way to travel, to the Cape. Six months later, the scene is repeated at the other end, and the train brings everyone and everything back to the Transvaal. It is as if there is no reason to change habits and patterns, no reason to worry.

Life inside the volcano is more unsettled. "The average black in South Africa is very patient, really," says Marius Wiechers, a

law professor who has been involved for more than a decade with
the seemingly contradictory tasks of defending the South African
system before the outside world and trying to make it more benign and fair at home. A bearded, wrinkled, soft-spoken man, he
has a capacity, unusual in a society so isolated, for putting South
Africa's problems in a broad international and historical context.
He speaks of the alienating influence of new technologies, and his
mind wanders to Iran and the causes of the fundamentalist Islamic revolution there. "We have been relatively successful here,"
he muses. "Unlike Iran under the shah, in South Africa the fruits
and the benefits of technology and modernization have trickled
down. . . . The black has made some progress."

However, the blacks themselves,* even those who would
realize that Wiechers's intentions are good and his analysis respectable, shake their heads in a combination of amusement and contempt when they hear remarks like that. They believe that the
white government and white academics cannot really know about
black patience or a black sense of progress, because they have not
really asked. "The government is determined not to negotiate, not
to listen to anybody except its puppets," says Dr. Nthatho Motlana,
chairman of the "Committee of Ten" in Soweto, the gigantic African township on the outskirts of Johannesburg. "Any changes
that do take place in South Africa will take place because of the
kind of violence that can be brought to bear on this government. . . . Nobody wants violence, of course . . . we are all
reaching for peaceful change. We are all hoping the government
will listen and do the right thing before Armageddon."

Another black man, one who has made compromises and
avoided politics in order to advance in the white business world,
speaks of the gap more sorrowfully than defiantly. "The majority
of white South Africans haven't a clue of what's going on here,"
he insists. "They think they do, but they don't. They think they'll
stay in power forever."

Still, if the whites know so little, it is hard to understand how
they have maintained such effective control until now; South Af-

* The term "black" is used in this chapter, as it generally is in South Africa,
to refer jointly to black Africans, Indians and other Asians, and so-called
"Coloureds" of mixed race. The narrower terms are used to refer to each
specific group.

rica seems quiet and orderly, a place infected with the world's most serious case of business-as-usual. The black executive bristles when asked why this is so, and he leans forward across his shiny wooden desk, his voice lowering to a whisper: "You know, you can have a revolution going on, but never sense it on the surface. . . . All I can tell you is that something is going to blow up here sometime."

Dinner at the home of a Western diplomat is one of the few occasions when South African blacks and whites gather to discuss politics frankly; to do so publicly would, in many cases, make them the objects of suspicion and investigation, perhaps even banning or detention. Tonight the group includes a professor from Potchefstroom University, the intellectual center of pure Calvinist Afrikanerdom, and his wife; a woman activist from Soweto whose movements have been restricted by the government several times; and male and female journalists for an English-language newspaper.

They discuss the efforts of a parochial school (with the connivance of the press) to hide from the government the fact that it is admitting children of all races; the inquiries into ideological reliability at Potchefstroom, resulting in ostracism or even dismissal of those faculty members whose ideas are thought to have strayed too far from the orthodoxy of the Dutch Reformed Church; the need of Africans to smuggle letters out of the country to children studying abroad, whose political views will be automatically suspect.

As the evening wears on, two realizations emerge: whatever peaceful solutions to South Africa's problems may be found eventually, the English-speaking whites will play little part in them; it is really up to the more numerous Afrikaners and the Africans, both of whom have a historic claim to the land and the resources of the country, to work things through. But it may be too late for Afrikaner men and African men to deal constructively with each other; they are too embittered and too tense about what is at stake. Perhaps it is more likely the women, unliberated and behind the scenes though they may be in this sexist society, who can manage to communicate across the color line and understand each other's anxieties. On this occasion, the professor's wife reacts empathically when the woman from Soweto wonders aloud, with anguish in her voice and tears in her eyes, about the fate of "our beautiful South Africa."

When the emotional evening is over, everyone leaves to return to his or her own authorized quarters.

Some simple events or images in present-day South Africa are so haunting that they become instantly etched in one's memory. Among them is the sight of a police car arriving at a street corner in the city—any city—and disgorging four hefty, club-swinging, white officers, who pounce on an African man who seems to be doing nothing in particular and take him away. Passersby do not even pause to watch, but simply steer a wider arc around the brief disturbance. They probably assume it is a "pass arrest"—the man may be in an area where his pass does not authorize him to be, may not be carrying his pass, or may not have a pass at all. At their peak, there were said to be seventeen hundred such pass arrests in the country every day.

Another is the scene in the wealthy white suburbs of South African cities just after sundown almost every night: the domestic servants who do not live where they work are coming off duty after a long day, and they trudge along beside the high hedges or fences that line many of the streets, in the first part of what is bound to be a long journey to their homes in the "townships." They seem not to talk at all while they are on white turf, not to each other and not to anyone else; the silence is eerie and unnerving.

And then there is the "nonwhite" entrance—to liquor stores and some other public facilities. It is separate and distinctly not equal: smaller, narrower, less well painted, or somehow inconvenient, around the side or the back. There is even a nonwhite entrance to the Voortrekker Monument outside of Pretoria, the imposing but ugly tribute to the Great Trek and the Battle of Blood River, chapters in the white conquest of the country that are recounted in lifelike murals on the inside. The monument is open for visits by the country's 4.8 million whites six days a week and by South Africa's other 27.7 million people one day a week.

South Africans of all races and political persuasions are obsessed with time. In every conversation about the country's future,

certain fundamental questions lurk: What is the deadline for
peaceful change, before violence takes over? Is time running out?
The responses that people give themselves or get from others,
whether in the form of general projections or specific predictions,
can make an enormous difference in people's lives—what jobs they
take, where they send their children to school, how they plan for
their future, whether they stay in South Africa at all or look for a
place to emigrate.

When Donald Woods, the renegade editor of the *Daily Dispatch* of East London, fled South Africa in 1977 after being restricted by the government, he achieved a great deal of attention
with his precise timetable for the Armageddon that loomed for his
country. Well-armed guerrilla battalions were already gathering
in nearby nations, he said, and South Africa could not possibly
hold out longer than five more years. The country was the target
of scattered guerrilla attacks during that period, but the system
certainly survived.

During a visit to South Africa in 1982, just after Woods's
deadline had expired, conversations with a wide variety of South
Africans yielded a whole new set of predictions:

"We are entering into five years of political instability," said
an Afrikaner intellectual in Pretoria, assessing the impact of a new
constitution granting limited involvement in government to Coloureds and Indians; "the prerevolutionary stage is just beginning."
On the contrary, to take the counsel of a Coloured community
activist in Cape Town, "we are in the final part of the prerevolutionary stage. . . . The government has two years' space, and
then it will be too late."

A professor at Stellenbosch University was convinced there
was more time than that. "We can stay ahead of the process of
radicalization if we create social and economic opportunities for
the Coloureds and the Africans. We have to buy time. We need
ten years." Oddly enough, Nthatho Motlana, the chairman of the
Committee of Ten in Soweto, suggested the same deadline. The
spiral of violence would get progressively worse, he predicted,
and then "in ten years, I think, the balloon will go up."

A white liberal politician, estimating how long the Progressive Federal party had to make an impact on the system, guessed
that "the young blacks in Soweto say, 'The future belongs to me.'
They figure they'll take over in fifteen or twenty years." "Well, the

Africans may feel that time is on their side," observed a Coloured of moderate views, "but we don't feel that way. We think time is running against us, and something must be done soon."

One middle-class black in his late thirties, working as an executive for a mining company in Johannesburg, said he was convinced he would see major changes in his lifetime. "I think I will die in a very different South Africa. . . . By the time I am sixty years old, there will be a black prime minister." Would this come about peacefully? He had grave doubts. Well, then, would South Africa as it is known today be blown up? "Possibly," he said. "You know, we can always build another one."

An idealistic Afrikaner, enthusiastically involved in a multi-racial community-improvement project in a small town in the Cape, estimated that "it will take twenty to thirty years to make real gains" and achieve meaningful equality in some domains; "but do we have that much time? I don't know." A Johannesburg woman, the daughter of a South African diplomat, thought she was being pessimistic, but sounded optimistic compared to most others. "In forty years," she said, "it will be impossible to live in South Africa, especially for English-speaking whites. We'll have to make some other plans."

The political circumstances and the relationships between the races in South Africa developed very differently from those anywhere else in Africa, in part because the Europeans arrived so early—and then decided to stay. When Jan van Riebeeck landed at Table Bay in the Cape of Good Hope on April 6, 1652, with a party of about one hundred men and four women, he had in mind nothing so ambitious as a colony, but rather a "refreshment station" that could supply ships of the Dutch East India Company at the midpoint of their long voyage from Europe to the Far East. But his group found the soft Mediterranean-type climate congenial and the local inhabitants, the Khoikhoi (otherwise known as the Hottentots) and the San (the Bushmen), willing to trade cattle from their enormous herds for the iron, copper, trinkets, tobacco, and brandy the Dutch had brought along. The cattle thus acquired by the Dutch required land for grazing, which was rapidly appropriated; as they moved inland and found the soil and rainfall less certain, the settlers took larger and larger tracts, often as large as six thousand acres each.

Such large farms required a great deal of labor, which was provided not by the Khoisan (as the two local groups were sometimes jointly known), who were not amenable, but by slaves brought in from elsewhere in Africa and the Dutch East Indies. As word spread in Europe of the surprising opportunities available for white settlers at the tip of Africa—free farms and guaranteed profits from the trade with passing ships—landless Dutch and German peasants were easily lured to this promised land. They were joined after 1688 by French Huguenots, skilled farmers and wine-growers, who, having fled to Holland to escape religious persecution at home, happily accepted the offer of free passage to Cape Town. By the middle of the eighteenth century, there were perhaps five thousand whites living in the Cape, five times the number in the more highly developed Portuguese colonies of Angola and Mozambique. Despite their varied backgrounds, the new residents of the Cape, sharing a common Protestant religion and a frontier outlook on life, quickly became a rather well-assimilated and homogeneous group, eventually known as the Afrikaners. Over time they melded components of various languages into their own new one, Afrikaans. Although substantial socioeconomic differences developed within the community, their new ethnic identity became very strong; their sense of cohesion helped them establish and maintain control in the area.

Another new ethnic group was formed in southern Africa at the same time. The relationship between the white settlers and the Khoisan had been ambivalent from the beginning. Some of the indigenous people died during wars over cattle, but more of them perished as the result of diseases brought by the Europeans, such as smallpox, against which they had no immunities. Others, however, especially Khoisan women, intermarried or cohabited with the settlers, as did some freed slaves; the mixed population that resulted was the Cape Coloureds. They came to speak Afrikaans; as "brown brothers" of the Afrikaners, they shared a culture with them and sought to preserve an identity distinct from the other nonwhite groups in the region. Their customs and practices were also affected by the Malays who had been brought from the East Indies.

Eventually those Khoisan who had not been absorbed into the Coloured population virtually disappeared, but for a time the Khoisan's resistance of the white settlers' advance into the interior postponed the Afrikaners' contact with other black people in southern Africa, mostly Bantu-speaking tribes. Before long, however, the hardiest of the pioneers, called *trekboers*, or wandering farmers, began to set forth, usually in extended-family units, to find greener pastures.

These people, *Boers* for short, became folk heroes of the new South African civilization; setting out in ox-drawn wagons, they risked all in the hope of further improving their lives. They recognized no authority but the senior married male in their group, who generally saw himself as a successor to the Hebrew patriarchs of the Old Testament and dispensed divine justice to the members of his own family, as well as any African slaves and Coloured servants they had brought along. The Boers were a pastoral white tribe. Finally they clashed with the Xhosa, who were living a quite similar life as nomadic cultivators and grazers. The difference, in the view of the Boers, of course, was that they themselves were God's messengers, while the dark-skinned people they encountered, the members of different groups that often did not get along with each other, represented the forces of evil and darkness in the world.

Several inconclusive wars were fought, and the whites only began to prevail after the British, as a result of events in Europe, arrived in 1795 to take over the Cape Colony from the Dutch East India Company.* At first the British pleased the Boers by instituting strict controls on the nonwhites, restricting where they could live and requiring them to carry passes whenever they moved about. But within a few years, in the early part of the nineteenth century, the British were talking about abolishing slavery in their empire, and British magistrates in the Cape Colony began to take seriously complaints by servants and slaves against their masters. (In one especially notorious incident in 1815—recounted ever since as a way to stir hatred against the British—a Boer farmer, who refused to appear in court on charges of mistreating a ser-

---

* The Dutch monarchy was replaced in 1795 by a republic, inspired by the French Revolution. When the head of the royal Dutch government, the prince of Orange, fled into exile in England, he asked the British government to occupy his colonial possessions and look after them for him until he could be restored to the throne. The Cape Colony did return briefly to Dutch control between 1803 and 1806, but then went permanently back to the British.

vant, was killed by Coloured troops under British command, and several Boer neighbors who protested were hanged in public.) British missionaries came to be regarded as troublemakers who interfered with Boer efforts to expand their territory; meanwhile, English was imposed as the language of instruction and the courts, and British criminal procedure put into effect.

The Boers felt their way of life was genuinely threatened, and their response was to reach farther afield. Packing up all of their belongings, some four thousand people from the Cape Colony—the Voortrekkers—set out in the mid-1830s on what would come to be known as the Great Trek. Traveling in caravans over a period of years and making alliances with settlements of Coloureds and other groups as they went, they first conquered the Ndebele and settled temporarily on land made available to them by the Sotho. From there, unable to agree on an overall plan, they went off in various directions, many of them across the Drakensburg Mountains to Natal, the home of the Zulu people. Under the leadership of a chief named Shaka, who was a highly sophisticated military and strategic thinker, the Zulu had become a powerful, dominant force with their own language and complex social system.

It fell to one of Shaka's half brothers, Dingane, to deal with the colonialists from the Cape. Dingane was clumsy and indecisive. Having first agreed to a treaty allowing the Boers to settle in his territory, he abruptly changed his mind and massacred the advance party of seventy people that came to his capital in February 1838 to sign the treaty; his forces also killed the men, women, and children who had stayed behind at their encampment, bringing the death toll to about seven hundred. Ten months later, a Boer regiment under Andries Pretorius avenged the slaughter of its brethren, overwhelmingly defeating Dingane and his army at the Battle of Blood River, so named because of the quantity of Zulu blood spilled in the fighting. (About three thousand Zulu died, while only three Boers were wounded.) Every December 16, the anniversary of that victory is still celebrated as a national holiday in South Africa—the Day of the Covenant, a reference to the oath the Boers had sworn to God before the battle began, to keep the day holy if they won.

Having vanquished the Zulu, the Boers went on to proclaim the Republic of Natalia, with a capital at Pietermaritzburg. But local British merchants soon became uneasy. They persuaded the government in London to take over the republic, first as part of the Cape Colony, and later as a separate self-governing colony, with its capital eventually established in the thoroughly English city of Durban. Some of the Boers stayed on in Natal, but most of them packed up again, recrossed the mountains, and settled on the other side of the Vaal River. The Transvaal seemed to be sufficiently deep in the interior that it did not, for the moment, interest the British. Despite serious quarrels among factions, the Boers established yet another government there, with a weak central authority. Meanwhile, the *trekkers* who had headed in a different direction, to the fertile land between the Caledon and Orange rivers, established what came to be known as the Orange Free State; there, too, the British seemed indifferent.

But in 1868, children playing along the Orange River found some diamonds. The boom was immediate, and before long Kimberley became an important mining center. A number of ambitious Englishmen were now attracted to South Africa, including Cecil Rhodes, who made a fortune in diamonds by the time he was twenty-one and later dominated the politics of the Cape Colony. Then, in 1886, gold was discovered on the Witwatersrand ridge in the Transvaal. Johannesburg sprang up on that spot. There was an enormous influx of white miners from all over the world, but the Boers maintained tight, exclusive political control in the Transvaal.

The British began to talk of the need to "consolidate" the various South African republics. First and foremost, they had visions of the country's grand wealth, which they wanted to exploit and manage. They were also suspicious that the Germans, already ensconced in South-West Africa, wanted to create an anti-British alliance with the Transvaal and the Orange Free State. The Boers certainly would have preferred that to British control, especially when they saw what had happened to the Cape Colony, where Coloureds and Africans were voting with the English against the perceived self-interests of the Afrikaners. The Transvaal successfully resisted one British attempt at annexation between 1877 and 1881, but by the last years of the nineteenth century, with imperialist jingoism at its peak and Afrikaner nationalism building, war was inevitable.

The Anglo-Boer war that began in 1899 was a bitter and

brutal conflict. The Boers eventually resorted to guerrilla tactics, which they had learned from the Africans, to win hit-and-run victories against the superior, well-trained British troops. Because they had no formal supply system, the Boers lived off the land, and to this the British responded with cruel tactics: they destroyed the farms and the buildings on them, herding the women and children into unsanitary camps, where some twenty-six thousand died. The Boers surrendered in 1902. Under the terms of the peace treaty, they were promised self-government, and the British agreed not to extend the franchise to Africans, but to leave such questions to the various colonial legislatures.

The Union of South Africa was finally formed in 1910, as a dominion of the British Empire. From an economic and administrative standpoint, this made good sense, but it also sealed white political control over the Africans, Coloureds, and Indians. (The British had first brought Indians to Natal as indentured laborers to work in the cane fields. As they became more numerous, their protests against discrimination gave rise to the career of Mahatma Gandhi). It was only a matter of time before the relatively progressive practices of the Cape Colony were eliminated. Under the leadership of the South Africa party and prime ministers Louis Botha and Jan Smuts, reconciliation among the whites was the top priority. The official ideology was that the British victory was final and it was time to create a single united white people, incorporating the best of both the English and Afrikaner cultures.

In reality, the differences remained substantial, and they were never far from the surface. The most conservative forces in the Afrikaner community opposed South Africa's entry into World War I on the British side, for example, and some Boer commandos tried to thwart the South African takeover of the German territory of South-West Africa. (The Germans were offering their help to break the Union apart and reestablish Boer sovereignty in the Transvaal and the Orange Free State.) South Africa did participate eventually on the Allied side in the war, but in several postwar elections old and bitter conflicts between the Boers and the British were revived. Poor Afrikaners felt the need for greater protection from the competition of the blacks, and they did not trust the moderate politicians in power or the English-speaking elite that controlled South African business to look out for them. Despite their deeply ingrained conservatism, Afrikaners supported the creation of state-owned industries, such as the South African Iron and Steel Corporation, as a means of guaranteeing jobs and economic security for their own community. The Afrikaners were increasingly migrating into South Africa's cities from the countryside, as a result of the drought and depression of the 1930s, and in the urban areas they felt all the more need for protection against discrimination.

Again, with the outbreak of World War II, the white South African consensus was tested, and it almost failed. Afrikaner extremists expressed an open sympathy for some of Hitler's ideas, and when Parliament voted narrowly to enter the war on Britain's side, as Smuts had advocated, a key Afrikaner nationalist politician, J. B. M. Hertzog, resigned from the coalition government that had pulled South Africa through the Great Depression. Hertzog had advocated neutrality, but a number of Afrikaner leaders, including key members of the *Broederbond,* or "brotherhood," a semisecret society established in 1918 to promote Afrikaner supremacy, went further. Pro-Nazi organizations engaged in anti-British propaganda, carried out sabotage attempts, and otherwise tried to destroy the morale of the South African troops fighting on the Allied side. Some of these overt Nazi sympathizers, including a future South African prime minister, John Vorster, and other future cabinet ministers, were interned by the pro-British South African government during the war as security risks.

Afrikaner nationalism had grown in the interwar period and was now complemented by effective political organization. Soon after the war, in the 1948 election, the National party, previously a minority faction, managed to unite most elements of Afrikanerdom under a single banner. A large number of blacks had migrated to the cities, the crime rate was up, and African organizations were demanding a better break; poor whites were again feeling threatened. Campaigning on a platform that promised more rigid racial separation—apartheid—and white domination, the National party leader, Daniel F. Malan, came to power. At last the Boers had their revenge, and they set about restructuring the country's laws to take care of old grievances and fears.

The National party was imbued with all of the traditional anxiety and zeal of the *trekboers,* plus new international political concerns. The Dutch Reformed Church had provided a theological justification for "separate development" as God's will, and to do anything but enforce the doctrine strictly, the new rulers believed, would simply play into the hands of the godless Communists, who wanted access to South Africa's riches. The Afrikaner nationalists saw all this not just as a matter of racial superiority, but more important, as an issue of the survival of a people on a continent and in a world they knew was becoming increasingly hostile to them. Unlike the majority of English-speaking South Africans (many of whom retained British passports), the Afrikaners had no place else to go, no other country in the world where they or their children's generation would be welcome to flee in the event of a crisis. They were by now entirely different and distinct from the people in their ancestral homeland of the Netherlands; indeed, the Dutch scorned and mocked the Afrikaners and their language and, along with other Europeans, treated them as political and moral outcasts.

The Afrikaners' resentments toward their compatriots of English origin were straightforward and relatively simple to understand. They believed that the British had moved in on a land that the Afrikaners' forefathers had conquered, tamed, and rendered productive; that the British had displayed a cultural and social insensitivity almost unequaled in the annals of modern history; and that they had taken far more out of the country than they had ever put in. But the Afrikaners outnumbered the English, and were confident of their continuing ability to outsmart them politically.

The Afrikaners' feelings toward the African people who surrounded them were far more complex and ambivalent. They were, above all, dependent on the labor of these people who, according to their interpretation of the Bible, were inferior infidels. Admittedly, despite all the outward manifestations of contempt, some Afrikaners were awed by the Africans' command of their environment. And although the government exuded a complete certainty of its ability to control these people with darker skin, it was profoundly frightened by them. The fear produced a phenomenon well known in Afrikaner history: the retreat into the *laager*, the closed circle of covered wagons. Internal opponents were denounced as treasonous, external ones as enemies. In a particularly self-defeating exercise, the new government even curtailed white immigration from overseas, lest it pollute the *volk* with foreign, liberal, not to say subversive, ideas.

Within a few years, the main pillars of the apartheid system were erected. One of the first consisted of the Prohibition of Mixed Marriages Act of 1949 and the Immorality Acts of 1950 and 1957, which dealt with the Afrikaners' most fundamental concerns. They made marriages across racial lines illegal, and made sexual relations between whites and nonwhites a crime punishable by up to seven years in prison. In forays to enforce that law, South African police would actually lurk outside bedroom windows, stage raids on illicit sexual encounters, and attempt to persuade lovers to testify against one another in the hope of leniency from the courts.

The number of people prosecuted under the Immorality Acts has declined substantially over the years, but in 1981 there were still 212 prosecutions, mostly involving whites and Africans, and 124 of them resulted in convictions. In rare cases, mixed couples managed to circumvent the laws. In the conservative northern Transvaal town of Pietersburg, for example, live the notorious Ian and Sherrin Whiteley, he white and she Indian. When first detected as a couple in the late 1960s, they were arrested on an Immorality Act charge, but acquitted for lack of evidence after he spent three months in jail. They fled to Botswana, where they married, then moved on to Norway and to Britain. When Ian Whiteley wrote to the South African government a few years ago, offering to be reclassified as a nonwhite so that he and his wife could come home and live together, he received a letter back from the prime minister's office, saying that reclassification would not be possible but they were welcome to return as a couple anyway. This they did in 1981 and took up residence in a house at the edge of an Indian township near Pietersburg called Nirvana, where they found themselves treated with benign curiosity.

The Population Registration Act of 1950 introduced a system under which every person in the country would receive an official "racial classification." Boards were established to review ambiguous cases. Coloureds with especially dark skin had to live with the fear that they might be demoted to the category of Africans, and ostensibly white people who had kinky hair and a dark complexion might be asked to prove that they were not actually Coloureds. Neighbors and friends were welcome to raise doubt about each other's background, and the eventual rulings often separated husbands from wives and parents from children. Should a couple, one African and one white, have an illegal child, for example, they would have to live separately when they got out of prison and the child would have to be raised as a Coloured.

It has always been the children of South Africa who have suffered most from the classification laws. Those of ambiguous origins are liable to be taunted by their playmates or schoolmates for being too dark, too light, or otherwise different. A voluntary, unofficial school run by the Good Shepherd Community Center in the Coloured township of Eldorado Park near Soweto is filled with dozens of problem cases—mostly the children of mixed, unmarried couples, who cannot enroll in any official school at all because their classification is uncertain or under dispute. One by one, as their cases are settled (mostly with the declaration that they are "Coloured"), they set out on a track that will determine where they may live and how they spend the rest of their lives.

Many people seek to modify their classifications, because of the burdens they impose on them. In one recent twelve-month period monitored by the Institute for Race Relations, 1,189 people applied for an official change and 997 of them were successful (mostly Coloureds seeking to be declared white). One government proclamation issued in 1959 turned the classification of Coloureds into a precise and fine art, providing seven subcategories: Cape Coloured, Cape Malay, Griqua, Indian, Chinese, "other Asiatic," and "other Coloured."

The Group Areas Act, also passed in 1959 and revised seven years later, provided for the designation of every square inch of South African land for the exclusive use of one racial group or another. Not surprisingly, the cities were almost entirely reserved for whites—even the parts of them that had long been inhabited by other people. As the act was gradually implemented over a period of decades, great disruption occurred. Those few neighborhoods where members of different groups had lived peacefully side by side were destroyed. The government confiscated property and carried out the forced "removal" of people found to be living in the wrong area. One study estimated that 3.5 million black people were "removed" during a twenty-year period, most of them required to settle in rural "homelands" far from the places that they had actually come to regard as home. Another two million or more are scheduled for forced resettlement in the years to come.

One of the most tragic events was the destruction of "District Six" in Cape Town, the traditional heart of that city's Coloured community, and the expulsion of its residents to the more distant, dusty Cape Flats. The government also interpreted the Group Areas Act as requiring the elimination of small "black spots" in officially white areas, such as an anomalous African-owned suburb just west of central Johannesburg named Sophiatown, and rural villages like Mogopa or Driefontein, where for generations Africans had cultivated land they believed themselves to own. In all such cases, the Africans, regardless of their age or the state of their health, were forcibly resettled and the land was cleared and turned over to whites.

One of the major flaws in the Group Areas Act was that it failed to make provisions for urban blacks. Since the dogma of apartheid required that they be officially regarded as merely "temporary sojourners" in the cities, Africans working there generally had to rent unsatisfactory housing from local administration boards, without any hope of owning the premises where they lived. With nearly half of the country's black population urbanized, however, the illusion that they were temporarily in the cities became ever more difficult to maintain. One major concession in the early 1980s was a ruling permitting some Africans to purchase a ninety-nine-year "leasehold" on houses, though still not a "freehold" of the type allowed to other groups.

Closely related to the Group Areas Act is the complex web of regulations that constitute South Africa's system of "influx control"—regulating the travel of black people between areas, and especially into the cities. The requirement that Africans carry passes, and obtain official permits for their various movements and activities, gave the government a theoretical knowledge of where everybody was and what he was doing. According to the latest version of the pass laws, only Africans born in urban areas or those who had worked for the same employer for ten years or for different employers for fifteen years were entitled to live permanently in the cities and towns. All other Africans present were regarded as "migrant workers" and were allowed into the cities on one-year permits; it was difficult to establish permanence, because of the requirement that blacks in the cities break their stay for a month every year.

In a 1983 decision on a case brought by an African machine operator, the South African supreme court ruled that permanence could be established with ten consecutive years' worth of one-year permits, regardless of the annual month away, and that after that time African workers were entitled to bring their families to the city. The government soon amended the law, however, to require that people in those circumstances must have "approved" housing before their families can join them; the waiting list for such housing goes back almost fifteen years. Despite limited reform in some areas, the government also increased the penalties for illegal migration to the cities and for helping others to circumvent the rules. Influx control remained a key part of the system, even after other fundamentals began to be questioned.

One early device for preserving apartheid was the Suppression of Communism Act of 1950, establishing the basic process for banning organizations and individuals, which would later become broader and more elaborate under the Internal Security Act of 1976. Under these laws, as well as the Sabotage Act of 1962 and the Terrorism Act of 1967, the government gave itself the power to detain people indefinitely without trial and to conduct ambitious investigative and surveillance activities in the name of security. Critics claimed that despite South Africa's pretense of operating according to Western legal traditions, it gradually became a police state. The security police, virtually unsupervised by their superiors and unchecked by the courts, frequently intimidated ordinary citizens in their quest for information and sometimes employed torture during the interrogation of prisoners.

The Bantu Education Act of 1953 saw to it that Africans would receive an education different from, and inferior to, that of whites and other groups. The limited representation—by whites, of course—of Coloureds, Indians, and, in some cases, Africans in national and local legislative bodies was gradually eliminated by other laws. Another major ingredient in the structure was the Industrial Conciliation Act, passed in 1956, which did the opposite of what was implied by its title. It established "job reservation," the process by which all jobs were limited to members of specified races, the best and most remunerative categories being reserved for whites. Meanwhile, the government refused to institute a minimum wage for Africans, who were at the same time forbidden to strike. Job reservation eventually caused major problems for South Africa's industrial economy, but it kept working-class Afrikaners happy.

Through the 1950s and 1960s, under a series of prime ministers faithful to the doctrine of apartheid, the National party extended the reach and streamlined the operation of this elaborate system of discrimination. It made South Africa unique in the world for the extent to which a person's life was determined by his or her color. Satisfying the dream of one of the major architects of the system, Dr. Hendrik Verwoerd, and underlining their distinctness and separateness as a nation, South African whites voted narrowly in October 1960 to adopt a new constitution and make the country a republic. That decision took effect in March 1961, and a few months later South Africa withdrew from the British Commonwealth. Its isolation was thus guaranteed.

South Africa's isolation—its almost universal condemnation by the outside world—often causes its spokesmen to defend themselves by accusing others. The skill of mocking those who try to occupy a higher moral ground is actually taught. One incident that occurred in 1978 is especially telling.

At a training session for South African diplomats in the inner sanctum of the magnificent Union buildings in Pretoria, tempers are high. The diplomats, self-consciously sharpening their debating skills for overseas encounters, demand that a visiting American justify the "selective application" of Jimmy Carter's human rights policy to South Africa and a few other vulnerable states. What about violations of civil liberties elsewhere on the African continent? ("Have you heard the name Idi Amin?" is a favorite question.) And why don't American officials, and the American press, say more about the slaughter going on in Communist-ruled Cambodia? Why pick on South Africa?

Then comes the knockout punch: "Brrrrrrowning, Montana." It is the American desk officer from the Department of Foreign Affairs, speaking up from the back of the room. "What about Browning, Montana? How do you explain that?"

The American visitor is bewildered. He has never heard of Browning, Montana, and therefore can offer no explanation for anything. But the questioner is not satisfied; he suspects a cover-up.

Subsequent research explains the reference: South African diplomats have made themselves experts on the mistreatment of American Indians, a subject they feel provides effective ammunition for returning the fire of Americans who are critical of the South African political system. It gives them an opportunity to say, in effect, "Clean up your own backyard first, before you complain about us." In 1977, a white South African on a lecture tour to defend apartheid happened through Browning, a small town in western Montana. There he heard about the case of Clayton Hirst, a Blackfoot Indian who had died in a nearby jail in 1975, under mysterious circumstances, just two days after being arrested on charges of malicious mischief and booked on suspicion of burglary. Hirst's family claimed that he was murdered by his white jailers, and they sued the local officials in federal court for a breach of his civil rights.

This controversy on the American frontier was dutifully and amusedly reported by the lecturer to his government. Tired of hearing from others about Steve Biko (the leader of the South African "Black Consciousness" movement who died of brain damage in detention in 1977, after being beaten, denied medical treatment, and transported across the country nude and shackled), the South Africans wanted to do with Clayton Hirst and anyone else they could find what the Soviet Union once did with Angela Davis: create an international embarrassment for the United States. The people in the Union buildings thought that would help their own case in the forum of world opinion.

One of the central features in the grand design of the South African apartheid system is the creation of "homelands"—defined by tribe—in which the vast majority of the country's African population are to become citizens and supposedly find their true political, economic, and cultural fulfillment. At an earlier stage, when South Africa's rulers paid less attention to public relations and referred to all Africans as "Bantu," these were known as the "bantustans." According to the official ideology, only in such small "nation-states," removed from the urban areas, can each black group live peacefully, following its own customs, unbothered and undominated by any others. Once the land has been designated for each homeland—altogether, 13 percent of the country's land for 87 percent of its Africans, or 64 percent of the whole population—the white government looks for a suitably compliant black "leader" to put in charge or help elect. With advice, funds, and often manpower, from Pretoria, the new little pseudocountry moves toward "independence." It gets its own flag, national anthem, and other trappings of nationhood. Before, during, and after that process, the South African government rounds up members of the appropriate group, especially those in or near the cities who are unemployed or otherwise "unproductive," and ships them "home." Along the way, they lose their citizenship in South Africa.

The homelands are generally pathetic. The territory (often noncontiguous bits) selected for them is usually unproductive scrubland that can scarcely sustain the people already there, let alone the new ones who have been banished from the cities. An original plan to create booming "border industries" that would employ homeland blacks has largely failed, and so most of the new arrivals sit idle, living in inadequate shelters or resettlement camps, struggling to feed their children, and dreaming of ways to get back to the city. Those who do go back may end up in a squalid squatters' camp, where they live in dread of being picked up by the police and banished again.

Although some of the homelands have elaborate charters and written guarantees of the freedom their people will enjoy—meant to distinguish them from South Africa proper—the reality is sometimes very harsh. The homeland administrations often outdo the government in Pretoria with their bannings of individuals and organizations, the detention of opposition figures without trial, and the virtually unrestrained actions of security police. Recognized by no other government in the world outside South Africa, the homeland leaders occasionally seek to prove their legitimacy by putting on a show of opposition to their sponsors, but in reality most are desperate to win and keep the approval of the South African government.

The one homeland that was originally regarded as having a better chance than most to catch on and succeed was the one that, in 1976, became the first to accept its "independence," the Transkei, along the Indian Ocean coast between East London and Durban. It had long been regarded by many people as a distinct area in its own right, a genuine center of Xhosa culture, and the

British had at one point considered making it an independent country. It seemed at first as if the South Africans would encourage the Transkei to emulate Lesotho (formerly Basutoland), with which Transkei also shared a border. Lesotho, while dependent on South Africa because of its landlocked position, ran its own affairs; it maintained a distinct (and, from a South African view, prickly) foreign policy. Transkei could do nothing of the kind. It was an utter failure, and as its economic difficulties mounted, its "chief minister"-turned-president, Kaiser Matanzima (who had held on to power by locking up most of the people who opposed independence until the referendum on that issue was over), looked for someone to blame.

To South Africa's astonishment, Matanzima decided in 1978 to break "diplomatic relations" with Pretoria, and he announced plans to petition the International Court of Justice "on behalf of the oppressed black population of South Africa." The petition was never filed, but from his capital of Umtata, Matanzima kept up his refrain. By 1983 he was deriding the "so-called independence" that had been accepted by Transkei and some of the other homelands as a "mockery of true freedom." The attacks were so shrill, especially at the time of the 1983 referendum on South Africa's new constitution, that some people suspected Matanzima of following an elaborate script written in Pretoria to demonstrate that the homeland leaders were not under the effective control of the central government.

In other respects, Matanzima behaved in a way that made South Africa itself look like a utopia. He kept the Transkei under an almost continuous state of emergency, prohibiting students and other potential adversaries of his regime from congregating in public places or leaving their homes at any time except to attend school or church. To be absent from classes, or to advocate a boycott of them in any form, was made a crime. Any police officer could arrest or detain any Transkeian or visiting foreigner at will, and those convicted of contravening the emergency regulations could never be admitted to school there again or be employed as a teacher or lecturer at any Transkeian institution. Searches and seizures could be carried out without restriction, and when any case was in doubt, the burden of proof was on the accused. The only justification cited was the threat from the African National Congress.

In other homelands, too, the stories of repression and arbitrary action were legion. In Venda, one of the least viable of the pseudostates, as the elections approached in which a decision on independence would be taken, the chief minister detained indefinitely more than fifty people, including prominent legislators and magistrates. In Ciskei, the other homeland set aside for the Xhosa people—separated from the Transkei by a thirty-mile-wide "white corridor" of choice land—the "president for life," Lennox Sebe, maintained a reign of terror with the apparent connivance of the South African authorities. According to a report by the Centre for Applied Legal Studies at the University of the Witwatersrand in Johannesburg, Sebe's police and vigilantes routinely arrested opponents and took them to a soccer stadium, where they were beaten, tortured, and, in some cases, raped. When the leaders of various unions launched a boycott of a bus company partly owned by the Ciskei government, they were all detained, and the authorities conducted house-to-house searches for the members of one union; other people were interrogated and forced to pledge their allegiance to Sebe. Even Sebe's younger brother Charles, the Ciskei's director of state security, who carried out some of the most draconian measures and offered to help the South Africans conduct raids into neighboring countries, found himself in prison as a result of a family feud.

The most hopeless homeland—the smallest and the poorest and the one that most discredits the government's policy—is perhaps KwaNdebele, a collection of camps about sixty miles north of Pretoria to which at least two hundred thousand (some believe twice that many) Ndebele people have been "removed" in recent years. Because most of their ancestors had migrated to Zimbabwe in the nineteenth century, the Ndebele remaining in South Africa really had no geographical base or cultural center, but were scattered throughout the country, many of them on the tiny "black spots" in white areas that seemed especially irritating to the government. The area now arbitrarily designated as their home is totally arid and barren, capable of producing little more than dust. Yet the leader of KwaNdebele and the members of his "cabinet," mostly black entrepreneurs who stand to make money from granting business licenses in their new "country," insisted they would seek independence at the earliest possible date.

But, say the most ardent members of the South African government, there is at least one new, artificially created nation, BophutaTswana, the homeland for the Tswana people, that is actually on its way to success. "I tell you, that country will work," insisted Barend du Plessis, former deputy minister of foreign affairs (and later finance minister), pointing to the BophutaTwsana entry in the display of miniature flags that has become standard equipment on the desks of ranking South African officials. "Those people don't want to become part of white South Africa again, and they don't want to be ruled by Gatsha Buthelezi." (The threat of domination by the Zulu, South Africa's largest and traditionally most powerful black tribe, has been used effectively by the government to persuade others to accept separate status. National party spokesmen have especially played on the fears of members of other tribes that Buthelezi, the current Zulu leader, might be in charge of a black-ruled South Africa—even as they promote Buthelezi as a moderate alternative to more radical black spokesmen.)

It is not immediately obvious why BophutaTswana should be an exception to the rule, since it is composed of seven scattered fragments of territory, six of them near the Botswana border and the other two hundred miles away; however, a visit to its main attraction, the entertainment center of Sun City, offers something of a hint.

On the two-and-a-half-hour drive from Johannesburg to Sun City, the traveler is liable to feel as if he is doing something both illicit and ridiculous. There is a temptation to pretend one is leaving South Africa; but the fiction becomes harder to maintain as one repeatedly crosses into and out of BophutaTswana along the way. (The road was built more logically than the border was drawn, and there is no way to distinguish between the homeland and the mother country except for the minute signs off to the side, indicating "RSA border" or "BophutaTswana border.") After crossing the Crocodile River, its banks lined with blue gum trees, and sweeping through the boomtown of Rustenberg (which looks as though it could be on the California frontier of a hundred years ago), one discovers a sandstone pleasure palace rising out of nowhere at the foot of the Megaliesburg mountain range. It is at this legendary spot that Johannesburg promoter Sol Kerzner, of the Southern Suns hotel chain, put his boot in the sand in the late 1970s and said, "This is it."

Sun City is like a microcosm of Las Vegas, but more garish

234

and more intense, with everything condensed under two roofs. There, accessible in just an evening's excursion from Johannesburg, is an astonishing array of entertainments and experiences forbidden in South Africa proper: slot machines, a gambling casino complete with roulette wheels and blackjack tables, pornographic films, chorus-line extravaganzas, and public interracial mingling. Some of the white South Africans, dressed for excitement, seem to be having the time of their lives, while others, with dour, disapproving expressions on their faces, wander through all this looking bewildered, almost frightened. The centerpiece of the complex is the "superbowl," an indoor amphitheater where internationally famous entertainers come to perform. Because they can participate in a convenient charade and make believe they are not in South Africa, the likes of Frank Sinatra and Liza Minnelli are easy to attract to Sun City. Sinatra's visit in 1982 had all South Africa in a whirl, and his performances sold out far in advance. (He was said to gross $1.4 million for a two-week stand.) Other well-known figures from the worlds of sport, entertainment, and business are drawn to Sun City by golf tournaments with a million-dollar purse and glittery water sports events on its artificial lake. Starved for exposure to the famous and the celebrated, South Africans turn out in droves.

On the occasion of my visit, the star attraction was American country-and-western singer Dolly Parton, who has an avid following among South Africans, especially working-class Afrikaners who can identify with her songs and stories about a difficult childhood in a large, poor family. Parton did not appear to know exactly where she was, although she made a decent attempt to master the local lingo, asking her audience whether they lived "out there in the bushes." When she belted out her famous ballads, strutting back and forth in her most revealing costumes, she brought the house down. So did her warmup act, a stand-up comic popular in the "borscht belt" of the Catskill Mountains of New York and among the large Jewish community of Johannesburg.

Built at a cost of $85 million, Sun City has been a phenomenal success, not only for its investors but also for the treasury of the Republic of BophutaTswana, which is guaranteed a percentage of all the money taken in there. After platinum—30 percent of the world's supply comes from South African–controlled mines

inside the homeland, which also yield chrome and vanadium—
Sun City is the state's second largest money-earner. This financial
boon has allowed BophutaTswana to cut back to 6 percent (from
an initial figure of 30 percent) the amount of its revenue that
comes directly from the South African government.

That modicum of financial independence has permitted BophutaTswana's president, Lucas Mangope, to insist that the homeland he runs be taken more seriously than most. Its unique constitution, drafted by a group of South African legal scholars, includes
a bill of rights that would be regarded as subversive if it were proposed in South Africa itself. Mangope, insisting that he wanted
"to use apartheid to abolish apartheid," also appointed a commission to review all the laws inherited from South Africa with a
view toward eliminating discriminatory provisions, including the
ban on sexual contacts between races. His claim that he was creating a multiracial society was boosted when the mostly white town
of Mafeking petitioned to become part of BophutaTswana; but
Mangope lost some credibility when it was realized that the prior
government experience of one of the three whites named to his
cabinet was as a member of Ian Smith's white-supremacist regime
in Rhodesia.

In the capital of Mmabatho, Mangope built a monumental
headquarters for his government, and he took every other step he
could think of to make his homeland seem separate. There was a
foreign minister and a South African "ambassador" to Bophuta-
Tswana, a member of Parliament who had irritated Prime Minister P. W. Botha and, as punishment, was forced to accept the undesirable assignment. Most of the Tswana people in South Africa,
however, still refused to have anything to do with the homeland
that was supposed to be theirs. Among those Africans who did
live in BophutaTswana, or got thrown inside its borders by the
South African authorities, the majority remained dirt poor and
saw little chance to change their status. Of those who had jobs,
two-thirds commuted daily to work in South Africa.

The question is whether BophutaTswana, by being discern-
ibly different from most of the other homelands and by achieving
a modest degree of legitimacy in some areas, would have a permanent effect on South Africa. It seemed unlikely that the South
African government would permit the "consolidation" of Bophuta-
Tswana's territory into a single, contiguous unit anytime soon, or

that it would permit the fragments directly along the Botswana border to be incorporated into that real country, as has occasionally been suggested. Yet, Sun City in particular (along with similar resorts in some of the other homelands) could have a subtly subversive influence on the strict Calvinist nature of South African society. In a minor way, perhaps, narrow-minded whites would have their perspectives altered by mixing, whether intimately or at a greater distance, with the middle-class blacks also drawn there; the discovery of similarities could do damage to the official ideology concerning the differences. And some optimists believed that the BophutaTswana bill of rights, if allowed to function effectively, could set a precedent that would be difficult to disturb. But these were slender hopes that could take many years to be realized.

Cape Town is the city, and the setting, that used to be a physical embodiment of whatever optimistic hopes remained for South Africa. It is incomparably beautiful—mountains rising in its midst, and the finest Cape Dutch architecture serving as a reminder of Afrikaner strength and creativity.

Cape Town was long the place where people mingled more successfully despite the harsh rules and laws—where they sat together on buses notwithstanding differences of color; where the railroad station was integrated one day when some Africans and Coloureds simply decided to walk through the white lobby; and where the artistic abilities of Malays and other nonwhites were appreciated and exalted. Cape Town University was a "liberal" institution long before that was fashionable—right-wingers still consider it a hotbed—and even today it is the center of one of South Africa's few communities of Bohemians and nonconformists.

Even while Parliament was in session in Cape Town, making repressive laws, the townspeople always had a capacity to observe and to mock those laws at the same time. Perhaps the best contemporary example is the little café at the top of Table Mountain, at the end of the cable-car run, where people of all races are able to eat together in the same room and look out over one of the most breathtaking views in the world. The reason is explained in a tiny message on white paper, posted on the door to the café: "This is an international restaurant." (International restaurant is a category invented in the 1970s, at a time when South Africa was

trying to reach out to the world, to prevent embarrassing incidents involving foreign diplomats and businessmen.)

However, the Cape Town example has begun to fade. The
razing of District Six, the old Coloured section, and the Malay
quarter was trauma enough. Then, because there were no official
African areas close to the city, during the 1970s homeless and
mostly unemployed families that were resisting removal to the
homelands began to collect in squatters' camps at a spot known as
Crossroads. For a time they lived amid squalor and disease, and
the government, acutely aware of the additional damage Crossroads could do to the country's image, tried every possible method
of dispersing the squatters, at one point even setting fire to their
tar-paper shacks. But the people—eventually thirty thousand or
more—really had no place to go, and the attention given to their
plight by the press and by domestic and international organizations, especially church groups, restricted the government's options.

Before long, Crossroads became an established, well-organized community, complete with electricity and water service, a
primary school, a clinic where white medical students from Cape
Town University provided free care, and shops where one could
have shoes repaired or buy used furniture. After a group of elderly
residents set up a system of regular day-and-night patrols, crime
dwindled as a problem. In fact, Crossroads became so crowded
that another community developed down the road, called "New
Crossroads." In both places, almost every home, however makeshift, had a number—an address of sorts—that represented the
family's rank on the waiting list for a place in one of the official
townships for Africans. Some of the numbers went into the thousands.

After a third squatters' camp emerged in the vicinity, the
government panicked, sending in police and demolition squads to
destroy the makeshift shanties built by black people with nowhere else to go. Some rebuilt their shelters time after time, but it
was usually only a few days before they were torn down again.
In the aftermath of some of the raids, small children whose homes
had been destroyed while their parents were at work were left to
wander the streets alone. Early in 1985, after a clash with police
had cost the lives of eighteen squatters, the government finally relented and said that about forty thousand of the estimated hundred

thousand people in the Crossroads camps could stay. Gerrit Viljoen, the minister of cooperation, development and education,
agreed to permit the "upgrading and development" of Crossroads
as a permanent community, but insisted that the rest of the squatters would have to move to the new township of Khayelitsha, farther from Cape Town.

It is not very far away in miles from Crossroads, but Stellenbosch, an idyllic little town nestled between the mountains of the
Cape, is a world apart. Here some of the early settlers established
themselves and their vineyards, and not all that much has changed.
Wildflowers, thousands of varieties, dot every hillside. Here also
sits the university that is today the bastion of "liberal" Afrikanerdom—the people who, for the most part, believe that the South
African system must be made more humane and internationally
acceptable, but who are still reluctant to share power with the
blacks. Six consecutive prime ministers of South Africa were Stellenbosch alumni, and so the place would be taken seriously for
that reason, if no other. When one talks of Stellenbosch being "integrated," it means that students from white English-speaking
families have begun to attend (a fashionable and clever thing to
do for those who want to win acceptance among the Afrikaner
elite). In recent years the university has also begun admitting a
small number of carefully selected blacks, and the joke, told with
an uneasy laugh, is that Stellenbosch is just hedging its bets to be
sure it produces another prime minister someday.

The student union building is an open, free-flowing place fea-
turing rock 'n' roll, cheeseburgers, and Coca-Cola. Were it not for
the fact that nearly everything is written and spoken in Afrikaans,
it could be in southern California. In fact, most of today's students
at Stellenbosch, by all accounts and appearances, seem more interested in sports than in politics; their world appears to be an
optimistic one, undisturbed by any outward sign that South Africa
might be in genuine trouble.

One sure symbol of optimism is that the university recently
established a faculty of Afrikaans journalism. In the old Cape
Dutch house where it is based, a group of Stellenbosch professors—self-proclaimed "court intellectuals"—gathered one morning
to discuss with a visitor their vision of South Africa's future. In
heavily accented English, they boasted of the healthy, vibrant

debate in National party circles, the only circles, they said, within
which the country's policies could be constructively developed. In
fact, suggested one professor gravely, as the others nodded their
concurrence, the time may soon come when South Africa—after
decades of portraying itself as the last bastion of Western democratic principles in Africa—must become a one-party state, rather
like many of the black-ruled neighbors to the north whom it has
mocked.

If anything, the trend has been running in the opposite direction in recent years. Despite its ideology of militant unity on behalf of the *volk* and the *vaderland*, the Afrikaner community has
been deeply split over fundamental issues, and the gap may now
be too wide to repair. There had always been conflicts and rivalries
within the relatively small Afrikaner universe—the *Voortrekkers*
had differences over strategy and direction, and every attempt at
Boer self-government had to deal with a strong streak of individ-
ualism—but the latest division is probably more severe and profound than any previous one.

The argument began to emerge in the late 1960s, when
Willem de Klerk, a member of a prominent Afrikaner political
family and then a professor at Potchefstroom University, coined a
distinction between what he saw as two quite different world
views emerging among his people: a *verligte*, or enlightened, attitude, which perceived a need for white South Africans to adopt
a more benign and generous posture toward other people at home
and toward the world outside; and a *verkrampte*, or closed and
narrow, attitude, an ultraconservative approach, tinged with racism, which posited that the Afrikaners were God's chosen people
who need not make concessions to anyone.

The concept found an application in almost every area of
white South African life, entering into the conversation even of
children and lending itself easily to parody and humor. English-
speaking whites borrowed it, too, as a way of characterizing differences among themselves. There was a *verligte* lifestyle and a
verkrampte one, and most people instinctively knew the difference. It extended to the way people dressed, the kind of car they
drove, and how they spent their spare time. It had parallels in
South African religious life, with one branch of the Dutch Reformed Church collaborating more and more with the government

and the other expressing growing concern about the morality of apartheid. There were limits to the distinction, of course, and as de Klerk wrote, soon after being relieved of his job as editor of the nationalist newspaper *Die Transvaler* (on the grounds that he had gone too *verligte* himself), "The most *verlig* Afrikaner is not an integrationist. And who could be one in the face of the realities of South Africa?"

The social, philosophical, and religious connotations of the dispute between *verligtheid* and *verkramptheid* were translated into the practical political arena shortly after the resignation of Prime Minister John Vorster in 1978, in the midst of a scandal over the use of secret South African government slush funds to influence events at home and abroad. Vorster's successor was Pieter W. Botha, the National party leader in the Cape Province, who, despite his background as minister of defense, began saying a number of distinctly *verligte*-sounding things, as he set out to broaden the government's base. White South Africans would have to "adapt or die," he asserted, suggesting that even the Immorality Act might have to be reexamined in the light of new circumstances and attitudes. "There is a problem when people [of different races] really love each other," he said. (A parliamentary select committee examining the Immorality and Mixed Marriages acts declared in 1984 that they could no longer "be justified on scriptural or other grounds," and in April 1985, the government said it had decided to abolish the laws forbidding marriage and sexual relations across the racial lines.)

The *verkrampte* were infuriated. For a time, it seemed as if Botha's heresies would breathe new life into the Reconstituted National party, a small group on the right led by an ideologue named Jaap Marais, whose ideas harked back to the extremism expressed by Afrikaner dissenters during World War II. That might have helped Botha, because the HNP (the Afrikaans acronym for Marais's group) was so far out on the fringe as to discredit itself. But a more serious challenge emerged when Andries P. Treurnicht, a cabinet minister and the leader of the National party's influential Transvaal provincial caucus, walked out of Botha's government to form a new Conservative party, which he promised would fight to uphold the complete orthodox doctrine of apartheid in its original form. Taking seventeen other members of Parliament with him, Treurnicht had the nucleus of a major opposition movement; when he won a parliamentary by-election and his followers made a credible showing in several others, he began to loom as a formidable rival.

The issue was truly joined in 1982, when Botha and his minister for constitutional affairs, Jan Christiaan Heunis, unveiled their "new dispensation," a constitution that would create additional, separate chambers of Parliament for Coloureds and Indians (but no such participation in the central government for Africans). Each new chamber was assigned jurisdiction over its own community's affairs, but "general" legislation affecting the country as a whole would have to pass through all three, and the white chamber was assured a majority over the other two combined.

The new constitution was an ingenious piece of work, produced by Afrikaner academics groping for a way to create an impression of limited "power-sharing" for liberal and outside consumption without actually surrendering the white domination that was fundamental to the South African system. Critical to the new plan was the assumption that the country's 2.8 million Coloureds and 870,000 Indians would still be willing to go along with the government's divide-and-rule tactics, despite the risk that the large African majority would turn their wrath against them. The government was also gambling that the Coloureds and the Indians, once co-opted into the new scheme, would consider themselves to have a stake in the system—that they could be recruited and, above all, conscripted into the military to defend it.

In fact, as it was designed, the new constitution gave very little power to these "brown" minorities. Under its terms, a powerful new "executive president" would rule the country with broad latitude, so long as he enjoyed a majority in the white chamber of Parliament; the minority there would have no way of linking up with the members of the other two chambers to thwart government policy. The president (presumably to be the leader of the National party) was entitled to choose his own cabinet, to decide which issues would go before which chamber of Parliament, and to control a "president's council" to which Coloured and Indian objections to policy would be referred. Still, in white South African terms, Botha had taken a bold step, because, however limited the change might be in the short run, some government officials suggested—and many Afrikaners feared—that it could be the "starting point" in an "open-ended process."

That was just what Treurnicht and his allies warned, and they reviled the new constitution as a "deviation" from the essential framework necessary to preserve white rule; some even called it "white suicide." One of the most galling prospects for them was that there would be Coloured and Indian members of the joint cabinet under the new system. The Conservative party preferred to deal with those two groups by creating homelands for them similar to those for the Africans. For the Afrikaner purists, the essential truth about Botha's reform was that some nonwhites would, for the first time in South African history, be in a position, theoretical or real, to assert authority over some whites. To them, that image was the beginning of the end.

In the November 1983 referendum among white voters on the new constitution, Botha was opposed both by the Conservatives, who thought the reform went too far, and by most members of the Progressive Federal party, who thought it did not go far enough. At the same time, the plan found support from surprising quarters, including parts of the normally antigovernment English-language press, on the theory that it was "a step in the right direction." Some liberals cynically argued that it was worth putting the new system into effect in the precise hope that it would not work, that out of its deadlock or breakdown would emerge some new, more genuinely democratic institutions in which a broader group of South Africans could participate. In the event, between the boost from unexpected allies and the substantial defections from both conservative and liberal groups that opposed the constitution, 65 percent of the white electorate voted to endorse what Botha insisted upon calling his "evolutionary reform." Only in one district in the northern Transvaal was the government narrowly defeated.

Stunning as Botha's initial victory seemed to be, the bitterness of the referendum campaign only reinforced the existence of strong opposition to the government on the right within the Afrikaner community. "We accept the results of the referendum only as a battle lost in the total struggle of our people," said Treurnicht. He worried about the same thing that the liberals hoped for—that Botha, despite his denials, had a "hidden agenda" that would include some access to meaningful political power for Africans, perhaps even a fourth chamber of Parliament in which they could be separately represented. The more bitter became the split in Afrikanerdom, the greater the possibility that Botha might search for new political allies to his left, among English-speaking whites of a progressive bent. In that event, the split among the *volk* might be permanent, and South African white politics irreversibly changed.

The prime minister proceeded immediately to implement his plans, and the leadership of the Coloured Labour party—a previously powerful group that now appeared to represent only a minority of the mixed-race community—made it easier for Botha by deciding to forgo its own referendum and proceed directly to elections for the new Coloured chamber of Parliament. The Indian parties willing to participate in the scheme did the same. When elections for the new Coloured chamber of Parliament were held in August 1984, however, the overall turnout was only 30 percent of registered voters (as low as 4–6 percent in some urban areas, but up to 57 percent in rural districts). Then, in elections for the Indian chamber, 20 percent of the registered voters went to the polls. According to the organizers of the successful election boycott, when those who refused to register were taken into account, the combined rate of participation by Coloureds and Indians was about 16 percent. The government arrested or detained many opponents of the new constitution, but still there were demonstrations at the time of the Coloured and Indian elections. In some black townships, where anger over the new system coincided with other grievances, the protests turned violent. When the police responded with a show of force, dozens of people died.

Blaming the low voter turnout on "intimidation" and the demonstrations on "certain organizations and individuals," the government declared itself to have a sufficient mandate to implement the constitution. It swore in the members of the new chambers of Parliament (one of whom attained victory by receiving only 118 votes) and said that they would now be the sole legitimate representatives of the Coloured and Indian people. P. W. Botha was named executive president by an electoral college that consisted of fifty members of his own party, plus twenty-three Coloureds and thirteen Indians from parties that had chosen to cooperate; he was inaugurated on September 14, 1984.

If there was one place where the debate over P. W. Botha's constitutional reform seemed utterly irrelevant, that was Soweto, the vast township located just outside of Johannesburg that is

really one of Africa's largest cities. It holds more people than entire nearby countries, such as Botswana and Swaziland, probably
upward of two million (although the government's figures are
much lower).

Soweto epitomizes apartheid's failure. By all evidence, the
vast majority of the people who live there regard themselves not
as "temporary sojourners" in white South Africa at all, but as permanent city dwellers, confined to an area where they are doomed
to receive minimal services and maximum harassment. They frequently demonstrate that they do not accept the inferior status
imposed on them by the South African system. For example, when
the government, in what it regarded as an important step toward
self-management by urban blacks, held municipal elections in
Soweto in December 1983, fewer than a thousand people voted.
Among those who did, the majority declined to endorse David
Thebehali, the controversial, government-sponsored black "mayor"
of Soweto—the chairman of its community council—who was so
unpopular that the "city hall" containing his office had to be surrounded with a high chain-link security fence topped with barbed
wire. Although the elections were regarded as meaningless, and
Thebehali's replacement no better, the people of Soweto danced
in the streets to celebrate his defeat.

Until 1976 it was possible to believe that the South African
government would be able to control the situation in Soweto indefinitely. For a community that one might expect to be volatile,
there had been remarkably few protests and little organized resistance over time. But the student riots of that year, in which at
least 575, but perhaps as many as 1,000, people were killed,
seemed to electrify Soweto, and the place has not been the same
since. The initial grievance in 1976 was the requirement that Afrikaans be taught in African schools; students rebelled because they
regarded it as the language of their oppression. A host of other
complaints about the system were put forward during the confrontation. In the process, a generation of young urban Africans
was radicalized, and an unknown number slipped out of the country to seek training as guerrillas.

The government was careful to point out at the time that it
was able to quell the 1976 disturbances without resort to major
force; only the police were involved, and the military troops that
are kept on standby just outside the DMZ-like band of territory

that surrounds Soweto never had to be put into action. The army has occasionally participated in small-scale operations on the fringe of Soweto and other African townships since then, but the overall message is clear: the government feels capable of handling much larger flare-ups before its resources will be strained. Whether it can handle hit-and-run guerrilla assaults is another matter; in one episode during the late 1970s, the people who attacked a large police station in Soweto seemed to have an intimate knowledge of its layout and facilities, allowing them to do substantial damage and escape quickly. Although government security officials believe they know a great deal about what is happening in this gigantic, seething African township, it is at least plausible that an underground political and guerrilla-support network exists which they have been unable to detect and penetrate.

Soweto is in a valley, and often it is covered by a blanket of dense, dark smoke from the coal fires that are used for cooking in many of the smaller houses. To penetrate that blanket and understand what is really underneath is very difficult for an outsider. The busy, industrious, even prosperous side of Soweto is relatively easy to find. It is marked by a proliferation of banks and billboards and Kentucky Fried Chicken franchises. There is a handsome commercial college, built by the American Chamber of Commerce in Johannesburg as evidence of its commitment to progress; and nearby, a boxing academy, sponsored by a Japanese electronics firm that has had particular success with its products in South Africa. In Dube Village, the "Beverly Hills" of Soweto, as it is known locally, the children wear fine clothing and ride their well-polished bicycles alongside their parents' expensive cars on quiet, orderly streets. This is where many of the African businessmen, professionals, and writers of Johannesburg live. (One entrepreneur from this section fled Soweto in a panic during the 1976 riots; he checked into the Carlton Hotel downtown until the crisis subsided.)

A few of the facilities in Soweto are actually the object of considerable local pride. Baragwanath Hospital, for example, is said to be the largest medical facility in the Southern Hemisphere. It is an impressive and well-equipped institution, and although policemen are stationed at some bedsides—a hint of trouble past or future—a visitor cannot help being favorably impressed; clearly, the medical care for blacks is better here than anywhere else on the African continent (although considerably less good than what is available for whites who live in the same country).

One young African physician, who conducted a tour for some visitors, was almost boastful about the hospital where he works, but a bit ashamed to admit that he is still paid significantly less than whites on the staff who have the same training. After spending several hours together, it would have been convenient and natural for us to sit down for a cup of tea; but that is impossible, because the tearooms in the hospital are still segregated. Most white staff members retreat to their own special facilities when they take a break.

It is not that far away to another side of Soweto entirely. In Meadowlands, the people picking through garbage are a sign of a different reality. Elsewhere, the crowded African markets, where herbalists have stalls next to chicken vendors, prompt comparisons with distant places in West Africa. Yet nothing quite compared to the structure off in the corner of a field easily overlooked on quick visits to Soweto—"the milking shed," where for a time entire families lived in filthy stalls once occupied by cattle. Their furniture consisted of seats that had been stripped from buses, trucks, and cars abandoned nearby; other people lived in the shells of those vehicles, using thin blankets to protect them from the jagged edges. The children of this impromptu neighborhood of perhaps fifty people played in stagnant pools of water, their toys fashioned from bits of metal and tires. These families settled in this spot without permission—perhaps they had fled a distant homeland—and they were occasionally routed by the police, only to return when nobody was watching. Finally, "the milking shed" was torn down and its residents dispersed, but other equally grim places became homes for people with nowhere else to go.

Between these extremes lie the great mass of Soweto residents. They include the bulk of Johannesburg's laborers, thousands of them men who are brought in from afar without their families and truly regard themselves as temporary, living as they do in crowded "dormitories" that are breeding grounds of violence. The Zulu among them often intimidate the members of other groups, a tendency that the white government does nothing to discourage and cites as proof that people of different ethnic backgrounds must ultimately live apart from one another. A few of the mining companies, for whom most of these migrants work, have sought to improve their own images and the workers' conditions by building new, more spacious and modern facilities that go by the name of "men's residences"; for the most part, they have to be surrounded by fences to prevent the less fortunate from breaking in. Indeed, violent crime, stoked by heavy drinking and growing drug abuse, is one of Soweto's most severe problems. On a typical weekend, there may be twenty to thirty stabbing deaths. Crime is the scourge of the families that occupy mile after mile of identical, nondescript, small houses erected by the West Rand Administration Board to cope with Soweto's growth—until 1968, that is, when its budget for housing ran out. Growth is officially forbidden in Soweto now, but it continues unabated.

The question of who can really speak for Soweto and its diverse population has proved to be very complicated. Surely it was neither defeated "Mayor" Thebehali nor his successor, Ephraim Tshabalala, a wealthy businessman whose cooperation with what he called "my dear government" was enough to disqualify him among most of his intended public. Tshabalala resigned after only a year in office, when black anger was turned against people cooperating with the government; the man initially picked to be his successor was assassinated in his car, an armed guard at his side, in December 1984.

During the 1976 riots a group of community activists emerged that called itself the Soweto "Committee of Ten." Not having been elected, it had no greater formal claim to legitimacy than any other group, but its militant views appeared to have wide public acceptance.

The committee's best-known spokesman—and the member who seemingly most irritates the government—is Nthatho Motlana, a physician whose successful private medical practice has made it possible for him to build a well-appointed home in the Dube Village section of Soweto. Frequently invited to speak overseas, Motlana was unable to go, because the white government would not give him a passport and wanted him to take one instead from the homeland government of BophutaTswana, to which he has been officially assigned. That he would not do. So he stayed at home, spoke out frequently, and was occasionally detained, as were his wife and son.

Motlana is adamant on the question of African participation in South Africa's central government. "As long as we are told in

no uncertain terms that there is to be no representation for us in
the final seat of authority, there is no way we are going to cooperate," he says, during a pause at his clinic; "we will therefore
remain outside [the system] looking in." But having advocated
negotiations with the government, Motlana is the first to admit
that African spokesmen of his generation and his ilk are doomed
to obsolescence in South Africa, only to be replaced by others
who favor more violent solutions. Eventually, he says, "people like
ourselves [on the Committee of Ten], who had hoped to work
peacefully for change, are going to be consigned to the ash heap,
and the boys with the AK-47s, or some improved form of it, are
going to face up to the need to change things here." He tells the
story of a young man who had been trying to escape South Africa
to join guerrillas outside for training, but was caught, tried, and
sent to Robben Island. Motlana examined him after his release
from five years in prison and was surprised by his own impressions: "It's like nothing has happened to him. He still says that if
he gets half a chance, he is going to get out [and fight]. That is
the kind of spirit you will find here."

This presumed trend toward support for violence has ob-
scured the future prospects of a number of people who have been
prominent spokesmen for Africans for many years. One is Gatsha
Buthelezi, who is both a hereditary and elected leader among the
Zulu and is well known outside South Africa. He has tried to
walk a fine line as "chief minister" of KwaZulu, meant to be the
Zulu homeland, by accepting "self-government" but rejecting "independence." His critics complain that this is a distinction without a significant difference and that Buthelezi has really been
knowingly co-opted into the government's scheme of things.

Buthelezi is a large, imposing man, but until he is provoked
or insulted (as he often is these days), he is also a surprisingly
soft one. He speaks with studied reasonableness, in a tone that
carries a trace of his royal bearing. He is courtly, yet intense.
There are two schools of conventional wisdom about Buthelezi
that vie for acceptance in South Africa today; one, that he is the
only well-known black leader moderate enough and wise enough
to attract a substantial multitribal following and still have some
credibility with the white government; the second, that he is too
moderate and too acceptable to both the white government and
the West to have any credibility left among the increasingly mili-

tant majority of South African blacks. A third view is also possible: that Buthelezi has been the victim of some rather careful and clever government efforts to discredit him; that by subtly helping to promote his image as the government's man, the government has gone a long way toward putting him out of business altogether.

The moderation is certainly there. Buthelezi has forthrightly opposed the imposition of economic sanctions against South Africa, because they would hurt blacks first and in the long run, he believes, would probably not work at all. "It is easier for our black brothers elsewhere in Africa to recommend sanctions," he says, "when they won't have to live with them." He has also argued against the withdrawal of American business and investment in South Africa, because "nothing will come of it"; other Western businesses and banks will gladly and readily replace their U.S. counterparts. But it became difficult for Buthelezi to convince people that he had arrived at that position independently after the South African government began to disseminate his views—complete with his photograph—in advertisements in British and American newspapers.

To the surprise of many people—some accused him of merely trying to reestablish his credibility as a government opponent—Buthelezi took an especially strong stand against the new constitution establishing separate chambers of Parliament for the Coloureds and Indians, and he directly criticized the Reagan administration for encouraging Prime Minister P. W. Botha along that path. "Blacks will now think more earnestly about the seizure of power through the gun," Buthelezi wrote in one article for a U.S. audience, as if to say that Americans would now share the blame for whatever happened. Later, he warned that if white South Africans adopted Botha's new plan, he would reconsider his opposition to international sanctions and disinvestment. One reason for the intensity of Buthelezi's anger was that the decision of the Coloured Labour party to participate in the new constitutional scheme resulted in a weakening, if not the collapse, of the South African Black Alliance, a multi-ethnic coalition he had formed in the late 1970s, composed of his own Zulu-based Inkhata movement, the Labour party, and the Reform party of the Indian community. If that coalition did not remain healthy, Buthelezi lost part of his claim to be a leader of anyone but the more traditional people among South Africa's six million Zulu. Still, after all his bluster, Buthelezi seemed to fall back into line. He visited the United States early in 1985 and after a meeting with Ronald Reagan at the White House, denounced the threat of sanctions against South Africa; his opponents, at home and in the United States, said Buthelezi had become little more than a "messenger" for the South African government.

The apparent decline of moderate leaders like Buthelezi and the potential rejection of those in Motlana's position coincided with substantial growth in the strength of the broadest-based of the South African opposition movements, the African National Congress (ANC). Founded in 1912 on principles of nonviolence espoused by Gandhi and others, the ANC was the original anti-government organization in South Africa. Its mostly middle-class leadership relied for decades on polite forms of protest, including petitions and public meetings; but after the National party came to power in 1948, the ANC gradually turned to boycotts, strikes, and civil disobedience to press its demands for change in an increasingly repressive system. The so-called Defiance Campaign of the early 1950s, conducted jointly with Indians, resulted in at least eighty-five hundred arrests, which in turn led to the political mobilization of tens of thousands of others.

A few years later the ANC adopted its "Freedom Charter," which has had a central place in the philosophy and direction of antigovernment actions ever since. Asserting that "South Africa belongs to all who live in it, black and white," the document went on to endorse such basic democratic ideals as universal suffrage, racial equality, and individual freedoms of the sort enshrined in the American Bill of Rights. It invoked a multiracial struggle against apartheid, based on a fundamental confidence in the rule of law, as defined and elaborated in the Western tradition.

This essentially nonrevolutionary, ecumenical approach was the source of many debates within the ANC during its expansion. One faction, convinced that Africans must do more to help themselves and rely less on alliances with other racial groups, broke off and formed the Pan Africanist Congress (PAC). Others quarreled bitterly and continuously over the role to be played in the ANC by members of the small but militant Communist party of South Africa, which had been formed by whites but became a home for some of the country's best-known black opposition figures. (That issue has never been completely resolved. Some of the most prominent leaders of the ANC were originally anti-Communists, or at least non-Communists, but the group's increasing reliance on the Soviet Union and other Eastern-bloc nations for military and other help moved its center of gravity to the left and gave Communists a more prominent role in its deliberations.) When Chief Albert Luthuli won the Nobel Peace Prize in 1960 for his work as president of the ANC, it was largely on the basis of the organization's broad appeal across racial and ideological barriers.

Another event occurred in 1960 that was to have a major impact on the ANC. In Sharpeville, south of Johannesburg, on March 21, police fired into a crowd of unarmed Africans who were demonstrating against the pass laws, killing 67 and wounding 186, including 40 women and 8 children (most of them shot from behind as they tried to flee). The government reacted to the "Sharpeville Massacre," as it came to be known, not with regret or remorse, but with a further crackdown. It banned both the PAC (the actual organizer of the Sharpeville protest) and the ANC. Forced underground, the ANC formed a military wing, Umkhonto we Sizwe (Spear of the Nation), which exploded its first bombs against symbolic targets in 1961 on a symbolic date—December 16, the Day of the Covenant. But the South African security police became proficient at ferreting out the adversaries of the state during that period, and through the use of informers, found Umkhonto's headquarters in 1963 and arrested, among others, Nelson Mandela, who had become the ANC's underground leader. Mandela was sentenced to life imprisonment.

For a time the ANC seemed to be dormant, the main avenues of African protest against the government becoming labor union activity and the much more highly intellectualized Black Consciousness Movement, whose best-known spokesman was Steve Biko. Black Consciousness emerged as an important philosophical strain in South Africa during the late 1960s. The critical formative event was a walkout in 1968 by black students, led by Biko, from the previously multiracial National Union of South African Students (NUSAS), a radical but generally white-led organization. Biko and his colleagues established the South African Students Organization (SASO) for blacks only, upsetting and insulting their white friends, but asserting that it was time for South

African blacks to escape paternalism, to demonstrate self-reliance and restore self-confidence by establishing their own autonomous organizations. Much of the inspiration for the South African Black Consciousness Movement was drawn from the thinking of American advocates of "black power," such as Malcolm X, Stokely Carmichael, and Eldridge Cleaver.

Biko argued that racism had inflicted profound psychological damage on blacks (whom he defined as including Coloureds and Indians) and that, as a result, "integration" was often "a one-way course, with the whites doing all the talking and the blacks listening." His slogan was "Black man, you're on your own." After blacks and whites had each done the necessary work to fight racism in their own communities, Biko believed, they could come together again to build the nonracial South Africa of the future. Black Consciousness represented a new kind of threat both to the apartheid system and to its liberal critics.

After the Soweto uprising of 1976 and a government crackdown in 1977 against Black Consciousness organizations and moderate African opposition figures, the ANC began to experience a resurgence. Its ranks swelled by veterans of Soweto, it established camps to train guerrillas in Angola and Tanzania and mapped out routes for their reinfiltration into South Africa; it also appeared to strengthen its clandestine network within the country. Alongside its continued external political and diplomatic efforts, the ANC launched an "armed struggle" inside, particularly against military and police targets. Most of the attacks were small-scale—and many may have gone unannounced by the government and unnoticed by the press—until the ANC struck at the heart of South African ingenuity in mid-1980, when it simultaneously sabotaged three important, well-guarded plants that were converting coal into oil and thus helping the country become less dependent on imported energy sources.

It was from then on that the South African government seemed to treat the ANC as its primary enemy, sending military forces from time to time into neighboring countries, especially Mozambique, to destroy facilities that the organization was allegedly using for planning and training. In December 1982, South African troops staged a midnight raid on Maseru, the capital of Lesotho, killing a dozen citizens of that independent country, as well as about thirty South African refugees and exiles whose connection to the ANC was unclear. (The defense minister, Magnus Malan, did not even interrupt his seaside holiday in the Cape for these dramatic events; he merely took reports by telephone.) In other ways, too, the government demonstrated that it regarded the ANC as the real opposition. It arrested people who possessed its literature or even wore its colors, and it found a new way to condemn moderate black leaders—to say they were "doing the ANC's work." The official line was that the ANC was Communist-dominated, committed to violence and destruction as an exclusive tactic, and unacceptable as a partner in any discussions of the country's future.

The ANC did become more violent, especially after the Maseru raid. In one of the most controversial actions in its history, it exploded a car bomb outside a military headquarters building in downtown Pretoria at rush hour in May 1983. Among the nineteen people killed and more than two hundred injured were many black civilians. Yet, to the surprise of observers on all sides, the reactions of blacks to this event appeared to be largely favorable. A correspondent for the *New York Times* discovered that beyond the homeland leaders, it was difficult to find black South Africans who would condemn the attack. He quoted one black man as telling him that "people are jubilant" about the Pretoria bombing. "They long ago gave up any hope for peaceful change. What they are saying is that the African National Congress is finally hitting real targets," the man added.

Other evidence of the ANC's growing significance can be found in the almost inexplicable popularity among blacks in South Africa of Nelson Mandela, who has been in prison, first on Robben Island and, more recently, at Pollsmoor Prison near Cape Town, for more than twenty years. Although Mandela is said to have some influence over ANC policy from inside prison, most of the group's actions are decided upon at an exile headquarters in Lusaka, the capital of Zambia, by a collective leadership headed by Mandela's longtime associate, Oliver Tambo. Nonetheless, Mandela remains a well-recognized and highly respected name in unofficial South African politics. In the limited surveys of African opinion that have been conducted on a national basis, Mandela has repeatedly been ranked at the top. He was given a favorable rating by 76 percent of the Africans consulted in a poll for the *Johannesburg Star* in 1981, compared to 58 percent for Motlana and

39 percent for Buthelezi. Mandela outranked Buthelezi even in the Zulu leader's home territory of Natal, and in urban areas like Soweto various other soundings have shown the ANC to be picking up strength at the expense of organizations like Buthelezi's Inkhata. One survey of well-educated Africans on the Witwatersrand showed that 70 percent believed that "only violence" would lead to meaningful change in South Africa.

Mandela's following is based almost entirely on memories, rumors, legends, and indirect citations of his views. He is, in a word, a martyr. Once a Johannesburg lawyer, Mandela had a reputation as a spellbinding orator, but none of his oratory has been heard publicly in decades. Helen Suzman, the veteran legislator from the Progressive Federal party, has occasionally visited Mandela in prison and reported on his condition—he has, on the whole, been well treated—and his wife Winnie sometimes passes along political views that he is assumed to share. Winnie Mandela was banned for more than twenty years herself, and exiled to a remote farming village in the Orange Free State for some time. It was illegal for her to meet with more than one person at a time and for anyone to quote her within South Africa. But she made known her opposition to the new South African constitution and her conviction that only violence would dislodge the white-minority government.

That conviction has been taken up increasingly by others, including African religious leaders who might ordinarily be expected to be among the last to hold out for moderate, peaceful change in South Africa. For example, Bishop Desmond Tutu, the former secretary-general of the South African Council of Churches who won the Nobel Peace Prize in 1984, became Anglican bishop of Johannesburg in 1985 and Archbishop of all southern Africa in 1986, frequently refers to the "deteriorating" circumstances in his country and warns that the white rulers will not make significant changes until they feel genuinely threatened by black resistance. Some observers of South African politics believe that Tutu has achieved a standing that makes him a potential leader of the country. The fact that he has remained free of restrictions and has been able to travel widely outside the country has given him an international exposure and visibility that many others lack, and his mournful, low-key tone has helped enhance his reputation among people inside and outside South Africa who fear violence.

But Tutu has implied that he, too, now endorses the ANC as the true representative of black aspirations in his country. "The government has to come to terms with the fact that the black community now says, 'Our leader is Nelson Mandela and any other persons are just filling in,' " Tutu declared at one point.

Thus has the universal slogan of South African protest politics become "Free Nelson Mandela." Even some *verligte* Afrikaner politicians and journalists have urged that the ANC be included in future negotiations. Exactly what positions Mandela or his associates might take in any eventual bargaining with the government, or what policies might guide the ANC if it were ever to share or monopolize power in South Africa, nobody seems to know. The ANC still formally demands that the country be converted into a single nonracial state governed by a system of majority rule based upon universal suffrage. According to experts on the internal politics of the ANC, it would also urge a dramatic redistribution of income through a socialist system that was flexible enough to tolerate free enterprise. The extent to which the ANC would respect white ownership of property and encourage the growth of a pluralistic political system, however, would depend on internal rivalry and jockeying in the organization in years to come.

In some respects, the South African government's characterizations of the ANC ring truer all the time. Younger ANC members, trained at Communist universities abroad, espouse a strong radical ideology. With its strident articles, the ANC's official monthly, *Sechaba* (the word in several African languages for "the people" or "the land"), printed in East Germany, gives the impression that Marxist influence is very profound, if not dominant, inside the group.

On the other hand, the ANC continues to receive aid not only from Soviet-bloc nations (which have provided most of the weapons for its guerrilla activities), but also from the West and the Third World. Sweden, Norway, Denmark, Italy, and the Netherlands (especially significant as the ancestral home of many white South Africans) have all provided money, as did Canada for a time. Nigeria, Algeria, Egypt, Senegal, and Ivory Coast have been important benefactors of the organization, and Angola and Tanzania have provided training camps for *Umkhonto*. The United Nations, increasingly at odds with the South African government, has funded the ANC's New York office as well as various refugee and training programs linked to the group. A small number of ANC-connected South Africans have participated in educational programs in the United States, but otherwise the American government has been among the few in the world refusing any formal contact with this organization. People of Mandela's and Tambo's generation have long stressed their interest in the lessons for South Africa of American history and the U.S. constitutional system, but it is a safe guess that American ideas about South Africa's future do not figure prominently in the ANC's thinking today.

Estimates of the ANC's military strength vary widely, but it may have as many as seven thousand trained guerrillas outside the country, with a similar number still in training. Officially the South African government says there are no ANC fighters inside the country, but that seems no longer to be true.

In January 1985, in an interview with a British peer who is a member of the European Parliament, Mandela implied that the ANC might be willing to change its tactics if the South African government were to "legalize us, treat us like a political party and negotiate with us." P. W. Botha reacted by saying that if Mandela unconditionally renounced violence and promised not to engage in any illegal acts, he could be released from prison. But the next month, Mandela's twenty-three-year-old daughter read his reply to a crowd gathered in a sports stadium in Soweto: "What freedom am I being offered whilst the organization of the people [the ANC] remains banned? . . . What freedom am I being offered when I may be arrested on a pass offense? . . . Only free men can negotiate." (Some other imprisoned members of the ANC did accept the government's offer of conditional release. Dennis Goldberg, a Communist who had served twenty-one years of a life sentence for plotting to overthrow the government, agreed to leave the country and flew immediately to join his daughter in Israel. (Later he went to work for the ANC in London.)

In South Africa, as elsewhere in the world, the most meaningful protest is sometimes one that makes its point but also plays a subtle trick on the authorities. One recent example concerns a new township for Coloureds that was built near Johannesburg. The residents wanted to name the streets for Coloured youths who were killed during the 1976 riots that began in Soweto and spread to many other areas. But that idea was quickly vetoed by the white authorities. When the residents suggested naming them for saints instead, the government officials concerned with the matter, ever devout, were pleased. So the people proceeded to denote each street with a saint's name that coincided with the name of one of the dead from 1976. Thus, "St. Francis Street" is not named for St. Francis at all, but for a young man called Francis who died in a confrontation with the police in the year of the great radicalization.

The Coloured community has always occupied the most complicated position in the intricate political and racial fabric of South Africa. As one South African student of the Coloureds' politics puts it, they have, at different times, joined forces "with whites against blacks or with blacks against whites or with whites against whites, in varying combinations." Coloureds were, above all, different from everyone else; they were neither indigenous Africans nor outside settlers, but rather a combination of the two, the product of unique historical circumstances and racial mixing that would today be regarded as scandalous in South Africa. The traditional favorite line of Afrikaners is that "we created the Coloureds as a race."

For centuries, the Coloureds behaved as the "brown brothers" they were expected to be, using Afrikaans as their first language and otherwise living in a manner that stressed their cultural closeness to the "pure" Afrikaners. (Their cuisine, arts and architecture, and other folkways are quite similar.) The fact that Coloureds were geographically concentrated in one part of the country, the Cape, only reinforced the circumstances. Indeed, some current-day Afrikaner politicians whose careers began in the Cape, such as President P. W. Botha (who once served as minister for Coloured affairs), believed for many years that the only "black people" who had to be dealt with were the Coloureds; the ruling whites had relatively little direct experience of Africans until after World War II.

At various times, for reasons both ideological and practical, the Afrikaner political establishment tried to push the Coloureds away—removing the limited franchise they enjoyed in the Cape, forcing them to evacuate areas where they had lived for generations, and generally conveying the message that cultural kinship had nothing to do with political, social, or economic equality.

This was a painful process for most Coloureds, who felt little in common with, and generally spoke a different language from, the various African groups in the country. In fact, many Africans were hostile to the Coloureds, whom they resented for having a higher status and whom they often called by the derogatory names of Bushmen, Hottentots, or Albinos. "We suffer most from apartheid," one Coloured community organizer told a reporter recently. "Racism is not confined to whites only, and it is encouraged by the authorities because they benefit from dividing people."

Sometime in the mid-1970s the tables began to turn. Although the South African government did not relax the enforcement of the rules of "separate development" as they applied to the Coloureds—people of mixed race and Indians were removed from areas newly declared white just as ruthlessly as Africans—it did try to play on their ethnic and cultural affinities in order to lure them over to the white side of the great divide. When an advisory "president's council" was named, several Coloureds were offered seats on it and a few accepted. Coloured political, professional, and trade union associations were allowed to flourish, while their African counterparts were harassed and often suppressed. Desperate to expand the base of the regime without genuinely having to share power, National party theoreticians and Afrikaner intellectuals tried to co-opt the Coloureds into helping design a new system.

But at the same time the government was reaching out to the Coloureds, the Coloureds were backing off and beginning to form alliances with Africans. There were many reasons for this, including a growing disillusionment with the traditional, generally collaborationist leadership of the Coloured community; a gradual awakening to the fact that the second-class facilities accorded to Coloureds, while better than the third-class ones allowed to Africans, were still far short of the first-class ones reserved by the whites for themselves; and a cold-blooded political and strategic calculation by some of the younger leaders of the Coloured community that the long-range interests of their people would be better protected as blacks than as quasi-whites.

The Coloured Labour party, then a substantial and militant force, sabotaged the "Coloured Persons Representative Council," which the National party had offered as a palliative after stripping Coloureds of all representation in the white central govern-

ment. In fact, many members of the community began to reject
the use of the term "Coloured" altogether, as a divisive label imposed by the white power structure in its obsessive need to clas-
sify everyone racially.* The most dramatic shift began in 1976,
when Coloured students launched boycotts and strikes in solidarity with young African protesters. Some of the Coloured actions
went on long after quiet had temporarily returned to the African
townships, and after that, more Africans were willing to make
common cause with the Coloureds.

There are still sharp divisions among the Coloureds. Many
of their institutions, including a technical college teachers' union
led by Franklin Sonn, remain quite conservative and wary of
hasty alliances with potentially radical African organizations. The
man who led the Coloured Labour party into participation in the
government's new three-tier Parliament, the Reverend Allan Hen-
drickse, was a political detainee in the mid-1970s, but now says
he has been persuaded of the government's good faith; he became
a cabinet minister under the new constitution.

One Coloured man has emerged with what seems to be a very
broad constituency among Coloureds and, remarkably, among
Africans and some whites as well—a minister of the Dutch Reformed Church named Allan Boesak. Although the Coloured
branch of that church has traditionally been a bastion of cautious, even retrogressive, political attitudes, Boesak has become
an articulate and militant opponent of the apartheid system. Starting as the campus chaplain at the University of the Western
Cape—a showcase educational institution outside of Cape Town
intended exclusively for the use of Coloureds—Boesak was elected
a national leader of his church, a member of the executive committee of the South African Council of Churches, and president of
the World Alliance of Reformed Churches. Abandoning the usual

---

* The term of reference preferred by a growing number of Coloureds is
"blacks." When they do use the traditional term to define themselves and
draw inevitable distinctions, it is often cast as "so-called Coloureds." The
use of quotation marks around the word in writing—a sign of skepticism
about the official racial classification—has a parallel in gesture, a sort of
"Coloured salute": people discussing politics in Cape Town and its environs
now invariably scratch the air twice with their forefingers, as if to insert the
quotation marks, whenever they say the word "Coloured." "If my hands
were tied behind my back, I would not be able to make a speech," said one
young Coloured leader.

polite discourse of Coloured politics, he accused the government of "using Westminster-style democracy as a cover for totalitarian rule" and "using the system to cover up shameful acts of dishonesty."

Boesak was instrumental in the formation, in 1983, of the United Democratic Front (UDF), a broad alliance of some four hundred large and small, national and local organizations with a total membership of perhaps 2.5 million people. Its initial purpose was to fight the government's constitutional reform, but at its widely attended launching, held in Mitchell's Plain, a Coloured area on the outskirts of Cape Town, in August 1983, the UDF said it cherished "the vision of a united, democratic South Africa based on the will of the people" and promised "united action against the evils of apartheid, economic and all other forms of exploitation." "We stand for the creation of a true democracy in which all South Africans will participate in the government of our country," said the UDF's declaration; "we stand for a single nonracial, unfragmented South Africa, a South Africa free of bantustans and Group Areas."

The most notable feature of the UDF was that it included representatives of all South Africa's racial groups and many of its diverse opposition political tendencies, including labor unions. By welcoming whites, it went one major step beyond Buthelezi's ill-fated South African Black Alliance. The organizers did not include everyone, however, pointedly withholding invitations to Buthelezi's Inkhata (on the grounds that he and it were cooperating with the government's homelands system) and the Progressive Federal party (on the grounds that by staying in the whites-only Parliament, it was participating in a fundamentally undemocratic institution). The UDF's organizing convention did hear a message of greetings and solidarity smuggled out of prison by Nelson Mandela, and several other ANC activists were named as patrons or officers of the organization (as were the Reverend Beyers Naude, the much-banned and restricted Afrikaner leader of the Christian Institute, and Andrew Boraine, the former president of the National Union of South African Students, himself a frequent detainee). Even some of the former leaders of the Black Consciousness Movement agreed to join the UDF, and the organization's effectiveness was enhanced by the fact that it received international recognition and prestige from the start.

Other coalitions were springing up, too. For example, the South African Federal Union grouped various government-recognized black leaders, including the heads of the "independent" as well as semiautonomous homelands, urban councils, and business groups; but in many eyes it was tainted by the fact that so many of its members owed their standing to cooperation with the apartheid system. The most important rival to the UDF was the National Forum, organized by adherents of the Black Consciousness Movement. Embracing a militant socialist platform, the Forum, with about six hundred thousand members, argued that whites, as the "oppressors," had no meaningful role to play in South Africa's future.

Most influential within the National Forum is the Azanian People's Organization (AZAPO), formed in 1978 after other Black Consciousness groups were banned by the government. Azania is the name that some black nationalists would give to South Africa, and AZAPO rejects even the ANC for not doing enough to liberate the nation; it also takes a virulently anti-American stand, denouncing the United States as "a partner in crime" in South Africa. It was AZAPO that organized blacks to embarrass Senator Edward Kennedy and his hosts (Tutu and Boesak) by demonstrating against him during his visit to South Africa early in 1985.

How such a broad and potentially unwieldy coalition as the UDF could survive this kind of opposition and devise its own distinct, widely accepted policies remained to be seen. Like any new group, it seemed almost intoxicated at first, passing resolutions condemning the Reagan administration's policy of "constructive engagement," criticizing the cooperation between Israel and South Africa, pronouncing on the roles of business and of women in South Africa, and taking up any other topic that interested one of its member organizations. As for its basic view on how to organize South Africa's political future, the UDF advocated a national convention at which the various groups in the country would negotiate a truly democratic constitution that would implement the goals delineated in the Freedom Charter of the 1950s. (Others, including even some of the homeland leaders, also supported the idea of a national constitutional convention.) The temptation to identify the UDF with the ANC was obvious. They shared many of the same principles and goals, and the UDF's reluctance to spell out specific strategies and tactics or to condemn violence was taken by many as a sign of implicit support for the ANC. Indeed, the only long-range alternative to a national convention, said one UDF leader privately, is "civil war."

It came as a surprise that the South African government did not attempt to interfere with the formation of the UDF and for more than a year and a half tolerated its militant statements. The security police were blamed for issuing hoax pamphlets claiming that some of the early UDF meetings had been called off; later the government banned some of the front's regional gatherings as potentially inflammatory and arrested or detained UDF activists who urged a boycott of the elections for the new Coloured and Indian chambers of Parliament. Finally, as unrest swelled in the Eastern Cape region early in 1985, the government silenced the UDF altogether for a period of time, and sixteen leaders of the organization were arrested and charged with treason. Boesak himself, however, as a Coloured and a churchman, enjoyed a remarkable latitude. The security police did attempt to discredit him by revealing to the press that he had had an extramarital affair with a white woman on the staff of the South African Council of Churches. The information was published and Boesak was temporarily suspended by his church, but after an investigation he was exonerated and reinstated; before long the issue became the government's abuse of its powers to investigate the personal lives of its opponents.

For decades, first under one law and then under a tidier version less subject to appeal in the courts, the South African government has sought to control what the people of the country read and see. The standards are vague, if predictable: "Undesirable" publications, objects, films, or public entertainments include anything that, in the view of the censors, "is indecent or obscene or is offensive or harmful to public morals." Anything "harmful to the relations between any sections of the inhabitants of the Republic" is proscribed, as is material considered "prejudicial to the safety of the State, the general welfare or the peace and good order of the State." "Religious convictions or feelings" are to be protected as well, with "particular regard" to be paid to "the constant endeavor of the population of the Republic of South Africa to uphold a Christian view of life."

The result, over the years, has often been oppressive and

sometimes bizarre. Among the estimated twenty-eight thousand titles that have been banned are the entire works of some black South African writers and poets. (In one notorious trial during the 1970s, involving members of the South African Student Organization, the primary evidence of "subversion" offered by the prosecution consisted of plays and poems written by the accused.) Foreign black writers whose works could have revolutionary implications, such as Eldridge Cleaver and Franz Fanon, are excluded, but so are certain works of popular American novelists, such as Philip Roth and John Updike. A newspaper, the *World*—serving mostly the residents of Soweto—was shut down at one point under the Publications Act, and the same law was used to keep out a novel by Gore Vidal because of objections to his sexual allusions.*

Despite the elaborate network of laws intended to control expression in South Africa, many things slip past the censors undisturbed. Books written by South African whites, and especially by Afrikaners, seem to have an easier time than others, but it is still surprising that some of the recent works of writers like Nadine Gordimer and J. M. Coetzee, with their visions of a South Africa devastated by racial war and revolution, have been tolerated. Indeed, on the evidence of those freely circulating works—admittedly read mostly by well-to-do whites and, all the more, by South Africa's critics overseas—the country enjoys an artistic freedom that is unrivaled in most such formally restrictive societies. The latitude is limited compared to what exists in the West (of which South Africa claims to be a part), but broad compared to much of the rest of Africa.

One of the most surprising developments in recent years was that Gordimer, in cooperation with producers from Europe, managed to make films of several of her short stories dealing with themes that are regarded as especially sensitive in South Africa.

---

* Sometimes the censors make absurd, almost comical, mistakes. For example, as rehearsals were getting underway late in 1982 for the South African debut of playwright Athol Fugard's tense drama, *Master Harold . . . and the Boys,* the cast found that, although no edict had been issued against the performances, the script itself had been banned. In other words, South Africans would be free to see the play, but not to read it, not even for the purpose of preparing to act in it. The anomaly was corrected after the press had pointed it out.

In one of them, *Country Lovers*, a young white man and an African woman are seen kissing each other in the especially surprising setting of a farm in the Orange Free State, the part of South Africa where traditional rules and values have been most strictly preserved. Special permits are required every time the Gordimer films are shown, and their release for general viewing has been prohibited.

The domain in which South African artistic freedom flourishes most openly is on the stage, where the painful human repercussions of racial conflict have frequently been portrayed. Black theater companies have survived amid political repression by remaining small and off the beaten path. A few others, which are multiracial, including the Market Theatre in Johannesburg and the Space Theatre in Cape Town, have attracted great attention by presenting dramas dealing with blacks to fashionable, mostly white audiences.

One of the most powerful pieces staged at those theaters in recent years, little known outside of South Africa, was *Saturday Night at the Palace*, by Paul Slabolepszy, the gripping story of two young ne'er-do-well Afrikaners who stop at an all-night roadside food stand late one Saturday. At first their banter and their taunting of one another provoke belly laughs from the audience. But gradually, as they complain about their personal misfortunes and the unfair treatment they feel they have received from South African society, they discover a convenient scapegoat in "September," the elderly black man who is the attendant at the roadside stand. He has no pass or permit to be in this "white area," and so he is especially vulnerable to their abuse. As their treatment of him turns physically brutal, the audience's laughs turn to gasps, their smiles fade to a uniform gaze of horror. Few of the genteel, well-to-do people attending *Saturday Night at the Palace* would ever have participated in, or even observed, such a scene themselves, but some of them, having seen it so graphically portrayed, go away understanding it as an allegory of the way South African society treats black people in general.

There is an irony in the fact that some of these painfully gripping South African dramas find such a wide audience overseas, especially in Britain and the United States, where the intelligentsia tend to have a morbid fascination with the problems of South Africa. It is as if artistic depictions of the tension and human suffering there have become the nation's major cultural export. The effect is to call greater attention to South Africa among people who otherwise might not notice.

Ask some right-wing Afrikaners, and they will tell you that the real trouble began in their country with the advent of television. That, they will say, was when men started going around wearing earrings, people began to use drugs, and for a time interracial clubs found ways to skirt the law.

South Africa had no television at all until 1976. Complicated justifications were found for the government's long delay in authorizing a television network, but according to some analysts of National party thinking, the real reason was a heartfelt fear that television would have a subversive influence on black attitudes. It would be hard to screen out all programs that explicitly or implicitly challenged the South African way of life. Once the South African Broadcasting Corporation (SABC) did launch its video service, there were new items on the national agenda of contentious issues. It was easy enough to control the news that was broadcast and make sure the government's view on every issue carried the day, and to produce boring local programs that emphasized the country's values, but it was the American imports that raised questions. Even dubbed in Afrikaans, "Kojak" was not entirely trustworthy. "The FBI" was more what the government had in mind. Somehow "Dallas" slipped by the censors and became a runaway success.

Much more permissive, and therefore the center of a new controversy, was the special channel for Africans operated by BophutaTswana, called "Bop-TV." When it went on the air in 1983, it featured some of the sought-after American serials rejected by the SABC, and since many of the theoretical citizens of BophutaTswana lived in Soweto, its signal was sent to an SABC tower in Johannesburg for relay there. The SABC tried to keep the Bop-TV beam as narrow as possible, but there was still "spillage" into white areas. One of the newest fads in the white suburbs of Johannesburg was to try to foil the system by purchasing a UHF antenna to capture the forbidden signal.*

---

* Often SABC producers and commentators working in risky political territory struggled to present controversial views that challenged the South Afri-

"The price of gold goes over $400, and everyone breaks out his black tie." The Cape Town businessman meant to be humorous, but his epigram revealed a basic truth about the South African economy: the country is uniquely dependent upon gold for its financial strength and growth, and no amount of economic planning can erase its fundamental vulnerability to fluctuations in the gold price. South Africa produces half of the world's gold.

Gold is what has allowed the South African economy to expand at one of the fastest rates in the world in recent decades, and it has played a key role in attracting foreign investment. After the United States set the dollar free from the gold standard in 1971, the price of the precious metal quadrupled within three years, and South Africa's earnings from gold tripled in the same period. As a result, the national growth rate for 1974 was 8.3 percent. But when the gold price plunged from a high of $198 an ounce in 1974 to a low of $103 an ounce in 1976, the economy plunged with it. South Africa suffered a deep recession, and its economy registered no growth at all in 1977. The ups and downs have continued ever since, and recent calculations indicate that every decrease of $10 in the gold price reduces South Africa's annual foreign exchange earnings by some $220 million; thus its balance of payments swings wildly between surplus and deficit almost without warning.

Another basic truth is that the South African economy is uniquely linked to the nation's internal political situation and its international reputation at any given time. Domestic turmoil tends to make potential foreign investors uneasy. That was true in the wake of the Sharpeville massacre in 1960 and again after the Soweto and other riots of 1976. In both cases economic downturns already underway were prolonged by anxiety over the country's long-range stability. Even outside of crisis moments, the apartheid

---

can orthodoxy. On one occasion, when he was about to interview a visiting American journalist, an SABC man paused at the last moment, trying to find a way to neutralize the impact that the journalist's criticism of South Africa would have on the network's internal censors. In a flash of inspiration, he dashed out to the next room and returned with a bust of the late Prime Minister Hendrik Verwoerd, the architect of apartheid. Positioned creatively, Verwoerd would seem to be scowling down at the visitor in disapproval. The gimmick worked, and the interview made it onto the air virtually uncut.

system has tended to place structural limits on South Africa's economic performance. Inequality of educational opportunities, job reservation, and influx control, among other things, have impeded the development of the kind of skilled labor pool necessary for the South African economy to fulfill its potential and its leaders' expectations. The institutionalized racism also prevents black purchasing power and consumption from growing as fast as it might, thereby holding prosperity back even in the best of times.

In many respects, the South African economy has been in an anomalous situation for much of the twentieth century. It has been, on the one hand, strong and nearly self-sufficient—South Africa has consistently been the only major food exporter on the African continent—but on the other hand, seriously dependent on foreign capital to offset balance of payments deficits and stimulate growth. Moreover, South Africa is both a developed country and a developing country at the same time, its white population maintaining a standard of living similar to that in the major industrialized nations, but most of the rest living as do many people in the Third World. With the black population so much larger than the white, the average of the two, according to World Bank ratings in 1983, made South Africa an "upper middle-income country," a category that also included Portugal, Greece, Brazil, Israel, Mexico, and Malaysia. In other words, although South Africa has a dominant position in Africa—contributing 86 percent of its steel production, 60 percent of its rail traffic, and 20 percent of its overall output of goods and services—it still has far to go before it can be considered fully developed. (When only sub-Saharan Africa is taken into account, South Africa produces about 40 percent of the total goods and services.)

Another aspect of the anomaly is that while South Africa purports to be the ultimate practitioner of free-enterprise capitalism, public sector activities account for more than a quarter of its gross domestic product. With parastatal corporations responsible for the iron and steel industry, the manufacture of arms, the provision of electricity, and the development of energy resources, the government's role in the economy is much greater in practice than in theory. The main reason for growth of the public sector was the Afrikaners' effort over time to achieve economic equality with the English-speaking whites. Afrikaners still dominate the civil service and the parastatals, while the private sector remains

largely—but somewhat less than before—in the hands of the anglophone commercial class.

After the public sector, the most important shares of the
country's economy are held by private manufacturing (24 percent) and mining (14 percent). Because South African minerals
are in such demand around the world—not only gold, but also diamonds, coal, platinum, ferrochrome and ferromanganese, to name
a few—its mining industry has earned it a great deal of foreign
exchange. The rapid growth of manufacturing, by contrast, has
meant that South Africa must spend that money importing a vast
quantity of foreign-made industrial machinery and equipment.
Industrialization has also resulted in a major shift in the population; whereas only 25 percent of the people lived in towns or cities at the time the Union of South Africa was formed, that figure
today is at least 50 percent.

Agriculture, which now represents only 8 percent of the
gross domestic product, is one of the areas where the disparity
between whites and blacks is most obvious. Almost all of the
country's commercial agriculture is conducted on large, highly
modernized and mechanized white farms; blacks are involved
mostly in subsistence farming. As a result, the output of the
mostly white workers in commercial agriculture is twenty times
that of the black subsistence farmers. The output of subsistence
farming has scarcely grown at all over the years, although the
number of people depending on it has increased substantially.
Thus, rural blacks, especially those living in the homelands, have
been progressively impoverished; any increase in their income is
the result of money sent home by family members working in the
mines or industry in the cities.

For much of the twentieth century, whites actually increased
their share of South Africa's wealth. In 1970, the ratio of white to
African per capita income was 15 to 1. African wages grew much
faster than those of whites during the 1970s, and in 1975 one economist estimated that the ratio had shifted to 10 to 1. But that
figure concealed another statistic that tells just how great economic disparities in South Africa really are: rural Africans—perhaps a third of the country's total population—have an income
that is only one-eighth that of urban Africans. (In one sheep-
farming area, for example, black workers on white-owned farms
earn only $10 a month.) That puts the relationship between the

income of the average white and that of the average rural African at perhaps 40 or 50 to 1.

A study financed by the Carnegie Corporation of New York revealed in 1984 that South Africa has probably "one of the most unequal distributions of national wealth in the world." A third of all black South African children under the age of fourteen are stunted in growth because they do not have enough to eat, the study found, and in some areas nearly half the children need treatment for tuberculosis. The infant mortality rate in certain black communities is thirty-one times higher than among the nation's whites. All of these problems are most severe in the homelands, according to the Carnegie research; unemployment there, on the average, is over 25 percent. The most important thing to recognize, said the director of the study, Francis Wilson, an economics professor at the University of Cape Town, is that poverty in South Africa results not from insufficiency but from inequality.

The government has long contended that sustained economic growth is the only reliable path to progress for all South Africans, and that is one area where it has had the enthusiastic support of the titans of South African business, who otherwise tend to espouse a political liberalism at odds with the doctrine of apartheid. Harry Oppenheimer, former chairman of the giant Anglo-American Corporation of South Africa and a patron of the Progressive Federal party, is among the businessmen who have pressed the regime to make reforms that require a dismantling of some of its own foundations. He was one of the first, for example, to advocate the recognition of black trade unions, and he was the prime mover behind establishment of the Urban Foundation, which has worked to improve the quality of life for urban blacks through better housing and education and a loosening of influx control regulations.

To some extent, the recognition of black unions has backfired for both government and business. Workers joined up more quickly and in much larger numbers than most people had anticipated, in part because the unions were seen as a potential avenue toward black political power. Recruitment was particularly successful in the mines, where working conditions for Africans are often deplorable and wages have sometimes stayed at the same level for decades; about thirty-five thousand miners joined the National

Union of Mineworkers in less than a year, and before long it demanded a 30 percent wage increase from the Chamber of Mines, the association of mining companies. In some instances, the unions have sought a role in investigations of mine explosions and other disasters. In April 1985, Anglo-American fired thirteen thousand miners at the world's largest gold mine and two thousand at another, for participating in an illegal twenty-four-hour strike for higher wages; in discussions with union leaders, however, the company agreed to establish procedures for hiring some of them back.

Most of the successful black unions resist becoming multiracial organizations. Their members see themselves as having little in common with the relatively better-off white workers, and many of their leaders have been involved with the Black Consciousness Movement. Still, a number of different confederations have sprung up, and some of them have become affiliated with international organizations, such as the International Conference of Free Trade Unions. The unions are an obvious place for the African National Congress and other militant political groups to seek influence, and one of the unions' thorniest problems has been to decide whether it is worth the risk to have contact with, or demonstrate support for, the ANC. The largest grouping, the Federation of South African Trade Unions (FOSATU), has kept its distance from the ANC, which it respects as "a great populist liberation movement" of the past, but now accuses of encouraging "undirected opportunistic political activity." FOSATU takes the position that conditions are ripe in South Africa, with its vast industrial proletariat, for a pure workers' struggle. It is interested only in the politics of the workplace. The vision is militant and romantic at the same time, and hardly a comfort to the authorities, but it falls far short of the violence now espoused and practiced by some elements of the ANC.

Even if the success of the unions leads to industrial conciliation and a greater sense of participation for Africans in the long run, as liberal businessmen hope it will, there is little reason to believe that South Africa will achieve the levels of economic growth that seem necessary to sustain and extend prosperity. Just to keep up with population growth—2.6 percent a year among blacks and 1.4 percent a year among whites—the economy must continue to grow by at least 5 percent a year. But at that rate, unemployment

would still continue to rise, as it did throughout the mostly prosperous 1960s and 1970s. (African unemployment is estimated at
about 16 percent in the urban areas, but may be significantly
higher.) To stabilize the number of unemployed, South African
economist Charles Simkins has estimated, would take a steady
growth rate of some 6.7 percent a year, a virtually unattainable
goal. Ironically, that goal may be all the more difficult to reach if
those blacks who are working continue to make economic progress. South Africa's past record of uniquely rapid economic growth
was achieved in part because of the availability of cheap unskilled
and semiskilled black labor. Apartheid put artificial constraints on
the South African labor market. As the labor needs become more
sophisticated, as skilled workers become harder to find, and as the
costs of all black labor increase, South Africa's unusually large
profit margins will decrease and the economy is bound to slow
down.

Already South Africa has discovered it is not as wealthy as it
long assumed itself to be. In 1980 and 1981, Owen Horwood, then
finance minister, openly recruited foreign capital to prop up the
economy, and the next year the South Africans took the surprising step of going to the International Monetary Fund for a loan
of $1.07 billion (not their first such application, but their biggest
and most widely publicized). The IMF's approval of the request
in November 1982, with the concurrence of the Reagan administration but over the objections of sixty-eight other countries, provoked substantial controversy. The Congressional Black Caucus
and other liberal members of the U.S. Congress spoke out against
the move, and the United Nations General Assembly approved a
resolution asking the IMF not to underwrite South African security forces or the country's apartheid system. IMF documents later
leaked to the press revealed that South Africa may actually have
received privileged treatment from the fund, since it did not have
to abide by the same restrictive conditions imposed on most other
recipients of IMF loans; the documents also brought to light a
judgment by the fund's staff that apartheid had created "infla-
tionary pressures" and exacerbated unemployment in South Africa.

The IMF loan did not solve South Africa's economic problems. A year later inflation was still climbing, the South African
currency, the rand, had dropped substantially in value against
the dollar, and experts in and out of government were describing

the nation's economy as being in the worst shape since the Great Depression. In 1984 officials revealed enormous budget overruns in connection with South African military operations in Namibia and Angola, and the government was complaining that it would be very expensive to put the new constitution, with its separate chambers of Parliament for Coloureds and Indians, into effect. Apartheid had always been costly, but both the attempt to defend it at the frontiers and a limited effort to reform it were now adding to the bill.

The rand again lost half its value against the dollar in 1984, and so the price of many imports skyrocketed. The South African budget for 1984–85 reflected severe austerity measures, including higher sales taxes and subsidies to farmers to help them deal with the effects of the drought. Business taxes were substantially increased, and before long the major South African banks raised their prime lending rate to 25 percent. With the incidence of strikes increasing and business investment down, South Africa hardly seemed poised for a new era of prosperity. Vexed by all of this and widely criticized for his management of the economy for nearly a decade, Horwood resigned in the summer of 1984 and was replaced by an up-and-coming Afrikaner politician, Barend du Plessis.

One area where South Africa was always assumed to be especially vulnerable was its reliance on imported oil for 20 percent of its total energy, particularly in transportation and agriculture. Even after Arab oil producers instituted an embargo against South Africa in 1973, however, Iran continued to supply almost 90 percent of its needs. When the shah fell from power in 1979, that dependable source disappeared, but South Africa found it easy to buy its oil on the spot market instead, sometimes at higher prices. The government had also prepared well in advance for such an eventuality, by establishing a national oil stockpile and instituting one of the world's most effective synthetic fuels programs. By 1978 the parastatal South African Coal, Oil, and Gas Corporation (SASOL) was producing gasoline from coal that was competitive in price with that refined from imported oil. The strangely sweet smell of much of the car exhaust in South Africa is evidence enough that SASOL's new automotive fuel has caught on. In the event of an emergency, South Africa could also save on imported crude oil by reducing or eliminating its sale of oil and gasoline to neighboring African states and to the ships that stop in South African ports.

South Africa did manage to expand its foreign trade and diversify its international markets, even as the rhetoric against the trade ties with this pariah state escalated. Its new gold coin, the Krugerrand, was a major hit in financial markets around the world, and the country's "secret" trade with black-ruled African states blossomed to the point where it surpassed $1 billion for the first time in 1980. Recent figures indicate that South Africa conducts surreptitious trade with forty-seven other African nations; despite their public hostility, they apparently cannot get along without South Africa. The United States replaced Great Britain as South Africa's first-place trading partner in the late 1970s; what with the role of gold, American imports from South Africa were substantially greater in value than U.S. exports to that nation.*

Direct U.S. investment in South Africa has also played a key role in its economy. Although American investment there represents only one percent of all American investment worldwide, its dollar value increased steadily beginning in the mid-1960s, reaching about $2.3 billion in 1983. (British investment in South Africa is about three times as great.) More than half of the American investment is held by two automobile companies, Ford and General Motors, and two oil companies, Mobil and Caltex, but many other well-known firms have smaller stakes. The symbolic importance of the United States to South Africa has made American investment there highly visible and hotly debated. Indeed, many people in both countries have questioned whether American investment in South Africa has helped promote economic, and therefore eventual political equality, or increased the efficiency and furthered the aims of apartheid.

That is a hard question to answer with precision, but since 1977 many American corporations doing business in South Africa have sought to demonstrate their good intentions by subscribing to a code of behavior designed by the Reverend Leon Sullivan, a

---

* American trade may be important to South Africa, but South African trade cannot be said to be truly important to the United States, in dollar terms. U.S. trade with South Africa has remained fairly constant at about 1 percent of total U.S. world trade. American trade with the rest of Africa is about five times as great, and even when Nigerian oil is excluded from the figure, it is significantly greater than the trade with South Africa.

Baptist minister from Philadelphia who is a member of the board of General Motors. The "Sullivan Principles," as the code is known, prescribe equal and fair employment practices, equal pay for equal work regardless of race, desegregation of company facilities, plus training programs and amenities designed to improve the lives of black workers. As of April 1985, 149 of the approximately 300 U.S. companies known to be substantially involved in South Africa had committed themselves to formal implementation of the code. That the Sullivan Principles had brought about short-term benefits for many workers could not be doubted—quite a few executives now felt obligated to look at more than the balance sheet when they evaluated their companies' performance in South Africa—but the long-range impact was more problematic. Few companies were willing to go so far as setting up their own schools, housing developments, and the like; short of that, there seemed to be little they could do to shake the foundations of South Africa's institutionalized racism and its profound economic consequences.

On one level, South Africa purports to be asserting its political independence and economic self-sufficiency. To listen to many white South Africans, both government officials and private citizens, it is as if the country could wrap itself in a cocoon and ignore what is going on outside, only to emerge later and be recognized as a beautiful and righteous creature. South Africa has no real friends anyway, they argue, so what is the point of trying to satisfy those who cannot and will not be satisfied?

But South Africa cannot become a fortress, especially not in the late twentieth century. And like many individuals who claim to feel indifferent and superior, South Africa, as a country, really feels the opposite. White South Africans, in particular, crave acceptance and approval from outside; they insist that their unique circumstances deserve a fuller hearing and more sympathetic understanding from the world community. This is especially true of English-speaking whites, who generally do not share the Afrikaners' sense of divine mission; they want desperately to be taken seriously as an extension of Western civilization in a part of the world fraught with violence and inhumanity. (They also want a place to go, in the event the South African bubble should burst in their lifetime.) The genteel, carefully modulated activities of the business-supported South Africa Foundation, intended to "pro-

mote South Africa through personal contact at top level throughout the world," are but one example of the drive for greater international acceptance of South Africa.

Increasingly sophisticated studies of white opinion in South
Africa—probably more reliable than most inquiries into black
views—indicate that there is a widespread perception of a "threat"
from the outside. In one survey conducted in 1982 for the South
African Institute of International Affairs, more than 70 percent of
the respondents said they believed that the government was not
exaggerating the challenge to South Africa from international
Communism; that the newly independent nation of Zimbabwe,
despite its own weaknesses and problems, posed a threat to South
Africa's security; and that a war like the one in Namibia would
eventually develop within South Africa itself.

There were differences between Afrikaans- and English-
speaking whites—the former tended to be more pessimistic and
to take a harder line—but overall the majority of the people sur-
veyed believed that blacks in South Africa were treated relatively
well, and they favored military solutions to the surge of black nationalism and protest within the country. Not surprisingly, the
survey also revealed support for the government's instinct to lash
out and strike militarily against "terrorist bases" in nearby black-
ruled states, and for South African efforts to starve those countries into submission, if necessary, by withholding food and other
exports.

It is sentiments like that, built upon a general South African
tendency to retreat into the *laager* and protect itself, that lead
outsiders to take seriously the prospect that the country might
soon decide to produce, and even consider using, nuclear weapons. South Africa launched a nuclear power program in the 1970s
as another part of its effort to achieve self-sufficiency in energy
supplies, and in 1977 Soviet and Western intelligence analysts,
relying on data from satellites, simultaneously became convinced
that the government was on the verge of testing a nuclear weapon
in the Kalahari Desert. Western pressure called that off; but while
the government agreed to conduct itself in accord with "the spirit,
principles, and goals" of the Nuclear Non-Proliferation Treaty, it
refused to sign that treaty or to permit outside inspection of its
most sensitive nuclear facilities, such as the Valindaba uranium
enrichment plant near Pretoria. The Koeberg nuclear power sta-

tion near Cape Town has already been the object of an ANC attack, and the mystery over government intentions in this field has further complicated tensions in the region.

Some South African black leaders and Western observers fear that if Afrikaner extremists were to come to power in the midst of domestic turmoil, they would be prepared to risk a nuclear holocaust as part of their last stand against the dreaded threat from their black enemies. But the chairman of South Africa's Atomic Energy Corporation, Wynand L. de Villiers, dismisses such worries as foolish; insisting that South Africa wishes to explore only "civil applications" of nuclear technology, he says typically that "the world can think what it likes."

One part of world reaction to South Africa that has had a major domestic impact is the application of political, cultural, professional, and athletic boycotts to the country because of the apartheid system. South Africans have long since stopped worrying about links with the United Nations, but as other relationships are broken, for example, with the International Organization of Employers, based in Geneva, in 1983, the sense of isolation intensifies. White South Africans have been so upset over sports boycotts that they have gone to great lengths to foil them; a West Indian cricket team was apparently persuaded to break the boycott and tour South Africa early in 1983 only after the South African Cricket Union promised to pay its members $100,000 each. Indeed, it is probably only because of such boycotts that limited reforms have been achieved and the South Africans have moved toward integration of some sports.

After the creation of Sun City in BophutaTswana, the country's critics in the Western entertainment world, led by singer Harry Belafonte, saw a need to intensify their efforts to isolate South Africa culturally. Early in 1984, the British Medical Association withdrew from the World Medical Association to protest the continued membership in the group of both the Medical Association of South Africa and a medical association from the Transkei homeland. Actions such as these hardly endanger the South African system, but they do tend to make many South African whites— again, primarily the English-speaking minority—uncomfortable about the system they have helped to sustain over the years.

Ever on the lookout for new friends, the South African government has recently drawn close to two other embattled coun-

tries that are sometimes classified as "pariah states," Taiwan and
Israel. Both have been persuaded to lend aid, and therefore some
degree of legitimacy, to the otherwise internationally shunned
homelands. The shelves in the offices of South African cabinet
ministers are lined with books and articles about the achievements of Taiwan and its ability to survive the hostility of the People's Republic of China and various international organizations.
The friendship of Israel and South Africa is born of the isolation
that each country feels in its region, their growing cooperation on
military and technical matters, and the strong ties to Israel felt
by the South African Jewish community. Although they have attracted widespread attention only recently, the ties between Israel
and South Africa actually date back to the early days of Israeli
independence and National party rule in South Africa, both of
which began in 1948; in fact, the first Nationalist prime minister,
D. F. Malan, traveled to Israel in 1953. Many years later the
Israelis gave comfort to South Africa by providing aid to some
of the "independent" homelands, such as the Ciskei. There is an
irony in the links between Pretoria and Jerusalem, given the history of explicitly pro-Nazi feeling in South Africa during World
War II. But international politics does make strange bedfellows,
and many South African Jews no doubt regard Israel as their preferred place of escape in the event the South African system
should collapse. (There is already a substantial immigration between the two countries, in both directions.)

But the real issue for most white South Africans is how to
secure and cash in on the enduring friendship of the United
States. It is a fundamental, if mostly unwritten and unspoken, assumption of white South Africa that if and when the crunch finally
comes, the Americans will step in and rescue them from disaster.
For an American visitor to argue otherwise—to say that in the
post-Vietnam era the American people have become more cautious, or that black American soldiers are unlikely to cooperate in
putting down black South African rebels—is considered at best
ignorant and at worst insulting. The idea that most Americans do
not pay much attention to events in southern Africa is, to white
South Africans, inconceivable.

The standing of the United States among black and white
South Africans has varied greatly in recent years. Jimmy Carter,
his vice-president, Walter Mondale, and his UN ambassador, An-

drew Young, were regarded as public enemies by the ruling whites, and even by many of their liberal white opponents, while they were in power in Washington; South African blacks, however, regarded them as heroes for the pressure they put on the regime both privately and publicly. (Particularly controversial was the 1977 meeting in Vienna between Mondale and then South African Prime Minister John Vorster, in which Mondale, departing from his script, said the United States favored a system of one man, one vote for South Africa.) The situation was reversed during the Reagan administration, with the blacks resenting the policy of "constructive engagement" and most whites appreciating it. The feelings ran so strong that many well-known Coloured and African figures began refusing invitations to functions at the American embassy or consulates around the country, and some declined invitations to visit the United States that they would have readily accepted a few years earlier. On the other hand, one white cabinet minister summed up his view of the Reagan policy by saying, "Finally we have the feeling that we are in the company of decent people."

For the many South African whites who deplore the country's racial policies and the government's brutality, daily life is full of compromises and choices. Even to eat in a whites-only restaurant or to ride on a whites-only bus involves a certain degree of cooperation with the system, and there is virtually no one who manages to operate free of the constraints and the guilty conscience imposed by apartheid.

A small number of mixed couples, it is said, live almost completely underground, moving often, frequently hidden by friends, sometimes even concealing the existence of their illegal children, who are eventually smuggled out of the country for an education. Whites whose discontent takes more prosaic forms struggle to find ways to express it. Even to consider signing a petition for greater restraints on the country's security police, to be published in the newspapers on international Human Rights Day, sometimes becomes an agonizing decision, an occasion for soul-searching about the reactions of professional colleagues and friends. There is a constant fear of witch-hunting, of getting on a list of troublemakers to be watched or interrogated—or worse—in times of crisis. Those who end up being cautious are bound to be resentful of those who act more boldly, and vice versa. Friendships are often dissolved along the way.

With multiracial political parties banned—the last to go was the Liberal party, headed by author Alan Paton, which dissolved itself in 1968 rather than expel its nonwhite members—the official parliamentary opposition to the apartheid regime has fallen to the Progressive Federal party, or the "Progs." For years the symbol of that party (and sometimes its only member of Parliament) was Helen Suzman, who represented a liberal constituency in the Johannesburg suburbs and achieved worldwide fame for her ability to irritate and enrage the ruling establishment. Under a new, outspoken Afrikaner leader, Frederik van Zyl Slabbert, the Progs began to pick up more seats in Parliament during the late 1970s (they inherited a few members when the old United party split apart), but they were reviled by increasingly militant black leaders for continuing to participate in the all-white political system. Finally, in 1984, as the government implemented its new constitution, the Progs decided to defy the "Prohibition of Political Interference Act" and open membership to people of all races.

One outlet for opposition that has become popular among white middle-class women over the years is an organization called the Black Sash. Decades ago, when such forms of protest were still permitted, its members conducted mass marches and national demonstrations to call attention to injustices. Under newer regulations, they must protest singly and quietly, but they are still a common sight standing at urban intersections during rush hour, a black swatch of material draped across one shoulder, placards propped up against their bodies or a nearby post, so that motorists will be able to read them. In eight offices around the country, Sash members also counsel Africans who have been arrested for pass law violations on how to assert their rights. Once the organization had ten thousand members; now it is down to two thousand, but claims to be growing again.

A handful of other whites have gone much farther in their challenge to the system. At least half a dozen are in prison, having been convicted of sabotage or of having passed information on sensitive matters to the ANC. But one of the martyrs of South African protest in recent years was involved in much less dramatic activities. Neil Aggett was twenty-eight years old when he died in a police cell in Johannesburg in 1982 while being detained under the security laws. He was a white physician who earned a minimal income by treating patients in the emergency room of Baragwanath Hospital in Soweto at night, so that he could do organizing work for one of the black labor unions, without pay, in the daytime. By all accounts a humble, idealistic, self-effacing man, Aggett was one of the few whites who was genuinely regarded as a hero by black South Africans. At least fifteen thousand people risked official reprisals by marching behind his coffin at his funeral, and almost a hundred thousand workers nationwide paused from their tasks one day in a silent half-hour tribute to his memory. The police claimed that Aggett committed suicide while in custody, but fellow prisoners said that he had been subjected to physical and psychological torture beforehand that put him into a suicidal state. Although it was acknowledged that Aggett spent 110 hours in interrogation rooms during his last week alive, a magistrate exonerated the police of any culpability in his death. Aggett was the fifty-second person to die in detention under suspicious circumstances in South Africa, but the first white.

Many white South Africans who find it impossible to come to terms with the system, or to design a meaningful and effective form of protest, simply go into exile and live as more or less permanent external critics of their country. Some insist at first that they will return one day and help to change things, but very few do. Most go to Britain or the United States—there are said to be more than twenty thousand white South African exiles in London alone—where they soon get caught up in new lives and fade from public view at home or abroad. The rebellious journalist Donald Woods, for example, continued to receive attention for a few years after his escape from house arrest, but then faded from public view until the film *Cry Freedom* brought attention back to him.

Before a change in strategy that led it to detain many more people on unspecified security charges, the government kept dozens of its harshest critics—especially articulate whites who had contacts with the press—under harsh "banning orders" that restricted their movements and their communication with other people. The rules were often oppressive—no attendance at meetings, no "social gatherings" with more than one other person at a time, no travel outside a specified area, no visits to factories or schools—and strictly enforced, with several security officers sometimes assigned to follow a single banned person.

But Andrew Boraine, the former president of NUSAS and son of a Progressive member of Parliament, insisted that it was still possible to live a meaningful life of protest while under a ban. Resisting suggestions that he leave the country, as did many of his NUSAS predecessors and colleagues, Boraine took a job running an "alternative book shop" near Cape Town University, called "Open Books," which specialized in materials that argued against apartheid and other forms of racism. When asked to explain the pressures of living as a banned person and the reasons he did not leave, he said, "Look, this is still a great place, despite what's going on. I have a lot of friends, black and white . . . there are a lot of good times to be had, despite what the Group Areas and Immorality Acts and the rest say. . . . I know that the majority of the people in this country are on my side." Although he had twice been detained and harshly interrogated, and knew he was subject to that prospect again, soon after his banning order was lifted in 1983 Boraine was active in launching the United Democratic Front.*

Given the large number of young white people who appear to oppose the apartheid system, and who object to the military effort in Namibia, for years one heard surprisingly little talk in South Africa of draft resistance. (South Africa had no conscription until the early 1950s, but in 1968 military service was made compulsory for all white males.) Random interviews with young men of draft age produce mostly declarations of their intention and desire to serve their country. Nonetheless, the South African Defense Force now acknowledges that some three to four thousand, or 15 to 20 percent, of the approximately twenty thousand people called up to serve every year fail to report for duty. Most of them are assumed to have gone overseas or into hiding to avoid military service, but a few have become outspoken resisters and risked a six-year prison term to make a point. With military forces increas-

---

* The government's newer tactic of trying to obtain convictions in the courts for technical violations of the security laws and other statutes has affected people of all colors. One young African mechanic was sentenced to prison for drinking tea from a mug that had ANC slogans on it, and two reggae singers got a four-year sentence for including ANC songs in their performance at a Johannesburg music festival. Another African man was imprisoned for eight years for wearing clothes with the ANC's colors; a white woman was charged under the censorship laws for having a supply of T-shirts that supported athletic boycotts of South Africa.

ingly being used to quell disturbances in black townships and to search for subversives there, the level of resistance was expected to increase; even some of those who were willing to fight in Namibia were horrified by the idea of being sent into action against South Africa's black population. Only in 1983 did the South African Parliament enact a law providing for a narrowly defined form of conscientious objection. Those whose application for that status is approved must perform six years of community service, instead of two to four on active duty in the military.

For many years the only truly effective and open opposition to the National party government was provided by South Africa's English-language press. Since the Afrikaans press tended to identify with government policy, there were many stories revealing official foibles and foolishness that appeared only in the English-language newspapers. Indeed, this so bothered the Information Department of the government that it surreptitiously channeled official funds in the mid-1970s to support the launching of a right-wing English-language paper called *The Citizen*. Were it not for investigations by the more established press, that action and other abuses of the Information Department's secret slush funds might never have been revealed. Similarly, it was only because of extensive English-language press coverage that the membership and the activities of the Afrikaner *Broederbond* were exposed for open discussion in South Africa and abroad.

But through various legal actions, political threats, and economic pressures, the South African English-language press has been rendered somewhat more tame in recent years. Because of strict laws governing the coverage of security matters, vast areas of South African government policy and behavior, including most of its actions in Namibia and Angola, have gone virtually unreported at home, except when official statements were released in Pretoria or Cape Town. On occasions when the press has been able to communicate black views or plans to the white public, the government's reaction has been to subpoena the reporters involved and demand that they reveal their sources; the South African Society of Journalists has warned that if these tactics are successful, one of the few remaining informal channels of communication between blacks and whites will be cut off. At various times the government has threatened to enact legislation or issue decrees further restricting press freedom, only to withdraw them at the last moment on the basis of an implicit commitment by the press to censor itself and otherwise behave with greater restraint. (When the bulk of the English-language press supported P. W. Botha's plan for constitutional reform, there was a substantial warming of relations with the government.) Some of the few black journalists working for the mainstream South African press have been banned or detained, and their all-black organization, the Media Workers Association of South Africa, subjected to investigation and harassment. A few new publications have cropped up, such as the monthly magazine *Frontline,* to fill in with the kind of irreverent and skeptical reporting that used to appear in the daily English-language press, but these journals reach a very limited audience. The shift in the role of the press was underlined in April 1985 when the *Rand Daily Mail* of Johannesburg, once the country's leading opposition newspaper, closed down, the victim of financial crisis and government disapproval. All publications suffered with the emergence of the state-controlled SABC radio and television as the dominant news organization in South Africa—reliable vehicles for the government to use to influence the way the white minority, in particular, sees the world.

The South African government has put overt and often intense pressures in recent years on foreign journalists and South Africans working for foreign media. Returning to an attitude common in the 1960s, when foreign journalists were sometimes expelled for writing things the government did not like, politicians and officials took to warning foreign reporters of the "serious repercussions" of any stories critical of South Africa. The Johannesburg office of *New York Times* correspondent Joseph Lelyveld was ransacked in 1982 while he was away, and there were suspicions that the culprits were members of the security police looking for the identity of some of his news sources.

One special target of government action was Allister Sparks, former editor of the *Rand Daily Mail,* who later became a correspondent for the *Washington Post* and the *Observer* of London. A South African citizen, Sparks was charged under the country's internal security laws with quoting a banned person (Winnie Mandela) and publishing alleged untruths about the South African security police, even though the articles in question had appeared overseas, in a Dutch newspaper. At one point, security police raided Sparks's home and office, seizing documents, tapes, and a typewriter. His wife and a friend who is a free-lance journalist were charged with obstructing justice for allegedly concealing or removing some of the materials sought by the police, but all charges were dropped several months later.

Another category of white protest, on the Afrikaner radical right, is taken very seriously by the South African government. There is, for example, an organization called the Orange Workers, run by a former minister of the Dutch Reformed Church with an emblematic name that commands attention and respect in South Africa, Hendrik Verwoerd, Jr. The late prime minister's son and namesake seeks to establish zones in South Africa where whites can live completely apart from blacks, a kind of homelands for whites (and especially Afrikaners). The Orange Workers would go so far as banning the employment of all nonwhites in these zones, so they could not come to outnumber the whites, as they have everywhere else in South Africa. Improbable as it seems for a people who have become accustomed to having servants do all physical work for them, members of the Orange Workers commit themselves to doing all their own housework and other chores, and some have even designed houses with cement furniture that requires minimal upkeep.

One organization that takes such ideas of white separatism an important step farther is the Afrikaner Resistance Movement, led by another man with a classic Afrikaner name, Eugene Terreblanche. His followers, convinced that the government is not doing enough to defend the apartheid system, have accumulated and buried caches of weapons that they intend to use to protect the *vaderland*. The government arrested and prosecuted several members of the movement in 1982 and 1983, and for a time it seemed to be discredited. But early in 1984, after white voters had approved the new constitution granting limited political participation to Coloureds and Indians, Terreblanche's name turned up on a list of people invited by Carel Boshoff, brother-in-law of Hendrik Verwoerd, Jr., to help form a new organization to guarantee the Afrikaners' "retention of a separate cultural identity." Boshoff, a theologian, had been forced out as head of the *Broederbond* because of his extreme views and felt that a new, more militant group had to be created.

That alternative emerged in May 1984 as the *Afrikaner*

Volkswag ("People's Guard"), which rallied seven thousand people to launch a new drive against the government from the right.
The initial meeting featured attacks on journalists (who were
called "criminals" and "intellectual mafiosi"), pornography, the
new constitution, the integration of certain public facilities, and
the increasing use of English, rather than Afrikaans, for many official and business transactions. The call for a return to racial purity
and fundamental apartheid was highlighted in a tirade delivered
by Terreblanche. As six young men wearing swastika-like insignias
and heavy black boots stood at his side, he concluded his speech
by giving the Nazi salute.

It is difficult to know how widespread such extreme forms of
white protest might become, but P. W. Botha was clearly worried
about a continued hemorrhage of support from the National party
on the right. The day did not seem distant when a coalition of
right-wing forces might replace the Progressive Federal party as
the official opposition in the white Parliament.

One incident in January 1983 poignantly demonstrated South
Africa's ability to dominate the entire southern African region.
King Moshoeshoe II of Lesotho was about to open a meeting
of the Southern African Development Coordination Conference
(SADCC) in his capital of Maseru. But the proceedings were suddenly interrupted by three explosions. The bombs damaged the
water supply to an abattoir that had just been built with Dutch
aid as part of an attempt to help Lesotho, which is surrounded
entirely by South African territory, to achieve greater independence in its food supply and other aspects of its economy. The
thunderous, exquisitely timed explosions were set off by the
Lesotho Liberation Army (LLA), the military wing of a banned
leftist political party, which, despite its ideological incompati-
bility, was supported by South Africa as an exercise in destabili-
zation. If the members of SADCC—an organization formed to encourage regional cooperation and self-reliance as an alternative to
dependence on South Africa—had any illusions about their prospects for success, this was one more sobering experience. South
Africa's might is always close at hand.

It was after P. W. Botha became South African prime minister in 1978 and named the former chief of the nation's military,
Magnus Malan, to succeed him as defense minister that a new

aggressive regional policy was instituted in Pretoria. The assumption behind it was that most of the trouble in southern Africa was caused by Communist subversion, if not direct action by the Soviet Union, and that South Africa would have to counteract this "total onslaught." While taking a reformist line on some domestic issues, Botha adopted a bellicose stance outside South Africa's borders. He not only authorized strikes against suspected ANC bases and offices in neighboring countries, but also involved South Africa in direct and indirect efforts to destabilize their governments. Ideological considerations were secondary; the regimes would be weakened, whether that meant helping exponents of the right or the left. One of the most frequent philosophical justifications was the comparison to Israel and the claim that unless South Africa acted to preempt terrorism, it would soon find itself encircled and threatened in much the same way that Israel does. (This reasoning neglected an important difference between the two countries: the vast majority of the people living inside South Africa might be regarded as potential opponents of the rulers, which is not the case in Israel.) The fact that most of the governments in the region remained fundamentally dependent on South Africa—for food, energy, and transportation, not to mention jobs—made it easier to carry out this policy.

From the time of the civil war that engulfed Angola in the mid-1970s, South Africa maintained a more or less constant presence in the southern part of that country, establishing its own bases there and using them to interdict anti-South African guerrillas heading south for Namibia, to launch occasional raids deeper inside Angola, and to coordinate with the forces of Jonas Savimbi's National Union for the Total Independence of Angola (UNITA). It was scarcely a secret that the South Africans worked with and supplied Savimbi—even the chief of the South African Defense Force, General Constand Viljoen, said publicly, "I know him very well indeed. I think a lot of him"—and through Savimbi, they were able to calibrate the pressure on the leftist government in Luanda.

That policy paid off for South Africa late in 1983. The Angolan government, having first rejected a South African offer of a cease-fire, yielded under further military pressure and finally agreed to engage in negotiations with Pretoria, initially with American mediation. The result, formalized in February 1984 at a ceremony in Lusaka, Zambia, was an agreement on a phased withdrawal of South African forces from Angola and joint patrols by Angolan and South African troops to stop the flow of SWAPO guerrillas into Namibia.* South Africa's withdrawal from Angola took far longer than originally scheduled, and fighting continued in both Namibia and Angola—South Africa proved to be unable, or unwilling, to persuade Savimbi to curtail his guerrilla attacks—but the agreement stood as an extraordinary example of South Africa's capacity to convert a Marxist enemy into a partner of sorts. For P. W. Botha, the agreement with Angola represented vindication of his regional strategy, as well as the first step in a settlement of the crisis in Namibia on South African, rather than United Nations, terms.

South African intervention in the other former Portuguese colony in the region, Mozambique, was logistically less complicated, because of the countries' substantial common border. Whenever the SADF wanted to strike at suspected ANC bases there, it did so with impunity and with little resistance. Early one morning in January 1981, South African soldiers dressed in Mozambican uniforms drove unimpeded across fifty miles of Mozambican territory in armored cars; once in the capital of Maputo, they killed or captured the people they were looking for, and then drove home. South Africa later struck several times from the air against supposed ANC facilities in Mozambique, and it was also believed to be responsible for the letter bomb that killed Ruth First (an exiled South African historian and the wife of Joe Slovo, a key figure in the ANC) at her university office in Maputo.

Perhaps most significant was South African support for the Mozambique National Resistance movement (MNR or RENAMO), an antigovernment guerrilla operation that disrupted agricultural areas, hydroelectric dams, railroad lines, and oil pipelines in that country (especially a pipeline that was the major means of supplying imported oil to Zimbabwe). According to some Western intelligence reports, South Africa actually trained MNR forces at camps in the Transvaal and airlifted them and their supplies across Zimbabwean territory to forward bases inside Mozambique.

After just a few years of independence, it was clear that Mo-

---

* The Reagan administration had hoped for membership on the joint monitoring commission, but had to settle for observer status; the developments did provide justification for the opening of an American liaison mission in the Namibian capital of Windhoek for the first time.

zambique was failing as a nation. Despite substantial assistance from the Soviet Union, its socialist economic system was foundering, the victim of drought, floods, insurgency, and inefficiency. The shops were empty of goods, agricultural production had virtually ground to a halt, and tens of thousands of people were starving to death. Notwithstanding ideological differences between the two countries, one of the main sources of employment and income for Mozambican men remained jobs in the South African mines. Finally, in December 1983, having already toured Western Europe in search of aid that had been refused by the Eastern bloc, Mozambique's president, Samora Machel, was compelled to open negotiations with South Africa on Pretoria's terms.

The result, signed in March 1984, was a "nonaggression and good neighborliness" pact between Mozambique and South Africa. Known as the "Nkomati Accord" (for the river that forms the boundary between the two countries), it pledged South Africa to stop aiding the MNR in exchange for Mozambique's promise to control ANC activities there. But above all, it was another victory for Botha and a symbolic reaffirmation of South Africa's dominant position in the region; when Machel shook his hand at the border post of Komatipoort, Botha was in effect accepting the surrender of one of his country's most militant opponents. (In an explanation of the extraordinary turn of events, Maputo Radio said, "One does not sign a nonaggression pact with one's friends . . . as long as apartheid exists, Mozambique cannot have friendly relations with South Africa, but we can have, and we intend to have, good neighborly relations with South Africa. One can choose one's friends, but not one's neighbors.") It was clear that Mozambique hoped for a respite from South Africa's pressure, which it said had cost almost $4 billion, as well as friendly consideration, including debt rescheduling, from Western nations and banks. It also looked ahead to a revival of trade with South Africa and even a return of free-spending white South African tourists to the Indian Ocean beaches of Maputo, where they had been a fixture in colonial days, when the capital was known as Lourenço Marques.

Mozambican police raided the homes of several prominent ANC members, arresting people and confiscating weapons; it seemed obvious that South Africa would now have an easier time monitoring the activities of any exiles who remained there. Pretoria's formal assistance to the MNR was cut back, although a number of wealthy South African zealots stepped in with private assistance to the guerrilla organization, which continued to harass the Mozambican regime. The South African government had enough confidence in the prospects for stability in Mozambique, however, to lend millions of dollars to rebuild that country's railroads and the Maputo harbor, which it pledged to use again for a large percentage of the Transvaal's imports and exports. It also promised to build a meat-canning factory in Maputo. That city's name suddenly appeared on South Africa's highway signs, and groups of white tourists began to venture forth cautiously across the border.

South Africa pressured Lesotho to sign a similar pact, but that was hardly necessary. Since the kingdom's only border is with South Africa, the entry and exit of almost all people and goods are easy for the Pretoria regime to control, and the South Africans are in a position to create shortages in Lesotho simply by tightening up and slowing down the routine checks at all border posts, Lesotho could be strangled altogether in just a week. The Lesotho government talks a tough line publicly and takes certain steps that provoke South Africa's anger and fear, such as establishing relations with the Soviet Union, China, and North Korea; but privately it accedes to virtually every South African demand. South African agents are known to operate with impunity on Lesotho's soil. After South Africa's December 1982 raid on Maseru, Lesotho expelled the two dozen alleged ANC members who were on a list provided by Pretoria. Chief Leabua Jonathan, the prime minister, won a pre-independence election in 1965 largely because of South African help, and his conservative government stayed in power for two decades with South African connivance. But in January 1986, as unrest continued to mount within South Africa and government officials looked for outsiders to blame, the South Africans—complaining that Lesotho had once again allowed the ANC to build up its strength there and that the tiny country was developing too many relationships with the communist world— suddenly overthrew the 71-year-old Chief Jonathan. After a nine-teen-day South African blockade that severely frightened the people of Lesotho, they reacted with some relief to the appearance of a military council headed by Major General Justin Lekhanya, who had Pretoria's confidence and support. The South Africans immediately allowed three freight trains carrying vital food and supplies to cross the border, and Foreign Minister R. F. "Pik" Botha declared after meeting with a delegation from Maseru that "good neighborliness" would now be possible.

South African agents have also been accused of secret raids, kidnappings and assassinations inside the tiny kingdom of Swaziland, despite that country's promises to cooperate with Pretoria. After the Maseru raid, the Swazis, fearing a similar action in their country, rounded up three hundred South African refugees thought to be associated with the ANC and put them in a detention camp. Officials in Pretoria believed that ANC guerrillas, with or without Swazi government knowledge or permission, sometimes stored arms there or used the country as an infiltration route into South Africa from Mozambique. Soon after South Africa's agreements with Angola and Mozambique, the Swazi government made known a secret pact it had signed with Pretoria two years earlier.

For some time, however, the Swazis have been preoccupied with their own succession crisis. When King Sobhuza II died in 1982 at the age of eighty-three, leaving dozens of widows and scores of children, the royal family had to invoke a process for selecting a ruler that it had not used in almost eighty years. There were few people alive who remembered the rules. At first a progressive, modernizing prime minister appeared to be in control, but he was dismissed by the queen-regent under pressure from a council of elders. He was accused ultimately of treason, and the elders installed a more traditionalist government that would be more accommodating to the wishes of South Africa. The implication of outside influence was obvious, and supposedly independent Swaziland began to seem more and more like a fiefdom of South Africa.

From its size and location on the map, one might expect Botswana to pose a substantial security problem for South Africa. Indeed, although it is very sparsely populated with its own citizens (only three people per square mile), Botswana has a larger number of genuine South African refugees than any other country in the region. But its cautious government has kept tight control over the refugees and tried to prevent its territory from being used for the smuggling of arms or the launching of attacks into South Africa. If those activities took place, it was almost surely without the knowledge or connivance of Botswana's authorities.

Despite the fact that it is 80 percent desert, Botswana has done relatively well since independence; it is the world's fourth largest diamond producer, and coal, copper, and nickel are also mined there. Its multiparty system has functioned smoothly, and after its long-time president, Sir Seretse Khama, died in 1980, he was succeeded by his vice-president, Quett Masire, without any open signs of unrest or rancor. That is probably why South Africans rarely mention Botswana when they insist that Africans are unable to govern themselves.

Botswana, too, was urged by the South Africans to sign a formal nonaggression pact. Pretoria applied economic pressures— for example, delaying the transmission to Botswana of revenues due from the regional customs union—and South African Foreign Minister Botha complained that cooperation between the two countries' security services was "not satisfactory." "Should it become necessary," he said, "the South African forces would strike back over a wider front than just terrorist targets." But Botswana officials tried to demonstrate that a formal pact was unnecessary; when several suspected ANC members fled across the border after a shootout with South African police, they were promptly arrested by Botswana police officers. In 1985 and again in 1986, however, the South African Defense Force added Botswana to its hit list, striking at alleged ANC bases inside that country.

The expanded role of the South African military in the region has led to enormous increases in the South African defense budget—nearly 1,000 percent between 1970 and 1981, when it reached $2.76 billion, according to the London-based International Institute of Strategic Studies. Another 21.4 percent rise was announced in 1984, amidst indications that the country's military establishment has been running much of its regional policy. The military has been highly successful at violating arms embargoes and smuggling weapons into South Africa, and the country now has a booming arms industry of its own. A "State Security Council," chaired by the president and including military, police, and intelligence officials, increasingly functioned as a sort of inner cabinet in recent years. According to studies of its work, the council eroded the role of the rest of the cabinet and of Parliament in the formulation of national polices in both the foreign and domestic fields; most of its staff comes from the military.

Increasingly, South Africa came to regard itself, and to be portrayed by international analysts, as a "regional superpower."

There was little room for doubt that the SADF would be able to vanquish any outside attacker. In maneuvers held in September 1984, the military demonstrated that it was also capable of mobilizing and equipping thousands of civilian reservists within a few days to defend their country; in a crisis, South Africa could call upon four hundred thousand such reservists and trained commandos to supplement its standing army of more than eighty thousand men. No other military force on the continent could match that might, with the possible exception of faraway Nigeria, where the military was hardly about to try to become involved in South Africa.

The ever clearer impression of South African prowess contributed to a new smugness in the country's diplomatic affairs. Despite all the sympathetic support the regime obtained from the Reagan administration's policy of "constructive engagement," it did not hesitate to exclude or embarrass American representatives at various key moments in the negotiations for regional accords. Nor indeed did it give the United States any concessions in exchange for "constructive engagement." In a typical demonstration of South African cockiness, when the Labour party came to power in New Zealand and its new prime minister, David Lange, threatened to close the South African consulate in that country as a protest against apartheid, Pretoria beat him to it, shutting the consulate immediately and bringing its diplomats home.

For South Africans, the most important symbolic change was that P. W. Botha, suddenly regarded as a world statesman rather than a pariah, was welcomed on official visits to Britain, Switzerland, Austria, Belgium, West Germany, and Italy in 1984. The first such European tour by a South African leader since one by Field Marshal Jan Smuts in 1946, Botha's trip provoked a few demonstrations and statements of disapproval, but he was politely, and in some cases ceremonially, received. The journey had no great concrete result, but the impact at home was enormous; Botha's every move was minutely reported in the South African press, and the overall impression was that South Africa had achieved a new level of acceptability, if not quite approval, from the Western world of which it claimed to be a part.

None of this, however, could conceal the tense and precarious situation within South Africa. At least forty people died in the violence that accompanied and followed the elections for the

Coloured and Indian chambers of Parliament in August 1984, the most serious outbreak since the riots in Soweto and other black townships in 1976. In this case, the grievances varied—one was an increase in rents and electric rates for government-owned housing—but blacks who cooperated with the system, including "township councilors," and Asian traders were most often the targets. (Among the people attacked on this and previous occasions as "stooges" of the government was one of South Africa's best-known black union organizers, Lucy Mvubelo, general secretary of the National Union of Clothing Workers. Apparently because of her support for continued foreign investment in the country, she was targeted by a group called the South African Suicide Squad, and her home in Soweto was repeatedly firebombed.) The police, responding with rubber bullets and whips, demonstrated once again that they were firmly in control, but the government also showed a willingness to use the military to put down black unrest. There was a symbolic component in these events, too: the worst rioting and the largest number of deaths occurred in Sharpeville, scene of the 1960 massacre that give rise to modern-day black militancy in South Africa.

As if offended that anyone would try to spoil the aura of celebration around implementation of the new constitution, the government detained many people who had advocated a boycott of Coloured and Indian elections, including leaders of the United Democratic Front and other opponents of the constitution. It also issued a new edict, forbidding indoor gatherings of two or more people to discuss government policy (a proviso which, if strictly applied, could affect the meetings of corporate boards of directors, not to mention dinner parties). And in an attempt to squelch one of the few remaining forms of legal black protest—at funerals and memorial services—it extended the ban to cover meetings "in memoriam of anything."

There was a new flash of black anger in the final months of 1984, as labor unrest engulfed South Africa. First the gold mines were hit; several people were killed and hundreds injured in violence that accompanied negotiations over a new contract for mine workers. Then, in early November, some eight hundred thousand workers participated in a two-day general strike in the Johannesburg area. More than a dozen deaths were reported, and the state-owned Sasol Corporation fired six thousand workers, 90 percent of its black labor force, for taking part in the protest; most of them were sent off to the homelands. Union leaders were arrested again, and the unusually successful work stoppage was attributed by a cabinet member to "instigators, arsonists and radicals." A report by the country's Catholic bishops warned that as a result of the government's overreaction to such protests, "a kind of state of war is developing between the police and the people." As if to increase its own capacity to fight that war, the government announced plans to expand the civilian police by 45 percent and to make "riot control" a regular duty of the South African Defense Force.

Early in 1985 the center of black protest shifted to the economically depressed Eastern Cape region. On March 21, the twenty-fifth anniversary of the Sharpeville massacre, a group of blacks from one township on the outskirts of the white industrial city of Uitenhage set out to attend a memorial service in another nearby township for three people who had been killed in an earlier clash with police. When this group refused orders to disperse, the police fired into the crowd, killing at least nineteen people, including some children; a subsequent investigation revealed that many of them had been shot in the back. This incident led to a series of funerals that turned into protest rallies and new clashes between blacks and police; it also set off protest marches around the country, in which government opponents seemed willing to resort to civil disobedience for the first time in decades. The prospect was that confrontation would build in the Eastern Cape, where the Africans are particularly impoverished but well organized, the Coloureds are in the process of being radicalized, and hard-pressed lower middle class Afrikaners are beginning to show signs of a backlash against recent reforms.

As many whites began to feel the brunt of the protests more directly than before, there were new appeals for the country's rulers to compromise. Six employer groups, including the Afrikaner chamber of commerce, issued a statement urging that blacks be given a meaningful political role in national affairs and that most of the key elements of the apartheid system be dismantled. P. W. Botha, opening the first formal working session of the new tricameral Parliament in January 1985, hinted that he might use his new power as state president to force some of those issues into the open. He spoke of establishing "political structures" for urban blacks and said that "the question of citizenship" in South Africa had to be clarified. Botha also offered to establish an informal "forum" through which blacks who refused to participate in the South African system might nonetheless communicate with the white authorities. A week later, the government announced a moratorium on the forced relocation of blacks living in white areas, pending a review of policy. Botha's initiatives were attacked by the right wing as dangerous moves toward racial integration; black leaders dismissed them as vague and tentative. Botha seemed to validate the latter view when, panicked by the wave of unrest in the Eastern Cape, he authorized new restrictive measures against opposition figures only weeks after having seemed to promise new concessions.

One avenue of dissent and protest the government still seemed utterly unable to reach and control. Bombs continued to be discovered, and sometimes to explode in the heart of white South Africa, including electricity substations and government offices. It was no longer plausible to place all of the blame on neighboring black-ruled states that were harboring ANC guerrillas. It was just possible that a long, slow, inconclusive war was beginning at home.

P. W. Botha's introduction of the new tricameral parliamentary system coincided with—and, to a considerable extent, caused—the most devastating internal violence South Africa has experienced since the formation of a unified state in 1910. Indeed, South Africa's crisis entered an entirely new phase, with much of the rest of the world anxiously watching the macabre events far more closely than ever before, speculating aloud about when the denouement might come.

Unrest flared in every part of the country, and for the first time there were doubts about whether the white regime, even with the extraordinary force it had at its disposal, would be able to bring the situation under control. South Africa's formidable military machine came to be required almost full-time to help suppress domestic protest, despite an increase of 25 percent in recruitments into the police force. (This did not stop the military, of course, from continuing its mischief beyond South Africa's borders. In May 1985, for example, South African commandos were discovered attempting to blow up the Gulf Oil refinery in Angola's Cabinda enclave, about one thousand miles north of the Namibian border. The captured leader of the commandos, Captain Wynand du Toit, dismissed the official explanation by the government in Pretoria that this was only an intelligence-gathering mission; he said the raid was intended to sabotage American business interests in Angola, damage the Angolan economy, and create the impression that the South African–supplied UNITA guerrillas of Jonas Savimbi were doing well.)

One remaining form of nonviolent black protest the police and the military were utterly unable to control: economic boycotts of white merchants by black consumers, who have 47 percent of the total buying power in the country (compared to 40 percent for whites). In the coastal city of Port Elizabeth, for example, white-owned food, clothing, and furniture stores lost at least 30 percent of their business when the well-organized black community withdrew its patronage; meanwhile, black-owned businesses profited from an increase in sales. The government could not easily neutralize this tactic; it might arrest boycott leaders and harass black shopkeepers—and it did—but it could hardly force people to resume their old buying habits.

In July 1985, frustrated and fearful over the growth of violence, sensitive to charges by the right wing that the state was losing its grip, and indecisive about how to proceed with his own program of piecemeal reform, Botha imposed a state of emergency in thirty-six districts around the country, many of them in the eastern Cape. Under its terms, the police and the military were given virtually unrestricted authority to act when and where they saw fit. Later he added two more districts in the Cape Town area, and in some black townships that were not formally covered by the emergency, strict curfews were put into effect. All across South Africa, the government lashed out with a new ferociousness. Thousands of people who were identifiable as opponents of the regime, including activists from the United Democratic Front, were arrested without charges and detained without a hearing, in the naive belief that peace could somehow be achieved by taking them out of circulation. Conservatives inside and outside the government who felt that the unrest had reached an intolerable level were pleased that Botha had finally taken decisive action. They were soon startled, however, to discover that calm had not been achieved. On the contrary, one of the first

effects of the draconian application of the state of emergency was
that strife broke out in many other areas not covered by it, places
that had previously seemed at least temporarily immune from the
uproar. For example, Durban, the capital of Natal province, which
had often appeared to be unaffected by the national crisis, suddenly became a hotbed of protest.

As the state of emergency wore on, the daily death toll
steadily increased. And things began to happen that further
eroded the South African government's claim that the country
was a bastion of Western civilization where decency and humanity prevailed. In addition to the sixteen hundred or more
confirmed deaths and the thousands of detentions that occurred
in the period from late 1984 until mid-1986, more than a hundred
other South Africans mysteriously vanished, many of them suspected victims of clandestine elements within the state security
apparatus. A court in Port Elizabeth verified a young doctor's
charge that many political detainees were being routinely tortured while in jail, and the judge ordered immediate improvements; the doctor who brought the charges found herself ostracized as a troublemaker.

It was widely known that the police, when sweeping through
some black townships, arrested young children who refused to
end their school boycotts and return to classes; in some cases,
their parents had to search frantically for them in jail and then
plead for their release. But a report compiled by an American
group, the Lawyers Committee for Human Rights, with the help
of two South African organizations, Black Sash and the Detainees'
Parents Support Committee, charged that more than two hundred children had actually been killed and hundreds of others injured by the police at the height of the emergency. Some students
suspected of throwing stones at official vehicles, the report said,
were pursued with *sjamboks* (metal-tipped whips) and badly
beaten; children who tried to run away from confrontations with
the police were randomly shot at, often from behind. With the
government's unwitting assistance, an entire new generation of
black South Africans was being radicalized. Many children, out
of school for months or even years at a time, had little exposure
to the Western democratic ideals once unanimously embraced by
those who sought to change their country.

The most militant opponents of the government responded

298   AFRICA

to the emergency by trying to make the townships ungovernable.
They set out particularly to raise the price of collaboration with
the apartheid system. In Alexandra, a small and especially tense
township on the northern outskirts of Johannesburg, the entire
nine-member governing council finally had to resign and seek
police protection from the activists who became the real authorities in the community. Attempting to ambush the armored personnel carriers that often brought the government forces into
their neighborhoods, the residents of Alexandra dug ditches three
feet deep across their roads, and justice was dispensed by "people's courts." Before long, posses of armed men were formed on
the other side and attacked the homes and families of the anti-
government activists. Alexandra was at war. Reviving an old tactic that was little known in the outside world, black vigilantes in
Alexandra and elsewhere captured black township officials and
people suspected of being informers for the police and executed
them by using "the necklace"—a gasoline-filled tire that was
pulled over the culprit's body and set afire. (The room that
served as the clandestine headquarters for one of the "people's
courts" in Alexandra had two automobile tires painted on the
wall.)

Although the state-controlled television network generally
tried to downplay the extent and the seriousness of the new racial
confrontation in South Africa, the image of black collaborators
being burned alive in "the necklace" was one that it seemed to
want to broadcast, as if to stress the point that blacks could not
get along with each other and therefore could never be trusted to
participate in governing the country. (Viewers overseas were
equally horrified by this image, and there was evidence that
South African black protesters lost some of their support from
moderates in the United States after these executions were initially viewed on American television.) The government also stood
back with apparent satisfaction as rival tribes—especially the Zulu
and the Pondo—did open battle with each other in both urban
and rural areas.

Despite these developments, most of the blacks who died
during this period did so at the hands of government forces. With
virtually all public meetings banned, the outdoor funerals for
these victims became the major avenue of black political expression—the only place where leaders who were not in prison could

speak out and some foreign representatives could demonstrate their solidarity. The crowds attending the funerals became ever larger, reaching tens of thousands, and the speeches they heard were increasingly militant, demanding not merely justice but also vengeance. In December 1985, Winnie Mandela chose a funeral near Pretoria for twelve blacks who had been killed in a clash with the police as the opportunity to make her first public speech in twenty-five years. She proclaimed that "this is our country. . . . As you have had to bury our children today, so shall the blood of our heroes be avenged." Some funeral orators asserted that the country's economic system would have to be overthrown along with the white regime. Whereas the banner of the African National Congress had often been displayed at political funerals over the years, on at least one occasion—in Cradock, eastern Cape, at the funeral of two black activists who had disappeared and then been found murdered—it was now accompanied by the Soviet flag.

Before long, the funerals themselves were banned as a dangerous source of incitement, and in November 1985, the government, reeling from the adverse publicity it was receiving overseas, placed new restrictions on the coverage of unrest, particularly by foreign broadcasters. Access to black townships was also severely limited. Claiming that foreign television crews had sometimes encouraged violence and possibly even paid blacks to throw stones and start fires in front of their cameras, officials tightened accreditation rules and made it more difficult for foreign journalists to obtain South African visas; Law and Order Minister Louis Le Grange declared that anyone who wanted to cover incidents of unrest would first have to report to the local commanding police officer and ask permission.

The government's effort to claim that the crisis was being exaggerated by South Africa's outside critics was partially successful for a time. Many South African whites failed to perceive the gravity of the situation, if only because most of the violence was confined to the black townships. When there was trouble in Soweto, it seemed far away, a mere wisp of smoke on the horizon, for the white residents of the wealthy northern suburbs of Johannesburg. Indeed, in the crisis that began late in 1984, the death toll among blacks reached 950 just around the time when the death toll among whites reached 6. Thus, over the Christmas holidays in 1985, the white elite, including many of the liberal politicians and business and academic figures who were putting pressure on the government for change, followed their usual custom of heading for the splendid beaches of Natal and the Cape, seemingly secure in the assumption that they could put off worrying about the nation's future for at least a month. The idea of taking a long, relaxed vacation in the early stages of a civil war may seem absurd from afar, but no matter what other people around the world were saying, in South Africa few whites were yet convinced that the ultimate showdown was looming in their country. One event went a long way toward changing this—a bombing just before Christmas 1985 at a shopping center in the whites-only beach resort of Amanzimtoti, on the Indian Ocean coast south of Durban. The attack killed six whites and injured more than sixty others, including small children, who had the misfortune of being near the trash can where the bomb had been planted. It began to dawn on more whites that the battle was starting to be carried onto their turf, and that they themselves or members of their families might soon become random victims, as blacks had been for so long.

The external economic and other consequences of the deterioration of conditions inside South Africa were disastrous. As overseas confidence slipped, some investors in South African stocks panicked, and at one stage all trading on the Johannesburg foreign exchange and stock markets had to be suspended. The government found itself pleading to have both public and private foreign debts rescheduled; the rand fell to new all-time lows against the dollar (at one point it was worth barely thirty-five cents), and the international bankers who had traditionally ignored moral issues inside South Africa, so long as the profits and payments flowed freely, now became a new source of pressure on the regime. Some foreign companies operating in South Africa took matters in their own hands and began to cut back or withdraw entirely, hedging their bets for economic as well as moral and political reasons. Inevitably, a growing number of white South Africans—mostly English-speaking members of the business community—having already found ways to stash some of their money overseas, started to look for places to emigrate. Australia was a favorite destination.

Botha lifted the state of emergency after less than eight months, claiming that it had been a success and had decreased the level of violence; but in fact, the number of deaths continued to rise in 1986, despite (or perhaps because of) new regulations giving summary powers to control unrest to the minister of law and order. Indeed, from the point of view of the government, the state of emergency had been a disastrous failure; tensions were considerably greater inside the country than they had been a year earlier, and South Africa's international reputation had suffered even further. It could be argued that the only people who actually gained during the state of emergency were militant black leaders, whose constituency was broadened considerably as their worst prophecies seemed to come true.

More and more South Africans of all colors and ethnic origins became convinced that the system was foundering, that the regime's practical authority was gradually descending to the level of its moral authority. On May Day 1986, nearly 2 million black workers, responding to the call for a general strike from the Congress of South African Trade Unions, brought the country's economy virtually to a halt; COSATU promised other demonstrations of its strength in the future.

One more dramatic example of the disintegration of government authority came when a court lifted the long-standing ban on Winnie Mandela, ruling that people could no longer be banned without specific reasons being stated by the government—this after a period in which she had repeatedly outsmarted the police, until they finally found it necessary to drag her out of her home in Soweto, while reporters from around the world stood by and recorded the event. It was not only she who went free as a result of the court ruling, but also a number of other political activists who had been identified as "subversives" many years before. As they spoke up, they sounded astonishingly moderate compared to the young radicals who now held sway in the townships—leading many people to wonder whether Nelson Mandela, if released, might not also seem like a cool-headed politician and a reasonable negotiating partner.

Hints of a willingness to talk with Mandela, and to legalize the African National Congress, surfaced in London early in 1986, passed along by South African officials to a group of "eminent persons" named by the Commonwealth to study the South African dilemma and suggest some possible solutions. On several previous occasions, the Pretoria regime had talked about striking a deal with Mandela, but always on terms that he could not possibly accept—requiring him to accept citizenship in the Transkei homeland or to agree to leave South Africa altogether. Whenever the government said that Mandela would have to renounce violence as a weapon to achieve change, as a condition of his release, he replied that he could do so only if the government also renounced the use of violence against his people and if it lifted the ban on the ANC.

It was not clear, however, that P. W. Botha had the political maneuvering room to take any such bold gesture. To be sure, his own National party was deeply split, with a faction of younger and more enlightened Afrikaner activists advocating dramatic steps that might lead to negotiations with the black majority; they argued that even the most conservative Afrikaners in the rural areas would respond positively to more daring leadership. (The Progressive Federal party saw its own role diminish in this period, until its leader, Frederik van Zyl Slabbert, resigned from Parliament altogether rather than continue to try to work for change within a framework that still excluded black Africans.) But Botha, for his part, seemed to worry only about pressures from the right; his nightmare vision came true in May 1987, when the Conservative party captured enough seats to replace the PFP as the official opposition in the white chamber. Analysts of the South African military asserted that the conservatives in its ranks had their own limits, too; some feared that if Botha went too far with his reforms and still failed to quell the unrest, the Defense Force might actually attempt a coup d'état. And the policies of a military regime in South Africa would probably make all prior repression look mild by comparison.

Finally, in April 1986, Botha made good on a promise to reform the hated pass laws, abolishing the pass books themselves in favor of a common identity document for all South Africans (still denoting race) and in effect declaring that blacks would now be allowed to move freely within the country. But with the Group Areas Act unaffected, with tough rules against squatting still in place, with gross disparities in education remaining, without a major commitment to the construction of new housing for blacks in the cities—and above all, with the racial classification of every person a fundamental requirement of the South African system—the changes in the pass laws could have only a limited impact.

(They did not apply to the 8 million people deemed by the government to be citizens of the homelands, for example, and the issue of dual citizenship for the residents of the homelands remained under study.) Bishop Tutu warned blacks to "beware of the small print" in the government's new regulations, and indeed, hand in hand with this liberalization of one set of laws came a grant of new power and authority for the minister of law and order to take whatever emergency steps he found necessary to check the violence. Thus, while Botha scored points internationally (especially in Washington), it was not clear what the results of the latest reforms would be inside South Africa—although the downward spiral toward anarchy was bound to continue.

The month of May 1986 contained enough horrors to justify the most apocalyptic scenarios for South Africa's future. For reasons that were not entirely clear—perhaps because P. W. Botha wanted to convince his right-wing opponents that he could still be tough in defense of the nation—the South African military struck again beyond the country's frontiers, claiming to attack ANC facilities in Botswana, Zambia, and Zimbabwe. In fact, the dead and injured were all civilians, and there was an international chorus of outrage that the regime rejected as unacceptable interference in its affairs. (The United States, in a symbolic gesture, expelled the South African military attaché in Washington, and the South Africans retaliated by doing the same to the U.S. military attaché in Pretoria.)

But the right wing hardly seemed reassured: A few days later, militants from Eugene Terreblanche's Afrikaner Resistance Movement (AWB), giving Nazi-like salutes and waving their Swastika-like flags, took over a National party meeting in Pietersburg where Foreign Minister Pik Botha had been scheduled to speak; Afrikaner police had to tear-gas Afrikaner extremists to bring them under control. Botha's speech was cancelled, and the government was humiliated. Newly emboldened, the AWB promised to make itself heard and seen more often in opposition to the government's reform program.

Meanwhile, as a result of having advocated the release of Mandela and negotiations with the ANC, Harald Pakendorf, the editor of the Afrikaans-language daily *Die Vaderland*, was forced to resign by the newspaper's governing board, which included important figures in the ruling party. In the Crossroads squatter camp outside Cape Town, some thirty thousand people were left homeless as a result of violence between the radical leaders of the camp and conservative black vigilantes who appeared to have government support.

As the tenth anniversary of the Soweto uprising of 1976 approached, Botha—alleging that blacks planned to turn the commemoration into an "insurrection"—declared another state of emergency, this time covering the entire country. Thousands of activists were arrested, many taken from their homes in the middle of the night and put into prison without any formal charges. Some of those picked up were people who had previously filed charges of abuse against the police, and there was good reason to fear for their lives; complaining about the police would not be an option this time around, since Botha's latest restrictions indemnified the police and military from responsibility for their excesses.

Included in the emergency decree this time were draconian restrictions on the local and foreign press, banning photographs or recordings of civil unrest and forbidding the dissemination of "subversive statements." Even some of the government's remaining moderate critics were now pushed to join the international chorus of outrage. "South Africa is today a country without a free press, without the rule of law, without the full protection of the courts and without the basic human rights to speak freely, to assemble or to protest," wrote Ken Owen, editor of the Johannesburg newspaper *Business Day,* suggesting that the country had crossed "the line that separates authoritarian from totalitarian societies."

The "Eminent Persons Group" dispatched by the Commonwealth to seek a basis for a negotiated settlement in South Africa declared its mission hopeless and disbanded; its two chairmen, former Australian Prime Minister Malcolm Fraser and former Nigerian leader Olusegun Obasanjo, warned that an all-out racial war loomed in South Africa and urged the United States, Great Britain and West Germany to impose full economic sanctions on the Pretoria regime.

In the event, on June 16, 1986, the Soweto anniversary, the government was successful in maintaining relative calm and suppressing details of what was really happening inside the country. But a general strike called by black leaders was apparently successful, and millions of workers once again stayed away from jobs in protest. In many black townships, the government cut telephone service in order to restrict communication between its opponents and the outside world.

In the view of many South Africans, the turning point had finally been reached. Even so, the country's transformation would undoubtedly take many years, and thousands of additional lives would be lost along the way.

Visitors to South Africa, weary from the strain of talking race and politics almost all the time, are sometimes seized with simple insights, born of frustration. At a luncheon reception, I succumbed to the temptation to ask a distinguished, elderly Afrikaner woman journalist, "Why can't the most realistic white people just sit down with some widely supported black leaders and agree on an agenda of twelve major problems that the country needs to solve?"

"I'll tell you why," she said wearily. "Because even if they solved those twelve, then number thirteen would be the sharing of power. And that is what we cannot do, because that would be like signing our own death warrant."

NAMIBIA

In the early 1950s, Otillie Abrahams was sent to Cape Town for high school, because it was impossible for nonwhites to get a decent education in South-West Africa. She joined a militant student union that advocated her country's independence from South Africa. She was twelve years old.

At twenty-two, she was caught smuggling arms and helping plan a guerrilla war against South Africa. She barely escaped with her life. For the next five years, she and her husband were in and out of prisons in various African countries, as their governments took sides in the factional disputes within what had become the South-West Africa People's Organization (SWAPO). They went on to live the idyllic, if lonely, life of African intellectual exiles in Sweden.

Today they are back at home, the beneficiaries of an amnesty declared in 1978. While their former SWAPO brethren continued to fight a seemingly endless bush war with South African soldiers, the Abrahamses decided to look for another way to achieve independence for their country, which most people now know as Namibia.

Otillie Abrahams is hardly typical. She is known as the first black woman college graduate in her country, although her exact racial classification has been an issue for some time. Alternately considered a Coloured or a "Baster" (a smaller mixed-race group, regarded as the pioneers of civilization in Namibia), Abrahams was finally classified under the apartheid laws as a member of racial group number 69: "Other." She lives in Windhoek, the capital, among middle-class whites, rather than in the townships reserved for nonwhites on its fringes. That is now her privilege, as the regulations of "petty apartheid" begin to be lifted there.

Namibia is one of the most sparsely populated countries in sub-Saharan Africa. With an average of five people per square mile (compared with ninety-one per square mile in Kenya and two hundred and sixty-six in Nigeria), it is made up mostly of the Namib and Kalahari deserts and the high plateau in between—all the more desolate and forbidding as a result of the severe drought that has afflicted southern Africa for the past several years. But its million people could probably live in relative prosperity if the nation's mineral wealth were ever fully exploited and a substantial share of the proceeds kept within its borders. Namibia is rich in diamonds, copper, uranium, and other strategic minerals. (An old saw has it that the deposits are so rich that they sometimes disturb the instruments of airplanes flying tens of thousands of feet over Namibia.) The prices of those minerals have been depressed in recent years, but the vision of future wealth has helped make Namibia the most fought-over and negotiated-over territory in Africa today.

But Namibia has a symbolic importance for South Africa far beyond its minerals. Now that white-ruled Rhodesia has become the independent black-ruled nation of Zimbabwe, Namibia is the last geographical buffer between the apartheid state and the rest of Africa; it is also the last political distraction that stands in the way of a more intense focus by the outside world on the explosive situation in South Africa itself.

A hundred years ago, imperial Germany bargained with Britain and Portugal and staked out South-West Africa as probably its most valuable African property. The Germans ruled harshly and engaged many indigenous groups in armed conflict as they sought to assert their authority. When the Herero people resisted them, the kaiser sent his troops into action, and after three years of war, all but fifteen thousand of the eighty thousand Herero had been killed. "That nation must vanish from the face of the earth," wrote German General Lothar von Trotha at the time. But once having subdued the people, the Germans had little opportunity to develop the vast territory or to build anything there before it was occupied by South Africa, during World War I. Woodrow Wilson helped to block South African annexation of the country after the war, although the Treaty of Versailles placed it under South African administration—the rest of Germany's African empire being divided among Britain (Tanganyika and parts of Cameroon and Togo), France (the other parts of Cameroon and Togo), and Belgium (Rwanda and Burundi). The League of Nations later formalized South Africa's mandate.

For decades the South Africans ruled with indifference toward the indigenous peoples and without much attention from the outside world. When the South Africans repressed an uprising by the Bondelswarts in the 1920s, indiscriminately bombing civilians as well as combatants, the League complained but decreed no punishment. Legal trouble began only in 1946, when South Africa and the League's successor, the United Nations, began to quarrel over the country's status. The UN would not consent to South Africa's newest push for annexation, and South Africa would not agree to make it a "trusteeship" under the UN system. South Africa argued that it could still administer Namibia as a "sacred trust of civilization," even though its other obligations had disappeared with the League. The UN said that those obligations were still in force, and that South African conduct in Namibia violated the mandate.

In 1960, Ethiopia and Liberia, the only two countries in Africa that had never formally been Western colonies, brought a case against South Africa at the International Court of Justice in The Hague, challenging its right to be in Namibia and its performance there. The best legal minds of South Africa fought the court battle for years. For a time, the Pretoria government thought it was on such solid legal ground that it could even get away with making the disputed territory a fifth province of South Africa. The Court equivocated on the issue until 1971, but meanwhile the UN became angrier. In 1966, it formally revoked South Africa's mandate in South-West Africa. The General Assembly declared that the UN would have direct responsibility for the country until it became independent (a declaration it was in no position to enforce). The next year, it created a "Council for South-West Africa," and in 1968 it adopted for the country the nationalist name of Namibia. Repeatedly, ever since, the UN Security Council has demanded that South Africa grant immediate independence to Namibia, and South Africa's refusal has contributed to its growing diplomatic isolation within the United Nations and the world community.

South Africa also began to face a military challenge in Namibia in the late 1960s. SWAPO, previously a political protest movement, launched low-level guerrilla attacks in the Caprivi Strip, the knife-shaped piece of Namibia that juts eastward between Angola, Botswana and Zambia. But in 1973, once the United Nations recognized SWAPO as a "national liberation movement" and the "authentic representative of the Namibian people," the nationalist rebels began to attract Soviet and other Eastern-bloc aid, which helped them turn the skirmishes into a war. After Angola became independent from Portugal, in 1975, SWAPO obtained a new sanctuary; eventually, it brought together the offices it maintained in Zambia, Tanzania, and Zaïre, and established a headquarters in Luanda, the capital of Angola. When the UN General Assembly gave SWAPO its further imprimatur as the "sole legitimate" representative of the Namibian people, in 1976, that helped the group to rally additional African and other Third World support.

Most white South Africans have gradually come to accept the idea that Namibia will become independent—that it is not worth fighting an all-out war to hold on to South Africa's only colony, and that such a war would, in any event, probably be unwinnable. But the South African government has been haunted by the specter of another militant Marxist regime on its borders. Having already coped with the actions of Mozambique and the rhetoric of Zimbabwe, it fears that a SWAPO-ruled Namibia could eventually become a base for the ANC and other groups that want to overturn minority rule in South Africa. Given these fears, a smaller-scale guerrilla war has seemed tolerable, at least until arrangements can be made that are acceptable to the white South African political system and, with any luck, internationally as well.

Many South Africans, of course, would have liked to impose on Namibia the same farcical kind of "independence" that was accepted by Transkei, Ciskei, BophutaTswana and Venda. But Namibia is far too big, and too much an international cause célèbre, for any such status, and so the goal of the protracted military and diplomatic struggle has been to find some way to avoid simply handing over Namibia to SWAPO. Six years of negotiations under UN auspices by a "contact group" of five Western nations (the United States, Britain, France, West Germany, and Canada) produced many elaborate cease-fire and election formulas, but never an actual solution.

When the Reagan administration came into office in 1981, it asserted that its policy of "constructive engagement" toward South Africa might help reach a solution in Namibia. Its first step, taken in May 1981, was to propose a linkage between any Namibian settlement and the proposed withdrawal of Cuban troops from Angola. That linkage was eagerly seized upon by the South African government, and so at first the prospects of independence for Namibia seemed more remote than ever—the Angolans, supported by most of the rest of Africa, being unwilling to tie up what they regarded as a domestic matter in a negotiation involving South Africa. (The Angolans' justifications for the presence of the Cubans—eventually more than 50,000—included the constant incursions onto their territory by South Africa and the guerrilla war waged by Jonas Savimbi's UNITA with South African help.)

Once South Africa and Angola reached a cease-fire, with American help, hopes for peace in Namibia were raised again. The South Africans were leaving Angola, and Angola was helping to block SWAPO. Zambian President Kenneth Kaunda hosted a conference on the issue in Lusaka, and the South Africans began talking directly with SWAPO in the Cape Verde Islands (where the negotiations with Angola had first taken place). Each time there seemed to be new problems, although the South Africans began to hint that the linkage with the Cuban issue might be surmountable. The most important thing to South Africa, it became clear, was to circumvent the long-standing United Nations plan for Namibian independence; if it could do that, it might be able to force SWAPO to share power with various "internal" parties that seemed more acceptable in Pretoria.

In April 1985, defying American and other warnings, the South African government established another internal administration in Namibia; under the latest plan, Pretoria would retain control over the territory's foreign and defense affairs, but in all other respects "the leaders of the country"—leaders acceptable to South Africa—would be responsible for drafting a proposed independence constitution.

Meanwhile, for all the swirl of international diplomatic activity, in Namibia itself the economy has deteriorated. Taxes on mining companies provide the bulk of local revenues, but mineral prices are down, and so revenues are too. Some beef is exported, but even the fishing business is in a slump, and South Africa's annual economic and military subsidy to prop up Namibia is estimated at $1 billion or more. For the moment, war and politics are the country's only growth industries.

Windhoek is the center for both, and so, oddly, it has the aura of a boomtown. It is like an outpost where a few skyscrapers were built in anticipation of development that never occurred. Despite its size, its isolation, and its languor, Windhoek has a veneer of worldliness. There is a "Bangkok Massage" parlor, an exotic way to flaunt the permissiveness that has emerged in Namibian society as the South Africans have begun to let go. But the real symbol of the outside world is the Kalahari Sands Hotel. There, people just in from the bush stand baffled as they try to figure out how to use the escalator from the shopping level up to the hotel lobby. They are serenaded with "Winter Wonderland" through speakers, even as the temperature outside goes to 100°F. and beyond. Perhaps half the patrons of this hotel and its bar openly carry weapons; many of them are young, rowdy South African soldiers just back from "the border" (also known as "the operational area"), stopping to clean up and have some fun on their way home.

Windhoek also has quaint German churches, restaurants that serve heavy German food, and German street names that commemorate Bismarck, the *Bahnhof* (railroad station), and even

Hermann Göring's father, who lived there for a time. The main street is called Kaiserstrasse. Germans still make up almost a third of Namibia's white population, officially estimated at seventy-six thousand. They farm, run gem shops and other retail establishments, or work as professionals. They have seen many crises come and go in their beloved *Südwest,* and find it hard to imagine that they might ever have to flee. Most of them have lived here all their lives; they work and shop and pray in German and get most of their news of the world from a German-language daily newspaper published in Windhoek. Politically they are moderate, and they say privately that they believe the South Africans have made a mess of things in their beautiful land.

Most of the other whites in Namibia are Afrikaners, who tend to see themselves as political missionaries serving nobly on the front line of civilization. Some are descendants of the *dorsland-trekkers* ("travelers to the thirsty land"), men driven by a religious zeal who went north from South Africa in search of opportunity. They sometimes went as far as Angola, where they married Portuguese women and then returned to the frontier territory. There they could start ranches, or easily find other jobs, and count on greater tolerance of their "mixed marriages" with Portuguese Catholics than they could at home in South Africa. The frontier mentality still prevails for many Namibian Afrikaners, and they have a rigid view of the future that has seriously complicated South Africa's problems. The Namibian branch of the National party, to which most of them belong, is so right-wing as to be an embarrassment to its counterpart back home.

Namibia's black population is very diverse. The Ovambo, of the North, because they make up at least half the country's population, are often feared and resented by the other groups, especially the Kavango, Herero, and Damara. The Basters, who are mulatto, have held themselves apart as a group entitled to privilege. Nearly everyone has persecuted the San and the Khoikhoi, the original inhabitants of the area, who have been reduced to a presence and a status roughly comparable to that of the American Indian. Over the years, all of this conflict played into the hands of the South Africans.

It is almost as difficult in Namibia as in South Africa to keep everyone truly apart, but the interim governmental system established by Pretoria for the transition to independence turned out to be a highly sophisticated form of apartheid. "AG-8," the South African administrator-general's decree that served as the country's temporary constitution, provided for two separate "tiers" of government. The first tier was the national authority, but it actually had little responsibility for the matters that affect people's daily lives, such as education, housing, health, and agriculture. Those were reserved, for the most part, for the second tier, or ethnic authorities. There were eleven of those, each for a distinct tribal group, including one for all the whites.

Each ethnic authority was entitled to tax its own people as it saw fit, and that is the mechanism by which the whites continued to assure themselves the best schools and other services without even having to think of sharing them with other groups. The duplication is obvious, and the waste and corruption enormous. The Ovambo ethnic administration, for example, seeking to assert its jurisdiction in the north, where SWAPO is strongest, bought a fleet of Mercedes-Benzes for the use of all its top officials. Ovamboland is governed according to a sophisticated system of political patronage, with the local elite awarded privileges that will discourage them from flirting with SWAPO or otherwise challenging the established system. But the system of ethnic administrations has created less loyalty than it has scandal.

As much as the ethnic divisions have been formalized and strengthened in Namibia, Windhoek, the cosmopolitan capital, is a place where people of different colors actually mingle freely at political and social gatherings, where white families have been known to adopt and raise black children. A few years ago, the South African authorities began to recognize that some form of black rule was inevitable in Namibia, and set out on a good-will campaign to demonstrate that an independence on their terms would be preferable to one on SWAPO's terms. They began by improving the facilities available to the majority of the people. So it is that the slick new hospital designated for nonwhites has the only intensive-care unit in town.

The township where most of the Africans of Windhoek live is called Katatura, a Herero name that translates roughly as "the place to which we do not wish to go." (The name was originally an informal one; it is not clear whether the government knew what the word meant when it accepted the name officially.) In fact, the black people of Windhoek resisted their forced removal in 1959 from another part of town, the "old location," to make way for a construction project. On December 10 of that year, the South Africans shot and killed eleven of the protesters who refused to leave their homes, and wounded forty-four others. Those people are still revered as martyrs, and the older generation resents the very existence of Katatura, but today most of its residents live in relatively decent conditions. Even with a substantial immigration of rural Namibians into the capital (now that "influx control" has been lifted), there are none of the seething squatters' camps that have become so common on the outskirts of the black townships near Johannesburg, Cape Town, and other South African cities. In one of many local ironies, the best neighborhood in Katatura, with the nicest houses and the most modern amenities, has been informally dubbed "Soweto."

It is extraordinarily difficult to obtain reliable information about the war that has raged for years five hundred miles to the north. There are none of the traditional body counts or public announcements of military engagements, and strict censorship laws prevent both the South African and the Namibian press from displaying much initiative. As the mother of one young South African assigned to "the border" said, "We really don't find out anything. Some of our children just turn up wounded, and a few don't come back at all." But those numbers have remained small enough to discourage reckless curiosity or serious protest.

A visit to "Bastion," the SADF headquarters in Windhoek, before the South African–Angolan cease-fire, produced a briefing on operations in the war zone. Elaborate wall charts and detailed slides revealed a gradual decline in the number of "terrorist incidents" caused by SWAPO forces, but a continuation of "intimidation," both "hard" and "soft." Hard intimidation occurs when the guerrillas demand food and other help from the villagers, explained the South African briefing officer, and "soft intimidation is when they just go into the village and talk."

It is scarcely possible to make out the Namibian-Angolan border on the military's maps of the operational area, except that on the northern side there are many spots labeled "KUB" to indicate the location of Cuban troop concentrations or bases. As far as one can tell, the Cubans keep to the task of supporting the Angolan government, while Angolan forces fight their own bush war against Savimbi's rebels. The Cubans also maintain a distance from SWAPO, thereby minimizing direct contact with the South Africans. But the briefing officer made no attempt to conceal the frequency and ferocity of South African incursions into Angola in search of SWAPO bases. Especially effective were the members of the "Three-two Battalion," ex-Angolans and American and European mercenaries who joined up with the South Africans in Namibia after the civil war in Angola in 1975. They are known for taking no prisoners.

The picture that emerged was of a South African rout of the insurgent forces. The number of SWAPO fighters has apparently dwindled to fewer than a thousand inside Namibia, and perhaps five thousand in Angola who want to invade Namibia but are unable to do so, because the South Africans have succeeded in shrinking the border area where they can operate freely; the guerrillas have been known to fill out their ranks by kidnapping Ovambo schoolchildren and putting weapons in their hands.

While occasional boasts of success are good for morale, the South Africans have been uncharacteristically reluctant to acknowledge the extent to which they hold the upper hand in the Namibian military struggle, and there are several possible explanations for this reluctance. Certainly the government does not want to risk a decline in popular support for the war effort or to face the allegation that it has sent too many troops north. (The exact number is secret, but reliable estimates run to thirty-five thousand, with perhaps fifteen hundred stationed inside Angola for a number of years.) The need to contain the menace of a nearby Soviet-armed enemy has been politically useful for President P. W. Botha to feed his people's obsessive fear of Communism.

In any event, the SADF takes a dim view of the endless negotiations over Namibia. "We would not be happy with a negotiated settlement," the briefing officer at Bastion said. "Why should we give it away, when we're winning the war?"

In the meantime, the South Africans have begun to militarize Namibian society, creating a South-West Africa Territory Force as an alternative to SWAPO—the embryo of a non-SWAPO army for what it would consider an acceptably independent Namibia. To a degree, the tactic has worked. Many black Namibian soldiers are fighting at the border on the South African side; in Windhoek, they strut along the streets in military dress. As one local politician put it, "Until recently, our girls wouldn't even think of dancing with men in uniform. Now that's changed. The soldiers are becoming heroes. The army has become the chief employer, a symbol of economic security."

If the soldiers strut, the politicians sit and scheme—ever hopeful that an election is just around the corner and eager to be in the right position when it comes. In the daytime, they stop at Schneider's Coffee Shop to collect the latest rumors; at night, they gather at the Kalahari Sands to speculate on their country's future. If an outsider should be in town, whether from America, Germany, or just Johannesburg, they will converge upon him and seek his opinions, informed or otherwise, on the prospects for a resolution of Namibia's troubles.

At last count, Namibia had about forty political parties. If one added up all of their claimed memberships, the total would probably be more than twice the population of the country. There is a humor and a futility to some of their rivalries, exemplified by the informal competition to see which party can sew and sell the most caftans with its colors to the people in Katatura. There are figures such as Andreas Shipanga, once a dynamic leader of SWAPO, now the head of a breakaway faction called SWAPO Democrats. Although he appears to be ignored at home, he travels in the Western world at the expense of conservative American foundations and think tanks that have singled him out as an exemplary African leader. And there is a potential for tragedy and fratricidal bloodshed, given the fact that almost every party is thought to be able to mobilize thousands of armed partisans in a crisis.

The issue of independence and how to achieve it has divided many families in Namibia. For example, Otillie Abrahams and her husband have launched their own small political party, the Namibian Independence party. One of her sisters, Nora Chase, is secretary for foreign affairs and information of the South-West Africa National Union (SWANU), one of the original independence movements in the country, which could eventually line up with SWAPO. While Abrahams lives in town among the elite, Chase affects a more militant stance, living in a black township on principle. Two other sisters still work for the internal branch of SWAPO. So chaotic is the domestic political situation in Namibia that when the representatives of German foundations came to Windhoek late in 1982 looking for deserving recipients of political development grants who would be tied neither to South Africa nor to SWAPO, they finally gave up and took their money home.

For several years, one Namibian political figure who seemed to be charting a workable temporary compromise was Dirk Mudge, a rich white rancher who said he wanted to take the country out of South Africa's clutches but still assure a stable, pro-Western course of development. Mudge's multiracial coalition of ethnic parties, the Democratic Turnhalle Alliance (named for a historic meeting hall where it was formed), won the internal Namibian election sponsored by South Africa in 1978 (and boycotted by SWAPO), and as a result, Mudge became a sort of prime minister of the first-tier authority. But four years later, the most important black politician in the DTA, Peter Kalangula, an Ovambo leader, withdrew from the coalition, with the encouragement of the South African military. Increasingly, Mudge's administration began to look like a minority within a minority, and when the South Africans failed to find a way to replace him with Kalangula, they simply dismissed the first-tier national authority altogether and resumed direct rule of Namibia through an administrator-general reporting to Pretoria. But that administrator-general was himself rendered obsolete when South Africa moved unilaterally in 1985 to establish a new internal administration outside the United Nations framework.

The South Africans hope that a moderate reformist like Kalangula will be able to win the loyalty of Namibia's emerging black middle class and prevail in an election. Just the appearance of support from Pretoria, though, is enough to brand him a "collaborationist" and doom his prospects. And that, in turn, improves the chances of the current leader of SWAPO and its guerrillas, Sam Nujoma, to win a UN-supervised election, if one is ever held, even if he cannot win the war. Nujoma, by all accounts a man who has little tolerance for opposition or dissent, has not appeared publicly in Namibia in more than twenty years for fear of being killed; but he has come to be seen by the ordinary people as the hero who would liberate them. Thus the South Africans have virtually ensured the fulfillment of their worst prophecy, and that circumstance has become the main pretext for further delaying elections—and independence.

But even if elections should come anytime soon, and if SWAPO should come to power by democratic means, it is unlikely that much will change in Namibia for a long time. After nearly seventy years of rule, South Africa enjoys total economic control of the country. It does not consider sovereignty over Namibia's major port, Walvis Bay—which was a South African enclave even during German colonial days—to be a negotiable issue. (Indeed, it has strengthened its forces there and given Walvis Bay direct representation in South Africa's white Parliament.) The railroad lines, air routes, and roads, not to mention electricity and water supplies, can be easily controlled from South Africa. A simple decision in Pretoria is all it would take to cut off most of Namibia's food supply within days. A SWAPO government would have to take that into account before it tried to assert true independence from South Africa.

As Otillie Abrahams says, "With a little sabotage, the South Africans could starve us all in a month." In Uganda, after Idi Amin took power and the economy fell apart, she points out, "the people could go into the jungle and eat bananas. All we've got here is sand."

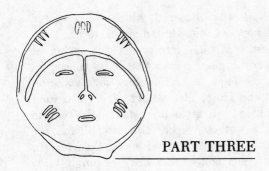

PART THREE

A
CONTINENTAL
SURVEY

Beyond the countries already discussed, which are relatively well known by some people in the United States, to the average American the rest of Africa often seems like one great blur, a profusion of exotic place names that have no special meaning or significance. There are flashpoints, such as Zaïre, Chad, Zimbabwe, or the Horn, that attract urgent attention in the news, but lacking context or immediate relevance to life on Main Street, U.S.A., they quickly fade into oblivion.

Public officials are often no more advanced than private citizens in their comprehension of this vast, seemingly mysterious continent. On one telling occasion, Richard Nixon was halfway through his meeting at the White House with a visiting official from Mauritius before he realized that he was not talking to someone from Mauritania. Those two African countries have little in common besides their place in the alphabet—one is an island in the Indian Ocean, the other a desert nation with an Atlantic coastline thousands of miles away—yet no one at the State Department or the National Security Council noticed when the president was given a briefing paper about the wrong place. Presumably, no harm was done and embarrassment was minimized. The man from Mauritius was no doubt honored to be received in the Oval Office, even under a cloud of confusion.

More than one president or secretary of state has complained of the difficulty of formulating a single "policy" toward a continent with so many separate and different countries. Indeed, no U.S. policy toward Africa could ever be rational or successful unless it took into account the variety and complexity of circumstances there. The policymaking process is rendered all the more awkward by a fundamental asymmetry: America is inevitably far more important to each individual African nation, however small it may be, than any one of them—or almost any combination of them—is to the United States. African statesmen will dutifully study the intricacies of the U.S. political system, while their American counterparts draw a blank on the names of African leaders or even capital cities, and out of uncomfortableness or insensitivity, poke fun at them for being hard to pronounce. Africans often compete with each other for American attention, and once they have learned how to play to basic political prejudices and ideological blind spots, may lead Washington into bad policy choices.

7

Zimbabwe:
Shattered Hopes

ONE AFRICAN COUNTRY that has received a great deal of attention in the West in recent years is Zimbabwe. The fifteen-year-
long drama of its transition from rebel colony to independent nation engaged people from all parts of the political spectrum in
every corner of the world.

Rhodesia, as the country was known for most of the period
from 1965 to 1980, became a symbol for many groups: among
others, African nationalists, who saw it as one of the last vestiges
of white domination on their continent; white South Africans and
their supporters in Europe and the United States, who regarded it
as an important buffer delaying the political and military onslaught
against Namibia and South Africa itself; and liberal Americans
and Europeans, who perceived Rhodesia as an opportunity to
steer a violent crisis toward a peaceful, democratic outcome. It
was also a sort of international litmus test, a likely indication of
where people stood on the grand issues of the day. Rhodesia became a topic of political dispute in many nations far from Africa;
some Americans who would have had a hard time finding it on

the map nonetheless took strong positions about what the outcome of the Rhodesian conflict should be.

A significant number of people in the United States and in Europe sympathized with the tiny white minority—250,000 people out of a total population of some 7.5 million—that encouraged the breakup of a federation uniting Southern Rhodesia (its official colonial name) with Northern Rhodesia and Nyasaland (later Zambia and Malawi). These Americans and Europeans admired the Rhodesian whites' renegade stance. Ian Smith, the right-wing, white farmer-politician who came to power by outmaneuvering old-line moderate political forces and then engineered a rebellion against the British crown, successfully portrayed his people as the underdogs in their own country and the region. With his "Unilateral Declaration of Independence" (UDI)* on November 11, 1965, he sought to evoke a spirit reminiscent of the American colonies' dramatic gesture against the same authorities 189 years earlier. "Good Old Smithy," as he came to be known, obtained open, public support only from South Africa and certain conservative political forces and commercial interests in the United States and Britain, but he had surreptitious backing from many other quarters. Above all, he could count on high morale and substantial solidarity among his white constituents. Few of them left. Instead, egged on by censored newspapers and a state-run broadcasting system about as objective as Radio Moscow, the Rhodesian whites dug in and, to the last, believed they would prevail against overwhelming odds. They hardly survived the "thousand years" that Smith had promised to them and future generations, but they did have a good dozen or so before their edifice began to crumble.

Cecil Rhodes would have been proud of them. Rhodes had traveled to South Africa from England in 1870, for health reasons, and he began a lucrative diamond- and gold-mining business there even before returning to attend Oxford University. Moved by contemporary beliefs in a "racial hierarchy" with "Anglo-Saxons" at the top and in Britain's imperial mission to colonize "fruitful waste ground" around the world, he devoted much of his short life to schemes for southern Africa.

The representatives of Rhodes who traveled north from South

* UDI was actually an event, but the term is also used in common parlance to connote an era and a regime.

Africa in 1888 to negotiate minerals concessions with a tribal king
(in exchange for weapons) at first promised to bring only ten
white men into the territory; but having bought out or otherwise
neutralized most of his rivals and the English humanitarians who
worried about the fate of the "natives," by 1890 Rhodes was dis-
patching a "Pioneer Column" northward, complete with police
protection. The settlers who established Fort Salisbury on his behalf were a microcosm of white British colonial society and, unlike
many other colonialists in Africa, they intended to stay. Each settler, as a reward for adventurousness, was authorized to stake fifteen gold claims and to grab enough land to create a three-thou-
sand-acre farm.

The black people who lived in what was then known as
"Zambesia" did not share the settlers' view of them as subjects,
but that did not matter; by 1893, after a brief war, the indigenous
blacks were at the mercy of the whites. The settlers' hegemony
was temporarily challenged by several black rebellions, but by
the turn of the century the colony's development was proceeding
apace, the clichés about the white man's "civilizing mission"
drowning out any nagging concerns over decency in race relations. For the most part, blacks and whites coexisted uneasily in
the country that would come to be known as Southern Rhodesia,
but for the settlers there was always an aura of romance and adventure about the place, equaled or exceeded only by the spirit
of the white settlers in Kenya. They had their occasional grievances with Rhodes—forcing him early on to establish a government and give them some representation in it, rather than admin-
istering the territory purely as a business enterprise—but they also
had reason to believe that they had stumbled into paradise. The
land was astoundingly fertile (permitting as many as three plant-
ings a year), the sky almost unremittingly clear, the climate moderate and benign. Some of the crops, tobacco and cotton, were
even drought-resistant.

Rhodes died in 1902, shortly before his forty-ninth birthday,
but his heirs in business and government made the country a
monument to his memory. A network of railroads was built to
connect the major population centers, and trade and other business boomed. Over the years, Salisbury, the capital, blossomed
into a grand colonial city, crossed by avenues broad enough for
a team of eight oxen and dotted with quiet parks full of jacaranda,

bougainvillea, and poinsettia. Salisbury sprawled over a vast area, but it never had a very large population.

From time to time there was talk, mostly by South African politicians, of trying to amalgamate South Africa and Southern Rhodesia, but the white Rhodesians invariably opposed the notion. Their dominance and privileges were even more clearly established, if less formally defined, than those of their counterparts in South Africa, and although they came to have a life style somewhat similar to that of Americans, they built a distinctly British society that they did not care to dilute with Afrikaner culture. Indeed, the image of a gracious, exclusive, if often dull and culturally dry, life in white Rhodesia attracted many immigrants— ten thousand or more a year for a time—who thought they could leave the crises and tensions of Europe behind. It also attracted overseas visitors threatened by the changes occurring in their own countries. Some of them became such ardent admirers that when they went home, they formed chapters of an organization called "Friends of Rhodesia." In reality very few Rhodesians became extremely wealthy, and life for the average middle-class white there was replete with struggle and insecurity; but the impression and the symbolism may have been more important than the reality.

This background is crucial to an understanding of Ian Smith and UDI. The sense that there was something special about Rhodesia, which made it immune to the ordinary imperatives of history, was reinforced by the British attitude in the late 1960s. Although the Labour party government of Harold Wilson was strongly opposed to Smith, it had a thin majority in Parliament at the time, and it ruled out in advance the use of military force to bring the Rhodesians into line. The British public was not about to accept extreme measures to punish their "kith and kin" in southern Africa. Indeed, while plodding through one abortive set of negotiations after another, Britain relied on a policy of economic sanctions and other subtle pressures to try to solve the problem. At first these tactics seemed to work, but before long Rhodesia bounced back; its farmers diversified their crops, its mining industry boomed, and its manufacturing sector became highly productive. The already enviable infrastructure was strengthened further. One of the ironies of the country's complex modern history is that the relative self-sufficiency developed under UDI as a means of avoiding majority rule became an important asset once majority rule was achieved.

Eventually Rhodesia's resilience was shattered by international economic conditions, especially the increase in the price of its imported oil, and by the guerrilla war against the Smith regime. Because black opposition had been stifled so effectively for so long, the fighting really only began in earnest in 1972. Three years later, the independence of Mozambique from Portugal under the radical auspices of Samora Machel permitted the opening of a new front. From that time on, with Joshua Nkomo's forces operating out of Zambia and another group, led at first by Ndabaningi Sithole and later by Robert Mugabe, out of Mozambique, the fall of white Rhodesia became inevitable. Smith's military leadership knew this was true, but their recognition was never shared with the public, lest the whites' extraordinary morale be shaken and an untimely exodus provoked; instead the whites fought on, and many unnecessary deaths resulted on all sides.

Once he was persuaded—by South African Prime Minister John Vorster, who came to see peace in Rhodesia as the best way to protect his own country, and by U.S. Secretary of State Henry Kissinger, who finally changed his mind about the future of southern Africa after the fall of Portugal's colonial empire—to accept the principle of majority rule, Smith tried to make the best deal possible. He chose to negotiate with black leaders of his own preference, including tribal chieftains, the outcast Sithole, and an old-line nationalist who had sat out the military struggle, Methodist Bishop Abel Muzorewa.

Changing the name of his state to "Zimbabwe-Rhodesia,"* Smith proceeded in 1978 to an "internal settlement" that ignored Nkomo and Mugabe; he held an election the next year that was certified as fair by observers from various corners of the Western

---

* Zimbabwe (literally, in the Shona language, "burial ground of the chiefs") had long since become the nationalist name for the country. It was taken from the "Great Zimbabwe," dry stone ruins spread over sixty acres near Fort Victoria, two hundred miles south of Salisbury, which are probably the remnants of a powerful, advanced civilization that went into abrupt economic and social decline in the fifteenth century. This evidence of a highly developed black monarchy in southern Africa before the arrival of European explorers and invaders was especially significant to African nationalists.

world, although it was boycotted by the externally based liberation movements. When Muzorewa won, as Smith had intended,
the white prime minister stepped down in favor of the black
bishop and proclaimed that the country's difficulties had been
solved. But this new arrangement got little international recognition. The problem was that not much had changed: whites still
held a greatly disproportionate number of seats in Parliament and
they continued to dominate the civil service, the police, the courts,
and the military. Tens of thousands of fighters still loomed in the
bush and beyond the borders, demanding a more genuine change.

The Rhodesian war was no closer to an end in May of 1979,
when the Conservatives won parliamentary elections in Britain,
and their new leader, Margaret Thatcher, became prime minister. Because of the position taken in her party's election manifesto, or platform, many people expected Thatcher to recognize
the Muzorewa government immediately. But she did not, largely
on the recommendation of her foreign secretary, a hereditary
peer, Peter Carrington, who knew Africa well; and indeed, when
Thatcher attended a Commonwealth Heads of Government Conference in Zambia in August of that year, she was persuaded to
launch a new British mediation effort.

The next month Lord Carrington convened a constitutional
conference at Lancaster House in London, the site of prior negotiations leading to the independence of other British colonies.
The result was a carefully crafted compromise: genuine black
majority rule would be assured in the new, legitimately independent nation of Zimbabwe, but the whites would have certain
guarantees, including a bill of rights and twenty reserved seats in
a one-hundred-member Parliament (still far out of proportion to
their numbers in the population). Smith, who formally attended
the conference as part of Muzorewa's delegation, accepted the
agreement in part because he felt confident that the bishop could
still win the coming election and would remain loyal to his mentor. Mugabe and Nkomo, who participated at Lancaster House as
the joint "Patriotic Front" that had been fighting the war, hesi-
tated for a time, but finally agreed under pressure from their African allies, especially hard-pressed Mozambique, and on the basis
of promises of British and American aid to the new Zimbabwe.

For a brief transitional period the country reverted to its
status as the British colony of Southern Rhodesia; Carrington dis-

patched another knowledgeable Conservative peer, Christopher Soames, to be its short-term governor. Lord Soames organized the new elections of February 1980, which most observers agreed were fair, despite intimidation and violence all around. Nearly all outsiders—most especially the South Africans, who thought they had superb intelligence from this country they had nurtured for fifteen years—expected Muzorewa to win. But almost a million more Africans voted than had done so in the previous "internal settlement" election, and Muzorewa, apparently rejected as a collaborationist, won only three seats. Nkomo's party, the Zimbabwe African People's Union (ZAPU), won twenty, assuring its virtually exclusive representation of the Ndebele tribe and its section of the country, while Mugabe's Zimbabwe African National Union (ZANU) took a majority of fifty-seven. Soames invited him to form a government, and formal independence ceremonies took place on April 18, 1980.

The task inherited by Mugabe was a very difficult one indeed. Not only did he have to try to reconcile an angry, impatient black majority with a bitter white minority that had ruled harshly, but he also had to do so in a way that would minimize white flight and inspire the confidence of outside investors. More daunting still was the need to fulfill the expectations of the people who had fought for independence, to give them some early, tangible evidence that their struggle and sacrifice had been worthwhile.

That need was made all the more complicated by the serious tribal and political divisions within Zimbabwe's black population, especially between the Shona-speaking majority led by Mugabe and the Ndebele tribe mostly loyal to Nkomo. These two groups had been adversaries since precolonial times, when the Ndebele, arriving from South Africa, conquered and persecuted the Shona, and once independence was achieved their bitter rivalry flared anew. To make matters worse, various subgroups of the Shona were now also at odds. Creating a single national army of reasonable size out of ethnically distinct, rival liberation armies, plus the force inherited from Smith, was an enormous challenge in itself. But on top of everything else, Mugabe had to chart a realistic relationship with the South African behemoth next door, while still remaining true to his principles and within the boundaries of what his more radical supporters would permit.

Mugabe had distinguished himself from other Zimbabwean

nationalist leaders over the years by his espousal of Marxism, and so many outsiders expected, and certain elements in ZANU demanded, an immediate transformation of the national economy along socialist lines. (It was Nkomo who had the material support of the Soviet Union, but Mugabe, with Chinese backing, who laid claim to ideological purity.) A few of his advisers advocated sweeping nationalization measures; while Mugabe took some limited steps in this direction—some of them symbolically important, such as the takeover of the previously independent newspapers—he mostly left control of the economy in the hands of the private sector. He shook up some companies with the establishment of a "Minerals Marketing Board," an effort to neutralize outside control over the country's natural resources and to assure that Zimbabwe received a fair price for what was extracted; but for the most part he was content to rely on old and well-accepted institutions, such as the Dairy Marketing Board, to set the tone for national economic well-being. (The minerals board was no more socialist in concept than the dairy board, but since it challenged powerful vested interests, it was seen in a different context.) Zimbabweans called each other "comrade," but those in the cities generally operated on the basis of the profit motive. Salisbury was renamed Harare, but it still functioned as the center of a colonial economy.

White interests went largely undisturbed. Despite some well-publicized instances of white farmers who were the victims of violence or who decided for other reasons to leave their land, the number of white commercial farmers actually increased for a time after Mugabe came to power. White civil servants and retired military personnel, including those who had helped administer and enforce the most draconian policies during the UDI period, had their pensions and other benefits guaranteed. The wealthiest white families still lived in great comfort, even splendor, with plenty of black servants. Indeed, one fact that tells a great deal about how limited was the initial transformation of Zimbabwe's economy is that three years after independence "domestic service" was still its third largest employment category.*

---

* Nothing could be a more poignant symbol than the grand home of Ian Smith in the still mostly white suburbs of Harare. There, in the midst of a finely sculpted garden and in a house filled with bric-a-brac and mementos

As Mugabe's honeymoon ended and tension began to grow in the country, more whites left Zimbabwe; they worried about their future in a nation where the independent judiciary and the bill of rights might not be respected after all. Some went to South Africa and formed an angry, highly vocal, anti-Zimbabwean pressure group. By the beginning of 1985, it was estimated that only 100,000 whites remained in the country—less than 2 percent of the population. Even more might have gone, if they had been permitted to take most of their assets with them. But like South Africa and many other embattled countries, Zimbabwe made it difficult for people simply to take their money and run, and so there was a certain hard core of angry, embittered white settlers who did little to make the new nation work, preferring to sit back and wait for their worst prophecies to be fulfilled.

Although these unhappy and outspoken remnants of Rhodesia often received a certain amount of attention from the international press, they were not necessarily typical of most of the whites who remained. Other elements in the community, believing that Zimbabwe could become a viable multiracial society, genuinely tried to do their part to make it so. Many young Englishmen, who could have easily moved on to more lucrative jobs elsewhere, stayed on in government ministries, often enduring great frustrations in dealing with ZANU partisans who seemed more interested in settling old scores than looking ahead. Then there were the likes of Judith Todd, daughter of the former moderate white Rhodesian prime minister, Garfield Todd; having been detained and expelled as a troublemaker during UDI, she returned to Zimbabwe in 1980 to work with ex-combatants who were trying to find a new role in the country. A few older stalwarts, such as Anthony Upfill-Brown, a financial manager and consultant who wore a black necktie for seven years to protest Smith's policies under UDI, were determined to stay, almost regardless of events. Having emigrated to Rhodesia from South Africa in 1957 because he believed that country was doomed by its racial tensions. Upfill-Brown insisted that Zimbabwean whites should devote their energies to "finding a *modus operandi* between capitalism and African socialism . . . and we should thank God that the Africans are kind enough and

of his controversial career, he graciously received visitors and held forth with impunity on the sins of the Mugabe government.

good enough to let us live here." Conciliatory sentiments emerged in the early 1980s in parliamentary by-elections for some of the seats reserved for whites; independents who did not owe their loyalty to Smith defeated members of his party, and some of the incumbents who had been elected under his standard switched to an independent status because they objected to his behavior. A few became ministers in Mugabe's cabinet.

One more benefit that independent Zimbabwe reaped from its recent turbulent past—another of its ironies—was that many upwardly mobile, middle-class blacks had been forced to go overseas for an education during UDI. The settlement of the conflict brought thousands of them back, and they were able to take up many of the positions left empty by departing whites. (At the time of independence, as some wealthy whites panicked and left, the returning black intelligentsia were also able to buy some of Harare's stateliest homes for very little money.) But they were far removed and emotionally remote from the concerns of the millions of penniless Zimbabweans—the bulk of the population—who had never had a share of the colonial prosperity, had no chance for an education anywhere, and were still waiting for their lives to change.

The government made a special effort to solve an old grievance by giving many ordinary peasants access to more land than just a subsistence plot. In part using foreign assistance money, it bought up abandoned white farms and other available land (paying market value to its owners, as required by the Lancaster House agreement) and resettled blacks, especially ex-combatants, on it to establish communal farms and other cooperatives. But the going was slow and the process disorganized. In some instances, whole villages of thatched huts were built before boreholes were available to supply them with water. Few people had any illusions that some new communal farming structure could match the output and efficiency of the old. Some resettlement occurred on an ad hoc basis, with defiant squatters simply moving onto available land, including some still officially owned by whites or already purchased by the government and awaiting allocation. Before long, the government admitted that it would have to find ways to create nonagricultural jobs in the rural areas, because there simply would not be enough land to satisfy everyone who

wanted some, and it would be years before many of the new farmers became genuinely productive.

Post-independence pressures were also felt in the cities, and
especially in Harare. Once the war ended, Zimbabwe's population
growth rate skyrocketed, and many families, as well as single
young men, gravitated to the urban areas to look for work or
charity. Squatters and beggars along the grand avenues and outside the hotels of Harare did not make the new rulers any more
comfortable than they did the old ones, and so the government
launched official "campaigns" to keep the streets clean of vagrants,
especially at holiday times. "While the Department of Social Services is considering long-term solutions to the problem of beggars," editorialized the government-controlled *Herald* just before
Christmas of 1982, "we would urge both the police and the department to [get] rid of this menace." The next year, in November, the government launched a crackdown on prostitution in
Harare and other major cities. Almost two thousand women were
arrested in the name of a "cleanup" campaign against vice and
crime that proved to be a classic case of excessive zeal. Among
those put in jail were foreign teachers, schoolgirls on their way
home, and women pulled out of movie theaters and supermarkets.
Drunken soldiers seized women who were out on dates and then
made advances to them, and members of the ZANU youth brigade
singled out their own targets. Upon examination of the problem,
government officials found that the real prostitutes had been
tipped off by the police, who then roamed the cities arresting
women at random. All were finally released, on Mugabe's orders.

If the anti-prostitution campaign was excessive, it nonetheless
helped direct attention to some of the new social problems of a
country suddenly no longer at war. According to one university
study, as much as 20 percent of Zimbabwe's urban population suffered from venereal disease of one sort or another. The incidence
of teenage pregnancy increased dramatically, and "baby dumping" became a serious law-enforcement problem in Harare. Young
women who gave birth to children they had no hope of supporting would simply abandon them, or even try to kill them. Those
who were caught were punished severely by the courts, and Sally
Mugabe, the prime minister's wife, complained, in terms that she
hoped less-educated women would understand, that "the gods and

spirits are watching us. They are not pleased with us." Encouraged by American aid, the government launched a major drive to promote family planning.

But for problems like this, the capital hardly changed with the advent of majority rule. It still looked like a grand colonial city, and streets named for such colonial explorers as Henry Morton Stanley and John Hanning Speke coexisted and intersected with others renamed for African leaders like Julius Nyerere and Samora Machel.

Many of the major economic problems faced by the new government stemmed from the fact that Zimbabwe was being reintegrated into an international economic system from which it had been estranged and insulated during the UDI period. For example, the Smith government, while it struggled to establish its legitimacy and maintain popular support among whites, had seen to it that inflation was almost nonexistent, and as goods entered the country under more normal market conditions, prices shot up. Zimbabwe found itself with underpaid workers and an artificially overvalued currency. Still, the country benefited from a booming agricultural sector, which produced the world's second-highest yields after the United States. Zimbabwe recovered quickly from the worst drought in a generation, and as a result it had its first post-independence trade surplus in 1984.

The effort to attract foreign investment—the only likely way to broaden the country's industrial base and hope to meet some of the majority's demands—proceeded slowly. The H. J. Heinz Company of Pittsburgh plunged in with a multimillion-dollar investment, but other corporations held back, on the grounds that the Zimbabwean government would not sign an "investment code" and give them explicit guarantees of the security of their capital. This was one of many areas where the Mugabe regime proved to be foolishly persistent rather than pragmatic: it insisted that anyone who read the new constitution and various government declarations would realize that such specific assurances were unnecessary. But many companies had, after all, been badly burned in other African countries and now worried over what they saw happening in Zimbabwe. And as Roger Riddel, chief economist of the Confederation of Zimbabwean Industries, put it, "When you're in Dallas, you don't read the Zimbabwean constitution."

Nonetheless, the government sacrificed opportunities for investment rather than compromise.

If the economic record of Mugabe's early years in power was mixed, the political record was even more problematic. The unity of the Patriotic Front had always existed more on paper than in fact, and soon after independence the relationship between Mugabe's and Nkomo's parties deteriorated substantially, almost to the point of outright civil war. For a time Nkomo and other members of ZAPU sat in Mugabe's cabinet, but their mutual distrust frequently boiled over into rhetorical attacks on one another. Substantially older than Mugabe and one of the earliest black nationalist leaders in Zimbabwe (during the guerrilla war, he called himself "Father Zimbabwe"), Nkomo felt he had been cheated out of a position that was rightfully his. An imposing figure who weighed more than three hundred pounds and carried a carved stick as a symbol of his authority, he attracted attention wherever he went and he always made his points forcefully. Mugabe and others feared he would try to seize power.

Mugabe's worst suspicions of treachery seemed to be confirmed when, early in 1982, large caches of Soviet arms were discovered on farms that had recently been bought up by Nkomo and his associates. After the prime minister arrested several of Nkomo's former military chiefs, now in the national army, and charged them with treason, vast numbers of soldiers originally loyal to Nkomo deserted in protest and began to roam the countryside in Matabeleland as bandits. Their attacks on white farmers, villagers, and foreign tourists created havoc and raised legitimate questions about the government's ability to maintain order. Mugabe escalated the tension in early 1983 when he sent the army's Fifth Brigade, composed entirely of Shona-speaking soldiers loyal to the prime minister and trained by North Koreans, to Matabeleland to quell the easily confused problems of dissidence and banditry. In the name of law and order, they brutally repressed a civilian population whose language and customs were virtually unknown to them. Murder, robbery, and rape were rampant. Fearing arrest and even execution, Nkomo fled the country, first to Botswana and later to Britain, increasing the attention that this Zimbabwean melodrama received in the international press.

Nkomo returned to Zimbabwe, after discovering during an

absence of several months that it was difficult to sustain his role
from as far away as London. Pledging his commitment to democratic processes, he managed to keep his seat in Parliament, although the government continued to be suspicious and hostile
toward him. But still Mugabe had difficulty containing the trouble in Matabeleland, where some of the guerrillas regarded ZAPU
figures other than Nkomo—especially Dumiso Dabengwa, a former ZAPU commander imprisoned by Mugabe—as their leaders,
and where surreptitious South African arms supplies (including
Communist-made weapons captured in Angola) and other mischief complicated the problem. Timing some of their boldest assaults for maximum impact at holiday times, the dissidents killed
at least forty whites and hundreds of blacks in an eighteen-month
period. But rather than deal with some of the genuine grievances
in the region, including a serious maldistribution of aid to relieve
the effects of the drought, Mugabe still reacted harshly and in-
sensitively. Again and again, troops went in to suppress the troublemakers. Symbolic figures like Sir Humphrey Gibbs, a farmer in
Matabeleland who was the former British governor-general of
Southern Rhodesia and a man known for racial tolerance, announced they were fed up with the violence and would leave the
country. Worried about the impact that reports of the violence
and departures were having on potential foreign investors, Mugabe's government resorted to punishing the bearers of the bad
news; it banned journalists from the affected areas. When reporters were finally welcomed back for a tour of the troubled provinces, villagers and missionaries only confirmed the worst suspicions about the government's treatment of the ethnic and political
minorities.

In other respects, too, Mugabe disappointed his international
supporters and admirers by resorting to authoritarianism rather
than conciliation. In fact, to put down some of his own political
opponents, as well as suspected saboteurs and foreign agents, he
relied upon the very same emergency laws and powers that Smith
had used to repress black activists during UDI. It did not seem
to bother Mugabe to detain people without charges or trial. After
a sabotage attack in 1982 damaged thirteen planes of the Zimbabwean air force, government security agents forced confessions
out of four white officers by torturing them. When a judge later
ordered the acquittal and release of these four men and two others,

the government used emergency legislation from the Smith era to arrest them anew on suspicion of being South African agents; the minister of home affairs, Herbert Ushewokunze, a member of ZANU's most militant faction, criticized the black judge who had released them for showing class bias. (Eventually, the government relented and set them all free.)

After being angered by critical remarks that Smith made during an overseas trip in 1982, Mugabe had the former white prime minister's home and farm searched; his personal firearms and his passport were seized and he was otherwise harassed. Smith was able to capitalize on the incident and portray himself as a victim of persecution. Late in 1983, the government's fury was surprisingly turned on Muzorewa, after the bishop returned from a trip to Israel and criticized the government's outspoken hostility toward that country. Muzorewa was detained on the grounds that he was engaged in a subversive plot with South African elements, and his case, too, received widespread attention when he went on a hunger strike to protest his treatment. All such actions heightened the worst fears about the turn that Mugabe's regime might take if ZANU were to carry out its promise to create a one-party state. Mugabe demoted Ushewokunze and otherwise resisted pressure by militants to abrogate the Lancaster House agreements; but when ZANU held a long-awaited party congress in August 1984, it created a Politburo from which some of the most important moderates were excluded.

During the buildup to parliamentary elections held in 1985, government officials and party workers became steadily more hostile toward the tribal and political minority. At one point in March 1985 Nkomo's stronghold of Bulawayo was sealed off, as soldiers and police searched for dissidents and weapons; more than fifty of Nkomo's leading supporters disappeared during the raids. Government workers sent to Matabeleland to register new voters would only accept those who professed an allegiance to ZANU, and only a ZANU membership card guaranteed people their freedom from police harassment.

In the fields of foreign policy and press relations, Zimbabwe seemed intent on pursuing a course bound to turn potential friends into likely adversaries. Certainly Mugabe's government did not have to emulate the likes of Zaïre and Liberia by establishing full-fledged relations with Israel, as Muzorewa advocated, but what it gained by banning all holders of Israeli passports from entering Zimbabwe, in the name of solidarity with the Palestinian cause, was hard to calculate. By prohibiting all foreign journalists based in South Africa from traveling to Zimbabwe, the government was expressing an understandable, if not entirely legitimate, exasperation with the coverage it had received in the international press; but it was also excluding many of the reporters who knew the region best and, in some cases, were most sympathetic to the problems and dilemmas faced by Zimbabwe. For reasons of proximity, airline schedules and other communication links, not to mention history, a certain natural traffic between Zimbabwe and South Africa is inevitable and necessary (as Mugabe implicitly recognized by continuing and encouraging the substantial trade between the two countries); that fact could not be changed by simple fiat. Indeed, the other five "front-line" states in the region joined Zimbabwe in formally proscribing South Africa–based correspondents, but immediately made it clear they would not enforce the rule, knowing that it could result in their getting no coverage at all.

Relations with South Africa became an issue in several other respects. There was ample reason to believe that the South African government was seeking to destabilize Zimbabwe, including by means of its aid to the guerrillas of the Mozambique National Resistance, who sabotaged the oil pipeline leading into Zimbabwe from the Indian Ocean port of Beira in December 1982. South African agents did seem to have a role in the disorders in the southern part of Matabeleland and in acts of sabotage against the Zimbabwean military. And South African government officials, rather than doing their part to help encourage the evolution of a peaceful multiracial society in Zimbabwe (perhaps as a model for change in Namibia or even their own country), took public delight in the troubles of their neighbor, as if they offered new proof of the inability of black Africans to govern themselves effectively. Even the liberal English-language press in South Africa jumped on the anti-Mugabe bandwagon, sometimes going so far as to compare the Zimbabwean leader to Idi Amin or Joseph Stalin. Because of South Africa's inordinate capacity to influence events in Zimbabwe, South African statements about the inevitable deterioration of the relationship took on the character of self-fulfilling prophecy.

One way that Mugabe attempted to ease his country's dependence on South Africa was to involve it in the affairs of a new regional organization, the Southern African Development Coordination Conference (SADCC, pronounced "Sadec"). The inspiration of the late president of Botswana, Sir Seretse Khama, SADCC was intended to achieve "economic liberation" from South Africa and "equitable regional integration"—the development of alternate rail and port facilities, the sharing of agricultural and industrial expertise, and the like. But initial reports and studies emerged slowly, and the ideological diversity among the member governments was only one of many problems; SADCC's close links to, and substantial aid from, the European Economic Community even brought charges of "neocolonialism." The capacity of SADCC member states to understand each other's problems, and even to help each other out occasionally, was a step forward, but the development of an economic counterweight to South Africa is a very distant goal indeed.

In Zimbabwe's case, more than 85 percent of its overseas exports still move through South Africa's railroads and ports; soon after the independence ceremonies in Harare, the South Africans demonstrated their muscle by withholding twenty-five locomotives that had been on loan to the Zimbabwean railways. (They were restored after pressure from the United States.) The ultimate test of relations between the two countries will come if and when Zimbabwe is asked to provide a haven for members of the African National Congress and other groups launching guerrilla raids inside South Africa. For all his anti-South African rhetoric, Mugabe has done nothing of the sort so far, and he has been careful not to act against South Africa in a way that would cause his own struggling nation economic harm.

Independent Zimbabwe's relationship with the United States almost defied prediction and analysis. The Carter administration gained points with the eventual rulers of the country by resisting substantial domestic pressures to recognize Ian Smith's "internal settlement," and although it had preferred an earlier "Anglo-American plan" for independence that the Carter State Department helped design, it lent important support to the Lancaster House conference and constitution. The United States opened the first foreign embassy in Zimbabwe, and it promised generous aid—$225 million over a three-year period—to help repair war damage and promote agricultural development. By the inevitable comparison to the Soviet Union, American credibility was excellent; Mugabe always resented the Soviets' persistent attempts over the years to promote Nkomo's prospects as the leader of the guerrilla struggle, and so there was no substantial Soviet presence in independent Zimbabwe. With the Reagan administration also eager to see Zimbabwe succeed, it seemed natural for Zimbabwean-American relations to flourish.

But beyond American concern over events in Matabeleland, the detention of Muzorewa, and other internal developments, a number of issues of great emotional significance to the United States emerged as problems in the relationship. When Zimbabwe, as a member of the United Nations Security Council, abstained in 1983 on the American-sponsored resolution condemning the Soviet Union for shooting down a South Korean civilian airliner—even as Mugabe was in Washington learning about the importance of the matter to the Reagan administration—there were calls in Republican circles to cut U.S. aid to Zimbabwe as a form of punishment. Then, just after Secretary of State George Shultz had overruled the director of the Agency for International Development and prevented such a cut, Zimbabwe not only supported, but actually cosponsored, the Security Council resolution denouncing the American invasion of Grenada. The final blow, if one were needed, came when Zimbabwean officials boycotted a memorial service in Harare for American and French members of the multinational peacekeeping force in Lebanon who had been killed in terrorist bomb attacks.

There were explanations for Zimbabwe's points of view, including the government's feeling that membership on the Security Council obligated it to represent not just its own position, but overall African attitudes (especially since another Security Council member from Africa, Zaïre, was reliably supporting the American line). Zimbabwe did not believe that the matter of the Korean airliner should be turned into an East-West crisis, with every nation in the Third World expected to choose sides. It worried about the precedent that might be established by approval of the U.S. occupation of Grenada (given the inclination of South Africa to stage raids into neighboring countries), and it saw the American action as being in a category with the Soviet invasion of Afghanistan. As for the boycott of the memorial service, that may well have been accidental or coincidental, but some members of Mugabe's government might have been reluctant to endorse the French and American, not to mention Israeli, presence in Lebanon. Zimbabwe deeply resented Israeli cooperation with South Africa, especially in the military field.

Still, in December 1983, on the pretext of making adjustments in aid programs to meet congressionally imposed limitations, the Reagan administration cut its economic assistance to Zimbabwe for fiscal year 1984 almost in half, from $75 million to $40 million. Official spokesmen denied that this represented punishment of Zimbabwe for its UN votes or other behavior, but it was clear that UN Ambassador Jeane Kirkpatrick and other critics of Zimbabwe had prevailed. It was probably foolish of the American government to react so fiercely, thereby provoking the Zimbabweans to a further, defiantly nationalistic defense of their right to vote and act as they pleased. Mugabe, in a news conference after the cut became known, said he still regarded the United States as a "friend," but he warned: "We are not on sale and will never be on sale to the highest bidder." Yet it was, at the very least, insensitive and unwise of Mugabe's government to provoke American anger at a time of international crisis and instability. The impression was created that Zimbabwe was not merely ungrateful to the United States—an all-too-familiar impression for Americans dealing with the Third World—but actually anti-American. Good judgment came up against national pride on both sides, and the result did no one any good.

Other actions of the Mugabe government were open to question on grounds of judgment and sensitivity. For example, just at the moment of the severest shortage of gasoline for ordinary citizens in December 1982, every minister and deputy minister in Mugabe's cabinet—all fifty-seven of them—rode out to the Harare airport, only one per car, to greet the visiting Ethiopian leader, Mengistu Haile Mariam. Whether such a rousing welcome ought to have been given to a man with such a questionable human rights record was one issue. Whether it was proper for members of the Zimbabwean government to flaunt their privileges in such a wasteful manner, when other people were waiting all night just to get a few gallons of gas, was another, more immediate question.

Yet prerogatives—even the prerogative to be wasteful—are part of what independence is all about. So it was that even as the basic demands and needs of hundreds of thousands of rural Zimbabweans went unmet, the government spent an estimated $65 million importing a large North Korean team, including ordinary laborers with no greater skills than many unemployed Zimbabweans, to build a giant monument in the capital to those who died in the guerrilla war. At the same time, the patronage system grew to exceed anything that had existed during the colonial era or UDI. Politicians and influential civil servants turned up with new luxury cars and other extravagances, and there were no government guidelines or regulations that defined the proper limits for the growing black elite.

Where Mugabe stood in the midst of all this was a great mystery. His style of governance seemed to be to sit back and observe while various factions struggled for dominance on various issues. Quiet, pensive, austere, and probably the best-educated head of any government in Africa, he was obviously torn personally between a commitment to Marxist and pan-Africanist principles on the one hand and, on the other, the urgent need to steer his country through difficult times in a pragmatic manner. But Mugabe's aloofness and his ostensible indifference to many of the excesses and outrages taking place within his government sometimes looked less like caution than like a failure of leadership. The dramatic, behind-the-scenes struggle for Mugabe's soul, and the mysterious, almost Kremlinlike aura of decision making in Harare, could not substitute indefinitely for decisiveness and decency.

If the energy that went into the debate over how to achieve a one-party state could only be applied to Zimbabwe's economic problems and its people's hunger, that would be an important step forward. Meanwhile, as the country's edge in resources and productivity began to be threatened by the worst drought in southern Africa in a century, Mugabe faced new pressures to rise above petty politics of the domestic and international varieties. The alternative was for Zimbabwe to drown in a sea of its own rhetoric and, in the process, to squander the enormous reservoir of international good will that it had at independence.

8

French
Connections

AMONG THE COUNTRIES that are especially poorly known in the United States are those of francophone Africa, and particularly the members of the French African Community (CFA), a customs union most of whose members share a currency that is tied to the French franc. Despite a great variety of political systems and economic circumstances among the thirteen participants in the CFA—some are ruled by avowed Marxists and others by staunch conservatives; a few are relatively prosperous and others continually on the verge of national bankruptcy—their ties to their former mother country have remained extraordinarily close.* By one count in the early 1980s, there were ten times as many French citizens living in West Africa as there had been twenty years earlier when most of these countries became independent. Among the estimated 470,000 Frenchmen, only about 12,000 were mili-

---

* The full members of the *Communauté Français Africain* are the People's Republic of Congo, Gabon, Cameroon, Central African Republic, Chad, Niger, Benin, Togo, Burkina Faso, Ivory Coast, Mali, and Senegal. Mauritania is part of the customs union, but maintains its own currency.

tary; the rest were working in or advising African governments, carrying on private business endeavors, or simply living the relatively good life reserved for Europeans in their former colonies.

African nationalism notwithstanding, there has been little stigma attached to this French presence, which helps preserve an attachment to French traditions and institutions, not to mention the Gallic way of life. Virtually all the telecommunications of the CFA countries are run by a French company, and most of their international phone calls are still routed through Paris. The CFA governments, regardless of their political orientation, tend to shop for what they need in France, and more than 80 percent of the foreign investment in their economies comes from there, too. One advantage of the arrangement for the CFA countries is that their currencies are tied to a stable Western currency, a fact that simplifies and enhances their international financial transactions; it also means that if the French franc slips in value against other currencies, the CFA franc suffers, too.

Outsiders make accusations of neocolonialism, but even the socialist government that came to power in France in 1981 was unconvinced; it saw little reason to loosen or restructure its ties with francophone Africa, and it felt no pressure from the Africans in that direction. On the contrary, more independent African countries have been applying to join the CFA all the time. That trend leads other Western countries, and especially the United States, to believe that much of French-speaking Africa is somehow not important or interesting—and, in any event, off-limits.

SENEGAL

One of the countries most tightly associated with France— economically, politically, and culturally—is Senegal, a nation of some six million people that is in many respects characteristic of the Sahel, the semidesert belt that lies below the Sahara but well above Africa's rich farmland and its known oil and mineral wealth. The poet-statesman who led Senegal to independence, Léopold Sédar Senghor, always boasted that he had done so without the slightest strain or waste of human and financial resources; he simply reached agreement on the details of his country's new status in the course of a dignified, hour-long conversation with then French President Charles de Gaulle.

There were obvious advantages to that procedure for both sides: Senegal stayed very much in the fold, trusted by French officials and businessmen as a stable, secure environment. Positioned at the westernmost point on the great bulge of Africa, it developed into a natural tourist haven. Plush hotels on idyllic beaches attracted first the French in search of all the comforts of home, but in a tropical setting, then American blacks in search of their roots. In Dakar's harbor sits Gorée Island, once a slave-trading station, now a museum beckoning visitors who are willing to take a glimpse at West Africa's tragic past. For black American visitors, Gorée provides a poignant opportunity to mock the slogan over the exit from the dungeons where their ancestors were kept, "The Doorway of No Return."

Dakar itself remains a little jewel in the Sahel, a deceptive oasis of charm and opulence, peopled by gracious men in long robes and statuesque women whose bodies and hair are wrapped in bright African cloth. A well-educated elite lives a life centered around Parisian-style shops and sidewalk cafés, where young graduates gather to debate political philosophy and read local newspapers filled with trivial news from France. As one American travel writer put it, Dakar is "sympathetic" and "serene"; it feels much farther away than it actually is from the turbulence and uncertainty that is the more common African reality. The gleaming white presidential palace, formerly home to the French colonial governor, and the well-manicured, quiet university campus contribute to the aura of serenity.

But at the other end of town, away from the grand boulevards and café society, sits another symbol, the Great Mosque, where thousands of Moslems come every day to pray on mats of straw. Most of them have migrated to Dakar from the countryside, and once one leaves the capital it is easy to understand why. Much of the rest of Senegal consists of vast stretches of desolate land, interrupted only by occasional stands of baobab trees and tiny villages where peasants eke out an existence trying to grow peanuts in poor, eroded soil. The rise and fall of the annual peanut harvest, depending as it does on mostly cruel, natural circumstances, largely determines Senegal's economic well-being. Inside the elegant government buildings of Dakar, officials confront a generally desperate financial situation. One study conducted by American and Senegalese experts estimated that the country could become self-sufficient in food production in the year 2010 at the earliest, and even then, only if it could count on enormous amounts of financial aid in the meantime.

Despite its precarious economy, Senegal has enjoyed unusual political stability. A federation with Mali fell into disarray soon after independence, but Senghor shrewdly built a personal power base that guaranteed his country a durable system. He was somewhat aloof from the masses, a Catholic leading a nation that was 85 percent Moslem, an African statesman married to a white Frenchwoman. And while Senghor was one of the most widely admired poets writing in French anywhere in the world, he did not even speak Wolof, the West African dialect that is the lingua franca of Senegal. Yet he extended patronage to the *marabouts*, or Moslem holy men, obtaining their loyalty in return, and he took a pragmatic approach to domestic, inter-African, and broader international politics.

Senghor called his political party "socialist," but he acted conservatively in many spheres: turning parts of Senegal's publicly managed economy back into private hands, calling for a larger Western military presence in Africa, and contributing Senegalese troops to international peacekeeping forces in Zaïre and Lebanon. During a visit to Washington in 1978, he broke ranks with many of his fellow Africans by publicly denouncing the Soviet and Cuban presence on the continent and complaining that the United States was not doing enough to counteract it. So it was not surprising that when there was a leftist-inspired coup attempt in Gambia, the finger-shaped English-speaking country that juts from the ocean into the heart of Senegal, in 1981, Senghor's handpicked successor did not hesitate for a moment to send out his troops to restore order and the old, trustworthy regime.

If Senghor was viewed as a bit of an eccentric, he was also revered in some circles as a senior African spokesman, a man who could do business with the world's giants even though he came from a small, sparsely populated, resource-poor country. Part of his prestige rested on his enunciation of "negritude," a philosophy of black consciousness that exalted Africa's cultural contributions and stressed its links to other great civilizations and continents. If

anything, Senghor thought he deserved an even more widely recognized leadership role in Africa and the Third World generally.
He was disappointed—even scornful—when people did not pick
up on his moderate suggestions for solving the problems of southern Africa. And when he saw U.S. ties with Nigeria growing to a
point where they overshadowed and perhaps excluded other countries he felt were equally important to America, such as his own,
he was insulted. Yet when Jimmy Carter traveled to West Africa
in 1978, Senghor consented to the stationing of some technicians
and the back-up plane for Air Force One at Dakar's airport, as if
that were the most Senegal could hope for.

In the late 1970s Senghor embarked on an experiment in
multiparty democracy, permitting some (but not all) of his bit-
terest opponents to challenge him openly in parliamentary and
presidential elections. But his truly unique contribution to African political history was in becoming the first leader of an independent black nation on the continent to relinquish power voluntarily and turn it over to a constitutional successor.

On the last day of 1980, at the age of seventy-four, Senghor
resigned in favor of his prime minister, a younger Moslem techno-
crat named Abdou Diouf. Admittedly, Diouf had been personally
selected by Senghor and groomed for the succession without ever
standing for election; still, it is significant that Senghor was willing to leave office without dying or being violently overthrown.
Within months Diouf moved to establish his own political identity. He lifted restraints on political activity, headed off a major
teachers' strike, and wiped out debts owed to the government by
peasants who could not afford to pay. Diouf also spoke out against
corruption and influence-peddling within his own ruling party,
promising to do something about it and also to extend more opportunities to the poor. Indeed, a number of top officials were put
on trial and sent to jail. The new president took a distinctly un-
Senghorlike, but politically popular, step when he ordered a review of Senegal's traditional education policies, including the
teaching of French rather than indigenous languages in the nation's schools. As for the country's severe problem of rapid population growth, however, Diouf followed a cautious, traditional Islamic approach, leaving it to men to declare how many wives
(and therefore how many children) they would like to have.

After two years, Diouf set out to legitimate his own rule. He
held presidential and legislative elections early in 1983, allowing
fourteen political parties to participate instead of just the four
that had been permitted by Senghor (one "liberal," one "conservative," one "socialist," and one "Marxist"). On the surface that
seemed like a major liberalization, but its practical effect was to
splinter the opposition and strengthen Diouf. A third of the eligible Senegalese did not bother registering, and of those who did,
only 55 percent cast ballots. Diouf won 83.5 percent of the presidential vote, and his party took 109 of the 120 seats in Senegal's
expanded National Assembly. The leading left-wing opposition
figures later criticized the electoral system, which they said had
stacked the deck in Diouf's favor, but he had enough political
strength in the country to push through a constitutional amendment, doing away immediately with the position of prime minister
and requiring elections within sixty days in the event of any future presidential departure from office. (The change enhanced
his own power, but weakened old-guard elements in the party.)

Diouf also began to recognize the grievances of the people
of the Casamance region, south of Gambia, members of minority
ethnic groups who have attempted to preserve their non-Christian,
non-Islamic traditional ways of life and, as a result, have been
neglected in post-independence development efforts. Casamance
is isolated from the rest of Senegal, there being only one ferry
crossing of the Gambia River. Seeking to quell separatist feelings
there, Diouf named more people from the region to his new cabinet and released many anti-government demonstrators from the
jail in the regional capital of Ziguinchor.*

Whether Diouf's maneuvers and his forging of alliances with

---

* The dissident movement in Casamance is one of the most unusual in
Africa. It goes back to 1943, when a twenty-three-year-old woman from the
region who was working as a housekeeper in Dakar heard "voices" beckoning her home; when she got there, she launched an effort at passive resistance to the French, who made her a martyr by deporting her to Mali. Even
in recent disturbances in Ziguinchor, women have played a leading role.
Lacking external assistance, Casamancian rebels attack their targets with
bows-and-arrows and knives, and they evoke fetishes and other magical
practices to protect themselves. One unspoken reason for the tough Senegalese intervention in Gambia in 1981 was a fear that a left-wing government
in Gambia would encourage separatism in Casamance and perhaps even try
to annex the region.

other conservative African leaders will keep Senegal as stable as it is proud, it is hard to know; with an economic crisis so severe as to provoke wildcat strikes and street violence, Senegal's future prospects came to be uncertain. But at least the nation faced its staggering problems with a government that seemed to be both competent and confident.

IVORY COAST

The other CFA country that inherited unusually close ties with France and maintained pretensions of African leadership is Ivory Coast. But unlike Senegal, Ivory Coast found that its economy grew to be strong and resilient, while its internal political stability became more precarious. The Ivorian leader, Félix Houphouët-Boigny, was as much a successful product of the French colonial system as Léopold Senghor. After being educated in Dakar, Houphouët-Boigny came home to be a prosperous rural paramedic and later, after inheriting land from an uncle, he became a successful coffee planter. Like Senghor, he represented his people in the postwar French constituent assembly in Paris, and Houphouët-Boigny even became a minister in the French government (although he had never been to France before the age of forty). That did not hurt his standing in Ivory Coast, however, because he achieved hero's status for helping push a bill through parliament outlawing forced labor in the French colonies.

Another important similarity to Senegal is that Ivory Coast was singled out very early by the French as a place they cared about and wanted to be able to stay in (or return to), unlike some of their other colonies, toward which they were more ambivalent. They built an infrastructure that would support investment and growth, and from the very earliest days after independence in 1960 Ivory Coast seemed to have excellent prospects, especially compared to its neighbor and rival to the east, Ghana. Ivory Coast was somehow one of the few places in Africa that did not conjure up the old stereotypes of the dark and savage continent, perhaps in part because its very name suggested whiteness. In July 1982, *National Geographic* trumpeted on its cover a feature entitled "The Ivory Coast—African Success Story." The article and pictures inside portrayed a nation that had comfortably integrated tribal customs with modern influences and advanced technology—the kind of place the West can understand and appreciate.

Ivory Coast's much-vaunted "success" is generally attributed to Houphouët-Boigny's cautious, moderate approach to his country's domestic and foreign affairs. Indeed, as a leader of a colonized people in the turbulent 1950s, he was so cautious as to oppose independence at first, preferring instead that Ivory Coast be granted some form of limited self-government within a new French federal system. When independence became inevitable, Houphouët-Boigny adapted quickly, using his *Parti Démocratique de la Côte d'Ivoire* as the unifying force for the country's dozens of competing tribes and ethnic groups. *Le Vieux* ("The Old One"), as he came to be known, was repeatedly reelected to five-year terms as president, always with nearly 100 percent of the vote.

Houphouët-Boigny's exclusive domination of Ivorian life and politics through his single party could hardly be defended in terms of democratic principles, but it did permit him to steer Ivory Coast's development in a direction that is unique in post-colonial Africa. Stubbornly resisting the automatic prestige attached to the rapid construction of industry in a developing country, Houphouët-Boigny concentrated instead on agriculture, especially the coffee and cocoa that grow profusely in various parts of Ivory Coast. Before long, the country was far out in front of other traditional cocoa producers, and for a time it was second only to Brazil in world coffee production. It also became a leader in the production of pineapples, bananas, palm oil, and cotton.

Here was an African state that was not only feeding itself, but also exporting large quantities of food in exchange for hard currency, which could, in turn, be used to support the gradual building of factories and for other forms of economic advancement. Ivory Coast enjoyed an enviable annual growth rate of 7 percent. The average annual per capita income of Ivorians reached $1,200 and, according to some outside studies, the money is much more evenly distributed than in most other African countries. The growth was deflated considerably when the international recession of the early 1980s drove down the prices of coffee and cocoa, but then Ivory Coast's dream of offshore oil discoveries came true; self-sufficiency in oil production was expected to produce a new

spurt of prosperity by the mid-1980s. Still, Houphouët-Boigny
was forced into budget cuts and other unaccustomed austerity
measures—all the worse when West Africa was hit by a drought
and brush fires in late 1982 and early 1983.

At first glance, one would detect nothing but an unmitigated
boom in Ivory Coast's dazzling capital, Abidjan. It has much of
the excitement of Lagos, albeit on a smaller scale, but with few
of the infuriating inconveniences. Indeed, what the Ivorians like
to call their "economic miracle" has added a layer of skyscrapers
onto what was already a sophisticated African metropolis with a
European flavor. Abidjan is so different from the capitals of other
nearby countries that its residents have been known to joke that
it is a nice place to live because it is "very convenient to Africa."
So many Frenchmen now make their homes in Abidjan—perhaps
sixty thousand or more out of a total population of almost two
million—that when they go on vacation, the city's traffic jams suddenly disappear. This expatriate community and its tastes have a
very important influence on life and life styles in Abidjan. The
shelves of supermarkets are almost indistinguishable from those
in Paris, and the truest American-style luxury opened some years
ago at the Hotel Ivoire: an indoor ice-skating rink to provide relief from Abidjan's torrid climate.

But beneath the glitter, Abidjan—and the rest of Ivory Coast—
have severe problems. The presence of such a large and affluent
European community has made it even harder than it would normally be to absorb into the economy the approximately ten thousand Ivorian high school and university graduates who turn up in
the capital each year. Because Houphouët-Boigny has paid less
attention than some of his counterparts in other countries to Afri-
canization of the top jobs in business and government, few new
opportunities become available. If the graduates were willing to
settle for something less, in many cases they would find their way
blocked by the entrenched Lebanese merchants and a growing
number of Nigerians who control local trade. Even menial labor
is not much of an alternative; immigrants from neighboring countries soak up most of those jobs at cut-rate wages. Indeed, there
are so many foreign Africans living in Ivory Coast now—about a
quarter of its more than 9.5 million inhabitants—that xenophobia
has set in. Not surprisingly, as in Lagos, the foreign workers are
frequently blamed for the dramatic increase in Abidjan's crime

rate. Some, especially Burkinabe and Ghanaians, are a target of persecution; in 1980 Mauritanian shopkeepers had to be evacuated from Abidjan to protect them from attacks and even murders at the hands of Ivorian nationalists. In a sign of the times, the president declared in 1983 that all foreign residents would have to register and carry identity cards.

As harder economic times arrived, tribalism also flared within Ivory Coast. Part of Houphouët-Boigny's genius was to handle the country's potentially explosive ethnic rivalries through a well-oiled paternalistic system; but once there were fewer favors to distribute, the president's Baoulé tribe was accused of having too much of the power and largesse. Corruption was late to be raised as an issue in Ivory Coast, but recently it has become a particular concern in the affairs of the dozens of poorly managed parastatal companies that control much of the country's business. In many instances, directors were found to be draining off public resources to support their own extravagant life styles, putting their relatives on the company payroll, and otherwise conspiring to avoid government supervision of their activities. Once he became aware of the magnitude of the problem, Houphouët-Boigny abolished some parastatals and brought most of the others under stricter control.

There has also been criticism of the government's handling of Ivory Coast's rich natural resources. Overcutting of the tropical rain forests, for example, could deplete the country's forest cover—and, in the process, dangerously alter its climate—before the end of the twentieth century. And because a pound of ivory sells on the black market for the equivalent of a month's salary, Ivory Coast's elephant population is diminishing at an alarming rate, due to the virtually unchecked activity of poachers.

A telling sign of growing economic anxiety is the Ivorian government's increasingly reckless borrowing and accumulation of foreign debt. In the 1970s, when coffee and cocoa were fetching premium prices on the world market, the hazards seemed remote, but now the repayment of some $9 billion in loans is a more daunting prospect for a small country. (The government barely prevented a crisis in 1984, when it obtained emergency help from the International Monetary Fund and convinced various other creditors to reschedule its debts.) One major source of debt was a sugar-production program launched by the government with the laudable goal of agricultural diversification, but without the necessary feasibility studies. By the time it was finished, Ivory Coast was producing sugar at a cost that was about three times its price on the world market.

An energy crisis began to compound the financial crisis in the early 1980s. Ivory Coast had relied almost exclusively on hydro-electric power for its development, seemingly a wise decision, until a severe drought began to affect the water level in its dams. The shortage of electricity became so severe that industrial production fell by 50 percent and many homes and businesses in Abidjan had power for only a fraction of the day.

Against this background, the country has begun to experience political unrest, especially among students who suddenly see a bleak future and therefore question the path their leaders have chosen. At one point the government sent police to raid a conference at the university in Abidjan that was discussing the issue of freedom of expression in Ivory Coast. In recent years, young Ivorians have seen little opportunity to become involved in Houphouët-Boigny's ruling party, and there simply are no alternative official channels for their political energies. As a result, looking east and west, some of them have become outspoken admirers of the military regimes of Jerry Rawlings in Ghana and Samuel Doe in Liberia. That, in turn, makes them seem more of a threat to the established order in Ivory Coast.

Political and economic frustration boiled over in the spring of 1983, when the national teachers' union went out on strike to protest a cutoff of government housing subsidies. The strike, which lasted two weeks (the longest since independence) and was joined by some doctors, dentists, pharmacists, and civil servants, caused a brief national crisis; Houphouët-Boigny found it necessary to appear on television twice in a week to defend his regime, and his party organized massive street demonstrations in Abidjan in support of the government. The president was apparently successful in turning public opinion against the strikers, portraying them as a spoiled, privileged class and accusing them of being manipulated by radical Ivorian exiles in league with Libya (although he later recognized the teachers' union and announced the discovery of corruption and favoritism in the state housing sector). Under a candid threat of severe reprisals and punishment, the teachers went back to work. But Ivory Coast's calm may have been permanently shattered.

Many of these problems would undoubtedly seem less serious if Houphouët-Boigny had tended to the question of political
succession as efficiently and convincingly as Senghor did. But for
the most part, relying on a Baoulé tradition of absolute respect for
the ruling chief, he ignored the issue. The president did liberalize
the Ivorian political system to some extent in 1980, loosening control over the party's political bureau, enlarging the National Assembly, and making it possible for anyone who wants to run for a
seat in it to do so. Already known to be in his eighties (his exact age is a secret), Houphouët-Boigny also agreed to the establishment of a vice-presidency, rather than continuing to insist that
the line of succession would run to his hand-picked speaker of the
National Assembly, Philippe Yacé. But then he repeatedly refused
to fill the new office, instead encouraging various members of the
Ivorian political oligarchy to compete openly with each other for
his favor. Since he would not say when he planned to make up his
mind, the prospect was an indefinite struggle.

Meanwhile, the country's politics and Houphouët-Boigny's
personal life were filled with intrigue worthy of a medieval court.
The president's first wife (the mother of his children) having retired to the village where she was born, his second wife, Marie-
Thérèse, became increasingly involved in politics and was believed to be a prime supporter of one of his possible successors,
the mayor of Abidjan. (The second wife was the cause of serious
personal strife between Houphouët-Boigny and his banker son,
Guillaume. The son had introduced her to his father as his own
prospective bride, but soon the father appropriated her for himself.) A third and little-known wife, a thirty-three-year-old woman
who had spent much of her time in one or the other of Houphouët-
Boigny's two homes in Europe, died under mysterious circumstances in 1981 at a luxurious villa in Abidjan. At least two members of the ruling circle who criticized the government's handling
of problems at the university died suddenly. At the same time, the
influence of several shadowy advisers to the president, including
one Frenchman of Algerian origin and another from the Antilles,
a Senegalese, and a Lebanese, has apparently increased.

In the course of dealing with the teachers' strike in the spring
of 1983, Houphouët-Boigny offered a new and revealing glance
into his own personal financial affairs. He admitted in a public
speech that he had billions of CFA francs tucked away in Switzer-

land, and he named the bank where they were on deposit. But as if to demonstrate faith in Ivory Coast's own financial institutions, he said he had billions there, too, and went on to acknowledge that he was the nation's largest producer of pineapples, avocadoes, and poultry. Hoping to be admired for his straightforwardness, he instead provoked new cries of outrage over his monopolization of wealth and power.

Undaunted and unconcerned about his regime's stability, Houphouët-Boigny went off a few weeks later on his first official visit to Washington in ten years. There he was received enthusiastically by Ronald Reagan, as he had been previously by Richard Nixon. The Reagan administration saw him as a successful practitioner of free enterprise, and it was pleased with his public and private warnings against the nefarious activities of Libyan leader Muammar al-Qaddafi. The Ivorian government marked the occasion with full-page advertisements in major American newspapers, touting "A Strong U.S. Ally in Black Africa" and extending an invitation to American business to invest in Ivory Coast and feel free to repatriate its profits. Going on to Canada, France, and Britain, Houphouët-Boigny stayed away for five months, but on his return showed no sign that he was thinking of retirement. He reduced the size of his cabinet from thirty-five to twenty-seven and shuffled some personnel, but named few young people to the top ranks.

An increasing amount of Houphouët-Boigny's energy has been spent in recent years converting his native village, Yamoussoukro, 166 miles northeast of Abidjan, into a kind of African Versailles. It has eight-lane highways on which nobody drives, a golf course where no one plays, and, on the site of the house where the president was born, a marble palace complete with golden rams and a crocodile-infested lake. Carpets were provided by the shah of Iran before he fell, and there is a guest palace for visiting heads of state. The airstrip is adequate to accommodate a Concorde supersonic jet. Yamoussoukro was barely a clearing in the forest when the president began his grand project, but now nearly a hundred thousand people live there. Finally, Ivory Coast's National Assembly made it official in March 1983, voting without a single dissent to move the nation's capital to Yamoussoukro. The decision seemed intended less to serve the goal of national unity (as with Abuja in Nigeria) than to satisfy the aging president's vanity. To those who objected to the diversion of resources for Yamoussoukro's development, Houphouët-Boigny replied that a young nation must make sacrifices to create its own history and cultural monuments.

CAMEROON

For many years it seemed as if the same syndrome of a strong political leader who refused to plan for the future might be a problem for Cameroon, a country of 10 million people strategically located at the hinge of the African continent. One man, Ahmadou Ahidjo, had been in power since before independence from France in 1960, and he had consolidated virtually all political forces within his single ruling party. He occasionally mused in public about wanting a "rest," but no one could really imagine his stepping down; nor did there seem to be any comfortable procedure that would permit him to do so. Although at least twenty years younger and from a very different background, Ahidjo was a kind of protégé of Houphouët-Boigny, who gave his blessing to Ahidjo's pragmatic regime by visiting Cameroon and touring rural development projects. But in November 1982, citing ill health, Ahidjo surprised his country by resigning as president. Like Senghor, he turned power over to a longtime prime minister, forty-nine-year-old Paul Biya, who was little known outside the country but had a reputation for honesty and competence.

Appearing in the Western press at the same time as reports of yet another coup d'etat in Upper Volta, the news of Ahidjo's voluntary departure did not attract much attention, and that has been true of Cameroon in general. Few outside reporters make extended visits to the country, using the international airport in Douala primarily as a transit stop on their way to and from other places where headlines are being made. But while few people were watching, Cameroon enjoyed considerable success as a young nation. In its first twenty years of independence, it nearly doubled its per capita gross national product. Like Ivory Coast, Cameroon first concentrated on agricultural development, then moved on to basic industry, and finally had the good fortune of offshore oil finds.

There were plenty of difficulties along the way. Cameroon is in many respects a microcosm of the African continent, a country composed of at least two hundred separate ethnic groups, each with its own language, none large enough to dominate the country's affairs. The land is almost as varied as the people who live on it, ranging from coastal swamps and tropical rain forests through savannas to desert areas. It would be hard enough to forge a single national identity under those circumstances, but Cameroon also has two—even three—separate colonial heritages with which to contend.

Originally a German protectorate, the country was split between France and Britain after World War I, and the two parts developed individually. Most of what had been British Cameroon voted to join a federation with French Cameroon (rather than Nigeria) just after independence, but there were still tensions. Officially the country conducts its affairs bilingually, in English and French (the only other language spoken by enough people to be considered a national language is Cameroonian "pidgin"), but the 20 percent anglophone minority is chronically discontented, much in the manner of the French-speaking minority in Canada. Very little English is actually used in the languid capital city of Yaoundé, where most of the political power is concentrated, or in Douala, where most of the country's financial business is transacted.

Even a quarter-century after independence, an excursion westward along the coast from Douala to Victoria is like a voyage across the English Channel. The nature of the roads, the uniforms of the police, the music, even the mannerisms of the people change once one has crossed the undemarcated cultural and linguistic frontier. Political discussions take place on one side at sidewalk cafés, on the other in pubs. Here and there a German-built castle can be seen in the hills, a remnant of an earlier era and yet another set of political and cultural traditions. (There are other reminders: hotelkeepers in some remote areas still speak only German, and the Goethe Institute does a booming business in Yaoundé among people who want to learn the language so they can better understand the country's past.)

For seventeen years, beginning five years before independence, the Cameroonian government fought a withering insurgency, based not so much on linguistic or tribal complaints as ideological differences. The rebels, who wanted to establish a Marxist system in Cameroon, were openly aided by China, and it was only with French assistance that Ahidjo finally prevailed in 1972. He not only neutralized much of the domestic opposition that remained by co-opting it into the government, but also turned the Chinese into friends. By the late 1970s Cameroonian shops were full of inexpensive Chinese consumer goods (whose Western equivalents would have been much more costly in terms of hard currency outlays), and China was building a palace of culture on a hill in the center of Yaoundé. The Chinese also constructed a dam in the north, and Ahidjo was able to play well enough on international rivalries to attract other substantial development aid from the United States, the Soviet Union, Saudi Arabia, Canada, and members of the European Community.

Although one of the two central banks of the French African Community is located in Yaoundé, Ahidjo managed to downplay Cameroon's French connection, and over the objections of French banking interests, he encouraged the Chase Manhattan Bank to open a branch in Douala. The First National Bank of Boston and Bank of America followed suit. Cameroon's ties with France remained very close, but the president cast himself as an individualist, staying away from the periodic summits of former French African colonies, for example, on the grounds that their symbolism was inappropriate.

Cameroon for years seemed the essence of stability compared to most of its close neighbors: Equatorial Guinea, where the regime of Nguema Masie Biyoto ruled by terror and reintroduced forced labor; Nigeria, where military coups and civil war had the country in disorder for years; the Central African Republic, where a despotic ruler crowned himself emperor and slaughtered schoolchildren; and Chad, where the ostensibly insoluble civil war was stoked by Libya and dragged on for decades. But Cameroon could not always keep as much distance as it wanted from these crises. Various parts of the country endured crosscurrents of refugees, and Ahidjo had to worry constantly that outspoken exile leaders from neighboring states who sought asylum in Cameroon would end up dragging his government into disputes. (The recurrent trouble along Cameroon's border with Nigeria was enough of a problem, aggravated as it was by the Cameroonians' envy of the Nigerians' wealth and influence in Africa.)

While not turning refugees away, Ahidjo tried to concentrate on preserving order at home. His style was autocratic and his tactics sometimes repressive (the government never liked to talk about how many political prisoners it might have), but he made material improvements in people's lives with such programs as urban renewal in the slums of Douala. In international policy, while he gained a reputation for being pro-Western, Ahidjo preferred to encourage and develop Cameroon's potential as a center of pan-Africanism. Toward that end, he provided government funds for an international relations institute and a journalism school in Yaoundé that would welcome students and faculty from throughout Africa. To some extent, this made the Cameroonian capital an arena for the exchange of ideas and the development of a new generation of African leaders and intellectuals. But it also made it a logical crossroads for the intelligence agents of various countries. Yaoundé became one of those places in the Third World where various competing powers watched each other watching each other.

As if to demonstrate that stability is always an elusive condition in Africa, Cameroon had a sudden bout of trouble beginning in the summer of 1983. Biya, the new president, fired several members of his cabinet, including his prime minister; announcing that he had uncovered and neutralized a plot against "the security of the republic," he then fell into an unseemly public feud with his mentor and predecessor, Ahidjo, who had at first maintained influence by remaining chairman of Cameroon's only political party. From his home on the French Riviera, Ahidjo suddenly became an open critic of his protégé, claiming that Biya had turned Cameroon into a "police state" where telephones were tapped and arbitrary interrogations carried out. The former president also contended that he had been tricked into stepping down in 1982 on the basis of a false report from his French doctors. The roots of the conflict, it turned out, were both personal (Biya would not permit Ahidjo to transfer his sizable fortune out of Cameroon) and regional (Moslem ethnic groups from the northern part of the country, the home of Ahidjo, resented the growing power of Christian southerners like Biya).

The situation deteriorated quickly. A Cameroonian court sentenced Ahidjo to death, in absentia, and then Biya, hoping to appear conciliatory, pardoned him. But in April 1984, units of the presidential guard, an elite unit that had been formed by Ahidjo, rebelled against Biya's orders that they be transferred. The army quelled the mutiny by mostly northern soldiers only after three days of fighting in the streets of Yaoundé. Ahidjo insisted he had nothing to do with the revolt, in which as many as a thousand people were estimated to have died, but the country seemed perilously divided. This time Biya showed little generosity; hundreds of guard members and civilian sympathizers were tried in secret by military tribunals and executed.

But within a few years, as calm returned to the country's political life, Cameroon was back on the short list of stable African countries where development was on track and investments would be safe.

GUINEA

There was a time when Guinea was regarded as a potential model for independent, black-ruled Africa; achieving independence early, as a kind of francophone counterpart to Ghana, it was led by Sékou Touré, a young, charismatic trade unionist, who was said to understand the need to meld the best parts of the French heritage with nationalistic impulses, in order to create a successful modern state. But in 1958, in the name of nationalism, Touré voted against joining the political and economic community envisioned for France's colonies under the new constitution prescribed by Charles de Gaulle for the Fifth French Republic. Touré said he would choose "poverty in freedom" over "riches in slavery." He probably did not realize just how accurate the first part of that statement would be.

The French were furious, and inasmuch as Guinea was the only African colony to resist the new arrangement, the reprisals were immediate and thorough. All of the French representatives in the capital city of Conakry, government officials and businessmen alike, pulled out immediately, taking with them everything from colonial archives and development plans to light bulbs and the dishes in the governor's palace. They emptied out pharmacies and burned the medications, rather than leave them behind. De Gaulle, offended and vengeful, persuaded other Western governments to take his side in the dispute, and so overnight Guinea found itself not only poor and backward, but also totally isolated in Africa and the rest of the world. Touré appealed for outside help, and the Soviet Union, sensing a rare opportunity, was alone in responding.

In retrospect, it is almost impossible to trace the exact course of Guinea's downward spiral. What appears to have happened, however, is that in accepting Soviet largesse, Touré also adopted all the least efficient and most repressive aspects of the Soviet economic and political system. Despite an extraordinary natural wealth in bauxite, iron ore, uranium, gold, copper, cobalt, manganese, diamonds, and hydroelectric power, Guinea went from poor to poorer. Almost no element of the new nation's economy functioned smoothly, and even the traditional network of market women was gradually restricted in favor of state-managed trading companies. Every bit of Soviet aid came with strings attached, and Guineans often found some of their own precious food resources being canned and shipped out in order to help pay off the country's debt to Moscow, while other food was being imported at premium prices. The government still must pay the Soviet Union an estimated $25 million a year, and some observers accuse the Russians of having smuggled out vast quantities of diamonds over the years. Meanwhile, Conakry became notorious as a headquarters for KGB activity in Africa, and the Soviets used Guinea as a base for reconnaissance aircraft. Conakry's airport was useful to the Soviets during the Cuban missile crisis of 1962, and later for shuttling Cuban troops to Angola.

Touré developed what was on paper one of the world's purest democratic systems, with the country divided into minute administrative units through which the citizens would theoretically be consulted constantly on every imaginable issue of national policy. In reality, the people of Guinea suffered an insidious, uncompromising repression, managed by Touré's immediate relatives and members of his clan. Touré relentlessly pursued his opponents and detractors, establishing detention camps whose population was carefully concealed; some of the inmates were tortured, others simply starved to death. He wrecked the independent trade union movement, his own former power base, and he broke the influence of Moslem, Christian, and traditional African religious leaders. Guinean exiles—perhaps a fifth of the population fled—told stories of purges and disappearances, but the president rejected appeals for objective, outside inspections with cries of self-righteous indignation. The persecution and executions often extended to members of the ruling circle who fell out of favor, including at least two former Guinean ambassadors to the United States and Diallo Telli, the first secretary-general of the OAU. The main precept of Guinea's system became worship of the paranoid Touré, who was known as the "Supreme Guide of the Revolution." Guinea nonetheless retained a circle of admirers and Touré-worshipers in the West, who paid attention to his theories and ignored his record.

By the calculation of most international organizations and knowledgeable observers, Guinea lost at least two decades of potential development; in the early 1980s its per capita annual income was still only about $230, and its six million people ranked among the world's very poorest. Touré, for reasons known only to himself, began to reconsider his economic decisions during the late 1970s, but it would take more than a change of heart to produce a change in national fortunes. Much of the country's resources were beyond the reach of potential investors, because few of the necessary roads and bridges or other means of transportation had ever been built or arranged; to construct them later was far more difficult and expensive, given inflation and the worldwide recession. Almost no one was being educated, and there was a chronic shortage of food. The country's agricultural development may have been permanently set back by neglect* and by damaging environmental practices, including the uncontrolled cutting of forests to produce firewood. The failure to replant trees led to severe erosion of the soil and may also have reduced the flow of several rivers in the region, on which many countries depend for their basic livelihood.

Belatedly recognizing these and other problems, Touré did make one of the Third World's most remarkable and awkward about-faces. Embracing Islam more fervently than before and still claiming to be true to his original principles of socialism and nonalignment—indeed, confidently offering himself as a political and philosophical successor to Yugoslavia's Tito—Touré opened his arms (and his country) to Western business and diplomacy. He reestablished relations with France in 1975 and welcomed French President Valéry Giscard d'Estaing for a visit in 1978. (In

---

* Guinea produced 100,000 tons of bananas in 1960, but only 162 tons in 1982.

1982, Touré traveled to France for the first time in twenty-four years.) Most dramatic was his flirtation, during repeated visits to the United States, with American business. Over time he virtually placed his country's future in the hands of the Chase Manhattan Bank, which sponsored investment seminars and other opportunities for American entrepreneurs to meet and negotiate personally with Touré. All of this culminated in a news conference that Touré gave at the Guinean embassy in Washington, after a meeting with President Reagan, during the summer of 1982. Dressed in his usual flowing white robes, the president sat in front of a gigantic portrait of himself and extolled the virtues of "my dear friend David Rockefeller," the former chairman of Chase, who had just been his host in New York.

Guinea still had some Soviet-bloc assistance, especially from Rumania, but Touré's principles had been adjusted to accommodate a new reality. Touré resumed diplomatic relations with some of the more conservative African states, including Senegal and Ivory Coast, and he came out of his self-imposed isolation to play a greater role in such multilateral organizations as the OAU and ECOWAS. (He was scheduled to host the annual OAU summit in Conakry in 1984.) He even took the bold step of opposing the Polisario guerrillas in their war with Morocco over Western Sahara. Internal economic liberalization was also an obvious need. The country resumed a more normal commercial life, complete with market stalls, kiosks, and other small entrepreneurial businesses. As a result, the World Bank took a new interest in Guinea and began to encourage greater Western aid and private investment.

Understandably, such dramatic changes caused turbulence in Guinea's political life, with the truest believers virtually being asked to trade one orthodoxy for another. Not only were outsiders suspicious of his fickleness, but Touré also had credibility problems at home. Some of his most trusted lieutenants felt he should remain true to his original principles. Others pressed for faster change, including an older half-brother, who was fired from his job as minister of the economy after he publicly compared Guinea unfavorably with other African countries that had made greater economic progress. (He later repented and was brought back into a lesser job.) With 90 percent illiteracy and an average life expectancy of only thirty-eight years, Touré's people were still far from the fulfillment they had been promised at independence. The best they could hope for in the short run was some relief from their hunger and despair.

The decline continued even during the period of economic opening, with government revenues falling by 30 percent between 1982 and 1983; Touré was ill and increasingly out of touch, and even the narrow Guinean elite and favored units within the military became restless. Touré resisted being taken out of the country for medical treatment, but finally in March 1984 he permitted Saudi Arabia to fly him to the Cleveland Clinic in Ohio for heart surgery. There he died on the operating table.

During several days of national mourning, Guinea remained calm and, on the surface, respectful of Touré's twenty-six years in power. Dignitaries from all over the world, including U.S. Vice-President George Bush, attended his funeral. But a week after Touré's death, anticipating a power struggle within the Touré family and the party politburo, a group of military officers bloodlessly took charge. They opened the doors of the prisons and detention camps, and only then did some of the horrors perpetrated by Touré in the name of the "revolution" become widely known. In death, the man who portrayed himself as a god was revealed to be a genuine villain. The new military regime promised the citizens true economic liberalization, under a free enterprise system, as well as free speech and the liberty to travel inside the country and abroad. The first signs were encouraging; but with hospitals that had no medications and other public facilities completely broken down, the soldiers had a daunting task ahead of them.

MALI • BURKINA FASO • NIGER

Other francophone West African states that have drawn Western attention in recent years include Mali, Upper Volta (now Burkina Faso), and Niger. All three are mostly Moslem societies that face classic postindependence political, social, and economic strains. They have also all suffered greatly from the drought in the Sahel.

Mali is the home of ancient civilizations—including the one that was based in Timbuktu—and in the precolonial era it had an active urban civilization that bustled with barter and trade. (It is said that in Mali every village boy wants to grow up to be a trader; that has traditionally been the route to status and power in the society.) Even now, in the midst of famine and severe national economic distress, the government has built a magnificent new museum (with French aid) to display the country's proud heritage; the new museum's electric bill alone is equal to the old museum's entire budget, and that fact is symbolic of Mali's problem of squaring ambition with reality.

Admittedly, Mali is one of those African countries that benefited little from the colonial era. While the French poured resources in and built the infrastructures of other, potentially more prosperous colonies, they neglected Mali. Its circumstances stayed about the same, or even declined. At independence, after the collapse of its federation with Senegal, the country had a rigid socialist philosophy, including collective farming, and bold hopes for industrialization, but limited natural wealth and know-how. Since the overthrow by the military of Mali's first postindependence leader, Modibo Keita, in 1968, the socialist purity has gradually fallen away, but still Mali promises far more than it can deliver to its people. All high school or university graduates get guaranteed government jobs, but they are paid so little that they must find some means, legal or otherwise, to supplement their salaries. Indeed, the overeducation of Malians came to be recognized as a problem, and the International Development Association, part of the World Bank, introduced a program to deemphasize higher education in favor of more basic vocational and agricultural skills.

It is a grim indication of Mali's prospects today that the country receives more in Western aid—some $200 million a year altogether, from various donors—than it collects from its own people in taxes.

Once again, in 1983, Mali turned to the dream of federation as a way out of its troubles, this time with the newly pragmatic regime of Guinea. Mali's president, Moussa Traoré, signed a merger agreement with Sékou Touré, pledging "full integration" of the two states. ("Mini-nations can never cope with the difficulties facing our world," Touré explained, but "bigger entities" can.) Integration with Guinea would give Mali a guaranteed route to the sea, but it was hard to imagine any other material gains that might result from a union with one of Africa's poorest and most poorly managed countries. The plan fell by the wayside when Touré died the next year.

Burkina Faso was even more economically depressed than Mali, and even more isolated from the west coast of Africa. It only became an official French colony in 1932, and when it was cut loose twenty-eight years later, it had little to show for the experience. An estimated 90 percent of its eight million people make their living through subsistence farming, and the level of economic activity of the rest is so low that foreign assistance accounts for almost half of the gross national product. Burkina Faso does earn some money (in years when there is a decent amount of rain) by exporting meat, peanuts, and cotton, but the vast percentage of the government's income actually comes from duties on imported goods. It is also typical of the country's plight that it depends heavily on the $70 million or so that is sent home to the national treasury each year by the million or more Burkinabe workers in Ivory Coast.

Some of Burkina Faso's problems are similar to those of Guinea. Little was done in the early years of independence to build the basic necessities for development, and outside the capital of Ouagadougou there are few good roads or decent means of communication. Education is the largest item in the national budget, but still the illiteracy rate remains very high. A relatively small elite has generally run the country. and has often been accused of draining off what few resources it has. There are so many overseas aid officials in the capital that they compete with each other for office space.

Burkinabe politics have been especially turbulent, in part because of the existence of a remarkably powerful labor movement. Almost half of the wage earners in the country belong to one of the four assertive national unions, whose support or opposition can cause a government to rise or fall. As a result, the government has changed often since independence, and seldom by a constitutional method. The military officers who took turns running the country in recent years were vulnerable to outside pressure and influence, and thus it is one country where the Libyan leader, Muammar al-Qaddafi, has been able to build a small but significant constituency. Indeed, a few months after the "People's Salvation Council" took power in late 1982, Qaddafi visited Ouagadougou. But the head of the council, an obscure army doctor named Jean-Baptiste Ouedraogo, was apparently unaware that Qaddafi was coming until just before the Libyan's plane touched down, and two weeks later he arrested the prominent members of the military faction sympathetic to Qaddafi, including Ouedraogo's own charismatic prime minister, Thomas Sankara, a military hero as a result of his performance during a border war with Mali in the mid-1970s. The subsequent expulsion of Libyan officials and technicians from Ouagadougou was regarded as a setback for Qaddafi's attempt to gain influence in sub-Saharan Africa.

But in the summer of 1983, on the twenty-third anniversary of the country's independence, Sankara, in turn, overthrew Ouedraogo and promised a new effort at achieving social justice in the country. Seeking to calm his neighbors' concerns over Libyan influence, however, Sankara moved quickly to promise that he would not be a "pawn" of Qaddafi. He also asked that Libyan planes suspend their flights to Ouagadougou with supplies that had not been requested. The influential teachers' union denounced Sankara as a dictator, but students and other young people seemed to be stirred by a head of state in his mid-thirties who composed his own "revolutionary music" for the guitar. Sankara frequently denounced "imperialists" and he increased contacts with Communist nations—even Albania sent an ambassador—but the most radical work done by his "Committees for the Defense of the Revolution" was to clean up the streets, dig wells, and repair potholes. The new leader refused to enrich himself.

Coups and countercoups aside, there was little change over time in the plight of the Burkinabe people, officially ranked among the very poorest in the world. Some hope was placed in the construction of a new railroad line that would make it possible to mine the country's extensive manganese deposits, and the discovery of gold, silver, and zinc led Sankara to nationalize all land and mineral rights. But it was still bound to be years before any significant improvement took place in the annual per capita income figure of $140.

Having survived at least one coup attempt and stayed in office for a year, in 1984 Sankara changed the name of his country from Upper Volta to Burkina Faso. In the language of the Mossi ethnic group, Burkina means "the land of men of integrity," and in the Dioula language, Faso is the description of a democratic form of government.* The country's task, as he defined it, was to transform "reactionary structures into citadels of revolution." In a typical gesture, he gave the Burkinabe people a New Year's gift at the end of 1984, announcing that workers would not have to pay any rent for their housing during 1985, regardless of who owned it. But in October 1987, Sankara's second in command, Blaise Compaoré, seized power and killed Sankara, whom he called "a traitor and a renegade."

Niger had every reason, at independence, to anticipate the same bleak fate as its destitute Sahelian neighbors. But the discovery of large deposits of uranium—and a boom in the world market for that mineral during the 1970s—turned what had seemed like a forlorn wasteland into a healthy economic oasis, at least for a time. Between 1974 and 1981, the price of uranium skyrocketed from $18 a kilogram to $81.50. Long-term purchase contracts, especially with France, kept Niger's mines operating in high gear. The government became wealthier than most of its francophone neighbors, and the capital city, Niamey, was transformed: squalid huts were replaced by luxury hotels and sumptuous office buildings, and a high-living new class of businessmen and bureaucrats gave it a night life that few had ever imagined in such a spot. Naturally enough, Niamey also became a center for black-market smuggling, especially into northern Nigeria; the combination of legal and illegal income created overnight fortunes.

As it happened, the start of the uranium boom coincided with the overthrow in 1974 of Hamani Diori, the traditionalist who had led the country during its early years. The colonel who came to power then, Seyni Kountché, was fortuitously given credit for the sudden prosperity, and that, in turn, allowed the country a spell of political stability that many other militarily

---

* African place name changes frequently cause problems for mapmakers and foreign ministries around the world, but the creation of Burkina Faso out of Upper Volta also created a touchy protocol question at the United Nations. The country was in the midst of a term on the Security Council when Sankara made the change, and it had already had an alphabetically-determined turn presiding for a month; the issue was whether it was entitled to another turn a few months later when the council started again at the top of the alphabet.

controlled nations in the region did not enjoy. Because some of the government's windfall from the uranium was spent on development projects, the peasants actually benefited, too. Niger is twice the size of Texas, but only 3 percent of its land is arable. Once money became available for sophisticated irrigation projects, however, that 3 percent of the land could be more wisely and productively cultivated.

But as if to demonstrate the precarious nature of African development, Niger's fortunes began to plunge soon after the world uranium market collapsed in the early 1980s. Whereas uranium accounted for half the country's national budget in 1979, that figure fell to 7 percent in 1982; and as world demand fell, so did Niger's output of uranium. Thus its hopes to become one of the world's most important producers of that mineral faded quickly. It was a classic case of how whipsawing commodity prices can hold a national economy hostage.

Once Niger's economy became shakier, so did its political stability and the security of its territory. Kountché, feeling threatened by ethnic rivalries and social unrest, began to shuffle the members of his cabinet, and he had his secret police arrest outspoken labor leaders and intellectuals; the new class of businessmen and bureaucrats who had profited from the uranium boom was another potential threat. But it was Kountché's fellow military, including the head of his presidential guard, who tried to overthrow him late in 1983 while he was in France, just as the IMF was approving new loans to help Niger's shattered economy. One suspicion was that the unsuccessful plotters had help from Libya.

Qaddafi had been known to declare more than once, "We consider Niger second in line after Chad." Indeed, Libya has laid a formal claim to some two hundred square miles in northern Niger, including one of the areas rich in uranium, and Qaddafi has tried to stir discontent among the nomadic Tuaregs who inhabit the area. The Libyan leader welcomed them as migrant workers in his country, and he also sought to increase his influence in Niger by building mosques, roads, and health facilities.

As Kountché lay dying of a brain tumor in a Paris hospital in November 1987, the Supreme Military Council announced in Niamey that it had named Ali Saibou, the Army chief of staff and Kountché's cousin, as his successor.

9

American
Clients

CERTAIN PROMINENT African countries have come to be regarded as special concerns of the United States. It is not that they have long-standing cultural ties with America, as Liberia does, or that they have developed close resource and trade relationships with the United States, as Nigeria has done. It is more that they are ruled by regimes that have come to identify with the American side of the East-West struggle and have become dependent on the United States for their economic and political survival.

The phenomenon is well known in the Third World generally, but it is especially dramatic in Africa, where new leaders often try to shore up their domestic position by demonstrating international contacts and support. Because the association may translate into friendly voting behavior at the United Nations and precious rhetorical support in other international forums, the United States eagerly accepts such new, if opportunistic, friends, and American leaders sometimes feel flattered by their attention and loyalty.

While the United States—or a particular administration—may

feel pride in, and even take credit for, the minor triumphs of client regimes, it is also bound to be held responsible for their excesses and failures. Indeed, once a close connection has developed, American prestige and honor may be on the line in surprising places, especially if the country in question covers a vast territory or is strategically located. If an administration in Washington holds back on providing some of the aid its client wants, then the United States may appear to be an unfaithful, unreliable friend; if it grants almost any request, then it becomes hostage to the whims, not to mention the repression, corruption and other misbehavior, of leaders it cannot control. The ensuing problems are classic ones: How much influence should the United States have over a government it supports? If American influence stands behind such a regime, even as it becomes unpopular with its own people, how should U.S. policymakers weigh short-term order and stability against the prospects of long-term unrest and instability? And how much contact should American representatives maintain with the opposition to leaders who are counting on U.S. support?

All of these issues are at stake in three important African nations that have, in recent years, aligned themselves with the United States: Zaïre, Somalia, and Sudan.

ZAÏRE

In Zaïre, the U.S. stake became apparent as soon as Joseph-Desiré Mobutu (later Mobutu Sese Seko) emerged on top of his rivals in that country's tumultuous politics in 1965. If by no other standard, the Mobutu regime is a success on the basis of staying in power; it is one of the longest-lasting governments in modern Africa. Nonetheless, by every rational criterion and according to virtually every expert analysis conducted by those inside and outside Zaïre, the regime has been on the verge of collapse for much of that time. That it has not collapsed is evidence of Mobutu's cunning and of his persistently reliable American support, despite ups and downs in the U.S.-Zaïrian relationship.

Mobutu's political and personal behavior is eccentric and contradictory. In the process of "Zaïrianizing" his country to make it more authentically African, he gave himself a new name (complete with connotations of sexual prowess)* and created an elaborate mystique surrounding his origins and his achievement of power; Zaïrian children can read all about it in comic-book form. Yet he has actually remained more aloof from the common people of his country than most leaders in Africa. Mobutu has complained often about the corruption in his society, but he has been its most corrupt member; indeed, during his time in power, he has become one of the richest men in the world, with a personal fortune estimated to be worth upward of $3 billion. (His properties include several chateaus in Belgium and other homes in France, Switzerland, Italy, Senegal, and Ivory Coast.)

Mobutu created a vast, overarching political party (the Popular Movement of the Revolution, of which he is "president-founder" and whose official philosophy is known as "Mobutuism") that was to control all elements of the country's affairs, but he promptly rendered it meaningless so it would not become a training ground for potential rivals or successors. He has locked people up and then let them out, seemingly on a whim, leaving even his closest associates wondering when they might fall out of favor and into prison. Although it was his original source of power, Mobutu has rendered the Zaïrian army largely ineffective at home, and when he has been under attack by insurgents, he has often had to call on outsiders, such as Belgium, France, and Morocco, for help. Yet he somehow manages to send off Zaïrian troops to help keep the peace in crisis spots elsewhere in Africa, such as the Central African Republic and Chad, ingratiating himself with their leaders and foreign sponsors.

The effect on the people of Zaïre of this form of rule has been devastating. The outward signs of despair in Kinshasa, the capital, are enough to convince even the most casual visitor that something is terribly wrong. Small children stand on street corners, barely clothed, clutching a crust of bread and a bottle of orange soda (probably their only nourishment for the day), begging passersby for a few coins to help them buy more. If they do not succeed that way, the urchins will invariably steal what they need instead. Indeed, anyone wearing a watch or any other piece of jewelry is

---

* The full name is Mobutu Sese Seko Koko Ngbendu wa za Banga, and one of several authorized translations is "the all powerful warrior who, because of his endurance and inflexible will to win, will go from conquest to conquest leaving fire in his wake."

liable to have it stolen on the spot. It takes a substantial bribe just to have a piece of luggage put on a conveyer belt for a departing flight at the Kinshasa airport. For years the only way to get an international phone call out of Zaïre was to bribe a hotel switchboard operator, who shared the proceeds with an accomplice at the central exchange; the state-owned telephone company got none of the money. Visitors are routinely advised not to bother trying to send out mail through the post office, because the stamps are liable to be removed and resold and the letters or postcards thrown away. On many streets there are ruins of never-completed construction projects, ambitious schemes that fell by the wayside because money ran out, materials were stolen or damaged, or investors simply gave up. At the same time, one sees a few skyscrapers housing luxurious office suites for government officials and private businessmen who are profiting massively from Mobutu's system; they come and go without apparent concern for the circumstances around them.

But the official statistics make it clear that things are even worse in Zaïre than they seem. The real wages earned by ordinary workers have declined almost constantly since independence, and they are now about 10 percent of what they were in 1960. Today's annual per capita income figure is only $170. Thousands of children die every year of malnutrition, and one estimate is that because of severe health problems, 50 percent of the children born in Zaïre never reach the age of five. The country ought to be rich and productive agriculturally. Indeed, in 1958, before independence, 41 percent of its exports were agricultural products, and Zaïre had no trouble at all feeding itself. But in that area, too, the performance has gone steadily downhill. By 1974, a relatively stable time in recent Zaïrian history, only 11 percent of exports were agricultural, and within a few years millions of dollars worth of food was being imported (much of it from South Africa). Most of the food that does come in, whether commercially or through aid programs, is unevenly distributed.

The Zaïrian economy has been declared bankrupt so many times now that the term has lost its meaning. Repeatedly the country has run out of foreign exchange and been unable to pay its bills. To some extent, this is the result of wildly varying commodities prices—the price of copper, for example, plunged drastically in the mid-1970s—but it is also due to extraordinary mismanagement and corruption in the national economy. More than once the IMF sent representatives to Kinshasa to take over the country's treasury and ministry of finance and try to make some order out of the chaos, but most left out of frustration. One IMF envoy, Erwin Blumenthal, a former German official, later reported that "there is no, I repeat no, chance on the horizon for Zaïre's numerous creditors to get their money back. . . . There has been and remains only one major obstacle to annihilate such prospects—the corruption of the team in power." That prognosis frightens the many private Western banks with large outstanding loans to Zaïre. Faced with little alternative, they keep rescheduling Zaïre's debts; with faint hope of recovering the principal within any reasonable time, they are now barely collecting the interest.

From time to time, Mobutu launches an "anticorruption campaign" that seems to be taken seriously by no one except the American embassy in Kinshasa. Typically, the only people caught and punished in such campaigns are lower-level bureaucrats; the corruption at the top continues unabated. Similarly, when Mobutu responded to IMF pressures for greater "economic efficiency" in 1984, he dismissed nearly seven thousand university and high school teachers, but did not begin to deal with some of the worst abuses.

This combination of irresponsibility, chaos, and fundamental human misery has led to many efforts within Congress to deny Mobutu his usual share of American largesse. At one public hearing after another, experts testify about his misdeeds and predict his demise. Angry congressmen, especially Democratic members of the Africa subcommittee of the House Foreign Affairs Committee, routinely vote to cut the authorization for aid to Zaïre, only to see it restored by House-Senate conference committees or Executive Branch maneuvers.

Mobutu has played his American connection with great skill, alternately biting the hand that feeds him (even to the point of expelling American ambassadors whom he accused of meddling in his country's internal affairs) and gently stroking it. He seems to have a keen sense of American domestic political trends. Thus, while he temporarily improved his record on human rights during the years of the Carter administration, he began to arrest and jail more of his opponents within days of Ronald Reagan's inauguration in Washington. At one point when Mobutu's international image was in decline, he arranged for Pope John Paul II to make Zaïre one of the main stops on his tour of Africa (on the eve of which Mobutu married a girlfriend in an elaborate Catholic ceremony). At another particularly tense moment in the standoff with his U.S. congressional critics, Mobutu made the dramatic gesture of resuming Zaïre's diplomatic relations with Israel (having been the first of many African leaders to break them off during the Middle East crisis of the early 1970s). That step delighted the United States at the same time that it somewhat diluted American leverage in Zaïre; Israel would now be an alternative supplier of military aid and training for Zaïre. By keeping up a fairly steady stream of anti-Soviet remarks, Mobutu has also maintained the friendship of China, which seems willing to ignore his domestic record.

Under serious economic pressure in 1983, just as he was applying for another $350 million loan from the IMF, Mobutu took a step calculated to please many of his international critics. He allowed the value of the country's currency (also known as the *zaïre*) to float. That amounted to a colossal 80 percent devaluation of the money, which had long been kept at an artificially high rate. (The official exchange rate went instantly from 6.06 *zaïres* to the dollar to 29.9 to the dollar.) The move also wiped out the huge black market that had complicated any attempts at economic planning and recovery in Zaïre, and it raised the prospect that the country's terms of trade might improve, because its exports would bring in more money. But it also dramatically raised the price of staple food items that must be brought to the city from the countryside at great expense.

In the same period, another notorious incident demonstrated how little respect Mobutu really had for American sensibilities. Just after his return from a triumphant state visit to Washington—during which President Reagan had praised him as a loyal friend—Mobutu found that a U.S. congressional delegation was meeting with ten former members of the Zaïrian Parliament who had previously been jailed for advocating the establishment of a second political party in the country. Furious, the president sent members of his own special brigade to attack and beat his audacious opponents as they left the hotel where they had met with the

American legislators; U.S. embassy officials stood by while this happened. Later the bloodied victims were once again arrested and detained. The congressmen's bipartisan written protest to Mobutu was met with silence. (One theory in Kinshasa was that the president's anger was ignited because the dissenters went to their meeting with the congressmen in Western-style dress of suits and ties, which has been illegal for Zaïrian men to wear ever since Mobutu designed his own "authentic" version of proper national dress, a kind of African adaptation of the Chinese "Mao suit.") A few months later, having just declared an amnesty for his political opponents, Mobutu did the opposite and arrested hundreds more, sending them into internal exile in the fashion of the Soviet Union.

Most of the time Mobutu behaves as if he is indifferent to his public image in the Western world. He closes down universities, rounds up the unemployed youths from Kinshasa's streets, and otherwise overreacts to the slightest signs of opposition. If there were ever a reliable test of the Zaïrian public's attitude toward Mobutu, he would almost surely have a low rating. Instead, he stages mock elections, in which the people have the option of voting for him with a green card or against him with a red one. In the 1984 election, many polling places had no red cards, and not surprisingly, Mobutu won with 99.16 percent of the vote.

The vexing issue for American policymakers of both parties is that having helped build Mobutu into such a behemoth, the United States has nowhere else to turn. At one point in the early 1980s, Nguza Karl-I-Bond, a former prime minister and foreign minister under Mobutu, appeared to have a chance of rallying the democratic, pro-Western forces opposing the regime. But Nguza's plan to have Mobutu's foreign friends prod him into voluntary exile for the sake of his country fizzled quickly, and by 1985 Nguza was back in the fold in Kinshasa; he became foreign minister again in 1988. With few alternatives on the horizon in a closed political system, and with Mobutu continuing to manipulate circumstances to maximize U.S. support, American policy was unlikely to change. Once the assumption was widely accepted that the United States needed Zaïre's minerals and its friendship, few people were willing to run the risk that this vast and significant country might fall into hostile hands.

SOMALIA

There is no apparent reason for American concern over minerals in Somalia, a desert land whose shape defines the Horn of Africa. Somalia is an odd place: 60 percent of its people are nomadic, and little of the country's economic or political life is formally recorded. (The Somali language has existed in written form for only a few years.) Statistics are often contradictory. Not much of value is thought to lurk beneath the Somali sands, although grazing livestock provides about 80 percent of the country's export earnings. Somalia's location is enough to assure it a great deal of international attention. Sitting at the entrance to the Red Sea and close to the oil fields of Saudi Arabia and other Arab states, Somalia has, in recent years, come to be regarded as part of the "arc of crisis" or "arc of instability" that sweeps across the map from the Himalayas to North Africa—a zone where many governments are fragile, military conflicts rage, and the East-West struggle seems often to be at stake.

Certainly the Horn of Africa fits that definition of crisis and instability. An ages-old conflict between Ethiopia and Somalia over possession of the Ogaden region has turned into a full-scale shooting war four times since 1960, and increasingly the United States and the Soviet Union (not to mention Cuba) have become involved. What has made the situation all the more complicated in recent years is a reversal of the long-standing alignments in the Horn.

Having been armed and emboldened by the Soviet Union, in the mid-1970s the Somali government helped the Western Somalia Liberation Front make a brash new attempt to wrest the Ogaden—to them, "western Somalia"—away from the Ethiopians. The front almost succeeded. But in 1977 the Soviets changed sides, taking up with the leftist junta that had overthrown Haile Selassie, the American-supported emperor. With the direct help of Russian and Cuban troops, the Ethiopians then pushed the Somalis back and humiliated them. Thus did the Somalis, once the closest Soviet friends in all of Africa, become the anti-Communist Cassandras of the continent. Still officially a revolutionary regime dedicated to the principles of "scientific socialism," the government of General Mohammed Siad Barre is, nonetheless, now second to no one in its warnings about the dangers that the Soviets and Cubans pose to African and world stability.

All of this has a special poignancy for an American visiting the laconic Somali capital of Mogadishu, where there are few amusements other than international and regional politics. Before 1977, when the Somalis were in their Soviet period, life in Mogadishu was unpleasant for Americans, who were followed, watched, and often harassed. But today Americans are treated as heroes— or, perhaps more accurately, as targets for aggressive affection. On the assumption that Americans will believe and accept almost any compliment, educated Somalis say coyly that they always liked the United States better anyway, that they simply went through a period of being foolishly enraptured by Soviet military aid. Now that they have seen the light, they want to embrace Americans—literally and figuratively—and they demand to be embraced in return. Protestations that the Somalis are trying to take a new relationship too far too fast fall on deaf ears; the advances only become more intense.

Just in case frequent speeches and official government declarations have not made the point sufficiently, the Somalis also resort to putting their message in public places where it cannot be missed. "Stop Russian and Cuban Aggression in Horn of Africa" reads the slogan scrawled crookedly on a white wall along the route into Mogadishu from the airport. Huge signs feature hideous, larger-than-life caricatures of Somalia's public enemy number one, Mengistu Haile Mariam, leader of Ethiopia's military government. Mengistu, fangs and all, is portrayed bayoneting the freedom-loving people of the Ogaden and otherwise suppressing the weak. Where the natural sandblasting effect of the desert winds and ocean breezes has worn away some of the graffiti, new ones have been splattered on top: "Africa Must Be Kept for the Africans!" "Down with International Imperialism." "Colonialists Only Understand the Barrel of the Gun."

Above all, the Somalis have learned how to exploit what they assume to be a general, hard-line American distrust of and contempt for Fidel Castro's government in Cuba. University students make the point about the dangerous Cuban presence in the Horn in the midst of casual conversation. An articulate "businessman" pays an unexpected visit to an American at his hotel, and the same subject comes up at once. Cabinet ministers have only one thing on their minds: the need for American aid to help Somalia fight the Soviet and Cuban menace. "If you abandon the entire area, it is like leaving meat for the lion," said one government official, as if he had taken his script from a conservative U.S. senator's prescription of Africa policies. "It is clear to us," said another, "that the U.S. government has never tried sincerely to stop the activities of the Soviet Union in the Horn of Africa." The basic, implicit argument seems to be that the United States has an opportunity to make a permanent new friend out of the new enemy of its old enemies. It is an argument that is all the more difficult to answer because it is pressed with the Somalis' innate air of superiority, of wisdom gained during centuries in the desert.

The American answer has, for the most part, been to say "yes" to Somali requests for aid. In exchange for U.S. access to the Soviet-built air and naval base at Berbera, on the Indian Ocean coast, first the Carter and then the Reagan administrations became very generous with their new friend on the Horn. Tens of millions of dollars were allocated, primarily to help Somalia deal with its refugee problem, the worst in Africa and one of the worst in the world. (The annual cost of caring for the refugees in Somalia is estimated at $120 million. Many of the refugees come from the Ogaden or other parts of Ethiopia; in 1978, when the flow was especially heavy, in some camps five hundred children were dying every day.) But there was also other economic and some military aid, including an authorization for Somalia to buy $40 million worth of American weapons every year.

Officially, those weapons and the other aid are meant to help Somalia defend itself from external attack (especially by the so-called Somalia Salvation Democratic Front, based in Ethiopia), and otherwise to strengthen the Somali economy and society. However, Ethiopia and some Somali dissidents accuse Siad Barre's government of using much of that money—and also diverting some of the refugee aid—to arm for new efforts to seize the Ogaden and to suppress dissent within Somalia. Indeed, Somalia's military capacity has grown exponentially since it adopted a Western orientation in 1977. The Pentagon is spending some $35 million to expand the Berbera facility and make it an important staging ground for the new U.S. Rapid Deployment Force. Somali troops have participated with Americans in regional military maneuvers, and in late 1983 the Somali defense minister set out on a tour of Washington and other Western capitals, seeking another $1.6 billion in military assistance over a five-year period.

Some American policymakers and members of Congress have urged that a greater degree of caution be exercised in the expansion of U.S.-Somali ties. They are innately suspicious of the kind of sudden change of heart that propelled Somalia in the American direction, and they warn that it could always happen again, in the other direction. But on the whole, the availability of Somalia as an American client has seemed almost too good a development for U.S. military and diplomatic planners to resist. And besides, Somalia has benefited from a growing constituency in the United States. Returned Peace Corps volunteers who served in Somalia and even former U.S. ambassadors there, enchanted as they are by the Somali people, have taken up their cause and argued that the American government should take this opportunity to correct a historic imbalance, a tilt toward Ethiopia that was always unfair.

The dream of recapturing the Ogaden is never far from the minds of most Somalis, no matter what they say. Most of the people who live in the Ogaden are not only ethnic Somalis, but they also function as if they were part of the economic, administrative, and social system of the Somali Democratic Republic. They send their products to market in Somalia or for export through the Somali port of Berbera; they receive most of their food and other supplies by the same routes. Disputes among themselves are invariably settled by arbitrators from Somalia, rather than by the courts of Ethiopia, the country in which they officially live. Ethiopia, in fact, under the emperor as well as his successors, has generally failed to supplant these traditional arrangements with its own. Ogadenis need no travel documents to move across the ill-defined border into Somalia, but they cannot and do not travel freely to other parts of Ethiopia. Many of the people who govern Somalia come from the Ogaden, or have family ties there; none of those who run Ethiopia do.

To the extent that Americans have thought about the rivalries in the Horn at all, they have traditionally sympathized and identified with the Ethiopian point of view. For many people, just the mention of Haile Selassie's name still conjures up a nostalgic vision of the brave little man who went before the League of Nations in Geneva in 1936 to protest the invasion of his struggling

African nation by the Italian fascists under Benito Mussolini. Indeed, for decades after World War II, the vindicated emperor returned the sympathy and various American material favors by welcoming U.S. communications bases and other military operations. Especially since little news ever seeped out about the famines and starvation that were rampant in Ethiopia, or about Haile Selassie's corrupt and despotic—even feudal—system, Ethiopia's thirty million people generally seemed closer, more interesting, and more important to Americans than the three million unknown Somalis next door. Over time, the United States came to endorse— and lend its prestige to—the Ethiopian incorporation of the Ogaden (even though the old border dispute there had never formally been settled). And it did the same with Haile Selassie's annexation of the Italian colony of Eritrea after World War II.

There is much to be said for correcting an imbalance, but the United States runs several risks if it goes too far in the Horn of Africa. One is that in Somalia, as in Zaïre, the American government has become identified with a regime whose ultimate stability and survival are far from assured. While the Somali population is relatively homogeneous, especially compared to those in other African nations, there remain serious rivalries among clans. Rather than being a conciliator, Siad Barre has kept wealth and power in the hands of his own clan and family—at one point, his ministers of health, planning, finance, and foreign affairs were all his relatives—and he has done little to alleviate the residual tensions between the northern region, once colonized by Italy, and the southern region, formerly a British colony. For that matter, he has done little to lift Somalia out of its status as a primitive desert society; he has launched few genuine development projects. Somalia under Siad Barre is a classically corrupt autocracy. Well-connected young men can avoid military service with a bribe to the right official. Hospitals get most of their medications on the black market. And while refugees languish in squalor, the wealthy build new villas.

When he came to power through a military coup in 1969, Siad Barre promised elections, but sixteen years later they still had not been held. Dissatisfaction with his iron-fisted rule has boiled over into riots on several occasions, especially in the northern city of Hargeisa, and there have been some signs of discontent and mutiny in the army. Few observers of Somalia seem to have much of a sense of who might follow Siad Barre in power, should he leave office by natural or other causes. If he is grooming any successors, they are not publicly identified as such. Indeed, little detail is known of his private actions and intentions, in part because of his eccentric habit of sleeping all day and working all night. A cabinet shuffle in 1984 seemed to indicate a turn toward free enterprise, but the government's intentions were hard to read. One bold move Siad Barre did take was to engage in conversations with South Africa; when South African Foreign Minister R. F. Botha visited Mogadishu in December 1984, he came away with an agreement on landing and overflight rights for South African Airways, among other things, in exchange for Somali access to South African military training and equipment.

A major concern about American policy in Somalia has to do with the sensibilities of the Kenyans. Siad Barre's regime has been no more willing than any other Somali government of recent memory to renounce its historic claims to "Greater Somalia." The maps of that larger nation that are displayed in government offices in Mogadishu still include Kenya's northeast province, where many ethnic Somalis live. The Kenyans, themselves the beneficiaries of American military assistance, are not amused. They prefer American to Soviet influence in Somalia, but they would not like to see Somalia strong enough or bold enough to provoke another border war with them in the name of a broader ethnic union.*

But the gravest risk of all is that the American-Somali embrace may damage the prospect of maintaining communication between the United States and Ethiopia. Having professed to care deeply about the Ethiopians during the decades of a close relationship with Haile Selassie, Washington virtually turned its back on them after the Mengistu regime came to power. This caused Mengistu to rely increasingly on Soviet, Cuban, East German, and other Communist assistance in confronting not only the old struggles in Eritrea and the Ogaden, but also a new insurgency in the Tigre region, which is demanding autonomy from the central government in Addis Ababa. (A more recent uprising among the Oromos, the largest population group in Ethiopia, calls into

---

* In July 1984, Kenyan President Daniel arap Moi visited Somalia, and Siad Barre told him that the "sensitive issues" of the past, including the disputed border, were no longer a problem.

question the country's very survival.) Some say that the Central Intelligence Agency has even yielded to the temptation to complicate Ethiopia's problems by sending covert help to various Ethiopian separatist groups, without much awareness of what alternatives they offer to existing policies.

To be sure, Mengistu's rule has been distasteful in the extreme. His "Red Terror" left many of the country's best-educated and most productive people dead; thousands of others barely escaped into exile. Terrible abuses were justified in the name of ideological purity. Nonetheless, without excusing any of his sins, it is possible to acknowledge some of the positive achievements of Mengistu. His cadres have dramatically increased the literacy rate in Ethiopia. The country's peasants have been given land from the vast holdings of the imperial family and its feudal nobles, and they are no longer required to hand over a portion of their meager earnings to the Coptic Church that once helped repress them. Access to basic health services is much greater than it was under Haile Selassie, and even if the new regime is not doing a better job of feeding its people than the old one did, at least it is admitting the problem and appealing for outside help, rather than hiding the truth for reasons of national honor, as the emperor did.

Mengistu and his colleagues did make it difficult for the Western world to help the starving Ethiopians. They delayed, or blocked altogether, the shipment of relief supplies to Eritrea and other parts of the country plagued by civil war, and in some instances refugees walking out of those areas in search of food were actually attacked by the Ethiopian air force. Despite the unambiguous diagnosis provided by doctors on the scene, the government sought to deny that Ethiopians in feeding camps in the North of the country were suffering from cholera (out of a fear that this would affect Ethiopia's export of coffee and meat); one camp was broken up and burned, its frail and hungry residents sent on a march for "resettlement" in another area. When Israel, with the help of the United States and illicit cooperation of Sudan, rescued thousands of Ethiopian Jews, the Falasha, from the famine, Mengistu reacted by claiming that they were not Jews at all and had been kidnapped.

Recent events in Ethiopia have been discouraging. After ten years of planning, Mengistu finally launched a "workers' party" on the Marxist-Leninist model. Even as people were once again starving to death around the country, he spent a fortune enlarging Addis Ababa's Revolution Square, adding statues of Soviet and other new heroes in preparation for an extravagant celebration of the emperor's overthrow. In a day-long speech on the occasion, he promised to tighten Ethiopia's alliance with the Eastern bloc and make it the first truly Communist state in Africa.

Still, U.S. congressional delegations that visit Ethiopia return with messages indicating a desire to retain the American connection in some fashion. Since the ties were close for so long, this would make sense; English remains the primary language of instruction in Ethiopia, and that renders a great deal of the Soviet propaganda directed at the people irrelevant. More important, the United States may be the only country in the world in a position to avert the starvation of millions of Ethiopians. For largely political reasons linked to the East-West struggle—and for fear of offending the new Americanophiles in Somalia—American leaders were initially reluctant to take any major humanitarian initiative to deal with the Ethiopian famine. Eventually, however, the United States became the largest contributor to Ethiopian relief, paying for a third of the external effort. In addition to the 416,000 tons of food worth $208 million pledged by the U.S. government, private American organizations also made major contributions. Even so, Mengistu kept up his attacks on "American imperialism," and when the United States tried to send food directly behind rebel lines in Eritrea and Tigre, he accused Washington of fueling secessionism. That was enough to make some American officials want to abandon the attempt to feed Ethiopians entirely and let Mengistu deal with his own problems or get more help from his friends in Moscow. Indeed, the Horn of Africa poses a special dilemma for American foreign policy: how to oppose a truly heinous regime without doing further harm to the people of the country it governs.

SUDAN

By gaining its independence in 1956, Sudan should have had a head start on solving the most severe problems of political and economic development, compared with some of its neighbors. But its early years were filled with chaos and strife, symbolized by

revolving-door governments, and Sudan seemed to lose the relative well-being it had enjoyed as a jointly administered British
and Egyptian colony.

Like Somalia, Sudan attained a measure of stability and continuity only after a military coup that took place in 1969. Like
Siad Barre, the military man who led Sudan's coup, Jaafar el
Nimeiry, leaned at first toward the Eastern bloc, but later decided
to side with the West, and especially with the United States. The
difference is that in Sudan the change was more gradual and it
took place, in part, under the influence of the late Egyptian president, Anwar el-Sadat. Eventually, because of its own special problems, Sudan became at least as dependent on the United States as
did Zaïre or Somalia. The turmoil along its borders—in Ethiopia,
Uganda, Zaïre, the Central African Republic, Chad, and Libya—
has guaranteed a flow of refugees and a frequent need for outside
support.

Although it is the largest country in Africa in terms of land
area (four times the size of Texas), Sudan has suffered an identity
crisis from the very beginning. The northern part, including the
capital city of Khartoum (where the White Nile and Blue Nile
rivers come together), is a gateway to the Middle East, the
home of a culture that has been greatly influenced by its location
just across the Red Sea from the Arabian peninsula. Its people
look Arabic, speak mostly Arabic or its variants, and feel little in
common with most of the rest of the people of the African continent. The South, by contrast, is authentically African. The Ni-
lotic people who live there tend to have darker skin, practice
Christianity or tribal religions, and have long resisted domination
by the Islamic forces to the North. Indeed, spearheaded by the
Anyanya guerrillas, they fought a seventeen-year-long civil war
in an attempt to establish themselves as a separate nation, and
Nimeiry's negotiation of a peaceful solution to that conflict in
1972 stood as the most important achievement of his regime.

Even if the conciliation were permanent—which it has not
been—the northern and southern sections of the Sudan would
still seem like different worlds, and it would be hard to imagine
ruling them jointly. The contrast between principal cities is typical: Khartoum is a teeming network of bazaars, a tattered place
of ancient rituals that is overcrowded, mysterious, and impene-
trable; a visitor has little sense of what is really taking place

around him. On the other hand, in Juba, the eerily silent administrative capital of the South, there seems to be almost nothing happening. Few of the streets are paved, electricity and water are uncertain commodities, and mosquitoes are more in evidence than people. It is easy to imagine that many of the residents have only recently emerged from the bush, where they fought their battles with the central government. Juba is not as dry and dusty as Khartoum, but it is mysterious in its own way. It seems frozen in a time warp, yet to experience even the most basic pangs of development.

Between and beyond these two centers lie vast wastes of territory, much of it uncharted, interrupted only occasionally by an oasis or a village. In these stretches of land, the Sudanese government has built monumental irrigation projects and tried to devise new and more efficient ways of growing cotton, the country's major export crop; but as the market price for cotton has declined, the efforts have become futile. At one point, sugar seemed like a reasonable alternative. With aid from Arab countries and technology imported from the West, gigantic sugar mills and refineries were constructed; but they cost far more than originally expected, often broke down, and came nowhere near fulfilling Sudan's own needs for sugar, let alone its ambitious goals for export. (Indeed, as late as 1981, the country was still spending a million dollars a day to import sugar.) Other development projects have been attempted with equal sincerity and energy, but usually to little avail, and so Sudan is another country that has repeatedly had to ask its creditors to reschedule its debts while it scrambles to find new ways to pay. The national reservoir of foreign exchange frequently goes dry, and, close though it may be to the great Middle Eastern oil reserves, Sudan often runs out of gasoline because of a failure to pay its bills.

Kuwait and Saudi Arabia have occasionally pitched in to help Sudan, and elaborate development plans have been drawn up for Sudan by the Arab Fund for Economic and Social Development, based in Kuwait. The original theory behind this was that Sudan could become a breadbasket for the Arab world, an insurance policy against Western food embargoes that might emerge in the event of any future oil embargoes. But as the Sudanese performance lagged, and as some Arab oil producers themselves began to feel an economic pinch because of market conditions, Sudan found that it could count less than expected upon its Arab brethren for financial assistance. Another factor contributing to their estrangement was that Nimeiry, having initially opposed Sadat's opening to Israel and the American-sponsored Camp David peace process, finally chose to support those initiatives.

In part out of gratitude for this and other ostensibly pro-American policies, in appreciation for Sudan's strategic location, and perhaps out of pity, the United States gradually came to fill the gap. Once the Libyan leader, Colonel Muammar al-Qaddafi, began to sponsor coup attempts and menace Sudan with cross-border raids, official American sympathies were genuinely engaged. By 1982, Sudan was receiving more American economic aid than any other country in sub-Saharan Africa—$160 million annually—in addition to some $100 million a year in military aid.

When American intelligence agencies became convinced that Qaddafi might attempt a full-fledged invasion of Sudan, the Reagan administration dispatched high-technology AWACS radar planes to Egypt to help protect Nimeiry and his army. It became increasingly clear that Sudan was in the American orbit, and Washington was willing to spend plenty of money and effort to keep it there. The only other aid that was obvious in Sudan was from China and various East European countries. The Chinese built a convention hall that made it possible for Sudan to host an OAU meeting, the Rumanians built the national legislative assembly building in Khartoum, and the Yugoslavs did the same for the regional assembly headquarters in Juba.

Surprisingly, there was virtually no protest and little controversy in the United States surrounding the enrollment of Sudan in the club of nations where American interests are perceived to be at stake. The reason may be that Sudan is even less well known to most Americans than are Zaïre and Somalia, and Nimeiry's connection with Sadat undoubtedly served him well with U.S. legislators. But there was an irony to this acceptance of Sudan into the fold, since it took place at a time when Nimeiry's position within his own country was weakening and there were new reasons to worry about the long-term stability and viability of his regime.

It was precisely Nimeiry's most notable accomplishment—peace between North and South—that began to fall apart in the early 1980s. The key to his success in ending the long internal struggle had been to convert the various southern provinces of

Sudan into a single, semiautonomous region that had its own elected government. Indeed, even though traditional ethnic rivalries had hardly abated (with the Dinka people maintaining their dominance in the area), the southern region was governed relatively democratically, while the North, and therefore the national administration, continued to function as a narrowly based autocracy. By no means was the South economically viable in its own right; on the contrary, it was able to raise only 20 percent of its necessary budget through local taxes. But the creation of a unified southern region gave its people a greater sense of representation and participation in national affairs than they had ever had before, and the discovery of oil in the region by Chevron, an American oil company, offered some hope for a lessening of the traditional dependence on the North.

But just when the system seemed to be functioning smoothly, Nimeiry took steps to change it. Pressed by opponents on various sides—including fellow members of the military dissatisfied with his authoritarian domination of the government, as well as Moslem fundamentalists who believed he was straying too far from tradition—Nimeiry yielded to a suggestion from his latest vice-president, Joseph Lagu, the one-time leader of the Anyanya guerrillas in the South, to redivide the southern region into three individual provinces responsible to the central government.

The southern regional assembly was strongly opposed to the plan, however, and when Nimeiry began to try to force the change, a new fledgling insurgency began in the South. While Khartoum denied the existence of any formal "Anyanya II" movement with clear military and ideological goals (it blamed "bandits" instead), there were enough serious incidents in the South to cause concern. Certainly plenty of weapons were available in the South, some left over from the civil war and others smuggled in from Uganda by the defeated forces of Idi Amin. Roving bands, some of them finding sanctuary in Ethiopia, attacked police stations and other central government offices, and at one point fourteen Arab merchants from the North were rounded up at a southern railway station and murdered. In addition, units of southern soldiers based in strategic locations mutinied rather than accept routine rotation for duty in the North. The situation became so precarious that Chevron considered abandoning its operations in Sudan altogether.

Nimeiry's primary response to the deepening crisis in Sudan was to retreat into his religion. In a true believer's turn to fundamentalism, he declared in 1983 that henceforth the country would be governed by Islamic rather than civil law. (He even released thirteen thousand prison inmates to give them a second chance under a new penal code.) Nimeiry presided over a public ceremony of alcohol obliteration and confiscation, and he declared that the rules against drinking alcohol would apply to non-Moslems as well as Moslems—although offending infidels would be subject to only thirty lashes as compared with forty lashes for Moslems caught drinking. He named Moslem mystics as his principal advisers, declared martial law, and blamed the country's problems on "Satan and his supporters."

All this might have been regarded as a clever political tactic to neutralize the Moslem Brotherhood, if it did not give the southern Sudan a new grievance against Khartoum. Politicians from that region were rejoined by the Catholic archbishop of the capital in protesting that the militant Islamicization of Sudan would intensify discrimination and repression against Christians and other non-Moslems. The protests were ignored by the president, however, and in an extended visit to the United States in the fall of 1983—during which he surprised the Reagan administration by bitterly denouncing Israel—Nimeiry apparently obtained American acquiescence in his harsh policies toward the new unrest in the South. It was even thought that American military advisers might be sent to help the new, desperate counterinsurgency effort in Sudan.

That did not happen, however, and perceiving the situation to be in a steep decline, the United States actually suspended aid to Sudan in February 1985. That brought Nimeiry to Washington again, to promise reforms and plead for a restoration of assistance; but in his absence, Khartoum was paralyzed by a general strike organized by doctors and other professionals. Nimeiry was in Cairo on his way home in April 1985, when he was overthrown in a coup led by his own defense minister, Abdelrahman Sawar-Dhahab.

Sawar-Dhahab insisted that his group of officers intended to hold power only briefly and would turn the government over to elected civilians within a year. Within weeks, thirty-five political parties had emerged. In Washington, the State Department said it felt reassured that U.S.–Sudanese ties would remain strong, although Sawar-Dhahab moved immediately to improve his country's relations with the Soviet Union, Libya, and Ethiopia. Muammar al-Qaddafi, for his part, declared that "Sudan is ours" and warned against American interference; it appeared that the rebels in the South, now called the Sudanese People's Liberation Army and suspected of having Libyan aid, would fight on for the time being.

The new military regime did keep its promise to move the country back toward civilian rule. In April 1986, just a year after taking power, it held elections for a national assembly, which was to write a constitution and decide upon a new form of government for Sudan. The big winner was Sadek el-Mahdi, a former prime minister and the great-grandson of the man who killed Charles Gordon, the British governor of Sudan, in 1885 and established the country's first independent government. Mahdi had been a major source of opposition to Nimeiry. Having lived in exile in Tripoli, Mahdi now counted on Qaddafi for military supplies to help put down the rebellion in the South. The bitter fighting there was said to have left some two million people homeless.

That same month, however, any illusion of a continuing constructive relationship between Khartoum and Washington was swept away in a rising tide of anti-Americanism. When President Reagan sent American planes to bomb Qaddafi's headquarters and other targets in Tripoli—in response to Libya's sponsorship of terrorism in Europe and the Middle East—the reaction in Khartoum was fierce. One U.S. Embassy employee was shot in the street; many non-essential American personnel and dependants were furtively evacuated from the country during the night.

But a new international political orientation could hardly keep Sudan together, and yet another internal upheaval was not about to guarantee its economic rehabilitation. Some 20 percent of the Sudanese people were still feeling the effects of famine in the late 1980s, and the country was stuck playing host to at least 650,000 refugees from war and famine elsewhere in the region. Extensive flooding in 1988 made the situation even worse. With a $9 billion foreign debt and a ban on new credit from the IMF (because of $200 million in overdue loans), there seemed to be little that any Sudanese government or outside patron could do to improve the nation's prospects.

10

Fallen Stars

THERE ARE a number of countries in Africa that came to independence aspiring to leadership, not only on their own continent, but also in the Third World as a whole. Such ambitious hopes were generally based on a richness in natural resources, the availability of both skilled and educated manpower, a relatively smooth transition from colonial status, an original and carefully designed philosophy of political and economic development, or a combination of those factors. These nations were relatively well prepared for independence, and life in the real world did not seem especially daunting to them. On the contrary, their leaders boasted about their prospects and often displayed a skeptical, even contemptuous, attitude toward outsiders who warned them about trouble ahead.

The reality has borne little resemblance to the aspirations of this group of countries. Their economic development has been limited or nonexistent; their political institutions fragile, if not chaotic; and their people usually hungry and frightened of repression. Their leaders, while preaching nationalism and self-sacrifice,

389

have often performed well at little other than self-enrichment. As a result of neglect, misfortune, unrealism, malfeasance, and, occasionally, sheer terror and torture, some of Africa's original showcases have become its most dramatic examples of failure.

GHANA

Nowhere is this more true than in Ghana. Its independence ceremonies in 1957, the first of their kind in sub-Saharan Africa, attracted international attention; dignitaries traveled to Accra, the capital, from all over the world to attend the historic event. Kwame Nkrumah, the ambitious Ghanaian who was an early leader of the "nonaligned movement," became well known around the world, a symbol of a newly proud and defiant continent. He advocated the development of pan-African institutions and the evolution of uniquely African systems of government. Nkrumah appeared on magazine covers in the West and was given repeated opportunities to explain his ambitious plans and dreams for Ghana.

There was little reason to be skeptical about Ghana's prospects. At independence, this new country was the world's leading exporter of cocoa, and it produced nearly 10 percent of the world's gold. It was also rich in diamonds, bauxite, and manganese, and was building an export trade in sought-after hardwoods, such as mahogany. The literacy rate was impressive, and unlike the Congo (later Zaïre) and other places that were poorly prepared for the transition from colonial status, Ghana had many well-trained citizens who seemed capable of managing its national affairs efficiently.

But somehow almost everything went wrong at once. In retrospect, it is clear that one of Nkrumah's earliest and biggest mistakes was to concentrate vast resources on major prestige projects—dams, smelters, and the like, and a plush headquarters building for the OAU, which then set up shop in Ethiopia instead—while the details of smaller scale agricultural development were neglected. Before long, the country's foreign currency reserves were sinking, and once world cocoa prices began to fall in the mid-1960s, the last hope for self-sufficiency disappeared. When in doubt, Nkrumah nationalized—everything from plantations and gold mines to the laundries in Accra. Growing economic hardship fueled political discontent, and Nkrumah, ever more concerned about his international reputation at the expense of domestic needs, resorted to repression in an effort to cover up Ghana's difficulties.

As his former supporters in the Western democracies began to criticize him for developing a system whose main characteristics were corruption and a cult of personality, Nkrumah turned increasingly to the Soviet bloc for inspiration and help. By the time he was overthrown in 1966, while on a visit to Peking, he had lost the support of the Ghanaian military and almost every other element of society. The Ghanaian people, and the outsiders who had placed so much faith in Ghana as a bulwark of a new kind of freedom, were thoroughly disillusioned and demoralized.

For more than a dozen years, those feelings were exacerbated during a succession of military regimes that promised to repair the damage done to Ghana since independence, but inevitably made things worse. There was a brief interlude of civilian rule, but that government, like others in Ghana, fell as soon as it took the economically necessary, but politically dangerous, step of devaluing the national currency, the *cedi*.

Under a series of military strongmen, Ghana's government became a prime example of a "kleptocracy"—rule by thieves. Those in power stole from the public and then turned around and tried to buy support by spending money they did not have and by creating jobs they could not pay for. As the official economy edged closer to collapse, the black market thrived; once a loaf of bread had come to cost one and a half times the daily minimum wage, dealing on the black market seemed the only way for the poor to survive. Eventually, much of Ghana's intellectual and professional elite left the country in disgust. Doctors quit the health service and found work overseas; university professors gave up their dedication to nation-building and sought jobs elsewhere in Africa or abroad. Grammar-school teachers fled to better-paying and more reliable jobs in booming Nigeria. Those who were left in Ghana resorted to theft and barter to get by.

It was against this background that a thirty-two-year-old military pilot named Jerry J. Rawlings seized power in Accra in the summer of 1979. He made it clear at once that his coup was different from all the others that had preceded it. Rawlings executed eight high-ranking military officers, including three previ-

ous heads of state, but he insisted that his primary goal was a
"moral revolution," a campaign to eradicate corruption and restore honor to Ghanaian society. Rawlings astonished observers
at home and abroad by promising that his Armed Forces Revolutionary Council would try to do its job quickly and delay by only
a few months the elections that had already been scheduled as
part of a return to civilian rule; then he astonished them again by
keeping his promise.

In July of 1979, a former Ghanaian foreign service officer,
Hilla Limann, won the presidential election, and on October 1
(the same day Nigeria returned to civilian rule) he took office with
Rawlings's blessing. For more than two years, Ghanaians would
once again feel officially optimistic about their country. Because
of his own background and the way he came to power, Limann
enjoyed a reservoir of good will in the West, and he seemed to
be in a good position to negotiate generous foreign aid agreements for his government; he gained approval in Washington by,
among other steps, condemning the Soviet invasion of Afghanistan; joining the boycott of the Moscow Olympics; urging that the
revolutionary government in Iran return its American hostages;
voting against granting observer status to the Palestine Liberation Organization in the World Bank and International Monetary
Fund; and publicly opposing the accession of Libyan leader
Muammar al-Qaddafi to the chairmanship of the OAU.

At one level, Limann made important steps toward domestic
reform: Ghana's lively press was allowed to function anew, the
Parliament acted more or less independently, and a variety of
political parties sprang up. But Ghana's economic crisis scarcely
subsided, and some of the steps that Limann took in an effort to
build his political base further undermined the economy. For example, by tripling the price paid to domestic cocoa farmers for
their product, he raised Ghana's production costs above the world
market price for cocoa; the more it sold, the more money it would
lose. Once again the *cedi* had become greatly overvalued, but
Limann refused to run the risk of another controversial devaluation and that cost his government a major loan from the IMF.
The country's infrastructure continued to deteriorate. Roads were
so bad that even those crops that still grew could not get to market; they just rotted in the fields. Above all, the flagrant corruption was unabated.

Once again, on New Year's Eve in 1981, Rawlings stepped in. With barely a dozen plotters and a handful of other soldiers, he staged a coup that Limann's government was powerless to quell. Already a national hero for some of the actions he had taken the first time around—freezing food prices and shutting Lebanese and Indian shops in Accra (which actually made goods more scarce)—Rawlings declared that the well-intentioned Limann regime had been "the most disgraceful in the country's history." He suspended the new American-style constitution, dissolved Parliament and the political parties, and put all power in the hands of a Provisional National Defense Council. As he had the first time around, Rawlings said his only goal was to do something about the fundamental issue of corruption and to build a new society that would allow Ghanaians to be as proud of their nation as they had been at independence.

But that proved very difficult to do. Ghana had become a country with so many problems that it was impossible to know which ones to try to solve first, and many of the proposed solutions only created new problems. The "people's defense committees" and "workers' defense committees" established by Rawlings as part of an effort to take government and decision making to the grass roots, for example, soon got out of hand, and before long he had to deal with their excesses (such as selling the products of nationalized industries for personal profit).

Rawlings also faced a number of severe economic and political difficulties that would have seemed insuperable even to the cleverest and most resourceful rulers in the world. Cocoa production declined still further, as farmers returned to growing subsistence crops rather than risk relying upon payments for their cocoa from the government. The production of other food, such as rice, cassava, yams, and poultry, also went down, leading to fears of widespread famine. A drought made things worse, and then fires ravaged the parched land, destroying crops and cattle. Empty shelves in grocery and other stores testified to the lack of foreign exchange. In 1982, Rawlings's first full year in power, Ghana's gross national product declined for the fifth year in a row and the decline began to pick up speed.

Just at the point when Ghana's economy seemed to be at rock bottom, in January 1983, the Nigerian government expelled hundreds of thousands—perhaps more than a million—Ghanaians who were working illegally in Nigeria. Their return home swelled Ghana's population by 10 percent almost overnight. Pleading that "our cities are dying," Rawlings persuaded at least 60 percent of these desperate people to return to the countryside; that only put more pressure on the scarce resources there. (Some of the returnees did bring enthusiasm—and vehicles—with them, thus providing a temporary boost of morale, and transportation, in the rural areas; but most of them bided their time until they could slip back into Nigeria and find work again.)

Rawlings remained popular among the urban workers, known officially as "the vanguard of the revolution," but he had many important adversaries. The Ghanaian middle class, which had survived with a surprising degree of comfort and privilege throughout the country's tribulations, found that it had to give up some of its luxuries (including multiple houses and expensive imported goods). The university students who traditionally talked a radical line while awaiting their own membership in the elite found their future prosperity threatened; they rioted against the austerity measures imposed by Rawlings. A number of prominent and outspoken Ghanaian exiles found a haven in Togo, just next door, where the ruler, Gnassingbe Eyadema, was hostile to Rawlings; those exiles, others in Ivory Coast, and unhappy factions within Ghana's military tried repeatedly to overthrow Rawlings, who charged that the U.S. Central Intelligence Agency was behind some of the plots. Somehow Rawlings survived in power, squelching at least five coup attempts in one twenty-seven-month period. From all appearances, unlike many other young leaders of military coups in Africa, he remained true to his principles, living modestly and resisting opportunities to make himself wealthy at the public's expense.

Faced with Ghana's hopeless circumstances and the real or imagined hostility of the West, Rawlings did turn quickly to the African bogeyman, Muammar al-Qaddafi, for help. He borrowed nearly $100 million from Libya to pay for oil that he needed to keep the country functioning (Libya sent some other oil free), and he obtained Qaddafi's help in establishing an "internal security" system to detect coup plots. Rawlings did manage to renegotiate the terms of Ghana's relationship with some of the multinational corporations that played a major role in its economy, but mostly he had to rely on economic assistance from Cuba and East

European nations. As many trappings of a Qaddafi-style regime
began to appear, Ghana's relations with some of its neighbors deteriorated badly. The association with Libya, predictably, also
made it more difficult to deal with some of Ghana's traditional
sources of outside aid, so by mid-1983 Rawlings was taking a
more moderate line in an effort to smooth their ruffled feathers.
He moderated some of his economic policies, even agreeing to a
massive devaluation of the *cedi*—in effect if not in name—as a
condition of badly needed assistance from the IMF. Countries attending a World Bank meeting in Paris praised Rawlings for taking "courageous and far-reaching" steps to halt the country's economic deterioration. Some of Rawlings's reforms did seem to help;
in 1984, after ten years of decline, Ghana's economy suddenly
showed a growth rate of 5 percent. But with the official daily minimum wage still at a level where it will buy only two eggs, Ghanaians had a long way to go before any noticeable improvement in
their country's fate and their own daily lives. It was a far cry from
the glory days of Kwame Nkrumah.

SIERRA LEONE

Another West African nation that came to independence with
great aspirations and pretensions to leadership was Sierra Leone.
It is a relatively small country, with about 3.5 million people,
and is only rarely mentioned in the Western, and especially the
American, press. Sierra Leone has some rich farmland and substantial deposits of diamonds and other minerals, but probably
its most important resource at the time of independence in 1961
was its "creole" culture.

Those who are known today as creoles are descendants of the
people who, beginning in 1787, settled Freetown, the capital,
under English guidance—freed slaves; "Nova Scotians," blacks
who had fought on the British side during the American Revolution and then retreated to Canada; "liberated Africans" from various parts of West Africa who had been about to be sold into slavery; and the human cargo of slave ships that were stopped in
mid-Atlantic and turned back. Thus, from the beginning, Freetown was an unusual place, a cosmopolitan city whose citizens
came originally from all over West Africa and had strong ideas

about their own freedom. Even after Sierra Leone formally became a British colony in 1808, the creoles had a special status; they enjoyed privileged access to the professions and to high positions in government and business. Gradually they let go of the latter, especially after Lebanese and Syrian merchants arrived from the Middle East, and the creoles have since evolved into a highly educated intellectual, professional, and social elite.

The parallel to Liberia, just next door, is obvious. The creoles of Sierra Leone have often held themselves aloof from the indigenous people of their country. But aware that they are greatly outnumbered by the members of certain ethnic groups, especially the numerically balanced Temne and Mende tribes, the creoles have never really sought to run their country's government or to monopolize power in the manner of the Americo-Liberians. Instead, their efforts have gone into building institutions like Fourah Bay College, which became one of West Africa's leading educational centers. The creoles also sustain a church that follows many of the tenets of the Church of England, down to using the Book of Common Prayer. And they have given Sierra Leone a language, Krio, a sort of pidgin English that has become the lingua franca of the country (while they themselves tend to prefer a cultured, British-accented form of English).

The center of the creole people and culture is still Freetown, located on a peninsula that is a geographical oddity for West Africa, because of the mountains and promontories that come almost to the shore of the Atlantic Ocean. Made famous by English novelist Graham Greene in *The Heart of the Matter,* Freetown is the product of a rich and unusual mixture of historical, cultural, and political forces. The City Hotel, one of the landmarks of the English colonial era in West Africa, is today shabby and down-at-heel, its bar populated more by restless American Peace Corps volunteers than by the famous adventurers and raconteurs of an earlier time. The broad avenues in the heart of the capital, lined with once-grand structures that are now crumbling, are harshly lit by incongruous modern streetlights, which were added in 1980 as part of a general face-lift, in preparation for the annual summit meeting of the OAU. Just a few blocks away is a frenzied market district, where pack animals and cars with their horns blaring compete to force their way through the throng. There a man carrying fifteen pillows on his head might be jockeying for space with another selling radios and watches. Freetown is, in its own way, one of the more exciting out-of-the-way places in Africa; its parks and cemeteries and grand churches, symbols of its traditions, alternate in the visitor's eye with seedy beer halls and disco parlors and modern hotels that began to fall apart from the day they opened their doors.

But the vibrancy and chaotic ferment of the capital contrast dramatically with the profound decay and disintegration that have overtaken Sierra Leone's political and economic system. The country was ruled beginning in the late 1960s by Siaka Stevens, a mine worker who became involved in union activities and served on a legislative council in the years before independence. Stevens originally came to power through a democratic election, but over time he changed the political structure, enhancing his own position and playing his opponents off against each other so that no one could effectively challenge him. His reelections in 1973 and 1977 were accompanied by violence and allegations of vote rigging; in each case he declared a state of emergency to justify excessive government actions. Finally, in 1978, purportedly to quell the violence of party politics, Stevens pushed through a new constitution, making Sierra Leone a one-party state governed by his so-called "All Peoples Congress."

Stevens was a vain man who liked to name public buildings and other facilities (including a Chinese-built soccer stadium) for himself. From his new twenty-five-bedroom presidential palace on a hill outside Freetown, he presided over the country as if he were a monarch. He talked often of his intention to retire, but for years took no effective steps to assure an orderly succession. One way that Stevens managed to extend the date he would actually have to surrender the reins of power was to conceal his true age from the public. (His opponents claimed to have proof, from his dental records, that Stevens was considerably older than he admitted, in his eighties rather than his seventies.)

His persistence in power led to talk that Sierra Leone was vulnerable to a coup, perhaps a violent one of the Liberian variety, in which the creoles and the Lebanese merchants in Freetown could be particular targets of accumulated rage. (One cynical theory held that in 1982, when his control of the country seemed to be slipping, Stevens actually stage-managed a false coup attempt in order to head off a real one. Several of the people implicated in the alleged plot at the time later turned up with lucrative jobs.) The leadership vacuum also raised the chilling prospect that tribal warfare of the sort that pitted the Mende and Temne against each other in the 1960s could break out again. Stevens's own doubts about Sierra Leone's future were revealed by the fact that he hired a band of highly trained mercenaries to whisk him out of the country in the event of a severe crisis.

Sierra Leone's agricultural potential has gone virtually undeveloped, and in most other respects its economy has deteriorated badly since independence. It is only the unofficial economy—through which about half of the diamonds mined each year leave the country illegally—that provides any money to finance the import of consumer goods to satisfy the exquisite tastes of the creole elite.

Corruption has become so pervasive as to deny the treasury the necessary funds to conduct some of the country's most basic business. Indeed, in 1982 an original way had to be found to select candidates for a much-postponed legislative election, because the government could not afford to pay for the usual process. Almost nobody in Sierra Leone can afford to live on his official income, and therefore everybody has to cheat—taking payoffs, doing private work while on the public payroll, and otherwise concealing the true amount and sources of income.

That kind of system is manageable while it lasts, as long as most people are scratching up enough money and goods to survive. But the workers at the bottom of the heap invariably suffer, and so the Sierra Leone Labor Congress became a center of opposition to the Stevens government, calling general strikes and organizing demonstrations to protest the working and living conditions of the urban poor in particular. But Stevens was invariably successful at diffusing such protests, through a combination of repression and exile. In fact, during recent years the only serious challenge to Stevens and his policies came from overseas organizations, most notably the Sierra Leone Alliance Movement based in London.

Even the outspoken Sierra Leone press has been forced into exile. For some time the only alternative to the government-controlled newspapers published in Freetown was an irreverent sheet called *The Tablet*. Edited by a brash young man named Pios

Foray, it took an uncommonly confrontational stance toward the Stevens government and published the only information available inside Sierra Leone about the activities and the arguments of exiled opposition figures. (Many of the articles were written secretly by employees of the government newspapers.) But finally even *The Tablet* became too much for Stevens to bear, and he sent government security agents to destroy its presses. After a harrowing escape from Sierra Leone, Foray and his production manager now publish the newspaper in the United States.

In January 1984, just as the eighth national convention of Stevens's party was beginning, students from Fourah Bay College marched downtown from their campus overlooking Freetown Harbor. They wanted to demonstrate calmly against the government's handling of the economy, but were spontaneously joined by the unemployed and poverty-stricken people of the capital; the result was a riot in which government offices and cars were stoned, Lebanese and Indian shops were attacked, and the regime's true unpopularity was made clear. Stevens, insulted, shut down the college, and only reopened it a few months later after student leaders had delivered an abject apology.

Perhaps the saddest commentary about a nation that once was so proud is the extent to which Sierra Leone is dependent upon, and ultimately influenced by, outside largesse and pressure. It is a pawn in classic struggles for influence in Africa, such as the one between North and South Korea. Communist North Korea, ever trying to expand its network of friends in the Third World, built a new, modern city hall in Freetown. South Korea, on the defensive, then provided a fleet of cars for Sierra Leone's government to use to chauffeur the visiting heads of state at the OAU conference in Freetown in 1980. Another example of the same phenomenon arose during the Carter administration's attempt to organize a boycott of the Moscow Olympics in 1980, as a reprisal for the Soviet Union's invasion of Afghanistan. Stevens, who had often taken pro-Western foreign policy stands, agonized publicly about whether to send any of the country's superb athletes to the Olympics. On hearing this, the Soviet government, desperate to increase participation from the Third World, first offered the Sierra Leone team free transportation, then gradually increased the ante to include free accommodations, sporting equipment, uniforms, travel clothing, and finally a supplementary travel allowance. At that point poverty prevailed over principle: Sierra Leone rejected the pleadings from Washington and sent its teams to Moscow.

UGANDA

No country in Africa had brighter prospects and more ambitious hopes at independence than Uganda. It was, in Winston Churchill's words, the "pearl of East Africa," a verdant, bucolic land where everything seemed to grow and the people were certain to prosper. The symbol of Uganda's fertility was the old saw that almost anywhere in the country, if you ate a piece of fruit and dropped the pit on the ground, a fruit tree would soon sprout. Kampala, the capital, was a booming, lively city built on hills, a symbol of the favorable projections for Africa's future and home to Makerere University, where the prospective leaders of many other countries flocked alongside Ugandans to receive a first-rate education. It was a cosmopolitan spot that made Nairobi look like a parochial backwater.

But for eight years in the 1970s Uganda became a horrific nightmare, a hell on earth that matched the most hideous caricature of Africa as a savage continent. It was ruled during that time by Idi Amin, a half-mad soldier-despot who killed for amusement and seemed to derive a perverse pleasure from running his country into ruin. The Amin era is an experience that Uganda struggles with today and from which it may never fully recover; it is a stain on the modern history of the African continent.

The seeds of disaster were present in Uganda from the beginning. Beneath the official optimism and bright appearances of its early years, Uganda in fact got off to a shaky start as an independent nation. It was a country not merely troubled by tribal rivalries, but actually composed of four separate kingdoms; their narrow interests were threatened by the establishment of a secular state that hoped to divert the people's loyalties. The most formidable obstacle to progress was the *kabaka*, or king, of Buganda, the largest of the kingdoms, from which the entire country derived its name. The man who came to power in Uganda in 1962,

Apollo Milton Obote, was by contrast a commoner, a poor farmer's son from outside the kingdom who tended his father's flocks before making his way to a Protestant mission school and, eventually, Makerere.

Obote spent considerable time in Kenya, where he learned a pragmatic political approach from master African statesmen like Jomo Kenyatta and Tom Mboya, and where he became an advocate of an effort at regional management and conciliation that would eventually be known as the East African Community. Obote faced the delicate job of honoring the *kabaka*'s role in the resistance against colonialism, but at the same time persuading him to step aside and allow the development of a modern democratic society. At first it worked, when Obote convinced the militant political party he had shaped to accept the traditional leader as the country's president (while Obote became prime minister), and he convinced the *kabaka* to accept an honorary position that carried no real power.

But after four years the delicate arrangement collapsed; in 1966 Obote's troops stormed the *kabaka*'s palace and forced him into exile. Thereafter Obote confronted another fundamental problem: how to assure economic development and political stability, yet still keep the military, to which he owed a new debt, from becoming restless. He abandoned his own commitment to democracy and resorted to blunt authoritarianism, abolishing the traditional kingdoms altogether, extending the life of a compliant Parliament by refusing to call elections, declaring a one-party state, detaining political opponents, and, although still in his early forties, arranging his own election as president for life. At the same time, Obote declared Uganda's adherence to a socialist philosophy in a document he called his "Move to the Left."

There are many factors that make such dramatic changes risky in a Third World country with high expectations and substantial exposure to the outside world. For one thing, if the new path does not succeed immediately in improving the lot of ordinary citizens, the leader who has enshrined himself at the center of the system may be held responsible, whatever the mitigating circumstances. But in this case, Obote had other problems. Uganda's neighbors (most notably Kenya, which was already embarked on its own avowedly capitalist path) were suspicious about what the conversion to socialism would mean, and the Ugandan army was dissatisfied over not having been adequately rewarded for keeping Obote in power.

While Obote was far away in Singapore in January 1971, attending a Commonwealth Conference, he was overthrown by Amin, who was at the time the Ugandan army chief of staff. The first reactions in the region and among Western nations ranged from indifference to satisfaction. Obote had become vaguely and unpredictably leftist. Amin, after all, had received some of his training from the Israelis, and his reputation with the Americans was that of a reliable, level-headed officer. The first outward signs of anything different were easily dismissed as quirks or madcap antics designed to attract attention in the press: his humbling of Englishmen still living in Uganda, for example, by insisting that they pay homage to him and carry him around Kampala in a sedan chair.

But soon Amin seemed to go off the deep end. He harassed the Asian business community in Kampala and eventually expelled all of the Asians from Uganda. He sang the praises of Hitler and proposed erecting a monument in his honor. He sent bizarre cables to heads of state around the world, sometimes offering to solve disputes but more often mocking and castigating them, especially the leaders of the United States. He made unpredictable allegations against members of his own government, at one point accusing the woman who was serving as his foreign minister (Elizabeth Bagaya, a traditional princess, lawyer, and former fashion model) of engaging in illicit sex in a public lavatory at an airport in Paris.

It is difficult to establish the precise moment—or week or month—when the situation in Uganda crossed the line from bizarreness and buffoonery to a reign of terror, but in retrospect Amin's rule stands out as a time when the light of civilization went out in Uganda, when all human values were abandoned and an anarchic brutality substituted for any rational system of government. The estimates of the number of people murdered during his reign vary widely, from a hundred thousand to half a million, but among the victims were businessmen, academics, professionals, and many other educated people on whom Uganda's progress depended. Many were killed in a bestial manner, their heads beaten in with sledge hammers in the secret underground chambers of the euphemistically named State Research Bureau. Altogether Amin employed an estimated fifteen thousand people as spies, torturers, informers, and enforcers for his elaborate network of security agencies. They tapped telephones, encouraged citizens to inform on each other, created computerized files on alleged opponents of the regime, and fostered a national atmosphere of paranoia. According to witnesses, Amin sometimes participated personally in the torture and slaughter, including in the notorious case of the disappearance of the Anglican archbishop of Uganda, Janani Luwum.

Amin took a fearsome toll on the Ugandan society, culture, and economy. The output of cash crops and manufactured goods ground to a halt. Inflation went wild, and an 8 percent annual growth rate disappeared as the country went broke. An estimated 65 percent of its technocrats were killed or fled into exile. The people who had no exit or could not afford to flee simply lived by their wits and tried to avoid calling attention to themselves. Many literally retreated into the forests and lived off the land, waiting for sanity to be restored to their nation. Meanwhile, Amin and his henchmen would pack suitcases full of dollars and take lavish trips overseas, squandering what little the country had left.

The accomplices in Uganda's ruin were many and varied. They included not only members of Amin's own minority Moslem tribe, but also an odd collection of foreigners who saw a cynical short-term opportunity for personal gain. There was an American doctor, for example, one John Marshall Branion, Jr., who fled the United States after being convicted of murdering his wife and turned up in Kampala as Amin's personal physician. A key figure in Uganda's labyrinthine security apparatus was Robert Astles, a British-born expatriate who formed an "anticorruption squad" whose main purpose appeared to be concentrating the benefits of corruption in the right hands. Astles' agents patrolled Lake Victoria in speedboats, arresting, and often killing, innocent fishermen along with suspected smugglers; Astles himself helped select the victims of some of Amin's most ruthless measures. The Palestine Liberation Organization, Libya, and the Soviet Union, each for its own reasons, sent aid to Amin, trained some of his enforcers, and otherwise helped keep him in power.

But Amin had other, unwitting accomplices, including the leaders of African nations who laughed at him long after his performance had lost any semblance of humor, or who declined to criticize him publicly because of an overdeveloped sense of noninterventionism. Indeed, many Africans treated Amin as a hero—a sort of bad boy who had made good by attracting so much attention to himself and to Africa. They derived a perverse satisfaction from seeing him on the cover of *Time* magazine and as the subject of documentary films, and they had to admire his ability to manipulate the outside world, especially the press, into giving credence to his every action and declaration. The nonaligned bloc at the United Nations greeted his outrages with silence. The OAU not only failed to condemn Amin's excesses, but it actually honored him with the chairmanship of the organization at a time when there were already grave doubts about his decency. Such indifference to Amin's brutality caused many in the outside world to scorn Africans for their unwillingness to discipline, or even criticize, one of their own.

It was not as if there was a great deal that anyone could really do about Amin. The United States Congress, in a rare gesture, voted economic sanctions against Uganda, but that served more as a moral judgment than as an actual blow that might cause his regime to collapse. (It provoked derision in some African quarters—complaints that the United States found it convenient to assert its economic power against a widely disliked black man who was an easy target, but not against a discriminatory white regime like the one in South Africa.) The Israelis, against whom Amin had turned viciously, did more to hurt and humiliate him than anyone else. In 1976, after an Air France plane carrying many Israeli passengers was hijacked to Uganda's international airport at Entebbe by Palestinians, Israeli commandos raided the airport and recaptured most of the hostages.

Ultimately, only Tanzania seemed willing to take direct action to undo Amin. It may never be known just how much outside encouragement or covert assistance the Tanzanians were given to move into Uganda, but Tanzanian President Julius Nyerere, who detested Amin for what he had done to the East African economy and to Africa's image generally, had apparently been waiting for a pretext to strike against Amin. The Ugandan bully gave it to him in late 1978, when, to conceal growing dissension within the ranks of his own army, Amin seized a quadrant of territory in northwest Tanzania that he claimed was part of Uganda. A few months later, Nyerere sponsored a full-scale invasion of Uganda; at the head of the column were some Ugandan dissident forces, who had theoretically requested and organized the action, but close behind was most of the Tanzanian army. At great expense to his own crippled economy (the cost was a million dollars a day at one point), Nyerere had his ill-trained, undisciplined forces press on to Kampala. They met token resistance from Libyan troops who had been sent to help Amin, but for the most part they were greeted as liberators by the long-suffering Ugandan people. Although they engaged in a certain amount of looting and pillaging themselves, the Tanzanians were a welcome relief.

Putting Uganda back on track proved to be a frustrating and disheartening experience. Obote had lived in Tanzania throughout Amin's rule, but for a time he held back from returning. The first man installed in Kampala by a council of Ugandan exiles with Tanzanian approval, Yusufu Lule, an educator who had once run Makerere University, lasted only ten weeks before he was pushed aside by rivals who felt he did not consult them sufficiently. The next interim president, like Lule a Baganda, was Godfrey Binaisa, a British-trained lawyer who had once been attorney general under Obote. But he, too, was unable to deal with the chaos and stem the residual violence, especially on the part of thousands of soldiers and security agents who still had weapons but no work; the members of the Tanzanian occupation force, unpaid and restless, also caused problems. Finally, in December 1980, elections were held. This time the Baganda people concentrated on backing a new Democratic party, but Obote had established his own party and easily won (some said stole) the presidency. He became one of the few leaders in modern Africa to have a second chance.

The country over which Obote resumed his rule was a shadow of its former self. Life in the once-glorious capital city remained perilous, with streets unpassable because of potholes, the water and electricity supply unreliable, and murder and assassination so common that diplomats had to travel in bulletproof cars. Roadblocks were everywhere, hotels were in a shambles, and many buildings were boarded up. Every night, during the curfew, shots rang out in the darkness. Two opposition movements, claiming they had no prospect of sharing power under Obote, took to the countryside and waged a guerrilla war against the new govern-

ment. The country embarked on a program of "moral rehabilitation," but it was not easy to restore human values and common
decency to a society that had gone so sour. Oddly enough, Uganda
did suddenly become one of the rare places in Africa where women
had great opportunities, largely because so many of the men who
had run the country were killed by Amin.

There has been some minor progress in Uganda. The agricultural sector of the economy began to recover—more food was produced, some of it actually exported legally—and there were fewer
shortages. After his years in Tanzania, Obote was disillusioned by
the socialist path to development and suddenly emerged as one
of Africa's most ardent capitalists. The annual national deficit
went down to 20 percent of government expenditures from its
previous high of 75 percent, and the IMF was sufficiently impressed with Obote's austerity measures to restore some aid. But
hundreds of thousands of Ugandans lived in displaced-persons
camps in pathetic conditions, on the verge of starvation, and even
more were camped on the other side of all the country's borders,
living as refugees. Many of the refugees were originally Rwandans, who emigrated to Uganda decades ago for political or economic reasons, but then were pushed back out because they were
regarded as being supportive of Amin.

In October 1983, on the twenty-first anniversary of independence, Obote sought to demonstrate his own stability and confidence by freeing 2,100 prisoners and political detainees, including soldiers loyal to Amin, and inviting other dissidents to return
from exile and help rebuild the country. But the violence was unabated; opposition members of Parliament were sometimes murdered in their homes, and one of Obote's key adversaries claimed
that Uganda had "never been in a worse state." The army seemed
out of control, and Obote unable to do anything about it. Some of
his most trusted aides fled, out of fear that he was about to turn
on them. Foreign diplomats and human rights organizations that
investigated the situation said there were at least ten thousand
political prisoners in Uganda at any given time, not including
those who might be scattered at military barracks around the
country. Estimates of the number of people killed by the military
or starved to death as a result of Obote's efforts to stamp out all
opposition ran as high as two hundred thousand. Finally Obote

was overthrown again by his own military in July 1985; rebel forces led by Yoweri Museveni took power less than a year later.

Meanwhile, Idi Amin was living in luxury in Saudi Arabia, with four wives and dozens of children, as a guest of that country's royal family.

TANZANIA

Tanzania's conquest of Uganda and rout of Idi Amin was out of character. If there was any field in which Tanzania was a clearly recognized, early leader in Africa, it was in the realm of conciliation, idealism, and respect for the rights of others. No one imagined it would become known for flexing its military muscle. Indeed, at independence, a reverence for principle and adherence to the high moral ground were about the only things that Tanganyika (the mainland part of what would later become Tanzania) had working in its favor. The country had few mineral or other natural resources, as far as anyone knew, and virtually no industry. The infrastructure was minimal. The British, having been awarded Tanganyika in the breakup of Germany's African empire after World War I, ruled it as a protectorate rather than a colony; never expecting to stay (as they intended to do in Kenya, for example), they did little to develop or improve the territory. Furthermore, most of Tanganyika's unhomogeneous population (divided into dozens of small ethnic groups that had little in common) was scattered across the countryside on tiny subsistence farms. The people were therefore difficult to mobilize or motivate.

High moral ground was not irrelevant as a qualification for leadership in Africa during the early 1960s. While other countries and their rulers pursued paths of self-aggrandizement, self-enrichment, and plain selfishness, Tanganyika stood out as a nation that would emphasize communal responsibility, be guided by ideals of self-sacrifice and self-reliance, and make a moral commitment to issues that were important to the entire continent, especially the liberation of the minority-ruled people of southern Africa.

This attitude was symbolized and represented by the new country's leader, Julius Nyerere, a gentle, spiritual man educated by Catholic missionaries, revered at home as *Mwalimu* (Swahili for "teacher"), and respected throughout most of the world as someone who was willing to share the necessary burdens with his countrymen. Nyerere was unique in Africa for his humble life style; he shunned the fancy cars, elaborate villas, and foreign bank accounts so common among his counterparts. He practiced what he preached. As a spokesman for the "front-line states" involved in the struggle for Zimbabwe's independence and other battles, he urged those who enjoyed freedom to make a commitment to those who did not. And Nyerere had a capacity to explain, so that others understood, why Africans objected to outside influence on their continent from East or West, why they felt suspicious of the former colonial powers' efforts to protect African security. He also displayed a healthy irreverence toward the OAU, which he candidly described as "a trade union for heads of state."

Tanganyika had warts, to be sure. Not everyone was comfortable with its early adherence to a one-party system, supposedly intended to assure purer democracy, or with the way in which Nyerere embraced the regime that came to power on the offshore island nation of Zanzibar in 1964, brutally slaughtering the Arab minority and turning the clock back on development efforts. (In a bold, pragmatic step, Nyerere soon merged Zanzibar and Tanganyika into the combined nation of Tanzania, conceding substantial autonomy to the island, but avoiding the emergence of a potentially hostile, destabilizing adversary just twenty-three miles off the Indian Ocean coast.) But on the whole, Nyerere and his system enjoyed a remarkably favorable press, and he was virtually worshiped by Africanists from the West, who flocked to the university in Dar es Salaam in the hope that they too could participate in the development of a social order that would be revolutionary and genuinely socialist, but not authoritarian. Young volunteers from the United States, Britain, and Scandinavia competed for the opportunity to help; those who had to settle for work in other nearby countries, such as Kenya, lived more comfortably but often felt envious of those who were getting to do the real thing in Tanzania.

Central to Nyerere's philosophy was the "Arusha Declaration" of 1967, named for the provincial city near the wild game parks along the Kenyan border where it was issued. It said that the old Western economic system would not be able to free Tanzania's people from poverty and that drastic steps were necessary to establish an alternate course: consolidation of government control over the means of production, a greater emphasis on improving the standard of living in rural areas, and the preparation of development plans that could be carried out without heavy dependence on foreign assistance. It also prescribed a code of conduct for government and party leaders: they were not to receive more than one salary, own rental properties or shares of stock in any private companies, or be directors of private firms. The emphasis on *ujamaa* ("familyhood"), Nyerere's theme since independence, would be strengthened, and in the name of communal cooperation a vast number of private interests, including the press, were nationalized soon after the Arusha Declaration. Nyerere was talking here not about Marxism-Leninism, but an egalitarian socialism supposedly rooted in traditional African village life, complete with decentralized decision-making processes.

Ironically, for a country that claimed to be determined to rely on itself, Tanzania soon became the most-aided country in all of Africa. As one Western ambassador in Dar es Salaam explained it, "Everyone has a different reason for giving. The British do it because it is a former British colony, the Germans because it is a former German colony, the Scandinavians because they are idealistic. The Russians do it to keep up with the Chinese, and the Chinese to keep up with the Russians." Even Iceland sent aid to Tanzania. The United States was eager to do its part, too, especially under Democratic administrations that were not especially bothered by Nyerere's hostility to private enterprise. The World Bank seemed to regard Tanzania as a worthy long-range demonstration project.

There were some aspects in which Tanzania made truly remarkable progress. Nyerere was successful, for example, in the promotion of Swahili as a national language (especially important in a country where so many different dialects were spoken, and ideologically preferable to English, which was regarded as a colonial language), and his effort to broaden his people's literacy—through universal primary education and adult training programs—was a model for the developing world. Whereas only about 20 percent of the country's adult population could read or write at the time of independence, by 1983 that figure was thought to be upward of 90 percent. Tanzania is also widely conceded to have the best rural health service in Africa, and as a result, the average life expectancy increased by 50 percent, from thirty-five years at independence to fifty-two years in the early 1980s.

Nonetheless, Tanzania must be regarded as a colossal failure, a disappointment to its own people and to its admirers around the world. For all the progress on paper and the certification by outside experts, the country seemed to grow steadily poorer. Nyerere admitted as much in 1977, when he issued a frank self-examination and critique on the tenth anniversary of the Arusha Declaration. Tanzania was "certainly neither socialist nor self-reliant," he concluded at the time, and the goal of making it so was "not even in sight." In what must have been a painful admission, the president declared that "the nature of exploitation has changed, but it has not been altogether eliminated. There are still great inequalities between citizens. . . . A life of poverty is still the experience of the majority of our citizens." Nyerere deplored Tanzania's continued dependence on foreign assistance and deficit financing for its development, and he complained that "mental paralysis" had led the people to insist on Western-style homes made of cement and tin roofs rather than accepting adequate traditional accommodations fashioned from burnt bricks and tiles. He acknowledged that the government had become the fastest growing sector of the Tanzanian economy, and worried over the failure of food production to keep up with population growth (which was itself racing out of control, thus exacerbating the difficulty of feeding and housing those in the rural areas).

As much as anyplace else in the developing world, Tanzania suffered from a decline in its terms of trade. Whereas at one point the country could buy a tractor with the proceeds from its export of five tons of tea, by the early 1980s it had to sell seventy tons of tea to buy one. In 1975, even after oil prices had begun to rise, a ton of Tanzanian coffee would pay for 147 barrels of crude oil; as the price of coffee declined, a ton bought only eighty barrels. In 1979, Tanzania spent more than 50 percent of its total export earnings just to make back payments on its international debt.

But not everything could be blamed on injustice in the world economy. What Nyerere did not admit is that while the government had succeeded in resettling almost the entire Tanzanian population into more than 7,500 "*ujamaa* villages" where they could receive government services, those villages really did not work. Many people had been forced into them at gunpoint and had never sufficiently overcome their feelings of dislocation to become productive. Indeed, only two of the registered villages had actually been certified as carrying out more than half of their economic activity collectively, as they were supposed to do. Outside investment was unwelcome in Tanzania and therefore nonexistent, so there were few alternative means of generating jobs and income. Many of the foreign-assistance projects were ill-planned and ineffective—some of the factories built with outside help closed within weeks—and much of the money flowed straight back to the donor countries through lucrative contracts to buy things that Tanzania did not really need. Even in idealistic Tanzania, it turned out, distinctly unidealistic corruption could flourish. Many of those likely to steal were government employees. The bloated bureaucracy sometimes seemed hardly to function at all, and visitors often found one office after another in government ministries empty and silent for days at a time.

"Our socialism, honestly, is the only thing holding us together," said a friend of the president in attempting to explain how the people accepted the sacrifices required of them. But Tanzania's socialism fell far short of its political promises. It proved to be undemocratic in practice, with a narrow elite controlling most of the decisions and resources. Nyerere rejected the notion that he held any political prisoners, but his jails were full of people accused of "economic crimes."

Dar es Salaam virtually fell apart during the 1970s. Hotels that were once well appointed declined into filthy disrepair, and shortages of such basic necessities as gasoline and cooking oil became a permanent condition. It was so rare to find butter in the capital that people traveling to Zanzibar (where, somehow, it was readily available) were often asked to bring back a supply for their friends and neighbors. For much of its early history as an independent nation Tanzania had seemed immune to the violent crime that plagued other African countries, but eventually the gangs of thugs that gathered on the street corners of Dar came to be indistinguishable from those in the big cities of other, nonsocialist nations around the continent. The port became ever more congested and inefficient, the airport chaotic.

After twenty years, the merger with Zanzibar was still not entirely accepted, especially on Zanzibar itself and its sister island of Pemba. While Zanzibari politicians agreed to the consolidation of their own single party and the mainland one into a single national party, the *Chama Cha Mapinduzi* ("Revolutionary party"), in the late 1970s, they resisted further steps toward meaningful unification. Many felt cheated by the government in Dar, their fertile and productive island bled for contributions to the war effort against Uganda, but not recompensed in terms of national services. The Zanzibari government continued to require passports (and vaccinations against certain diseases) of visitors from the mainland, and Radio Zanzibar—although controlled by the island government, whose president is at the same time a vice-president of Tanzania—sometimes blasted the national administration.

Zanzibar remained a very separate, distinct place. Its elegance has long since faded, but elaborately carved wooden doors, brass chests, and narrow, winding passageways are reminders of an ancient culture that bears little relationship to the broken hopes of the mainland. An island-wide color television network is a sign of skewed priorities today. For years Zanzibar town was a surprising microcosm of conflicts in the world community: Soviet and Chinese consulates, on the same street, offered outdoor photographic displays reflecting their respective points of view concerning border disputes in East Asia, and they literally tried to drown each other out with propaganda messages transmitted on public-address systems. The Indians and Egyptians asserted themselves there as leaders of the Third World, and the United States used its consulate as a challenging training ground for young diplomats.* Zanzibar's economy is still based entirely on its rich clove crop, and it tries to hold on to as much of the proceeds as possible. When the price of cloves improved in the early 1980s, the leader of the Zanzibari government, Aboud Jumbe, asserted his own reckless independence by ordering a $5 million executive jet to transport him to the mainland for affairs of state. (Jumbe was removed by Nyerere in 1984, ostensibly for encouraging separatist sentiment on Zanzibar.)

Nyerere's feud with Kenya over tourist revenues and other trade issues, one of the factors that led to the breakup of the East African Community, cost Tanzania dearly. The establishment of

---

* The American consulate on Zanzibar, open almost continuously since 1837, was closed in 1979 as part of a State Department economy move, but a USIA post was later reopened there by the Reagan administration.

a separate airline and countless other facilities that had previously been shared by the three East African countries had an initial price tag of at least $100 million. The penalties of a closed border and of the rupture of all communication links between the two countries were incalculable; certainly almost everyone who had to choose to do business with one or the other preferred Kenya. An independent Tanzanian tourist industry proved to be difficult to develop. Few vacationers want to visit Dar es Salaam, and the Tanzanian game parks, while less despoiled than those in Kenya, are much harder and more expensive to reach directly from overseas. The new Kilimanjaro jetport near Moshi, in northern Tanzania, is an asset, but the cheapest airfares to it or Dar from London were generally about twice as much as the lowest fares between London and Nairobi.

The Tanzanian military action against Idi Amin was in some respects a great humanitarian gesture—it certainly did a great deal for the morale and self-respect of the Tanzanian elite—but it was a disaster for the national treasury. Plenty of African and other countries wanted Nyerere to invade Uganda—even if they did not say so publicly—but none of them seemed willing to contribute substantially to that military cause. One estimate of the war's cost to Tanzania was more than half a billion dollars. During the conflict, foreign exchange reserves quickly fell below the level needed to meet an emergency, and they never recovered; the government easily used up its lines of credit around the world. The effect on plans for major hydroelectric projects and other ambitious development schemes was obvious, and the multi-million-dollar program to move the national capital from Dar es Salaam to the interior city of Dodoma seemed doomed.

But the real change after the war in Uganda was the end of illusions about and within Tanzania. The country lost its image as a conciliator that could not easily be drawn into using the crass methods of the rest of the world; Tanzania's hungry and poorly disciplined soldiers behaved just as badly as any others elsewhere in Africa. Thoughts of the Arusha Declaration did not do them much good in moments of bitterness or panic on the dangerous streets of Kampala. Indeed, the Tanzanian army became a center of corruption, not to mention discontent with and even rebellion against Nyerere's regime. In early 1983 a group of officers stationed near the Uganada border mutinied; before they could articulate their grievances, their rebellion was put down, but it sent a chill through the ranks of the government. A year earlier another army officer had led a group of Tanzanians in hijacking one of the few planes of the national airline; they flew it to Kenya, Saudi Arabia, Greece, and Britain, along the way radioing a description of the plight of the poor in Tanzania and a demand for Nyerere's resignation.

Although he had talked for years about retiring, on the grounds of sheer fatigue, Nyerere was not about to yield to that kind of pressure.* Nor did he renounce the socialist principles that had guided him since independence. But faced with the threat of famine and mass starvation for several years running, the president did find it necessary to compromise in important ways. Having spoken out repeatedly and forcefully against the kinds of conditions imposed by the IMF in granting loans to Third World countries (he once even sponsored a conference—in Arusha—to rally opposition to the IMF), Nyerere finally found himself agreeing to some of those same conditions, including a substantial devaluation of the Tanzanian shilling and cuts in government spending and in the subsidies that held down the cost of certain goods on the domestic market. He also agreed to dismantle some of the three hundred parastatal organizations that had been established since independence, and to reduce the size and scope of others; often run by young, untrained ideologues, most of these state enterprises ended up costing more than they earned and became an additional drag on the economy.

In a major turnabout, Nyerere declared in 1983 that Tanzania would once again permit "large-scale farming" on a public or private basis, with foreign and local individuals and companies free to invest in private commercial farms "within the framework of national land policies." The Tanzanian government appeared willing as well to listen to the free-enterprise-oriented ideas for development offered by the Reagan administration. After a period of great warmth during the Carter administration—Nyerere allowed the Peace Corps to return to Tanzania in 1979, after an

* For some time it was assumed that Prime Minister Edward Sokoine, author of some controversial economic policies, would succeed Nyerere; after Sokoine was killed in an automobile accident in 1984, the heir apparent became Salim Ahmed Salim, a Zanzibari who had once been the Third World's candidate for secretary-general of the United Nations. But Salim fell victim to squabbles within the ruling party.

absence of ten years—relations with Washington cooled after Reagan's election in 1980; but a new pragmatism was forced upon a country whose per capita annual income was still only $270 and whose average annual growth rate since independence had been a mere 1.7 percent.

Nyerere also launched a crackdown on Tanzania's flourishing black market, in an effort to convince the IMF and other outside donors and lenders that the government could gain effective control over the economy. In its initial phases, more than a thousand people were detained as "economic saboteurs," and nearly $2 million in proceeds from smuggling, illegal currency dealings, and other rackets was seized by the police. "We shall confiscate their ill-gotten property and give them hoes to work on the land for a very long time," said Nyerere of the people arrested. In one particularly controversial aspect of the campaign, substantial amounts of money were confiscated from churches and mosques around the country, on the grounds that it represented the proceeds of illegal activity. Religious groups protested that this was not true.

Many observers applauded Nyerere for taking actions that involved a tacit admission that so much had been wrong in the management of the country, but there were new grounds for severe criticism: the accused were brought before tribunals to face the charges against them, but they had no access to legal counsel and no opportunity to appeal the verdict. The only relief offered to those found to be falsely accused was an apology. The plan was to send those declared guilty to "reeducation camps" where they would have to work on the land; the camps were to be established with the money seized during the investigations.

As it became known that many of the new detainees, along with others who had been held without trial previously, were being asked to pay bribes to prison officials to obtain special privileges or release, Tanzania lost even more of its special credit as a leader among developing nations. Many who once admired and defended Tanzania now argued that Nyerere could not be permitted indefinitely to substitute prestige for performance, that he could not simply continue to blame outside forces for his inability to improve the lot of his people. Within Tanzania, hard questions were asked about whether too much of the country's intellectual energy had been directed southward—toward solving the crises in southern Africa—and too little inward, where the problems were intractable enough in their own right.

When Nyerere stepped down as president (but not as party chairman) in November 1985, in favor of Ali Hassan Mwinyi, head of the Zanzibari island government, Tanzania had still experienced relatively little in the way of true economic development. The country's friends and supporters were becoming less tolerant of its failures.

ZAMBIA

Zambia started its life as a nation much richer than Tanzania, because it had some of the world's most extensive and purest deposits of copper. It also had a substantial agricultural base, maintained in part by white settlers who had come to spend their lives and make their fortunes in the British colony of Northern Rhodesia; because the transition to independence was achieved peacefully there, unlike a number of other places in southern Africa, Zambia seemed to have a unique chance to become a successful multiracial state.

But Zambia suffered important disadvantages at the time of independence in 1964. It was a landlocked country, and the only real hope for improvement in the lot of its six million people, many of whom were desperately poor, was to arrange for reliable access to the sea for the export of Zambia's copper and the import of basic necessities. That was difficult to achieve, however, given the fact that so many of Zambia's neighbors were in turmoil, or would be soon. The only choices were routes that went through white-ruled Southern Rhodesia (later Rhodesia, and eventually Zimbabwe) or South Africa, which were considered ideologically unacceptable; one through Angola, whose security could not be assured because of the independence struggle and later the civil war there; and another through Tanzania, where a new railroad had to be built through the wilderness. The existence of almost perpetual trouble on one or more of these routes doomed Zambia to a frustrating economic life. Even after China spent millions of dollars constructing the Tan-Zam Railroad, maintenance problems made it unreliable; it was usable for less than 40 percent of the freight traffic in and out of Zambia.

The dependence on copper—and, to a lesser extent, on cobalt—was a serious problem for Zambia. Everything was fine as long as the world price of these minerals held up; but when it began to fall in the early 1970s, so did the nation's fortunes. Zambia still counts on copper and cobalt for more than 90 percent of its foreign exchange income; as the country's president, Kenneth Kaunda, likes to say, "We were born with a copper spoon in our mouth." As the price got lower and lower, the copper mines began to operate at a loss, and the money they brought in was barely enough to pay for imported oil and to make interest payments on the ever larger national debt. (By the 1980s, according to the IMF, Zambia was one of the five most indebted nations in the Third World.) The fifty-five thousand Zambians who worked in the copper mines began to feel severely threatened themselves, and their powerful unions called frequent strikes to dramatize their grievances. Each strike in turn cost the country millions of dollars in lost income.

Compounding these difficulties of the international marketplace was Zambia's inevitable involvement in the wars on its borders. First it was drawn into Mozambique's struggle for independence from Portugal, and for many years it was caught up in the battle over Namibia. But it was the Rhodesian war that took the most serious toll on Zambia. One of the major contending forces in that conflict, Joshua Nkomo's Zimbabwe African People's Union (ZAPU), had its headquarters and thousands of soldiers in Zambia; since the ZAPU fighters were more numerous than the Zambian army, it often seemed as if they ran the country where they were guests. Zambia had trouble feeding its own people, let alone Nkomo's force and the accompanying Zimbabwean refugees. And whenever the white-minority Rhodesian regime, headed by Ian Smith, wanted to strike at its enemies inside Zambia, it did so with impunity—sometimes in the heart of Lusaka, the capital. Despite its large quantities of Soviet arms, Zambia seemed incapable of defending itself.

For all the pain these military struggles caused Zambia, they proved to be perversely convenient for Kaunda. For years he managed to blame regional conflicts for Zambia's troubles, for its penury and the decline in most Zambians' standard of living since independence. Kaunda, known to many as "KK," was another of the towering figures of the African nationalist movements that came to life toward the end of the colonial era. Like Julius

Nyerere, he counted on the high road of moral purpose and benign statesmanship to carry himself and his country far, and he
had his own custom-tailored philosophy, a blend of Christian pre-
cepts and African socialism that he called "humanism," which he
said would guide his people to eventual fulfillment. A devoutly
religious man and a spellbinding orator, Kaunda could burst into
tears in the midst of a speech as easily as he could move his listeners to do so. He lived humbly and worked long hours, in the
fashion of Nyerere. He had an uncanny capacity to prevent tribal
conflicts from arising, but once he had established himself as a
national leader, he acted almost as if he believed he had a divine
right to his position. He was intolerant of opposition or criticism.

Kaunda also had a streak of pragmatism that allowed him to
make compromises that Nyerere probably never would have considered. Twice he ignored the wishes and feelings of his counterparts in other "front-line states" and met privately with South African prime ministers—with John Vorster in 1975 and with P. W.
Botha in 1982—in a bold attempt to solve the problems of the region. The meetings were heavy with drama, the first taking place
in a railroad car over Victoria Falls on the Zambian-Rhodesian
border and the second in a trailer straddling the South Africa–
Botswana border; but they were light on substance. Indeed, from
a political and public relations standpoint, the South African leaders probably gained more from the meetings than did Kaunda,
who characteristically came home hopeful but empty-handed. One
meaningful compromise that probably did help keep the peace at
home was Kaunda's continuation of special tax and production incentives for the country's seven thousand commercial farmers, an
increasing number of them blacks. Although Zambia was no longer
almost self-sufficient in food production, as it had been during the
1960s, it would have had to import an even larger percentage of its
food if its private farmers had not stayed in business.

Yet Kaunda's pragmatism was hardly enough to keep Zambia politically stable and economically optimistic. The "peace dividend" that many Zambians expected after the war ended in Zimbabwe never materialized. On the contrary, things only became
progressively worse, and when a severe drought spread across
southern Africa in the early 1980s Zambia was one of the countries hardest hit. Meanwhile, anyone who looked carefully at the
country saw an economic horror show: a declining gross domestic

product, acute shortages of basic goods, and government-run enterprises, including cooperative farms, that were grotesquely inefficient.

After converting his country into a one-party state in 1972, Kaunda became increasingly authoritarian, shuffling the members of his cabinet and his lieutenants in the United National Independence party (UNIP) frequently enough to prevent anyone from being considered a likely successor. In a great charade of national solidarity, Kaunda was reelected to his fifth term as president in 1983, with 93 percent of the voters casting their ballots for him; but increasingly those Zambians who spoke up privately said that UNIP could probably never survive in power if the country were a multiparty democracy. The discontent came to a head in 1980, when a group of well-armed mercenaries, apparently hired by politicians opposed to Kaunda, were discovered on a farm near Lusaka shortly before they had planned to attack and seize strategic installations in the capital and along the copper belt in the northern part of the country. In 1984, student discontent boiled over into major riots. Demonstrating at first over requirements concerning meal cards, the students complained that Kaunda was too lenient with corrupt associates, and they deplored the fact that he spent almost $2 million importing Mercedes-Benz limousines from South Africa for a meeting of SADCC, when Zambia's own car-assembly plants were operating well below capacity because of a lack of foreign exchange to bring in spare parts.

For a time Kaunda's sole reaction to the political and economic discontent was to clamp down further on any opposition to him. He charged the coup plotters with treason (they were later sentenced to death) and imposed a dusk-to-dawn curfew on Lusaka for a time. Resorting to a common African cure for student protest, he closed the university. However, he took the unusual step of recruiting some regional tribal chiefs onto the UNIP central committee, in the hope that traditional elements in Zambian society might be willing to help bolster his regime. Kaunda also announced that the party would consider a reform of the constitution that would let independent candidates run for election to Parliament. He tried to stir the national spirit by declaring that "the lean days I have been talking about have come" and by asking for new sacrifices from the public. Under pressure from the IMF, he put a national ceiling on all salary increases, devalued the currency, and withdrew government subsidies from many products. Kaunda cleverly used some of the money he obtained from the IMF to put consumer goods into the shops, and he purchased them from the easiest source, South Africa.

When he traveled to the United States in the spring of 1983, Kaunda exuded his old public confidence, but he privately admitted that his country was in grave difficulty. In press conferences and other appearances he preferred to talk about what the United States must do to solve the racial difficulties in Namibia and South Africa; in meetings behind the scenes he discussed the requirements of international bankers for further loans to prevent Zambia's collapse. Pride and principle could not motivate the country indefinitely, and they certainly could not feed the people. Twenty years after independence, Zambia was in bad condition.

11

Desperate Cases

FOR MUCH of the rest of Africa, there is little good will or good fortune available to squander. A number of countries have had bitter, painful experiences since independence, and they see faint hope for improvement in the near future. Some nations appear to have declined into a kind of hell on earth, and the path back has been hard to find; others are desperately dependent on outside help just to survive from one day to the next. Many are mini- or micro-states that struggle to be noticed at all.

CENTRAL AFRICAN REPUBLIC

Once the French territory of Oubangui-Chari, the Central African Republic, or CAR, is a pathetically poor, land-locked nation of some 2.5 million people. Indeed, only a tiny handful of those people have ever had the slightest sense of physical or economic well-being, despite the fact that the country has vast natural resources, including diamonds, uranium, manganese, timber, and rich agricultural soil, which, if ever developed in a careful, equitable manner, would give it great potential. But with no railroads, only 265 miles of paved roads, and the vast majority of the population trapped in subsistence farming, development has seemed a dim prospect. What little infrastructure there was at independence in 1960 has virtually disappeared; for example, there is no longer any telephone system at all to speak of.

During the years immediately before and after independence, control of the country was passed among a number of relatives who belonged to the small local elite based in the capital of Bangui. But the critical event that would shape the experiences and the image of the CAR for years to come occurred on New Year's Eve in 1965, when the army commander-in-chief, Jean-Bédel Bokassa, overthrew his particularly ineffectual cousin, David Dacko, then serving as president. Bokassa, a man with many wives, a great deal of money, and close ties with both the French and (surreptitiously) the South Africans, imposed an increasingly harsh regime on the docile nation. Within a few years he had proclaimed himself president for life and then, in a 1977 ceremony that cost $25 million and attracted worldwide attention as a bit of absurd comic opera in the jungle, had himself crowned Emperor Bokassa I of the newly christened "Central African Empire."

It took some time for all the tales of horror to emerge into the outside world, but eventually it became clear that Bokassa, even before his imperial days, had ruled with a selfish vengeance and a mad rage. He accumulated a fleet of five black Mercedes-Benz limousines and other trappings of great wealth; yet when his country needed money, he always went begging for aid, especially from the French, rather than dip into his own pocket. Bokassa was known to lock foreign diplomats inside his palace and other government buildings, so they would have to listen to his long, rambling, incoherent speeches, which usually followed long bouts of drinking. Some escaped through the windows. He was also known to imprison and personally assault foreign correspondents whose stories he did not like. On one occasion, after burglars broke into his home, Bokassa went directly to the local prison, where he beat a number of inmates to death, gouged out their eyes, and put them on public display as examples to other potential criminals. He also practiced cannibalism, installing a special "cold room" just off the imperial kitchen to store the human bodies he intended to consume.

What finally undid this despot were the reports, confirmed by a panel of investigating African jurists, that Bokassa and his imperial guard had personally massacred hundreds of schoolchildren who protested an order that they buy uniforms made from cloth produced at a factory owned by one of his wives. Finally French President Valéry Giscard d'Estaing (who had received diamonds and other gifts from Bokassa when he went hunting in the CAR) withdrew his support from his regime, and in 1979 French paratroopers flew into the capital of Bangui, overthrew him, and put Dacko back in power. After Dacko rigged elections to keep himself in office, he was pushed aside again, in September 1981, this time by the latest army commander-in-chief, André Kolingba.

Bokassa's successors were less brutal, but almost as corrupt and as indifferent to the poor, and so the CAR saw few changes. France's socialist president, François Mitterrand, urged reform, but even in its absence, treated this central African backwater as a colony. Paris continued to subsidize at least half the CAR's annual budget, paid the salaries of most of its civil servants, and regularly sent an inspector-general to supervise the country's finances. French military advisers and combat troops remained close at hand, the better to maintain some role in any further changes that might occur. (The French, in fact, apparently helped prevent a CAR opposition figure, Ange Patasse, from overthrowing Kolingba, but they also protected Patasse from the government's revenge against him, helping install him in exile in Togo.) Caught in Libya at the time of the 1979 coup against him, Bokassa had tried but failed to get into France. Instead, the French persuaded President Félix Houphouët-Boigny of Ivory Coast to take him in and there Bokassa lived comfortably, although officially under house arrest, for four years—until Houphouët-Boigny threw him out in 1983, when he learned of a plot to put Bokassa back in power in the CAR. At the Abidjan airport, where he was about to board a private flight for Bangui (his lawyer and a number of French journalists were already on board), Bokassa was seized and sent instead to Paris. Embarrassed French officials allowed him to take up residence, with a wife and fifteen of his children, in his country chateau.

EQUATORIAL GUINEA

Equatorial Guinea is one of Africa's smallest countries, only ten thousand square miles split between the mainland enclave once known as Rio Muni, wedged between Cameroon and Gabon, and several islands off the coast, the largest of which was originally known as Fernando Pó. The country's three hundred thousand people had a per capita annual income of about $320 at independence in 1968, not bad by African standards at the time. Having been a Spanish colony since 1778, Equatorial Guinea was expected to capitalize on its European connections and its small corps of well-educated citizens to make early progress as a nation.

However, Nguema Masie Biyoto (formerly Francisco Macías Nguema), who came to power in United Nations–supervised elections at independence, immediately closed the country off from the outside world, taking such extreme measures as having every boat that could be found destroyed, and turned it into a virtual concentration camp. During eleven years of paranoid dictatorship, the "Unique Miracle," as Masie called himself, killed at least fifty thousand people and enslaved forty thousand others on state-run plantations. Tens of thousands more, including most of the intellectuals, escaped into exile, cutting the population almost in half. Even with this smaller base, annual per capita income plunged to just $60 (the lowest in the world), as cocoa production was drastically cut and nearly a hundred thousand acres of land previously under cultivation reverted to jungle. After Spanish teachers fled his reign of terror, Masie closed all the country's schools. He eventually closed all the churches, too, and put most of the Catholic priests and nuns in prison. Under a typically repressive rule that he imposed, it became a capital crime to be a journalist.

In one of their more cynical actions in Africa of recent years, the Soviet Union, Cuba, and several other Communist-ruled countries helped keep Masie in power, in exchange for liberal use of Equatorial Guinea's ports and airfields. But their support was no help when finally Masie's nephew, Colonel Teodoro Obiang Nguema, angered because his brother had become one of Masie's random victims, decided to overthrow his uncle and seize power in 1979. Obiang evaluated the conditions he inherited at the time: "Our country is totally devastated, totally subjected to misery. . . . Our capital city is almost without electricity and water. Our hospitals are totally abandoned and without medical supplies. This is a place where there is nothing, absolutely nothing." Masie made sure that was true when, as he was about to be captured in his native village after holding out against Obiang for four days, he set fire to all of the money in the national treasury, an estimated $105 million. He was subsequently executed.

Obiang adopted a pro-Western stance and won immediate recognition of his new government from Spain. King Juan Carlos and Queen Sofia visited Equatorial Guinea soon after he took charge, and Pope John Paul II included the country (whose population is 90 percent Catholic) on the itinerary of his 1982 tour of Africa. That same year an overwhelming majority of Equatorial Guineans voted to approve a new constitution, one of the most liberal in Africa, with guarantees of human rights, an independent judiciary, and universal suffrage. As a result, the World Bank and twenty-nine countries agreed jointly to finance a $150 million plan to begin rebuilding the country. But with the literacy rate still at only 16 percent, the government had to import foreigners—mostly Spaniards—to take on the most important jobs. Many exiles were reluctant to return home, because they felt that Obiang was trying to monopolize power in the hands of the Mongomo clan (to which Masie had also belonged, along with most of the military). But after Obiang wrote into the new constitution a guaranteed seven-year presidential term for himself, members of the military also became discontented and repeatedly attempted to overthrow him.

Spanish and other aid notwithstanding, Equatorial Guinea made little progress toward economic recovery or political cohesion during the several years after it was rid of one of the world's most bestial rulers. Health and sanitation conditions declined even further, and much of the international food aid sent to Equatorial Guinea was sold on the black markets of neighboring countries. With the population of some of the smaller islands talking about establishing independent governments, and with Gabon eager to extend its borders, there was some question as to whether the country would survive at all.

CHAD

Similar doubt arose over the years as to the survival of Chad, a poverty-stricken and land-locked, but much larger, desert country that is strategically located in the transition zone between North Africa and sub-Saharan Africa. The lines that define Chad on most Western maps are meaningless, because Libya has occupied a substantial slice of the country, the Aozou strip, for years, on the basis of a treaty signed during World War II between Italy (which then ruled Libya) and the pro-Nazi Vichy government of France (which governed Chad). The rest of Chad has been the object—and the potential prize—of one of the world's most intractable civil wars, in which the internal and external alliances shift as frequently and unpredictably as the desert sands. Since the boundaries of Chad were among the most irrational in Africa, it was inevitable that strife would become its only growth industry.

For fifteen years after independence in 1960, Chad was ruled by a man from the Christian, Westernized southern part of the country, François Tombalbaye, who enjoyed the support of the French but, as time went on, fewer and fewer of his own people. Tombalbaye once boasted that he had survived more plots against his life than any other leader in Africa. But his luck ran out in 1975, when he was overthrown and killed in an army coup. The general who came to power at the time, Félix Malloum, never achieved genuine authority over the country, especially the nomadic northern areas, where the leaders of two rival rebel groups, Goukouni Oueddi and Hissene Habre, temporarily formed a coalition to oppose and harass the central government. Before long, members of the southern elite who had run the country since independence were being assassinated in the eastern section of Chad, and Moslems were being massacred in the South. The capital city of N'Djamena, formerly a tranquil French colonial outpost named Fort Lamy, was reduced to ruins after several battles took place there.

As the French began to lose interest and influence in Chad, despite their control of the meager cotton industry and other dwindling resources, the vacuum was increasingly filled by Muammar al-Qaddafi of Libya. The greater his presence in Chad, the more worried became other Chadian neighbors, especially Sudan, Nigeria, Niger, and Cameroon, and so the old civil war suddenly became the subject of international attention and rhetoric. Qaddafi shifted sides from time to time and withdrew his troops at one point, but eventually a situation evolved in which he was backing Oueddi. The latter had briefly run the government, but then had to settle for becoming the leader of most of the rebels in the North against Habre, who had declared himself president of the country and now enjoyed the backing of France and the United States. Qaddafi lost his chance to be head of the OAU because of his position in Chad. The Reagan administration, having decided to draw the line on what it regarded as Qaddafi's expansionist goals in Africa, provided logistical support and other aid to Habre's embattled government; but finally it was left to France to intervene militarily and urge a negotiated settlement. As the civil war reached yet another stalemate, Chad was effectively partitioned in two. In the autumn of 1984, France and Libya reached agreement on a mutual withdrawal of forces, but the peace was bound to be fragile.

Meanwhile, the most basic necessities were unavailable to most of the people of Chad, who cared far more about trying to eke out a meager existence than about choosing between two (for them) virtually indistinguishable leaders. The number of Chadian doctors working in the country dwindled to perhaps half a dozen. Even in the capital, water became a scarce commodity. The average life expectancy remained only forty-four years. With such basic problems haunting daily life, it was no surprise that the university was closed indefinitely, since there was no money to pay salaries or buy books and equipment. Outsiders continued to argue over who should rule Chad, but Chad itself fell apart.

BENIN • CONGO

A number of Africa's smallest states have tried over the years to find salvation in Marxism. Among the most dramatic examples of this trend were Benin (formerly Dahomey) and the People's Republic of the Congo (most often identified by adding the name of its capital, as in Congo-Brazzaville, to avoid confusion with its neighbor, Zaïre, once ruled by Belgium and also then known as the Congo). The two had many things in common, beyond their French colonial heritage and their continued membership in the French African Community despite ideological differences with most of its other members. Each one lived in the shadow of a much larger, potentially more powerful next-door neighbor, in Benin's case Nigeria and in Congo's case Zaïre, and each one sometimes had to find much of its income through illicit trade in the neighbor's resources and products. Both, with Soviet inspiration and assistance, developed enormous parastatal sectors that created new problems worse than the old ones. And both eventually had the good fortune of oil discoveries that made otherwise hopeless economies suddenly seem viable.

In more recent years, although their official Marxist rhetoric has scarcely diminished, both Benin and Congo-Brazzaville have become much more pragmatic, making compromises to attract Western investment, reaching a rapprochement with the socialist government of France, and forgoing Soviet closeness for better relations with China and other nations willing to provide aid with fewer strings attached.

In Benin, Mathieu Kerekou, who presided over a grand radicalization of his sliver of a country after seizing power in 1972, sought to advertise his new moderation in the early 1980s by dismissing the Marxist-Leninist extremists in his cabinet, making high-profile visits to Paris, and inviting American banks to help reorganize the economy for more efficient development efforts. Benin's fledgling offshore oil industry was minimal compared to that of Nigeria (whose economic ups and downs have a disproportionate effect on tiny Benin), but it was enough to cover domestic needs and even to permit small-scale exports. Furthermore, the government was wise enough to keep its oil income in a separate account, lest it overextend itself in the manner of some other African countries with newfound wealth. The increased prosperity did raise the prospect that some of the self-exiled Beninois intellectuals who had long been playing a key role in other West African countries might come home and devote more energy to their own.

Congo-Brazzaville went through twenty years of official "scientific socialism," but its subsequent transformation was so thorough and so fast as to earn it the label of Africa's only "Marxist-capitalist" country. Just a few years after the overthrow of Marien

Ngouabi—who had turned the Congo into a sort of African Albania, complete with a red flag adorned with a crossed hammer and hoe—another military leader, Denis Sassou-Nguesso, a dapper man who favored a French life style, began to downplay his own doctrinaire Marxist credentials and invited Western oil companies in to see what they could do. What they did was to make the Congo the fourth largest oil producer in black Africa, after Nigeria, Gabon, and Angola. As a result, the country's annual average per capita income skyrocketed to $1,200. State-run farms were quickly dismantled and available credit channeled to the growing private sector instead.

Brazzaville, the African headquarters of the Free French during World War II, still bears the name of the French explorer, Savorgnan de Brazza, who founded it, and it is still a relatively quiet, laconic place with mostly unpaved streets; but compared to Kinshasa, the gigantic, tense Zaïrian capital just across the Congo River, it is a fount of hope and optimism. Indeed, both Brazzaville and Pointe Noire, the country's port on the Atlantic coast, are booming with new construction (which tends to be completed, unlike most of the buildings in Kinshasa), and roads are being built to the interior, which should permit the development of a timber industry out of the country's lush equatorial forests. Two-thirds of Congo's 1.9 million people still live in a narrow strip of land along the railway between Brazzaville and Pointe Noire in the southern part of the country; development of the interior and the North would require a substantial population shift.

Relations with Washington were not only restored by Sassou-Nguesso after a long hiatus, but Congolese have also begun to turn up among groups of Africans sent on tours of the United States by the State Department. American marketing professors have been invited to give management seminars in Brazzaville for aspiring Congolese entrepreneurs. But all of this has caused trouble among hard-liners in the ruling party; whether Marxist ideology can coexist indefinitely with a capitalist boom remains to be seen.

GAMBIA

One of Africa's microstates, Gambia, surrounded on three sides by Senegal, finally dealt with its serious security problems in 1982 by allowing itself virtually to be swallowed by its seven-teen-times-larger neighbor. The result, the confederation of Sene-gambia, is an experiment that, if it succeeds, might well be emu-lated elsewhere in Africa.

For years after Gambia—a finger-shaped former British colony along the Gambia River, populated by only 600,000 people—became independent in 1965, it was cited as one of the most democratic nations in Africa. In reality, despite the existence of several opposition political parties, no one had a serious prospect in Gambia's elections of upsetting Sir Dawda Jawara, the Scot-tish-trained veterinarian who was regarded as the father of his country. But unrest grew among the poor and youthful segments of the population, who resented the corruption of the elite, and in the summer of 1981, while Jawara was off in London attending the wedding of Prince Charles, a young man whose Marxist party had been banned led a violent uprising. Gambia had no army, only a police force, and it took more than fifteen hundred troops from Senegal a week of tough fighting to put down the rebellion and make Gambia safe for Jawara's return. The damage was sub-stantial, especially in the port city of Banjul, Gambia's capital, where looting and arson were widespread; unofficial estimates were that as many as two thousand people may have died in the conflict, and more than one thousand were arrested.

Within months Jawara and President Abdou Diouf of Sene-gal had devised their plan for confederation (which had origi-nally been suggested twenty years earlier, but scoffed at on both sides). While Gambia was assigned disproportionate representa-tion in the confederal cabinet—four ministers out of nine, in-cluding finance and economic affairs—foreign policy and defense matters were left entirely to Senegalese representatives. What was especially noteworthy and challenging about the effort was that notwithstanding certain elements of ethnic and religious her-itage that the two had in common, an English colonial culture was being merged into a French one. Certain problems were bound to arise.

The Gambians were worried about losing their identity, which had become all the more distinct since the world-famous saga, *Roots*, by American black author Alex Haley, had been set there. It had attracted a certain amount of American tourism. Another concern was that the Gambian currency, pegged to the British pound, would have to disappear in favor of the CFA franc used by Senegal, traditionally stable because of its tie to the French franc but suffering in the early 1980s as a result of the French currency's weakness. But the greatest crisis looming for Gambia was the inevitable pressure for joint customs regulations with Senegal. Banjul (once Bathhurst) had been an active port since the early 1800s, and one of the Gambians' most reliable sources of income since independence was their so-called "border trade," a sophisticated form of smuggling. Because Gambia had notoriously low import duties, a vast amount of electronic equipment came into the country—according to some estimates, at least one transistor radio and two stereo sets for every citizen every year—only to be quietly and unofficially "reexported" at a considerable profit by Banjul trading companies to nearby countries, which collected no duties at all. Since Senegal was one of the main losers in this system, it was bound to try to use the new confederal arrangement to share in Gambia's proceeds.

But with both economies in bad condition—at the time of the union, Gambia was spending a fifth of its annual revenues to import rice to feed its people—it was unlikely that either Senegal or Gambia would achieve a financial bonanza from their new relationship. The hope was that both countries would feel more secure and that as mutual suspicions receded, some of the obvious duplication of services and other waste could be eliminated.

TOGO

Farther down the West African coast, between Benin and Ghana, lies Togo, which has sought to avoid obscurity in recent years by acting as a peacemaker in disputes among other African states. There is an irony in this, for the highly ambitious and visible Togolese president, Gnassingbe Eyadema, originally came to power in 1967 in the second of two violent military coups that his country experienced in its early years of independence.

But Eyadema did manage to compile an enviable diplomatic record. He negotiated a rapprochement between Nigeria and several of the French-speaking nations that had recognized Biafra during the Nigerian civil war. He served as an intermediary at one point among various combatants in Chad's internal strife. He

persuaded Nigeria to extend its deadline for illegal foreign workers to get out in 1983, and then, after arranging for the shipment
of American relief supplies to Togo, fed hundreds of thousands
of Ghanaians on their way home. At one stage, Eyadema even
helped negotiate a solution to a conflict between Egypt and
Libya. And one of his most important achievements was hosting
the meetings in Togo's capital that resulted in the Lomé Convention, under which Third World nations obtained preferential treatment from the European Economic Community. Although he was
unpopular among many French socialists because of his repression of domestic opposition, Eyadema persuaded President François Mitterrand to begin an African tour by visiting Togo on the
sixteenth anniversary of the coup that originally brought him to
power, thus conferring additional legitimacy on his own rule.

For years Eyadema behaved as if his country's exports of
phosphate and agricultural commodities, such as cocoa, would
be adequate to finance anything he wanted to do. On that assumption, he tried to create jobs with flamboyant development
projects, such as an oil refinery on the outskirts of Lomé and a giant electric steel-making plant. Both were early failures, as were
a textile factory and a twenty-five-story hotel in Lomé built to be
the most luxurious in all of West Africa; despite Togolese efforts
to promote tourism on its handsome beaches, especially among
wealthy Nigerians, its room occupancy rate hovered around 25
percent. (The hotel was also part of an effort to encourage a move
of the permanent headquarters of the OAU from Addis Ababa to
Lomé, but that too failed.)

But those were just some of the elements of Togo's economic
malaise. Political and financial disputes with Ghana, which led to
closing of the common border; the decline of Nigeria's economy;
greater competition from the newly pragmatic government of Benin to supply goods to Nigeria; and severe internal corruption—all
of these contributed to Togo's accumulation of a billion-dollar external debt. As bankruptcy loomed, Eyadema traveled to the
United States in the autumn of 1983, where he was granted the
prestige of a half-hour meeting with Ronald Reagan in the White
House Oval Office and also met with the heads of American corporations that were potential investors in Togo. One thing that
aided him in his country's difficult hour was his ability to point to
Togo's almost unblemished pro-Western voting record during a

two-year term on the United Nations Security Council. A personal friendship and business partnership with conservative West German politician Franz-Josef Strauss also helped keep Togo afloat, with Eyadema in charge.

DJIBOUTI

Djibouti, one of the last African states to become independent (in 1977), is in a particularly unenviable position. Once known as French Somaliland, and later as the Territory of the Afars and the Issas, it is located in one of the most unstable spots on the globe—on the western shore of the Bab-el-Mandeb strait, across from Saudi Arabia, wedged between Somalia and Ethiopia, its northern coastline alongside that of the rebellious Ethiopian province of Eritrea. Djibouti is dirt poor. Among its population of 450,000, at least 40 percent of the potential work force is unemployed, and in recent years it has had to accept a tide of some thirty thousand refugees from Ethiopia.

Both Ethiopia and Somalia have traditionally laid claim to the area that is now known as Djibouti (it is included on the maps of "Greater Somalia" in Mogadishu), and it is probably only the Western stake and visible presence there that protected it from being gobbled up. American naval vessels operating in the Indian Ocean and the Persian Gulf have often made it a point to refuel in Djibouti's deep-water port, and the French, after granting independence, left four thousand troops more or less permanently stationed in the new country. Indeed, no one tried to hide the fact that these troops and the other eight thousand Frenchmen who stayed on in Djibouti had a key role in running the nation's affairs. They owned most of the shops in the sleepy capital—one of the hottest spots on earth—supervised the police, and taught a traditional French curriculum in Djibouti schools. In most places overseas, visas to visit Djibouti can be obtained only from the nearest French consulate. The French also kept a substantial supply of their own military equipment on hand in Djibouti and serviced and maintained the equipment of Djibouti's national army. They pointedly refused, however, to touch the twenty armored personnel carriers and two patrol boats that Libya presented as a gift to the Djibouti armed forces; thus the Libyan equipment was unusable, except once a year during the Independence Day parade.

Few Djiboutians or Frenchmen believed that this forlorn outpost had any hope of standing on its own feet anytime soon, although a new effort by the United Nations High Commissioner for Refugees to repatriate some of the Ethiopians from camps in Djibouti offered the possibility of some relief. Local officials had to be prevented from pushing the refugees back across the border, especially given the repression that some of the Ethiopians were bound to face at home.

MAURITIUS

While not technically a part of the African continent, Mauritius, an island nation east of Madagascar, came to be considered an African colony during its years of British rule, and it opted for participation in the affairs of the OAU and other African councils after being granted independence in 1968. A country with a rich mix of European, Indian, and African heritage—it was settled by the Dutch and the French before the British turned up there in 1810, and the majority of the islanders regard themselves as Hindus—Mauritius suffered in recent years from dramatic population growth and an international glut of sugar, its main export. Mauritians are entitled to free education up to the university level, and so they have an unusually high literacy rate, but there are very few interesting economic opportunities at home. When even just a few dozen of the country's nearly one million people get jobs overseas, it is headline news in the local press.

What was most significant about Mauritius in recent years was the successful functioning of its democratic system in two major elections held within a fourteen-month period in 1982 and 1983. In the first, a leftist coalition symbolized by Paul Berenger, a young activist who came home from Paris to lead a peaceful political revolution, swept to victory in almost every parliamentary seat, displacing the moderate administration of Sir Seewoosagur Ramgoolam, a physician and patriarch who had run Mauritius since before independence. But before long, Berenger, who was finance minister in the new government, quarreled with his own political allies. In part because of discontent over controversial recommendations of the IMF for austerity measures, which Berenger wanted to accept, the coalition fell apart. In a new election, Berenger and his party were humiliated, and he lost his seat in Parliament. The remaining socialists who had originally worked with him then formed a new alliance with Ramgoolam's party and other, more conservative political elements. That new government sought to deal with some of Mauritius's economic problems by tightening the country's already controversial links with South Africa; more Mauritians would be permitted to travel to South Africa for medical treatment at preferential rates, and South African tourism in Mauritius would be further encouraged. The new coalition also moved to ease a conflict with Britain and the United States over the Western military facilities on the island of Diego García. The dispute over Diego García, once administered jointly with Mauritius by British colonial authorities (although more than a thousand miles away), was a popular nationalist cause on Mauritius, but it was costing the country cooperation and aid from the West.

RWANDA • BURUNDI

Two countries with an especially tragic modern history and a difficult road ahead are the twin nations of Rwanda and Burundi. Originally a single kingdom nestled in the mountains of east-central Africa, they were first colonized by Germany and then, after World War I, ruled by Belgium. The Belgian record there was similar to that in the Congo, and Burundi, for example, did not have a single college graduate in its population at the time of independence in 1962. But the most acute problem, which was exploited rather than ameliorated by the Belgians, was tribalism. For generations, perhaps centuries, the majority Hutu people had been held in a kind of feudal serfdom by the kings and lords of the Tutsi aristocracy. According to the traditional racial stereotype, the Hutu were short and stocky, the Tutsi tall and lanky. The Hutu tended to till the land, and the Tutsi raised and herded cattle. Because the numbers were so unbalanced—about 85 percent to 15 percent—the Tutsi, fearing a rebellion, made their repression of the Hutu ever more severe in the colonial period.

In 1959, as independence approached, tribal tensions erupted into bloodshed in Rwanda. The Hutu overthrew the old Tutsi monarchy and slaughtered an unknown number of the minority tribesmen they had hated for so long, driving tens of thousands more into neighboring countries, especially Uganda. When some of the Tutsi attempted to return and take charge again in 1963, there was still more fighting, but the Hutu retained control. Meanwhile, in Burundi, the tensions took longer to boil over; but finally, in 1972, the Tutsi, who were still in power there, fearing that the Hutu were planning an uprising similar to the earlier one in Rwanda, made a preemptive strike. They systematically killed a vast number of the Burundi Hutu—probably more than one hundred thousand, perhaps as many as two hundred thousand—while the world community hardly uttered a protest. Many Hutu who survived fled Burundi and became refugees in Rwanda, Tanzania, and Zaïre.

Eventually, leaders who put an emphasis on tribal conciliation came to power in both countries, although Burundi is still governed largely by the Tutsi and Rwanda by the Hutu. Jean-Baptiste Bagaza, a Tutsi who seized power in the Burundian capital of Bujumbura in 1976, welcomed thousands of Hutu back and abolished most of the unjust taxes and regulations that had burdened them for so long. Many Hutu at last came to own the land they farmed in Burundi, and some were given access to education and government jobs. Burundi achieved a reputation for using its foreign assistance wisely and fairly, and by following a relatively pragmatic line in international affairs, it attracted help from various sources. One of the Burundi government's greatest challenges was to find a way to deliver services to its people, 95 percent of whom lived in small, scattered family settlements rather than villages; a new constitution adopted in 1981 seemed to indicate that Burundi would attempt to follow the questionable Tanzanian model. Bagaza was himself overthrown in September 1987, while he was attending a conference in Quebec. He was succeeded by Pierre Buyoya, who promised to respect freedom of religion more than Bagaza had. Less than a year later, the slaughter of the Hutu in Burundi began again.

The military man who took over in Rwanda in 1973, Juvenal Habyarimana, allowed some Tutsi back into positions of influence, but he was somewhat less forthcoming about readmitting exiles, because Rwanda is even more overpopulated than Burundi. (The two nations are of about equal size; Burundi has about 4.5 million people and Rwanda 5.9 million, which translates to more than five hundred people per square mile.) Although Rwanda is known as the "land of a thousand hills," nearly every inch of the country is under cultivation. Through terracing of the land, even steep inclines have been rendered productive. Rwanda produces coffee, tea, beans, sorghum, and so many bananas that the national drink is homemade banana beer; for the most part it has been able to feed itself since independence. But as health and nutrition have improved, the population has grown at a rate of more than 4 percent a year. If it continues at that rate, Rwanda's population could double by the year 2000, a circumstance that would be intolerable. It is this pressure on the land that has prevented some forty-five thousand Rwandan (mostly Tutsi) refugees from returning home from Uganda, where their lives are increasingly in danger. In many cases, the Rwandans' cattle have already severely overgrazed the land available to them in Uganda, and because they have a reputation of having supported Idi Amin while he was in power, Ugandan President Milton Obote was reluctant to extend special help to them. Faced with his own food crisis in Uganda, Obote even tried to drive out Rwandans who had long since established Ugandan citizenship and forgotten the Rwandan language. Those who do come home to Rwanda are often driven back across the border.

Rwanda, too, has relied on its wits to bring in aid from various sources. The North Koreans constructed the Parliament building in the capital of Kigali. The West Germans trained part of the army, and the United States developed a population-control center. The Chinese built roads north to the Rwandan jungles where some of the world's rarest gorillas live, and the European Community paved some of the red-earth roads winding south around the hills toward the Burundi border.

At first glance, Rwanda and Burundi look like a paradise that has remained benignly untainted by the advances of Western civilization. With only a few flights a week that can bring outsiders to Kigali or Bujumbura, their hospitality has not been strained. But unless population growth can be stemmed immediately, they will face adversities almost impossible to surmount.

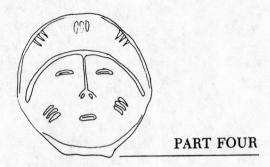

PART FOUR

THE
CRISIS
AHEAD

12

The Prognosis for Africa

No OTHER PART of the world has changed as dramatically and as thoroughly in the post-World War II era as has Africa. The sub-Saharan part of the continent (including the offshore islands usually associated with it) has evolved from a colonial hodge-podge into forty-six separate, independent countries. Having had virtually no voice in world affairs before the mid-twentieth century, Africa now has nearly a third of the votes in the United Nations General Assembly and substantial influence over many UN specialized agencies, as well as a considerable presence in other international organizations. And Africa has been transformed from a collection of largely rural, agricultural-based societies that had little connection with the international economy into a network of increasingly urban, sophisticated systems that are intimately linked with the outside world. Sub-Saharan Africa's population has grown geometrically—from 210 million in 1960 to some 500 million today—and it is continuing to grow by an overall rate of at least 3.2 percent a year, faster than anyplace else on earth. At that rate, the population will double by the year 2005.

It would be comforting and encouraging to be able to say that Africa has made great strides since the end of the colonial era, that the majority of its people have reaped the benefits of nationhood and growth. But as the preceding discussions of individual countries have indicated, that is far from the case. And when Africa is examined as a whole, the record and the outlook are even worse.

Africans in ever increasing numbers are going hungry. Although many parts of the continent are fertile and potentially productive, per capita food output has declined since independence. In fact, since 1960 Africa's grain imports have increased seven times. Still, the World Bank estimates that 60 percent of the people eat fewer calories each day than are officially estimated to be necessary for survival. It is no surprise, then, that the United Nations Secretary-General has found that 5 million children die in Africa every year and another 5 million are crippled by malnutrition and hunger. A drought of moderate proportions in the early 1970s is thought to have taken at least three hundred thousand lives; the far more severe drought of the early 1980s, covering a much wider area, caused twenty-four African countries to face what the UN Food and Agricultural Organization (FAO) calls "catastrophic food shortages." In 1983 alone, just in Ethiopia, more than three million people depended on emergency food supplies for their survival. The prospects for early improvement in the situation are not bright. The FAO estimates that most African countries will not achieve self-sufficiency in food supplies before the year 2000, and probably not for some time after that.

According to the World Bank, twenty-one of the world's thirty-four poorest countries are located in Africa. The poverty does not result from a lack of foreign assistance or available credit in the past. On the contrary, Africa's dismal performance may be owing in part to an overreliance on outside funding, which often reduces the incentives for domestic production. Foreign aid, bilateral and multilateral, accounted for 42.5 percent of Africa's total capital inflows in 1980; for the very poorest nations on the continent, that figure was 80 percent. Sub-Saharan Africa's total external debt was $5 billion in 1970; by 1982 it was more than fourteen times as large, or $72 billion, and still growing, because many countries had to keep borrowing in order to pay the interest on previous loans. In just the bleak three-year period between

1980 and 1983, according to the calculations of the Economic Commission for Africa, the continent's average annual per capita income fell by 18 percent.

The one obvious exception to this dreary outlook is South Africa. But there, the internal disparities skew all of the statistics, and the possibility of unrest and upheaval threatens to undo economic progress and bring about political and social chaos.

Political instability has already accompanied economic decline in much of Africa. Few leaders have stepped aside voluntarily since independence, and Africa's coup-per-country rate is the highest in the world. By one tally, more than seventy leaders were overthrown in twenty-nine countries during a twenty-five-year period. The rate has stepped up in recent years; there have been at least twenty successful coups since 1977. Only fifteen African nations have never undergone a successful coup, and half of Africa's people now live under military rule. The fact that most members of the original generation of African elder statesmen who led their nations to independence were so reluctant to step aside or train successors has made it all the harder for a newer generation to fill their shoes. Less automatically revered and respected, the younger leaders have often resorted to repression or official violence to keep themselves in power. Many have made their party the only party; fewer than ten African countries now have effective opposition parties or movements that can function openly, and while some one-party states, such as Kenya and Ivory Coast, have experienced a good deal of open democratic competition, that is the exception rather than the rule.

Meanwhile, Africa is home to about half of the world's estimated 10 million refugees. While others in Southeast Asia, the Middle East, or Central America generally command far more attention from the press, those in Africa often live in the most miserable and desperate conditions. Some are the victims of long-standing petty ethnic rivalries or border disputes, others of serious wars that seem to be permanent fixtures of the African landscape. In recent years Africa has had several wars raging at any given time, the most intractable being the Somali-Ethiopian conflict on the Horn, the struggle between Morocco and the Algerian-backed Polisario guerrillas for possession of the former Spanish colony of Western Sahara, and the battle between South Africa and SWAPO guerrillas over Namibia. If the vast resources devoted to war, and otherwise to military buildups, had been diverted to social programs or food production, the continent might be in somewhat better condition.

Dismayed, disgusted, and increasingly disillusioned with Africa's record of corruption and disorder, many of the continent's benefactors have begun to throw up their hands and turn away. On the whole, it is a sorry picture, far from the dreams and promises that accompanied independence. "Our ancient continent is now on the brink of disaster, hurtling toward the abyss of confrontation, caught in the grip of violence," says one former secretary-general of the OAU. "Gone are the smiles, the joys of life." With little hope for substantial improvement soon on any front, the future of Africa's nations and people looks bleak.

Africa's proudest and most ambitious hopes in the early years of the postcolonial era focused on the Organization of African Unity (OAU). The brainchild of ardent pan-African nationalists like Kwame Nkrumah and Sékou Touré, the OAU was expected to create a new African identity, to reassert a common heritage and history over the more recent and diverse experiences of colonialism. As Nkrumah put it in the book that became his political manifesto, *Africa Must Unite*, "The forces making for unity far outweigh those which divide us. In meeting fellow Africans from all parts of the continent I am consistently impressed by how much we have in common. . . . I can best describe it as a sense of one-ness in that we are Africans." To further that spirit, the signatories of the OAU charter, drawn up in Addis Ababa in 1963, pledged to "coordinate and harmonize" their policies in fields ranging from health and education to defense and security. "Nonalignment with regard to all blocs" was a key principle in the OAU credo, and above all, the members promised to respect the borders inherited from the colonial powers and not to interfere in each other's internal affairs.

Viewed in retrospect, it was a major accomplishment for the OAU simply to bring together in a common cause and organization African leaders as different and disparate as Haile Selassie and Kwame Nkrumah, Léopold Senghor and Julius Nyerere. At the start, the OAU was the only forum that promoted useful communication between anglophone and francophone African countries, as well as between the Arab states of North Africa and the black states south of the Sahara (although the latter was a benefit of temporary and questionable value, since the North African presence in the OAU eventually became the source of its most profound difficulties). To a degree, the OAU also succeeded in creating and building upon the kind of African identity and pride that Nkrumah originally had in mind. It gave very small states a share in what would become a very loud, and sometimes clear, voice.

As a result of OAU initiatives, African diplomats at the United Nations often managed to adopt a unified stance on issues of international importance. The consensus extended not only to controversies concerning white-minority rule in southern Africa— an obvious, even convenient rallying point—but also to broader topics, such as votes involving international economic issues. Indeed, the African bloc at the UN was the envy of other regional groupings for the extent of the unity it often seemed to achieve. The Africans invariably agreed in advance, for example, on which African countries would be put forward as candidates for seats on the Security Council or the presidency of the General Assembly; only rarely did disagreements on such matters surface publicly.

At one point, in Lagos in 1980, the OAU adopted a comprehensive "plan of action" for African development, emphasizing regional cooperation and self-reliance. It was the first time that Africans had spoken up clearly and jointly on the issue, instead of accepting economic strategies imposed by international institutions or individual nations providing aid. Similarly, for a short time in 1981, the OAU, on its own initiative, organized a multinational African peacekeeping force to try to deal with the civil war in Chad and the Libyan intervention there, rather than standing aside while outside parties acted.

Those were short-lived and superficial successes, however. For the most part, the OAU's history is a tale of empty rhetoric, an inability or unwillingness to deal with crises, and a failure to address the important issues concerning Africa's future. While routinely and resoundingly criticizing South Africa, the OAU has remained silent about the abuses of human rights and other excesses in the black-ruled states of Africa. It virtually lost its moral authority as an organization when it did nothing to condemn, let alone punish or halt, the outrages committed by Idi Amin in Uganda, Jean-Bédel Bokassa in the Central African Republic, and Nguema Masie Biyoto in Equatorial Guinea. In fact, Amin was permitted to take his turn as head of the OAU at a moment when his massacre of Ugandan citizens was reaching its peak; in an exhibition of indifference bordering on cynicism—and an incident that hurt Africa's standing with other parts of the world—Amin's fellow heads of state greeted him with a standing ovation after he was elected to lead the organization.

Automatic rotation of the chairmanship of the OAU, without any regard to the qualifications, the merit, or even the decency of the person taking over the job, did a great deal to discredit the organization among many of its own members, as well as outside observers. Election to that position was desirable for a variety of reasons: it assured a head of state a great deal of publicity and prestige and therefore, even if only temporarily, a likely improvement in his political fortunes at home. For a year, a man who might ordinarily be paid little attention in the world arena was officially entitled to speak for all of Africa. The chairmanship also guaranteed the holding of an OAU summit in one's capital—often an occasion to build a new conference center, hotels, and deluxe villas to house the visiting dignitaries. That, in turn, meant a sudden increase in construction jobs and other economic activity, as well as a chance to acquire a new fleet of imported cars that would eventually be available for the use of government officials. Invariably, foreign assistance was available to make all this happen, and there were opportunities for corrupt politicians and bureaucrats in the host country to enrich themselves along the way.

What happened at those summits was another matter entirely. Amid the overdeveloped protocol and false cordiality of their annual meetings, in the name of "noninterference" in the internal affairs of sovereign states the African leaders went out of their way not to offend each other. They did nothing to mediate or resolve the major disputes tearing Africa apart—the Biafran secession from Nigeria in the 1960s, the Angolan civil war, the conflicts in the Shaba province of Zaïre, and the recurrent fighting in the Horn—and they took no practical steps to ease Africa's food crisis or its refugee problem.

The lack of useful dialogue on the pressing issues of the day culminated in 1982 with the OAU's inability even to convene its nineteenth summit meeting, scheduled for the Libyan capital of Tripoli. It had been a questionable, probably foolish, decision in the first place to give the controversial Libyan leader, Muammar al-Qaddafi, his turn at the OAU helm. Qaddafi was despised in the West; some of that feeling was bound to be transferred to an OAU led by him. But Qaddafi insisted upon his right to the honor, and he was in a position to buy support within the organization.*

Several months before the Tripoli summit was scheduled to begin, the OAU's then secretary-general admitted the Sahrawi Arab Democratic Republic (SADR), the Polisario's name for Western Sahara, to full membership in the organization, on the grounds that more than half of the OAU's members had already recognized its legitimacy. Other members had very strong feelings on that issue, however, and they refused to send representatives to any summit in which the Polisario would also be participating. Thus, in August 1982, the OAU failed to muster the quorum of two-thirds of its members necessary to convene officially. Another attempt was made to hold the summit in Tripoli in November of the same year, after the Polisario agreed not to attend; but this time Egypt, Sudan, and Somalia refused to go because of their general opposition to Qaddafi, and fifteen other countries boycotted the meeting as a result of a dispute over who would represent Chad. Once again the summit failed to convene. The striking feature of both disputes was that they involved no negotiation at all, just the stubborn confrontation of two prefabricated blocs. They also involved fundamentally North African problems. Who controls Western Sahara is, arguably, an issue not very important to most of sub-Saharan Africa. If Libya were not a member of the OAU, most of the continent would be opposed to Qaddafi's involvement in Chad.

Finally the OAU's nineteenth annual meeting was held in June 1983, almost a year late, in Addis Ababa. Ethiopia's military leader, Mengistu Haile Mariam, was chosen as chairman in Qaddafi's place, and the Libyan decided to absent himself altogether.

---

* Former Nigerian Foreign Minister (and later United Nations Ambassador) Joseph Garba explained in an interview that the smallest African countries were uniquely vulnerable to the blandishments—and cash advances—of wealthy North African regimes like those in Libya and Algeria. "Countries like the Seychelles or São Tomé and Principe will often surprise you in the OAU," he said, "by taking strong positions [on issues that seem remote to them] and being very vocal. . . . Someone gives them a million dollars once in a while, and they're happy."

Although in the end this summit, which took place in the OAU's twentieth anniversary year and in the city of its birth, was its best-attended one ever, the truth was that the organization had virtually ceased to exist as an instrument of African solidarity. Qaddafi sought to blame the United States and France for discouraging attendance at the meetings in Tripoli and otherwise sowing discord in Africa. There was some basis for the charge, since the Reagan administration in particular had publicly expressed its view that Qaddafi was an "inappropriate" leader for the OAU and had shaped much of its Africa policy around its opposition to him. And it was no secret that the governments in Washington and Paris had urged some of their African friends not to go to Tripoli.

But Africa hardly needed help in dividing itself. For lack of open discussion and debate on a genuinely African agenda, the continent had essentially split along ideological lines. There were no overtly pro-Soviet and pro-American blocs (although there were several countries that might fall into those two categories), but "radicals" on the one hand and "moderates" or "conservatives" on the other, with a group of flexible nationalists in between who believed in genuine nonalignment. The membership of these two categories shifts occasionally with events in Africa and elsewhere, but the dichotomy reflects the basic reality of intra-African politics today.

While there is still an external facade of unanimity on some issues, the OAU seems destined to fade still further. It has lost even its ability to prevail upon members to meet their financial commitments to the organization. Some African states ran as many as four years behind in their required contributions to the OAU's "Special Liberation Fund" for southern Africa, and in 1982 the secretary-general complained that only ten of the fifty member states had paid their dues for the year, and not all of those had done so in full. Some countries have failed to make any payments since 1970. By 1984 the OAU had an operating deficit of $45.5 million. There was a serious possibility that the OAU might disappear altogether, or split into two, ideologically defined, rival units. (President Mobutu of Zaïre, for one, suggested launching a new organization that would exclude the countries of North Africa.)

Potentially more useful as a serious effort to solve African problems have been a number of regional organizations formed in recent years to promote economic cooperation and development. The most ambitious of these is the Economic Community of West African States (ECOWAS), a common market formed in 1975 and now composed of sixteen former British, French, and Portuguese colonies that had found themselves competing unnecessarily as individual countries and as linguistic or subregional blocs. Some of the smaller member countries feared initially that Nigeria would dominate ECOWAS and try to turn it into a sphere of economic influence, but in practice the organization functioned relatively democratically. It took early steps toward the establishment of West Africa as an important regional market. In more recent years, ECOWAS explored experimental ideas such as permitting non-oil-producing members suffering from chronic shortages of foreign exchange to barter their products for crude oil from oil-producing member states. There was also an attempt to deal jointly with the problem of pollution along the West African coast, something that individual states with short coastlines could not hope to do for themselves.

Another group with similar aspirations is the Economic Community of Central African States, formed by ten mostly French-speaking countries in 1983 at the suggestion of Omar Bongo, the president of Gabon. Since four of its members are relatively successful oil producers, and the group as a whole has a trade surplus, its prospects for mutually lowering tariffs and otherwise coordinating economic policies were thought to be good. Indeed, it seemed likely that the new Central African organization would lead to the abolition of some smaller, less effective groupings in the region, such as the African "Great Lakes" Community, which had included only giant Zaïre and tiny Rwanda and Burundi.

One organization with a more specialized and urgent purpose is the Permanent Inter-State Committee on Drought Control in the Sahel, the band of semi-arid territory just south of the Sahara. Created by eight countries whose economies had been ravaged by drought, this group hoped to coordinate external aid efforts and to halt the spread of the desert through such controllable human practices as overcultivation, overgrazing, and deforestation. At least 20 percent of Africa's land surface is desert now, and scientists have estimated that unless various forms of "desertification" are halted and land-use patterns change, that figure could rise to

45 percent in fifty years. The Sahel is the frontier where that change would occur.

The Southern African Development Coordination Conference (SADCC) is different from the other regional economic groupings, in that its nine members are specifically trying to ease their vulnerability to economic, political, and military manipulation by South Africa. With a customs union and other forms of economic integration still far off for the black-ruled states of southern Africa, SADCC's early efforts concentrated more on schemes to develop transportation and communication in each of the member countries, so that they would have alternatives to depending on South Africa. (For the time being at least, a country like Lesotho did not dare to disturb the customs union grouping it with South Africa, Botswana, and Swaziland, because it was the source of 70 percent of Lesotho's government revenues.) But with South Africa successfully putting pressure on several SADCC members to modify their political and military policies, the goal of self-sufficiency seemed distant.

Economic integration was obviously an elusive goal in Africa. Many countries had little interest in or need for each other's products, and undertakings to permit the free movement of labor among member states of an organization like ECOWAS backfired on those where conditions were better (as Nigeria learned during the oil boom). Still, the regional economic organizations distinguished themselves from the crumbling fifty-one-member OAU by concentrating on a few real, rather than purely rhetorical issues. International funding organizations like the World Bank were impressed with these attempts at coordination and seemed prepared to take greater risks in Africa as a result.

Quite apart from the chaotic, and often ineffective attempts to achieve intra-African unity and stability, individual African countries and leaders have generally failed to develop stable political institutions or systems of their own that will promote civil order and economic development. The collapse of Nigeria's elaborate new democracy at the end of 1983 was a poignant demonstration that Western-style representative government was not really making dramatic headway in Africa, as previously imagined. At the same time, with a growing number of countries abandoning their Soviet-inspired philosophical and economic structures—Guinea, Congo-Brazzaville, and Mozambique, among others—it became clear that the Communist world had also failed to inspire imitations in Africa. The effort to fashion a uniquely African alternative, perhaps incorporating features of various other systems, simply has not gone far.

As a result, most African countries suffer from chronic political crisis. With few relevant traditions or proven institutions to build upon, many states function on the basis of an ad hoc, easily manipulated, and perilously fragile political structure. The stability of a nation's daily life may depend largely, or even entirely, on the personality and skill of individual leaders. If they are ruthless and cruel like Amin, greedy like Mobutu, or utterly unable to plan ahead like Haile Selassie or, it seems, Houphouët-Boigny, then their countries automatically, if not immediately, face the consequences. If the leadership changes often, as it has in Ghana and Burkina Faso, among other places, then national policy and priorities may shift so unpredictably as to rob a political system of any clear, recognizable character.

Their rhetoric to the contrary notwithstanding, few African leaders have made genuine attempts to develop a politically active citizenry, to involve a broad cross-section of the people in major national decisions. As a result, most countries on the continent, whatever the official ideology, are run by a narrow elite that is aloof from the masses of its own people. The elite tends to keep itself in power through patronage, bribery, and other forms of corruption. Even when angry young rebels come to power, as Samuel Doe and Jerry Rawlings did in Liberia and Ghana respectively, they often find that they must turn eventually to the elite to keep the country running from one day to the next. But so long as political competition and the opportunity to participate in public affairs are so restricted, the ordinary people are bound to distrust their governments.

A number of historical circumstances contribute to Africa's general condition of political underdevelopment. First among them is the colonial legacy. The European colonial powers, for the most part, cared little about constructing stable political institutions that they could pass along at independence. On the contrary, fearing nationalism, they often encouraged the very forces, such as tribalism, that prevented those institutions from developing.

With few exceptions (Nigeria is one), the European rulers

failed to integrate Africans into their colonial administrations or to train indigenous people to take over from them. (Some would contend that this was a deliberate policy and that the French, for example, used it to make sure they would be invited back to run their former colonies.) Another problem inherited from the colonial era is that the political boundaries passed on at independence, while they had once seemed practical as a way of defining European spheres of influence, had little to do with African realities. The grouping of different, sometimes mutually antagonistic tribes and linguistic groups into the same country was bound to cause trouble, as was the mixture of vast and tiny individual states that emerged side by side, especially in West Africa. Many African states are nations in name only, and broader federations would probably make more sense; but few would be likely to find the courage to dilute their sovereignty once they have tasted it.

Tribalism is itself a barrier to the development of national identity and pride in the modern African state. With loyalties still focused on traditional or sectarian leaders, as they are in many African countries, it has been more difficult for modern institutions or structures to assert themselves. In some places, the government has come to be associated with the alienating influence of modernization; thus, in a traditional society like Sudan, a political leader sometimes tries to buttress his authority and assert his legitimacy by reverting to Islamic law and other fundamentalist doctrines.

The surge in educational progress after independence has ironically contributed to political instability in Africa. With so few of the indigenous people having access to higher education at home or abroad during colonial rule, it was natural that there would eventually be a degree boom. The trouble was that only the members of the first wave of that boom had access to the kind of government jobs to which they felt they were entitled. Subsequent generations of educated young Africans have often found themselves unemployed or underemployed, and therefore restless and all the more easily attracted to radical ideologies. Migration to the urban areas by the rural population is a related phenomenon that has accompanied and complicated independence. The larger the cities become, the more quickly social services decline and food becomes scarce, turning many African capitals and provincial centers into cauldrons of discontent. Needless to say, the urban poor are far more easily stirred to protest than disadvantaged people in rural areas. They are also harder to hide.

Many African thinkers have criticized Western analysts for judging African progress on the basis of Eurocentric and sometimes racist standards. But the fact remains that for many African states, the most serious political problem is the absence of any clear succession process. The emergence of charismatic and sometimes ruthless nationalist leaders—the "fathers" of their nations—during the period just before independence was understandable, and it was to be expected that they would want to centralize authority at the start in order to achieve some of their basic objectives. But in far too many cases, the preservation of personal power became a substitute for the advancement of genuine national interests, and it was usually at that stage that the violation of human rights and other forms of political repression were introduced. In the process, many men who had fought for freedom from colonial repression became authoritarian rulers themselves, and before long they were putting their brethren in prison and building up unnecessarily large police and military establishments to help them stay in office. The ruler's opponents, in turn, became convinced that violence was the only way to achieve change, and they were usually right. The syndrome is what Ugandan opposition leader Paul Ssemogerere calls "Africa's real nightmare," and it is hard to imagine a greater threat to development and progress for the continent.

On the basis of more than two decades of experience, it has become easier to define the political formula that seems to improve the performance of independent African countries: a mixed economy; a strong but pragmatic central government led by wise and skillful politicians who know how to accommodate regional, tribal, and other potentially divisive forces; the development of reliable, adjustable institutions; and some degree of public participation in selecting the government and making national decisions. As Ssemogerere has said, "There should be a model of governance that can effectively discourage violence as a means of gaining and retaining power," and African countries must find a way "to make resignation and retirement an attractive option" for their leaders. Whether the mechanism is a traditional one, a multiparty democracy, or some other device still unknown, Africans will have to deal with this problem before they can proceed to solving others.

It will be hard to solve Africa's political crisis in any effective, enduring way without also taking steps to deal with the continent's profound economic crisis. The gravity of Africa's economic difficulties is almost impossible for outsiders to envision, let alone understand.

"Africa is at a low point," said Luis de Azcarate, a World Bank official concerned with sub-Saharan Africa, in February 1984. The majority of African nations are officially classified by the World Bank as "low-income countries." What is worse, their income has declined substantially since independence. Most did less well in the 1970s than in the 1960s, and they have continued to slip further in the 1980s. Should the trend continue, according to the bank's development report for 1983, "there is now a real possibility that [per capita income in Africa overall] will be lower by the end of the 1980s than it was in 1960." Whereas sub-Saharan Africa's gross domestic product (GDP) grew at an average rate of 5 percent a year during the 1960s, that rate declined steadily through the 1970s. By 1982 growth had stopped altogether, and preliminary estimates indicated that Africa's overall GDP shrank 2.3 percent in 1983.

The averages conceal the worst horrors: out of twelve countries in the world that have actually seen their per capita income fall since 1960, nine are in sub-Saharan Africa. With population increasing rapidly in most parts of the continent, the decline is accelerating; African income is in effect racing backward. (The estimated rate of decline in per capita income for 1983 was 5.4 percent.) The volume of Africa's exports is plunging, and the prices its primary products command are the lowest they have been since World War II.

When annual per capita income is less than $300, as it is in eleven African countries, according to the World Bank's figures for 1982, the daily life of the average citizen is very marginal indeed. Often it is not a question of what to eat, but whether there is any food at all, any way of assuring that one's children will survive from one day to the next. It is natural, then, that the average life expectancy at birth in Sierra Leone is thirty-eight years, in Angola forty-three, and in Chad forty-four. Even when local conditions seem to be improving, an economic downturn in the industrial world or a new increase in the price of imported oil, when translated down to the African grass roots, can mean the difference between life and death for tens of thousands of people. There are a few bright spots in recent statistics—Botswana has a growth rate of 11 percent a year, thanks to its diamond mines, and per capita income there has almost reached the $1,000 mark; underpopulated Gabon, because of its rich oil deposits, has achieved a startling per capita income figure of $3,340—but in an important country like Zaïre, run by one of the richest men in the world, the average annual income is still only $170 per person.*

There is no real mystery about how Africa became so poor. Some of the same conditions that led to political instability after independence—in particular, the creation of so many small, separate national economic units—guaranteed financial disaster. The shortage of indigenous administrators, technicians, and entrepreneurs in most countries was an obvious handicap, as was the lack of decent roads and other basic elements of infrastructure. At independence, few people were involved in modern wage-earning activities, and most of those in agriculture were subsistence farmers who could contribute little to the national economy. The geography and climate were mostly inauspicious. Much of the soil was poor and dry and had been improperly cultivated. The terrain was daunting. Tropical conditions encouraged the spread of disease in humans and animals, and discouraged many people from searching for minerals or taking chances with investment. The colonial authorities were indifferent to these problems, or unimaginative in dealing with them.

But some of the blame lies with the poor performance of the new nations themselves. Regardless of the political and economic philosophies they would eventually choose to follow, most African countries made the same early mistakes. They expanded their public sectors too far and too fast; parastatal organizations were in charge of everything from running the railroads and the airlines to setting the prices of agricultural and other commodities. The obvious result was not the hoped-for accountability and con-

* By comparison, the annual per capita income in Libya is $7,500, in Denmark $11,240, in the United States $16,400, and in Switzerland $16,380.

trol over the economy, but inefficiency and corruption in the extreme. Simple transactions that could have been accomplished overnight became matters of great bureaucratic complexity and took weeks or months instead. Paperwork became an end unto itself, and political interference often made it impossible for state enterprises to do anything but drain off dwindling reserves from the national treasury. The newly independent nations tried to cut their high import bills by establishing industries that could manufacture the goods they ordinarily imported, a strategy known as "import substitution." But because these fledgling industries were protected by high tariffs or quotas, they never had reason to become efficient or competitive, and they, too, were a drag on the struggling new economies. The tendency to pour great resources into prestige projects—conference centers, luxury hotels, and the like—compounded an already precarious financial situation.

When the going got rough, the new governments borrowed—in massive quantities. But even when foreign loans and overseas assistance were taken into account, there was usually far too little revenue to cover expenses, and so officials began to fund their nation's deficits by borrowing more from their own banks. That contributed to the already rampant inflation—worse in Africa than in most other parts of the world—which, in turn, tended to lessen the buying power of the local currency. But devaluation was usually resisted as a matter of national pride and as a means of insuring the flow of cheap imports for city dwellers. Instead, the governments simply printed more and more money that was worth less and less, tacitly encouraging the development of black markets on which it was exchanged for hard currency at rates that corresponded more to its real value. On those rare occasions when a surplus did develop in an African nation, it was often squandered on military hardware. In all of Africa, excluding Egypt and Libya, expenditures on arms increased by a factor of thirteen between 1970 and 1979, reaching a total of $2.3 billion at the end of that decade.

But in retrospect, the most critical mistake appears to have been independent Africa's severe neglect of its own agricultural development. Many nationalist leaders regarded the expansion of agriculture for export purposes as an undesirable idea inherited from the colonial powers; it did not seem like the sort of thing that a modern state would do.* Income taxes were hard to impose on rural peasants and impossible to collect from the wealthy urban elite, and so some governments, desperate for new sources of revenue, heavily taxed agricultural exports. They also held down the prices paid to agricultural producers, so that the cities could be guaranteed cheap food. As a result, more and more people flocked to the cities, and those who stayed in the countryside had little incentive to grow food for anyone but themselves.

It was not as if taking the emphasis off agriculture strengthened industry. On the contrary, the further impoverishment of the rural areas and the crowding of unskilled people with high expectations into the urban slums reduced incomes generally. That hurt the domestic market for locally manufactured goods, which could not, in any case, compete effectively with comparable, usually higher-quality products from overseas. Exports grew slowly, so there was little money available for the basic imports necessary to keep local industry functioning; before long, the paltry reserves of foreign exchange were being spent on importing food. Expanding food imports are part of a seemingly endless downward spiral in Africa; they contribute to trade deficits, which in turn worsen the debt burden, making it harder to attract and spend money for future development efforts.

Even when some countries have awakened to the need to improve agriculture, they have gone for large-scale irrigation projects, rather than building up the small-holder farming that offers the promise of going beyond subsistence and contributing to food self-sufficiency. This tendency has been reinforced by publicity-conscious aid donors, both individual countries and multilateral organizations, which focus on technologically advanced, large-scale projects at the expense of old-fashioned, sometimes primitive agriculture. In the Sahel, for example, small-scale, rain-fed farming is responsible for 95 percent of the local grain production, but gets only 25 percent of the aid; the rest goes to irrigation schemes, which have done little or nothing to improve the region's food production. In fact, most studies have shown that where agricul-

---

* Kwame Nkrumah called agriculture "a code word for bondage." Ghana's leading crop, cocoa, he said, was "contaminated by capitalism."

tural successes have been achieved in Africa—in Ivory Coast, Kenya, Malawi, Zimbabwe, and Cameroon, for example—they have been mostly on small farms.

For many African economies that had been limping along through the 1970s, a major blow came at the end of that decade in the form of the second wave of oil price increases. The prices of many minerals and other commodities exported by African nations fell at the same time, so their incomes went down while their expenses were going up. When the dust settled, the terms of trade had seriously deteriorated for most African countries. Oil gluts later caused prices to slump, and that offered a bit of relief to the poorest countries, but at the same time made things harder for African oil exporters like Nigeria. The ensuing world recession of the early 1980s hurt Africa once again. The markets for African exports contracted, so there was a new shortage of the foreign exchange necessary to pay for imports. Local manufacturing slowed down, cutting government revenues, which in turn caused existing development projects to deteriorate for lack of maintenance. With foreign currency reserves low (most countries had enough to cover about two months' worth of imports at a time), African governments had to borrow still more and slow down their repayment of old debts.

That kind of vulnerability in the world marketplace has led Africans to join others from the Third World in pressing for the creation of a "new international economic order," a fundamental restructuring that would stabilize commodity prices and transfer some of the wealth of the industrialized North to the developing South. Serious international discussions were held on this issue from time to time, including the major "North-South summit" in Cancun, Mexico, in 1981, but little progress was made, especially after some of the industrialized countries began to experience their own financial hardships and conservative economic philosophies came to the fore in the United States, Great Britain, West Germany, and elsewhere.

Lacking new international economic rules, which do not seem to be anywhere on the near horizon, most African countries have been forced to rely on the International Monetary Fund, which invariably attached strict conditions to its credit agreements with Third World governments. Typically, the IMF requires a country getting its help, regardless of its economic system, to create free-market conditions. It must devalue its currency, freeze wages, increase prices of local agricultural products, cut consumer subsidies, raise interest rates, and decrease imports. IMF-imposed austerity measures generally cause hardship, not to mention riots in the streets, and they often create further resentment against the international financial system and the Western nations that dominate it. As Tanzanian President Julius Nyerere, an opponent of the organization, said late in 1983, "When did the IMF become an international ministry of finance? When did nations agree to surrender to it their power of decision making?"

Yet a growing number of African nations have had no choice but to accept the IMF's terms, especially because many donor countries and private banks have also begun to insist that a country have the IMF seal of approval before it can qualify for their grants or loans. But some sign with the IMF and then have a hard time meeting its conditions. Seven African countries, including Tanzania, ran afoul of the IMF's stringent guidelines in 1982 alone, and for a time grants that had already been awarded to them were cut off. Even those who have complied may have problems meeting their economic growth targets or keeping their budget deficits and inflation rates within acceptable limits. Critics of the fund argue that this is because the IMF cannot, through its recommendation of austerity or by any other means, change the structural features of the world economy that reinforce and perpetuate underdevelopment in the Third World. On the contrary, they contend, the IMF has tended to preserve that structure.

If there is a reasonable substitute for the IMF approach, it is not yet publicly known or, more important, funded. A number of countries may soon experience life without the IMF, however, since the Western nations, led by the United States, have cut back on their contributions and there will be less to go around.

One of the most chilling stories to come out of Africa in recent years, as reported by the *Christian Science Monitor*, relates to a diplomatic reception at the American embassy in the capital of a small West African country. When the food arrived, the formality of the occasion dissolved into chaos. The African guests, some of them government officials or professionals, grabbed as much food as they could and stuffed it into bags to take home with them. It was an awkward moment for the hosts. Many of the guests were being impolite and some greedy, but the underlying truth of the matter was that most them were simply hungry.

That is how bad things have become in the wake of Africa's severest drought within memory. The last period of good rains in the Sahel occurred in 1968, and the cumulative effect in that region has been tragic. Mauritania, for example, produced food to cover only one-tenth of its needs in 1983 and was expected to do worse in 1984. Ghana, wracked by political and economic chaos and stretched to the limit by the return of hundreds of thousands of people expelled from Nigeria, had many of its crops destroyed by a virtual epidemic of brush fires; when emergency food supplies did arrive, it was hard to get them to the villages that needed them most, because Ghana's roads had deteriorated to the point of being impassable and there was not enough fuel and spare parts to keep supply trucks moving. In some badly stricken parts of northern Ethiopia, there are no roads at all; where there are, the fighting between government forces and insurgents often makes it impossible for relief convoys to get through. Zimbabwe's 1983 maize crop was half its normal size, and Namibia has lost much of its livestock. Even South Africa, a land of surplus, had to import corn in 1983. In Mozambique, at least one hundred thousand people have died in a famine and tens of thousands more have left their villages in the interior to wander aimlessly about the country in search of food.

The growing African famine was scarcely noticed in the West until a five-minute video tape on conditions in Ethiopia was broadcast in Britain and the United States in October 1984. Suddenly the images of emaciated children stirred governments and private organizations to action, and before long the international community was awakening to the extent of the crisis: more than twenty countries requiring millions of tons of food to prevent rampant starvation. The United Nations Development Program spoke of a need for billions of dollars in outside contributions, and the Food and Agriculture organization predicted the problem would extend well beyond 1985. One Washington research group, The Worldwatch Institute, issued a report warning that population growth and soil erosion in Africa would cause the situation to become steadily worse for the rest of the twentieth century.

One major problem, of course, is the inability of meteorologists to predict accurately the continuation, the end, or the recurrence of drought conditions. Thus, it is hard to prepare for emergencies or to take steps to prevent starvation. African nations have simply come to live with the knowledge that their margin of survival gets thinner all the time, and that every environmental catastrophe has a bitter price in lives. Scientific studies have shown that some of the climatic disasters may be caused or at least exacerbated by human activities. Nomadic peoples have overgrazed the land available to them. Forests have been stripped for fuel. More than half of the world's uncultivated farmland is in Africa, yet fertile soil is now becoming exhausted and depleted, because population pressures prevent it from lying fallow long enough; fertilizers are often unknown or unaffordable. As dryness prevents the normal growth of plants and trees, ground water evaporates more rapidly and erosion becomes more severe. Foreign assistance has scarcely touched these fundamental ecological and land-use problems.

Africa's drought and its other economic miseries have naturally been accompanied by severe health problems. The continent's high birth rate becomes more understandable in light of its infant mortality rate—in the tropical parts of Africa, 155 per 1,000, the highest in the world. Children under five represent about 15 percent of Africa's population, but in all parts of the continent except southern Africa they represent 50 percent or more of all reported deaths. The leading cause of illness and death in African children is diarrhea, mostly caused by parasites, bacteria, and viruses. In the developed world, diarrheal disease is relatively easy to cure, but in Africa the problem is complicated by poor sanitation and a lack of diagnostic and treatment capabilities. Most of the 1.5 million deaths in the world from malaria each year occur in the tropical zones of Africa, and again it is children who are most at risk. In addition, African children are frequent victims of measles, polio, meningitis, and tuberculosis. Hepatitis has also become a common African illness. Vaccines are readily available to treat some of these diseases, but delivery to those who need them is difficult because of a break in the "cold-storage chain"; refrigeration is unavailable in most parts of rural Africa.

One indicator of economic and social development in some African countries, as in other nations of the Third World, is increased cigarette consumption. That, in turn, brings an increase in lung cancer and other smoking-related diseases, stressing health-care systems in a new way.

The paucity of medical personnel is still a problem in Africa as well. In 1970 the continent had only 1.36 doctors per 10,000 population, the lowest ratio in the world. The figure has improved since, but not nearly enough to meet fundamental needs. Indeed, many young Africans who go abroad to medical school, with the help of scholarships from their governments, end up staying over-seas where they can practice sophisticated modern medicine rather than coming back home where they often face grim conditions and depressing prospects. Doctors are a significant part of the intellectual exodus that complicates Africa's needs.

Despite scientific advances, hunger and poor nutrition have made Africans more vulnerable to infectious diseases and other serious illness in recent years. The pathetic signs of protein defi-ciency in children—swollen stomachs, pencil-thin arms, and yel-lowing or reddening hair—are becoming a more frequent sight in African villages. Blindness is also an increasing problem, often the result of a chronic deficiency of vitamin A. In addition, the World Health Organization (WHO) reports an alarming growth of anemia, generally brought on by iron deficiency, among preg-nant women in the Third World, but especially in Africa. (One out of six women between the ages of fifteen and forty-nine in the developing world is pregnant, according to WHO, compared to one out of seventeen in developed countries.)

Livestock diseases seemed to be under control in most Afri-can countries during the early years of independence, but veteri-nary services and education have fallen into neglect, and so rin-derpest, the major infectious disease afflicting cattle, has once again become a menace. Similarly, a lack of money for pesticides has led to renewed infestation of crops by insects; one major vic-tim is cassava, a turnip-like root that is the staple food of many poor people in Africa.

One problem complicates all the other aspects of Africa's political, economic, health, and social crisis: refugees. One of every two hundred Africans is a refugee, and in Somalia the ratio is thought to be as high as one in seven. Barely able to meet the needs of their own people, African governments are continually faced with hordes of others who pour across their borders, usually without warning. Nonetheless, according to the United Nations High Commissioner for Refugees (whose office provides financial support for most of the refugees), African countries have been uncommonly tolerant of refugee influxes, in part because the borders inherited from colonial times were not true dividing lines in the first place; those who flee may still be welcomed by members of their own ethnic group. Indeed, some people who are merely "displaced" within their own countries, but do not fit the formal definition of refugees, may be living in more alien circumstances than others who have actually crossed borders, so the refugee problem is even greater and more complex in Africa than the official statistics indicate.

In a few countries—again, Somalia is a leading example—international refugee assistance may allow a higher standard of living for the new arrivals than that enjoyed by the permanent residents of a nation. As a result, to avoid social tensions, local inhabitants have to be incorporated into refugee welfare programs. In the more typical case, however, local resources are simply strained further until refugees can be repatriated or achieve self-sufficiency in their new environments.

"We are undergoing a second colonization," a Tanzanian professor complained to *Time* magazine recently. "Our present leaders are just like the old tribal chiefs who signed pacts with colonizers for a few beads. Friendship and military pacts are now penciled up in return for guns, aid, or cash loans. Africa is up for grabs."

Certainly the current generation of African leadership, while often quite opportunistic, is far more wary than the helpless elders who during preceding centuries bargained away ancestral lands in exchange for trinkets. But it is true that Africa today is uniquely dependent on outside interest and investment for its survival from one disaster to the next, and anyone who did not know a great deal about the intervening history could be excused for concluding that nothing much has changed since the colonial era. In some cases, things have changed—for the worse—and then reverted to an earlier stage.

This is an especially tempting conclusion to reach in some of the former French colonies in Africa. There are twice as many Frenchmen living in Africa now as there were just before independence, many of them in key management positions in government and business. In Libreville, the booming capital of Gabon, a quarter of the population is French, and in Ivory Coast they are estimated to hold 80 percent of the jobs requiring college degrees. Even after the installation of a socialist government in Paris at the beginning of the 1980s, France remained the primary defender of the status quo in francophone Africa. More than ten thousand of its troops are stationed in various parts of the continent, and it was only after the government of François Mitterrand, with some prodding from Washington, drew the line on Libyan expansion into Chad in the summer of 1983 that the regime of Hissene Habre managed to stay in power there.

Doubtless most of the countries that have welcomed a continuing French presence reaped genuine benefits in terms of political stability and limited economic progress, but some have also sacrificed flexibility. French business has had a competitive advantage in those nations, because of the common language and a currency tied to the French franc. It is widely assumed that French nationals working in African governments pass inside information to their compatriots in business. As a result, other potential investors and trading partners stay away, rather than help some of these small countries diversify their economic relations.

For some years it seemed as if the only real competition for the French in Africa was coming from the Soviet Union and its Cuban and Libyan surrogates. It was dogma in American foreign policy during the 1970s that Soviet influence was rising to a danger point in Africa and posing a serious threat to Western interests. Some U.S. officials conjured up a map of Africa on which a number of countries that were important for different reasons—including Angola, Mozambique, Guinea, and Ethiopia—were colored red, because putatively Marxist regimes were in power there and had signed various agreements with the Kremlin.

It was true, of course, that the Soviet Union had an early advantage in Africa, having publicly and forcefully identified itself with anticolonial aspirations long before the United States did, and having supported the push for black-majority rule in southern Africa early on. But apart from the initial Soviet intervention in the civil war in Zaïre (then the post-Belgian Congo) during the 1960s, and its direct involvement, at different times, on both sides of the fighting in the Horn, there were few instances where Soviet military personnel actually set foot on the continent. To be sure, Moscow frequently provided arms to African nationalist movements and underwrote the massive Cuban presence in Angola and Ethiopia, but Soviet and Cuban actions and goals in Africa were not always congruent.

Increasingly, as the Soviets proved to be parsimonious with economic aid to their presumed African clients, those countries turned toward Western sources and connections instead; their rhetoric often stayed the same, while their actions changed dramatically. The Soviets sometimes justified their lack of concern for Africa's economic predicament by arguing that it was a colonial legacy and therefore not their worry; but the real reason may have been a desire to preserve their own reserves of hard currency. Many Africans who had contact with Soviet advisers and technicians in their countries, like others before them who studied at Patrice Lumumba University in Moscow, complained that the Soviets actually behaved like the worst racists of the colonial era and had a great deal of trouble understanding African realities or priorities.

The Chinese have been far more successful in Africa on a personal level, in part because they style themselves as citizens of the Third World who can understand and identify with the peasants and other poor people in Africa's developing nations. China has devoted half of its entire foreign aid budget to Africa in recent years, and while some of that money has gone for military purposes, most of it is for less visible but more essential development projects at the grass roots. The Chinese were willing to take risks where the West was not—for example, by funding and building the TanZam Railroad through Tanzania and Zambia after traditional donors had refused to do so. As an indication of the significance that China places on Africa, Premier Zhao Ziyang spent a month touring the continent in early 1983, exploring commercial relations and other issues. If any philosophy could be said to guide China's choice of African friends, however, it was probably anti-Sovietism. Thus, despite the risk of ideological inconsistency, Beijing developed close ties with the conservative traditionalist regimes in Zaïre, Somalia, and Morocco, not to mention the South African–supported UNITA movement of Jonas Savimbi in Angola.

At the same time, the Chinese maintained a major stake in Tanzania and Mozambique, despite those countries' friendship with the Soviet Union.

The most significant comeback of the early 1980s in Africa was actually made by Israel. In the early days of African independence, the Israelis had a major presence on the continent, building large hotels and government quarters, training military units, and sharing the agricultural expertise gained in the cultivation of the Negev desert. But many African states broke relations with Israel after it seized the Egyptian-held Sinai peninsula—officially regarded as African soil—during the Six-Day War of 1967, and still others did so after the Arab-Israeli conflict of 1973. In black African states with a large Islamic population, there was a growing feeling of solidarity with the Arab, and especially the Palestinian, cause; the North African presence in the OAU created substantial pressure on other African leaders, leading them to believe that hostility toward Israel might earn them a guaranteed supply of oil and extensive new aid from wealthy Arab oil-producing countries.

That aid mostly failed to materialize, however, and it became more difficult to maintain pro-Arab feelings in Africa as rising oil prices devastated one economy after another. The military adventures and territorial ambitions of Muammar al-Qaddafi also hurt the Arab cause in Africa and led many countries to look again at Israel as a potential friend, notwithstanding the substantial ties that had developed between Israel and South Africa during the 1970s. Israel resumed surreptitious commercial relations with black-ruled African states over time, but it became more feasible to conduct those dealings openly after Israel returned the Sinai peninsula to Egypt in 1982. The major breakthrough came the next year, when Zaïre reestablished diplomatic relations with Israel, just at a time when the U.S. Congress was cutting American aid to the Mobutu regime because of human rights abuses. Israel, eager to extend its acceptance and influence in the Third World, provided Zaïre advanced military assistance and training and, in a peculiar twist, put its excellent contacts on Capitol Hill in Washington at Mobutu's service. Ironically, Mobutu's gesture pleased and outmaneuvered the United States at the same time.

Liberia followed Zaïre's lead, with an eye not only on military training and development assistance, but also on Israel's intelligence information about Qaddafi's activities in West Africa. A number of other African nations, including Ivory Coast, Cameroon, and Kenya, were said to be considering reestablishment of relations with Israel, but felt constrained to move slowly. Israel was especially eager to have a formal relationship with Nigeria, but the strong Moslem influence in that country made it an elusive goal; nonetheless, most of the four thousand Israeli technicians working in Africa were believed to be in Nigeria, helping revive its agricultural sector. Israeli President Chaim Herzog's visit to Zaïre and Liberia early in 1984, the first such trip in twenty years, was a symbolic statement of Israel's new acceptability on the continent.

Another indication of the growing complexity of Africa's international relations—and its desperation for aid from any source— is the enthusiastic welcome that has been given in recent years to representatives of former European colonial powers who had especially bad records on the continent, including Germany, Portugal, and Spain. The ceremonial president of West Germany, Carl Carstens, for example, visited Niger and Ivory Coast in 1983 to demonstrate support for their conservative governments and join their warnings about Libyan expansionism. A number of African governments would like to take advantage of German nostalgia for the continent by obtaining aid from the Bonn government. Portugal is hardly in a position to offer much aid, but its socialist government took on a role as mediator between South Africa and the former Portuguese colonies of Angola and Mozambique.

Japan, sensing excellent commercial opportunities, also began to take a greater interest in Africa. For business reasons, the Japanese had long been accorded the status of "honorary whites" in South Africa, but now they understood the necessity of diversifying their relationships on the continent.

None of these resumed or expanded contacts guaranteed Africa more sympathetic consideration and assistance from the major actors on the world scene, however. On the contrary, with Africa seemingly relegated to the status of a strategic backwater, far from the center of international confrontation and diplomacy, its problems were easily overlooked or ignored. Not surprisingly, they became worse.

By comparison to almost every other region of the developing world, Africa's postindependence record looked dismal. It was the only part of the Third World whose per capita food production actually declined during the decade of the 1970s. Whereas expenditure on debt consumed 8.7 percent of the gross domestic product of low-income Asian countries in 1983, that figure was 42.2 percent for similarly placed nations in Africa. Fewer than 10 percent of married African women are estimated to be using modern methods of contraception, and so Africa's population problem is by far the world's worst in the long run. African governments also seem to be doing less about it than others; the per capita expenditure on population control programs in sub-Saharan Africa during 1980 was only 29 cents, compared to an average of 62 cents per capita in developing countries generally. Half the population of the Third World is now thought to be literate, but in Africa only a third of the adult population has achieved literacy. The average life expectancy in Africa in 1982 was forty-nine years; according to the World Bank, this was "ten years less than in other countries at the same income level" elsewhere in the world.

In 1984, the World Bank established a new program and a special office to deal with Africa's grave difficulties. "While Africa faces deep-seated problems," said Ernest Stern, the bank's senior vice-president for operations at the time, "the combination of strong action on policy reforms, coupled with appropriate external support, can, in our view, turn the situation around . . . in a relatively short period of time." Many close observers of Africa viewed that projection with great skepticism.

A number of European countries became alarmed in the late 1980s about Africa's slide into the economic abyss. François Mitterrand, just after his reelection as president of France in 1988, offered to cancel a third of the debts owed to his country by African nations with per capita incomes of less than $500 a year. When the issue was taken up at the annual Western economic summit in Toronto a few weeks later, other countries said they would consider doing the same, or at least reduce interest rates or extend repayment schedules on existing loans to the poorest African governments.

Meanwhile, there were grave warnings of famines yet to come in Africa. Drought conditions made it difficult for most governments to recuperate from the 1984–85 crisis and made a mockery of some countries' best-intentioned agricultural policy reforms, which had not yet had an opportunity to work. Moreover, the UN Food and Agriculture Organization (FAO) said that as vast swarms of locusts infesting North Africa moved south into the Sahel, they could destroy as much as a third of the food crops in such countries as Senegal, Burkina Faso, Mali, Niger, and Chad. Unless the African governments organized public information campaigns to teach people in remote areas to spot and report the swarms of locusts, the FAO warned, tons of crops could be destroyed in a matter of days.

The fight against such nature-induced problems is hampered in Africa by three complicated and complementary issues: wars, arguments over the effect of pesticides on the environment, and painful decisions about priorities in times of economic crisis. The latest plague of locusts appears to have developed in Sudan, where the areas worst afflicted were unreachable because of the civil war; as they spread to Ethiopia, Chad, and Western Sahara, the locusts were again protected because they were in zones of military conflict. The agent most effective against locusts, dieldrin, is banned in the United States and some other countries, because it is believed to be a carcinogen that ends up in milk and other foods once it enters the life cycle of plants and animals. Some development experts contend that since substitute pesticides are less useful, Africa cannot afford the luxury of Western-style environmentalism; but just pausing to argue over the matter causes a critical loss of time. In any event, the West African regional locust-control center, based in Dakar, suffered a financial crisis so severe that it suspended operations early in 1988. Its member states, hard-pressed at home on more fundamental problems, simply could not afford to keep such a cooperative effort going.

If Africa needed any new problems to worry about, it found one in 1988: the dumping of Western nations' toxic wastes in some of the poorest continent's very poorest countries, often with the complicity of African government officials and local entrepreneurs. Guinea, for example, discovered that 15,000 tons of incinerator ash from Philadelphia had been deposited on an offshore island by a Norwegian ship; it arrested a Norwegian honorary consul and held him until the government in Oslo agreed to remove the ash. Three Congolese government officials were arrested after they were found to have signed a contract with a New Jersey firm that would permit the dumping of up to 50,000 tons of pesticide residue and sludge a month. A similar scheme was said to be under consideration in Benin, and a ship with more ash from Philadelphia was reported to be heading for the Cape Verde Islands.

As is often the case, it was Nigeria that brought this problem to the attention of other Africans, complaining that this was hardly an appropriate way for countries to solve their financial problems. At a meeting of the OAU, the Nigerian foreign minister singled out Guinea and Guinea-Bissau for accepting waste that amounted to an "attack on Africa's dignity." Only a few days later, Lagos newspapers revealed that Nigeria was itself actually a major importer of toxic waste. Reporters found that a dump in a Niger River port town contained 3,800 tons of waste from Italy, including 150 tons of dangerous polychlorinated biphenyl, or PCB. In the uproar that followed, a spokesman for President Ibrahim Babangida said that anyone found guilty of such outrages in Nigeria in the future would risk execution by firing squad.

The symbolism of Africa's new role as a dumping ground for refuse from the developed nations was especially poignant and upsetting.

13

AIDS in Africa .

THE VISITOR to a major African capital had a startling experience when he was taken out to dinner by his host, a physician at the local university hospital, in mid-1987. Nearly everyone in the city's best restaurant seemed to know the man and greeted him enthusiastically—not just the other patrons, including businessmen, lawyers, and government officials, but also the entire staff. At each stop along the sumptuous buffet, he was treated as a celebrity. Waiters tripped over each other to make him welcome and comfortable. His table was constantly visited during dinner. Finally, as his guest looked at him in puzzlement about the obsequious display, he leaned over and explained in a confidential tone: "They're all my patients. They all have AIDS."

Such an experience was not uncommon in the late 1980s in many of the major cities of Central and East Africa, where between 8 and 10 percent of the urban population is believed to be infected with the human immunodeficiency virus (HIV) that causes AIDS. It is the particular pattern of AIDS in Africa that has immobilized health systems and panicked those in charge of

managing the economies: because the disease appears to be transmitted primarily through heterosexual practices and blood transfusions, women and men are affected in almost equal numbers, as
are virtually all socioeconomic groups in the urban areas. Thus,
many nations risk the imminent loss of a significant number of
both blue-collar and white-collar workers, not to mention some of
the most highly educated and productive members of their elite.
The consequences for economic development and social order are
profound.

The short history of AIDS in Africa, and of knowledge and
research about it, is very troubled. The first reports that the continent might have a serious problem with the disease appeared in
the Western scientific literature only in late 1983 and early 1984,
well after alarm had begun to spread in the United States and
other developed countries about a syndrome that appeared to
infect primarily homosexual men, hemophiliacs, intravenous drug
abusers, and Haitian immigrants.

In fact, the first known African cases of AIDS were identified
two years earlier among well-to-do Africans visiting or living in
Europe, whose symptoms were similar to those of Haitians with
the disease. But investigation soon revealed substantial numbers
of people with AIDS or seemingly related afflictions and symptoms in such cities as Kinshasa and Kigali, the capitals of Zaïre
and Rwanda respectively. And once more information was available for comparison, it became clear that "slim disease," a wasting, life-threatening illness that had begun to sweep through
Uganda, and to a lesser extent Tanzania, during the early 1980s
was probably AIDS. Eventually, more than 80 percent of prostitutes in Nairobi tested positive for HIV; indeed, the rapid spread
of the virus among that high-risk group in Kenya's booming capital has been compared to the earlier situation among homosexual
men in San Francisco. In Zambia, after the revelation that President Kenneth Kaunda's son had died of AIDS, any remaining
complacency about the disease quickly disappeared.

Yet at first, the attempts to analyze and understand AIDS in
Africa came across to some people (especially to sensitive African
political leaders) as an effort to assign responsibility for an international problem to the poorest continent, and later, almost in
missionary fashion, to stigmatize Africans for their social behavior.
Indeed, certain researchers hypothesized at one stage that HIV

had actually originated in Africa, having mutated from a virus commonly found among African green monkeys, also known as vervets. How it was thought to spread to humans was never entirely clear, although one theory implicated bites from pet monkeys and the exposure to blood and internal secretions that might occur during the preparation of monkeys for smoking or other forms of cooking in some societies. Beneath the science lurked the implication of some bizarre and improper form of contact between humans and animals in Africa.

The argument that AIDS had come from Africa was buttressed for a time by the discovery that blood serum specimens frozen and banked years (or even decades) earlier in several African countries showed a high prevalence of weakly positive results in HIV tests, which were admittedly still in their early stages of refinement. One suggestion was that the disease had lain dormant and undetected in Africa for many years. (It later turned out that similar results could also be produced with specimens banked in the United States as early as the late 1950s and the 1960s, but it was very difficult to evaluate the significance of such retrospective findings.)

Although there was no reason to believe that such speculation about Africa as the birthplace of this modern-day scourge was explicitly motivated by racism, Africans often interpreted it that way and reacted angrily. As they saw it, AIDS had first come to light as a symptom of decadent Western behavior, particularly in the United States, and this was just an effort to use scientific verbiage to pass the buck and blame the victims. (This attitude no doubt made Africans particularly susceptible to belief in the theory—whose origin appears to lie with disinformation spread by the KGB, the Soviet intelligence agency—that HIV was actually manufactured by the U.S. Army in a germ-warfare laboratory at Fort Detrick, Maryland, with the specific intent of using it against blacks and other minorities at home and in the Third World. To this day, many sophisticated and well-educated Africans stand by that explanation for the international AIDS pandemic.)

However temporary the credibility given to the African-monkey-virus theory about the origin of AIDS, it had the effect of putting a stigma on Africans living abroad. After it was revealed publicly that seven African students in India had tested positive for HIV, there was an outbreak of public hysteria: university officials immediately expelled several Kenyan students, and others from Tanzania, after having their beds and eating utensils destroyed, were put under police surveillance and then driven out of the town where they were studying and eventually forced to return home. All 16,000 foreign students in India, more than half of them Africans, were soon required to be tested for the AIDS virus, a move that provoked public demonstrations and many instances of private discrimination. In Belgium, where more than half the known AIDS cases involved Zaïrians, all African students must be tested (and are often expelled if they test positive); the many Belgians who routinely travel back and forth to their former colony of Zaïre are not subjected to the same requirement on their return to Belgium, however. In Cuba and some East European countries, African students testing positive for HIV have often been sent home. And Egypt, always on uneasy terms with its African neighbors, apparently refused entry to a handball team from Cameroon until its members could prove they were not AIDS carriers.

African physicians and clinical investigators were rarely included in the early scientific meetings or written symposia examining the nature of the disease on their own continent. (It was September 1988 before the first such meeting was held in Africa.) As outside scientists struggled to understand and explain the spread of AIDS in Africa, they produced other, questionable theories. For a time, it was fashionable to suggest that HIV was spread by insects common in tropical areas, such as mosquitoes and bedbugs. Another focus was on certain African cultural practices, such as female circumcision and infibulation, ritual scarification, and the therapeutic bloodletting and enemas administered by traditional doctors among some tribal groups. Because of the unhygienic circumstances associated with these practices and the likelihood of exposure to contaminated blood, it was argued, Africans would likely be at greater risk to AIDS than others might be. However, the data actually demonstrated little direct correlation between these practices and the disease—largely because such customs are now more prevalent in rural areas and AIDS, with a few exceptions, is more common in African cities.

Another sensitive issue in the study of AIDS in Africa involved accusations of greater sexual promiscuity on the part of Africans than other people. Understandably, given the pattern of the disease's spread in the West, researchers at first looked for evidence of homosexual or bisexual practices in the countries most seriously affected. But although homosexuality is thought to be common in the all-male compounds of migrant labor camps and in situations like the South African mines (where workers are separated from their families for long periods of time), it is still illegal in many African countries and there seems to be less of the overt, sequential homosexual activity found in other parts of the world. Africans are, in any event, reluctant to talk about the subject. (Male prostitutes are active in cities like Nairobi, however, and most scholars acknowledge that this is an issue on which little research has been done, in part because of the cultural and political obstacles to getting accurate information.) And the disease seems to spread in Africa primarily by heterosexual intercourse.

What does appear to be true among heterosexuals, as among homosexuals—in Africa as elsewhere—is that people who have a large number of sexual partners are more likely than monogamous individuals to contract AIDS. It is no secret that in many of the affected African countries, prosperous upper- and middle-class men, among others, tend to have many sexual liaisons at the same time, whether or not they are married. Indeed, among the elite of Zaïre and Rwanda, it is commonly joked that men often take a long time to arrive home from work because they must make a stop at their *"deuxième bureau,"* or "second office." Some confide that their schedule becomes especially complicated when they have to fit in occasional visits to their *troisième* (third) or *quatrième* (fourth) as well. In Kenya, polygamous marriages are still quite common among the Kikuyu and other groups, and women are traditionally not considered marriageable until they have become pregnant. There, as in other countries, prostitutes do a thriving business with both a local and tourist clientele.

It would be a difficult task to prove conclusively that all of this amounts to greater promiscuity than exists in, say, Paris, Rome, Bangkok, Manila, Rio, or even New York. What can be said, however, is that other sexually transmitted diseases, such as genital ulcers and chlamydia, are rampant in African cities, and the medical disruptions associated with those diseases may cause increased susceptibility to the transmission of AIDS. In one African study, a third of AIDS patients said they had had at least one sexually transmitted disease during the three years preceding their illness.

Despite the widespread suffering from AIDS in Africa and the obvious need for outside help, for several years many countries were reluctant to make information available or to cooperate with international study of the disease. Furious over being made scapegoats, they reacted by denying there was a problem. In late 1986, only seven African nations were willing to submit official figures on AIDS cases to the World Health Organization (WHO); a year later, thirty-six countries on the continent were cooperating with WHO, but it was not clear how many governments were truly prepared to take the political risks associated with an aggressive AIDS reporting and prevention program. Some regimes were apparently worried about the effects on tourism if they were publicly candid about AIDS. In a few instances, they accused Western scientists of obtaining and publishing information about the epidemiology of the disease in Africa without permission, creating a "scientific black market."

African diplomats are still reluctant to talk openly about the subject, and a few African scientists have reinforced that reticence with claims that the problem of AIDS in Africa was being blown out of proportion by the Western media. One West African physician working in London wrote to the British medical journal, *The Lancet,* in mid-1987 that after a six-week tour of twenty-six cities and towns in sixteen sub-Saharan countries, he had found no basis for the widespread hysteria and was convinced that AIDS was nowhere near becoming a catastrophe in Africa. "Why do the world's media appear to have conspired with some scientists to become so gratuitously extravagant with the untruth?" he asked, concluding that "journalistic hyperbole" was once again doing great harm to Africa.

It is almost certainly true that some outsiders have been shrill and have exaggerated the place of AIDS on the list of serious public health problems in Africa. As to morbidity and mortality, malaria, diarrheal diseases, and malnutrition still stand as greater threats on the continent, as in other parts of the Third World, at this time. But it would be foolish to underestimate the scope or the urgency of the AIDS issue in Africa, or to lose any time in dealing with it.

The exact number of cases in Africa is not known. WHO officially counted 14,000 people with AIDS in Africa as of July 1988, but the agency itself admitted that the true figure might be ten times that; and some researchers believe that upwards of 5 million Africans may now be infected with HIV.* In Uganda, which has been more open to discussion of the issue than most, the number of acknowledged cases went from 17 in 1983 and 29 in 1984 to 1,138 in 1987; according to some speculation, half of all Ugandan adults may have AIDS by the year 2000. In one hospital in Central Africa, more than a third of the patients in internal medicine wards have AIDS, and another, in Zaïre, reports that a quarter of its recorded deaths are now related to the disease. Perhaps most worrisome of all is the dramatic growth in the rate of AIDS infection among children, many of whom are infected before or at birth. Between 2 and 15 percent of pregnant women test positive for HIV in some areas of Central and East Africa, and a Nairobi study showed that more than half of the infants born to virus-infected mothers had HIV antibodies at birth. In one hospital serving the poor of Kinshasa, the death rate within the first few months of life of babies born to women who tested positive for HIV was almost twenty times higher than it was among those born to women who tested negative.

One of the most compelling explanations for at least part of the spread of AIDS in Africa is also one of the simplest—that the disease has followed the path of the heavy trucks that haul food and other material from the Indian Ocean ports of Mombasa, Kenya, and Dar es Salaam, Tanzania, into the interior of the continent. From Mombasa, the trucks head northwest to Nairobi and then on around Lake Victoria into Uganda, Rwanda, and Burundi; from Dar es Salaam, southwest across Tanzania and then the full length of Zambia. Along the way, there are plenty of bars and prostitutes catering specifically to the rough-and-tough drivers; at least 30 percent of the drivers tested, according to some reports, are infected with HIV. To the extent that this urban disease has reached small towns and rural areas, they invariably lie along or near the truck routes. One particularly poignant and pathetic ex-

---

* By contrast, the number of people in the United States thought to be infected with the virus stood between 1.5 and 2 million in 1988, and there were about 70,000 actual AIDS cases.

ample is the Rakai district in southeastern Uganda, where AIDS
has affected entire villages and people desperately turn to itiner-
ant prophets for a miracle cure.

Another, less systematic means of spread into remote regions
relates to the tradition in some countries that the widow of a dead
man must return to the village of her birth. Since many such
widows today are young and may carry the AIDS virus themselves, they are quite likely to pass it along further after they return home. The facilities for diagnosis and treatment are, of course,
less adequate in rural areas than in the cities, and so the reporting
of cases is bound to be less reliable. It is when the disease is widely
disseminated through an entire country that genuine devastation
will result.

But nowhere in Africa—in urban or rural areas, in large countries or small—has anyone been equipped so far to handle the
magnitude of the AIDS problem. Some nations still have only one
doctor for every 25,000 people and ordinarily spend an average of
$10 per person per year, or even less, on all health-care costs. (In
Tanzania, where rural health care is better than in most African
countries, the per capita budget for health is down to $1 a year.)
Just the test to confirm a single suspected case of HIV infection
now costs about $20, and the price of caring for ten AIDS patients
in the United States (some $450,000) is more than the entire an-
nual budget of a large hospital in Zaïre.

The cost of the tests most frequently used to screen for HIV—
and the time they take to perform—are a major barrier to dealing
with one of the most common sources of the disease, AIDS-infected
blood donors and contaminated blood. Transfusions are used very
widely (almost recklessly) in Africa, sometimes as a substitute for
expensive medications that cannot be obtained; since blood banks
may be limited or nonexistent, relatives of people who are seriously ill or about to have surgery will often turn up at the hospital
to make their blood available on the spot. Yet if the blood being
transfused is not to be trusted, it may create more problems than
it solves. WHO, as part of its ambitious program for dealing with
AIDS in Africa, has provided money to some countries for the
screening of blood donors, but what is really needed is the development of a reliable new, cheap, rapid HIV test. (One test that
has been developed in the United States and employed experi-

mentally in Zaïre takes only five or ten minutes to perform and can be done in the operating room; its cost is less than half that of the ELISA or Western Blot tests commonly used around the world, but unfortunately, it also seems to be considerably less accurate.)

For the time being, the major focus and the main hope for dealing with AIDS in Africa lies with public education about the disease and how it is spread. In several countries, graphic posters and simply written pamphlets warning about AIDS have been widely disseminated, with some success. In Uganda, the slogan that seems to have caught on is "Love Carefully." The Family Life Movement of Zambia, with the cooperation of that country's ministry of health, distributes a four-page flyer entitled "AIDS and You." It warns that "the most common means of transmission in Zambia is between men and women during sexual intercourse, from the man to the woman or the woman to the man" and adds concisely, "the best advice is to stick to one healthy partner." To confront the disease, the pamphlet concludes, requires "a return to the sexual morality proposed by our best Zambian traditions as well as Christianity, Islam, and Hinduism." In Rwanda, the national radio has been particularly active in the education and prevention effort.

Meanwhile, the U.S. Agency for International Development (USAID) has launched an ambitious effort to distribute condoms on the continent. Although they are regarded with suspicion in some societies where birth control has been slow to take hold and it is sometimes difficult to store condoms effectively in hot and humid tropical climates, there are indications that they have begun to catch on in certain afflicted countries. USAID and other national and international assistance agencies are also encouraging the use of disposable or sterile needles and syringes in Africa, so that the growing immunization programs against other diseases do not have the accidental effect of transmitting HIV.

There is, however, far to go. The appearance of a second virus, dubbed HIV-2, in Africa has raised many new questions. Initial epidemiological studies show that it is widespread in West Africa, particularly in Senegal, Ivory Coast, and Guinea-Bissau, where there have been relatively few cases of AIDS thus far. While HIV-2 seems to have fewer serious effects at the moment than does the original virus (now often called HIV-1), some scientists believe it may evolve into something equally lethal; as a result, there is a debate over what resources should be devoted to screening for HIV-2.

Indeed, there are many debates and problems yet to come. If AIDS compromises recent improvements in infant mortality rates and thus comes to be perceived by the African public as a major killer of children, it may also set back many African countries' halting, but urgently necessary, programs to reduce the rate of population growth. And AIDS has an explosive potential in South Africa, where most of the cases reported so far have been among whites and have followed the patterns of the disease in the developed world; if blacks and whites there find cause to blame each other for the disease, it could open up new areas of conflict between them. (Black miners in South Africa who test positive for HIV, according to some reports, have been quietly deported to neighboring countries.) Yet wise policy and courageous political leadership, supported by culturally sensitive help from the outside, could actually make African countries the leaders in this fight against a serious international problem.

14

American Policy

In the spring of 1982, a number of American embassies in Africa received mysterious phone calls from the United States. The caller wanted to know about the quality of the hunting in each country, and the laws controlling it. A bit of detective work by a few enterprising foreign service officers revealed that the calls were coming not from an anonymous American tourist who wanted to figure out where to go on his vacation, but from—or on behalf of—a businessman from San Luis Obispo, California, with good friends in the White House. He was Theodore C. Maino, the sixty-nine-year-old president of a construction company, and he was in other ways openly shopping for an embassy to which he might be named by President Ronald Reagan. Maino's *curriculum vitae* made it clear that he was a solid citizen, with wartime service in the Naval Reserve, six years on the local school board, and a stint as foreman of a county grand jury in 1961–62. He was a member of the Boy Scouts of America, Rotary International, and the Mzuri Safari Club and Foundation. (*Mzuri* is the Swahili word for "good" or "nice.") America's newly recruited diplomat, in other words, was a big-game hunter.

Maino nearly became the U.S. ambassador to Kenya; that was where he wanted to go and where some of his well-placed friends wanted to send him. But officials in the Africa bureau of the State Department thought better of it and urged that he be dispatched to a less strategically important country where he could have almost as good a time but his lack of diplomatic experience and relevant knowledge might be less noticeable. So it was that Maino went off to serve his country in the unsuspecting southern African nation of Botswana (which, as it happens, has strict controls on the hunting of game). His brief tenure at the embassy in Gaborone was undistinguished but mostly harmless; part of his time, alas, was spent in a hospital in nearby South Africa, recovering from illness.

The fleeting diplomatic career of Theodore Maino might have passed virtually unnoticed had it not coincided with those of Robert H. Phinny and Keith Brown, who were, at the same time, the Reagan administration's ambassadors to Swaziland and Lesotho respectively. Phinny, whose prior job had been to manage the investments of his in-laws, the Gerber family (of baby food fame), demonstrated at his Senate confirmation hearing—attended by only one senator—that despite State Department briefings, he knew very little about the ancient kingdom to which he was being assigned. (One story that made the rounds was that Phinny had not listened carefully while being offered an ambassadorship and accepted, thinking he was going to Switzerland, rather than the "Switzerland of Africa," as Swaziland is sometimes known.) Brown, a prominent Colorado Republican who had developed the Rocky Mountain ski resort in Vail, began running off to South Africa for rest and recreation with old friends as soon as he arrived in Lesotho—logging trips to Johannesburg, Durban, and Cape Town within the first six weeks. His widely circulated letters home reflected white South African sensibilities and attitudes. Brown wrote, for example, about Lesotho's "natives," their quaint villages, and their attire. His wife, in her own letters on embassy stationery, intended for distribution among family and friends, complained that it was boring in Lesotho's tiny capital city of Maseru on the weekends, and she made fun of the prominent women there for being overweight. (She was apparently unaware that in the local culture, obesity is a traditional sign of prosperity.)

Every American president in memory has named political

ambassadors, and many have made mistakes. But during the Reagan administration, Africa seemed to be singled out as a particular dumping ground for people with little experience or even interest. And by putting this trio into the "BLS countries" (Botswana, Lesotho, and Swaziland) in the midst of a crisis area—in each case replacing a career officer who had African experience—the United States seemed to be demonstrating that it had little regard for African sensibilities.

Indeed, there was virtually no evidence during the early 1980s that the long-standing and fundamental American attitude toward Africa had changed. The continent was still being treated as a backwater, a place of marginal interest to the United States except when the great global struggle between East and West could be invoked. For a time, especially when things were going badly elsewhere, the Reagan administration was content to claim foreign policy successes in southern Africa; but when that claim went sour, in light of events inside South Africa, the continent came into national focus again only as the scene of a disastrous drought. Despite having the most highly qualified assistant secretary of state for African affairs in decades, Chester A. Crocker, the United States continued to shape policy on the basis of simplistic images and short-sighted prejudices.

It need not be that way. The United States can develop an Africa policy that is consistent with national principles and transcends partisan differences.

The first step is to recognize that the United States and the American people have enduring interests on the African continent. These interests are economic, political, strategic, humanitarian, and, above all, practical.

America's economic interests go far beyond the traditional concern about strategic minerals in South Africa, Zaïre, and elsewhere, or the more recent preoccupation with access to the oil reserves of Nigeria. An Africa that is stable and develops in an orderly fashion can also be the source of other raw materials and a booming market for industrial and other finished goods—in other words, a continent where normal trade can be conducted to the mutual benefit of both sides. Furthermore, as a number of American corporations have discovered, Africa—all of Africa, not just white-ruled South Africa—can provide excellent opportunities for private investment. All of this is true without regard to the political system that has been chosen by any particular country or the rhetoric its leaders employ.

But Africa does matter politically as well. If the United States genuinely cares about advancing the cause of freedom in the world, as it often says it does, then Africa, with some fifty independent countries, is certainly a place that merits attention. That alone would be a reason for Americans to pay close attention to the evolution of events in South Africa. More broadly, the large bloc of African votes in the United Nations and other international forums can be significant to the West; Africans are in a position to advance or impede international peacekeeping efforts in the Middle East and other parts of the world.

Far too much has been made, particularly by South Africa and its friends, of the strategic importance to the West of the Cape sea route for transporting U.S. and European oil imports and other goods. Yet there are realistic considerations of Western security that come into play in Africa. In the unlikely event that all or most of Africa were to fall under the control or influence of forces hostile to the West, the implications would be grave. If Western aircraft were prohibited from overflying much of Africa, for example, that would inhibit the defense of many other parts of the world. If Africa were to become the home of many Soviet air, sea, and land bases (as it is now often erroneously claimed to be), this would inevitably compromise Western military interests. Simply put, Africa is a large piece of strategic real estate.

The humanitarian considerations are, for some people, the most compelling concerns in Africa. According to the tenets of all religions and any but the most callous political philosophies, it is a fundamental responsibility of the rich to help feed the poor. A vast number of people in Africa are not merely poor, but facing starvation and death. Human considerations aside, the existence of such a large mass of hungry, desperate people is potentially a powerful destabilizing factor in international affairs. They can be ignored or neglected only at the peril of the entire world.

Once having recognized these more or less permanent interests, Americans (and for that matter the citizens of other Western nations) have a set of well-defined principles that can be applied in Africa. Perhaps the most important is self-determination, the right of the people of any country to assert control over their own national life, free of outside interference and domination. In Africa, as in other parts of the Third World, this implies a respect for and understanding of nationalism and a newly achieved sense of sovereignty. Africans are no different from other people in their desire to be masters of their own fate as much as possible; nothing annoys them more than the tendency of outsiders, however well-intentioned, to tell them what is best for them—what system of government and economic management they should select.

At the same time, African governments, like others, must be encouraged to respect the human rights and instincts toward individual self-determination of their own citizens. Whatever standards are applied to one kind of regime must be applied to all others, without regard to the color, the politics, or the international affiliations of the rulers. Thus, if American pressure for change in South Africa is to be credible and respected, it has to be matched by a parallel concern for civil liberties and freedom of political participation everywhere else on the continent—not only in Marxist-oriented countries like Ethiopia and Angola, but also in avowedly pro-Western states like Zaïre, Liberia, and Somalia. This does not mean that anyone has the right to impose on African states uniquely Western institutions such as Westminster-style parliaments or two-party systems, any more than the Soviet Union should get away with imposing "dictatorships of the proletariat"; but it is entirely reasonable to press African rulers to respect the right of their people to have control over their own daily lives, in a manner consistent with the history, culture, and current needs of their own society.

One of the gravest drawbacks of American policy in Africa, as it has evolved over the years, is that there is often confusion between the interests of a regime in power and the interests of an entire nation. Typically, the United States has identified with a narrowly defined elite, as it did for decades in Ethiopia and for more than a century in Liberia, forgetting that if a regime is detested, those same feelings will almost surely be transferred to its American or other backers. (In the event, when the old order was overthrown in Liberia, the American connection survived; but in Ethiopia and other revolutionary situations around the world—Nicaragua and Iran come readily to mind—American symbols have been the first things to go.)

Although it can require a degree of patience and sophistication that does not often characterize American foreign policy, the

United States must somehow learn not to expect regular expressions of love and devotion from friendly nations in Africa. Indeed, those rulers who are most obsequious in their praise for the United States may well be the ones who are most in trouble at home. Policymakers in Washington have to understand (and perhaps explain to the American public) that for complicated historical and political reasons, closeness to the United States may sometimes be taken as a mixed blessing in the developing world. This means that even those rulers who have made a rational and cautious choice to pursue an American connection must retain their right to criticize their friends publicly and, when necessary, forcefully.

A related issue is the importance of not simplistically judging and labeling every regime on the basis of its rhetoric or its short-term decisions. When the leader of a military coup proclaims his devotion to "socialism," for example, or a government establishes direct air service between its capital and Moscow, this does not necessarily mean that the country in question has suddenly decided to join the Soviet bloc. Indeed, the tendency of U.S. spokesmen to pick up on such actions and blow them out of proportion may well become a self-fulfilling prophecy, impelling the leader under attack to prove his importance as a deserving object of American denunciation by taking further steps that will anger the United States. The vast majority of African governments resent being pushed by Washington—or, for that matter, by Moscow—to choose sides in the great East-West struggle; they believe they can decide what to do without divine guidance from one of the superpowers.

One factor that has distorted American policy in Africa in recent years is the hostility between the United States and Muammar al-Qaddafi's Libya. As a bogeyman, Qaddafi has received a status previously held only by Fidel Castro. Indeed, it often seems as if a central premise of U.S. policy on the continent is that no friend of Qaddafi's could be all good, no enemy of his all bad. This is a foolish line to take, not only because it gives Qaddafi a status he does not deserve, but also because it contorts American choices and behavior. What is more, on some occasions it has made the United States vulnerable to manipulation, by both the supporters and the opponents of Qaddafi.

As a general matter, America could be far more careful and

prudent in the selection of friends and allies in Africa. Admittedly, American clients have no monopoly on corruption and brutality—Idi Amin, after all, was propped up by the Soviet Union—but they have been among the worst. Some American friendships, with dictators like Mobutu Sese Seko of Zaïre and Mohammed Siad Barre of Somalia, are understandable and probably inevitable, but often there is no outward sign that U.S. officials are attempting to persuade these rulers to moderate their behavior. To be sure, what they are doing is far from unique, but the behavior does take on a special significance when it appears to have an American endorsement.

Nonetheless, it is on the issue of financial and political corruption that the United States often seems hypocritical and condescending. American statements on corruption in Africa and elsewhere in the Third World sometimes sound as if they are coming from a nation that has never before heard of such behavior. But the truth is that there is plenty of the same kinds of corruption in the United States—from the Watergate affair to the indictments of public officials at all levels—and the Africans, like everyone else, have heard and read all about these incidents.

What can the United States do to help Africa and win greater credit and credibility at the same time? It can, for a start, do a great deal more to promote and assist genuine development, both by being more generous and by paying more attention to the true needs and desires of the people who are supposedly being helped. This is not simply a matter of altruism, but also of self-interest. It is well known that a large amount of overseas development aid comes back to the donor country in the form of construction and other contracts; beyond that, however, a more highly developed Africa is a better customer for American goods, and a more economically prosperous Africa is less likely to be the scene of potentially destabilizing crises. The United States has a great deal of expertise to offer, in agriculture as well as in technical fields; too often, though, the aid projects that get pushed are those that are particularly useful to certain powerful members of Congress and the special interests they represent. Worse, in recent years, far more of U.S. overseas assistance has gone for military than for economic purposes.

Above all, the United States has to relearn lessons it once taught others about the value of multilateral institutions that

Americans helped design in the period after World War II, such as the World Bank. Many American aid dollars could be spent far more effectively than they are now if they were channeled through such institutions. When the United States reneges on its commitments to the World Bank and its subsidiary, the International Development Association (which lends money to the very poorest countries at concessionary rates), it is hard to persuade struggling nations of America's good intentions. Among the wealthy, developed nations of the world, the United States is one of the few where there is a bitter battle every year over how much to help the world's poor.

The area of American policy in Africa that attracts the most attention and controversy, and on which the United States is most often judged, is the attitude toward the Republic of South Africa. South Africa, as the classic pariah state, is a topic of debate around the world, but there are special dimensions to the American relationship with the apartheid regime.

For one thing, the ruling white minority in South Africa seems to have decided long ago that it has something in common with the white majority in America, and for many white Americans the feeling is mutual. For black Americans and others who took part in the civil rights struggle in the United States, it is understandable that there would be an instinct to bring American moral force to bear on one of the world's most intractable problems. Indeed, it sometimes seems as if there is a morbid fascination in the United States with the complex and tragic situation in South Africa; it appeals at the same time to the noble and the nasty sides of the American public character.

The most recent U.S. policy toward South Africa—the so-called "constructive engagement" practiced by the Reagan administration—has catered to the sense of a special connection between the whites of the two countries. In the process, by all reliable accounts, it has alienated much of the black majority in South Africa, and therefore, in cold political terms, has probably damaged the long-range interests of the United States in southern Africa. After four years, it also moved black Americans and liberal activists to a level of outrage and action that had eluded them for some time. The result was the "Free South Africa Movement," which began demonstrations outside the South African embassy in Washington on the eve of Thanksgiving, 1984, and brought out thousands of people willing to be arrested in a protest fraught with symbolism.

Perhaps the most telling complaint against "constructive engagement" was that it gave the white regime a great deal—from material advantages such as the lifting of restrictions on the shipment of certain materials to South Africa to intangibles like greater international credibility—but it did not demand anything in return. It was a case of the carrot without the stick, and for all the noble intentions expressed by the State Department, it appeared to have done little to improve the lot of nonwhite South Africans. On the contrary, there was some evidence that the circumstances had deteriorated in South Africa during the period of "constructive engagement." The forced removal of blacks from the cities to the artificially created homelands actually increased, and while bannings of opposition figures were down, arrests and detention of critics of the regime went up. If anything, tensions were greater than they had been before. This led the late Percy Qoboza, a distinguished black South African journalist, to label the Reagan administration policy "constructive instigation."

The evidence was compelling enough to cause concern among conservative Republicans who ordinarily would have been expected to support the president on most issues of foreign policy. The then chairman of the Senate Foreign Relations Committee, Republican Richard Lugar of Indiana, asked the president in 1985 to show where he stood by denouncing apartheid "much more sharply and more often," and one group of thirty-five Republican House members gave the South Africans plenty of warning that they would support diplomatic and economic sanctions unless there was some improvement in the racial situation there. With a number of cities and states enacting legislation requiring their employees' pension funds to sell the stocks of companies with investments in South Africa, the issue was achieving a new bipartisan visibility.

What has emerged is a broad consensus that the United States must adopt a new, tougher policy toward South Africa, one that reflects widely shared American values and can attract the respect of a broad cross-section of South Africans of all races. It could begin with the demands made in January 1985 by the *Afrikaanse Handelsinstitut*, the Afrikaans-speaking chamber of com-

merce, and five other employer organizations: meaningful political participation for all black South Africans; the end of job
reservation and establishment of the right of all groups to own
shops or conduct business anywhere in the country; universal citizenship in South Africa, instead of the "homelands"; the right of
all workers to organize and join free and independent trade unions;
administration of equal justice with court safeguards and a cut-
back in the state's power to detain people without charges; and
an end to the forced removal of people from the areas where they
live. Americans would probably add an objection to the Group
Areas Act, which prevents the kind of integration that is essential
if South Africa is to have any future as a multiracial society.

It is important, of course, to recognize the limits of American
pressure and influence in South Africa, as in any other country;
the United States cannot force South Africa to do something that
it does not have the will or capacity to do. But there is a record
of successful American and other outside pressures on South Africa: it was the threat of boycotts that caused the South Africans
to integrate some of their sports. It was the "Sullivan principles,"
designed by a black American pastor on the board of General
Motors, that brought fundamental decency to many factory floors.
And it was the international outcry after the death of Black Consciousness leader Steve Biko in detention that brought some reform, albeit temporary, to South African police practices. The
dispatch of integrated delegations of South African businessmen
and academics to the United States, to warn against sanctions and
disinvestment, says something about just how much outside attitudes still matter to South Africans.

What, then, of the demands for imposition of controls over,
or the complete withdrawal of, American investments in South
Africa, or for sanctions against the Pretoria regime if it does not
soon take meaningful steps toward a more just society?

The debate over disinvestment is one of the more frustrating
elements of any discussion of American policy in Africa, because
there are many different interpretations of what its effect would
be. One survey of black workers in South African industry, funded
in part by the U.S. State Department, found them overwhelmingly
opposed; so are many moderate politicians, black and white, such
as Gatsha Buthelezi and Helen Suzman. The argument usually
made for this view is that blacks would be the first to be hurt by

disinvestment—that foreign investment, by promoting general economic progress, provides jobs for blacks and makes more likely the prospects for eventual political change. There is also a widely held belief that if American companies pull out, their investments will quickly be bought at bargain-basement rates by others—the British, French, Japanese, or white South Africans—who feel less pressure to demand change in the system.

On the other side, a number of South African black leaders argue that disinvestment is the only way to shock the country into fundamental change, and America must lead the way. Whatever temporary harm blacks may suffer, they insist, will be worth the ultimate rewards of freedom.

It does seem useful to make a distinction between existing investment in South Africa and new investment there. The United States can exert leverage for change by putting strict controls on any new American investment in the South African economy, requiring, for example, that some of the most appalling practices of the system be ignored or defied. But if all existing investment were to be removed at one time, then America's only remaining leverage would be rhetorical—not a form that the South Africans are likely to respect. However, the threat of disinvestment in the event that things took a decided turn for the worse in South Africa (say, if the new right-wing Conservative party or the military were to come to power), or if substantial progress were not made soon, can be a meaningful element in American policy.

Many American businesses have already found that their capital is at risk in South Africa and have opted to withdraw their involvement in the apartheid economy; more will undoubtedly be doing so. As for the dilemma that institutions and individuals face on the issue of whether to maintain holdings in U.S. firms that operate in South Africa, they may find it useful to be selective—to sell their shares in any companies that perform in a regressive manner (for example, automatically dismissing any workers who are detained on political charges), but to hold on to the shares of companies that have genuinely played a constructive role in fighting injustice. Indeed, some companies whose presence is especially meaningful to the South African regime could be pressed to defy the law by constructing multiracial housing estates for their employees and otherwise promoting racial conciliation.

The issue of sanctions has been at the center of debate over

American policy in South Africa. With the Reagan administration imposing punitive economic measures against Nicaragua—and, from time to time, against Poland and the Soviet Union—the argument that sanctions would be pointless in the South African case became harder to sustain. After bipartisan majorities in both houses of Congress had voted for limited economic sanctions in the summer of 1985, President Reagan, under substantial political pressure, took his own steps in an executive order in September of that year. Except that his order imposed a ban on the sale of Krugerrand gold coins in the United States, Reagan's sanctions essentially lifted favors that had been granted during the previous five years, putting the substance of American policy back where it was at the end of the Carter administration.

A year later, in the fall of 1986, Congress approved a far more ambitious package of sanctions, including trade restrictions, bans on certain kinds of investment in and loans to South Africa, and, perhaps most important symbolically, the suspension of South African Airways' lucrative direct air service between Johannesburg and New York. In addition, the Comprehensive Anti-Apartheid Act of 1986 authorized educational, legal, and other assistance to blacks in South Africa and called on the president to launch an international effort to end apartheid. Reflecting various currents of opinion and concern among members of the unusual coalition that passed the sanctions bill by overwhelming majorities in both the House and Senate, the act required the Executive Branch to prepare reports on health conditions in the South African homelands, on the role of the South African Communist party, and on how to reduce American dependence on strategic minerals from South Africa.

This sweeping legislation—described by supporters as the belated triumph of a good cause and by detractors as a hodgepodge of dramatic, well-intentioned gestures that would have little practical effect—was made possible by a major change in the climate of opinion on South Africa in the United States. One basic factor was that ordinary Americans had been able for some time to have a glimpse on the nightly television news of the nature and the scope of violence in South Africa; the impact was not unrelated to what had happened when the reality of the Vietnam war was brought into American living rooms courtesy of broadcast technology. While the imposition of a national state of emergency and severe press restrictions by the South African government helped cut those images off, that very tactic intensified the anger felt by the minority of Americans who paid close attention. The fact that certain members of the Reagan administration still insisted that "constructive engagement" had been a success (even if that newly unfashionable term was no longer favored to describe the policy) emboldened its opponents, including disillusioned moderate Republicans, even further. (Others had their own motives for supporting the sanctions bill, including the establishment of antiracist credentials that would be helpful in pressing for aid to "freedom fighters" against Marxist regimes elsewhere and the potential improvement of the Republican party's prospects among black voters.)

When the act reached his desk, President Reagan, demonstrating consistent principles but foolish domestic and international politics, vetoed it. (In formal statements and impromptu responses to questions, the president was still using lines that could not help but please the South African government—suggesting that much of the violence in South Africa arose out of tribal rivalries and warning primarily against the "calculated terror" and Communist sympathies of the ANC.) During the Senate debate over whether to override the veto, televised live in South Africa, Foreign Minister R. F. Botha actually telephoned senators in the cloakroom in the hope of influencing their votes; but in a strong symbolic gesture, the veto was overridden and the Reagan administration thus became obligated to implement sanctions it had strongly opposed.

In a sense, that was another major turning point in U.S. policy. Black South Africans were able to see, if they cared to, that many Americans, including more than two-thirds of the members of Congress, were ready to put significant pressure on the white government for change. (The appointment in the same period of Edward Perkins, a black career diplomat known to have reservations about constructive engagement, as U.S. ambassador to South Africa served to underscore the point.)

Whether the sanctions had their intended effect became the subject of another fierce debate. A year after they were enacted, on September 30, 1987, in a report required by Congress, Reagan insisted that sanctions "are not the best way to bring freedom to" South Africa, that they "put a brake on any inclination toward fundamental reform by the South African government," and that they had only a "minimal" impact on the South African economy. (Some South African liberals, including Helen Suzman, made the same point in eloquent speeches and writings.) But Senator Edward M. Kennedy of Massachusetts, one of the leading proponents of sanctions, offered his own assessment in *The Washington Post* that the act had "moved the United States into the forefront of the worldwide effort to end apartheid," restoring American credibility in the rest of Africa and hastening "the breakup of the monolithic Afrikaner community." Kennedy and his allies pushed on, in an effort to tighten the sanctions further.

In August 1988, the House of Representatives passed a tough new sanctions bill, requiring all American companies, institutions, and individuals to withdraw all investments from South Africa, and banning virtually all U.S.–South African trade; although it had influential sponsors, it seemed unlikely to pass the Senate, in light of the ongoing negotiations in Southern Africa.

An observer looking in from outside could not help but be confused, however. For at the same time Congress was voting for sanctions against South Africa, it was approving aid for Jonas Savimbi to continue his South African–sponsored guerrilla war in Angola (consistent with administration policy). Some conservative Republican senators argued (contrary to administration policy) that the United States should go further and help RENAMO, the South African–supplied movement seeking to wrest control of Mozambique from Frelimo in a particularly brutal war that had spilled over into Zimbabwe and Malawi.

Those are precisely the kinds of steps that the United States should not take in Southern Africa. Even if some of the governments in the area are not Washington's favorites ideologically, it is important that American policy contribute to regional stability— and that politically, economically, and perhaps even militarily, it help other legitimate governments establish their true independence and protect their territorial integrity from South African assaults. Additional sanctions and other economic pressures on South Africa may well be needed to help push a recalcitrant regime toward meaningful reform and compromise with its own people; but other, perhaps more subtle and imaginative measures will also be necessary.

There will always be some Americans who argue, whether on

anti-Communist, humanitarian, or other grounds, that the United States must be careful not to weaken the South African state further, lest it become vulnerable to outside powers or react defensively and turn still more harsh and repressive internally. But the danger is that any appearance of an American reluctance to offend the government in Pretoria—or of a tendency to see it, as Ronald Reagan did, against all evidence to the contrary, as a tried and true "friend"—will be interpreted by black South Africans and others in Africa as a sign of the United States' indifference to their plight. The fact that the United States brokered an agreement in 1988 among South Africa, Angola, and Cuba that seemed likely to lead to independence for Namibia and withdrawal of the Cubans from Angola obviously helped the American reputation; but still there remained a substantial agenda for change within South Africa itself.

The problems of South Africa and of the rest of the continent are so severe, and potentially so important to the Western world, in political, economic, and human terms, that America cannot afford to be indifferent. Least of all can the United States return to attitudes and approaches that have long since been discredited by history.

Epilogue

DEVELOPMENTS IN AFRICA since this book was first published in 1985 have hardly been such as to assure peace, prosperity, economic growth, and political stability on the continent. On the contrary, it often seems as if Africa is doomed to a downward spiral whose end point is far beyond anything the experts have ever been willing to predict.

In South Africa, the failure of moderate reform to keep up with the rising anger and frustration of the black majority continued to have profound effects. With each new development, the various forces in that country's inexorable political drama appeared to grow further apart. The National party government tried desperately to hold the center against challenges from all sides, but the center became steadily smaller and more narrowly defined; only on the issues of independence for Namibia and the departure of foreign forces from Angola did there appear to be significant progress.

In June 1988, President P. W. Botha renewed South Africa's sweeping nationwide state of emergency for a third year, leading many to believe that draconian restrictions on political expression and major expansions of police power were becoming permanent fixtures of life in this country that still claimed to adhere to Western democratic standards. The government had already squelched the multiracial United Democratic Front (UDF) and put some of its leaders on trial for treason, and it had even begun to tie educational subsidies to the suppression of antigovernment demonstrations by university authorities. Among other things, the new emergency decree restricted the political activities of the Confederation of South African Trade Unions (COSATU) and closed various loopholes that had permitted other groups to defy the government. Botha insisted these steps were necessary so that "daily lives can continue without fear, intimidation, and terror"; but it became hard to see how he was truly protecting anything but white privilege and power, albeit temporarily.

As part of the effort to make life safer in South Africa, the government tightened further its restrictions on the press, making it illegal to quote any organization that has been banned (such as the UDF) or any of its spokesmen. It became an offense even to cite members of the law-abiding Detainees' Parents Support Committee and others who attempted to protest, or just to publicize, the detention of people without trial. Earlier the government had temporarily closed down one of South Africa's newest and most outspoken opposition newspapers, the weekly *New Nation*, for publishing "propaganda" that allegedly encouraged the revolutionary overthrow of the government. (The newspaper's founding editor, Zwelakhe Sisulu, the son of prominent anti-apartheid activists, was detained without charges beginning in late 1986 because of his journalistic activities; in July 1988, suffering from severe depression, he was transferred to a hospital.) "After this," editorialized *The Star* in Johannesburg, a more establishment, mainstream publication, "no other newspaper is safe."

Under the latest renewal of the state of emergency, the government also tried to establish an official registry of journalists, requiring all free-lance reporters and various news agencies operating in South Africa to provide the Ministry of Home Affairs with their names, the names of their clients, and other details about themselves and their work. The home affairs minister would have the authority to remove from the registry, and thereby end the journalistic career of, anyone he considered a threat to public order. The new procedure was initially expected to damage the low-budget, alternative, opposition press and its reporters, many of whom work part-time for overseas news organizations that do not maintain full-time correspondents in South Africa; it was also aimed at small-scale news agencies providing information from rural areas and black townships where other reporters find it difficult to work. Having already successfully restricted the work of foreign broadcasters and expelled many Western correspondents whose reporting it did not like, the government was now moving against a domestic menace in the press field. But after international protests and under pressure from mainstream news organizations in South Africa, the government backed down three months later. The home affairs minister, Stoffel Botha, said, however, that the principle of government control over free-lance journalists remained "a matter of grave concern."

Nonetheless, Botha pushed ahead with his plan for a "national forum" that would theoretically recruit blacks into helping draft a new constitution providing for "participation by all South African citizens in the process of government." Eventually, Botha said, this could lead to having blacks in the national cabinet, in roles limited to "matters affecting their communities." However, most black leaders with any real constituency, including Zulu Chief Gatsha Buthelezi, refused to take part in the forum on Botha's terms. Indeed, it was not clear that the black councilmen who were supposed to select some of the black members of the forum would themselves be able to be elected, given opposition plans to organize boycotts of municipal elections in the townships. The Coloured and Indian chambers of Parliament went along with Botha's plan, but members of the Conservative party, now the official opposition in the white chamber, complained that the forum would amount to the "destruction of all the whites have built up over the last 300 years."

No such destruction could be imagined in the other "reform" legislation proposed by Botha. For example, despite having done away with most aspects of the "influx control" laws regulating the movement of blacks into urban areas, the government now proposed to strengthen the Group Areas Act, which restricts where people may live, and to toughen the penalties against those who violate it. Under the new law, the state would have the power to evict any black living in an area officially reserved for whites, without any obligation to provide alternative housing; anyone found guilty of illegally owning or occupying property in a place designated for another racial group could be sentenced to five years in prison and a fine of more than $4,000.

The legislation was apparently intended to eliminate multiracial "gray areas," such as the high-rise Johannesburg suburb of Hillbrow, where middle-class blacks had begun to live unobtrusively in apartments officially designated for whites; such areas are anathema to apartheid purists, particularly those in the Conservative party. In a companion bill, Botha promised that some multiracial residential areas would eventually be authorized, through referenda among residents, with a veto power in the hands of the white central government; but there was no assurance that the existing, impromptu ones like Hillbrow—some of the most interesting neighborhoods in South Africa—would survive.

Thus continued an inevitable South African process: tiny steps forward, always accompanied by cynical steps backward. South African Transport Services announced triumphantly in mid-1988 that racial segregation would be ended on local train service (in favor of a price-differentiated class system); but meanwhile, tens of thousands of black people whose only crime was to live in apartments they could afford faced brutal eviction and dislocation under a new, politically motivated stiffening of one of the original bulwarks of apartheid, the Group Areas Act. Although South Africa withdrew its troops from Angola in August 1988, that same month the government banned the activities of the End Conscription Campaign, which had lobbied against compulsory military service. And new regulations were put into effect, making it possible for the government to restrict its political opponents without telling them it has done so.

Increasingly, for a substantial number of people in South Africa, such legalisms were irrelevant; they were involved in a newly radical resistence that really did have the violent overthrow of the white regime as its goal. Within the African National Congress, the balance of power and influence appeared to have swung strongly, if temporarily, in the direction of militant members of its military wing, with the result that there were many more bombings inside South Africa with civilian targets and victims. One of the goals, said guerrilla leaders based in Lusaka, Zambia, was to persuade white South Africans that their government could no longer be counted upon to assure their safety. Indeed, for all its detentions and other security measures and with all of its incursions into neighboring countries, the white regime seemed to have remarkably little control over what was happening at home. The point was eloquently made on July 2, 1988, when there was an especially bold attack outside a rugby stadium in Johannesburg: 220 pounds of explosives packed inside a BMW detonated just as a rugby match was ending, killing 2 whites and injuring 67 other people.

Still the government refused to grant status to the ANC as anything but a band of terrorists devoted to "godless communism." When a group of white politicians and activists traveled to Dakar, Senegal, for a meeting with members of the ANC—who took a moderate approach and reiterated their interest in working toward a multiracial South Africa—the reaction within the government and among its supporters was to be outraged rather than intrigued. In what was apparently intended as a trial balloon, late in 1987 Botha did release seventy-seven-year-old Govan Mbeki, one of Nelson Mandela's original codefendants, after he had served twenty-four years in prison; but as soon as Mbeki attempted to speak out on the current situation in South Africa, he had restrictions imposed on his movements and his actions. On the occasion of Mandela's seventieth birthday in 1988, there were many pleas for his release—including one from the influential pro-government Afrikaans-language newspaper, Beeld—but the government's only response was to ban demonstrations, concerts, and other activities planned in Mandela's honor. (Later, when Mandela proved to be suffering from tuberculosis, he was moved from prison to a medical clinic for whites, and the government appeared to be looking for a face-saving way to release him.)

As far as protests and civil disobedience were concerned, the Botha government did appear for a time to gain the upper hand. With their parents concerned about the long-term consequences of boycotts, students in many of the black townships began drifting back to school. (The government acknowledged holding 250 children under the age of sixteen in detention; human rights groups said the numbers were actually much higher.) As a rent strike in Soweto entered its third year, with an estimated compliance rate of 75 percent, local authorities struck back by simply turning off the electricity and water just as winter temperatures in the Johannesburg area neared the freezing range.

Once the government had seemingly gained greater control over civil strife and the stories of violence in South Africa had begun to disappear from the evening news and the front pages in most Western countries, the nation's economy appeared to bounce back; gold production shielded the country from the worst effects of the worldwide stock market crash in October 1987, but the long-range projection for South Africa's international economic relations was quite bleak. Leon Sullivan, the black American minister on the board of General Motors, whose famous principles promoting racial equality in the workplace had for years been the crutch that allowed many American companies to stay in South Africa, declared that he had personally despaired of achieving peaceful change there through economic growth; he urged businessmen to resort to disinvestment after all. Many took his advice, and other governments began to follow the lead of the United States Congress in imposing economic sanctions. During 1987, according to the Investor Responsibility Research Center, fifty-one firms announced they were closing down their operations in South Africa, and another eleven said they would do so soon. Even Japanese businessmen, ever pragmatic in such circumstances, started to hedge their bets in South Africa.

Not about to be beaten easily, the South African government established an "unconventional trade" department in several of its ministries, the purpose being to help exporters and importers devise strategies to circumvent sanctions.

Another cause for South African economic distress was the continuing war in Namibia and Angola, estimated to cost Pretoria more than $2 billion a year, not to mention growing casualties among white draftees. With Cuban units inside Angola having been reinforced and sent closer to the Namibian border, South African troops found themselves no longer able to operate with impunity in southern Angola. Indeed, for the first time, the Cubans were fighting alongside SWAPO guerrillas as well as Angolan government forces, and in one battle near the Calueque Dam, along the Namibian-Angolan border, in June 1988, at least a dozen South African soldiers were killed.

Whether as a result of these setbacks, of P. W. Botha's recognition that he could not effectively fight simultaneous wars inside and outside his country, of the persuasiveness of U.S. State Department officials who had been searching for a solution to these issues they had linked in 1981, or of some other cause, South Africa agreed once again to formal talks on Namibia and Angola—this time with representatives of both the Angolan and Cuban governments participating, and with the United States mediating and the Soviet Union observing. After preliminary meetings in Brazzaville, London, and Cairo, the negotiators agreed at a session in New York in July 1988 on broad principles governing the withdrawal of Cuban and South African troops from Angola and the granting of black majority rule in Namibia under United Nations supervision. Many details remained to be worked out—including the timetable for and verification of the Cubans' withdrawal as well as the fate of Jonas Savimbi's UNITA guerrillas, who fought the Angolan government with aid from South Africa and the United States—but the initial agreement reflected hopes that the newly cordial Soviet-American relations inaugurated by Mikhail Gorbachev and Ronald Reagan would have a positive effect far away in Southern Africa.

Elsewhere in the region, the South African struggle cast a long shadow. In Mozambique, the RENAMO rebels—generally dubbed "right-wing" because of their sustained support from the South African government and from extreme conservative interests in the United States—brought terror and devastation to the rural population, as they continued their effort to overthrow the nominally Marxist government in Maputo. The guerrillas routinely attacked provincial villages, burning crops and houses, raping women, and slitting the throats of anyone who resisted them; they also ambushed humanitarian relief convoys, preventing any recovery from the severe famine that already afflicted the nation.

Hundreds of thousands of Mozambicans fled the country into nearby Malawi and Zimbabwe. In Malawi alone, there were estimated to be more than 600,000 refugees from Mozambique, competing for scarce resources at a time when some of the most important agricultural crops were suffering from infestation by insects. Malawian hospitals were crowded with Mozambican patients, water supplies were strained, and human congestion literally caused some farmland to be taken out of production. Zimbabwe, perceiving a threat to its own physical and economic security from attacks on railroad lines and cross-border raids by RENAMO, deployed at least 10,000 of its own troops in Mozambique.

Late in 1986, Mozambique weathered the severest kind of political crisis when its first president, Samora Machel, and some of the senior members of his government were killed in a plane crash just inside the South African border on their way home from a meeting in Zambia. (South Africa was at first widely suspected of assassinating Machel, but independent inquiries convinced most people that the accident was caused by technical failures in the Soviet-made presidential aircraft.) Frelimo, the ruling party that had emerged from the independence struggle against the Portuguese, avoided a power struggle and quickly selected Joaquim Chissano, a close ally of Machel who was then forty-seven years old, as his successor. A political moderate, Chissano continued Machel's efforts to break Mozambique's dependence on the Soviet Union, develop broader ties in the West, and introduce economic reforms.

A dramatic change was signaled in September 1988, when South African President P. W. Botha actually visited Mozambique (as well as Malawi), and Chissano promised to return the favor. Botha promised to stop aiding RENAMO, and Chissano praised him for his reforms to apartheid.

In Zimbabwe, ethnic tensions finally began to ease in a way that seemed likely to help bring greater political stability. Robert Mugabe's ruling party gained an even stronger hold on Parliament in the 1985 elections, and planning intensified to create a one-party state. Joshua Nkomo, at the age of seventy-one, finally agreed to fold his own party into Mugabe's, and at the end of 1987 he accepted a secondary role in the leadership of a country he had long dreamed of running; he took a ministerial portfolio in the cabinet that would apparently permit him to bring more patronage jobs and greater economic development to Matabeleland. Mugabe, meanwhile, became state president of a stronger central government.

A study released in May 1986 by the Lawyers Committee for Human Rights, an American group, had charged that summary executions, torture, beatings, arbitrary arrests, and officially condoned mob violence were then still being routinely used in Zimbabwe to keep the Ndebele ethnic minority under control. (Two men who were thought to be primary sources for the study were arrested by Mugabe's government at the time.) But the accord between Mugabe and Nkomo was expected to reduce violence in the countryside and make the government feel less threatened. With fewer reports of guerrilla attacks on white farmers, Zimbabwe hoped to have better prospects of attracting additional foreign investment; the issues of land reform and white domination of the economy remained grievances for those who had fought for independence, however.

The periodic explosion of land mines along the Zimbabwean–South African border shattered the provisional calm between those two countries, leading the Pretoria government to harbor new suspicions that the ANC was operating in Zimbabwe after all, and therefore to make new threats against Mugabe. The inclusion of Zimbabwe on South Africa's hit list in May 1986 launched a new era of overtly hostile relations between neighbors.

Even ever-cautious Botswana, whose capital city of Gaborone lies only twelve miles from the porous South African border, found itself drawn into the struggle. The South African military and police often sent patrols into Botswana, allegedly to gather information, and on some occasions carloads of South Africans drove across the frontier with the clear intention of stirring up trouble. When it could, Botswana arrested and interrogated these people, but tried to be cautious about provoking a confrontation with Pretoria bigger than it could handle.

Liberia continued to be a source of embarrassment for its American sponsors. After Thomas Quiwonkpa, whom many regarded as a potentially promising reformer, was killed in the course of his attempted coup against Samuel Doe, the regime rounded up most of its usual suspects, including the outspoken liberal Ellen Johnson-Sirleaf. (She was imprisoned and threatened with death for a time, but finally, after being released, escaped the country and went into exile in the United States.) One opposition group, the Liberia Action Party (LAP)—with which Johnson-Sirleaf and some of her friends were allied—had been allowed to contest the presidential election of October 15, 1985. Most people who observed the process closely within Liberia were convinced that the LAP candidate, Jackson Doe (no relation to Samuel), had actually won; but after some ballot boxes were burned and the counting of votes from others was substantially delayed (among other irregularities), Samuel Doe was declared the unequivocal winner. The Reagan administration accepted the official results and continued sending aid to Liberia, despite warnings that more crises loomed in the future there.

Once confirmed in office and given an American stamp of approval, Doe became steadily more despotic. Despite occasional declarations that he supported a free press and wanted to encourage investigative reporting, Doe frequently jailed journalists whose work embarrassed him and his associates. After another attempted coup in early 1988, he shut down two of the country's eleven daily newspapers and suspended the daily broadcast on local radio of African news from the BBC and the Voice of America. Yet another coup attempt in July 1988 resulted in the death of Doe's former second-in-command, J. Nicholas Podier, and the arrest of two Americans who allegedly conspired with him to overthrow Doe. Foreign journalists who reported what was really happening in Liberia were promptly told they were unwelcome to return.

The Liberian economy disintegrated almost completely in Doe's hands. Having vastly expanded the number of people on the public payroll and once again raised all salaries, he minted more than 120 million "Doe dollars" that had no real value, but helped give the impression that the bills were being paid. The value of Liberia's only legitimate currency, the U.S. dollar, skyrocketed on the black market. Despite having put Americans in key places in most government ministries, there was little the United States could do about the economic or human rights abuses in Liberia; Washington was in effect the hostage of its own client state.

There was a certain irony to the fact that the same military officers who had removed Nigeria's civilian regime at the end of 1983 decided in August 1985 that after twenty months in charge of one of the world's most ungovernable countries, Mohammed Buhari, although one of their own, also had to go. Complaining particularly of the curbs that Buhari had placed on freedom of the press, other human rights abuses, and his inability to deal with Nigeria's economic difficulties, they quietly (and bloodlessly) removed him while he was off in his hometown observing a Moslem religious holiday.

Buhari's successor was Major General Ibrahim Babangida, a charismatic forty-four-year-old war hero who lost no time winning popular support. In a television and radio broadcast the day after taking power, intended to explain yet another coup d'état to the weary Nigerian public, Babangida complained calmly that Buhari had been "too rigid and uncompromising in his attitude to issues of national significance," and that Buhari's chief of staff had "arrogated to himself absolute knowledge of all problems and solutions." One of Babangida's first steps was to curb the powers of the Nigerian Security Organization, which had come to be greatly feared; he also declared a fifteen-month "state of economic emergency" and, with oil prices plunging ever further, opened new negotiations with the IMF. How well he would manage to keep other promises—to encourage a return to small-scale farming, to sell off selected state enterprises, and to streamline Nigeria's notorious government bureaucracy—was bound to have an effect on how long a turn Babangida would have in office.

As for Nigeria's future, some people in and out of government began to speak of the need to try a "diarchy," in which civilians and the military would devise a constitutional means of sharing power; but to their credit, Babangida and his advisers kept their promise and began to prepare yet another transition back to civilian rule, despite the hazards of recent experience. The question was whether Babangida would be able to stay in power long enough to hand it over in an orderly fashion. The major threat to the country's stability this time seemed to come from its pitiful economic condition, a great comedown from the heady days of the oil boom. The average per capita income plunged by half over a period of four years, and creditor nations and banks began to clamor for repayment of $27 billion in outstanding loans. Still, the Nigerians, true to form, continued construction of a mammoth steel works in the interior and kept building the new federal capital at Abuja, complete with three luxury hotels with a total of more than 2,000 rooms. Symbolically, the occupancy rate at the new Hilton there ran below 6 percent.

Siaka Stevens of Sierra Leone, one of post-colonial Africa's most durable and stubborn leaders, finally stepped down toward the end of 1985. But rather than passing authority on to his vice-president, S. I. Koroma, who longed to be his successor, "Pa" Stevens anointed the armed forces chief of staff, Major General Joseph Saidu Momoh, a man in his forties, at a party convention. In an election held several months later to legitimate the choice, Momoh supposedly received 98 percent of the votes cast. Sierra Leone thus became the first country in Africa where the military took power without staging a coup, and Stevens died knowing that he had assured continuity even if he had done little to deal with the country's epidemic corruption.

Drought and economic hardship did nothing to cure the lethal rivalries that sometimes erupted in West Africa. An old hostility reemerged in December 1985 between Burkina Faso and Mali. While the frontier was unguarded, Malian forces launched air and ground attacks deep inside Burkinabe territory, ostensibly seeking to take over an area thought to be rich in minerals and natural gas. But the man who was then Burkina's leader, the late Thomas Sankara, responded in kind with an attack into Mali, and before long, mutual African friends were negotiating a cease-fire, pending a ruling on the border demarcation from the International Court of Justice.

There was a surprising turn toward peace in the far northwestern corner of the continent, as Morocco and the Polisario front agreed in August 1988 to a referendum to determine the future of the Western Sahara. This end to a thirteen-year-old war appeared to be a by-product of the reconciliation between Morocco and Algeria, which had supported and armed the Polisario.

Zaïre continued to be in a class by itself for its capacity to survive economic and political conditions that would quickly have caused major disruption in other, less resilient nations. Its president, Mobutu Sese Seko, made another of his ostentatious pilgrimages to the United States in the summer of 1988 "to say good-bye to President Reagan" and to talk with private bankers, as well as the World Bank and the IMF, about rescheduling his country's multibillion dollar debt once again. A regular visitor to Capitol Hill, he also claimed to be seeing some 200 members of Congress to fight a bill that would end military aid to Zaïre and make further economic aid dependent on improvements in the human rights situation there. For his capacity to manipulate his

American friends and adversaries, Mobutu was not to be under-estimated.

Julius Nyerere stepped down from the presidency of Tanzania, as promised, in November 1985, although he retained the chairmanship of the ruling party. (*Mwalimu* pointedly told interviewers that "our policies are determined by the party and carried out by the government," and he promised that he would be keeping a careful eye on affairs of state.) The party's compromise choice to succeed Nyerere was another former schoolteacher, Ali Hassan Mwinyi, the sixty-year-old president of Zanzibar's island government—a man who had dutifully worked his way up through the hierarchy and had served in several cabinet positions, but was little known outside Tanzania. As a Moslem, Mwinyi might be expected to bring the country closer to the Arab world; as a Zanzibari presumably committed to the permanent union of the restive island with the mainland, he was in a position to calm domestic political rivalries; and as an economic reformer, he was likely to achieve more stable relations with the IMF in an attempt to improve Tanzania's disastrous financial condition.

Another period of tribal conflict and civil chaos culminated in Uganda in July 1985 with Milton Obote being overthrown again, this time by a group of senior military officers pledging reconciliation; they appointed Obote's own defense minister, Paulo Muwanga, as their prime minister. Five months later, the new government announced a peace treaty with the "National Resistance Army," which had begun as a ragtag guerrilla force in 1980 and eventually became the main military threat to Obote's new regime. But the leader of that movement, a highly educated forty-one-year-old man from western Uganda named Yoweri Museveni (who had also once been in an Obote cabinet), renounced the peace treaty and marched into Kampala in February 1986, declaring himself president. Museveni had at one time been aided by Libya, but also appeared to be an admirer of the United States; thus, no one was sure what to expect of his rule in Uganda. He did promise to control human rights violations, to return Uganda to parliamentary democracy, and to reorganize the economy through private and public development projects.

One of Museveni's first challenges was yet another rebellion, this one led by Alice Lakwena, an Acholi woman in her twenties who believed herself to be possessed of supernatural powers. She organized peasants, former soldiers, and other Ugandans into the so-called Holy Spirit Mobile Force. Perhaps as many as 8,500 of her followers—fortified only with sticks, stones, and oils they were told had magical powers—perished in battle, but not before creating a serious threat to Uganda's stability once again. Finally, Lakwena (the name means "messiah" in the Acholi language) was arrested in Kenya at the end of 1987, after she and seven of her soldiers crossed the border on bicycles and on foot, seeking refuge.

Even after this bizarre and pathetic opposition had been dealt with, there were said to be other small guerrilla groups lurking in the bush, remnants of Uganda's decades of travail. In an attempt to establish a historical record and promote reconciliation, Museveni convened a Commission of Inquiry to conduct public hearings on the atrocities of both the Amin and Obote regimes, which turned out to be equally brutal; hundreds of thousands of people had been massacred, and farmers around the country were encouraged to collect the skulls and bones of the dead and turn them over to the government. But about half of Uganda's population remained illiterate, and the fear was that with the economy still in appallingly bad condition, the poor and hopeless would be willing victims of new demagogic appeals. Graft and corruption were so serious, especially in Kampala, that some new government buildings, under construction for a decade or more, looked as if they might never be completed. Augustine Ruzindana, a former banker named inspector general of the government by Museveni, told a visiting reporter that "Uganda is spending a lot of money on agriculture, education, and health, yet it makes no impact because it disappears."

In the Horn of Africa, Ethiopia and Somalia took tentative, and surprising, steps to end their long-standing border disputes and other mutual hostilities. They restored diplomatic relations in April 1988, but only for a cynical reason: because both governments needed to pull their military forces away from the border to deal with internal threats to their survival.

Ethiopia, for its part, was on the verge of total dismemberment. Mengistu Haile Mariam, the harsh military leader who had created Africa's first truly communist state, drastically reduced the food supply and so alienated the public with his crude collectivization efforts that people seemed willing to support virtually any rebel movement that promised an alternative. In Eritrea, the former Italian colony that Haile Selassie had annexed after World War II, separatists were edging closer to victory after a decades-long war, with the prospect that Ethiopia's access to the sea would be cut off altogether. In other regions, too, the Mengistu regime appeared to be losing its effort to hold the line against guerrilla fighters, despite the regime's sweeping arrests and summary executions of its opponents. Notwithstanding a repetition of the famine that crippled Ethiopia in the mid-1980s and attracted world-wide attention to starvation in Africa, Mengistu ordered all foreign relief workers out of Eritrea and Tigray provinces, declaring that their tasks would be taken over by local agencies and charities; the assumption was that he simply did not want outsiders to be able to observe his desperate efforts to reassert control.

In the northern region of Somalia, a less well-publicized conflict also reached critical proportions. The Somali National Movement, with some 10,000 men in its army, made substantial inroads against the American-backed government of Mohammed Siad Barre, and although few journalists were able to get to the area of the fighting, reports reached Nairobi in June 1988 that at least 25,000 northern Somalis had fled across the border to seek refuge in Ethiopia. Later the number grew to more than 300,000. Foreigners, including oil exploration workers and aid personnel from Western countries, had to be airlifted out of Hargeisa, the north's main city.

The challenge to Siad Barre seemed to be motivated less by ideology than by rivalries among Somalia's clans and widespread disgust over the imprisonment and torture of anyone who expressed the slightest dissent against the regime. Although outside experts and former advisers to Siad Barre were predicting the government's imminent collapse, official statements insisted that "the bandits have been totally wiped out" and the situation in the northern part of the country is "very normal." But Somali diplomats recalled home from overseas refused to go, and Amnesty International reported widespread detention without trial and torture of political prisoners in Mogadishu, the capital.

Source Notes/Bibliography

THIS BOOK is the result of an abiding interest in and many voyages to Africa, reaching back more than twenty years. I lived in South Africa and Kenya as a journalist for nearly a year, and I have visited seventeen other African countries, some of them several times. I have also spent a great deal of time during these years with Africans based in or traveling through the United States, as well as with people responsible for formulating American and other Western policy toward Africa and scholars who have made the continent the principal focus of their work. I have participated in many conferences in the United States and abroad dealing with African affairs and have occasionally lectured at home and in Africa on U.S. policy there.

My major source material, therefore, has been my own personal observations, reporting, and interviews, along with my prior writings on African topics. I have particularly borrowed from and built upon articles I have written over the years about South Africa, Namibia, Kenya, and Liberia for the *Atlantic*, about West Africa for *Foreign Policy* magazine, about Somalia for *Saturday Review*, and about Tanzania for the *New Republic*. I have also drawn on my writings about Africa and Africa policy in the *Washington Post*, the *New York Times*, the *Boston Globe*, the *Chicago Tribune*, and other newspapers.

Inevitably, during my six years of intermittent work on this project, I have devoured, clipped, or consulted many books and magazine or newspaper articles by others. I have relied heavily on these scholarly and journalistic resources to fill in my gaps and extend my reach. Most useful has been the coverage of Africa in the *New York Times,* the *Washington Post,* the *Christian Science Monitor,* the *Wall Street Journal, Le Monde,* and the *Guardian,* along with the *Economist, Time, Newsweek, Foreign Policy,* and *Foreign Affairs.* I have also had regular access to the local press of several African countries. Among the many special-interest publications that I used were *Africa News, Africa Confidential, West Africa, Africa Report, New African, Africa Now, Frontline,* and *Africa Notes.* My knowledge was enhanced, in particular, by the work of Leon Dash, David Ottaway, Jay Ross, Glenn Frankel, William Claiborne, Blaine Harden, and Allister Sparks in the *Washington Post;* of Joseph Lelyveld, Anthony Lewis, John Burns, Allan Cowell, James Brooke, Sheila Rule, and Clifford May in the *New York Times;* of David Lamb and Charles Powers in the *Los Angeles Times;* and of Colin Legum and Paul van Slambrouck in the *Christian Science Monitor.*

For economic and social data I have generally relied upon the World Bank, International Monetary Fund, and United Nations, as well as various agencies of the U.S. government and African embassies in Washington. Other useful sources included the Investor Responsibility Research Center, TransAfrica, the South Africa Foundation, the Congressional Black Caucus, the Africa subcommittees of the Senate Foreign Relations Committee and House Foreign Affairs Committee, and the Foreign Agents Registration Unit of the U.S. Department of Justice.

Inasmuch as my methods and purpose were more journalistic than scholarly, I have not attempted to provide detailed footnotes, but sought wherever feasible to offer reference points in the text itself. It does seem useful, however, to give the reader some additional information about sources, and suggestions for further reading, chapter by chapter.

There are many ways to trace the impact of African culture on Western civilization, as mentioned in the Introduction, including the frequent exhibitions of African art that now tour the United States. One especially appealing resource is *African Folktales,* selected and retold by Roger D. Abrahams (Pantheon, 1983). Serious students of this subject would also want to consult *Flash of the Spirit: African and Afro-American Art and Philosophy,* by Robert F. Thompson (Random House, 1981).

For "Ignorance and Insults," I found the writings about Africa in early twentieth-century American popular publications especially helpful; my citations of racist attitudes are minor and mild compared to what is available. The description of African efforts in Washington is based upon interviews and other encounters with ambassadors and other diplomats, as well as some of the public relations firms working on their behalf.

Many historical studies of African-American relations have been published over the years. In "An Undistinguished History," for details of the early period, I relied especially on *Along the Afric Shore: An Historic Review of Two Centuries of U.S. Relations with Africa*, by Russell Warren Howe (Barnes & Noble Import Division, Harper & Row, 1975). A more recent and more comprehensive work is *The United States and Africa: A History*, by Peter Duignan and L. H. Gann (Cambridge University Press, 1984). Duignan and Gann, senior fellows of the Hoover Institution at Stanford University, are also the authors of *Burden of Empire: An Appraisal of Western Colonialism in Africa South of the Sahara* (Praeger, 1967, and Hoover Institution Press, 1971). Another interpretation of Africa's emergence and the American role there can be found in *Let Freedom Come: Africa in Modern History*, by Basil Davidson (Atlantic-Little, Brown, 1978).

Those interested in the role of Western explorers and white settlers in Africa would find four other books helpful: *Africa Explored: Europeans in the Dark Continent, 1769–1889*, by Christopher Hibbert (W. W. Norton, 1982); *No Man's Land: The Last of White Africa*, by John Heminway (Dutton, 1983); *Africa And Its Explorers: Motives, Methods, and Impact*, edited by Robert I. Rotberg (Harvard, 1970), and *Angola Under the Portuguese: The Myth and the Reality*, by Gerald Bender (University of California Press, 1978).

A classic pre-independence overview of Africa from an American perspective is *Inside Africa*, by John Gunther (Harper, 1955). Journalist David Lamb recorded his impressions from four years of work on the continent in *The Africans* (Random House, 1982). British journalist Martin Meredith did the same in *The First Dance of Freedom: Black Africa in the Postwar Era* (Harper & Row, 1985). The ups and downs of recent U.S. policy, especially in the Congo crises of the 1960s, are discussed in *From the Congo to Soweto: U.S. Foreign Policy Toward Africa since 1960*, by Henry F. Jackson (Morrow, 1982); *JFK: Ordeal in Africa*, by Richard D. Mahoney (Oxford, 1983); and *The Congo Cables: The Cold War in Africa—From Eisenhower to Kennedy*, by Madeleine G. Kalb (Macmillan, 1982). An essential reference for understanding Reagan administration policy toward southern Africa is the article by Chester A. Crocker, eventually assistant secretary of state for African affairs, "South Africa: Strategy for Change," in *Foreign Affairs*, Winter 1980–81.

Because of its close and unusual relationship with the United States, Liberia has been the subject of many academic studies over the years. Still one of the most useful (with applications to other places in Africa and elsewhere in the Third World) is the controversial *Growth Without Development: An Economic Survey of Liberia,* by Robert W. Clower et al. (Northwestern University Press, 1966).

The best recent sources on Nigeria are the writings of Jean Herskovits, especially her articles in *Foreign Affairs* and *Foreign Policy* and her 1982 pamphlet for the Headline Series of the Foreign Policy Association, *Nigeria: Power and Democracy in Africa.* Those seeking to understand the tortured evolution of this important country since independence would also want to consult one or more of the studies of the civil war during the late 1960s, including *The Brothers' War: Biafra and Nigeria,* by John de St. Jorre (Houghton Mifflin, 1972), or *The International Politics of the Nigerian Civil War,* by John J. Stremlau (Princeton, 1977). A chilling investigation of the attitude of Britain and the United States toward the Biafran war can be found in *The Brutality of Nations,* by Dan Jacobs (Knopf, 1987). To understand the social and cultural conflicts besetting Nigeria and many other African nations, it is valuable to read the fiction of Chinua Achebe and the drama of Wole Soyinka. Soyinka's autobiography, *Aké: The Years of Childhood* (Random House, 1983), is also a useful reference.

For an ongoing appreciation of Kenyan politics, a dependable source is the *Weekly Review,* published in Nairobi, which may be the most candid and subtle publication in all of black-ruled Africa. Any serious student of Kenya must also read some of the early writings of Jomo Kenyatta, especially *Facing Mount Kenya* (Random House, 1962), his explanation of the cultural heritage and political aspirations of his Kikuyu people, as well as one of many biographies of him, such as *Kenyatta,* by Jeremy Murray-Brown (Dutton, 1973). A superb explanation of the intrigue surrounding Kenyatta's later years and his death is *The Kenyatta Succession,* by Kenyan journalists Joseph Karimi and Philip Ochieng (TransAfrica Book Distributors, Nairobi, 1980). For an increasingly bitter view of life in independent Kenya, there are the writings of Ngugi wa Thiong'o (formerly James Ngugi), especially *Petals of Blood* (Dutton, 1978) and *Detained: A Writer's Prison Diary* (Heinemann, 1981). *Politics and Public Policy in Kenya and Tanzania,* edited by Joel Barkan (rev. ed., Praeger, 1984), compares the systems in those two countries.

There is a vast literature available, of course, on South Africa and its relationship to the West. Two books that take up the urgent and ultimate questions about that country's future are *How Long Will South Africa Survive?* by R. W. Johnson (Oxford, 1977) and *South Africa: Time Running Out* (The Report of the Study Commission on U.S. Policy Toward Southern Africa; University of California Press,

1981). *Up Against Apartheid: The Role and the Plight of the Press in South Africa,* by Richard Pollak (Southern Illinois University Press, 1981), looks at a critical element of the conflict there. *Cry, the Beloved Country,* by Alan Paton (Scribner's, 1982), remains the classic statement of the South African tragedy, but many other writers—including Nadine Gordimer, André Brink, J. M. Coetzee, and Athol Fugard—have more recently defined the problem in fiction and drama. A less well-known, but effective and amusing, fictional treatment of apartheid is *A Separate Development,* by Christopher Hope (Scribner's, 1980). One recent warning of the prospects for racial conflagration is contained in *South Africa at War: White Power and the Crisis in Southern Africa,* by Richard Leonard (Lawrence Hill & Co., 1983). An Afrikaner intellectual's protest against the system is *Apartheid Must Die,* by Willie Esterhuyse (Tafelberg, Cape Town, 1981). Two recent books that look at the crisis in South Africa from opposite perspectives are *Waiting: The Whites of South Africa,* by Vincent Crapanzano (Random House, 1985), and *Freedom Rising,* by James North (Macmillan, 1985). Another important analysis, by a veteran foreign correspondent, is *Move Your Shadow: South Africa, Black and White,* by Joseph Lelyveld (Times Books, 1985). An excellent analysis of South Africa's regional foreign policy and the effect of the American policy of "constructive engagement" can be found in the *Economist,* March 30, 1985, pp. 17–34. For an offbeat and irreverent interpretation of current affairs in South Africa, the monthly magazine *Frontline* is superb.

There have also been many chronicles of the long struggle that converted Rhodesia into Zimbabwe. One that attracted considerable attention was *Under the Skin: The Death of White Rhodesia,* by David Caute (Northwestern University Press, 1983). Other than contemporary journalistic accounts and V. S. Naipaul's tale of a visit to Ivory Coast—"The Crocodiles of Yamoussoukro" in *Finding the Center: Two Narratives* (Knopf, 1984)—there are few useful popular sources in English about much of French-speaking Africa. Most studies of the Horn of Africa tend to be partisan, with the authors taking the side of either Ethiopia or Somalia. Sudan is the subject of *African Calliope,* by Edward Hoagland (Random House, 1979), and Zaïre has been treated in great detail in books concerning American policy in Africa (including those mentioned above).

Among the most relevant books by or about the first generation of leaders of independent Africa are *The Riddle of Violence,* by Kenneth Kaunda of Zambia (Harper & Row, 1980), and *We Must Run While They Walk: A Portrait of Africa's Julius Nyerere,* by William Edgett Smith (Random House, 1972). A selection from Nyerere's writings and speeches can be found in *Freedom and Development* (Oxford, 1974).

In compiling my chapter on the prognosis for Africa, I relied primarily on recent newspaper and magazine accounts of the economic and political crisis, as well as my own reporting. One early and prescient description of Africa's food crisis was *The Politics of Starvation*, by Jack Shepherd (Carnegie Endowment for International Peace, 1975). A number of World Bank studies are also relevant to this subject, including the "Berg Report"—*Accelerated Development in Sub-Saharan Africa: An Agenda for Action* (1981), written by a team led by Elliot Berg—and *Toward Sustained Development in Sub-Saharan Africa: A Joint Program of Action* (1984). The Committee on African Development Strategies, a joint project of the Council on Foreign Relations and the Overseas Development Council, issued a report in December 1985 summarizing the African development crisis and calling for a new "compact" between African nations and the Western world to deal with it. *How Can Africa Survive?*, by Jennifer Seymour Whitaker (Harper & Row, 1988), is an excellent new synthesis.

For my chapter on AIDS in Africa, I have relied primarily on coverage of the issue in *Science* magazine, especially Thomas C. Quinn *et al.*, "AIDS in Africa: An Epidemiologic Paradigm" (vol. 234, pp. 955–963, Nov. 21, 1986); David Dickson, "Africa Begins to Face Up to AIDS (vol. 238, pp. 605–607, Oct. 30, 1987); and Peter Piot *et al.*, "AIDS: An International Perspective" (vol. 239, pp. 573–579, Feb. 3, 1988).

The American interests in Africa and options for Western policy there have been discussed in many articles in recent years in *Foreign Policy* and *Foreign Affairs*. Also useful are *Africa and the United States: Vital Interests*, edited by Jennifer Seymour Whitaker (New York University Press, 1978); *U.S. Foreign Policy in Sub-Saharan Africa: National Interest and Global Strategy*, by Robert M. Price (Policy Papers in International Affairs, Institute of International Studies, University of California, Berkeley, 1978); *Suffer the Future: Policy Choices in Southern Africa*, by Robert I. Rotberg (Harvard, 1980); and *The United States and South Africa: Realities and Red Herrings*, by Helen Kitchen and Michael Clough (Significant Issues Series, Center for Strategic and International Studies, Georgetown University, vol. 6, no. 6, 1984). For an extensive critique of the Reagan administration's policy of "constructive engagement" toward South Africa, see "South Africa: Why Constructive Engagement Failed," by Sanford J. Ungar and Peter Vale, in *Foreign Affairs*, Winter 1985/86 (vol. 64, no. 2), pp. 234–258.

Appendix

THE FOLLOWING CHARTS are intended as a quick reference for basic information about each country in sub-Saharan Africa, as well as a basis for comparison among countries.

The historical information is drawn from *Political Handbook of the World 1982–1983* (New York: McGraw-Hill, 1983); *Columbia Lippincott Gazetteer of the World* (New York: Columbia University Press, 1962); *Columbia Encyclopedia* (New York: Columbia University Press, 1975); and *The Europa Handbook 1984: A World Survey* (London: Europa Publications, 1984). The names of current leaders are drawn from *Chiefs of State and Cabinet Members of Foreign Governments* (Washington: Central Intelligence Agency, March 1988), updated from news reports. Figures on country and capital populations, as well as population growth rates, are from *Demographic Yearbook 1985* (New York: United Nations, 1987) and *Africa South of the Sahara 1988* (London: Europa Publications, 1987). Country population figures are 1985 mid-year estimates; capital populations are based on the most recent available census data. Population growth rate estimates are for 1980–85. Information on land area and currency is from *Political Handbook*. Main exports, language, religion, and ethnic groups are primarily

519

from *The World Factbook 1984* (Washington: Central Intelligence Agency, 1984); *National Geographic Atlas of the World* (Washington: National Geographic Society, 1981); and *Political Handbook.* (Statistics on ethnic groups and religion are, in some cases, incomplete.) *The World Bank Atlas 1987* (Washington: World Bank, 1987) is the primary source for data on per capita income, average annual growth rate, and life expectancy. Annual growth rate covers the period 1973–85; per capita income data are for 1985; life expectancy figures are for 1984. *World Development Report 1987* (Washington: World Bank, 1987) is the main reference for information on infant mortality and average daily caloric intake. (The infant mortality rate is expressed in terms of deaths of children under a year old, per 1,000 births; in some countries, the rate continues to be quite high among older children, but statistics are difficult to obtain. Caloric intake refers to the average daily supply per capita.) Both sets of data are for 1985 (except as noted), and caloric intake figures can be assumed to have declined since then in many African countries, as a result of drought conditions and other adverse economic developments. *The World Factbook 1987* (Washington: Central Intelligence Agency, 1987) and *FAO Production Yearbook 1986,* Volume 40 (Rome: Food and Agricultural Organization, 1987) were used to supplement those two sources, as were U.S. State Department country background notes and the U.S. Commerce Department's series on foreign economic trends.

ANGOLA

Colonial or other former name	
Capital	Luanda
Former colonial power(s)	Portugal
Date of independence	November 11, 1975
Leader at independence	Agostinho Neto
Current leader	José Eduardo dos Santos, president
Form of government	one-party centralized rule
Country population	8.7 million
Capital's population	approx. 1.3 million
Land area	1,246,700 sq. km (481,353 sq. mi)
Population per square km	7
Annual population growth rate	2.5%
Main exports	oil, coffee, diamonds, fish
Average annual growth, GNP, 1973–85	n.a.
Currency	kwanza
Per capita income	n.a.
Infant mortality rate (per 1,000 births)	143
Life expectancy at birth (years)	43
Average daily caloric intake	1,969
Language(s)	Portuguese (official); various Bantu languages
Religions	40% Roman Catholic, 20% Protestant, 40% indigenous beliefs
Ethnic groups	30% Ovimbundu, 23% Kimbundu, 15% Bakongo, 2% Mestiço and white

BENIN

Colonial or other former name	Dahomey
Capital	Porto-Novo (official), Cotonou (de facto)
Former colonial power(s)	France
Date of independence	August 1, 1960
Leader at independence	Hubert Maga
Current leader	Mathieu Kerekou, president
Form of government	people's republic
Country population	4.0 million
Capital's population	144,000
Land area	112,622 sq. km (43,475 sq. mi)
Population per square km	35
Annual population growth rate	2.8%
Main exports	palm products, cotton, cocoa
Average annual growth, GNP, 1973–85	5.6%
Currency	CFA franc
Per capita income	$270
Infant mortality rate (per 1,000 births)	115
Life expectancy at birth (years)	49
Average daily caloric intake	2,173
Language(s)	French (official), Fon, Yoruba, Bariba, Fulani
Religions	70% animist, 15% Moslem, 15% Christian
Ethnic groups	Fon, Adja, Yoruba, Bariba

BOTSWANA

Colonial or other former name	Bechuanaland
Capital	Gaborone
Former colonial power(s)	Great Britain (protectorate)
Date of independence	September 30, 1966
Leader at independence	Sir Seretse Khama
Current leader	Quett Masire, president
Form of government	democracy
Country population	1.13 million
Capital's population	59,657
Land area	600,372 sq. km (231,804 sq. mi)
Population per square km	2
Annual population growth rate	4.3%
Main exports	diamonds, cattle, copper, nickel
Average annual growth, GNP, 1973–85	11.0%
Currency	pula
Per capita income	$840
Infant mortality rate (per 1,000 births)	71
Life expectancy at birth (years)	58
Average daily caloric intake	2,219
Language(s)	English (official), Setswana
Religions	15% Christian, 85% indigenous beliefs
Ethnic groups	94% Tswana, 5% San, 1% European

BURKINA FASO

Colonial or other former name	Upper Volta
Capital	Ouagadougou
Former colonial power(s)	France
Date of independence	August 5, 1960
Leader at independence	Maurice Yaméogo
Current leader	Blaise Compaoré
Form of government	military regime
Country population	7.9 million
Capital's population	442,223
Land area	274,200 sq. km (105,869 sq. mi)
Population per square km	29
Annual population growth rate	1.6%
Main exports	livestock, peanuts, cotton, sesame
Average annual growth, GNP, 1973–85	2.7%
Currency	CFA franc
Per capita income	$140
Infant mortality rate (per 1,000 births)	144
Life expectancy at birth (years)	45
Average daily caloric intake	1,924
Language(s)	French (official), tribal languages
Religions	65% indigenous beliefs, 25% Moslem, 10% Christian
Ethnic groups	Mossi, Gurunsi, Senufo, Lobi, Bobo, Mande, Fulani

BURUNDI

Colonial or other former name	Urundi
Capital	Bujumbura (formerly Usumbura)
Former colonial power(s)	Germany, Belgium
Date of independence	July 1, 1962
Leader at independence	Michel Micombero
Current leader	Pierre Buyoya, president
Form of government	military regime
Country population	4.7 million
Capital's population	172,201
Land area	27,834 sq. km (10,759 sq. mi)
Population per square km	169
Annual population growth rate	2.7%
Main exports	coffee, tea, cotton, hides, skins
Average annual growth, GNP, 1973–85	3.5%
Currency	Burundi franc
Per capita income	$240
Infant mortality rate (per 1,000 births)	118
Life expectancy at birth (years)	47
Average daily caloric intake	2,116
Language(s)	Kirundi, French, Swahili
Religions	67% Christian, 32% indigenous beliefs, 1% Moslem
Ethnic groups	85% Hutu, 14% Tutsi, 1% Twa

CAMEROON

Colonial or other former name	French and British Cameroons
Capital	Yaoundé
Former colonial power(s)	Germany, France, Great Britain
Date of independence	January 1, 1960
Leader at independence	Ahmadou Ahidjo
Current leader	Paul Biya, president
Form of government	one-party presidential regime
Country population	10.1 million
Capital's population	700,000
Land area	475,442 sq. km (179,558 sq. mi)
Population per square km	21
Annual population growth rate	3.5%
Main exports	coffee, oil, tea, cotton
Average annual growth, GNP, 1973–85	7.1%
Currency	CFA franc
Per capita income	$810
Infant mortality rate (per 1,000 births)	89
Life expectancy at birth (years)	54
Average daily caloric intake	2,089
Language(s)	French and English (both official), tribal languages
Religions	50% indigenous beliefs, 33% Christian, 17% Moslem
Ethnic groups	200 tribes

CAPE VERDE ISLANDS

Colonial or other former name	
Capital	Praia
Former colonial power(s)	Portugal
Date of independence	July 5, 1975
Leader at independence	Aristides Pereira
Current leader	Aristides Pereira, president (Pedro Pires, prime minister)
Form of government	one-party parliamentary regime
Country population	326,000
Capital's population	57,748
Land area	4.033 sq. km (1,557 sq. mi)
Population per square km	81
Annual population growth rate	1.9%
Main exports	fish, bananas, salt, flour
Average annual growth, GNP, 1973–85	6.7%
Currency	Cape Verde escudo
Per capita income	$430
Infant mortality rate (per 1,000 births)	60 (1983)
Life expectancy at birth (years)	64
Average daily caloric intake	2,614
Language(s)	Portuguese, Creole
Religions	predominantly Catholic
Ethnic groups	71% Creole (mulatto), 28% African

CENTRAL AFRICAN REPUBLIC

Colonial or other former name	Ubangi-Shari
Capital	Bangui
Former colonial power(s)	France
Date of independence	August 13, 1960
Leader at independence	David Dacko
Current leader	André-Dieudonné Kolingba
Form of government	military regime
Country population	2.6 million
Capital's population	473,817
Land area	622,984 sq. km (240,325 sq. mi)
Population per square km	4
Annual population growth rate	2.5%
Main exports	cotton, coffee, diamonds, timber
Average annual growth, GNP, 1973–85	0.6%
Currency	CFA franc
Per capita income	$270
Infant mortality rate (per 1,000 births)	137
Life expectancy at birth (years)	49
Average daily caloric intake	2,050
Language(s)	French (official), Sangho
Religions	25% Protestant, 25% Catholic, 24% indigenous beliefs, 10% Moslem
Ethnic groups	34% Baya, 28% Banda, 21% Mandja, 10% Sara

CHAD

Colonial or other former name	
Capital	N'djamena (formerly Fort-Lamy)
Former colonial power(s)	France
Date of independence	August 11, 1960
Leader at independence	François N'Garta Tombalbaye
Current leader	Hissene Habre, president
Form of government	centralized presidential rule (civil war)
Country population	5.0 million
Capital's population	402,000
Land area	1,284,000 sq. km (495,755 sq. mi)
Population per square km	4
Annual population growth rate	2.3%
Main exports	cotton, meat, fish, animal products
Average annual growth, GNP, 1973–85	n.a.
Currency	CFA franc
Per capita income	$78 (1986)
Infant mortality rate (per 1,000 births)	138
Life expectancy at birth (years)	44
Average daily caloric intake	1,504
Language(s)	French (official), Chadian Arabi, Sara, Sangho
Religions	52% Moslem, 43% indigenous beliefs
Ethnic groups	200 distinct groups

COMOROS

Colonial or other former name	
Capital	Moroni
Former colonial power(s)	France
Date of independence	July 6, 1975
Leader at independence	Prince Said Mohamed Jaffar
Current leader	Ahmed Abdallah Abderemane, president
Form of government	Islamic republic
Country population	444,000
Capital's population	17,267
Land area	1,860 sq. km (838 sq. mi)
Population per square km	239
Annual population growth rate	3.1%
Main exports	perfume, oils, vanilla, copra, cloves
Average annual growth, GNP, 1973–85	4.0%
Currency	CFA franc
Per capita income	$280
Infant mortality rate (per 1,000 births)	92 (1983)
Life expectancy at birth (years)	55
Average daily caloric intake	2,090
Language(s)	Arabic, Shaafi Islam, Malagasy, French
Religions	86% Shirazi Moslem, 14% Catholic
Ethnic groups	Antalote, Cafre, Makoa, Oimatsaha, Sakalava

CONGO

Colonial or other former name	French Congo
Capital	Brazzaville
Former colonial power(s)	France
Date of independence	August 15, 1960
Leader at independence	Fulbert Youlou
Current leader	Denis Sassou-Nguesso, president
Form of government	one-party people's republic
Country population	1.9 million
Capital's population	302,459
Land area	342,000 sq. km (132,046 sq. mi)
Population per square km	6
Annual population growth rate	2.6%
Main exports	oil, lumber, tobacco, veneer, ply-wood, coffee, cocoa
Average annual growth, GNP, 1973–85	7.7%
Currency	CFA franc
Per capita income	$1,020
Infant mortality rate (per 1,000 births)	77
Life expectancy at birth (years)	57
Average daily caloric intake	2,549
Language(s)	French (official), Lingala, Kikongo
Religions	48% animist, 47% Christian, 2% Moslem
Ethnic groups	48% Kongo, 20% Sangha, 12% M'Bochi, 17% Teke

DJIBOUTI

Colonial or other former name	French Somaliland
Capital	Djibouti
Former colonial power(s)	France
Date of independence	June 27, 1977
Leader at independence	
Current leader	Hassan Gouled Aptidon, president
Form of government	one-party system
Country population	456,000
Capital's population	200,000
Land area	23,000 sq. km (8,996 sq. mi)
Population per square km	20
Annual population growth rate	6.7%
Main exports	hides, skins
Average annual growth, GNP, 1973–85	n.a.
Currency	Djibouti franc
Per capita income	$450
Infant mortality rate (per 1,000 births)	140
Life expectancy at birth (years)	48
Average daily caloric intake	n.a.
Language(s)	French (official), Somali, Afar, Arabic
Religions	94% Moslem, 6% Christian
Ethnic groups	60% Somali (Issa), 5% Afar

EQUATORIAL GUINEA

Colonial or other former name	
Capital	Malabo (formerly Santa Isabel)
Former colonial power(s)	Spain
Date of independence	October 12, 1968
Leader at independence	Francisco Macias Nguema Biyogo
Current leader	Teodoro Obiang Nguema Mbasogo, president
Form of government	military rule
Country population	392,000
Capital's population	34,980
Land area	28,051 sq. km (10,832 sq. mi)
Population per square km	14
Annual population growth rate	2.2%
Main exports	cocoa, coffee, wood
Average annual growth, GNP, 1973–85	n.a.
Currency	epkwele
Per capita income	$250
Infant mortality rate (per 1,000 births)	143
Life expectancy at birth (years)	43
Average daily caloric intake	n.a.
Language(s)	Spanish (official), pidgin English, Fang
Religions	predominantly Catholic
Ethnic groups	Fang, Bubi and others

ETHIOPIA

Colonial or other former name	Abyssinia
Capital	Addis Ababa (formerly Finfinnie)
Former colonial power(s)	occupied by Italy (1935–1941)
Date of independence	
Leader at independence	
Current leader	Mengistu Haile Mariam
Form of government	military regime
Country population	43.3 million
Capital's population	1,460,000
Land area	1,221,900 sq. km (472,400 sq. mi)
Population per square km	35
Annual population growth rate	2.4%
Main exports	coffee, hides, skins
Average annual growth, GNP, 1973–85	2.2%
Currency	birr
Per capita income	$110
Infant mortality rate (per 1,000 births)	168
Life expectancy at birth (years)	44
Average daily caloric intake	1,681
Language(s)	Amharic (official), Tigrinya, Orominga, Arabic, English
Religions	40–45% Moslem, 35–40% Ethiopian Orthodox, 15–20% animist, 5% other
Ethnic groups	40% Oromo, 32% Amhara & Tigre, 9% Sidamo, 6% Somali, 6% Shankella

GABON

Colonial or other former name	
Capital	Libreville
Former colonial power(s)	France
Date of independence	August 17, 1960
Leader at independence	Leon M'Ba
Current leader	El Hadj Omar Bongo, president
Form of government	one-party presidential rule
Country population	1.2 million
Capital's population	251,400 (1975)
Land area	267,667 sq. km (102,317 sq. mi)
Population per square km	4
Annual population growth rate	1.6%
Main exports	oil, wood, manganese, uranium concentrates, gold
Average annual growth, GNP, 1973–85	0.9%
Currency	CFA franc
Per capita income	$3,340
Infant mortality rate (per 1,000 births)	117
Life expectancy at birth (years)	50
Average daily caloric intake	n.a.
Language(s)	French (official), Fang, Myene, Bateke
Religions	55–75% Christian, less than 1% Moslem, remainder animist
Ethnic groups	25% Fang, 10% Bapounou, others

GAMBIA

Colonial or other former name	
Capital	Banjul (formerly Bathurst)
Former colonial power(s)	Great Britain
Date of independence	February 18, 1965
Leader at independence	Sir Dawda Jawara
Current leader	Sir Dawda Jawara, president
Form of government	democracy
Country population	643,000
Capital's population	49,181
Land area	10,403 sq. km (4,361 sq. mi)
Population per square km	62
Annual population growth rate	1.4%
Main exports	peanut, palm products, cotton
Average annual growth, GNP, 1973–85	0.6%
Currency	dalasi
Per capita income	$230
Infant mortality rate (per 1,000 births)	174
Life expectancy at birth (years)	42
Average daily caloric intake	2,229
Language(s)	English (official), Mandinka, Wolof, Fula
Religions	85% Moslem, 14% Christian, 1% indigenous beliefs
Ethnic groups	37.7% Mandinka, 16.2% Fula, 14% Wolof

GHANA

Colonial or other former name	Gold Coast
Capital	Accra
Former colonial power(s)	Great Britain
Date of independence	March 6, 1957
Leader at independence	Kwame N. Nkrumah & J. B. Danquah
Current leader	Jerry John Rawlings
Form of government	revolutionary council
Country population	13.6 million
Capital's population	964,879 (1984)
Land area	238,537 sq. km (92,098 sq. mi)
Population per square km	57
Annual population growth rate	3.3%
Main exports	wood, gold, diamonds, manganese, bauxite, aluminum
Average annual growth, GNP, 1973–85	−0.6%
Currency	new cedi
Per capita income	$390
Infant mortality rate (per 1,000 births)	94
Life expectancy at birth (years)	53
Average daily caloric intake	1,747
Language(s)	English (official), Akan, Mole-Dagbani, Ewe, Ga-Adangbe
Religions	42% Christian, 38% indigenous beliefs, 12% Moslem, 7% other
Ethnic groups	Akan, Ashanti, Ewe, Ga, Mossi-Dagomba

GUINEA

Colonial or other former name	
Capital	Conakry
Former colonial power(s)	France
Date of independence	October 2, 1958
Leader at independence	Ahmed Sékou Touré
Current leader	Lansana Conté, president
Form of government	military rule
Country population	6.0 million
Capital's population	525,671
Land area	245,857 sq. km (94,925 sq. mi)
Population per square km	24
Annual population growth rate	2.0%
Main exports	bauxite, alumina, diamonds, coffee, pineapples
Average annual growth, GNP, 1973–85	0.0%
Currency	syli
Per capita income	$320
Infant mortality rate (per 1,000 births)	153
Life expectancy at birth (years)	38
Average daily caloric intake	1,728
Language(s)	French (official), tribal languages
Religions	75% Moslem, 24% indigenous beliefs, 1% Christian
Ethnic groups	40% Foulah, 25% Malinke, 10% Soussou

GUINEA-BISSAU

Colonial or other former name	
Capital	Bissau
Former colonial power(s)	Portugal
Date of independence	September 10, 1974
Leader at independence	Luis de Almeida Cabral
Current leader	João Bernardo Vieira, president
Form of government	republic
Country population	890,000
Capital's population	109,214
Land area	36,125 sq. km (13,948 sq. mi)
Population per square km	25
Annual population growth rate	1.9%
Main exports	peanuts, palm kernels, shrimp, fish, lumber
Average annual growth, GNP, 1973–85	1.9%
Currency	Guinean peso
Per capita income	$170
Infant mortality rate (per 1,000 births)	250
Life expectancy at birth (years)	38
Average daily caloric intake	n.a.
Language(s)	Portuguese (official), Creole, African languages
Religions	65% indigenous beliefs, 30% Moslem, 5% Christian
Ethnic groups	30% Balanta, 20% Fula, 14% Manjaca, 13% Mandinga

IVORY COAST

Colonial or other former name	
Capital	Abidjan/Yamoussoukro
Former colonial power(s)	France
Date of independence	August 7, 1960
Leader at independence	Félix Houphouët-Boigny
Current leader	Félix Houphouët-Boigny, president
Form of government	one-party presidential regime
Country population	9.7 million
Capital's population	951,216 (1976)
Land area	322,463 sq. km (124,503 sq. mi)
Population per square km	30
Annual population growth rate	4.0% (1985)
Main exports	cocoa, coffee, tropical woods, cotton, palm oil, bananas
Average annual growth, GNP, 1973–85	3.2%
Currency	CFA franc
Per capita income	$772
Infant mortality rate (per 1,000 births)	105
Life expectancy at birth (years)	52
Average daily caloric intake	2,505
Language(s)	French (official), Dioula and other tribal languages
Religions	63% indigenous beliefs, 25% Moslem, 12% Christian
Ethnic groups	Agni, Baoulé, Krou, Senoufou, Mandingo, 40,000 French, 30,000 Lebanese

KENYA

Colonial or other former name	
Capital	Nairobi
Former colonial power(s)	Great Britain
Date of independence	December 12, 1963
Leader at independence	Jomo Kenyatta
Current leader	Doniel T. arap Moi, president
Form of government	one-party presidential rule
Country population	20.3 million
Capital's population	1,100,000
Land area	582,646 sq. km (224,081 sq. mi)
Population per square km	35
Annual population growth rate	4.1%
Main exports	coffee, tea, sisal
Average annual growth, GNP, 1973–85	4.3%
Currency	Kenya shilling
Per capita income	$290
Infant mortality rate (per 1,000 births)	91
Life expectancy at birth (years)	54
Average daily caloric intake	2,151
Language(s)	English and Swahili (official), indigenous languages
Religions	38% Protestant, 28% Catholic, 26% indigenous beliefs, 6% Moslem
Ethnic groups	21% Kikuyu, 14% Luhya, 13% Luo, 11% Kalenjin

LESOTHO

Colonial or other former name	Basutoland
Capital	Maseru
Former colonial power(s)	Great Britain
Date of independence	October 4, 1966
Leader at independence	King Moshoeshoe II
Current leader	Maj. Gen. Justin Lekhanya, chief of military council
Form of government	constitutional monarchy
Country population	1.5 million
Capital's population	106,000
Land area	30,355 sq. km (11,716 sq. mi)
Population per square km	50
Annual population growth rate	7.1%
Main exports	labor to South Africa, wool, mohair, wheat, cattle
Average annual growth, GNP, 1973–85	4.6%
Currency	maioti
Per capita income	$480
Infant mortality rate (per 1,000 births)	106
Life expectancy at birth (years)	50
Average daily caloric intake	2,358
Language(s)	Sesotho, English (official), Zulu, Xhosa
Religions	80% Christian, 20% indigenous beliefs
Ethnic groups	99.7% Sotho

LIBERIA

Colonial or other former name	
Capital	Monrovia
Former colonial power(s)	settler regime of freed American slaves
Date of independence	July 26, 1847
Leader at independence	
Current leader	Samuel K. Doe, president
Form of government	military rule
Country population	2.2 million
Capital's population	208,629 (1978)
Land area	111,369 sq. km (38,250 sq. mi)
Population per square km	20
Annual population growth rate	3.5%
Main exports	iron ore, rubber, diamonds, lumber, coffee, cocoa
Average annual growth, GNP, 1973–85	1.4%
Currency	U.S. dollar
Per capita income	$470
Infant mortality rate (per 1,000 births)	127
Life expectancy at birth (years)	50
Average daily caloric intake	2,311
Language(s)	English (official), Niger-Congo languages
Religions	43% traditional, 21% Moslem, 35% Christian
Ethnic groups	Kpelle, Bassa, Gio, Kru, Grebo, Mano, Krahn, Americo-Liberians

MADAGASCAR

Colonial or other former name	Malagasy Republic
Capital	Antananarivo (formerly Tananarive)
Former colonial power(s)	France
Date of independence	June 26, 1960
Leader at independence	Philibert Tsiranana
Current leader	Didier Ratsiraka, president
Form of government	military rule
Country population	9.9 million
Capital's population	406,366 (1975)
Land area	587,041 sq. km (226,658 sq. mi)
Population per square km	17
Annual population growth rate	2.8%
Main exports	coffee, vanilla, sugar, cloves
Average annual growth, GNP, 1973–85	−0.7%
Currency	Malagasy franc
Per capita income	$250
Infant mortality rate (per 1,000 births)	109
Life expectancy at birth (years)	52
Average daily caloric intake	2,469
Language(s)	Malagasy (official), French
Religions	over 50% indigenous beliefs, 41% Christian, 7% Moslem
Ethnic groups	Merina, Bétsileo, Betsimisáraka

MALAWI

Colonial or other former name	Nyasaland
Capital	Lilongwe
Former colonial power(s)	Great Britain
Date of independence	July 6, 1964
Leader at independence	Hastings Kamuzu Banda
Current leader	Hastings Kamuzu Banda, president
Form of government	centralized presidential rule
Country population	7.3 million
Capital's population	150,000
Land area	118,484 sq. km (45,747 sq. mi)
Population per square km	62
Annual population growth rate	3.1%
Main exports	tobacco, tea, peanuts, sugar, cotton
Average annual growth, GNP, 1973–85	2.6%
Currency	kwacha
Per capita income	$170
Infant mortality rate (per 1,000 births)	156
Life expectancy at birth (years)	45
Average daily caloric intake	2,448
Language(s)	English, Chichewa
Religions	15% Moslem, 10% Protestant, 10% Catholic, 65% indigenous beliefs
Ethnic groups	Chewa, Nyanja, Tumbuka

MALI

Colonial or other former name	French Sudan
Capital	Bamako
Former colonial power(s)	France
Date of independence	September 22, 1960
Leader at independence	Modibo Keita
Current leader	Moussa Traoré, president
Form of government	military rule
Country population	8.2 million
Capital's population	404,000 (1976)
Land area	1,240,000 sq. km (478,841 sq. mi)
Population per square km	7
Annual population growth rate	3.6%
Main exports	livestock, peanuts, dried fish, cotton. skins
Average annual growth, GNP, 1973–85	1.0%
Currency	Mali franc
Per capita income	$140
Infant mortality rate (per 1,000 births)	174
Life expectancy at birth (years)	46
Average daily caloric intake	1,788
Language(s)	French (official), Bambara
Religions	90% Moslem, 9% indigenous beliefs, 1% Christian
Ethnic groups	50% Mande, 17% Peul, 12% Voltaic, 6% Songhai, 5% Tuareg and Moor

MAURITANIA

Colonial or other former name	
Capital	Nouakchott
Former colonial power(s)	France
Date of independence	November 28, 1960
Leader at independence	Moktar Ould Daddah
Current leader	Maaouiya Ould Sid Ahmed Taya, premier
Form of government	military rule
Country population	1.9 million
Capital's population	134,986
Land area	1,030,700 sq. km (398,000 sq. mi)
Population per square km	2
Annual population growth rate	3.0%
Main exports	iron ore, processed fish, cattle
Average annual growth, GNP, 1973–85	2.3%
Currency	ouguiya
Per capita income	$410
Infant mortality rate (per 1,000 births)	132
Life expectancy at birth (years)	46
Average daily caloric intake	2,078
Language(s)	Hasanya Arabic, French, Toucouleur, Fula, Sarakole, Wolof
Religions	nearly 100% Moslem
Ethnic groups	40% mixed Moor/black, 30% Moor, 30% black

MAURITIUS

Colonial or other former name	
Capital	Port Louis
Former colonial power(s)	Holland, France, Great Britain
Date of independence	March 12, 1968
Leader at independence	Sir Seewoosagur Ramgoolam
Current leader	Anerood Jagnauth, prime minister
Form of government	unicameral parliamentary system
Country population	1.0 million
Capital's population	136,323
Land area	2,045 sq. km (787 sq. mi)
Population per square km	489
Annual population growth rate	1.3%
Main exports	sugar, molasses, tea, tobacco
Average annual growth, GNP, 1973–85	3.3%
Currency	Mauritian rupee
Per capita income	$1,070
Infant mortality rate (per 1,000 births)	25
Life expectancy at birth (years)	66
Average daily caloric intake	2,740
Language(s)	Creole, French, English, Hindi, Urdu, Tamil
Religions	51% Hindu, 30% Christian, 17% Moslem
Ethnic groups	68% Indo-Mauritian, 27% Creole

MOZAMBIQUE

Colonial or other former name	
Capital	Maputo (formerly Lourenço Marques)
Former colonial power(s)	Portugal
Date of independence	June 25, 1975
Leader at independence	Samora Machel
Current leader	Joaquim Chissano, president
Form of government	people's republic
Country population	13.9 million
Capital's population	903,621
Land area	801,590 (303,769 sq. mi)
Population per square km	17
Annual population growth rate	2.9%
Main exports	cashews, cotton, sugar, mineral products
Average annual growth, GNP, 1973–85	n.a.
Currency	metical
Per capita income	$90
Infant mortality rate (per 1,000 births)	123
Life expectancy at birth (years)	59
Average daily caloric intake	1,678
Language(s)	Portuguese (official), indigenous languages
Religions	65% animist, 20% Christian, 10% Moslem
Ethnic groups	Mokonde, Makua-Lomue, Tsonga, lower Zambezi groups

NAMIBIA

Colonial or other former name	South-West Africa
Capital	Windhoek
Former colonial power(s)	Germany, South Africa
Date of independence	
Leader at independence	
Current leader	
Form of government	ruled by South Africa
Country population	1.6 million
Capital's population	97,000
Land area	824,292 sq. km (318,827 sq. mi)
Population per square km	2
Annual population growth rate	2.8%
Main exports	diamonds, uranium, meat, fish products
Average annual growth, GNP, 1973–85	3.7%
Currency	South African rand
Per capita income	n.a.
Infant mortality rate (per 1,000 births)	n.a.
Life expectancy at birth (years)	49
Average daily caloric intake	n.a.
Language(s)	Afrikaans, German, English, various tribal languages
Religions	70% Lutheran, 18% Catholic, 12% animist
Ethnic groups	51% Ovambo, 9.7% Kavango, 7.7% Herrero, 7.5% Afrikaner and English, 6.9% mixed

NIGER

Colonial or other former name	
Capital	Niamey
Former colonial power(s)	France
Date of independence	August 3, 1960
Leader at independence	Hamani Diori
Current leader	Ali Saibou, president
Form of government	military regime
Country population	6.1 million
Capital's population	225,314
Land area	1,267,000 sq. km (490,100 sq. mi)
Population per square km	5
Annual population growth rate	2.9%
Main exports	uranium, livestock, cow hides, skins
Average annual growth, GNP, 1973–85	3.5%
Currency	CFA franc
Per capita income	$200
Infant mortality rate (per 1,000 births)	140
Life expectancy at birth (years)	43
Average daily caloric intake	2,250
Language(s)	French (official), Hausa, Djerma
Religions	80% Moslem, remainder indigenous and Christian
Ethnic groups	56% Hausa, 22% Djerma, 8.5% Fulani, 8% Tuareg

NIGERIA

Colonial or other former name	
Capital	Lagos (moving to Abuja)
Former colonial power(s)	Great Britain
Date of independence	October 1, 1960
Leader at independence	Sir Abubaker Tafawa Balewa
Current leader	Maj. Gen. Ibrahim Babangida, head of state
Form of government	military rule
Country population	95 million
Capital's population	1,061,000
Land area	923,768 sq. km (356,700 sq. mi)
Population per square km	103
Annual population growth rate	3.4%
Main exports	oil, cocoa, palm products, rubber, timber, tin
Average annual growth, GNP, 1973–85	0.3%
Currency	naira
Per capita income	$760
Infant mortality rate (per 1,000 births)	109
Life expectancy at birth (years)	50
Average daily caloric intake	2,038
Language(s)	English (official), Ibo, Hausa, Yoruba
Religions	47% Moslem, 34% Christian, 18% indigenous beliefs
Ethnic groups	Hausa, Fulani, Yoruba, Ibo

RWANDA

Colonial or other former name	
Capital	Kigali
Former colonial power(s)	Germany, Belgium
Date of independence	July 1, 1962
Leader at independence	Gregoire Kayibanda
Current leader	Juvenal Habyarimana, president
Form of government	military rule
Country population	6.1 million
Capital's population	117,749
Land area	26,338 sq. km (10,169 sq. mi)
Population per square km	232
Annual population growth rate	3.3%
Main exports	coffee, tea
Average annual growth, GNP, 1973–85	5.4%
Currency	Rwanda franc
Per capita income	$290
Infant mortality rate (per 1,000 births)	127
Life expectancy at birth (years)	47
Average daily caloric intake	1,919
Language(s)	French (official), Kinyarwandu, Swahili
Religions	65% Catholic, 9% Protestant, 1% Moslem, indigenous beliefs
Ethnic groups	85% Hutu, 14% Tutsi, 1% Twa

SÃO TOMÉ & PRINCIPE

Colonial or other former name	
Capital	São Tomé
Former colonial power(s)	Portugal
Date of independence	July 12, 1975
Leader at independence	Manuel Pinto da Costa
Current leader	Manuel Pinto da Costa, president
Form of government	one-party parliamentary system
Country population	108,000
Capital's population	40,000
Land area	964 sq. km (372 sq. mi)
Population per square km	112
Annual population growth rate	4.9%
Main exports	cocoa, copra, coffee, palm oil
Average annual growth, GNP, 1973–85	3.2%
Currency	dobra
Per capita income	$310
Infant mortality rate (per 1,000 births)	63
Life expectancy at birth (years)	63
Average daily caloric intake	2,435
Language(s)	Portuguese
Religions	Catholic, Evangelical Protestant, Seventh Day Adventist
Ethnic groups	Portuguese-African mixture, African minority

SENEGAL

Colonial or other former name	
Capital	Dakar
Former colonial power(s)	France
Date of independence	April 4, 1960
Leader at independence	Léopold Sédar Senghor
Current leader	Abdou Diouf, president
Form of government	republic
Country population	6.4 million
Capital's population	850,000 (1975)
Land area	196,192 sq. km (75,750 sq. mi)
Population per square km	33
Annual population growth rate	2.8%
Main exports	peanuts, phosphate, fish
Average annual growth, GNP, 1973–85	2.0%
Currency	CFA franc
Per capita income	$370
Infant mortality rate (per 1,000 births)	137
Life expectancy at birth (years)	46
Average daily caloric intake	2,342
Language(s)	French (official), Wolof, Pulaar, Diola, Mandingo
Religions	75% Moslem, 20% indigenous beliefs, 5% Christian
Ethnic groups	36% Wolof, 17.5% Fulani, 16.5% Serer, 9% Toucouleur, 9% Diola

SEYCHELLES

Colonial or other former name	
Capital	Victoria
Former colonial power(s)	France, Great Britain
Date of independence	June 29, 1976
Leader at independence	James R. Mancham & France-Albert René
Current leader	France-Albert René, president
Form of government	socialist one-party state
Country population	65,000
Capital's population	23,334
Land area	227 sq. km (171 sq. mi)
Population per square km	286
Annual population growth rate	0.6%
Main exports	cinnamon, vanilla, copra, fish
Average annual growth, GNP, 1973–85	n.a.
Currency	Seychelles rupee
Per capita income	$2,100
Infant mortality rate (per 1,000 births)	26
Life expectancy at birth (years)	70
Average daily caloric intake	2,289
Language(s)	Creole, English, French
Religions	90% Roman Catholic
Ethnic groups	Seychellois (mixture of Asian, African & European)

SIERRA LEONE

Colonial or other former name	
Capital	Freetown
Former colonial power(s)	Great Britain
Date of independence	April 27, 1961
Leader at independence	Sir Milton Margai & Sir Albert Margai
Current leader	Maj. Gen. Joseph Saidu Momoh, president
Form of government	one-party republic
Country population	3.6 million
Capital's population	469,776
Land area	71,740 sq. km (27,699 sq. mi)
Population per square km	50
Annual population growth rate	1.8%
Main exports	diamonds, iron ore, palm kernels, cocoa, coffee
Average annual growth, GNP, 1973–85	1.9%
Currency	leone
Per capita income	$370
Infant mortality rate (per 1,000 births)	175
Life expectancy at birth (years)	38
Average daily caloric intake	1,817
Language(s)	English (official), Mende, Temne, Krio
Religions	70% indigenous beliefs, 25% Muslim, 5% Christian
Ethnic groups	30% Temne, 30% Mende, 2% Creole

SOMALIA

Colonial or other former name	British/Italian Somaliland
Capital	Mogadishu (formerly Mogadiscio)
Former colonial power(s)	Great Britain & Italy
Date of independence	July 1, 1960
Leader at independence	
Current leader	Mohammed Siad Barre, president
Form of government	military regime
Country population	4.6 million
Capital's population	500,000
Land area	637,657 sq. km (246,199 sq. mi)
Population per square km	7
Annual population growth rate	3.0%
Main exports	livestock, hides, skins, bananas
Average annual growth, GNP, 1973–85	2.5%
Currency	Somali shilling
Per capita income	$270
Infant mortality rate (per 1,000 births)	152
Life expectancy at birth (years)	46
Average daily caloric intake	2,072
Language(s)	Somali (official), Arabic, Italian, English
Religions	Sunni Moslem (almost entirely)
Ethnic groups	Somalis

SOUTH AFRICA

Colonial or other former name	Union of South Africa
Capital	Pretoria/Cape Town
Former colonial power(s)	Holland, Great Britain
Date of independence	May 31, 1910
Leader at independence	Jan Smuts, Louis Botha
Current leader	Pieter Willem Botha, president
Form of government	republic controlled by white minority
Country population	33.0 million
Capital's population	Pretoria 443,059/Cape Town 776,617
Land area	1,233,404 sq. km (435,868 sq. mi)
Population per square km	26
Annual population growth rate	2.5%
Main exports	gold, wool, diamonds, metallic ores
Average annual growth, GNP, 1973–85	2.4%
Currency	rand
Per capita income	$2,010
Infant mortality rate (per 1,000 births)	78
Life expectancy at birth (years)	54
Average daily caloric intake	2,979
Language(s)	Afrikaans and English (official), Zulu, Xhosa, Sotho, Tswana
Religions	Christian, Hindu, Moslem
Ethnic groups	73.8% African, 14.7% white, 8.6% Coloured, 2.6% Asian

SUDAN

Colonial or other former name	Anglo-Egyptian Sudan
Capital	Khartoum
Former colonial power(s)	Egypt, Great Britain
Date of independence	January 1, 1956
Leader at independence	
Current leader	Sadek el-Mahdi
Form of government	parliamentary regime
Country population	21.5 million
Capital's population	561,000
Land area	2,505,813 sq. km (967,757 sq. mi)
Population per square km	9
Annual population growth rate	2.9%
Main exports	cotton, gum arabic, peanuts, sesame
Average annual growth, GNP, 1973–85	4.0%
Currency	Sudanese pound
Per capita income	$330
Infant mortality rate (per 1,000 births)	112
Life expectancy at birth (years)	48
Average daily caloric intake	2,003
Language(s)	Arabic (official), Nubian, Ta, Bedawie, Nilotic, English
Religions	70% Sunni Moslem, 20% indigenous beliefs, 5% Christian
Ethnic groups	52% black, 39% Arab, 6% Beja, 3% other

SWAZILAND

Colonial or other former name	
Capital	Mbabane
Former colonial power(s)	Great Britain
Date of independence	September 6, 1968
Leader at independence	King Sobhuza II
Current leader	Prince Sotsha Dlamini, prime minister
Form of government	monarchy
Country population	706,137
Capital's population	38,636 (1982)
Land area	17,363 sq. km (6,703 sq. mi)
Population per square km	41
Annual population growth rate	3.4%
Main exports	sugar, asbestos, wood & forest products, citrus, canned fruit
Average annual growth, GNP, 1973–85	4.2%
Currency	lilangeni
Per capita income	$650
Infant mortality rate (per 1,000 births)	156
Life expectancy at birth (years)	54
Average daily caloric intake	2,562
Language(s)	English (official), siSwati, Afrikaans
Religions	57% Christian, 43% indigenous beliefs
Ethnic groups	70% Nguni, 25% Sotho, 5% Tsonga

TANZANIA

Colonial or other former name	Tanganyika and Zanzibar
Capital	Dar es Salaam
Former colonial power(s)	Germany, Great Britain
Date of independence	December 9, 1961
Leader at independence	Julius Nyerere
Current leader	Ali Hassan Mwinyi, president
Form of government	one-party republic
Country population	22.2 million
Capital's population	1,090,000
Land area	945,087 sq. km (364,886 sq. mi)
Population per square km	23
Annual population growth rate	3.2%
Main exports	coffee, cotton, sisal, cashew nuts, diamonds, cloves, tea
Average annual growth, GNP, 1973–85	1.7%
Currency	Tanzanian shilling
Per capita income	$270
Infant mortality rate (per 1,000 births)	110
Life expectancy at birth (years)	52
Average daily caloric intake	2,335
Language(s)	Swahili, English
Religions	35% Christian, 35% Moslem, 30% indigenous beliefs
Ethnic groups	100 distinct tribes

TOGO

Colonial or other former name	Togoland
Capital	Lomé
Former colonial power(s)	Germany, Great Britain, France
Date of independence	April 27, 1960
Leader at independence	Sylvanus Olympio
Current leader	Gnassingbé Eyadéma, president
Form of government	one-party republic
Country population	3.0 million
Capital's population	230,000 (1977)
Land area	56,000 sq. km (21,853 sq. mi)
Population per square km	54
Annual population growth rate	3.0%
Main exports	phosphates, cocoa, coffee, palm kernels
Average annual growth, GNP, 1973–85	1.7%
Currency	CFA franc
Per capita income	$250
Infant mortality rate (per 1,000 births)	97
Life expectancy at birth (years)	51
Average daily caloric intake	2,236
Language(s)	French (official), Ewe, Mina, Dagomba, Kabye
Religions	70% indigenous beliefs, 20% Christian, 10% Moslem
Ethnic groups	Ewe, Mina, Kabye

UGANDA

Colonial or other former name	
Capital	Kampala
Former colonial power(s)	Great Britain
Date of independence	March 1, 1962
Leader at independence	Milton Obote
Current leader	Yoweri Museveni, president
Form of government	republic with centralized presidential system
Country population	15.5 million
Capital's population	458,423 (1980)
Land area	236,036 sq. km (91,104 sq. mi)
Population per square km	66
Annual population growth rate	3.4%
Main exports	coffee, cotton, tea
Average annual growth, GNP, 1973–85	n.a.
Currency	Uganda shilling
Per capita income	$230
Infant mortality rate (per 1,000 births)	108
Life expectancy at birth (years)	51
Average daily caloric intake	2,083
Language(s)	English (official), Luganda, Swahili, Bantu, Nilotic
Religions	33% Catholic, 33% Protestant, 16% Moslem
Ethnic groups	Baganda, Teso, Nkore, Soga, Kiga, Ruanda, Lango, Gisu, Acholi

WESTERN SAHARA

Colonial or other former name	Spanish Sahara
Capital	El Aaiún
Former colonial power(s)	Spain
Date of independence	Polisario declared gov't in exile on Feb. 28, 1976
Leader at independence	Mohammed Lamine Ould Ahmed
Current leader	Mohammed Abdulaziz
Form of government	ruled by Morocco
Country population	155,000
Capital's population	93,000
Land area	266,770 sq. km (102,703 sq. mi)
Population per square km	0.6
Annual population growth rate	2.8%
Main exports	phosphates, fish, handicrafts
Average annual growth, GNP, 1973–85	n.a.
Currency	Moroccan dirham
Per capita income	n.a.
Infant mortality rate (per 1,000 births)	n.a.
Life expectancy at birth (years)	n.a.
Average daily caloric intake	n.a.
Language(s)	Hassanya Arabic, Moroccan Arabic
Religions	Moslem
Ethnic groups	Tekna (Arab and Berber), Reguibat, Moorish, Tuareg

ZAIRE

Colonial or other former name	Belgian Congo
Capital	Kinshasa (formerly Léopoldville)
Former colonial power(s)	Belgium
Date of independence	June 30, 1960
Leader at independence	Joseph Kasavubu and Patrice Lumumba
Current leader	Mobutu Sese Seko, president
Form of government	republic with centralized presidential system
Country population	30.4 million
Capital's population	2,400,000 (1976)
Land area	2,345,409 sq. km (905,063 sq. mi)
Population per square km	13
Annual population growth rate	2.9%
Main exports	copper, zinc, cobalt, lead, tobacco
Average annual growth, GNP, 1973–85	−0.9%
Currency	zaïre
Per capita income	$170
Infant mortality rate (per 1,000 births)	102
Life expectancy at birth (years)	51
Average daily caloric intake	2,154
Language(s)	French (official), English, Lingala, Swahili, Kingwana, Kikongo
Religions	50% Catholic, 20% Protestant, 10% Kimbanquirt, 10% Moslem
Ethnic groups	Kongo, Mongo, Luba, Mangbetu-Azande, Lulua, Lunda, Bwaka

ZAMBIA

Colonial or other former name	Northern Rhodesia
Capital	Lusaka
Former colonial power(s)	Great Britain
Date of independence	October 24, 1964
Leader at independence	Harry Nkumbula, Kenneth Kaunda
Current leader	Kenneth Kaunda, president
Form of government	republic with one-party presidential system
Country population	6.6 million
Capital's population	538,469
Land area	752,614 sq. km (290,586 sq. mi)
Population per square km	9
Annual population growth rate	2.7%
Main exports	copper, zinc, cobalt, lead, tobacco
Average annual growth, GNP, 1973–85	0.5%
Currency	kwacha
Per capita income	$400
Infant mortality rate (per 1,000 births)	84
Life expectancy at birth (years)	51
Average daily caloric intake	2,137
Language(s)	English (official) & 70 indigenous languages
Religions	50–75% Christian, 1% Moslem and Hindu
Ethnic groups	Bemba, Lozi

ZIMBABWE

Colonial or other former name	Southern Rhodesia
Capital	Harare (formerly Salisbury)
Former colonial power(s)	Great Britain
Date of independence	April 18, 1980
Leader at independence	Robert Mugabe and Joshua Nkomo
Current leader	Robert Mugabe, president
Form of government	one-party state
Country population	8.3 million
Capital's population	681,000
Land area	390,580 sq. km (150,873 sq. mi)
Population per square km	21
Annual population growth rate	3.1%
Main exports	gold, tobacco, asbestos, cotton, copper
Average annual growth, GNP, 1973–85	3.2%
Currency	Zimbabwe dollar
Per capita income	$650
Infant mortality rate (per 1,000 births)	77
Life expectancy at birth (years)	57
Average daily caloric intake	2,054
Language(s)	English (official), Shona, Sindebele, Ndebele
Religions	50% syncretic, 25% Christian, 24% indigenous
Ethnic groups	77% Shona, 19% Ndebele, 4% other

Index